ACTS

ACTS
A Handbook on the Greek Text

Martin M. Culy
Mikeal C. Parsons

Baylor University Press
Waco, Texas USA

This volume is the forty-third published by the Markham Press Fund of Baylor University Press, established in memory of Dr. L. N. and Princess Finch Markham of Longview, Texas, by their daughters, Mrs. R. Matt Dawson of Waco, Texas, and Mrs. B. Reid Clanton of Longview, Texas.

Cover Design: Pamela Poll

Library of Congress Cataloging-in-Publication Data

Culy, Martin M.
The Acts of the Apostles : a handbook on the Greek text / Martin M. Culy, Mikeal C. Parsons.— 1st ed.
p. cm.
ISBN 0-918954-90-8 (pbk. : alk. paper)
1. Bible. N.T. Acts—Commentaries. I. Parsons, Mikeal Carl, 1957- II. Title.

BS2625.53.C85 2003
226.6'077—dc22

2003018700

Printed in the United States of America on acid-free paper

Contents

Table of Contents

Preface

This volume is intended for Greek scholars and students at the intermediate and advanced level, as well as for students of Acts itself. We have used and tested earlier versions of the book with such students with great success. Pastors whose Greek skills have gotten a bit rusty since seminary tell us the volume has proven invaluable in their expository preaching on the book of Acts. The commentary is not intended to excuse the student from the hard work of syntactic analysis (the inadvertent errors inevitably associated with a work like this preclude its naive acceptance), but rather to help immerse (or reimmerse) the student or pastor into the delightful mysteries of Greek grammar.

We have attempted to allow our different areas of expertise to complement each other in this book. Martin Culy, Associate Professor of New Testament at Briercrest Biblical Seminary in Saskatchewan, Canada, is a trained linguist who has been involved in Bible translation for many years and more recently in teaching Greek at the college and seminary level. Mikeal Parsons, Professor of Religion at Baylor University in Waco, Texas, has spent nearly two decades engaged in the interpretation of the Lukan writings and has taught Greek on the doctoral level for the past fifteen years. This work has been a labor of love for those who are preparing to serve or are already engaged, for the sake of the Church and to the glory of God, in the interpretation of the sacred Scriptures and the proclamation of the Good News that God was in Christ reconciling the world to Himself.

Gloria Deo!

Martin Culy
Briercrest Biblical Seminary

Mikeal Parsons
Department of Religion
Baylor University

Acknowledgments

Preparing a reference work of any sort for the book of Acts is a daunting task. The sheer size of the text invariably leads the writer to wish that he or she had chosen Philemon instead! While commenting on technical aspects of the Greek text may seem to be a more straightforward challenge than writing a traditional commentary, the overwhelming mass of details involved in such an endeavor can lead to paranoia regarding inevitable errors in the final product. In seeking to weed out such errors, we have been significantly aided by our advanced Greek students who have used portions of this handbook at various stages of its development as a textbook in courses at the undergraduate, masters, and doctoral levels at Briercrest Bible College, Briercrest Biblical Seminary, and Baylor University. We gratefully acknowledge the helpful input of Andy Arterbury, Tony Creech, Jason Davis, Derek Dodson, Aimee Efird, Eddie Ellis, Chad Hartsock, Derek Hogan, Tyler Horton, Annie Judkins, Pamela Kinlaw, Darlene McLeod, Justin Rattermann, James Stewart, Tamara Vaags, Ed Watson, Susan Wendel, and Brenda Zwicker. We also wish to thank Jason Whitlark, who provided timely and invaluable assistance at the end of the project, and Chris Culy, who spent much of one summer checking the parsing against standard reference works.

In addition, we received significant institutional support for which we are immensely grateful. To the Baylor University Sabbatical and Research Committees we express appreciation. Thanks to Dr. Randall O'Brien, Chair of the Religion Department, Dr. Wallace Daniel, Dean of the College of Arts & Sciences, Dr. David L. Jeffrey, Provost and Vice-President for Academic Affairs, Dr. Donald D. Schmeltekopf, Provost Emeritus, and Dr. Robert B. Sloan, President—all of Baylor University—who, as usual, have given unfailing support in various ways to this and other projects. Thanks also to Dr. Paul Magnus, President of Briercrest Family of Schools, and Dr. Dwayne Uglem, Dean of Briercrest Biblical Seminary, for their commitment to fostering an environment in which faculty are encouraged in practical ways to pursue research projects. We are deeply grateful to Dr. Carey Newman, Director, and

Diane Smith, Production Manager, both of Baylor University Press, who have worked enthusiastically and diligently to make this the best book it could be. Finally, a heartfelt thanks to our families who indulged us while we worked on this project. We dedicate this volume to them—Heidi, Mikeal Joseph, and Matthew Quincy; Jo-Anna, Chris, Calvin, and Charissa.

Introduction

Anyone seeking to master the intricacies of Koine Greek in order to better understand the New Testament writings will find the Acts of the Apostles an appropriate point of departure. With 18,382 words, Acts is the second longest book in the New Testament. Only its companion piece, the Gospel of Luke, is longer (with 19,428 words; Morganthaler, 164). Of the 5,436 unique vocabulary words in the New Testament, 2,038 are found in Acts (second again only to Luke with 2,055). A systematic study of this important New Testament book will thus pay rich dividends for subsequent study of the other New Testament writings. This volume attempts to guide students through the intricacies of the Greek text of Acts. By working through the text systematically, readers will not only gain a firmer grasp of the peculiar shape of Acts' grammar, but given Acts' length and complexity, the student will also become better equipped to approach the other New Testament documents with increased confidence, particularly the other narrative literature (which together with Acts contain 82,773 of the 137,490 words of the NT; see Morganthaler, 164).

Probing the Grammar of Acts

In addition to parsing all verb forms, we have attended to important grammatical issues. Our guiding principle has been to deal only with those points that are "exegetically significant." This principle has turned out to be extremely difficult to apply, since any feature of the grammar, when misunderstood, becomes exegetically significant! As a general rule, we have sought to anticipate where students of Greek with at least an intermediate knowledge of the language may encounter difficulties. What distinguishes this work from other analytical guides to the Greek New Testament (most of which are single volumes covering the entire NT) is the detailed and comprehensive attention paid to the text of Acts. Many of the more complex issues related to Greek syntax tend to be ignored by the standard commentaries. In contrast, we have attempted to offer an explanation wherever significant questions may arise.

Anyone who is only superficially aware of the textual traditions of the Acts of the Apostles will know that the so-called "Western" text of Acts (approximately ten percent longer than the "Alexandrian" text) is a peculiarity, perhaps even an anomaly, in the textual history of the New Testament. In fact, several recent studies have argued that the Western text holds priority or at least equal footing with the Alexandrian text, predominately represented in the critical editions of Nestle-Aland and the United Bible Societies (see, e.g., Boismard and Lamouille; A. C. Clark; and W. A. Strange). While we have worked from the NA^{27}/ UBS^{4} text, we have not presumed, with very few exceptions, to evaluate textual variants for their status as "original" readings. Rather, when we have treated textual variants, we have simply explored those readings (widely agreed on as being secondary in nature) for evidence that might shed light on particular grammatical questions. Our assumption has been that, in some cases, the textual tradition represents the efforts of scribes, whose knowledge of Greek grammar far exceeds (with notable exceptions!) that of even the most accomplished Greek grammarian of the modern era, to "smooth out" grammatical difficulties in the text. While such textual tampering may present a nuisance or hindrance for the text critic seeking to reconstruct the "original text," for the grammarian they provide indirect evidence of ancient discomfort with grammatical or lexical features of the text. We have also occasionally taken note of issues of text segmentation and punctuation variants (now nicely catalogued in the Fourth Revised Edition of the UBS text), where those points affect interpretation.

This book is not a commentary of the traditional sort, which seeks, through philological and cultural analysis of text and context, to elucidate the theological meaning of the document under consideration. (Ironically, many of the scholarly commentaries produced in the past century may also fail to qualify by that definition!) Nor does it attempt to deal with the traditional issues often associated with the task of a commentary, such as authorship, date, provenance, and so forth. Rather, this volume serves as a "prequel" to commentary proper. Properly understood, the vocabulary and grammar of any document, including that of the sacred Scriptures, provide the foundation upon which exegesis can construct, or better reconstruct, the message of the text. Rarely have we found, at least in the case of Acts, that these grammatical observations *prove* any particular exegetical decision. We have found, however, that careful attention to such issues frequently renders interpretive options unlikely or improbable, some of which until now have found a more or less secure position in the history of interpretation. It is on these points that we have engaged the rich commentary tradition on Acts that extends back at least until the time of John Chrysostom, the "golden-mouth" preacher/bishop of the fourth century C.E. Our interaction with these commentaries, however, is selective and illustrative and should by no means be understood as an attempt to engage the secondary literature in an exhaustive manner. Our task has not been to *correct* the commentary tradition, but rather to examine the grammatical foundations of certain popular interpretations.

Since our approach to the functions of verb tenses and participles is superficially inconsistent—we list functions for the latter but not for the former—some explanation is in order. Traditional grammatical analyses of New Testament texts have a long history of blurring the boundaries between form and function. Most New Testament Greek grammars describe the tense system as being formally fairly simple (only six tenses), but functionally complex. The aorist tense, it is often said, can function in a wide variety of ways that are associated with labels such as, "ingressive," "gnomic," "constative," "epistolary," "proleptic," and so forth. Similar functional complexity is posited for the other tenses.

In recent years, as biblical scholars have become more conversant in modern linguistics, there has been a move toward abandoning such labels in recognition of the fact that such "functions" are not a feature of the tenses themselves but rather are derived from the context. Indeed, the positing of such "functions" typically stems not from a careful analysis of Greek *syntax*, but rather from grappling with the challenges of *translating* Greek verbs into English.

Another important development with regard to the Greek verbal system has been a move toward abandoning systems that define Greek tenses in terms of temporal reference and arguing for an aspectual basis for the tenses. Perhaps most influential in recent years has been the work of Stanley E. Porter. In what follows, we will assume that Porter is essentially correct in describing the Greek tenses in the following terms.

The aorist tense is aspectually perfective (or completive), i.e., authors use this tense to depict the action as complete. Used in narrative texts like Acts, the aorist functions as the default or least marked tense. Consequently, it is typically used to present information within a narrative as background material and is the tense used to carry the story along. The imperfect and present tenses, on the other hand, are both aspectually imperfective, i.e., they indicate that the author is portraying the action as incomplete or in progress. They are semantically more marked than the aorist tense and thus often serve on the discourse level to identify foreground material. Finally, the perfect and pluperfect tenses are aspectually stative, i.e., they focus on the verbal process as a state of affairs or condition. They are semantically the most marked of the tenses and are often used to highlight material within a discourse that is particularly significant (Porter uses the term "frontground" to describe their discourse function).

In light of this theoretical perspective and our desire to avoid confusing issues of translation with issues of syntax, we have chosen to avoid tense labels such as ingressive, iterative, and so forth, in an effort to help mitigate the tendency of some to maintain that the aorist, for example, *emphasizes* the beginning of an action. On the contrary, Koine Greek had other tools that allowed writers to emphasize semantic features such as this. By dispensing with these labels, we do not intend to communicate that such semantic features are insignificant to readers of the Greek New Testament. Instead, we want to emphasize that such nuances are essentially translation issues rather than syntactic issues. (Failure to distinguish between syntactic and translation issues has, for example, led many scholars to identify syntactically adjectival participles as adverbial because the English translation requires an adverbial rendering; see Culy 2004.) In short, Greek verb tenses do not *denote* semantic features such as ingressive, iterative, and so forth; they certainly do not *emphasize* such notions; at best they *allow* for ingressive or iterative translations. We have not, however, left the reader completely without guidance. In the commentary that follows, readers can refer to our translation to determine the verbal nuance that we deemed most appropriate given contextual factors.

Finally, as with tense "functions," traditional discussions of the function of participles have been somewhat misleading. In describing how a participle functions, scholars are typically seeking to identify the semantic relationship between the participial clause and the clause it modifies. Such an identification must rely, in large part, on pragmatic features within the context. At this point, however, we are hedging our bets. Daniel B. Wallace (1996) has demonstrated that there is some correlation between the combination of tenses used with participles and the verbs they modify and the function of the participle. For example, when writers want to introduce an event that serves as an attendant circumstance of an aorist verb they use an aorist participle (typically preceding the main verb). Our own analysis has revealed that when writers want to introduce an event that serves as an attendant circumstance of an imperfect or present tense verb they use a present participle, i.e., a participle that is *aspectually equivalent* to the main verb, as in the case of aorist participles. Similar correspondences prevail with other functions of the participle suggesting that context is not the sole determiner of a participle's function. We have, therefore, chosen to follow the traditional practice of noting the participle's most likely function.

Current Research on Acts

"A storm center" (van Unnik). "Shifting sands" (Talbert 1976). "A fruitful field" (Gasque). These are but a few of the epithets used to describe the scholarly interpretation of the Acts of the Apostles in the twentieth century. The spate of commentaries in English and collected essays over the past decade suggests continued and sustained interest in Acts (*commentaries:* Barrett; Fitzmyer 1998; Johnson; Polhill; Talbert 1998; Witherington 1998; *collected essays:* Keathley; Marconi et al.; Marshall and Peterson; Moessner; Neyrey; Parsons and Tyson; Richard; Thompson and Phillips; Tyson 1988; Verheyden; Witherington 1996).

Since van Unnik, surveyors of the Lukan landscape have typically categorized the scholarship on Acts in terms of interest in Luke the historian, Luke the theologian, and more recently, Luke the litterateur. The move from form and source criticism (Dibelius et al), which focused on Luke as an historian, to redaction criticism (Conzelmann et al), which focused on Luke as a theologian, to the newer literary studies, which focused on Luke as a creative writer (Tannehill et al), have been well documented in the surveys of Acts research (see esp. Powell). The attention Acts has generated has not always been positive. As an historian, though he had his defenders (see Ramsey, Gasque, Marshall, Hemer), Luke was routinely criticized for his unreliable depictions of various characters (e.g., Vielhauer on Paul) and events (eg., Knox on the Jerusalem conference). As a theologian, Luke was accused, among other things, of advocating a triumphalistic "theology of glory" that was inferior to Paul's "theology of the cross" and of replacing the pristine eschatology of early Christianity with a three-stage salvation history—an "early Catholicism" shaped by the delay of the Parousia that represented a degenerative step away from the primitive Christian kerygma, proclaiming the imminent return of Jesus (so Käsemann). Even Luke's abilities as a writer have been called into question from time to time (see Dawsey).

This rubric of Luke as historian, theologian, and writer, remains useful for describing works that have appeared particularly within the last decade or so, albeit with certain new nuances. Given the sea of literature and the already very competent surveys of scholarship, the following summary focuses mainly (though not exclusively) on book-length studies of Acts or Luke/Acts (but not Luke alone) that have appeared since Gasque's summary or research was written. This section also overlaps to some limited extent with Mark Powell's fine summary of Acts scholarship.

Luke the Historian

While the question of the identity of the author of the Lukan writings no longer invigorates scholarly discussion as it once did, there are still those who give ample attention to defending or refuting the traditional attribution to Luke the physician (see the discussion in Fitzmyer 1989, 1998). Others have departed from the traditional question of authorship to examine the social location of the implied author of Luke/Acts (Robbins in Neyrey) or, accepting the common authorship of Luke and Acts, have probed its implications for the study of the genre, literary patterns, and theological themes of the Lukan writings (Parsons and Pervo).

Nor can the question of Luke's historical reliability be considered resolved. On the one hand are those many erudite scholars who continue, in the spirit of William Ramsay, to defend Luke's reliability. In addition to Hemer and Witherington (1998), many of the contributors to the multi-volume series on *The Book of Acts in Its Ancient Literary Setting* have as one of their goals the defense of Luke's historical accuracy (see Winter). On the other hand, Gerd Lüdemann, in his attempts to separate tradition from redaction in Acts, has claimed that while Luke preserves individual and isolated facts accurately, much of his chronology and framework are secondary, and Lüdemann rejects out of hand all reports of the miraculous. Such presuppositions on the part of the interpreter inevitably and profoundly shape the conclusions drawn about the historicity of a narrative like Acts (see appendix in Talbert 1997). Critical evaluation of the historicity of Acts continues with the work of the Acts Seminar, a group of scholars convened by Robert Funk and the Westar Institute, to evaluate the reliability of early Christian history as depicted by Luke, in ways analogous to what the Jesus Seminar (sponsored by the same institute) attempted with the historical Jesus.

More recently, some have turned away from questions of history in Acts to the place of Acts in history. In a collection of essays edited by Jerome Neyrey, various contributors examine sociological aspects of the Lukan writing, from the role of ritual and ceremony in Acts to the significance of the social relations in pre-industrial cities or the countryside to the importance of the social values of honor/shame for reading the Lukan writings. Others have employed sociological criticism to examine Luke/Acts as a document of "political legitimation" for the early Christian movement (Esler). Still others have examined the cultural context of Acts for understanding such topics as magic and miracle in Luke/Acts (Garrett). These studies have profitably used the narrative of (Luke and) Acts to open up the sometimes unspoken cultural codes, mores, and values that nevertheless pervade the text and shape our reception of it. Finally, others have attempted to situate (Luke/)Acts in its larger literary and intellectual environment (see, e.g., Alexander; Squires). Attention to the reception of Acts in subsequent history, especially in the "premodern" period, fits also under this rubric of "Acts in history" (one eagerly awaits, for example, the contribution on Acts in the Ancient Commentary on Scripture series). The relationship between Acts and history is much more broadly conceived these days than it once was.

Luke the Theologian

Studies on various aspects of Lukan theology continue to pour out, confirming Charles Talbert's (1976) observation a quarter century ago that Hans Conzelmann's theological synthesis no longer held a consensus among scholars. Conzelmann's failure has not totally discouraged others from making similar attempts to synthesize Luke's theology (e.g. Fitzmyer 1989; Jervell; Pokorny), although far more prevalent are studies that deal with specific aspects of Luke's theology (Marshall and Petersen; see the bibliography in Verheyden, 22-45). One notes also that these studies employ a plethora of methodologies to characterize Luke's theology.

The end of the twentieth century has also witnessed a turn in some quarters of biblical scholarship from theology understood in redaction-critical terms to ideology shaped by advocacy criticism. This turn has had its impact on Acts scholarship. Feminist scholars have examined anew the Lukan writings for their perspective on gender. In *The Women's Bible Commentary,* Jane Schaberg reaches the radical conclusion that Luke (and by extension Acts) is the "most dangerous book in all the Bible" (Schaberg in Newsom and Ringe). This view is balanced by more judicious studies of gender in Luke (in addition to various articles, see the book-length studies by Seim; Reimer; Arlandson). The question of Luke's "anti-Judaism" has been taken up again by Joseph Tyson (1999). Though calling Tyson himself a "advocacy critic" would be a misnomer, he does chronicle the anti-Jewish (both intentional and inadvertent) attitudes prevalent in much of the history of Lukan scholarship, though given Luke's characterization of the Christian movement in Acts as a Jewish sect one might rightly question Tyson's assertion that Luke himself was anti-Jewish in any modern sense of the term. Again, interest in the theological shape of Acts has not diminished, but there is little agreement on the most appropriate methods for describing that theology and for assessing its hermeneutical value for contemporary communities.

Luke the Writer

The explosion of new literary approaches in New Testament studies that began in the 1980s has certainly left its mark on the study of Acts. In the last decade alone, too many narrative and literary-critical studies have appeared to enumerate (but see especially Brawley; Darr; Gowler; Kurz; Matson; Shepherd; Tannehill). Despite the widely acknowledged achievements of these studies in refocusing our attention on the narrative as a whole (and the attendant issues of plot, characterization, and intertextuality, *inter alia*), the limitations are well known as well. Drawing its methodology largely from the secular field of literary criticism, narrative criticism uses terminology to describe techniques and literary phenomena that might be appropriate for nineteenth- and twentieth-century novels, but not necessarily appropriate for first-century narratives. This problem is often acknowledged but seldom addressed.

Given this oft-cited criticism of applying modern theory to ancient narrative, it is surprising, perhaps, to note the lack of studies that attend to Acts from the perspective of ancient rhetorical criticism. Such studies are not altogether missing, especially on the speeches in Acts (Soards; Witherington 1998). These studies (as well as numerous articles) have advanced convincing arguments regarding Luke's knowledge of rhetorical conventions in the speeches. Thus, it would appear that studies that read the narrative portions of Acts in light of ancient rhetoric, and especially in light of ancient *progymnasmata* (elementary rhetorical exercises for speaking and writing), would hold great promise in further illuminating Luke's rhetorical strategies employed not only in the composition of the Third Gospel (see e.g., Robbins in Moessner; and Fearghail), but Acts as well.

The study of the author of Acts as a writer continues to include consideration of the text's genre, although no consensus has been reached. In addition to those who maintain Acts represents anything from a *sui generis* to a *genus mixtum*, advocates for (Luke/)Acts as ancient biography (see recently Talbert 1988), some form of ancient historiography (Sterling), or a kind of ancient novel (Pervo) can still be found. Finally, while the search for oral and/or written sources in Acts has subsided, the interest in Luke's use of Scripture as a key to his hermeneutic and theology has increased (in addition to Brawley and Moessner already cited; see Bock; Evans and Sanders). How best to appreciate Luke's literary prowess is no less contested than are issues of history and theology in relation to the Lukan writings.

Conclusion

Long ago W. C. van Unnik rightly warned against the biblical scholar playing the role of prophet in trying to predict the future shape of Lukan studies (van Unnik). Given what transpired in the intervening decades between van Unnik's caveat and now, his words seem even more prudent. Nevertheless, it is safe to say that work on Luke as historian, theologian, and writer, with all of their mutations noted above, will continue well into this century. Studies that explore the rhetorical shape of social conventions (e.g., hospitality, friendship, and benefaction) in terms of how they illuminate Lukan theological perspectives will be especially welcome.

A HANDBOOK ON THE GREEK TEXT OF ACTS

Acts 1:1–14

[1]I wrote my first book, Theophilus, about all the things that Jesus began both to do and to teach [2]until the very day he was taken up, after he had given commands through the Holy Spirit to the apostles, whom he had chosen. [3]After he had suffered, he showed that he was alive by many proofs and by appearing to them for forty days and telling them things about the kingdom of God.

[4]While he was with them, he commanded them not to depart from Jerusalem but to wait for what the Father had promised, "which you heard from me. [5]For John baptized with water, but you will be baptized with the Holy Spirit, not many days from now." [6]Then those who were gathered asked him, "Lord, are you going to restore the kingdom to Israel at this time?" [7]But he said to them, "It is not for you to know the times or seasons that the Father has established by his own authority. [8]But you will receive power when the Holy Spirit comes upon you, and you will be my witnesses in Jerusalem, throughout Judea and Samaria, and to the end of the earth."

[9]When he had said these things, while they were watching, he was lifted up and a cloud took him up from their sight. [10]And as they were staring into the sky, while he was going, two men dressed in brilliant clothes stood among them! [11]They said, "Galileans, why are you standing (there) staring at the sky? This Jesus, who was taken up from you into the sky, will come (back) in the very same manner that you saw him go into the sky."

[12]Then they returned to Jerusalem from the mountain called 'The Olive Grove,' which is near Jerusalem—(just) a sabbath day's journey away. [13]When they entered (the city), they went up to the upstairs room where they were staying—Peter, John, James, Andrew, Philip, Thomas, Bartholomew, Matthew, James (the son) of Alphaeus, Simon the Zealot, and Judas (the son) of James. [14]All of them devoted themselves together to prayer along with the women, Mary the mother of Jesus, and his siblings.

1:1 Τὸν μὲν πρῶτον λόγον ἐποιησάμην περὶ πάντων, ὦ Θεόφιλε, ὧν ἤρξατο ὁ Ἰησοῦς ποιεῖν τε καὶ διδάσκειν,

μὲν. The author of Acts frequently uses μὲν (especially to begin sections) without a δέ (see Barrett, 65).

πρῶτον. In classical Greek, this term was typically used to refer to the first in a series. In the Koine period, however, it was often used interchangeably with πρότερος to identify something as "earlier, former" (see also 7:12; 12:10). The use of πρῶτον here, then, does *not* imply that Acts is the second volume of a multivolume series (*pace* Barrett, 65). For a similar introduction to a multivolume work see Philo, *Quod Omnis* 1: Ὁ μὲν πρότερος λόγος ἦν ἡμῖν, ὦ Θεόδοτε, περὶ τοῦ δοῦλον εἶναι πάντα φαῦλον.

λόγον. Here, "book, account." Louw and Nida (33.51) suggest that λόγος may denote a more formal treatment of the subject matter than γράμμα.

ἐποιησάμην. Aor mid ind 1st sg ποιέω.

πάντων. Luke is clearly being hyperbolic here (see 1:18).

Θεόφιλε. Vocative.

ὧν. Genitive by attraction to πάντων. Sometimes a relative pronoun takes the case of its antecedent rather than the case it would bear as a constituent of the relative clause (in the present instance we would expect the relative pronoun to be accusative as the object of the two infinitives). This phenomenon, known as attraction, occurs eighteen times in the Book of Acts (see also 1:21, 22; 2:22; 3:25; 6:10; 7:16, 17, 45; 9:36; 10:39; 13:38; 17:31; 20:38; 22:10, 15; 24:13; 26:2) and a total of more than fifty times throughout the NT. Attraction appears to be a stylistic device with no pragmatic function.

ἤρξατο. Aor mid ind 3rd sg ἄρχω. Unlike many other scholars, Witherington (10) argues that the verb ἤρξατο in this construction does not necessarily imply that the present work is a continuation of a previous work. In his view, ἤρξατο ὁ Ἰησοῦς ποιεῖν τε καὶ διδάσκειν means nothing more than "Jesus did and said."

ποιεῖν. Pres act inf ποιέω (complementary).

διδάσκειν. Pres act inf διδάσκω (complementary).

1:2 ἄχρι ἧς ἡμέρας ἐντειλάμενος τοῖς ἀποστόλοις διὰ πνεύματος ἁγίου οὓς ἐξελέξατο ἀνελήμφθη·

ἄχρι ἧς ἡμέρας. In this construction, known as an internally headed relative clause, the head noun or antecedent (here, ἡμέρας) is actually inside the relative clause that modifies it, though it gets its case from the main clause (in this instance, the case comes from the preposition ἄχρι). A more "typical" Koine construction would have been ἄχρι ἡμέρας ἧς (cf. 1:22). The placement of the noun probably intensifies the expression: "until the *very* day."

ἐντειλάμενος. Aor mid dep ptc masc nom sg ἐντέλλομαι (temporal).

ἀποστόλοις. In Acts, the term ἀπόστολος is reserved for the Twelve, except in 14:4, 14, where it is applied to Paul and Barnabas.

διὰ πνεύματος ἁγίου. This prepositional phrase must modify ἐντειλάμενος rather than ἐξελέξατο. In order to modify the latter it would have to follow the relative pronoun οὓς, which marks a clause boundary. While this proposition is unusual, it is consistent with Luke's theme of God's servants being empowered by the Holy Spirit.

ἐξελέξατο. Aor mid ind 3rd sg ἐκλέγω. The middle voice is "indirect" or "benefactive," i.e., the action of the verb is performed for the subject's benefit.

ἀνελήμφθη. Aor pass ind 3rd sg ἀναλαμβάνω.

1:3 οἷς καὶ παρέστησεν ἑαυτὸν ζῶντα μετὰ τὸ παθεῖν αὐτὸν ἐν πολλοῖς τεκμηρίοις, δι' ἡμερῶν τεσσεράκοντα ὀπτανόμενος αὐτοῖς καὶ λέγων τὰ περὶ τῆς βασιλείας τοῦ θεοῦ·

οἷς. The antecedent of the relative pronoun is τοῖς ἀποστόλοις. Dative indirect object of παρέστησεν.

παρέστησεν. Aor act ind 3rd sg παρίστημι.

ἑαυτὸν. The accusative direct object of παρέστησεν, which is transitive in this verse.

ζῶντα. Pres act ptc masc acc sg ζάω. The participle functions as the complement in an object-complement double accusative construction. In this construction, the second accusative (either a noun, adjective, or participle) complements the direct object in that it predicates something about it (Wallace 1985, 93). We have not maintained Wallace's distinction between object-complement and person-thing double accusatives since in some cases the latter is appropriately labeled "object-complement" while in others the two accusatives represent a different syntactic phenomenon altogether (see 8:25 on πολλάς κώμας and 13:32 on ὑμᾶς).

μετὰ τὸ παθεῖν. Aor act inf πάσχω. The construction μετά τό plus infinitive is used to indicate antecedent time, that is, the event of the infinitive precedes the event of the main verb (Wallace 1996, 595). Eight of the fifteen occurrences of this construction in the NT are found in Luke/Acts (see 7:4; 10:41; 15:13; 19:21; 20:1; Luke 12:5; 22:20; Robertson 1934, 1074). παθεῖν may be an example of synecdoche (see 1:22 on τοῦ βαπτίσματος Ἰωάννου), with "suffering" being used to refer to the entire experience leading up to and including Jesus' death (cf. Barrett, 69).

αὐτὸν. The accusative pronoun is an example of what has generally been called either the "accusative subject of the infinitive" or the "accusative of general reference." Neither label is fully satisfactory. The former has in its favor the fact that the accusative noun is the conceptual "subject" of the infinitive verb. The latter has in its favor the fact that, strictly speaking, only finite verbs can take a "subject." Some linguists have argued that in infinitive constructions that are not part of a prepositional phrase, as here (μετὰ τὸ παθεῖν αὐτὸν), "raising" has occurred. The noun that we expect to be the "subject" of the infinitive has been "raised" from the infinitive (or lower) clause to the main clause, where it functions syntactically as the direct object of the verb. It is, therefore, placed in the accusative case. While such an analysis may account for most infinitival constructions, it cannot explain the accusative case marking where the infinitive clause is part of a prepositional phrase, as in the present verse. It cannot be said that the "subject of the infinitive" takes its case from the preposition since it always bears accusative case even when used with a preposition that takes a noun in a different case (see, e.g., 2:1 where the "subject of the infinitive" follows the preposition ἐν and is still in the accusative rather than the dative case). In what follows, we use the label "accusative subject of the infinitive" because it is, for the most part, a helpful description of the phenomenon.

ἐν πολλοῖς τεκμηρίοις. Instrumental/means modifying παρέστησεν.

τεκμηρίοις. The term τεκμήριον referred to conclusive evidence that was irrefutable (cf. Quintilian, *Inst. Or.* 5.9.3; cited in Witherington 1998, 108; LN 28.45).

δι' ἡμερῶν τεσσεράκοντα. The prepositional phrase need not indicate continuous action. Jesus appeared from time to time over the course of a forty-day period (cf. Moule, 56; BDF §223.1).

ὀπτανόμενος. Pres dep ptc masc nom sg ὀπτάνομαι (means, not manner; contra Rogers and Rogers, 229).

λέγων. Pres act ptc masc nom sg λέγω (means).

τὰ. Although the neuter article could be construed as substantival, it is better to view it as a "nominalizer"—a word (or affix) that changes the following word, phrase, or clause into a substantive. The case of the nominalizer is determined by its syntactic role in the sentence. As the direct object of the participle λέγων, the substantival expression τὰ περὶ τῆς βασιλείας τοῦ θεοῦ is placed in the accusative case.

τῆς βασιλείας τοῦ θεοῦ. Barrett (70) notes that "Kingdom of God is used several times in Acts as a general term covering the whole of the Christian proclamation (1.3; 8.12; 19.8; 20.25 [here without God]; 28.23, 31)."

1:4 καὶ συναλιζόμενος παρήγγειλεν αὐτοῖς ἀπὸ Ἱεροσολύμων μὴ χωρίζεσθαι, ἀλλὰ περιμένειν τὴν ἐπαγγελίαν τοῦ πατρὸς ἣν ἠκούσατέ μου,

συναλιζόμενος. Pres dep ptc masc nom sg συναλίζομαι (temporal). It is unclear whether this participle should be taken in its regular sense, "to be gathered together with someone" (cf. Josephus, *Jewish War* 3.429), as an orthographic variant of συναυλιζόμενος ("to spend the night with someone" or "to stay with someone"), or as related to the noun ἅλας (thus, "to eat salt with someone" or "to eat together," cf. Barrett, 71–72; see also Bruce, 101). On the whole, there is little rationale for not taking the verb in its usual sense. The singular form is appropriate since it modifies a singular main verb, and it is difficult to argue that this rare verb should be used in the perfect rather than the present tense (contra Bruce, 101).

παρήγγειλεν. Aor act ind 3rd sg παραγγέλλω.

χωρίζεσθαι. Pres pass inf χωρίζω (indirect discourse).

περιμένειν. Pres act inf περιμένω (indirect discourse).

τοῦ πατρὸς. The article may function as a possessive pronoun here ("my"; Wallace 1996, 215). The genitive noun denotes either the source of τὴν ἐπαγγελίαν, or the agent (subjective genitive) of the implicit event expressed by τὴν ἐπαγγελίαν ("God promised").

ἣν ἠκούσατέ μου. As is typical in Hellenistic texts, the preceding indirect discourse gives way to direct discourse (which continues through v. 5; cf. 23:22; 25:4–5; BDF §470.2).

ἠκούσατέ. Aor act ind 2nd pl ἀκούω. The second accent comes from the enclitic μου. A clitic is a word that appears as a discreet word in the syntax but is pronounced as if it were part of another word. *En*clitics "give" their accent to the *preceding* word.

μου. Genitive of source.

1:5 ὅτι Ἰωάννης μὲν ἐβάπτισεν ὕδατι, ὑμεῖς δὲ ἐν πνεύματι βαπτισθήσεσθε ἁγίῳ οὐ μετὰ πολλὰς ταύτας ἡμέρας.

ὅτι. Introduces the reason why the disciples should wait.

ἐβάπτισεν. Aor act ind 3rd sg βαπτίζω.

ὕδατι. Dative of instrument or location. A decision between the two options cannot be made through reference to the syntax. If ἐν πνεύματι ἁγίῳ were parallel (it is not since it has a preposition), it would lend support to the instrumental view.

ἐν πνεύματι. Probably instrumental. The fronting (see 3:13 on ὑμεῖς) of part of the prepositional phrase (ἁγίῳ is left behind) highlights the contrast between John's baptism and Jesus' baptism.

βαπτισθήσεσθε. Fut pass ind 2nd pl βαπτίζω.

οὐ μετὰ πολλὰς ταύτας ἡμέρας. Litotes—a figure of speech in which a statement is made by negating the opposite idea. For example, "she is *not* a *bad* tennis player" means "she is a *good* tennis player" (see also 4:20; 5:26; 12:18; 14:28; 15:2; 17:4, 12; 19:11, 23, 24; 20:12; 21:39; 25:6; 26:19, 26; 27:14, 20; 28:2; and perhaps 14:17). Here, "not after many days" means, "not many days from now" or "very soon."

1:6 Οἱ μὲν οὖν συνελθόντες ἠρώτων αὐτὸν λέγοντες, Κύριε, εἰ ἐν τῷ χρόνῳ τούτῳ ἀποκαθιστάνεις τὴν βασιλείαν τῷ Ἰσραήλ;

Οἱ. The article modifies the participle συνελθόντες as a nominalizer (see 1:3 on τὰ; see also 2:41; 8:4, 25; 11:19; 15:3, 30; 23:16).

μὲν οὖν. According to Levinsohn (1987, 139), when οὖν occurs in the narrative of Acts, it makes "explicit the close consequential relationship that exists between the elements it links. The second event is the direct result of the first, and closely conforms with its demands and implications." Here, the disciples' question naturally follows Jesus' statement in vv. 4–5 (142). Furthermore, μέν οὖν is always prospective, that is, it always anticipates an additional event or proposition (usually introduced by δέ) to follow the event or proposition that it introduces (see Levinsohn 1987, 141–50). "In 1:4–6, the disciples' initial response to Jesus' charge not to depart from Jerusalem, but to wait for the promise of the Father (v 4), does not conform to his goal in giving the directive. The use of *men* in v 6 both indicates this and anticipates their compliance. It is clear from 1:12–2:1 that the disciples did comply. However, there is no specific sentence, introduced by *de*, which spells it out" (145).

συνελθόντες. Aor act ptc masc nom pl συνέρχομαι (substantival). There is nothing in the context to suggest that the article should be taken substantivally and the participle temporally ("they, then, when they had assembled"; contra Barrett, 75). The obligatory position of μὲν οὖν necessitates that the article be separated from the participle it modifies.

ἠρώτων. Impf act ind 3rd pl ἐρωτάω. Barrett (75) states that the imperfect is used because the action of questioning is incomplete until the answer is given. The fact that this verb is used in the aorist tense in analogous passages, however, makes such a claim questionable.

λέγοντες. Pres act ptc masc nom pl λέγω (attendant circumstance, redundant). The redundant participle reflects a common Semitic idiom. Although most "attendant circumstances" are introduced with an aorist participle that precedes an aorist main verb, where the main verb is imperfect, a participle introducing an "attendant circumstance" will be present tense, as here.

Κύριε. Vocative.

εἰ. Introduces a direct question.

ἀποκαθιστάνεις. Pres act ind 2nd sg ἀποκαθιστάνω.

τῷ Ἰσραήλ. Dative of advantage.

1:7 εἶπεν δὲ πρὸς αὐτούς, Οὐχ ὑμῶν ἐστιν γνῶναι χρόνους ἢ καιροὺς οὓς ὁ πατὴρ ἔθετο ἐν τῇ ἰδίᾳ ἐξουσίᾳ,

εἶπεν. Aor act ind 3rd sg λέγω.

ὑμῶν. The genitive functions as the predicate of the main verb and should probably be viewed as "possessive." It may be better, however, to view ἐστιν with a genitive predicate pronoun as an idiom meaning something like "to be one's prerogative."

ἐστιν. Pres act ind 3rd sg εἰμί. In the present indicative (except εἶ), the verb εἰμί is an enclitic, that is, it (usually) loses its accent to the preceding word (see 1:4 on ἠκούσατέ).

γνῶναι. Aor act inf γινώσκω. The infinitival clause could be viewed as either epexegetical, explaining what does not belong to the apostles (so Rogers and Rogers, 230), or as the subject of the main verb: "To know times and seasons is not for you."

χρόνους ἢ καιροὺς. One should probably not look for a difference in meaning between the two near synonyms (cf. LN 67.78; Barrett, 78; BDF §446). The use of both (as a doublet; see 2:43 on τέρατα καὶ σημεῖα) probably emphasizes the fact that any knowledge related to the time of the restoration of Israel is not the prerogative of the disciples.

ἔθετο. Aor mid ind 3rd sg τίθημι.

ἐν τῇ ἰδίᾳ ἐξουσίᾳ. Barrett (78) argues that the prepositional phrase should be understood as "*within* his own authority" rather than "*by* his own authority." Such an interpretation is consistent with the use of τίθημι with ἐν in Acts (5:4, 25; 7:16) and elsewhere in the NT (Rom 9:33; 2 Cor 5:19; 1 Pet 2:6). In each of these cases, however, the noun in the prepositional phrase is appropriately viewed as a location. Such a sense is difficult to maintain with the noun ἐξουσίᾳ. It is, therefore, probably better to view the prepositional phrase as instrumental.

1:8 ἀλλὰ λήμψεσθε δύναμιν ἐπελθόντος τοῦ ἁγίου πνεύματος ἐφ᾽ ὑμᾶς καὶ ἔσεσθέ μου μάρτυρες ἔν τε Ἰερουσαλὴμ καὶ [ἐν] πάσῃ τῇ Ἰουδαίᾳ καὶ Σαμαρείᾳ καὶ ἕως ἐσχάτου τῆς γῆς.

ἀλλὰ. The conjunction introduces a strong contrast between what the followers can expect (v. 8) and what they cannot (v. 7; cf. 2:16).

λήμψεσθε. Fut mid dep ind 2nd pl λαμβάνω.

δύναμιν. The context makes it clear that some sort of "*divine* power" is in view. The full import of this expression is only seen as the "acts of the apostles" are subsequently recounted.

ἐπελθόντος. Aor act ptc neut gen sg ἐπέρχομαι. Genitive absolute, temporal. The genitive absolute is used when the subject of the participle (which must also be in the genitive case) is different from the subject of the main clause (see Healey and Healey; cf. 7:21 on ἐκτεθέντος; 19:30 on αὐτὸν). Although genitive absolute constructions typically occur prior to the finite clause they modify, here the the genitive absolute follows the finite clause (cf. 4:37; 13:24).

τοῦ ἁγίου πνεύματος. Genitive subject (see above on ἐπελθόντος).

ἐφ' ὑμᾶς. Although it is a common practice in Koine Greek, strictly speaking the inclusion of the preposition is redundant, since its sense has already been expressed by the compound verb.

ἔσεσθέ. Fut ind 2nd pl εἰμί. The second accent comes from the enclitic μου (see 1:4 on ἠκούσατέ).

μου μάρτυρες. It is difficult to label the function of the genitive pronoun in this noun phrase. Rogers and Rogers (230) argue that it should be called either possessive or objective. The head noun, μάρτυρες, carries an implicit verbal idea ("to bear witness"), while the genitive pronoun is the one concerning whom testimony is offered. "Genitive of reference" may be appropriate.

μάρτυρες. Predicate nominative.

ἔν. The accent comes from the enclitic τε (see 1:4 on ἠκούσατέ).

ἕως. The preposition is often used to denote "extension up to or as far as a goal" (LN 84.19).

ἐσχάτου τῆς γῆς. Although the NRSV renders this phrases "the *ends* of the earth," perhaps in accord with the English idiom, the singular ἐσχάτου may indicate that Luke had a particular place in mind (Rome or Spain). If this is an indirect reference to Rome, which was widely known as the ὀμφαλός ("navel, center") of the ancient world, the relegation of the world's political center to geographical obscurity ("the end of the earth") would have been highly ironic (see Parsons 1998).

1:9 καὶ ταῦτα εἰπὼν βλεπόντων αὐτῶν ἐπήρθη, καὶ νεφέλη ὑπέλαβεν αὐτὸν ἀπὸ τῶν ὀφθαλμῶν αὐτῶν.

εἰπὼν. Aor act ptc masc nom sg λέγω (temporal).

βλεπόντων. Pres act ptc masc gen pl βλέπω. Genitive absolute (see 1:8 on ἐπελθόντος), temporal. While the events expressed by the aorist participle, εἰπών, precede the event of the main verb, the event expressed by the present participle is contemporaneous with the event of the main verb.

αὐτῶν. Genitive subject (see 1:8 on ἐπελθόντος).

ἐπήρθη. Aor pass ind 3rd sg ἐπαίρω.

ὑπέλαβεν. Aor act ind 3rd sg ὑπολαμβάνω.

ἀπὸ. Separation.

τῶν ὀφθαλμῶν αὐτῶν. A metonym for "their sight." Metonymy is a figure of speech in which one term is used in place of another with which it is associated. In the expression, "he was reading the prophet Isaiah" (Acts 8:28), the writer ("the prophet Isaiah") is used as a metonym for his writings ("the book that the prophet Isaiah wrote").

1:10 καὶ ὡς ἀτενίζοντες ἦσαν εἰς τὸν οὐρανὸν πορευομένου αὐτοῦ, καὶ ἰδοὺ ἄνδρες δύο παρειστήκεισαν αὐτοῖς ἐν ἐσθήσεσι λευκαῖς,

ὡς. Temporal (see 18:5).

ἀτενίζοντες. Pres act ptc masc nom pl ἀτενίζω (imperfect periphrastic; the imperfect of εἰμί plus a present participle is analogous to a simple imperfect verb).

ἦσαν. Impf ind 3rd pl εἰμί.

τὸν οὐρανὸν. This term (in the singular or plural) can refer to either the "sky" or "heaven" (cf. LN 1.5, 1.11).

πορευομένου. Pres dep ptc masc gen sg πορεύομαι. Genitive absolute (see 1:8 on ἐπελθόντος), temporal.

αὐτοῦ. Genitive subject (see 1:8 on ἐπελθόντος).

ἰδοὺ. This particle (often preceded by καί in narrative texts) is used to seize the listener's/reader's attention and/or emphasize the following statement (LN 91.13; cf. Porter 1989, 123).

ἄνδρες δύο. "When *idou* or *kai* (. . .) *idou* is used in connection with the introduction of a new participant . . . the subject always precedes the independent verb of the sentence" (Levinsohn 1987, 7).

παρειστήκεισαν. Plprf act ind 3rd pl παρίστημι. The use of the pluperfect verb (along with καί at the beginning of this clause) probably implies that the followers of Jesus were so engrossed in his departure that they failed to notice that two "men" had been standing among them for some time (cf. Levinsohn 1987, 93).

ἐν ἐσθήσεσι λευκαῖς. As with the English preposition "in," ἐν can be used by itself to express "*dressed* in" or "wearing."

λευκαῖς. The description of the clothes as "white" or "bright" helps identify the men as angels (Barrett, 83).

1:11 οἳ καὶ εἶπαν, Ἄνδρες Γαλιλαῖοι, τί ἑστήκατε [ἐμ]βλέποντες εἰς τὸν οὐρανόν; οὗτος ὁ Ἰησοῦς ὁ ἀναλημφθεὶς ἀφ' ὑμῶν εἰς τὸν οὐρανὸν οὕτως ἐλεύσεται ὃν τρόπον ἐθεάσασθε αὐτὸν πορευόμενον εἰς τὸν οὐρανόν.

οἵ. This form must be a relative pronoun rather than an article functioning like a pronoun (cf. 12:15) since there is no clitic (see 1:4) from which the article could have received the accent.

εἶπαν. Aor act ind 3rd pl λέγω.

Ἄνδρες. This vocative noun is used throughout Acts (29 times) as a formal opening to a speech. When it is followed by another vocative noun identifying the referents (elsewhere in Acts except 7:26; 14:15; 19:25; 27:10, 21, 25), it should be left untranslated.

Γαλιλαῖοι. Vocative.

ἑστήκατε. Prf act ind 2nd pl ἵστημι. In the NT, the perfect form of this verb is deponent and functions like a present tense verb (except perhaps in Rom 3:31).

[ἐμ]βλέποντες. Pres act ptc masc nom pl [ἐμ]βλέπω (manner). There is no reason to take ἑστήκατε [ἐμ]βλέποντες as a periphrastic construction (contra Dietrich, 209–10; cf. 26:22 on μαρτυρόμενος).

τὸν οὐρανόν. See 1:10.

ἀναλημφθεὶς. Aor pass ptc masc nom sg ἀναλαμβάνω (attributive).

οὕτως . . . ὃν τρόπον. The combination of the adverb and the relative expression makes the statement particularly emphatic (see below; cf. 27:25).

ἐλεύσεται. Fut mid dep ind 3rd sg ἔρχομαι.

ὃν τρόπον. The internally headed relative clause (see 1:2 on ἄχρι ἧς ἡμέρας) probably produces an intensive expression: "in the *very* same manner."

ἐθεάσασθε. Aor mid dep ind 2nd pl θεάομαι.

πορευόμενον. Pres dep ptc masc acc sg πορεύομαι. The participle functions as the complement in an object-complement double accusative construction (see 1:3 on ζῶντα).

τὸν οὐρανόν. See 1:10.

1:12 Τότε ὑπέστρεψαν εἰς Ἰερουσαλὴμ ἀπὸ ὄρους τοῦ καλουμένου Ἐλαιῶνος, ὅ ἐστιν ἐγγὺς Ἰερουσαλὴμ σαββάτου ἔχον ὁδόν.

Τότε. The adverb "indicates that the event it introduces is in 'close chronological sequence' with the event that led up to it. This means that no *unnecessary* action, delay or debate separates them" (Levinsohn 1987, 152).

ὑπέστρεψαν. Aor act ind 3rd pl ὑποστρέφω.

καλουμένου. Pres pass ptc neut gen sg καλέω (attributive).

Ἐλαιῶνος. Although typically identified as a "predicate genitive," the genitive noun actually serves as a complement in an object-complement double case construction that is used with a passive verb ("X is called 'Y' by someone"; cf. 1:23 on Βαρσαββᾶν; 3:2 on Ὡραίαν; 7:58 on Σαύλου; 8:10 on Μεγάλη; 9:11 on Εὐθεῖαν; 10:1 on Ἰταλικῆς; 10:18 on Πέτρος; 10:32 on Πέτρος; 11:15 on Πέτρον; 12:12 on Μάρκου; 12:25 on Μάρκον; 13:1 on Νίγερ; 27:8 on Λιμένας; 27:14 on Εὐρακύλων; and 27:16 on Καῦδα).

ὅ. The antecedent of this neuter nominative singular relative pronoun is the neuter genitive ὄρους.

ἐστιν. Pres act ind 3rd sg εἰμί. On the loss of accent, see 1:7 on ἐστιν.

σαββάτου ἔχον ὁδόν. Lit. "having a sabbath's journey." A "sabbath's journey" was equivalent to 2000 cubits (= 1120 meters; Barrett, 85) or about 3/4 of a mile.

ἔχον. Pres act ptc neut nom sg ἔχω. The neuter nominative (ἔχον ὁδόν) serves as a predicate of ἐστιν in apposition to ἐγγὺς Ἰερουσαλήμ.

1:13 καὶ ὅτε εἰσῆλθον, εἰς τὸ ὑπερῷον ἀνέβησαν οὗ ἦσαν καταμένοντες, ὅ τε Πέτρος καὶ Ἰωάννης καὶ Ἰάκωβος καὶ Ἀνδρέας, Φίλιππος καὶ Θωμᾶς, Βαρθολομαῖος καὶ Μαθθαῖος, Ἰάκωβος Ἁλφαίου καὶ Σίμων ὁ ζηλωτὴς καὶ Ἰούδας Ἰακώβου.

εἰσῆλθον. Aor act ind 3rd pl εἰσέρχομαι. The location (Jerusalem; v. 12) is left implicit.

ἀνέβησαν. Aor act ind 3rd pl ἀναβαίνω.

οὗ. The genitive relative pronoun without an antecedent functions like a locative adverb: "where" (cf. 2:2; 7:29, 52; 12:12; 16:13; 20:8; 25:10; 28:14).

ἦσαν. Impf ind 3rd pl εἰμί.

καταμένοντες. Pres act ptc masc nom pl καταμένω (imperfect periphrastic; see 1:10 on ἀτενίζοντες).

ὅ. The article should not be mistaken for a relative pronoun. The accent comes from the enclitic τε (see 1:4 on ἠκούσατέ).

Ἁλφαίου. Genitive of relationship; a shortened form of υἱός Ἁλφαίου.

ὁ ζηλωτής. Nominative in apposition to Σίμων. The term need not carry a partisan sense (see 21:20; 22:3; Bruce, 106).

'Ιακώβου. Genitive of relationship; a shortened form of υἱός 'Ιακώβου. On the identity of this "James," see Fitzmyer 1998, 215.

1:14 οὗτοι πάντες ἦσαν προσκαρτεροῦντες ὁμοθυμαδὸν τῇ προσευχῇ σὺν γυναιξὶν καὶ Μαριὰμ τῇ μητρὶ τοῦ'Ιησοῦ καὶ τοῖς ἀδελφοῖς αὐτοῦ.

ἦσαν. Impf ind 3rd pl εἰμί.

προσκαρτεροῦντες. Pres act ptc masc nom pl προσκαρτερέω (imperfect periphrastic; see 1:10 on ἀτενίζοντες).

ὁμοθυμαδόν. Ten of the eleven NT occurrences of this word are found in Acts (2:26; 4:24; 5:12; 7:57; 8:6; 12:20; 15:25; 18:12; 19:29; Romans 15:6). Barrett (88–89) notes that although the term can be used to denote unanimity, it often simply means "together." Its prevalence in Acts and the contexts in which it occurs (here, e.g., with προσκαρτεροῦντες), however, suggests that Luke was focusing on "unity of purpose."

τῇ προσευχῇ. Dative complement of προσκαρτερέω.

γυναιξὶν. It is unclear whether this term refers to "wives," or to "women" in general. Given the fact that the subject, "all these," refers to a list of men, a reference to "wives" is superficially the most natural way to take σὺν γυναιξὶν (cf. Barrett, 89). Furthermore, the reading of codex Bezae (σὺν ταῖς γυναιξὶν καὶ τέκνοις, "with their wives *and children*") makes it clear that at least one early scribe understood the term this way, although it is possible that the Western scribe was uncomfortable with a text that afforded women independent status as followers of Jesus and thus sought to reduce their role. Given the fact that Acts is the second of two volumes, however, and the fact that Luke spends a significant amount of time in the first chapter refreshing the memory of Theophilus, it would also be natural to "assume that Luke means the same women he had mentioned at the end of his first volume—female disciples (cf. Luke 23:55; 24:1, 9, 22)" (Witherington 1998, 113).

τῇ μητρὶ. Dative in apposition to Μαριάμ.

ἀδελφοῖς. Here, ἀδελφοῖς refers to literal "siblings" (cf. 1:15) or, less likely, "relatives" (see Fitzmyer 1998, 216–17; Barrett, 90).

Acts 1:15–26

[15]In those days Peter stood up among the believers—the crowd of

people together numbered one hundred and twenty people—and said, [16]“Fellow believers, it was necessary for the Scripture to be fulfilled that the Holy Spirit foretold through the mouth of David concerning Judas, who became a guide for those who arrested Jesus. [17]For he had been included among us and received a share of this ministry.” [18]So then, this man purchased a field using the money earned from his unjust deed and after becoming prostrate he burst open in the middle and all his insides poured out. [19]And it became known to all those living in Jerusalem so that that field was called, in their own dialect, *Hakeldama*, that is ‘Field of Blood.’ [20]“For it is written in the Book of Psalms, ‘Let his house become deserted, and let there be no one who lives in it’; and ‘Let another take his office.’ [21-22]Therefore, from the men who accompanied us during all the time in which the Lord Jesus went about with us—beginning with the baptism of John until the day he was taken up from us—it is necessary for one of these to become a witness of the resurrection with us.”

[23]So, they put forward two men, Joseph called Barsabbas, who was (also) called Justus, and Matthias. [24]And they prayed and said, “You Lord, who know the hearts of all people, show the one that you have chosen from these two men [25]to receive a place in this ministry of apostleship from which Judas turned away in order to go to his own place!” [26]And they cast lots for them and the lot indicated Matthias and he was included among the eleven apostles.

1:15 Καὶ ἐν ταῖς ἡμέραις ταύταις ἀναστὰς Πέτρος ἐν μέσῳ τῶν ἀδελφῶν εἶπεν ἦν τε ὄχλος ὀνομάτων ἐπὶ τὸ αὐτὸ ὡσεὶ ἑκατὸν εἴκοσι·

ἐν ταῖς ἡμέραις ταύταις. This temporal phrase is used to indicate that what follows is background information separate from the main storyline (also 6:1; 11:27; Sweeney, 246–47).

ἀναστὰς. Aor act ptc masc nom sg ἀνίστημι (attendant circumstance; less likely temporal). “A circumstantial participial clause [= attendant circumstance] is not just a convenient means of expressing peripheral information without specifying its relation to the nuclear part of the sentence. Placed at the beginning of a sentence, it also indicates continuity of situation and even unity of topic between the independent clauses which are contiguous to it” (Levinsohn 1987, 67).

ἀδελφῶν. This familial term should probably be viewed as a technical term for “believers,” in this case with no gender distinction intended.

εἶπεν. Aor act ind 3rd sg λέγω.

ἦν τε ὄχλος ὀνομάτων ἐπὶ τὸ αὐτὸ ὡσεὶ ἑκατὸν εἴκοσι. The abrupt narrative aside introduced by τε, rather than δέ, is unusual (cf. Barrett, 95; cf. Levinsohn 1992, 104).

ἦν. Impf ind 3rd sg εἰμί.

ὀνομάτων. A metonym (see 1:9 on τῶν ὀφθαλμῶν αὐτῶν) for "people" (cf. 18:15).

ἐπὶ τὸ αὐτὸ. This phrase is often used in the sense of "altogether" (cf. Bruce, 108). Here, the sense could also be "in that place" (cf. 2:44). Although Omanson argues for a technical meaning, "in church fellowship" (also in 2:1, 47; 1 Cor 11:20; 14:23), the data is insufficient to substantiate a technical sense.

1:16 Ἄνδρες ἀδελφοί, ἔδει πληρωθῆναι τὴν γραφὴν ἣν προεῖπεν τὸ πνεῦμα τὸ ἅγιον διὰ στόματος Δαυὶδ περὶ Ἰούδα τοῦ γενομένου ὁδηγοῦ τοῖς συλλαβοῦσιν Ἰησοῦν,

Ἄνδρες. See 1:11.

ἀδελφοί. See 1:15.

ἔδει. Impf act ind 3rd sg δεῖ (impersonal).

πληρωθῆναι. Aor pass inf πληρόω. According to Wallace (1996, 600), δεῖ is one of several impersonal verbs that take a subject infinitive. Since, strictly speaking, impersonal verbs do not take a "subject," it may be better to label the infinitive complementary.

τὴν γραφὴν. Accusative subject of the infinitive (see 1:3 on αὐτὸν).

προεῖπεν. Aor act ind 3rd sg προλέγω.

διὰ στόματος Δαυὶδ. Instrumental/intermediate agent.

γενομένου. Aor mid dep ptc masc gen sg γίνομαι (attributive, not genitive absolute; contra Rogers and Rogers, 230).

ὁδηγοῦ. Predicate genitive. As part of an equative construction (X equals Y), the predicate (Y, ὁδηγοῦ) must agree in gender, number, and case with the noun it describes (X, Ἰούδα).

τοῖς συλλαβοῦσιν. Aor act ptc masc dat pl συλλαμβάνω (substantival). Dative of advantage.

1:17 ὅτι κατηριθμημένος ἦν ἐν ἡμῖν καὶ ἔλαχεν τὸν κλῆρον τῆς διακονίας ταύτης.

ὅτι. Causal. Barrett (97) notes that although the ὅτι may introduce "the content of what the Holy Spirit said; more probably it explains why a vacancy occurred: this was because he had been counted among us."

κατηριθμημένος. Prf pass ptc masc nom sg καταριθμέω (pluperfect periphrastic; the imperfect of εἰμί plus a perfect participle is analogous to a pluperfect verb).

ἦν. Impf ind 3rd sg εἰμί.

ἔλαχεν. Aor act ind 3rd sg λαγχάνω.

τῆς διακονίας ταύτης. Partitive genitive.

1:18 Οὗτος μὲν οὖν ἐκτήσατο χωρίον ἐκ μισθοῦ τῆς ἀδικίας καὶ πρηνὴς γενόμενος ἐλάκησεν μέσος καὶ ἐξεχύθη πάντα τὰ σπλάγχνα αὐτοῦ·

The fact that the fate of Judas would not have been new information to the followers of Jesus, and the explicit reference to "*their* language" in v. 19, both suggest that vv. 18-19 are the narrator's comments (cf. v. 15) rather than Peter's (Witherington 1998, 121).

μὲν οὖν. See 1:6.

ἐκτήσατο. Aor mid dep ind 3rd sg κτάομαι. While Wallace (1996, 424–25) may be correct in viewing κτάομαι as a true middle (the semantics of the verb imply something done in the subject's interest), the fact that the verb *always* occurs in the middle suggests that the voice does not serve a specific function (contra Wallace, who takes ἐκτήσατο as a "causative middle").

ἐκ. Denotes the means by which Judas acquired the field (cf. Barrett, 98).

ἀδικίας. Genitive of production/means (Wallace 1996, 125, n. 143) or attributive genitive: "his unrighteous reward" (cf. Bruce, 109).

πρηνὴς. Predicate adjective. The term denotes "being stretched out in a position facedown and headfirst" (LN 17.20). For an explanation of why the common gloss "swollen" should be avoided, see BDAG, 863.

γενόμενος. Aor mid dep ptc masc nom sg γίνομαι (temporal).

ἐλάκησεν μέσος. Lit. "the middle burst open," with the nominative μέσος serving as the syntactic subject.

ἐλάκησεν. Aor act ind 3rd sg λακάω.

ἐξεχύθη. Aor pass ind 3rd sg ἐκχέω. The singular verb is used with a neuter plural subject.

πάντα. The hyperbole makes the narrative more vivid (cf. 1:1, 19; 2:12; 3:9, 18; 7:51; 8:10; 20:31; 24:5; 25:24; 26:7, 20).

1:19 καὶ γνωστὸν ἐγένετο πᾶσι τοῖς κατοικοῦσιν Ἰερουσαλήμ, ὥστε κληθῆναι τὸ χωρίον ἐκεῖνο τῇ ἰδίᾳ διαλέκτῳ αὐτῶν Ἁκελδαμάχ, τοῦτ᾽ ἔστιν Χωρίον Αἵματος.

γνωστὸν. Neut nom predicate adjective.

ἐγένετο. Aor mid dep ind 3rd sg γίνομαι.

πᾶσι. More hyperbole (cf. 1:18 on πάντα).

τοῖς κατοικοῦσιν. Pres act ptc masc dat pl κατοικέω (substantival).

Ἰερουσαλήμ. Accusative of location (cf. 2:14; 8:25, 40; 9:32, 35; 14:21; 19:10, 17). Although the place where the subject lives (κατοικέω) is typically introduced by the preposition εἰς (2:5; 7:4) or ἐν (1:20; 7:2, 4), the location is sometimes simply expressed in the accusative case (cf. 2:9–11, 14; 19:10, 17).

κληθῆναι. Aor pass inf καλέω. Used with ὥστε to indicate result.

τὸ χωρίον. Accusative subject of the infinitive (see 1:3 on αὐτὸν).

διαλέκτῳ. The following word (Ἁκελδαμάχ is transliterated from Aramaic) makes it clear that the reference is to the Aramaic language.

αὐτῶν. Since a language, as an abstract idea, cannot be possessed, it is probably better to treat this as a subjective genitive: "their language" or "the language that they speak."

τοῦτ᾽ ἔστιν. Cf. 4:36 on ὅ. Although the retention of the accent can indicate emphasis (see 2:13 on εἰσίν), here the retention is conditioned by the elision of the final *omicron* in τοῦτο (an optional process; see 2:16).

ἔστιν. Pres act ind 3rd sg εἰμί.

Αἵματος. Genitive of content or attributive genitive ("Bloody Field").

1:20 Γέγραπται γὰρ ἐν βίβλῳ ψαλμῶν, Γενηθήτω ἡ ἔπαυλις αὐτοῦ ἔρημος καὶ μὴ ἔστω ὁ κατοικῶν ἐν αὐτῇ, καί, Τὴν ἐπισκοπὴν αὐτοῦ λαβέτω ἕτερος.

Γέγραπται. Prf pass ind 3rd sg γράφω.

Γενηθήτω. Aor pass impv 3rd sg γίνομαι.

ἔπαυλις. Only here in the NT ("property in which a person was expected to reside, either as the result of ownership or legal contract"; LN 7.4).

ἔστω. Pres act impv 3rd sg εἰμί.

ὁ κατοικῶν. Pres act ptc masc nom sg κατοικέω (substantival).

ἐπισκοπὴν. Although this term was later used to denote an official church office (cf. 1 Tim 3:1), the sense here is most likely more general: "the position of one who has responsibility for the care of someone" (LN 35.40; cf. 53.69).

λαβέτω. Aor act impv 3rd sg λαμβάνω.

ἕτερος. Substantival.

1:21–22 δεῖ οὖν τῶν συνελθόντων ἡμῖν ἀνδρῶν ἐν παντὶ χρόνῳ ᾧ εἰσῆλθεν καὶ ἐξῆλθεν ἐφ' ἡμᾶς ὁ κύριος 'Ιησοῦς, ἀρξάμενος ἀπὸ τοῦ βαπτίσματος 'Ιωάννου ἕως τῆς ἡμέρας ἧς ἀνελήμφθη ἀφ' ἡμῶν, μάρτυρα τῆς ἀναστάσεως αὐτοῦ σὺν ἡμῖν γενέσθαι ἕνα τούτων.

δεῖ. Pres act ind 3rd sg δεῖ (impersonal). The complementary infinitive (γενέσθαι) does not appear until the end of v. 22.

τῶν. The article modifies ἀνδρῶν rather than συνελθόντων.

συνελθόντων. Aor act ptc masc gen pl συνέρχομαι (attributive, modifying ἀνδρῶν). This cannot be a genitive absolute (see 1:8 on ἐπελθόντος) participle since it is part of an articular noun phrase.

ἡμῖν. Verbs with a συν- prefix take a dative complement.

ἀνδρῶν. Genitive of reference or partitive genitive (see below on τουτῶν).

ᾧ. Dative by attraction (see 1:1 on ὧν) to χρόνῳ.

εἰσῆλθεν καὶ ἐξῆλθεν ἐφ'. The conjoined verb phrase (lit. "went in and out among") is best understood as an idiomatic expression meaning something like "to go about with" (cf. LN 83.9).

εἰσῆλθεν. Aor act ind 3rd sg εἰσέρχομαι.

ἐξῆλθεν. Aor act ind 3rd sg ἐξέρχομαι. On the use of the aorist tense, see 10:38 on διῆλθεν.

ἐφ'. The preposition with the accusative may denote association (a rare usage; here, as part of an idiom) or subordination ("over us"; so Bruce 111).

ἀρξάμενος. Aor mid ptc masc nom sg ἄρχω. This participle functions adverbially (modifying εἰσῆλθεν καὶ ἐξῆλθεν). It appears to agree with the subject of the main verbs, ὁ κύριος 'Ιησοῦς, in gender, number, and case. It may, however, be an idiomatic usage (see 10:37).

ἀπὸ. Used with ἄρχω, this preposition marks the starting point in a span of time.

τοῦ βαπτίσματος 'Ιωάννου. This expression may refer to Jesus' baptism by John, or it may be an example of synecdoche meaning "John's ministry." Synecdoche is a figure of speech in which one term is used in place of another with which it is associated. Unlike metonymy (see 1:9 on τῶν ὀφθαλμῶν αὐτῶν), with synecdoche the association specifically relates to a part-whole relationship. Here, a part of John's ministry ("baptism") would be used to refer to the whole.

ἕως. Used with ἄρχω, this preposition marks the endpoint in a span of time.

ἧς. Genitive by attraction (see 1:1 on ὧν) to ἡμέρας.

ἀνελήμφθη. Aor pass ind 3rd sg ἀναλαμβάνω.

ἀφ'. Denotes separation.

μάρτυρα. Predicate accusative. As the predicate of the infinitive γενέσθαι, μάρτυρα must agree with the (accusative) subject of the infinitive (ἕνα).

ἀναστάσεως. Objective genitive.

γενέσθαι. Aor mid dep inf γίνομαι (complementary; see 1:16 on ἔδει).

ἕνα. Substantival accusative subject of the infinitive (see 1:3 on αὐτὸν).

τουτῶν. Partitive genitive. The demonstrative picks up ἀνδρῶν from v. 21 (Barrett, 102, mistakes the attributive participle συνελθόντων for the referent).

1:23 καὶ ἔστησαν δύο, Ἰωσὴφ τὸν καλούμενον Βαρσαββᾶν, ὃς ἐπεκλήθη Ἰοῦστος, καὶ Μαθθίαν.

ἔστησαν. Aor act ind 3rd pl ἵστημι. Codex D reads ἔστησεν, which makes Peter the one who put forward the two candidates (in conformity with later church practice). The scribe of Codex D, or its exemplar, may have been uncomfortable with the implication from the text that the process of choosing church leaders was both communal and democratic; or perhaps, the change from a plural to singular verb was simply an attempt to enhance the status of Peter.

δύο. Substantival.

Ἰωσήφ. Accusative in apposition to δύο.

καλούμενον. Pres pass ptc masc acc sg καλέω (attributive).

Βαρσαββᾶν. The accusative noun serves as a complement in a passive object-complement double case construction (cf. 1:12 on Ἐλαιῶνος).

ἐπεκλήθη. Aor pass ind 3rd sg ἐπικαλέω.

᾿Ιοῦστος. Predicate nominative. This second name is Roman.

Μαθθίαν. Accusative in apposition to δύο.

1:24 καὶ προσευξάμενοι εἶπαν, Σὺ κύριε καρδιογνῶστα πάντων, ἀνάδειξον ὃν ἐξελέξω ἐκ τούτων τῶν δύο ἕνα

προσευξάμενοι. Aor mid dep ptc masc nom pl προσεύχομαι (attendant circumstance; see 1:15 on ἀναστάς).

εἶπαν. Aor act ind 3rd pl λέγω.

Σὺ. The pronoun could be either vocative ("You, Lord . . . show") or the nominative subject of ἀνάδειξον ("You show, Lord, . . .").

κύριε. On the position of the vocative, see 10:13 on Πέτρε.

καρδιογνῶστα. Vocative or nominative in apposition to Σὺ or Σὺ κύριε ("You, Lord, the one who knows the hearts . . .").

ἀνάδειξον ὃν ἐξελέξω ἐκ τούτων τῶν δύο ἕνα. While the meaning is clear enough, the syntax of the relative clause is difficult to determine. The substantival adjective ἕνα could be viewed as either (1) the accusative object of the verb ἀνάδειξον ("show *the one* whom you have chosen from these two"), (2) an accusative in apposition to the relative clause ("show he whom you have chosen, *the one* of these two" or "show he whom you have chosen from these two, *the one*"), or (3) an internal head of the relative clause (see 1:2 on ἄχρι ἧς ἡμέρας; "show *the precise one* whom you have chosen from these two"). For a fourth possible analysis, see 1:25. If (1) is correct, this would be a rare example of a relative clause preceding the substantive that it modifies. Since the vast majority of relative clauses *follow* the noun they modify, and no language is known to use relative pronouns where the relative clause precedes the head noun, this analysis should be abandoned. Option (2) is disallowed by the fact that the relative clause (probably) continues into the next verse with the complementary infinitive λαβεῖν. This verse is thus best viewed as another example of an internally headed relative clause (see 1:2 on ἄχρι ἧς ἡμέρας). As such, the expression is probably intensive: "show *the very/precise one* whom you have chosen from these two."

ἀνάδειξον. Aor act impv 2nd sg ἀναδείκνυμι.

ἐξελέξω. Aor mid ind 2nd sg ἐκλέγω.

ἕνα. Substantival.

1:25 λαβεῖν τὸν τόπον τῆς διακονίας ταύτης καὶ ἀποστολῆς, ἀφ' ἧς παρέβη Ἰούδας πορευθῆναι εἰς τὸν τόπον τὸν ἴδιον.

λαβεῖν. Aor act inf λαμβάνω. The function of the infinitive depends on where the relative clause in the prior verse ends. If the analysis offered above is correct, then the infinitive should be viewed as complementary (to ἐξελέξω). It would also be possible (though less likely), however, to treat the infinitive as epexegetical to ἐξελέξω (cf. Rogers and Rogers, 231), with ἕνα functioning as the accusative subject of the infinitive (see 1:3 on αὐτὸν). Verses 24b–25a would then read: "show he whom you have chosen from these two, the one who will take the place . . ." The syntax does not appear to allow for taking the infinitive as denoting purpose (contra Rogers and Rogers, 231): "show the one (ὃν) you have chosen from these two so that the one (ἕνα) might take the place . . ."

τόπον. Accusative object of the infinitive λαβεῖν.

τῆς διακονίας ταύτης καὶ ἀποστολῆς. Most recent scholars treat this phrase as a hendiadys (two conjoined nouns are used to refer to a single idea, with one noun functioning like an adjective): "this apostolic ministry" (cf. Barrett, 103; Fitzmyer 1998, 228). Strictly speaking, however, the presence of the demonstrative ταύτης separating the two nouns probably disallows this view (διακονίας καὶ ἀποστολῆς or διακονίας καὶ ἀποστολῆς ταύτης would be potential examples of hendiadys), though it makes little difference for the sense of the phrase. The combination of the demonstrative with the conjunction indicates that the καί is epexegetical: "this ministry, even apostleship" (cf. Wallace 1996, 288; for an analogous construction, see Rom 1:5).

παρέβη. Aor act ind 3rd sg παραβαίνω.

πορευθῆναι. Aor pass dep inf πορεύομαι (purpose).

τὸν τόπον τὸν ἴδιον. The irony set up by the contrast between this phrase and τὸν τόπον τῆς διακονίας ταύτης καὶ ἀποστολῆς reveals a strong indictment of Judas on the lips of Peter.

1:26 καὶ ἔδωκαν κλήρους αὐτοῖς καὶ ἔπεσεν ὁ κλῆρος ἐπὶ Μαθθίαν καὶ συγκατεψηφίσθη μετὰ τῶν ἕνδεκα ἀποστόλων.

ἔδωκαν κλήρους αὐτοῖς. Lit. "they gave lots to/for them." It is more typical to use the word βάλλειν to denote "casting" lots (cf. Luke 23:34; and LXX Esth 3:7 where ἔπεσεν also occurs). Typically, when the verb δίδωμι is used with the noun κλῆρος in the LXX, κλῆρος carries the sense of "a share, portion." Here, however, the following statement (καὶ ἔπεσεν ὁ κλῆρος) makes it virtually certain that ἔδωκαν κλήρους refers to the casting of lots. Some have suggested that the unusual expression indicates that a vote was taken, and that the vote was in favor (ἔπεσεν ὁ κλῆρος; lit. "the lot fell upon") of Matthias. Advocates of this interpretation argue that the verb συγκατεψηφίσθη could carry the sense of "chosen *by a vote*." The prayer in v. 24, however, strongly suggests that the decision was left up to God rather than being decided by vote (Witherington 1998, 125).

ἔδωκαν. Aor act ind 3rd pl δίδωμι.

κλήρους. The use of "lots" to decide God's will was looked upon positively within the Jewish (and Greco-Roman) culture. Proverbs 16:33 seems to approve of the practice ("The lot is cast into the lap, but the decision is the Lord's alone"), and lots were often used in the OT (see, e.g., Lev 16:8; Judg 20:9; Prov 18:18) without any negative assessment of the practice.

αὐτοῖς. Dative indirect object (if the pronoun is part of an idiomatic expression—lit. "to give lots to") or dative of advantage (if the preceding expression refers to voting = "to cast lots for").

ἔπεσεν. Aor act ind 3rd sg πίπτω.

συγκατεψηφίσθη. Aor pass ind 3rd sg συγκαταψηφίζομαι.

μετὰ. Association.

Acts 2:1–13

[1]When the Day of Pentecost arrived, they were all together in the
same place. [2]Suddenly, there was a noise from the sky, like a strong
blowing wind, and it filled the whole house where they were staying.
[3]Divided tongues (that looked) like fire appeared to them, and they
came to rest upon each one of them. [4]And they were all filled with the
Holy Spirit and began to speak with other languages as the Spirit was
giving them the ability to speak.

[5]Now, there were Jews living in Jerusalem, pious men from every
nation under heaven. [6]When they heard this noise, a crowd of people
came together and were bewildered because each one of them heard
them speaking in their own language. [7]They were completely astounded
and said, "Aren't all of these people who are talking Galileans? [8]So
how is it that each of us hears (them speaking) in our own native language? [9]Parthians, Medes, Elamites, those living in Mesopotamia, Judea,

Cappadocia, Pontus, Asia, [10]Phrygia, Pamphylia, Egypt and the parts of Libya adjacent to Cyrene, those who live in Rome— [11]both Jews and proselytes—Cretans and Arabs, we hear them speaking of God's greatness in our own languages!" [12]All of them were completely bewildered and were saying to one another, "What does this mean?" [13]Others, though, mockingly said, "They are drunk!"

2:1 Καὶ ἐν τῷ συμπληροῦσθαι τὴν ἡμέραν τῆς πεντηκοστῆς ἦσαν πάντες ὁμοῦ ἐπὶ τὸ αὐτό.

συμπληροῦσθαι. Pres pass inf συμπληρόω. Used with ἐν τῷ to denote contemporaneous time (see Wallace 1996, 595; cf. 8:6; 9:3; 11:15; and perhaps 3:26; 4:30).

τὴν ἡμέραν. Accusative subject of the passive infinitive (see 1:3 on αὐτὸν).

πεντηκοστῆς. Genitive of identification. On the day of Pentecost, the fiftieth day after Passover, the Jews celebrated the Feast of the Grain Harvest (see Exod 23:16; 34:22; Lev 23:15–21; cf. Acts 20:16).

ἦσαν. Impf ind 3rd pl εἰμί.

πάντες. Substantival subject of ἦσαν. The referent could be either the band of apostles or the whole group of believers (1:15). In favor of the former view is the fact that (1) 1:15–26 functions as background information, with 2:1 resuming the main story line that left off in 1:14 where the focus was on the eleven apostles (see 1:15 on ἐν δὲ ταῖς ἡμέραις ταύταις); (2) the focus of this pericope is on the apostles (see 2:14, 37); and (3) the expression "Galileans" (2:7) links this group to the "men of Galilee" in 1:11, who were probably the apostles (Sweeney, 245–48).

ὁμοῦ ἐπὶ τὸ αὐτό. The adverb (ὁμοῦ) and prepositional phrase ἐπὶ τὸ αὐτό; and perhaps the adjective πάντες, see above) together form a complex predicate expression: "They were *all together in one place.*"

ἐπὶ τὸ αὐτό. In contrast to 1:15, where this phrase occurs with ὡσεὶ, in this case the phrase should be understood more literally: "in the same place."

2:2 καὶ ἐγένετο ἄφνω ἐκ τοῦ οὐρανοῦ ἦχος ὥσπερ φερομένης πνοῆς βιαίας καὶ ἐπλήρωσεν ὅλον τὸν οἶκον οὗ ἦσαν καθήμενοι

ἐγένετο. Aor mid dep ind 3rd sg γίνομαι.

ἐκ. Denotes source.

ἦχος. Predicate nominative with the impersonal verb ἐγένετο.

ὥσπερ. The conjunction indicates an analogy or comparison between the connected ideas.

φερομένης. Pres pass ptc fem gen sg φέρω (attributive). The genitive noun phrase (φερομένης πνοῆς βιαίας) modifies an implicit ἦχος: "like *the sound* of a strong blowing wind." It should not be mistaken for a genitive absolute (see 1:8 on ἐπελθόντος; contra BAGD, 899).

πνοῆς. Genitive of production: "like the sound *produced by* a strong blowing wind."

ἐπλήρωσεν. Aor act ind 3rd sg πληρόω. The subject is ἦχος.

οὗ. See 1:13.

ἦσαν. Impf ind 3rd pl εἰμί.

καθήμενοι. Pres dep ptc masc nom pl κάθημαι (imperfect periphrastic; see 1:10 on ἀτενίζοντες).

2:3 καὶ ὤφθησαν αὐτοῖς διαμεριζόμεναι γλῶσσαι ὡσεὶ πυρός καὶ ἐκάθισεν ἐφ' ἕνα ἕκαστον αὐτῶν,

ὤφθησαν. Aor pass ind 3rd pl ὁράω. In the passive voice, this verb means "to appear" (see Wallace 1996, 165, n. 72).

διαμεριζόμεναι. Pres mid/pass ptc fem nom pl διαμερίζω. Given its position and its tense (participles introducing an attendant circumstance are typically aorist when modifying an aorist verb), διαμεριζόμεναι should probably be taken as an attributive participle.

ὡσεὶ. The conjunction indicates an analogy or comparison between the connected ideas.

ἐκάθισεν. Aor act ind 3rd sg καθίζω. In Greek, a singular verb is often used with a plural subject (in this case, γλῶσσαι). Here, the use of the singular probably stems from the distributive sense: "a tongue sat on each one of them." The slight awkwardness of the construction was smoothed out by the scribes of Codex א and D, which read ἐκάθισαν.

αὐτῶν. Partitive genitive.

2:4 καὶ ἐπλήσθησαν πάντες πνεύματος ἁγίου καὶ ἤρξαντο λαλεῖν ἑτέραις γλώσσαις καθὼς τὸ πνεῦμα ἐδίδου ἀποφθέγγεσθαι αὐτοῖς.

ἐπλήσθησαν. Aor pass ind 3rd pl πίμπλημι.

πάντες. Substantival.

πνεύματος. Genitive of content. The phrase "filled with the Holy Spirit" also occurs at 4:8, 31; 9:17; 13:9.

ἤρξαντο. Aor mid ind 3rd pl ἄρχομαι.

λαλεῖν. Pres act inf λαλέω (complementary).

γλώσσαις. Dative of instrument (cf. 2:6, 8, 11; 10:46; 19:6). This is the only place in the NT where the fact that the languages were "other" (ἑτέραις) languages is made explicit.

καθὼς. The conjunction introduces a subordinate clause that indicates that the speaking took place *as* the Spirit enabled the followers of Christ to do so.

ἐδίδου. Impf act ind 3rd sg δίδωμι. Here, as is common, the verb δίδωμι is used as part of a causative construction: "X caused/allowed Y to do something."

ἀποφθέγγεσθαι. Pres dep inf ἀποφθέγγομαι (direct object; lit. "the Spirit was giving to speak to them").

2:5 Ἦσαν δὲ εἰς Ἰερουσαλὴμ κατοικοῦντες Ἰουδαῖοι, ἄνδρες εὐλαβεῖς ἀπὸ παντὸς ἔθνους τῶν ὑπὸ τὸν οὐρανόν.

Ἦσαν. Impf ind 3rd pl εἰμί.

δὲ. In Acts, the conjunction δέ is typically used (on the discourse level rather than the sentence level) to introduce new developments in the story. The fact that 2:5 marks the first such usage is striking: "The rhetorical effect of not using δέ to introduce the [earlier] incidents is to indicate that, as far as Luke is concerned, the story only starts to develop after Jesus has ascended to heaven and the Holy Spirit has come upon those assembled in the upper room" (Levinsohn 1992, 37). The first part of Acts (1:1–2:4), then, sets the stage for the rest of the book in which Luke describes "the progress of Christianity from Jerusalem to Rome" (Levinsohn 1987, 106). "*De* appears only with the introduction of the Jews who will form the congregation for the apostles' message (2:5)" (105).

κατοικοῦντες. Pres act ptc masc nom pl κατοικέω (attributive or imperfect periphrastic; see 1:10 on ἀτενίζοντες).

Ἰουδαῖοι. One important manuscript (Codex א) omits this word, while others (e.g., Codex C and E) move it to improve the style. The scribe of Codex א may have viewed the term as contradictory to the phrase "from every nation," and/or as redundant since everyone knew that Jews lived in Jerusalem. If the omission were original it would suggest that pious Gentiles were included in the events of Pentecost. Otherwise, Luke may have intended to echo the catalogue of nations in Genesis 10 (see Scott).

ἄνδρες. Nominative in apposition to Ἰουδαῖοι.

ἀπὸ παντὸς ἔθνους τῶν ὑπὸ τὸν οὐρανόν. More Lukan hyperbole (cf. 1:18 on πάντα). Read in conjunction with the participle κατοικοῦντες, the prepositional phrase denotes the places from which the Jews had migrated to Jerusalem.

τῶν ὑπὸ τὸν οὐρανόν. The article functions as an adjectivizer. An adjectivizer is a word (or affix) that changes the following word, phrase, or clause into an adjective (cf. nominalizers; 1:3 on τὰ). The whole expression, τῶν ὑπὸ τὸν οὐρανόν, functions like an attributive adjective modifying ἔθνους. Normally, the case, number, and gender of the adjectivizer is determined by the noun that the expression modifies (here the genitive singular ἔθνους). In this case, the article is plural in agreement with the sense of παντὸς ἔθνους.

2:6 γενομένης δὲ τῆς φωνῆς ταύτης συνῆλθεν τὸ πλῆθος καὶ συνεχύθη, ὅτι ἤκουον εἷς ἕκαστος τῇ ἰδίᾳ διαλέκτῳ λαλούντων αὐτῶν.

γενομένης τῆς φωνῆς ταύτης. Lit. "When this noise occurred."

γενομένης. Aor mid dep ptc fem gen sg γίνομαι. Genitive absolute (see 1:8 on ἐπελθόντος), temporal.

φωνῆς. Genitive subject (see 1:8 on ἐπελθόντος). It is unclear whether this refers to the sound of those speaking in tongues, or to the sound of the "strong blowing wind" (with the ὅτι indicating why they were bewildered but not why they came together).

συνῆλθεν. Aor act ind 3rd sg συνέρχομαι.

συνεχύθη. Aor pass ind 3rd sg συγχέω.

ὅτι. Causal.

ἤκουον. Impf act ind 3rd pl ἀκούω. The plural verb agrees with the distributive subject "each one."

διαλέκτῳ. Dative of instrument, or perhaps manner (cf. 2:4, 8, 11).

λαλούντων. Pres act ptc masc gen pl λαλέω (genitive complement of ἀκούω in an object-complement "double genitive" construction; see

1:3 on ζῶντα; cf. 2:11; 6:11, 14; 8:30; 10:46; 11:7; 14:9; 15:12; 22:7). The object of ἀκούω often occurs in the genitive case, as here (αὐτῶν). The participle should not be treated as a genitive absolute (see 1:8 on ἐπελθόντος).

2:7 ἐξίσταντο δὲ καὶ ἐθαύμαζον λέγοντες, Οὐχ ἰδοὺ ἅπαντες οὗτοί εἰσιν οἱ λαλοῦντες Γαλιλαῖοι;

ἐξίσταντο . . . καὶ ἐθαύμαζον. The conjoined near synonyms should probably be viewed as a doublet (see 2:43 on τέρατα καὶ σημεῖα) that intensifies the idea ("they were completely astounded").

ἐξίσταντο. Impf mid ind 3rd pl ἐξίστημι.

δὲ. The use of δέ here, rather than καί, is somewhat surprising. When a sentence refers to the same subject as the previous sentence, any changes in the subject's circumstances, state or attitude are typically viewed as the next step in a sequence of events. The conjunction καί is therefore expected (Levinsohn 1987, 91). Although Levinsohn (91–92), following Newman and Nida (37), argues that Luke "may be conveying a change of attitude from the initial bewildered 'excitement' (v. 6) to the reaction of amazement and questioning that followed," a simpler explanation is possible. By using the doublet, ἐξίσταντο . . . καὶ ἐθαύμαζον (see above), Luke would have been left with two contiguous καίs had he followed the normal rules. The δέ in this verse, then, may simply be a necessary substitute for καί.

ἐθαύμαζον. Impf act ind 3rd pl θαυμάζω.

λέγοντες. Pres act ptc masc nom pl λέγω (attendant circumstance, redundant; see 1:6 on λέγοντες).

ἰδοὺ. See 1:10.

οὗτοί. See below. The second accent comes from the enclitic εἰσιν (see 1:4 on ἠκούσατέ).

εἰσιν. Pres act ind 3rd pl εἰμί. On the loss of accent, see 1:7 on ἐστιν.

λαλοῦντες. Pres act ptc masc nom pl λαλέω. The participle could be viewed as either substantival, modified by ἅπαντες οὗτοι (which has been fronted [see 3:13 on ὑμεῖς] for emphasis), or attributive, modifying a substantival οὗτοι.

Γαλιλαῖοι. Predicate nominative.

2:8 καὶ πῶς ἡμεῖς ἀκούομεν ἕκαστος τῇ ἰδίᾳ διαλέκτῳ ἡμῶν ἐν ᾗ ἐγεννήθημεν;

ἡμεῖς. The explicit subject pronoun is emphatic.

ἀκούομεν. Pres act ind 1st pl ἀκούω.

ἕκαστος. Nominative in apposition to ἡμεῖς.

τῇ ἰδίᾳ διαλέκτῳ ἡμῶν ἐν ᾗ ἐγεννήθημεν. This phrase, lit. "in our very own language in which we were born," is an idiomatic expression used to refer to one's mother tongue.

διαλέκτῳ. Dative of instrument (cf. 2:4, 6, 11).

ἡμῶν. The use of the genitive pronoun is unnecessary with τῇ ἰδίᾳ. It probably makes the statement convey an even stronger sense of incredulity: "our *very* own language."

ἐγεννήθημεν. Aor pass ind 1st pl γεννάω.

2:9–11 Πάρθοι καὶ Μῆδοι καὶ Ἐλαμῖται καὶ οἱ κατοικοῦντες τὴν Μεσοποταμίαν, Ἰουδαίαν τε καὶ Καππαδοκίαν, Πόντον καὶ τὴν Ἀσίαν, Φρυγίαν τε καὶ Παμφυλίαν, Αἴγυπτον καὶ τὰ μέρη τῆς Λιβύης τῆς κατὰ Κυρήνην, καὶ οἱ ἐπιδημοῦντες Ῥωμαῖοι, Ἰουδαῖοί τε καὶ προσήλυτοι, Κρῆτες καὶ Ἄραβες, ἀκούομεν λαλούντων αὐτῶν ταῖς ἡμετέραις γλώσσαις τὰ μεγαλεῖα τοῦ θεοῦ.

Πάρθοι . . . Μῆδοι . . . Ἐλαμῖται . . . οἱ κατοικοῦντες . . . οἱ ἐπιδημοῦντες . . . Ἰουδαῖοί . . . προσήλυτοι, Κρῆτες . . . Ἄραβες. The long list of nominatives all function as a large nominative absolute construction that serves as the topic of the sentence but not the subject of the main verb (ἀκούομεν, v. 11).

οἱ κατοικοῦντες. Pres act ptc masc nom pl κατοικέω (substantival).

Μεσοποταμίαν, Ἰουδαίαν . . . Καππαδοκίαν, Πόντον . . . Ἀσίαν, Φρυγίαν . . . Παμφυλίαν, Αἴγυπτον . . . τὰ μέρη. Accusatives of location; see 1:19.

Λιβύης. Partitive genitive.

τῆς κατὰ Κυρήνην. The article functions as an adjectivizer (see 2:5 on τῶν ὑπὸ τὸν οὐρανόν), changing the prepositional phrase into an attributive modifier.

οἱ ἐπιδημοῦντες. Pres act ptc masc nom pl ἐπιδημέω (substantival).

Ἰουδαῖοί. The second accent comes from the enclitic τε (see 1:4 on ἠκούσατέ).

ἀκούομεν. Pres act ind 1st pl ἀκούω.

λαλούντων. Pres act ptc masc gen pl λαλέω (genitive complement of ἀκούω in an object-complement "double genitive" construction; see 2:6 on λαλούντων).

αὐτῶν. Genitive object of ἀκούομεν.

γλώσσαις. Dative of instrument (cf. 2:4, 6).

τὰ μεγαλεῖα. The substantival neuter plural noun may be the direct object of λαλούντων, or an accusative of reference.

θεοῦ. Subjective genitive: "the mighty deeds that God has done"; not possessive (see 1:19 on αὐτῶν).

2:12 ἐξίσταντο δὲ πάντες καὶ διηπόρουν, ἄλλος πρὸς ἄλλον λέγοντες, Τί θέλει τοῦτο εἶναι;

ἐξίσταντο . . . καὶ διηπόρουν. The conjoined verbs form a doublet (see 2:43 on τέρατα καὶ σημεῖα) that serves to emphasize their amazement.

ἐξίσταντο. Impf mid ind 3rd pl ἐξίστημι.

πάντες. Substantival. Once again, this term should be understood as hyperbole (see ἕτεροι, v. 13; cf. 1:18 on πάντα).

διηπόρουν. Impf act ind 3rd pl διαπορέω.

λέγοντες. Pres act ptc masc nom pl λέγω (attendant circumstance or, less likely, result).

Τί θέλει τοῦτο εἶναι. An idiomatic expression of amazement (lit. "What does this wish to be?").

Τί. Predicate accusative (of εἶναι, in agreement with an unexpressed accusative subject of the infinitive; cf. 1:22 on μάρτυρα).

θέλει. Pres act ind 3rd sg θέλω

τοῦτο. The demonstrative pronoun should be viewed as the nominative subject of the main verb θέλω rather than the accusative subject of the infinitive (see 1:3 on αὐτὸν).

εἶναι. Pres act inf εἰμί (complementary).

2:13 ἕτεροι δὲ διαχλευάζοντες ἔλεγον ὅτι Γλεύκους μεμεστωμένοι εἰσίν.

ἕτεροι. There is no need to be surprised by the use of this term following the adjective πάντες in v. 12 (contra Barrett, 125; Haenchen, 174). The use of ἕτεροι here makes it clear that the earlier expression was hyperbolic.

διαχλευάζοντες. Pres act ptc masc nom pl διαχλευάζω (manner; Wallace 1996, 628).

ἔλεγον. Impf act ind 3rd pl λέγω. "With verbs of saying an alternation is frequently found between the aorist and the imperfect" (Porter 1994, 34; see also BDF §329).

ὅτι. Introduces direct discourse.

Γλεύκους. Genitive of content.

μεμεστωμένοι. Prf pass ptc masc nom pl μεστόω (perfect periphrastic; the present tense εἰσίν with the perfect participle forms a perfect periphrastic construction equivalent to a finite perfect verb).

εἰσίν. Pres act ind 3rd pl εἰμί. The retention of the accent here (see 1:7 on ἐστιν may indicate emphasis [Robertson 1934, 233–34; cf. 2:29; 5:25; 19:2]).

Acts 2:14–41

[14]Peter stood up, along with the eleven, raised his voice and declared
to them, "Judeans and all who live in Jerusalem, pay attention to my
words! Let this be known to you: [15]These people are not drunk as you
suppose, for it is only 9:00 a.m.! [16]Instead, this is (exactly) what was
said through the prophet Joel:

> [17]And, in the last days, says God, I will pour out my Spirit upon all
> people, and your sons and your daughters will prophesy, your young
> men will see visions, and your old men will dream dreams. [18]In-
> deed, in those days I will pour out my Spirit upon (all) my ser-
> vants—both male and female—and they will prophesy. [19]And I
> will cause wonders in the sky above and signs on the earth be-
> low—blood, fire and smoky vapors. [20]The sun will be turned into
> darkness and the moon into blood before the great and marvelous
> day of the Lord comes. [21]And *everyone* who calls upon the name
> of the Lord will be saved.

[22–23]Israelites, listen to these words! Jesus the Nazarene—a man who
was commended to you by God through miracles, wonders, and signs
that God did through him in your midst, just as you yourselves know—
this is the man who, delivered by the fixed intention and foreknowledge of God, you crucified and killed by the hands of lawless men.
[24](He is the one) who God raised up, when he had destroyed the pains
of death, because it was not possible for him to be held by it. [25]For

David said concerning him,

> I saw the Lord before me at all times; since he is at my right hand I will not be shaken. 26Therefore, my heart was glad and my tongue was full of joy. Moreover, my flesh will live in hope, 27since you will not abandon my soul to Hades, nor will you allow your holy one to experience decay. 28You have made known to me the ways of life; in your presence you will fill me with gladness.

29Brothers, it is possible to say to you with confidence concerning the patriarch David that he both died and was buried, and his tomb is among us to this day. 30Therefore, since he was a prophet and knew that God had sworn an oath to him to put one of his offspring on his throne, 31he foresaw this and spoke of the resurrection of the Christ, for he was neither abandoned in Hades nor did his body see corruption. 32God raised this Jesus, (and) all of us are his witnesses. 33So then, after he was exalted to the right side of God, and after receiving the promise from the Father—the Holy Spirit—he poured him out, as you yourselves (now) see and hear. 34For David did not go up into heaven, but he himself says, 'The Lord said to my Lord, "Sit at my right hand 35until I put your enemies under your feet."' 36Therefore, let all the people of Israel know with certainty that God has made him both Lord and Christ—this Jesus whom you crucified."

37When they heard (this), they were deeply convicted and said to Peter and the rest of the apostles, "What should we do, brothers?" 38Peter (responded) to them, "Repent, [he said,] and be baptized, each of you, in the name of Jesus Christ for the forgiveness of your sins and you will receive the gift of the Holy Spirit. 39For the promise is for you and your children and for all those in the future, as many as the Lord our God calls to himself." 40With many other words he testified and exhorted them, saying, "Be saved from this crooked generation!" 41So then, those who accepted his message were baptized and on that day (about) 3,000 people were added (to the group of believers).

2:14 Σταθεὶς δὲ ὁ Πέτρος σὺν τοῖς ἕνδεκα ἐπῆρεν τὴν φωνὴν αὐτοῦ καὶ ἀπεφθέγξατο αὐτοῖς, Ἄνδρες Ἰουδαῖοι καὶ οἱ κατοικοῦντες Ἰερουσαλὴμ πάντες, τοῦτο ὑμῖν γνωστὸν ἔστω καὶ ἐνωτίσασθε τὰ ῥήματά μου.

Σταθεὶς. Aor pass ptc masc nom sg ἵστημι (attendant circumstance;

see 1:15 on ἀναστὰς).

ἐπῆρεν τὴν φωνὴν αὐτοῦ. A common expression in Luke's writings (see 14:11; 22:22; Luke 11:27) denoting the manner in which the speaker spoke.

ἐπῆρεν. Aor act ind 3rd sg ἐπαίρω. The use of σύν rather than καί after ὁ Πέτρος makes the subject singular rather than plural (cf. 5:1 on ἐπώλησεν).

ἀπεφθέγξατο. Aor mid dep ind 3rd sg ἀποφθέγγομαι. In the NT this verb only occurs in Acts (2:4, 14; 26:25). Elsewhere, it is typically used with oracle-givers, diviners, prophets, exorcists, and other "inspired" speakers (cf. LXX Mic 5:1; Zech 10:2; Ezek 13:9, 19; Philo, *Mos.* 2, 33). A connotation of *inspired* speech may be present in Acts, particularly given the context of 2:4, or the term may simply be used as a verb of speaking in which the focus is "upon verbal sound rather than upon content" (LN 33.76), with any connotation of inspiration deriving from the context rather than the verb itself.

Ἄνδρες. See 1:11.

Ἰουδαῖοι καὶ οἱ κατοικοῦντες. Vocative.

οἱ κατοικοῦντες. Pres act ptc masc nom pl κατοικέω (substantival).

Ἰερουσαλὴμ. Accusative of location (see 1:19).

τοῦτο. The (nominative subject) demonstrative refers forward to the speech that follows.

γνωστὸν. Predicate adjective.

ἔστω. Pres act impv 3rd sg εἰμί.

ἐνωτίσασθε. Aor mid dep impv 2nd pl ἐνωτίζομαι.

μου. Subjective genitive (the agent of an implicit verbal idea: "words that I speak"; not possessive [see 1:19 on αὐτῶν]).

2:15 οὐ γὰρ ὡς ὑμεῖς ὑπολαμβάνετε οὗτοι μεθύουσιν, ἔστιν γὰρ ὥρα τρίτη τῆς ἡμέρας,

οὐ. The negativizer has been fronted for emphasis (see below on ὑμεῖς).

γὰρ. The γάρ probably introduces a statement that provides loose support for Peter's plea for attention.

ὡς. This adverb introduces the second half of the comparative clause. Here, the comparison precedes the topic.

ὑμεῖς. The explicit subject pronoun lends emphasis to the claim that they are misinterpreting the events. The terms "emphasis" and "focus" are used in their technical senses throughout the commentary. *Emphasis* "highlights an item of information which will be surprising to the hearer." In contrast, *focus* draws the readers' attention to information that is "of particular interest or significance" (Callow, 52).

ὑπολαμβάνετε. Pres act ind 2nd pl ὑπολαμβάνω.

οὗτοι. Although the masculine plural demonstrative pronoun could refer to the Eleven, it is almost certainly a reference to all of the occupants of the upper room, both men and women, given the context (see 1:14; 2:1, 17; contra the NIV).

μεθύουσιν. Pres act ind 3rd pl μεθύω.

ἔστιν. Pres act ind 3rd sg εἰμί.

γάρ. Causal; introduces the grounds for the conclusion expressed in the first clause (Cotterell and Turner, 211–12).

ὥρα τρίτη τῆς ἡμέρας. Lit. "the third hour of the day."

ὥρα. Predicate nominative.

2:16 ἀλλὰ τοῦτό ἐστιν τὸ εἰρημένον διὰ τοῦ προφήτου Ἰωήλ,

ἀλλὰ. The conjunction introduces a contra-expectation proposition ("Contrary to what you may think . . .").

τοῦτό. The demonstrative is used loosely to refer to what the people had been observing. The second accent comes from the enclitic ἐστιν (see 1:4 on ἠκούσατέ).

ἐστιν. Pres act ind 3rd sg εἰμί.

τὸ εἰρημένον. Prf pass ptc neut nom sg λέγω (substantival).

διὰ τοῦ προφήτου Ἰωήλ. Instrumental/intermediate agent (see Wallace 1996, 433–34).

2:17 Καὶ ἔσται ἐν ταῖς ἐσχάταις ἡμέραις, λέγει ὁ θεός, ἐκχεῶ ἀπὸ τοῦ πνεύματός μου ἐπὶ πᾶσαν σάρκα, καὶ προφητεύσουσιν οἱ υἱοὶ ὑμῶν καὶ αἱ θυγατέρες ὑμῶν καὶ οἱ νεανίσκοι ὑμῶν ὁράσεις ὄψονται καὶ οἱ πρεσβύτεροι ὑμῶν ἐνυπνίοις ἐνυπνιασθήσονται·

Καὶ ἔσται . . . ἐκχεῶ. The use of καὶ ἔσται plus a future finite verb is a periphrastic future construction (probably a Hebraism; Bruce, 121; cf. v. 21; 3:23).

ἔσται. Fut ind 3rd sg εἰμί.

λέγει. Pres act ind 3rd sg λέγω.

ἐκχεῶ. Fut act ind 1st sg ἐκχέω.

ἀπὸ τοῦ πνεύματός. The use of this partitive prepositional phrase is probably governed more by the verb (you pour out *some* of something) than any theological concerns (cf. Barrett, 136). Alternatively, it may indicate source (you pour out something *from* something). The second accent on πνεύματός comes from the enclitic μου (see 1:4 on ἠκούσατέ).

μου. Genitive of relationship.

σάρκα. Synecdoche (see 1:22 on τοῦ βαπτίσματος Ἰωάννου) for "people."

προφητεύσουσιν. Fut act ind 3rd pl προφητεύω.

ὑμῶν. Genitive of relationship.

ὁράσεις. Cognate accusative.

ὄψονται. Fut mid dep ind 3rd pl ὁράω.

ὑμῶν. Genitive of relationship.

ἐνυπνίοις. Cognate dative.

ἐνυπνιασθήσονται. Fut pass dep ind 3rd pl ἐνυπνιάζομαι.

2:18 καί γε ἐπὶ τοὺς δούλους μου καὶ ἐπὶ τὰς δούλας μου ἐν ταῖς ἡμέραις ἐκείναις ἐκχεῶ ἀπὸ τοῦ πνεύματός μου, καὶ προφητεύσουσιν.

τοὺς δούλους μου καὶ τὰς δούλας μου. Although this conjoined noun phrase may refer to two new groups of referents, it more likely functions as a summary statement of what precedes: "Indeed, I will pour out my Spirit on *all* of my servants, and they will prophesy!" (cf. Arichea, 442). This interpretation is supported by the addition of γε and μου (twice) to the LXX reading.

μου. Genitive of relationship.

ἐκχεῶ. Fut act ind 1st sg ἐκχέω.

ἀπὸ τοῦ πνεύματός. See v. 17.

μου. Genitive of relationship.

προφητεύσουσιν. Fut act ind 3rd pl προφητεύω.

2:19 καὶ δώσω τέρατα ἐν τῷ οὐρανῷ ἄνω καὶ σημεῖα ἐπὶ τῆς γῆς κάτω, αἷμα καὶ πῦρ καὶ ἀτμίδα καπνοῦ·

δώσω. Fut act ind 1st sg δίδωμι.

αἷμα καὶ πῦρ καὶ ἀτμίδα καπνοῦ. This conjoined accusative noun phrase stands in apposition to the preceding noun phrase, τέρατα . . . καὶ σημεῖα. Verses 19–20a form a chiasm with αἷμα καὶ πῦρ καὶ ἀτμίδα καπνοῦ referring to events on earth and 20a returning to the topic of what will take place in the heaven/sky above (Arichea, 443).

καπνοῦ. Attributive genitive.

2:20 ὁ ἥλιος μεταστραφήσεται εἰς σκότος καὶ ἡ σελήνη εἰς αἷμα, πρὶν ἐλθεῖν ἡμέραν κυρίου τὴν μεγάλην καὶ ἐπιφανῆ.

μεταστραφήσεται. Fut pass ind 3rd sg μεταστρέφω.

πρὶν ἐλθεῖν. Aor act inf ἔρχομαι. Used with πρὶν (or πρὶν ἤ) the infinitive denotes subsequent time, that is, the event of the main verb precedes the event of the infinitive (Wallace 1996, 596).

ἡμέραν. Accusative subject of the infinitive (see 1:3 on αὐτὸν).

ἐπιφανῆ. The accusative singular adjective (from ἐπιφανής) denotes that which is readily apparent or conspicuous and, therefore, "wonderful."

2:21 καὶ ἔσται πᾶς ὃς ἂν ἐπικαλέσηται τὸ ὄνομα κυρίου σωθήσεται.

καὶ ἔσται . . . ἐπικαλέσηται. See v. 17.

ἔσται. Fut ind 3rd sg εἰμί.

πᾶς. Indefinite relative clauses (see below) normally occur without an overt antecedent (see, e.g., Luke 8:18; 9:48; 18:17). The use of πᾶς with the indefinite relative clause here is probably emphatic (cf. Luke 12:8).

ὃς ἂν ἐπικαλέσηται. The use of ὃς ἄν (together these form an indefinite relative pronoun) with a subjunctive verb (aor mid subj 3rd sg ἐπικαλέω) forms an indefinite relative clause. The indefinite relative pronoun introduces a contingency or condition (like a third class condition) and can appropriately be rendered, "whoever, whatever." (Note: Grammarians have often referred to ὅστις as an "indefinite relative pronoun." This is a misnomer since this relative pronoun is used with a definite antecedent approximately 90% of the time in the NT; Culy 1989, 20, 30–31, n. 4.)

σωθήσεται. Fut pass ind 3rd sg σῴζω.

2:22–23 **Ἄνδρες Ἰσραηλῖται, ἀκούσατε τοὺς λόγους τούτους· Ἰησοῦν τὸν Ναζωραῖον, ἄνδρα ἀποδεδειγμένον ἀπὸ τοῦ θεοῦ εἰς ὑμᾶς δυνάμεσι καὶ τέρασι καὶ σημείοις οἷς ἐποίησεν δι' αὐτοῦ ὁ θεὸς ἐν μέσῳ ὑμῶν καθὼς αὐτοὶ οἴδατε, τοῦτον τῇ ὡρισμένῃ βουλῇ καὶ προγνώσει τοῦ θεοῦ ἔκδοτον διὰ χειρὸς ἀνόμων προσπήξαντες ἀνείλατε,**

Ἄνδρες. See 1:11.

Ἰσραηλῖται. Vocative.

ἀκούσατε. Aor act impv 2nd pl ἀκούω.

Ἰησοῦν τὸν Ναζωραῖον. This accusative noun phrase is brought to the front of the sentence where it serves as the topic: "Jesus the Nazarene—a man . . ." In a topic construction, the referent that is in focus is placed at the beginning of the sentence. If the topic has a syntactic relationship to the clause that follows, it is placed in the case it would bear in that clause, even though it is typically picked up with a demonstrative pronoun within the clause. In this case, Ἰησοῦν τὸν Ναζωραῖον and the resumptive τοῦτον in v. 23 serve as the direct object of ἀνείλατε.

ἄνδρα. Accusative in apposition to Ἰησοῦν τὸν Ναζωραῖον.

ἀποδεδειγμένον. Prf pass ptc masc acc sg ἀποδείκνυμι (attributive).

ἀπὸ. Introduces the agent of the passive verb.

εἰς. Introduces the indirect object of ἀποδεδειγμένον.

δυνάμεσι καὶ τέρασι καὶ σημείοις. Dative of instrument. The stacking of near synonyms emphasizes that Jesus performed all kinds of miraculous deeds.

οἷς. Dative by attraction (see 1:1 on ὧν) to δυνάμεσι καὶ τέρασι καὶ σημείοις (it normally would have been accusative as the object of ἐποίησεν).

ἐποίησεν. Aor act ind 3rd sg ποιέω.

δι' αὐτοῦ. Instrumental/intermediate agent.

καθὼς αὐτοὶ οἴδατε. This rhetorically powerful clause implies that the listeners were slow to accept the implications of what they knew to be true.

οἴδατε. Prf act ind 2nd pl οἶδα.

τοῦτον. The demonstrative is resumptive and should probably be taken as modifying ἔκδοτον. Like its antecedent (Ἰησοῦν τὸν Ναζωραῖον, v. 22), the demonstrative is moved to the front of the construction to serve as the topic: "*Jesus the Nazarene*—a man . . . *this is the man who* . . ." On "fronting," see 3:13, 14 on ὑμεῖς.

ὡρισμένῃ. Prf pass ptc fem dat sg ὁρίζω (attributive).

βουλῇ καὶ προγνώσει. Although most scholars treat this phrase as a dative of instrument, it may be better to call it dative of rule ("in conformity with"; Wallace 1996, 158): "in accord with the intention and foreknowledge."

τοῦ θεοῦ. Subjective genitive.

ἔκδοτον. Substantival.

διὰ χειρὸς. Instrumental/intermediate agent of προσπήξαντες. Theoretically, it could introduce the agent of the verbal adjective ἔκδοτον.

προσπήξαντες. Aor act ptc masc nom pl προσπήγνυμι (attendant circumstance, or perhaps means).

ἀνείλατε. Aor act ind 2nd pl ἀναιρέω.

2:24 ὃν ὁ θεὸς ἀνέστησεν λύσας τὰς ὠδῖνας τοῦ θανάτου, καθότι οὐκ ἦν δυνατὸν κρατεῖσθαι αὐτὸν ὑπ' αὐτου.

ὃν. The antecedent is τοῦτον . . . ἔκδοτον.

ἀνέστησεν. Aor act ind 3rd sg ἀνίστημι.

λύσας. Aor act ptc masc nom sg λύω (means or temporal).

τὰς ὠδῖνας τοῦ θανάτου. The use of τὰς ὠδῖνας makes for a vivid expression: "the childbirth-like/intense pains of death."

καθότι. This term is distinctively Lukan (Luke 1:7; 19:9; Acts 2:24, 45; 4:35; 17:31).

ἦν. Impf ind 3rd sg εἰμί.

δυνατὸν. Predicate adjective.

κρατεῖσθαι. Pres pass inf κρατέω. Subject of ἦν, or complementary to the verb phrase ἦν δυνατὸν if ἦν is taken impersonally.

αὐτὸν. Accusative subject of the infinitive (see 1:3 on αὐτὸν).

ὑπ'. Introduces the agent of the passive infinitive.

αὐτοῦ. The antecedent must be the masculine τοῦ θανάτου.

2:25 Δαυὶδ γὰρ λέγει εἰς αὐτόν, Προορώμην τὸν κύριον ἐνώπιόν μου διὰ παντός, ὅτι ἐκ δεξιῶν μού ἐστιν ἵνα μὴ σαλευθῶ.

λέγει. Pres act ind 3rd sg λέγω.

εἰς αὐτόν. The prepositional phrase denotes reference.

Προορώμην τὸν κύριον ἐνώπιόν μου διὰ παντός. This clause should probably be understood as a strong statement of confidence. If it carries the same meaning as the Hebrew text (שִׁוִּיתִי יְהוָה לְנֶגְדִּי תָמִיד), then it is probably an idiomatic expression referring to obedience to divine law (see Craigie, 157).

Προορώμην. Impf mid ind 1st sg προοράω. In the middle voice, particularly with ἐνώπιόν μου, the sense of the verb is clearly "to see before one."

ἐνώπιόν. The second accent comes from the enclitic μου (see 1:4 on ἠκούσατέ).

διὰ παντός. A fairly common idiomatic expression (see, e.g., Matt 18:10; Luke 24:53; Acts 10:2; 24:16), meaning "always," that may have come from διὰ παντὸς νυκτὸς καὶ ἡμέρας.

ὅτι. The conjunction introduces a causal clause that (probably) provides the reason for the following (result) clause. It is less likely that it supplies the reason for the confidence expressed in the first clause: Προορώμην τὸν κύριον ἐνώπιόν μου διὰ παντός.

ἐκ δεξιῶν μού. This set expression carries a locative sense (cf. 2:24; Luke 20:42).

μού. In this case, the pronominal enclitic μου (see 1:4 on ἠκούσατέ) has taken the accent of the enclitic ἐστιν that follows.

ἐστιν. Pres act ind 3rd sg εἰμί. On the loss of accent, see 1:7 on ἐστιν.

ἵνα. The conjunction, with the subjunctive, (probably) supplies the result of the preceding statement. It is also possible, however, that ἵνα μὴ was used to express a strong negative analogous to the Hebrew בַּל (Barrett, 145).

σαλευθῶ. Aor pass subj 1st sg σαλεύω.

2:26 διὰ τοῦτο ηὐφράνθη ἡ καρδία μου καὶ ἠγαλλιάσατο ἡ γλῶσσά μου, ἔτι δὲ καὶ ἡ σάρξ μου κατασκηνώσει ἐπ' ἐλπίδι,

διὰ τοῦτο. Introduces a reason for the joy expressed in the previous verse.

ηὐφράνθη. Aor pass ind 3rd sg εὐφραίνω.

ἡ καρδία μου. Synecdoche (see 1:22 on τοῦ βαπτίσματος Ἰωάννου) for "I."

ἠγαλλιάσατο. Aor mid ind 3rd sg ἀγαλλιάω.

ἡ γλῶσσά μου. See ἡ καρδία μου above.

γλῶσσά. The second accent comes from the enclitic μου (see 1:4 on ἠκούσατέ).

ἔτι δὲ καὶ. "Moreover, besides."

ἡ σάρξ μου. See ἡ καρδία μου above.

κατασκηνώσει ἐπ' ἐλπίδι. This expression (lit. "will live upon hope") means something like "will continue to have hope," or perhaps, "will remain safe."

κατασκηνώσει. Fut act ind 3rd sg κατασκηνόω.

2:27 ὅτι οὐκ ἐγκαταλείψεις τὴν ψυχήν μου εἰς ᾅδην οὐδὲ δώσεις τὸν ὅσιόν σου ἰδεῖν διαφθοράν.

ὅτι. Causal. This verse provides a reason for the final statement of v. 26.

ἐγκαταλείψεις. Fut act ind 2nd sg ἐγκαταλείπω.

τὴν ψυχήν μου. Synecdoche (see 1:22 on τοῦ βαπτίσματος Ἰωάννου) for "me."

δώσεις. Fut act ind 2nd sg δίδωμι. The verb is used as part of a causative construction (see 2:4 on ἐδίδου) with the infinitive: "You will not *allow* . . . to."

τὸν ὅσιόν. Accusative subject of the infinitive (see 1:3 on αὐτὸν). The second accent comes from the enclitic σου (see 1:4 on ἠκούσατέ).

σου. Genitive of relationship.

ἰδεῖν διαφθοράν. An idiom (lit. "to see corruption") meaning something like "to experience death." Notice that in order to derive a messianic interpretation from the Hebrew Scriptures, writers of the NT often took an idiomatic Hebrew expression and interpreted it literally. (Here, the writer is dependent upon the LXX reading to make the messianic application. The Hebrew text reads, "You will not allow your holy one to see the Pit"). In Ps 16:10 (LXX), the expression οὐδὲ δώσεις τὸν ὅσιόν σου ἰδεῖν διαφθοράν almost certainly referred to the psalmist's confidence that God would preserve him from death. In the case of the Messiah, God allowed him to *die* but did not allow his body to *rot* in the grave (ἰδεῖν διαφθοράν).

ἰδεῖν. Aor act inf ὁράω (complementary; the infinitival clause functions as the clausal direct object of δώσεις).

2:28 ἐγνώρισάς μοι ὁδοὺς ζωῆς, πληρώσεις με εὐφροσύνης μετὰ τοῦ προσώπου σου.

ἐγνώρισάς. Aor act ind 2nd sg γνωρίζω. The second accent comes from the enclitic μοι (see 1:4 on ἠκούσατέ).

ὁδοὺς ζωῆς. Genitive of destination: "paths that lead to life."

πληρώσεις. Fut act ind 2nd sg πληρόω.

εὐφροσύνης. Genitive of content.

μετὰ προσώπου σοὺ. The preposition probably denotes association here.

2:29 Ἄνδρες ἀδελφοί, ἐξὸν εἰπεῖν μετὰ παρρησίας πρὸς ὑμᾶς περὶ τοῦ πατριάρχου Δαυὶδ ὅτι καὶ ἐτελεύτησεν καὶ ἐτάφη, καὶ τὸ μνῆμα αὐτοῦ ἔστιν ἐν ἡμῖν ἄχρι τῆς ἡμέρας ταύτης.

Ἄνδρες. See 1:11.

ἀδελφοί. Here the term does not refer to believers (cf. 1:15).

ἐξὸν. Pres act ptc neut nom sg ἔξεστι (impersonal). On the function of the participle, see 24.5 on εὑρόντες. Although ἔξεστι generally means "it is lawful/permissible" in the NT, here the sense is probably "it is possible or appropriate."

εἰπεῖν. Aor act inf λέγω (complementary; see 1:16 on ἔδει).

μετὰ παρρησίας. The prepositional phrase describes the manner of the infinitive.

ὅτι. Introduces indirect discourse.

καί . . . καί. "both . . . and."

ἐτελεύτησεν. Aor act ind 3rd sg τελευτάω.

ἐτάφη. Aor pass ind 3rd sg θάπτω.

ἔστιν. Pres act ind 3rd sg εἰμί. The retention of the accent here (see 1:7 on ἐστιν) may indicate emphasis (cf. 2:13 on εἰσίν).

2:30 προφήτης οὖν ὑπάρχων, καὶ εἰδὼς ὅτι ὅρκῳ ὤμοσεν αὐτῷ ὁ θεὸς ἐκ καρποῦ τῆς ὀσφύος αὐτοῦ καθίσαι ἐπὶ τὸν θρόνον αὐτοῦ,

ὑπάρχων. Pres act ptc masc nom sg ὑπάρχω (causal).

εἰδὼς. Prf act ptc masc nom sg οἶδα (causal).

ὅρκῳ. Dative of instrument, or perhaps the dative complement of ὤμοσεν.

ὤμοσεν. Aor act ind 3rd sg ὀμνύω or ὄμνυμι.

ἐκ καρποῦ τῆς ὀσφύος. The prepositional phrase functions like a substantive, though it is not formally marked as such. It modifies an unexpressed noun ("one") that would have been in the accusative case and functioned either as the object of the infinitive, if it is transitive, or subject of the infinitive (see 1:3 on αὐτὸν), if it is intransitive. The unusual construction led a number of scribes to alter the text.

καρποῦ τῆς ὀσφύος. An idiomatic expression (lit. "fruit of the loins/waist/genitals") denoting "a descendant, offspring."

καθίσαι. Aor act inf καθίζω (indirect discourse). If ὅρκῳ is viewed as the dative complement of ὤμοσεν, then the infinitive would be epexegetical (cf. Rogers and Rogers, 233).

2:31 προϊδὼν ἐλάλησεν περὶ τῆς ἀναστάσεως τοῦ Χριστοῦ ὅτι οὔτε ἐγκατελείφθη εἰς ᾅδην οὔτε ἡ σὰρξ αὐτοῦ εἶδεν διαφθοράν.

προϊδὼν. Aor act ptc masc nom sg προοράω. This participle introduces an attendant circumstance (see 1:15 on ἀναστὰς) of the main verb (ἐλάλησεν). As such, it also expresses the result of the two causal participles in the previous verse (προφήτης ὑπάρχων καὶ εἰδὼς). The diaeresis over the *iota* indicates that the vowel is not part of a diphthong, but rather is syllabic.

ἐλάλησεν. Aor act ind 3rd sg λαλέω.

ὅτι. Causal.

ἐγκατελείφθη. Aor pass ind 3rd sg ἐγκαταλείπω.

εἶδεν διαφθοράν. See 2:27.

εἶδεν. Aor act ind 3rd sg ὁράω.

2:32 τοῦτον τὸν Ἰησοῦν ἀνέστησεν ὁ θεός, οὗ πάντες ἡμεῖς ἐσμεν μάρτυρες·

τοῦτον τὸν Ἰησοῦν. The use of the demonstrative and the sentence-initial position of the noun phrase bring Jesus back into focus (see 2:15 on ὑμεῖς). The construction may be intensive (see v. 36).

ἀνέστησεν. Aor act ind 3rd sg ἀνίστημι.

οὗ. The genitive relative pronoun (genitive of reference) probably refers to the preceding statement (neuter) or (less likely) to Jesus (masculine).

πάντες ἡμεῖς. The use of the adjective πᾶς with the overt subject pronoun, and their position before the verb, makes the expression particularly emphatic.

ἐσμεν. Pres act ind 1st pl εἰμί. On the loss of accent, see 1:7 on ἐστιν.

μάρτυρες. Predicate nominative.

2:33 τῇ δεξιᾷ οὖν τοῦ θεοῦ ὑψωθεὶς, τήν τε ἐπαγγελίαν τοῦ πνεύματος τοῦ ἁγίου λαβὼν παρὰ τοῦ πατρός, ἐξέχεεν τοῦτο ὃ ὑμεῖς [καὶ] βλέπετε καὶ ἀκούετε.

τῇ δεξιᾷ. Dative of location. "At the right" is the place of honor and authority. Barrett (149), however, argues that the dative should be understood as instrumental here ("by means of his right hand"). If his analysis were correct, δεξιᾷ would be an example of metonymy (see 1:9 on τῶν ὀφθαλμῶν αὐτῶν): "by his power."

ὑψωθεὶς. Aor pass ptc masc nom sg ὑψόω (temporal).

τοῦ πνεύματος. Epexegetical genitive: "the promise which is the Holy Spirit" (Wallace [1996, 99] calls this a genitive of apposition).

λαβὼν. Aor act ptc masc nom sg λαμβάνω (temporal).

ἐξέχεεν. Aor act ind 3rd sg ἐκχέω.

τοῦτο. Neuter accusative direct object of ἐξέχεεν.

βλέπετε. Pres act ind 2nd pl βλέπω.

ἀκούετε. Pres act ind 2nd pl ἀκούω.

2:34 οὐ γὰρ Δαυὶδ ἀνέβη εἰς τοὺς οὐρανούς, λέγει δὲ αὐτός, Εἶπεν [ὁ] κύριος τῷ κυρίῳ μου, Κάθου ἐκ δεξιῶν μου

ἀνέβη. Aor act ind 3rd sg ἀναβαίνω.

οὐρανούς. See 1:10.

λέγει. Pres act ind 3rd sg λέγω.

αὐτός. Intensive.

Εἶπεν. Aor act ind 3rd sg λέγω.

Κάθου. Pres dep impv 2nd sg κάθημαι.

ἐκ δεξιῶν μου. See 2:25.

2:35 ἕως ἂν θῶ τοὺς ἐχθρούς σου ὑποπόδιον τῶν ποδῶν σου.

θῶ τοὺς ἐχθρούς σου ὑποπόδιον τῶν ποδῶν σου. Lit. "I place your enemies as a footstool of your feet." The idiom means "to put someone under one's control."

θῶ. Aor act subj 1st sg τίθημι. The subjunctive verb is used with ἕως ἂν to form an indefinite temporal clause.

ὑποπόδιον. Complement in an object-complement double accusative construction.

2:36 ἀσφαλῶς οὖν γινωσκέτω πᾶς οἶκος Ἰσραὴλ ὅτι καὶ κύριον αὐτὸν καὶ Χριστὸν ἐποίησεν ὁ θεός, τοῦτον τὸν Ἰησοῦν ὃν ὑμεῖς ἐσταυρώσατε.

γινωσκέτω. Pres act impv 3rd sg γινώσκω.

πᾶς οἶκος Ἰσραήλ. Lit. "the whole house of Israel."

ὅτι. Introduces the clausal complement of γινωσκέτω. Luke uses the fronted (see 3:13 on ὑμεῖς) καὶ κύριον καὶ Χριστὸν, the redundant pronoun αὐτόν, the intensive demonstrative τοῦτον, and the overt subject pronoun ὑμεῖς to finish the speech with a rhetorical flourish.

καί . . . καί. "both . . . and."

κύριον . . . Χριστὸν. The accusative nouns function as complements in an object-complement double accusative construction (see 1:3 on ζῶντα).

ἐποίησεν. Aor act ind 3rd sg ποιέω.

τοῦτον τὸν Ἰησοῦν. Intensive: "this very Jesus."

ὑμεῖς. The overt fronted (see 3:13 on ὑμεῖς) subject pronoun clearly identifies the agents of Jesus' crucifixion, helps bring the speech to its climax, and implicitly calls for a response from the listeners.

ἐσταυρώσατε. Aor act ind 2nd pl σταυρόω.

2:37 Ἀκούσαντες δὲ κατενύγησαν τὴν καρδίαν εἶπόν τε πρὸς τὸν Πέτρον καὶ τοὺς λοιποὺς ἀποστόλους, Τί ποιήσωμεν, ἄνδρες ἀδελφοί;

Ἀκούσαντες. Aor act ptc masc nom pl ἀκούω (temporal).

κατενύγησαν τὴν καρδίαν. Lit. "They were stabbed (in) the heart."

κατενύγησαν. Aor pass ind 3rd pl κατανύσσομαι.

τὴν καρδίαν. Accusative of reference (cf. LXX Ps 108:16, where the dative τῇ καρδίᾳ is used).

εἶπόν. Aor act ind 3rd pl λέγω. The second accent comes from the enclitic τε (1:4 on ἠκούσατέ).

τε. This conjunction indicates a close relationship between the two clauses: "and so they said" (BDF §443.3).

ποιήσωμεν. Aor act subj 1st pl ποιέω (hortatory). Although some use the label deliberative subjunctive, such a label masks the fact that the deliberative subjunctive "is merely the hortatory subjunctive turned into a question" (Moule, 22; cf. Porter 1994, 58).

ἄνδρες. See 1:11.

ἀδελφοί. See 2:29.

2:38 Πέτρος δὲ πρὸς αὐτούς, Μετανοήσατε, [φησίν,] καὶ βαπτισθήτω ἕκαστος ὑμῶν ἐπὶ τῷ ὀνόματι Ἰησοῦ Χριστοῦ εἰς ἄφεσιν τῶν ἁμαρτιῶν ὑμῶν καὶ λήμψεσθε τὴν δωρεὰν τοῦ ἁγίου πνεύματος.

Πέτρος δὲ πρὸς αὐτούς. The verb, εἶπεν, is left implicit.

Μετανοήσατε. Aor act impv 2nd pl μετανοέω.

[φησίν]. Pres act ind 3rd sg φημί.

βαπτισθήτω. Aor pass impv 3rd sg βαπτίζω.

ἐπὶ τῷ ὀνόματι. It is unclear why the preposition ἐπί is used with βαπτίζω (only here in NT) rather than the expected εἰς or ἐν.

εἰς ἄφεσιν. The prepositional phrase denotes purpose. On the theological issues involved with this phrase see Wallace 1996, 369–71. It is likely that repentance and baptism were viewed as a single complex act leading to the forgiveness of sins (cf. 2:41; 18:8; 22:16).

λήμψεσθε. Fut mid dep ind 2nd pl λαμβάνω.

τοῦ ἁγίου πνεύματος. Epexegetical genitive (cf. 2:33).

2:39 ὑμῖν γάρ ἐστιν ἡ ἐπαγγελία καὶ τοῖς τέκνοις ὑμῶν καὶ πᾶσιν τοῖς εἰς μακράν, ὅσους ἂν προσκαλέσηται κύριος ὁ θεὸς ἡμῶν.

ὑμῖν . . . τοῖς τέκνοις . . . πᾶσιν τοῖς εἰς μακράν. Dative of advantage or possession (with εἰμί). The position of ὑμῖν makes it emphatic.

ἐστιν. Pres act ind 3rd sg εἰμί. On the loss of accent, see 1:7 on ἐστιν.

τοῖς εἰς μακρὰν. The article functions as a nominalizer (see 1:3 on τὰ).

προσκαλέσηται. Aor mid dep subj 3rd sg προσκαλέομαι. The subjunctive is used with the indefinite relative pronoun ὅσους ἄν.

2:40 ἑτέροις τε λόγοις πλείοσιν διεμαρτύρατο καὶ παρεκάλει αὐτοὺς λέγων, Σώθητε ἀπὸ τῆς γενεᾶς τῆς σκολιᾶς ταύτης.

λόγοις. Dative of instrument.

διεμαρτύρατο. Aor mid dep ind 3rd sg διαμαρτύρομαι.

παρεκάλει. Impf act ind 3rd sg παρακαλέω.

λέγων. Pres act ptc masc nom sg λέγω (attendant circumstance, redundant; see 1:6 on λέγοντες).

Σώθητε. Aor pass impv 2nd pl σῴζω.

2:41 οἱ μὲν οὖν ἀποδεξάμενοι τὸν λόγον αὐτοῦ ἐβαπτίσθησαν καὶ προσετέθησαν ἐν τῇ ἡμέρᾳ ἐκείνῃ ψυχαὶ ὡσεὶ τρισχίλιαι.

οἱ. The article modifies the participle (cf. 1:6).

μὲν οὖν. See 1:6.

οἱ ἀποδεξάμενοι. Aor mid dep ptc masc nom pl ἀποδέχομαι (substantival).

ἐβαπτίσθησαν. Aor pass ind 3rd pl βαπτίζω.

προσετέθησαν. Aor pass ind 3rd pl προστίθημι.

ψυχαὶ ὡσεὶ τρισχίλιαι. This whole construction is the nominative subject of προσετέθησαν.

ψυχαί. Synecdoche (see 1:22 on τοῦ βαπτίσματος Ἰωάννου) for "people."

Acts 2:42–47

[42]Now, they were devoting themselves to the teaching of the apostles and to fellowship, to the breaking of bread and to prayer. [43]Fear came upon every person, and many signs and wonders were being done through the apostles. [44]All those who believed were in the same place and shared everything. [45]They were selling their properties and possessions and distributing (the proceeds from) them to all, as anyone had a need. [46]And everyday they continued (meeting) together in the temple. They broke bread house by house and shared (their) food with gladness and humility. [47]They praised God and had favor before all the people. And the Lord added new converts daily in that place.

2:42 ἦσαν δὲ προσκαρτεροῦντες τῇ διδαχῇ τῶν ἀποστόλων καὶ τῇ κοινωνίᾳ, τῇ κλάσει τοῦ ἄρτου καὶ ταῖς προσευχαῖς.

ἦσαν. Impf ind 3rd pl εἰμί.

προσκαρτεροῦντες. Pres act ptc masc nom pl προσκαρτερέω (imperfect periphrastic; see 1:10 on ἀτενίζοντες and 1:14 on προσκαρτεροῦντες).

τῇ διδαχῇ . . . τῇ κοινωνίᾳ . . . τῇ κλάσει . . . ταῖς προσευχαῖς.

Dative objects of προσκαρτερέω (cf. 1:14).

τῶν ἀποστόλων. Subjective genitive.

τῇ κοινωνίᾳ. It is unclear whether this term refers to close mutual relations among the believers (cf. LN 34.5), sharing resources with the less fortunate (cf. LN 57.98), a combination of these, or something different. The lack of contextual clues suggests a general sense of close association.

τῇ κλάσει τοῦ ἄρτου. It is unclear whether this expression should be taken in the secular sense of "eating together" or in the cultic sense of "celebrating the Lord's Supper" (so Witherington 1998, 160–61; see also 2:46 on κλῶντές . . . ἄρτον).

τοῦ ἄρτου. Objective genitive.

ταῖς προσευχαῖς. Lit. "prayers."

2:43 Ἐγίνετο δὲ πάσῃ ψυχῇ φόβος, πολλά τε τέρατα καὶ σημεῖα διὰ τῶν ἀποστόλων ἐγίνετο.

Ἐγίνετο . . . ἐγίνετο. Impf dep ind 3rd sg γίνομαι.

ψυχῇ. Synecdoche (see 1:22 on τοῦ βαπτίσματος Ἰωάννου) for "person." The dative may be viewed as locative (and thus idiomatic: "fear was upon every soul" = "everyone was afraid") but probably not as a dative of possession, since "fear" cannot be possessed (contra Wallace 1996, 149).

τέρατα καὶ σημεῖα. This conjoined noun phrase may have been used as a doublet (two or more synonymous words used to express a single idea) that served to emphasize the supernatural aspect of the events.

διὰ τῶν ἀποστόλων. Instrumental/intermediate agent.

Textual note. The ending of this verse appears in many variations. The substance of the variants, however, remains fairly constant. The main difference between many readings and the UBS[4]/NA[27] text is the addition of "in Jerusalem" and the more emphatic reading "*great* fear" in many manuscripts.

2:44 πάντες δὲ οἱ πιστεύοντες ἦσαν ἐπὶ τὸ αὐτὸ καὶ εἶχον ἅπαντα κοινά

οἱ πιστεύοντες. Pres act ptc masc nom pl πιστεύω (substantival).

ἦσαν. Impf ind 3rd pl εἰμί.

ἐπὶ τὸ αὐτὸ. This prepositional phrase should probably be taken as "in the same (place)" (cf. 2:1), though as elsewhere in Acts (1:15; 2:47; 4:26) the expression is somewhat ambiguous.

εἶχον. Impf act ind 3rd pl ἔχω.

ἅπαντα. Substantival accusative object of εἶχον. The expression is clearly hyperbolic in light of v. 45.

κοινά. The accusative adjective could stand in apposition to ἅπαντα and have a function comparable to the predicate of an equative clause. It may be better, however, to interpret it as an accusative of manner.

2:45 καὶ τὰ κτήματα καὶ τὰς ὑπάρξεις ἐπίπρασκον καὶ διεμέριζον αὐτὰ πᾶσιν καθότι ἄν τις χρείαν εἶχεν·

καὶ τὰ κτήματα καὶ τὰς ὑπάρξεις. The first term probably refers to real estate while the second term refers to possessions in general (cf. LN 57.16, n. 8). This analysis is supported by the καί . . . καί ("both . . . and") construction, which probably disallows viewing the phrase as a doublet (see 2:43 on τέρατα καὶ σημεῖα). In either case, the meaning is essentially the same: all types of possessions were sold to meet the needs of the community.

ἐπίπρασκον. Impf act ind 3rd pl πιπράσκω.

διεμέριζον. Impf act ind 3rd pl διαμερίζω.

καθότι. See 2:24.

εἶχεν. Impf act ind 3rd sg ἔχω.

2:46 καθ' ἡμέραν τε προσκαρτεροῦντες ὁμοθυμαδὸν ἐν τῷ ἱερῷ, κλῶντές τε κατ' οἶκον ἄρτον, μετελάμβανον τροφῆς ἐν ἀγαλλιάσει καὶ ἀφελότητι καρδίας

καθ' ἡμέραν. The preposition is used distributively to form a common idiomatic expression meaning "daily" or "every day."

προσκαρτεροῦντες. Pres act ptc masc nom pl προσκαρτερέω (attendant circumstance).

ὁμοθυμαδὸν. See 1:14.

κλῶντές . . . ἄρτον. Fitzmyer (1998, 271, 272) sees a distinction between the use of this expression to refer to the Lord's Supper and the following phrase μετελάμβανον τροφῆς to refer to common meals (cf. v. 42).

κλῶντές. Pres act ptc masc nom pl κλάω (attendant circumstance).

The second accent comes from the enclitic τε (see 1:4 on ἠκούσατέ).

κατ' οἶκον. The preposition is used distributively (cf. καθ' ἡμέραν above).

μετελάμβανον. Impf act ind 3rd pl μεταλαμβάνω. The verb means "to receive a share in, to have a share of" (LN 57.129).

τροφῆς. Genitive complement of **μετελάμβανον.**

ἐν ἀγαλλιάσει καὶ ἀφελότητι καρδίας. The prepositional phrase (the preposition governs both dative nouns) denotes manner.

ἀφελότητι καρδίας. This idiom (lit. "simplicity of heart") could indicate either "humility" (cf. LN 88.55) or "generosity" (cf. Bruce, 133; see James 1:5 where the adverb ἁπλῶς carries this sense). It is also possible that the whole expression (ἐν ἀφελότητι καρδίας) was used in place of ἐν ἁπλότητι καρδίας (see Eph 6:5; Col 3:22), which seems to mean "with sincerity."

2:47 **αἰνοῦντες τὸν θεὸν καὶ ἔχοντες χάριν πρὸς ὅλον τὸν λαόν. ὁ δὲ κύριος προσετίθει τοὺς σῳζομένους καθ' ἡμέραν ἐπὶ τὸ αὐτό.**

αἰνοῦντες. Pres act ptc masc nom pl αἰνέω (attendant circumstance of μετελάμβανον, v. 46).

ἔχοντες. Pres act ptc masc nom pl ἔχω (attendant circumstance of μετελάμβανον, v. 46).

προσετίθει. Impf act ind 3rd sg προστίθημι.

τοὺς σῳζομένους. Pres pass ptc masc acc pl σῴζω (substantival).

καθ' ἡμέραν. See 2:46.

ἐπὶ τὸ αὐτό. The uncertainty over how this prepositional phrase should be understood led scribes to make a number of changes to the text (the UBS[4]/NA[27] text is supported by 𝔓[74vid] 𝔓[91vid] ℵ A B C *al*). Some scribes (D E Ψ 33 *Byz al*) added the phrase (ἐν) τῇ ἐκκλησίᾳ, a reading that would apparently support the sense "in that place" for ἐπὶ τὸ αὐτό. Some of those who added (ἐν) τῇ ἐκκλησίᾳ, however, took ἐπὶ τὸ αὐτό (with the meaning "together") as the beginning of the following verse ("Peter and John went up *together*"; E Ψ 33 *Byz al*). Omanson, following Barrett (173), treats the phrase as a technical expression meaning something like "in church" (see 1:15).

Acts 3:1–10

[1]Now, Peter and John were on their way up to the temple at the hour

of prayer, the ninth (hour), [2]and there was a certain man, who had been crippled since the time of his birth, and he was carried (around by others). Every day someone would place him by the door of the temple, which is called Beautiful, in order to beg alms from those going into the temple. [3]When he saw Peter and John about to enter the temple, he started asking (them) for alms. [4]Peter looked at him, along with John, and said, "Look at us!" [5]Now, he was paying attention to them because he was expecting to get something from them; [6]but Peter said, "I do not have any silver or gold, but I will give you what I have. In the name of Jesus Christ of Nazareth, [get up and] walk!" [7]He grabbed him by the right hand and pulled him up, and immediately, his feet and ankles became strong (again). [8]He jumped up, stood (there), and then began walking. He went with them into the temple, walking and leaping and praising God. [9]All the people saw him walking and praising God. [10]Then they recognized him—that he was the one who sat (and begged) for alms at the Beautiful Gate of the temple—and they were utterly astonished at what had happened to him.

3:1 Πέτρος δὲ καὶ Ἰωάννης ἀνέβαινον εἰς τὸ ἱερὸν ἐπὶ τὴν ὥραν τῆς προσευχῆς τὴν ἐνάτην.

δὲ. The δέ marks the following pericope as a new development in the overall story (see 2:5). It provides a smooth discourse level transition (contra Barrett, 177).

ἀνέβαινον. Impf act ind 3rd pl ἀναβαίνω.

τὴν ἐνάτην. Accusative in apposition to τὴν ὥραν τῆς προσευχῆς.

3:2 καί τις ἀνὴρ χωλὸς ἐκ κοιλίας μητρὸς αὐτοῦ ὑπάρχων ἐβαστάζετο, ὃν ἐτίθουν καθ' ἡμέραν πρὸς τὴν θύραν τοῦ ἱεροῦ τὴν λεγομένην Ὡραίαν τοῦ αἰτεῖν ἐλεημοσύνην παρὰ τῶν εἰσπορευομένων εἰς τὸ ἱερόν·

χωλὸς. Predicate adjective of ὑπάρχων.

ἐκ κοιλίας μητρὸς αὐτοῦ. A metonymic expression (lit. "from his mother's womb"; see 1:9 on τῶν ὀφθαλμῶν αὐτῶν) meaning "since the time of his birth."

ὑπάρχων. Pres act ptc masc nom sg ὑπάρχω (attributive modifying the anarthrous ἀνήρ [see 3.3 on Πέτρον καὶ Ἰωάννην]; cf. Rogers and Rogers, 234). It would also be possible to view the participle as adverbial (attendant circumstance). The presence of the explicit participle, along with the two imperfect verbs, highlights the fact that this man had been in a sorry state for a very long time (Barrett, 179).

ἐβαστάζετο. Impf pass ind 3rd sg βαστάζω. The verb is best translated with a "customary" connotation rather than a progressive one (contra Wallace 1996, 544). This notion is made clear from the following context (καθ' ἡμέραν). Rogers and Rogers (234) state that the man was being carried as the apostles were going up to the temple. This analysis seems to be ruled out by the fact that the encounter with the apostles takes place when the lame man is sitting down (see v. 7).

ἐτίθουν. Impf act ind 3rd pl τίθημι. The following expression, καθ' ἡμέραν, necessitates the use of the imperfect verb (cf. Wallace 1996, 548).

καθ' ἡμέραν. See 2:46.

πρός. The author of Acts uses τίθημι with the preposition πρός as an expression meaning "to place at" (cf. 4:37).

τοῦ ἱεροῦ. Here, ἱερός clearly refers to the whole temple complex.

λεγομένην. Pres pass ptc fem acc sg λέγω (attributive).

Ὡραίαν. The accusative noun serves as a complement in a passive object-complement double case construction (cf. 1:12 on Ἐλαιῶνος).

τοῦ αἰτεῖν. Pres act inf αἰτέω. The genitive articular infinitive introduces a purpose statement. NT examples of this construction are almost exclusively found in Matthew, Luke and Acts (Wallace 1996, 591, n. 4).

τῶν εἰσπορευομένων. Pres dep ptc masc gen pl εἰσπορεύομαι (substantival).

τὸ ἱερόν. See above.

3:3 ὃς ἰδὼν Πέτρον καὶ Ἰωάννην μέλλοντας εἰσιέναι εἰς τὸ ἱερὸν, ἠρώτα ἐλεημοσύνην λαβεῖν.

ὅς. The antecedent is τις ἀνήρ (v. 2).

ἰδών. Aor act ptc masc nom sg ὁράω (temporal).

Πέτρον καὶ Ἰωάννην. "When a participant is first mentioned, reference to him or her by name is typically *anarthrous*. However, once (s)he has been introduced, subsequent references to him or her by name within the same incident are *arthrous*" (Levinsohn 1992, 100).

"Anarthrous references to particular, known participants either mark the participant as locally salient [i.e., the focus of attention] or highlight the speech which he utters" (99). In the present passage, "each time attention switches to Peter, references to him are anarthrous (vv. 4, 6; see also v. 3). From the perspective of the story as a whole, Peter, rather than the lame man, is the salient participant [i.e., the character to whom the reader's attention is directed]" (103).

μέλλοντας. Pres act ptc masc acc pl μέλλω. The participle functions as the complement in an object-complement double accusative construction (see 1:3 on ζῶντα). The verb is used here with an infinitive to express an imminent event.

εἰσιέναι. Pres act inf εἴσειμι (complementary). The unusual form probably derives from the verb εἰσίημι ("to enter"), which merged with εἴσειμι at some point in time.

ἱερὸν. See v. 2.

ἠρώτα. Impf act ind 3rd sg ἐρωτάω.

λαβεῖν. Aor act inf λαμβάνω (indirect discourse).

3:4 ἀτενίσας δὲ Πέτρος εἰς αὐτὸν σὺν τῷ Ἰωάννῃ εἶπεν, Βλέψον εἰς ἡμᾶς.

ἀτενίσας. Aor act ptc masc nom sg ἀτενίζω (attendant circumstance; see 1:15 on ἀναστὰς).

δέ. See 2:5.

εἶπεν. Aor act ind 3rd sg λέγω. On the use of the singular verb, see 2:14 on ἐπῆρεν.

Βλέψον. Aor act impv 2nd sg βλέπω.

3:5 ὁ δὲ ἐπεῖχεν αὐτοῖς προσδοκῶν τι παρ' αὐτῶν λαβεῖν.

ὁ. The article functions like a personal pronoun here (cf. 5:8; 7:2, 25; 8:31; 9:29, 40; 10:22; 12:15; 16:31; 19:2-3; 22:14, 27; 28:5, 6, 21). The construction article + δέ is frequently used in reported speech to indicate a shift in speaker (see, e.g., 5:8; 7:2; 8:31; 10:22; 12:15; 16:31; 19:2–3.

ἐπεῖχεν. Impf act ind 3rd sg ἐπέχω.

προσδοκῶν. Pres act ptc masc nom sg προσδοκάω (causal).

λαβεῖν. Aor act inf λαμβάνω (complementary).

3:6 εἶπεν δὲ Πέτρος, Ἀργύριον καὶ χρυσίον οὐχ ὑπάρχει μοι, ὃ δὲ ἔχω τοῦτό σοι δίδωμι· ἐν τῷ ὀνόματι Ἰησοῦ Χριστοῦ τοῦ Ναζωραίου [ἔγειρε καὶ] περιπάτει.

εἶπεν. Aor act ind 3rd sg λέγω.

Ἀργύριον καὶ χρυσίον. Neuter nominative subject of ὑπάρχει.

ὑπάρχει. Pres act ind 3rd sg ὑπάρχω.

μοι. Dative of possession (with ὑπάρχω).

ὃ. The neuter accusative singular relative pronoun introduces a "headless relative clause," that is, a relative clause with no expressed antecedent: lit. "that which I have."

τοῦτό. The resumptive demonstrative pronoun helps increase the tension in the story as it nears its climax. The second accent comes from the enclitic σοι (see 1:4 on ἠκούσατέ).

δίδωμι. Pres act ind 1st sg δίδωμι.

ἐν τῷ ὀνόματι. Probably should be viewed as metonymy (see 1:9 on τῶν ὀφθαλμῶν αὐτῶν) for "by the authority."

τοῦ Ναζωραίου. Strictly speaking, the genitive expression is not a genitive of source ("Jesus Christ, from Nazareth"), but stands in apposition to Ἰησοῦ Χριστοῦ ("Jesus Christ, the Nazarene").

ἔγειρε. Pres act impv 2nd sg ἐγείρω. The text-critical question of whether the original text included this verb with the conjunction καί (the two words are omitted by א B D *al*) has little bearing on the sense of the passage.

περιπάτει. Pres act impv 2nd sg περιπατέω.

3:7 καὶ πιάσας αὐτὸν τῆς δεξιᾶς χειρὸς ἤγειρεν αὐτόν· παραχρῆμα δὲ ἐστερεώθησαν αἱ βάσεις αὐτοῦ καὶ τὰ σφυδρά,

πιάσας. Aor act ptc masc nom sg πιάζω (attendant circumstance; see 1:15 on ἀναστὰς).

τῆς δεξιᾶς χειρὸς. Although verbs that denote touching or taking hold of something often take their direct object in the genitive case (see Wallace 1996, 131), here the direct object is the accusative αὐτόν and the genitive τῆς χειρὸς (fem gen sg of χείρ) indicates "by the right hand."

ἤγειρεν. Aor act ind 3rd sg ἐγείρω.

ἐστερεώθησαν. Aor pass ind 3rd pl στερέοω.

3:8 καὶ ἐξαλλόμενος ἔστη καὶ περιεπάτει καὶ εἰσῆλθεν σὺν αὐτοῖς εἰς τὸ ἱερὸν περιπατῶν καὶ ἁλλόμενος καὶ αἰνῶν τὸν θεόν.

ἐξαλλόμενος. Pres dep ptc masc nom sg ἐξάλλομαι (manner). "He jumped to his feet."

ἔστη. Aor act ind 3rd sg ἵστημι.

περιεπάτει. Impf act ind 3rd sg περιπατέω.

εἰσῆλθεν. Aor act ind 3rd sg εἰσέρχομαι.

περιπατῶν. Pres act ptc masc nom sg περιπατέω (manner).

ἁλλόμενος. Pres dep ptc masc nom sg ἅλλομαι (manner).

αἰνῶν. Pres act ptc masc nom sg αἰνέω (manner).

3:9 καὶ εἶδεν πᾶς ὁ λαὸς αὐτὸν περιπατοῦντα καὶ αἰνοῦντα τὸν θεόν·

εἶδεν. Aor act ind 3rd sg ὁράω. The singular verb is used with a collective singular subject.

πᾶς ὁ λαὸς. Hyperbole (cf. 1:18 on πάντα).

περιπατοῦντα. Pres act ptc masc acc sg περιπατέω. The participle functions as the complement in an object-complement double accusative construction (see 1:3 on ζῶντα).

αἰνοῦντα. Pres act ptc masc acc sg αἰνέω (see above on περιπατοῦντα).

3:10 ἐπεγίνωσκον δὲ αὐτὸν ὅτι αὐτὸς ἦν ὁ πρὸς τὴν ἐλεημοσύνην καθήμενος ἐπὶ τῇ Ὡραίᾳ Πύλῃ τοῦ ἱεροῦ καὶ ἐπλήσθησαν θάμβους καὶ ἐκστάσεως ἐπὶ τῷ συμβεβηκότι αὐτῷ.

ἐπεγίνωσκον. Impf act ind 3rd pl ἐπιγινώσκω.

αὐτὸν. The use of the direct object pronoun makes the expression more forceful: "they recognized *him*, that *he* was . . ." rather than simply "they recognized that he was . . ." (cf. 4:13). The beginning of the verse could appropriately be rendered, "Then it dawned on them that he was. . ."

ὅτι. Epexegetical (not complementary, see above on αὐτὸν).

ἦν. Impf ind 3rd sg εἰμί. Wallace (1996, 552) views this an example of the "imperfect retained in indirect discourse."

πρὸς. Introduces the purpose of the crippled man's sitting at the Beautiful Gate.

ὁ καθήμενος. Pres dep ptc masc nom sg κάθημαι (substantival). Predicate nominative.

ἐπλήσθησαν θάμβους καὶ ἐκστάσεως. Lit. "they were filled with astonishment and amazement."

ἐπλήσθησαν. Aor pass ind 3rd pl πίμπλημι.

θάμβους καὶ ἐκστάσεως. Genitive of content. The conjoined nouns (lit. "astonishment and amazement") form a doublet (see 2:43 on τέρατα καὶ σημεῖα) that emphasizes the onlookers' utter amazement.

ἐπὶ. Causal.

τῷ συμβεβηκότι. Prf act ptc neut dat sg συμβαίνω (substantival).

Acts 3:11–26

[11]While he was clinging to Peter and John, all the people ran together
to them at the porch called Solomon's (Porch), amazed. [12]When Peter
saw (this), he responded to the people: "Israelites, why are you amazed at this? Why are you staring at us as if by our own power or piety we
have made him walk? [13]The God of Abraham, Isaac, and Jacob, the God
of our ancestors, glorified his servant Jesus, whom you handed over and disowned before Pilate, although he had decided to release him.
[14]You rejected the holy and righteous one, and requested that a man
who was a murderer be given to you. [15]You killed the author of life,
whom God raised from the dead, whose witnesses we are. [16]By faith in
his name, his name strengthened this man, whom you see and know; and the faith that comes through him gave him this perfect health before all of you.

[17]And now, brothers, I know that you acted in ignorance, just as your
leaders did. [18]But God thus fulfilled the things he foretold through the
mouth of all the prophets, namely that his Christ would suffer. [19]There-
fore, repent and turn (to God) so that your sins might be wiped out,
[20]and so that refreshing times may come from the Lord's presence and
he might send the Christ who has been chosen for you, Jesus. [21]He must
remain in heaven until the time when all the things God spoke of through the mouth(s) of his holy prophets long ago are restored.

[22]Moses said, 'The Lord your God will raise up for you a prophet like me from your brothers. Obey him in everything that he says to you.
[23]And it will be that every person who does not obey that prophet will
be cut off from the people.' [24]All the prophets who spoke, including

Samuel and those who came after him, also announced these days. [25]You are descendants of the prophets and members of the covenant that God established with your ancestors when he said to Abraham, 'All the families of the earth will be blessed through your seed.' [26]God raised up his servant, first of all for your benefit, and sent him to bless you by turning each of you from your wicked ways."

3:11 Κρατοῦντος δὲ αὐτοῦ τὸν Πέτρον καὶ τὸν Ἰωάννην συνέδραμεν πᾶς ὁ λαὸς πρὸς αὐτοὺς ἐπὶ τῇ στοᾷ τῇ καλουμένῃ Σολομῶντος ἔκθαμβοι.

Κρατοῦντος. Pres act ptc masc gen sg κρατέω. Genitive absolute (see 1:8 on ἐπελθόντος), temporal.

αὐτοῦ. Genitive subject (see 1:8 on ἐπελθόντος).

συνέδραμεν. Aor act ind 3rd sg συντρέχω. The singular verb is used with a collective singular subject.

πᾶς ὁ λαὸς. See v. 9.

καλουμένῃ. Pres pass ptc fem dat sg καλέω (attributive).

Σολομῶντος. Possessive predicate genitive.

ἔκθαμβοι. Nominative in apposition to πᾶς ὁ λαὸς. Here the plural is used to modify the collective singular subject. The people's amazement is once again emphasized.

3:12 ἰδὼν δὲ ὁ Πέτρος ἀπεκρίνατο πρὸς τὸν λαόν, Ἄνδρες Ἰσραηλῖται, τί θαυμάζετε ἐπὶ τούτῳ ἢ ἡμῖν τί ἀτενίζετε ὡς ἰδίᾳ δυνάμει ἢ εὐσεβείᾳ πεποιηκόσιν τοῦ περιπατεῖν αὐτόν;

ἰδὼν. Aor act ptc masc nom sg ὁράω (temporal).

ἀπεκρίνατο. Aor mid dep ind 3rd sg ἀποκρίνομαι. Wallace (1996, 421) suggests that the middle voice (the only use of the middle with this verb in twenty occurrences in Acts) may imply "a vested interest on the part of the speaker."

Ἄνδρες. See 1:11.

τί. The two rhetorical questions carry the force of rebukes: "You should not be surprised!" "You should not be staring at us!"

θαυμάζετε. Pres act ind 2nd pl θαυμάζω.

ἀτενίζετε. Pres act ind 2nd pl ἀτενίζω.

δυνάμει ἢ εὐσεβείᾳ. Dative of means.

πεποιηκόσιν. Prf act ptc masc dat pl ποιέω (substantival; lit. "those who have made"). The participle cannot be adverbial since it does not have the same subject as the main verb. The dative case comes from ἡμῖν, the referent of the ὡς clause. Like δίδωμι (see 2:4 on ἐδίδου), ποιέω can be used in causative constructions.

περιπατεῖν. Pres act inf περιπατέω (complementary in a causative construction).

αὐτόν. Accusative subject of the infinitive (see 1:3 on αὐτὸν).

3:13 ὁ θεὸς Ἀβραὰμ καὶ [ὁ θεὸς] Ἰσαὰκ καὶ [ὁ θεὸς] Ἰακώβ, ὁ θεὸς τῶν πατέρων ἡμῶν, ἐδόξασεν τὸν παῖδα αὐτοῦ Ἰησοῦν ὃν ὑμεῖς μὲν παρεδώκατε καὶ ἠρνήσασθε κατὰ πρόσωπον Πιλάτου, κρίναντος ἐκείνου ἀπολύειν·

ἐδόξασεν. Aor act ind 3rd sg δοξάζω.

παῖδα. This term can be used to refer to a "child" or a "servant."

Ἰησοῦν. Accusative in apposition to τὸν παῖδα.

ὑμεῖς. The explicit fronted pronoun shifts the focus (see 2:15 on ὑμεῖς) to the listeners. Following Levinsohn (1987, 3) we consider the unmarked, or "normal" order of the major constituents of the Greek clause to be verb-subject-object. Anything that precedes the verb is "fronted."

παρεδώκατε. Aor act ind 2nd pl παραδίδωμι.

ἠρνήσασθε. Aor mid dep ind 2nd pl ἀρνέομαι. On the meaning of this term, cf. 7:35 on ἠρνήσαντο.

κρίναντος. Aor act ptc masc gen sg κρίνω. Genitive absolute (see 1:8 on ἐπελθόντος), either concessive or temporal. It should not be mistaken for an attributive modifier of the genitive Πιλάτου since it has a subject pronoun.

ἐκείνου. Genitive subject (see 1:8 on ἐπελθόντος).

ἀπολύειν. Pres act inf ἀπολύω (indirect discourse with a verb of cognition).

3:14 ὑμεῖς δὲ τὸν ἅγιον καὶ δίκαιον ἠρνήσασθε, καὶ ᾐτήσασθε ἄνδρα φονέα χαρισθῆναι ὑμῖν,

ὑμεῖς. The explicit fronted (see 3:13 on ὑμεῖς) pronoun maintains the focus (see 2:15 on ὑμεῖς) on the listeners.

τὸν ἅγιον καὶ δίκαιον. The fronted (see 3:13 on ὑμεῖς) position of this noun phrase probably highlights the contrast in character between Jesus and the murderer (φονέα).

ἠρνήσασθε. Aor mid dep ind 2nd pl ἀρνέομαι. On the meaning of this term, cf. 7:35 on ἠρνήσαντο.

ἄνδρα. Accusative subject of the passive infinitive.

φονέα. Accusative in apposition to ἄνδρα.

ᾐτήσασθε. Aor mid ind 2nd pl αἰτέω.

χαρισθῆναι. Aor pass inf χαρίζομαι (indirect discourse).

3:15 τὸν δὲ ἀρχηγὸν τῆς ζωῆς ἀπεκτείνατε, ὃν ὁ θεὸς ἤγειρεν ἐκ νεκρῶν, οὗ ἡμεῖς μάρτυρές ἐσμεν.

τὸν . . . ἀρχηγὸν τῆς ζωῆς. The fronted expression is again in focus (see 2:15 on ὑμεῖς).

ἀπεκτείνατε. Aor act ind 2nd pl ἀποκτείνω.

ἤγειρεν. Aor act ind 3rd sg ἐγείρω.

οὗ. The genitive relative pronoun is either masculine (with τὸν ἀρχηγὸν τῆς ζωῆς as its antecedent) or, more likely, neuter (with the preceding statements as its antecedent).

μάρτυρές. Predicate nominative. The second accent comes from the enclitic ἐσμεν (see 1:4 on ἠκούσατέ).

ἐσμεν. Pres act ind 1st pl εἰμί. On the loss of accent, see 1:7 on ἐστιν.

3:16 καὶ ἐπὶ τῇ πίστει τοῦ ὀνόματος αὐτοῦ τοῦτον ὃν θεωρεῖτε καὶ οἴδατε, ἐστερέωσεν τὸ ὄνομα αὐτοῦ, καὶ ἡ πίστις ἡ δι' αὐτοῦ ἔδωκεν αὐτῷ τὴν ὁλοκληρίαν ταύτην ἀπέναντι πάντων ὑμῶν.

The language of this verse is notoriously difficult to decifer (cf. Barrett, 198–200). First, why is the preposition ἐπί used? The prepositional phrase ἐπὶ τῇ πίστει τοῦ ὀνόματος αὐτοῦ is typically rendered "by faith in his name." The preposition ἐπί, however, is not typically used in an instrumental sense (some scribes solved this problem by omitting it; see א* B). It would be more natural to take the preposition as causal or as denoting "in response to." Second, why is ὀνόμα(τος) αὐτοῦ included twice? The inclusion of τὸ ὄνομα αὐτοῦ after the verb ἐστερέωσεν is probably intended to make crystal clear to the listener that Jesus ("his name" should probably be read as a metonym for "him"; see 1:9 on τῶν ὀφθαλμῶν αὐτῶν) is responsible for the miracle. It may be possible to further minimize the apparent redundancy by reading the genitive τοῦ ὀνόματος as subjective rather than objective: "because of the faithfulness of his name, his name strengthened this man, whom you see and know." Third, what is the meaning of ἡ πίστις δι' αὐτοῦ? The preposition διά probably introduces the means of the faith(fulness).

τοῦτον. The fronting (see 3:13 on ὑμεῖς) of the demonstrative pronoun places the healed man in focus (see 2:15 on ὑμεῖς).

θεωρεῖτε. Pres act ind 2nd pl θεωρέω.

οἴδατε. Prf act ind 2nd pl οἶδα.

ἐστερέωσεν. Aor act ind 3rd sg στερεόω.

ἡ δι' αὐτοῦ. The article functions as an adjectivizer (see 2:5 on τῶν ὑπὸ τὸν οὐρανόν), changing the prepositional phrase into an attributive modifier.

ἔδωκεν. Aor act ind 3rd sg δίδωμι.

3:17 καὶ νῦν, ἀδελφοί, οἶδα ὅτι κατὰ ἄγνοιαν ἐπράξατε, ὥσπερ καὶ οἱ ἄρχοντες ὑμῶν·

καὶ νῦν. See 4:29 on καὶ τὰ νῦν.

οἶδα. Prf act ind 1st sg οἶδα.

ἐπράξατε. Aor act ind 2nd pl πράσσω.

ὥσπερ. See 2:2.

3:18 ὁ δὲ θεὸς ἃ προκατήγγειλεν διὰ στόματος πάντων τῶν προφητῶν παθεῖν τὸν Χριστὸν αὐτοῦ ἐπλήρωσεν οὕτως.

ὁ . . . θεὸς. Nominative subject of ἐπλήρωσεν.

ἃ. The relative pronoun (accusative direct object of ἐπλήρωσεν) introduces a headless relative clause (see 3:6 on ὅ): lit. "that which he foretold."

προκατήγγειλεν. Aor act ind 3rd sg προκαταγγέλλω.

πάντων. More Lukan hyperbole (cf. 1:18 on πάντα).

παθεῖν. Aor act inf πάσχω (epexegetical). Wallace (1996, 606–7) prefers to call this infinitive "appositional."

τὸν Χριστὸν. Accusative subject of the infinitive (see 1:3 on αὐτὸν).

ἐπλήρωσεν. Aor act ind 3rd sg πληρόω.

3:19 μετανοήσατε οὖν καὶ ἐπιστρέψατε εἰς τὸ ἐξαλειφθῆναι ὑμῶν τὰς ἁμαρτίας,

μετανοήσατε καὶ ἐπιστρέψατε. It is unclear whether the conjoined verbs should be viewed as a doublet (so Barrett, 203; see 2:43 on τέρατα καὶ σημεῖα). In 26:20, the same verbs are used together but clearly do not form a doublet since ἐπιστρέφειν is modified by ἐπὶ τὸν θεόν. Overall, it seems better to treat the first verb here as indicating "turning away" from sin and the second as indicating "turning to" God (though the verbs are not always used in this way; see, e.g., LXX Joel 2:14 where they are used with God as the subject).

μετανοήσατε. Aor act impv 2nd pl μετανοέω.

ἐπιστρέψατε. Aor act impv 2nd pl ἐπιστρέφω.

ἐξαλειφθῆναι. Aor pass inf ἐξαλείφω. Used with εἰς τό to denote purpose.

τὰς ἁμαρτίας. Accusative subject of the infinitive (see 1:3 on αὐτὸν).

3:20 ὅπως ἂν ἔλθωσιν καιροὶ ἀναψύξεως ἀπὸ προσώπου τοῦ κυρίου καὶ ἀποστείλῃ τὸν προκεχειρισμένον ὑμῖν Χριστόν Ἰησοῦν,

ὅπως. Introduces (with the subjunctive verbs) a second and third purpose (or motivation) of the imperative verbs in v. 19.

ἔλθωσιν. Aor act subj 3rd pl ἔρχομαι.

ἀποστείλῃ. Aor act subj 3rd sg ἀποστέλλω.

τὸν προκεχειρισμένον. Prf pass ptc masc acc sg προχειρίζομαι (attributive). The articular participle could also be taken substantivally, in which case Χριστόν Ἰησοῦν would be in apposition to the substantive participle ("the one who was chosen for you, Christ Jesus").

ὑμῖν. Dative of advantage.

Ἰησοῦν. Accusative in apposition to Χριστόν (but see above on προκεχειρισμένον).

3:21 ὃν δεῖ οὐρανὸν μὲν δέξασθαι ἄχρι χρόνων ἀποκαταστάσεως πάντων ὧν ἐλάλησεν ὁ θεὸς διὰ στόματος τῶν ἁγίων ἀπ' αἰῶνος αὐτοῦ προφητῶν.

ὃν δεῖ οὐρανὸν μὲν δέξασθαι. Lit. "whom it is necessary for heaven to welcome."

δεῖ. Pres act ind 3rd sg δεῖ (impersonal).

οὐρανὸν. Accusative subject of the infinitive (see 1:3 on αὐτὸν).

δέξασθαι. Aor mid dep inf δέχομαι (complementary; see 1:16 on ἔδει). Used with ἄχρι, the verb δέχομαι carries the sense "remain where one is received" (see Barrett, 205).

χρόνων . . . πάντων. Lit. "times of the restoration of all things."

ὧν. Probably genitive of reference rather than genitive by attraction to πάντων (see 1:1 on ὧν).

ἐλάλησεν ὁ θεὸς διὰ στόματος τῶν ἁγίων ἀπ' αἰῶνος αὐτοῦ προφητῶν. This expression is also found in Luke 1:70 and Odes of Solomon 9:70. The unusual word order in the phrase τῶν ἁγίων ἀπ' αἰῶνος αὐτοῦ προφητῶν (supported by 𝔓[74] א* A B* C) led to numerous variant readings, though the sense is clear enough. The syntax of the phrase is complicated by the position of αὐτοῦ, which probably rules out taking ἁγίων as an attributive adjective modifying προφητῶν. More likely, ἁγίων is substantival and αὐτοῦ modifies either ἁγίων ("through the mouth of his holy ones of old, the prophets") or προφητῶν ("through the mouth of the holy ones of old, his prophets").

ἐλάλησεν. Aor act ind 3rd sg λαλέω.

προφητῶν. Genitive in apposition to τῶν ἁγίων.

3:22 Μωϋσῆς μὲν εἶπεν ὅτι Προφήτην ὑμῖν ἀναστήσει κύριος ὁ θεὸς ὑμῶν ἐκ τῶν ἀδελφῶν ὑμῶν ὡς ἐμέ· αὐτοῦ ἀκούσεσθε κατὰ πάντα ὅσα ἂν λαλήσῃ πρὸς ὑμᾶς.

εἶπεν. Aor act ind 3rd sg λέγω.

ὅτι. Introduces direct discourse here.

ὑμῖν. Dative of advantage.

ἀναστήσει. Fut act ind 3rd sg ἀνίστημι. On the meaning of the verb, see v. 26 on ἀναστήσας.

ὡς ἐμέ. The comparison could mean either (1) God will raise up a prophet as he raised up me (so Barrett, 186); or (2) God will raise up a prophet like me. The fact that the fronted (see 3:13 on ὑμεῖς) noun Προφήτην is the topic (see 2:22 on Ἰησοῦν τὸν Ναζωραῖον) of the sentence and the comparison in LXX Deut 18:15 is more clearly "a prophet like me" (προφήτην ἐκ τῶν ἀδελφῶν σου ὡς ἐμὲ ἀναστήσει σοι κύριος ὁ θεός σου; see also 7:37) makes option (2) more likely.

αὐτοῦ. Genitive object of ἀκούσεσθε.

ἀκούσεσθε. Fut mid ind 2nd pl ἀκούω. The future functions like an imperative (cf. 18:15 on ὄψεσθε).

κατά. The preposition with the accusative noun denotes reference.

πάντα ὅσα. This emphatic construction makes it clear that absolute obedience is called for.

λαλήσῃ. Aor act subj 3rd sg λαλέω.

3:23 ἔσται δὲ πᾶσα ψυχὴ ἥτις ἐὰν μὴ ἀκούσῃ τοῦ προφήτου ἐκείνου ἐξολεθρευθήσεται ἐκ τοῦ λαοῦ.

ἔσται. Fut ind 3rd sg εἰμί. ἔσται plus a future finite verb (ἐξολεθρευθήσεται) forms a periphrastic future construction (cf. 2:17).

πᾶσα . . . ἥτις. This emphatic construction again makes it clear that absolute obedience is mandatory (cf. v. 22 on πάντα ὅσα).

ψυχὴ. Synecdoche (see 1:22 on τοῦ βαπτίσματος Ἰωάννου) for "person."

ἀκούσῃ. Aor act subj 3rd sg ἀκούω.

τοῦ προφήτου. Genitive object of ἀκούσῃ.

ἐξολεθρευθήσεται. Fut pass ind 3rd sg ἐξολεθρεύω. It is unclear whether the verb refers to execution or severe ostracism (suggested by the following prepositional phrase; cf. LN 20.35).

ἐκ. See 1:8 on ἐφ' ὑμᾶς.

3:24 καὶ πάντες δὲ οἱ προφῆται ἀπὸ Σαμουὴλ καὶ τῶν καθεξῆς ὅσοι ἐλάλησαν καὶ κατήγγειλαν τὰς ἡμέρας ταύτας.

τῶν καθεξῆς. The article functions as a nominalizer (see 1:3 on τὰ). In terms of syntax, τῶν καθεξῆς ("those in order/succession" = "successors") is part of the larger noun phrase Σαμουὴλ καὶ τῶν καθεξῆς that is governed by the preposition ἀπό. It is, therefore, in the genitive case. The phrase ἀπὸ Σαμουὴλ καὶ τῶν καθεξῆς appears to be a fairly rare idiomatic expression used to introduce a list with a starting point (the noun following ἀπό), a middle non-specific portion (καθεξῆς), and no final item (cf. Gregory of Nyssa, *Contra Eunomium* 3.1.12.9; Georgius Monachus, *Chronicon breve* 110.505.44).

ἐλάλησαν. Aor act ind 3rd pl λαλέω.

κατήγγειλαν. Aor act ind 3rd pl καταγγέλλω.

3:25 ὑμεῖς ἐστε οἱ υἱοὶ τῶν προφητῶν καὶ τῆς διαθήκης ἧς διέθετο ὁ θεὸς πρὸς τοὺς πατέρας ὑμῶν λέγων πρὸς Ἀβραάμ, Καὶ ἐν τῷ σπέρματί σου [ἐν]ευλογηθήσονται πᾶσαι αἱ πατριαὶ τῆς γῆς.

ὑμεῖς. The explicit fronted (see 3:13 on ὑμεῖς) subject pronoun places the rhetorical spotlight back on the audience as Peter begins to drive home his point.

ἐστε. Pres act ind 2nd pl εἰμί. On the loss of accent, see 1:7 on ἐστιν.

τῶν προφητῶν καὶ τῆς διαθήκης. The conjoined genitive nouns clearly function differently. The first denotes relationship while the second is descriptive. This distinction necessitates using two separate terms to render υἱοὶ in English.

ἧς. Genitive by attraction (see 1:1 on ὧν) to διαθήκης (it normally would have been accusative as the object of διέθετο; cf. Heb 8:10).

διέθετο. Aor mid ind 3rd sg διατίθημι/διατίθεμαι.

λέγων. Pres act ptc masc nom sg λέγω (temporal).

ἐν. Instrumental.

ἐνευλογηθήσονται. Fut pass ind 3rd pl ἐνευλογέω.

3:26 ὑμῖν πρῶτον ἀναστήσας ὁ θεὸς τὸν παῖδα αὐτοῦ ἀπέστειλεν αὐτὸν εὐλογοῦντα ὑμᾶς ἐν τῷ ἀποστρέφειν ἕκαστον ἀπὸ τῶν πονηριῶν ὑμῶν.

ὑμῖν. Dative of advantage construed with ἀναστήσας, or perhaps dative indirect object of ἀπέστειλεν.

πρῶτον. The adverb should probably be taken with the contiguous pronoun ὑμῖν ("first of all, for your benefit," contrasting what follows with the preceding statement about πᾶσαι αἱ πατριαὶ τῆς γῆς; cf. Barrett, 213) rather than with the participle ἀναστήσας or the verb ἀπέστειλεν.

ἀναστήσας. Aor act ptc masc nom sg ἀνίστημι (attendant circumstance). The verb should be taken in the same sense as in v. 22 ("to raise up to do something") rather than as "to raise from the dead."

παῖδα. See 3:13.

ἀπέστειλεν. Aor act ind 3rd sg ἀποστέλλω.

εὐλογοῦντα. Pres act ptc masc acc sg εὐλογέω (attributive). The participle cannot be adverbial since it does not have the same subject as the verb (see Culy 2004). The accusative case (in agreement with αὐτὸν) makes Jesus the agent of blessing.

ἀποστρέφειν. Pres act inf ἀποστρέφω. The infinitive construction (ἐν τῷ ἀποστρέφειν) can be understood in several ways: (1) it may denote contemporaneous time (cf. 2:1) and thus indicate that the blessing will occur in conjunction with repentance: "to bless you as each of you turn from your wicked ways"; or (2) the preposition may introduce the means of the blessing (so Wallace 1996, 598). In this interpretation the sense of the infinitive can be either (a) transitive ("by turning each of you") or, less likely, (b) intransitive ("by each of you turning").

ἕκαστον. Either the direct object of the infinitive or the accusative subject of the infinitive (see above and 1:3 on αὐτὸν).

Acts 4:1–12

1While they were speaking to the people, the priests, the captain of
the temple, and the Sadducees approached them. 2They were irate because (the apostles) were teaching the people and proclaiming, with
respect to Jesus, the resurrection from the dead. 3So they arrested them
and put them in jail until the next day; for it was already evening. 4But
many of those who had heard the message believed. Indeed, the number of men (that believed) was about 5,000.

5Now, on the next day, their leaders, elders, and scribes were gathered in Jerusalem. 6Annas, the high priest, Caiphas, John, Alexander,
and all those who were from the high priestly family (were also there).
7They made them stand before them and started asking, "By what power
or by what name did you do this?"

8Then Peter, filled with the Holy Spirit, said to them, "Rulers of the
people and elders, 9since we are being interrogated today because of a
good deed (done) for a sick man, (to find out) how this man has been
cured, 10let it be known to all of you, and to all the people of Israel, that
by the name of Jesus Christ of Nazareth—whom you crucified *but* God
raised from the dead—by this (name), this man stands before you,
healthy. 11This (Jesus) is the stone that was despised by you, the build-
ers, that has become the cornerstone. 12There is salvation in no other
person; for there is no other name under heaven that has been *given to*
people by which we must be saved."

4:1 Λαλούντων δὲ αὐτῶν πρὸς τὸν λαὸν ἐπέστησαν αὐτοῖς οἱ ἱερεῖς καὶ ὁ στρατηγὸς τοῦ ἱεροῦ καὶ οἱ Σαδδουκαῖοι,

Λαλούντων. Pres act ptc masc gen pl λαλέω. Genitive absolute (see 1:8 on ἐπελθόντος), temporal. The use of the genitive absolute allows Luke to paint a vivid picture in which Peter's speech is interrupted by the religious authorities.

αὐτῶν. Genitive subject (see 1:8 on ἐπελθόντος).

ἐπέστησαν. Aor act ind 3rd pl ἐφίστημι.

αὐτοῖς. Dative complement of ἐπέστησαν.

4:2 διαπονούμενοι διὰ τὸ διδάσκειν αὐτοὺς τὸν λαὸν καὶ καταγγέλλειν ἐν τῷ 'Ιησοῦ τὴν ἀνάστασιν τὴν ἐκ νεκρῶν,

διαπονούμενοι. Pres dep ptc masc nom pl διαπονέομαι (causal modifier of ἐπέστησαν).

διδάσκειν. Pres act inf διδάσκω. Used with διὰ τό to indicate cause.

αὐτοὺς. Accusative subject of the infinitive (see 1:3 on αὐτὸν).

καταγγέλλειν. Pres act inf καταγγέλλω. Used with διὰ τὸ to indicate cause.

ἐν. The preposition probably denotes reference/respect, "with reference to Jesus," though it may (perhaps) be understood instrumentally, "by means of (the story of) Jesus" (so Barrett, 220).

τὴν ἐκ νεκρῶν. The article functions as an adjectivizer (see 2:5 on τῶν ὑπὸ τὸν οὐρανόν), changing the prepositional phrase to an attributive modifier.

4:3 καὶ ἐπέβαλον αὐτοῖς τὰς χεῖρας καὶ ἔθεντο εἰς τήρησιν εἰς τὴν αὔριον· ἦν γὰρ ἑσπέρα ἤδη.

ἐπέβαλον αὐτοῖς τὰς χεῖρας. An idiom (lit. "they laid hands on them") meaning "to arrest" (LN 37.110) or "to attack" (Barrett, 574).

ἐπέβαλον. Aor act ind 3rd pl ἐπιβάλλω.

ἔθεντο εἰς τήρησιν. Or, "took them into custody" (Barrett, 221).

ἔθεντο. Aor mid ind 3rd pl τίθημι.

εἰς. Denotes extent of time.

τὴν. The article functions as a nominalizer (see 1:3 on τὰ), changing the adverb αὔριον into a substantive.

ἦν. Impf ind 3rd sg εἰμί.

ἑσπέρα. Predicate nominative.

4:4 πολλοὶ δὲ τῶν ἀκουσάντων τὸν λόγον ἐπίστευσαν, καὶ ἐγενήθη [ὁ] ἀριθμὸς τῶν ἀνδρῶν [ὡς] χιλιάδες πέντε.

τῶν ἀκουσάντων. Aor act ptc masc gen pl ἀκούω (substantival). Partitive genitive.

τὸν λόγον. Strictly speaking, τὸν λόγον could be the direct object of either ἀκουσάντων or ἐπίστευσαν. The word order favors the former.

ἐπίστευσαν. Aor act ind 3rd pl πιστεύω.

ἐγενήθη. Aor pass dep ind 3rd sg γίνομαι. The use of this verb leaves it unclear whether the writer intended to say that (1) there were 5,000 men there on that particular day who believed, or (2) including the men who believed on that day, the number of male believers, which had previously been placed at 3,000 (see 2:41), now rose to 5,000 (cf. Barrett, 221).

τῶν ἀνδρῶν. As Barrett (222) notes, this expression should probably not be viewed as a generic reference that could also include women. For some reason, only the men were counted.

[ὡς]. The use of brackets in the UBS[4]/NA[27] text indicates the difficulty, given the variation in the textual tradition, of determining whether ὡς should be traced to Luke or to scribes attempting to imitate him.

4:5 Ἐγένετο δὲ ἐπὶ τὴν αὔριον συναχθῆναι αὐτῶν τοὺς ἄρχοντας καὶ τοὺς πρεσβυτέρους καὶ τοὺς γραμματεῖς ἐν Ἰερουσαλήμ,

Ἐγένετο. Aor mid dep ind 3rd sg γίνομαι. "The word ἐγένετο 'it happened,' followed by a temporal expression and sometimes an infinitival subject, is a device that Luke often uses to indicate that the prior events form the background for the following foreground events. . . . In Acts, the infinitival subject of ἐγένετο typically presents an event which is the specific circumstance for the following foreground events" (Levinsohn 1992, 170–71, 174; cf. Gault, 393).

τὴν. The article functions as a nominalizer (see 1:3 on τὰ), changing the adverb αὔριον into a substantive.

συναχθῆναι. Aor pass inf συνάγω. The infinitival clause (συναχθῆναι αὐτῶν τοὺς ἄρχοντας καὶ τοὺς πρεσβυτέρους καὶ τοὺς γραμματεῖς ἐν Ἰερουσαλήμ) functions as the subject of ἐγένετο (see also 9:32 on κατελθεῖν).

αὐτῶν. The antecedent of the pronoun is syntactically unspecified, but clearly must be "the Jews" as a group.

τοὺς ἄρχοντας καὶ τοὺς πρεσβυτέρους καὶ τοὺς γραμματεῖς. Accusative subject of the infinitive (see 1:3 on αὐτὸν).

γραμματεῖς. Experts in the Jewish Law.

4:6 καὶ Ἅννας ὁ ἀρχιερεὺς καὶ Καϊάφας καὶ Ἰωάννης καὶ Ἀλέξανδρος καὶ ὅσοι ἦσαν ἐκ γένους ἀρχιερατικοῦ,

Ἅννας ὁ ἀρχιερεὺς καὶ Καϊάφας καὶ Ἰωάννης καὶ Ἀλέξανδρος καὶ ὅσοι ἦσαν ἐκ γένους ἀρχιερατικοῦ. The whole construction serves as the nominative subject of ἐπυνθάνοντο (v. 7).

ἦσαν. Impf ind 3rd pl εἰμί.

γένους. Genitive following ἐκ (from γένος).

4:7 καὶ στήσαντες αὐτοὺς ἐν τῷ μέσῳ ἐπυνθάνοντο, Ἐν ποίᾳ δυνάμει ἢ ἐν ποίῳ ὀνόματι ἐποιήσατε τοῦτο ὑμεῖς;

στήσαντες. Aor act ptc masc nom pl ἵστημι (attendant circumstance or temporal).

αὐτοὺς. Once again (see v. 5), the antecedent is unspecified in the syntax. Here, the referents are clearly Peter and John.

ἐπυνθάνοντο. Impf mid ind 3rd pl πυνθάνομαι.

Ἐν/ἐν. Instrumental.

ἐν ποίῳ ὀνόματι. Or, "by whose authority?" (cf. 3:6 on ἐν τῷ ὀνόματι).

ἐποιήσατε. Aor act ind 2nd pl ποιέω.

4:8 τότε Πέτρος πλησθεὶς πνεύματος ἁγίου εἶπεν πρὸς αὐτούς, Ἄρχοντες τοῦ λαοῦ καὶ πρεσβύτεροι,

τότε. Peter's reply gets straight to the point (Levinsohn 1987, 152; see 1:12).

πλησθεὶς. Aor pass ptc masc nom sg πίμπλημι (attributive). The participle could also be taken as attendant circumstance ("Then Peter was filled with the Holy Spirit and said . . ."; cf. 13:9) or temporal ("Then, after Peter was filled with the Holy Spirit, he said . . .").

πνεύματος. See 2:4.

εἶπεν. Aor act ind 3rd sg λέγω.

Ἄρχοντες καὶ πρεσβύτεροι. Vocative.
τοῦ λαοῦ. Genitive of subordination.

4:9 εἰ ἡμεῖς σήμερον ἀνακρινόμεθα ἐπὶ εὐεργεσίᾳ ἀνθρώπου ἀσθενοῦς ἐν τίνι οὗτος σέσωται,

εἰ. Introduces a first class condition; here appropriately rendered, "since." The relationship between the protasis and apodosis (v. 10) is one of cause and effect (see Kruger, 101–5; cited in Porter 1989, 319).

ἀνακρινόμεθα. Pres pass ind 1st pl ἀνακρίνω.

ἐπὶ. Causal.

ἀνθρώπου. The genitive noun is the object of the implicit verbal idea in εὐεργεσίᾳ.

ἀσθενοῦς. Genitive (from ἀσθενής) in agreement with ἀνθρώπου.

ἐν τίνι. "How?" (lit. "with what"; cf. Matt 5:13//Luke 14:34; Mark 9:50). It may also be possible to take the phrase instrumentally with τίνι being masculine rather than neuter: "by whom" (cf. Matt 12:27// Luke 11:19).

σέσωται. Prf pass ind 3rd sg σῴζω.

4:10 γνωστὸν ἔστω πᾶσιν ὑμῖν καὶ παντὶ τῷ λαῷ Ἰσραὴλ ὅτι ἐν τῷ ὀνόματι Ἰησοῦ Χριστοῦ τοῦ Ναζωραίου ὃν ὑμεῖς ἐσταυρώσατε, ὃν ὁ θεὸς ἤγειρεν ἐκ νεκρῶν, ἐν τούτῳ οὗτος παρέστηκεν ἐνώπιον ὑμῶν ὑγιής.

γνωστὸν. Predicate (neuter) nominative.

ἔστω. Pres act impv 3rd sg εἰμί.

ὅτι. See 28:22.

ἐν τῷ ὀνόματι. The prepositional phrase probably denotes the instrument/means by which the man was healed (on the meaning of the phrase, see 3:6).

ἐσταυρώσατε. Aor act ind 2nd pl σταυρόω.

τοῦ Ναζωραίου. Lit. "the Nazarene." Genitive in apposition to Ἰησοῦ Χριστοῦ.

ἤγειρεν. Aor act ind 3rd sg ἐγείρω.

ἐν τούτῳ. The demonstrative pronoun is resumptive and focuses the listener's/reader's attention on Jesus (or his name). The syntactic antecedent of τούτῳ could be either τῷ ὀνόματι (neuter dative; the prepositional phrase would then introduce the instrument/means of the healing) or, less likely, Ἰησοῦ Χριστοῦ (masculine dative).

παρέστηκεν. Prf act ind 3rd sg παρίστημι.

ὑγιής. Predicate adjective.

4:11 οὗτός ἐστιν ὁ λίθος, ὁ ἐξουθενηθεὶς ὑφ' ὑμῶν τῶν οἰκοδόμων, ὁ γενόμενος εἰς κεφαλὴν γωνίας.

οὗτός. The antecedent is Ἰησοῦ Χριστοῦ (v. 10). The second accent comes from the enclitic ἐστιν (see 1:4 on ἠκούσατέ).

ἐστιν. Pres act ind 3rd sg εἰμί. On the loss of accent, see 1:7 on ἐστιν.

ὁ λίθος. Predicate nominative.

ὁ ἐξουθενηθείς. Aor pass ptc masc nom sg ἐξουθενέω (attributive or substantival in apposition to ὁ λίθος). The editors of the UBS[4]/NA[27] text indicated their preference for the latter by inserting a comma.

ὑφ'. Introduces the agent of the participle ἐξουθενηθείς.

τῶν οἰκοδόμων. Genitive in apposition to ὑμῶν.

ὁ γενόμενος. Aor mid ptc masc nom sg γίνομαι (attributive or substantival in apposition to ὁ λίθος).

εἰς κεφαλὴν γωνίας. The preposition εἰς with an accusative noun is frequently used as a substitute for a predicate modifier to indicate equivalence (cf. 5:36; 7:5, 21; 8:20; 11:29; 13:22, 47; 19:47; and probably 7:53). The construction usually occurs in OT quotations, and thus typically reflects a Semitic influence (see Wallace 1996, 47).

κεφαλὴν γωνίας. Lit. "head of the corner."

4:12 καὶ οὐκ ἔστιν ἐν ἄλλῳ οὐδενὶ ἡ σωτηρία, οὐδὲ γὰρ ὄνομά ἐστιν ἕτερον ὑπὸ τὸν οὐρανὸν τὸ δεδομένον ἐν ἀνθρώποις ἐν ᾧ δεῖ σωθῆναι ἡμᾶς.

ἔστιν. Pres act ind 3rd sg εἰμί. The verb εἰμί, which is usually enclitic in the present indicative (see 1:7 on ἐστιν), does not lose its accent when preceded by οὐκ.

ἐν ἄλλῳ οὐδενί. The adjective οὐδενί could be either masculine and refer to Jesus, or perhaps neuter (referring to ὄνομα). In the latter case, the preposition would introduce the instrument/means of salvation. In the former case, it would introduce the agent (a function of ἐν that is questioned by Wallace 1996, 373–74).

ἡ σωτηρία. Nominative subject or predicate nominative (with impersonal ἔστιν).

ὄνομά. Predicate nominative (with impersonal ἐστιν). The second accent comes from the enclitic ἐστιν (see 1:4 on ἠκούσατέ).

ἐστιν. Pres act ind 3rd sg εἰμί. On the loss of accent, see 1:7 on ἐστιν.

ὑπὸ τὸν οὐρανὸν. Barrett (232) rightly compares this expression (lit. "under heaven" or "under the sky") with the English expression "under the sun." It sets Jesus (or his name) off as the unique means of salvation for humankind.

δεδομένον. Prf pass ptc neut nom sg δίδωμι (attributive).

ἐν ἀνθρώποις. The prepositional phrase could be understood as locative (among humankind) or as introducing the indirect object (a rare usage analogous to the simple dative; Codex D omits the preposition). It is also possible, however, that δίδωμι ἐν may be an idiomatic expression that means something like "to dole out" or "to distribute" (see 2 Cor 8:1; cf. LXX Gen 49:21; 2 Kgs 19:7; 2 Chr 11:11; Isa 46:13; Ezek 23:46; Sir 47:10).

ἐν ᾧ. Instrument/means.

δεῖ. Pres act ind 3rd sg δεῖ (impersonal).

σωθῆναι. Aor pass inf σῴζω (complementary; see 1:16 on πληρωθῆναι).

ἡμᾶς. Accusative subject of the infinitive (see 1:3 on αὐτὸν).

Acts 4:13–22

[13]When they saw the boldness of Peter and John, and realized that they lacked education and were laymen, they were amazed and recognized them—that they had been with Jesus. [14]And when they saw the man standing with them, who had been healed, they had nothing to say against (them). [15]So they commanded them to depart from the Council and began conferring with one another, [16]saying, "What should we do with these men? For, it is obvious to all those living in Jerusalem that an extraordinary sign has occurred through them, and we are not able to deny it. [17]But in order that this may not spread further among the people, let us warn them not to speak in this name any more with anyone."

[18]So they summoned them and ordered them that under no condition were they to speak or teach in the name of Jesus. [19]But Peter and John responded and said to them, "Is it right before God to obey you rather than God? You be the judge! [20]For we simply must tell about the things we have seen and heard!"

[21]Then, after threatening them more, they released them because they could not find a way to punish them, on account of the people, since everyone was glorifying God because of what had happened. [22]For the man on whom this sign of healing had been performed had been (crippled) for more than forty years!

4:13 Θεωροῦντες δὲ τὴν τοῦ Πέτρου παρρησίαν καὶ Ἰωάννου καὶ καταλαβόμενοι ὅτι ἄνθρωποι ἀγράμματοί εἰσιν καὶ ἰδιῶται, ἐθαύμαζον ἐπεγίνωσκόν τε αὐτοὺς ὅτι σὺν τῷ Ἰησοῦ ἦσαν,

Θεωροῦντες. Pres act ptc masc nom pl θεωρέω (temporal).

καταλαβόμενοι. Aor mid ptc masc nom pl καταλαμβάνω (temporal).

ἄνθρωποι. Predicate nominative.

ἀγράμματοί. "Pertaining to one who has not acquired a formal education (referring primarily to formal training)" (LN 27.23). The second accent comes from the enclitic εἰσιν (see 1:4 on ἠκούσατέ).

εἰσιν. Pres act ind 3rd pl εἰμί. On the loss of accent, see 1:7 on ἐστιν. The tense reflects what would be used in direct discourse (see Wallace 1996, 458, 537–39).

ἰδιῶται. "A person who has not acquired systemic information or expertise in some field of knowledge or activity" (LN 27.26).

ἐθαύμαζον. Impf act ind 3rd pl θαυμάζω.

ἐπεγίνωσκόν. Impf act ind 3rd pl ἐπιγινώσκω. The second accent comes from the enclitic τε (see 1:4 on ἠκούσατέ).

αὐτοὺς. The use of the direct object pronoun makes the expression more forceful: "they recognized them, that they . . ." rather than simply "they recognized that they . . ." (cf. 3:10; Barrett, 234).

ὅτι. Epexegetical (not complementary, see above on αὐτοὺς).

ἦσαν. Impf ind 3rd pl εἰμί. The tense reflects what would be used in direct discourse (see Wallace 1996, 458, 552–53).

4:14 τόν τε ἄνθρωπον βλέποντες σὺν αὐτοῖς ἑστῶτα τὸν τεθεραπευμένον οὐδὲν εἶχον ἀντειπεῖν.

τόν ἄνθρωπον. The direct object is fronted (see 3:13 on ὑμεῖς), temporarily placing the healed man in focus (see 2:15 on ὑμεῖς).

βλέποντες. Pres act ptc masc nom pl βλέπω (temporal). The participle could also be taken causally: "And since they saw the man . . ."

ἑστῶτα. Prf act ptc masc acc sg ἵστημι. The participle functions as the complement in an object-complement double accusative construction (see 1:3 on ζῶντα). The distinction between this use of the participle and an attributive participle is illustrated in this verse where the participial complement is anarthrous (see 3:3 on Πέτρον καὶ ' Ιώαννου) and the attributive participle is articular modifying an articular head noun (τόν ἄνθρωπον).

τεθεραπευμένον. Prf pass ptc masc acc sg θεραπεύω (attributive).

εἶχον. Impf act ind 3rd pl ἔχω.

ἀντειπεῖν. Aor act inf ἀντιλέγω (epexegetical to οὐδὲν).

4:15 κελεύσαντες δὲ αὐτοὺς ἔξω τοῦ συνεδρίου ἀπελθεῖν συνέβαλλον πρὸς ἀλλήλους

κελεύσαντες. Aor act ptc masc nom pl κελεύω (temporal).

αὐτοὺς. Accusative subject of the infinitive (see 1:3 on αὐτὸν), not the direct object of (the intransitive) κελεύσαντες.

ἀπελθεῖν. Aor act inf ἀπέρχομαι (indirect discourse; not epexegetical since αὐτοὺς is not the direct object of κελεύσαντες).

συνέβαλλον. Impf act ind 3rd pl συνβάλλω.

4:16 λέγοντες, Τί ποιήσωμεν τοῖς ἀνθρώποις τούτοις; ὅτι μὲν γὰρ γνωστὸν σημεῖον γέγονεν δι' αὐτῶν πᾶσιν τοῖς κατοικοῦσιν 'Ιερουσαλὴμ φανερόν καὶ οὐ δυνάμεθα ἀρνεῖσθαι·

λέγοντες. Pres act ptc masc nom pl λέγω (attendant circumstance; redundant, see 1:6 on λέγοντες).

ποιήσωμεν. Aor act subj 1st pl ποιέω (hortatory; see 2:37 on ποιήσωμεν).

τοῖς ἀνθρώποις. Dative of reference/respect.

ὅτι. The ὅτι introduces a substantival clause (see Wallace 1996, 453–54) that functions as the subject of an implicit verb (ἐστιν is added by Codex D).

γνωστὸν. Neuter nominative modifier of σημεῖον meaning "extraordinary, unusual" or "well known, remarkable" (LN 58.55, 28.32).

σημεῖον. Nominative subject of γέγονεν.

γέγονεν. Prf act ind 3rd sg γίνομαι.

δι' αὐτῶν. Instrumental/intermediate agent.

τοῖς κατοικοῦσιν. Pres act ptc masc dat pl κατοικέω (substantival).

φανερόν. Predicate (neuter) adjective.

δυνάμεθα. Pres dep ind 1st pl δύναμαι.

ἀρνεῖσθαι. Pres dep inf ἀρνέομαι (complementary).

4:17 ἀλλ' ἵνα μὴ ἐπὶ πλεῖον διανεμηθῇ εἰς τὸν λαὸν ἀπειλησώμεθα αὐτοῖς μηκέτι λαλεῖν ἐπὶ τῷ ὀνόματι τούτῳ μηδενὶ ἀνθρώπων.

διανεμηθῇ. Aor pass subj 3rd sg διανέμω. Used with ἵνα to introduce a negative purpose clause.

ἀπειλησώμεθα. Aor mid subj 1st pl ἀπειλέω (hortatory).

λαλεῖν. Pres act inf λαλέω (indirect discourse).

ἐπὶ τῷ ὀνόματι. Although expressions like ἐν τῷ ὀνόματι 'Ιησοῦ, using the preposition ἐν, are common in the epistles (1 Cor 5:4; 6:11; Eph 5:20; Phil 2:10; Col 3:17; 2 Thes 3:6; Jas 5:10, 14; 1 Pet 4:14, 16) and do occur in the book of Acts (10:48; 16:18), Luke appears to use ἐπί in roughly the same way (2:38; 4:17, 18; 5:28, 40) more frequently (but see note on v. 18).

μηδενὶ ἀνθρώπων. Dative indirect object (the genitive ἀνθρώπων is partitive): lit. "to no one of men."

4:18 καὶ καλέσαντες αὐτοὺς παρήγγειλαν τὸ καθόλου μὴ φθέγγεσθαι μηδὲ διδάσκειν ἐπὶ τῷ ὀνόματι τοῦ 'Ιησοῦ.

καλέσαντες. Aor act ptc masc nom pl καλέω (attendant circumstance or temporal; see 1:15 on ἀναστὰς).

παρήγγειλαν. Aor act ind 3rd pl παραγγέλλω.

καθόλου. "at all" or "under no condition."

φθέγγεσθαι. Pres dep inf φθέγγομαι (indirect discourse).

διδάσκειν. Pres act inf διδάσκω (indirect discourse).

ἐπὶ τῷ ὀνόματι. The preposition may be equivalent to ἐν here (see v. 17), or it may reflect something akin to the English expression "to teach on (a particular subject)."

4:19 ὁ δὲ Πέτρος καὶ 'Ιωάννης ἀποκριθέντες εἶπον πρὸς αὐτούς, Εἰ δίκαιόν ἐστιν ἐνώπιον τοῦ θεοῦ ὑμῶν ἀκούειν μᾶλλον ἢ τοῦ θεοῦ, κρίνατε·

ἀποκριθέντες. Aor pass dep ptc masc nom pl ἀποκρίνομαι (attendant circumstance).

εἶπον. Aor act ind 3rd pl λέγω.

δίκαιόν. Predicate adjective (neuter nominative). The second accent comes from the enclitic ἐστιν (see 1:4 on ἠκούσατέ).

ἐστιν. Pres act ind 3rd sg εἰμί. On the loss of accent, see 1:7 on ἐστιν.

Εἰ. Introduces a direct question (cf. 1:6; 7:1; but see note below).

ὑμῶν. Genitive object of ἀκούειν.

ἀκούειν. Pres act inf ἀκούω (subject; but see note below).

τοῦ θεοῦ. Genitive object of ἀκούειν.

κρίνατε. Aor act impv 2nd pl κρίνω.

Note: Verse 19 could also be taken in the following way: "You must decide whether it is right before God to obey you rather than God!" In this case, Εἰ would introduce an indirect question and ἀκούειν would be epexegetical.

4:20 οὐ δυνάμεθα γὰρ ἡμεῖς ἃ εἴδαμεν καὶ ἠκούσαμεν μὴ λαλεῖν.

οὐ δυνάμεθα . . . μὴ λαλεῖν. This construction (lit. "we are not able not to tell") probably represents a litotes (see 1:5 on οὐ μετὰ πολλὰς ταύτας ἡμέρας) meaning, "We must by all means tell . . ."

δυνάμεθα. Pres dep ind 1st pl δύναμαι.

ἃ. The neuter accusative relative pronoun introduces a headless relative clause (see 3:6 on ὃ). The relative pronoun is the direct object of εἴδαμεν καὶ ἠκούσαμεν not λαλεῖν (which has the implied antecedent of ἃ as its direct object).

εἴδαμεν. Aor act ind 1st pl ὁράω.

ἠκούσαμεν. Aor act ind 1st pl ἀκούω.

λαλεῖν. Pres act inf λαλέω (complementary to δυνάμεθα).

4:21 οἱ δὲ προσαπειλησάμενοι ἀπέλυσαν αὐτούς, μηδὲν εὑρίσκοντες τὸ πῶς κολάσωνται αὐτούς, διὰ τὸν λαόν, ὅτι πάντες ἐδόξαζον τὸν θεὸν ἐπὶ τῷ γεγονότι·

οἱ. The article probably functions like a personal pronoun (see 3:5), though it could conceivably be taken as a nominalizer (see 1:3 on τὰ) making the participle substantival (see v. 24 on οἱ ἀκούσαντες).

προσαπειλησάμενοι. Aor mid ptc masc nom pl προσαπειλέω (temporal or attendant circumstance; but see note on οἱ above).

ἀπέλυσαν. Aor act ind 3rd pl ἀπολύω.

μηδὲν. The adjective modifies the nominalized clause (τὸ πῶς κολάσωνται αὐτούς; see below) rather than being an accusative of respect (contra Barrett, 238).

εὑρίσκοντες. Pres act ptc masc nom pl εὑρίσκω (causal).

τὸ πῶς κολάσωνται αὐτούς. The article functions as a nominalizer (see 1:3 on τὰ), changing the interrogative clause into a substantive that serves as the direct object of εὑρίσκοντες (cf. 1 Thes 4:1; BDF §267).

κολάσωνται. Aor mid subj 3rd pl κολάζω. The subjunctive is used with a potential event.

ἐδόξαζον. Impf act ind 3rd pl δοξάζω.

τῷ γεγονότι. Prf act ptc neut dat sg γίνομαι (substantival).

4:22 ἐτῶν γὰρ ἦν πλειόνων τεσσεράκοντα ὁ ἄνθρωπος ἐφ' ὃν γεγόνει τὸ σημεῖον τοῦτο τῆς ἰάσεως.

ἐτῶν . . . πλειόνων τεσσεράκοντα. There are several ways that this expression can be analyzed. Barrett (239) treats ἐτῶν . . . πλειόνων as a descriptive genitive noun phrase with τεσσεράκοντα being a genitive of comparison. He accordingly renders the clause: "the man . . . was more than forty years old." There are two problems with this analysis. First, it does not account for the use of γάρ. What relevance could the man's age have to the popular reaction to the miracle? Second, it does not account for the forefronting of the word ἐτῶν. It is more likely that the writer has left the man's state (crippled) implicit. The expression ἐτῶν . . . πλειόνων would then be a genitive introducing duration of time (a rare use of the genitive, but see the reading of D* in 1:3: τεσσεράκοντα ἡμερῶν for δι' ἡμερῶν τεσσεράκοντα; see also BDF §186). This results in the rendering: "For the man . . . had been that way over the course of more than forty years!"

γὰρ. Introduces the reason for such a widespread reaction to the miracle.

ἦν. Impf ind 3rd sg εἰμί.

γεγόνει. Plprf act ind 3rd sg γίνομαι. As is common in the NT, the pluperfect occurs without an augment (cf. 14:23; 20:16; Bruce, 155).

τῆς ἰάσεως. Epexegetical genitive.

Acts 4:23–31

[23]After they had been released they went to their own people and

reported everything that the chief priests and elders had said to them.
[24]Those who heard it together lifted (their) voice to God and said, "Master, you who made the sky and earth and sea and all that is in them,
[25](You) who, through the mouth of our ancestor David, your servant—
by the Holy Spirit—said, 'Why did the nations rage and the people plan
foolish things? [26]The kings of the earth took their stand and the rulers
assembled together against the Lord and against his Christ' [27]—and
certainly in this city, both Herod and Pontius Pilate, with the Gentiles
and the people of Israel, assembled together against your holy servant
Jesus, whom you annointed, [28]to do what (you by) your power and plan
foreordained to happen. [29]And now, Lord, (please) take note of their
threats and allow your servants to speak your message with great boldness [30]by stretching out your hand so that there will be healing and
signs and wonders through the name of your holy servant Jesus."
[31]While they were praying the place where they had gathered began
to shake, and all of them were filled with the Holy Spirit and began
speaking the message of God with boldness.

4:23 Ἀπολυθέντες δὲ ἦλθον πρὸς τοὺς ἰδίους καὶ ἀπήγγειλαν ὅσα πρὸς αὐτοὺς οἱ ἀρχιερεῖς καὶ οἱ πρεσβύτεροι εἶπαν.

Ἀπολυθέντες. Aor pass ptc masc nom pl ἀπολύω (temporal).

ἦλθον. Aor act ind 3rd pl ἔρχομαι.

τοὺς ἰδίους. Probably a reference to the Christian community as a whole (Barrett, 242).

ἀπήγγειλαν. Aor act ind 3rd pl ἀπαγγέλλω.

εἶπαν. Aor act ind 3rd pl λέγω.

4:24 οἱ δὲ ἀκούσαντες ὁμοθυμαδὸν ἦραν φωνὴν πρὸς τὸν θεὸν καὶ εἶπαν, Δέσποτα, σὺ ὁ ποιήσας τὸν οὐρανὸν καὶ τὴν γῆν καὶ τὴν θάλασσαν καὶ πάντα τὰ ἐν αὐτοῖς,

οἱ . . . ἀκούσαντες. This construction could be analyzed in one of two ways: (1) the two constituents could be taken together as a substantival participial phrase ("those who heard it"); or (2) the article could function like a pronoun (see 12:15) with the participle functioning temporally: "they, when they heard it." The latter is supported (a) by the writer's frequent use of a pronominal article followed by δέ to begin a speech (here a prayer; see 12:15); and (b) possibly by the variant reading in Codex D that seems to support a temporal sense: οἱ δὲ ἀκούσαντες καὶ ἐπιγνόντες τὴν τοῦ θεοῦ ἐνεργείαν. The (major) weakness of this view is that the writer does not generally use a pronominal article with an adverbial participle at the beginning of a sentence (see, e.g., 2:37; 5:5, 21; 7:12, 54).

ἀκούσαντες. Aor act ptc masc nom pl ἀκούω (substantival, but see above).

ὁμοθυμαδὸν. See 1:14.

ἦραν. Aor act ind 3rd pl αἴρω.

εἶπαν. Aor act ind 3rd pl λέγω.

Δέσποτα. This vocative noun (cf. κύριος) emphasizes the fact that God is in absolute control of all that he created, including the Jewish authorities.

σὺ ὁ ποιήσας. Vocative; or perhaps an equative clause with a nominative subject (σύ) and a predicate nominative (ὁ ποιήσας): "You are the maker . . ."

ὁ ποιήσας. Aor act ptc masc nom sg ποιέω (substantival). The articular participle either stands in apposition to the pronoun or is a predicate nominative (see above).

τὰ. The article functions as a nominalizer (see 1:3).

4:25 ὁ τοῦ πατρὸς ἡμῶν διὰ πνεύματος ἁγίου στόματος Δαυὶδ παιδός σου εἰπών, Ἱνατί ἐφρύαξαν ἔθνη καὶ λαοὶ ἐμελέτησαν κενά;

ὁ τοῦ πατρὸς ἡμῶν διὰ πνεύματος ἁγίου στόματος Δαυὶδ παιδός σου εἰπών. The unusual word order in the UBS[4]/NA[27] text (supported by 𝔓[74] ℵ A B E Ψ 33 *al*) appears to have spawned several improvements, including ὃς διὰ πνεύματος ἁγίου διὰ τοῦ στόματος λαλήσας Δαυὶδ παιδὸς σου (D) and ὁ διὰ στόματος Δαυὶδ παιδός σου εἰπών (*Byz al*). As Omanson notes, it would be very difficult to explain how the complicated text reflected in UBS[4]/NA[27] could have arisen through scribal additions to one of the simpler texts.

ὁ . . . εἰπών. The article modifies the participle εἰπών and marks the beginning of a long participial clause (with nine genitives!) of which εἰπών is the head. The whole clause (and the following subordinate clauses in this verse) stands in apposition to the previous participial clause in v. 24 (ὁ ποιήσας τὸν οὐρανὸν καὶ τὴν γῆν καὶ τὴν θάλασσαν καὶ πάντα τὰ ἐν αὐτοῖς) and thus further identifies the σύ of v. 24. It can thus be taken either as vocative or as a predicate nominative.

τοῦ πατρὸς. Genitive of means ("by our father") or possession (modifying στόματος).

ἡμῶν. Genitive of relationship.

διὰ πνεύματος ἁγίου. Instrumental/intermediate agent.

στόματος. Genitive of means (perhaps in apposition to τοῦ πατρὸς: "(You) who, by the Holy Spirit, through our ancestor—that is, through the mouth of David your servant—said."

Δαυὶδ. Genitive of possession.

παιδός. Genitive in apposition to Δαυὶδ. On the meaning, see 3:13.

σου. Genitive of relationship.

εἰπών. Aor act ptc masc nom sg λέγω (substantival; see above).

Ἱνατί. A shortened form (crasis) of ἵνα τί γένηται meaning "why?" (lit. "in order that what might happen").

ἐφρύαξαν. Aor act ind 3rd pl φρυάσσω. According to Louw and Nida (88.185), φρυάσσω means "to show insolent anger, to rave, to be incensed." Barrett (246) notes that "it suggests a haughty, insolent, abusive attitude."

ἐμελέτησαν. Aor act ind 3rd pl μελετάω.

κενά. Substantival.

4:26 παρέστησαν οἱ βασιλεῖς τῆς γῆς καὶ οἱ ἄρχοντες συνήχθησαν ἐπὶ τὸ αὐτὸ κατὰ τοῦ κυρίου καὶ κατὰ τοῦ Χριστοῦ αὐτοῦ.

παρέστησαν. Aor act ind 3rd pl παρίστημι.

τῆς γῆς. Genitive of subordination (Wallace 1996, 103).

συνήχθησαν. Aor pass ind 3rd pl συνάγω.

ἐπὶ τὸ αὐτὸ. The LXX expression probably means "together" here, following the Hebrew יחד (but see 2:44), though it is somewhat redundant with a συν- verb.

κατὰ. See v. 27 on ἐπὶ τὸν ἅγιον παῖδά σου.

4:27 συνήχθησαν γὰρ ἐπ' ἀληθείας ἐν τῇ πόλει ταύτῃ ἐπὶ τὸν ἅγιον παῖδά σου Ἰησοῦν ὃν ἔχρισας, Ἡρῴδης τε καὶ Πόντιος Πιλᾶτος σὺν ἔθνεσιν καὶ λαοῖς Ἰσραήλ,

συνήχθησαν. Aor pass ind 3rd pl συνάγω.

γὰρ. The conjunction marks vv. 27–28 as parenthetical.

ἐπ' ἀληθείας. An adverbial expression meaning, "certainly."

ἐπὶ τὸν ἅγιον παῖδά σου. It is unclear whether the switch from κατά (v. 26) to ἐπί changes the sense of the action, reflects a shift in Greek usage in the NT period, or simply reflects the use of a synonym for stylistic purposes. Louw and Nida (90.34) state that ἐπί with the accusative or dative can serve as "a marker of opposition in a judicial or quasijudicial context," while κατά with the genitive can serve as "a marker of opposition, with the possible implication of antagonism" (90.31).

παῖδά. See 3:13. The second accent comes from the enclitic σου (see 1:4 on ἠκούσατέ).

Ἰησοῦν. Accusative in apposition to παῖδά.

ἔχρισας. Aor act ind 2nd sg χρίω.

λαοῖς. Dative, as part of the noun phrase (ἔθνεσιν καὶ λαοῖς Ἰσραήλ) governed by σύν.

4:28 ποιῆσαι ὅσα ἡ χείρ σου καὶ ἡ βουλή [σου] προώρισεν γενέσθαι.

ποιῆσαι. Aor act inf ποιέω (purpose).

ἡ χείρ σου . . . ἡ βουλή [σου]. Synecdoche (see 1:22 on τοῦ βαπτίσματος Ἰωάννου) for "you."

προώρισεν. Aor act ind 3rd sg προορίζω. Singular verbs are sometimes used with compound subjects. The present case may be explained by the fact that both subject nouns refer (by synecdoche) to the same referent: God.

γενέσθαι. Aor mid dep inf γίνομαι (complementary).

4:29 καὶ τὰ νῦν, κύριε, ἔπιδε ἐπὶ τὰς ἀπειλὰς αὐτῶν καὶ δὸς τοῖς δούλοις σου μετὰ παρρησίας πάσης λαλεῖν τὸν λόγον σου,

καὶ τὰ νῦν. Within a speech, this expression seems to indicate that the speaker is about to make his or her main point (cf. 5:38; 7:34; 10:5; 13:11; 20:22, 25, 32; 22:16; 27:22; see also 17:30 on τὰ νῦν).

κύριε. Vocative.

ἔπιδε. Aor act impv 2nd sg ἐφοράω/ἐπεῖδον (request).

δὸς τοῖς δούλοις. Lit. "give to your servants." The imperative verb δὸς together with the infinitive λαλεῖν forms a causative construction (see 2:4 on ἐδίδου).

δὸς. Aor act impv 2nd sg δίδωμι (request).

μετὰ παρρησίας πάσης. Introduces the manner in which they desire to speak.

λαλεῖν. Pres act inf λαλέω (complementary; the infinitival clause functions as the clausal direct object of δὸς).

4:30 ἐν τῷ τὴν χεῖρά [σου] ἐκτείνειν σε εἰς ἴασιν καὶ σημεῖα καὶ τέρατα γίνεσθαι διὰ τοῦ ὀνόματος τοῦ ἁγίου παιδός σου Ἰησοῦ.

ἐν τῷ τὴν χεῖρά [σου] ἐκτείνειν. The numerous textual variants make little or no difference for the sense of the verse.

τὴν χεῖρά ἐκτείνειν. An idiom meaning, "to show one's power."

ἐκτείνειν. Pres act inf ἐκτείνω. The use of ἐν τῷ with an infinitive probably introduces the means of the main verb (δὸς; v. 29) though it may denote contemporaneous time ("as you stretch out your hand"). Either way, the infinitive expresses a second request of the speaker.

σε. Accusative subject of the infinitive ἐκτείνειν (see 1:3 on αὐτὸν).

εἰς ἴασιν καὶ σημεῖα καὶ τέρατα γίνεσθαι. Since the preposition εἰς is not followed by the neuter singular article τό it cannot modify the infinitive γίνεσθαι (see 1:3 on αὐτὸν). Consequently, ἴασιν καὶ σημεῖα καὶ τέρατα cannot be viewed as a single conjoined noun phrase. Instead, εἰς ἴασιν should be taken as introducing the first purpose of the preceding infinitival construction, with the first καί then introducing a second purpose (indicated by γίνεσθαι): "stretch out your hand for healing and to do signs and wonders."

σημεῖα καὶ τέρατα. See 2:43.

γίνεσθαι. Pres dep inf γίνομαι (purpose; see above).

παιδός. See 3:13.

Ἰησοῦ. Genitive in apposition to τοῦ ἁγίου παιδός.

4:31 καὶ δεηθέντων αὐτῶν ἐσαλεύθη ὁ τόπος ἐν ᾧ ἦσαν συνηγμένοι, καὶ ἐπλήσθησαν ἅπαντες τοῦ ἁγίου πνεύματος καὶ ἐλάλουν τὸν λόγον τοῦ θεοῦ μετὰ παρρησίας.

δεηθέντων. Aor pass dep ptc masc gen pl δέομαι. Genitive absolute (see 1:8 on ἐπελθόντος), temporal.

αὐτῶν. Genitive subject (see 1:8 on ἐπελθόντος).

ἐσαλεύθη. Aor pass ind 3rd sg σαλεύω.

ἦσαν. Impf ind 3rd pl εἰμί.

συνηγμένοι. Prf pass ptc masc nom pl συνάγω (pluperfect

periphrastic; see 1:17 on κατηριθμημένος).

ἐπλήσθησαν. Aor pass ind 3rd pl πίμπλημι.

τοῦ ἁγίου πνεύματος. See 2:4.

ἐλάλουν. Impf act ind 3rd pl λαλέω.

μετὰ παρρησίας. See v. 29.

Acts 4:32–35

[32]Now, the heart and soul of the whole group of believers was one; and no one at all claimed any of their possessions as their own, but they had all things in common. [33]With great power the apostles were testifying to the resurrection of the Lord Jesus, and all of them were experiencing God's favor in abundance. [34]There was not anyone in need among them, for all who were owners of properties or homes were selling (property) and then bringing the proceeds of the sales [35]and placing it at the feet of the apostles; and (the money) was then distributed to each person as needs arose.

4:32 Τοῦ δὲ πλήθους τῶν πιστευσάντων ἦν καρδία καὶ ψυχὴ μία, καὶ οὐδὲ εἷς τι τῶν ὑπαρχόντων αὐτῷ ἔλεγεν ἴδιον εἶναι ἀλλ' ἦν αὐτοῖς ἅπαντα κοινά.

Τοῦ . . . πλήθους τῶν πιστευσάντων. This genitive noun phrase may be taken in one of two ways: (1) it may modify καρδία καὶ ψυχὴ directly ("The heart and soul of the group of believers was one"), or (2) it may be taken as a genitive of reference ("With reference to the group of believers, [their] heart and soul was one"). In favor of the latter is the fact that the verb separates the genitive noun phrase from καρδία καὶ ψυχὴ making it less likely that they make up a single (discontinuous) constituent. This discontinuity, however, may be explained by the fact that the theme (not always the syntactic subject) of the sentence normally precedes the verb in Greek. In this instance, the theme happens to be a genitive noun phrase (cf. Levinsohn 1987, 7).

δὲ. The conjunction, in this case, introduces a new section concerned with the communal practices of the early Christians (Levinsohn 1987, 109).

πλήθους. Neuter genitive singular of πλῆθος.

τῶν πιστευσάντων. Aor act ptc masc gen pl πιστεύω (substantival). Genitive of identification.

ἦν. Impf ind 3rd sg εἰμί. The singular verb is used with a compound subject here, probably because the compound subject refers to a single referent (see below on καρδία καὶ ψυχή).

καρδία καὶ ψυχή. The conjoined nouns should probably be taken as a doublet (see 2:43 on τέρατα καὶ σημεῖα) used to emphasize the depth of the believers' unity.

μία. Predicate adjective.

τι. Accusative of respect/reference. The substantival adjective should probably not be taken (syntactically) as the accusative subject of the infinitive εἶναι since it is outside the infinitive clause's boundaries.

τῶν ὑπαρχόντων. Pres act ptc neut gen pl ὑπάρχω (substantival).

αὐτῷ. Dative of possession (with εἰμί).

ἔλεγεν. Impf act ind 3rd sg λέγω.

ἴδιον. Predicate accusative adjective (see 1:22 on μάρτυρα).

εἶναι. Pres act inf εἰμί (indirect discourse).

ἀλλ'. This conjunction is found only three times outside of the reported speeches of Acts (see also 5:13; 18:20). In each case, it provides a contrast to a negated statement (here, "no one [οὐδὲ] at all claimed any of their possessions as their own"). "The first element states what did not happen, and the second describes the corresponding event which did take place" (Levinsohn 1987, 156). In the present case, the contrasting clauses state two sides of the same coin, thus emphasizing the importance of communal sharing within early Christianity.

ἦν. Impf ind 3rd sg εἰμί.

αὐτοῖς. Dative of possession (with εἰμί).

ἅπαντα. Substantival nominative subject of ἦν.

κοινά. Predicate adjective.

4:33 καὶ δυνάμει μεγάλῃ ἀπεδίδουν τὸ μαρτύριον οἱ ἀπόστολοι τῆς ἀναστάσεως τοῦ κυρίου Ἰησοῦ, χάρις τε μεγάλη ἦν ἐπὶ πάντας αὐτούς.

δυνάμει μεγάλῃ. Dative of manner.

ἀπεδίδουν. Impf act ind 3rd pl ἀποδίδωμι. The verb phrase ἀπεδίδουν τὸ μαρτύριον (lit. "they were giving testimony") is equivalent to the verb μαρτυρέω.

τῆς ἀναστάσεως. Genitive of reference/respect.

χάρις . . . αὐτούς. Lit. "great grace was upon all of them."

χάρις. This expression, given the context and the modifier μεγάλη, should probably be understood as the favor of God expressed in a variety of ways, rather than the favor of the surrounding community (cf. Barrett, 254).

ἦν. Impf ind 3rd sg εἰμί.

πάντας αὐτούς. Given the context of v. 32, this expression probably refers to the entire Christian community rather than just the apostles.

4:34 οὐδὲ γὰρ ἐνδεής τις ἦν ἐν αὐτοῖς· ὅσοι γὰρ κτήτορες χωρίων ἢ οἰκιῶν ὑπῆρχον, πωλοῦντες ἔφερον τὰς τιμὰς τῶν πιπρασκομένων

γάρ. The conjunction marks this clause as evidence of God's abundant favor (v. 33): "*This was seen in the fact that* there was not anyone in need among them."

ἐνδεής. Predicate adjective ("needy" = ἔχω χρείαν).

ἦν. Impf ind 3rd sg εἰμί.

γάρ. Introduces the reason for the previous claim.

κτήτορες. Predicate nominative plural of κτήτωρ ("owner"; only here in the NT).

ὑπῆρχον. Impf act ind 3rd pl ὑπάρχω.

πωλοῦντες. Pres act ptc masc nom pl πωλέω (attendant circumstance).

ἔφερον. Impf act ind 3rd pl φέρω.

τῶν πιπρασκομένων. Pres pass ptc neut gen pl πιπράσκω (substantival). Genitive of source.

4:35 καὶ ἐτίθουν παρὰ τοὺς πόδας τῶν ἀποστόλων, διεδίδετο δὲ ἑκάστῳ καθότι ἄν τις χρείαν εἶχεν.

ἐτίθουν. Impf act ind 3rd pl τίθημι.

διεδίδετο. Impf pass ind 3rd sg διαδίδωμι. The implicit subject is presumably αἱ τιμάι (from v. 34).

ἑκάστῳ. Dative indirect object.

καθότι . . . εἶχεν. Lit. "as anyone had a need."

εἶχεν. Impf act ind 3rd sg ἔχω.

Acts 4:36–5:11

[36]Now, Joseph, who was called Barnabas by the apostles —which is translated 'son of encouragement'—a Levite, a Cypriot by birth, [37]since

he had a field, he sold it and brought the sum of money and set it at the feet of the apostles. [5:1]But a certain man named Ananias, with his wife Sapphira, sold a property [2]but kept some of the proceeds for himself—his wife was also aware of this—and brought part (of the money) and placed it at the feet of the apostles. [3]Peter said, "Ananias, why has Satan filled your heart so that you tried to deceive the Holy Spirit and kept some of the proceeds from the land for yourself? [4]While it was yours didn't it remain (yours)? After it was sold wasn't it (still) under your authority? Why is it that you planned this thing? You did not lie (only) to people, but (also) to God!" [5]When Ananias heard these words he dropped dead; and great fear came upon all those who heard (about this incident). [6]The young men got up and wrapped him up, and (then) took him out and buried him.

[7]Now, after an interval of about three hours his wife came in, not knowing what had happened. [8]Peter said to her, "Tell me, did you sell a field for such an amount?" And she replied, "Yes, for that amount." [9]Peter (said) to her, "Why did you both agree to tempt the Spirit of the Lord? The feet of those who buried your husband are at the door and they will carry you out (as well)!" [10]Immediately, she collapsed at his feet and died. When the young men came, they found her dead and carried her out and buried her beside her husband. [11]And great fear came upon the whole church and upon all those who heard about these things.

4:36 Ἰωσὴφ δὲ ὁ ἐπικληθεὶς Βαρναβᾶς ἀπὸ τῶν ἀποστόλων, ὅ ἐστιν μεθερμηνευόμενον υἱὸς παρακλήσεως, Λευίτης, Κύπριος τῷ γένει,

ἐπικληθεὶς. Aor pass ptc masc nom sg ἐπικαλέω (attributive).

Βαρναβᾶς. Complement in a subject-complement double nominative construction (see below on υἱὸς).

ἀπὸ. Introduces the agent (a rare use) of ἐπικληθεὶς.

ὅ. The use of the neuter nominative relative pronoun with a verbal expression referring to interpretation or translation (sometimes simply ὅ ἐστιν: "that is") is a fairly common idiom (an "interpretive relative phrase") in the NT (see Matt 1:23; 27:33; Mark 3:17; 5:41; 7:11, 34; 12:42; 15:16, 22, 34, 42; John 1:38, 41, 42; Col 1:24; Heb 7:2; Rev 21:17; Culy 1989, 37–39, 158).

ἐστιν. Pres act ind 3rd sg εἰμί. On the loss of accent, see 1:7 on ἐστιν.

μεθερμηνευόμενον. Pres pass ptc neut nom sg μεθερμηνεύω (periphrastic; the use of the present tense of εἰμί with a present participle forms a present periphrastic construction).

υἱός. Used with the passive verb, the nominative noun functions as a complement in a "subject-complement double nominative" construction, in which ὅ is the subject of the construction (cf. 5:39; 8:10; 10:18; 32; 42; 13:1; 20:9; 25:14; 26:8; 27:14; 28:1; and 1:12 on Ἐλαιῶνος).

παρακλήσεως. Attributive genitive. It is unclear whether this term refers to "encouragement" (cf. Phil 2:1) or "exhortation" (2 Cor 8:4). In the latter case, the description "son of exhortation" would probably indicate that Barnabas was a noted preacher (see the discussion in Barrett, 358–59). Such a view, however, does not seem consistent with the fact that Paul was the primary speaker when he and Barnabas worked as a team (14:12).

Λευίτης . . . Κύπριος. Nominatives in apposition to Ἰωσήφ.

τῷ γένει. Dative of respect/reference.

4:37 ὑπάρχοντος αὐτῷ ἀγροῦ πωλήσας ἤνεγκεν τὸ χρῆμα καὶ ἔθηκεν πρὸς τοὺς πόδας τῶν ἀποστόλων.

ὑπάρχοντος. Pres act ptc masc gen sg ὑπάρχω. Genitive absolute (see 1:8 on ἐπελθόντος), causal. Here, the dative of possession construction necessitates using the genitive absolute since the syntactic subject of ὑπάρχω (ἀγροῦ) is different than the subject of the main verb. Although genitive absolute constructions normally occur at the beginning of a sentence, this one follows the extended topic construction in v. 36 (cf. 13:24).

αὐτῷ. Dative of possession.

ἀγροῦ. Genitive subject (lit. "a field being to him"; see 1:8 on ἐπελθόντος).

πωλήσας. Aor act ptc masc nom sg πωλέω (attendant circumstance).

ἤνεγκεν. Aor act ind 3rd sg φέρω.

ἔθηκεν πρὸς. There does not appear to be a distinction between πρός and παρά when used with τίθημι (although UBS[4]/NA[27] reads πρός, following ℵ E 36, there is far stronger external support for παρά: 𝔓[57] 𝔓[74] A B D Ψ *Byz*; cf. 5:2 and the textual variants of 5:10).

ἔθηκεν. Aor act ind 3rd sg τίθημι.

5:1 Ἀνὴρ δέ τις Ἁνανίας ὀνόματι σὺν Σαπφίρῃ τῇ γυναικὶ

αὐτοῦ ἐπώλησεν κτῆμα

Ἀνὴρ δέ τις Ἁνανίας. The fronted subject marks a change in focus.

ὀνόματι. Dative of reference.

Ἁνανίας. Nominative in apposition to Ἀνὴρ.

τῇ γυναικί. Dative in apposition to Σαπφίρῃ.

ἐπώλησεν. Aor act ind 3rd sg πωλέω. The use of σύν rather than καί with Ἁνανίας makes the subject singular rather than plural (cf. 2:14 on ἐπῆρεν).

5:2 καὶ ἐνοσφίσατο ἀπὸ τῆς τιμῆς, συνειδυίης καὶ τῆς γυναικός, καὶ ἐνέγκας μέρος τι παρὰ τοὺς πόδας τῶν ἀποστόλων ἔθηκεν.

ἐνοσφίσατο. Aor mid ind 3rd sg νοσφίζω. Used in the middle voice, νοσφίζω denotes "to misappropriate funds for one's own benefit" (LN 57.246).

συνειδυίης. Prf act ptc fem gen sg σύνοιδα. Genitive absolute (see 1:8 on ἐπελθόντος), attendant circumstance; see Levinsohn 1992, 181. Genitive absolutes usually occur at the beginning of a sentence. Its placement here marks the participial clause as a parenthetical comment (cf. 27:2 on ὄντος).

τῆς γυναικός. Genitive subject (see 1:8 on ἐπελθόντος).

ἐνέγκας. Aor act ptc masc nom sg φέρω (attendant circumstance).

μέρος τι. Lit. "a certain part."

ἔθηκεν. Aor act ind 3rd sg τίθημι.

5:3 εἶπεν δὲ ὁ Πέτρος, Ἁνανία, διὰ τί ἐπλήρωσεν ὁ Σατανᾶς τὴν καρδίαν σου, ψεύσασθαί σε τὸ πνεῦμα τὸ ἅγιον καὶ νοσφίσασθαι ἀπὸ τῆς τιμῆς τοῦ χωρίου;

εἶπεν. Aor act ind 3rd sg λέγω.

Ἁνανία. Vocative.

διὰ τί. Introduces a rhetorical question.

ἐπλήρωσεν. Aor act ind 3rd sg πληρόω. The weakly attested textual variants, ἐπήρωσεν (א*, "disabled, maimed") and ἐπείρασεν (𝔓[74], "tempted"), are easily explained as scribal attempts to smooth out what may well be a Hebraic idiom (lit. "to fill the heart to do something") meaning, "to cause someone to dare to do something" (Aquila uses ἐτόλμησαν to translate מָלֵא לֵב in Eccl 8:11, while the LXX uses ἐτόλμησε to translate מְלָאוֹ לִבּוֹ in Esth 7:5; see Metzger, 327–28).

ψεύσασθαί. Aor mid dep inf ψεύδομαι (result). The second accent comes from the enclitic σε (see 1:4 on ἠκούσατέ). On the meaning of this verb, see below on τὸ πνεῦμα τὸ ἅγιον.

σε. Accusative subject of the infinitive.

τὸ πνεῦμα τὸ ἅγιον. The verb ψεύδομαι/ψεύδω, which occurs only nine times in the NT, can take addressees (the person lied to) in a number of forms. Indeed, the three examples of this construction in the NT are all different. Here, the addressee is in the accusative case (cf. LXX 2 Kgs 4:16; Ps 65:3); in the following verse (5:4), the addressee is in the dative case (see also LXX 1 Kgs 13:18; Pss 17:45; 77:36; 80:16; 88:36); and in Col 3:9, the addressee is introduced with the preposition εἰς. The three forms may not be interchangeable. It is possible that only the dative noun marks an addressee. In such a construction ψεύδομαι would then refer to the actual utterance of the lie. When used with εἰς the sense of the verb may be "to lie against" (cf. LXX Susanna 1:55, 59). This construction would then emphasize that the utterance is in opposition to someone else. When used with an accusative noun the sense of the verb may be "to deceive" (Barrett, 266–67), "to deny" (cf. LXX Job 6:10, 18), or perhaps even "to fail" (cf. LXX Hos 9:2; Hab 3:17). Where the context involves an actual spoken lie, the emphasis may be on the consequences or implications of lying.

καὶ. Epexegetical.

νοσφίσασθαι. Aor mid inf νοσφίζω (result). On the meaning of this verb, see v. 2.

5:4 οὐχὶ μένον σοὶ ἔμενεν καὶ πραθὲν ἐν τῇ σῇ ἐξουσίᾳ ὑπῆρχεν; τί ὅτι ἔθου ἐν τῇ καρδίᾳ σου τὸ πρᾶγμα τοῦτο; οὐκ ἐψεύσω ἀνθρώποις ἀλλὰ τῷ θεῷ.

οὐχὶ . . . ἔμενεν. Lit. "While it remained yours, did it not remain (yours)?"

οὐχὶ. Introduces a question expecting a positive answer (Rogers and Rogers, 238).

μένον. Pres act ptc neut nom sg μένω (temporal).

σοὶ. Dative of possession.

ἔμενεν. Impf act ind 3rd sg μένω.

πραθὲν. Aor pass ptc neut nom sg πιπράσκω (temporal).

ὑπῆρχεν. Impf act ind 3rd sg ὑπάρχω.

τί ὅτι. Probably a shortened form of τί γέγενοεν ὅτι ("Why has it happened that . . .").

ἔθου . . . τοῦτο. Lit. "you put this thing in your heart" (see 19:21 on ἐν τῷ πνεύματι).

ἔθου. Aor mid ind 2nd sg τίθημι.

ἐψεύσω. Aor mid dep ind 2nd sg ψεύδομαι. See v. 3.

ἀλλὰ. See 1:8; 2:16.

5:5 ἀκούων δὲ ὁ Ἀνανίας τοὺς λόγους τούτους πεσὼν ἐξέψυξεν, καὶ ἐγένετο φόβος μέγας ἐπὶ πάντας τοὺς ἀκούοντας.

ἀκούων. Pres act ptc masc nom sg ἀκούω (temporal).

ὁ Ἀνανίας. The use of the full noun phrase to refer to Ananias, rather than the expected articular pronoun, highlights this verse as the climactic event of this episode (Levinsohn 1992, 119).

πεσὼν ἐξέψυξεν. More lit. "he fell down and died."

πεσὼν. Aor act ptc masc nom sg πίπτω (attendant circumstance).

ἐξέψυξεν. Aor act ind 3rd sg ἐκψύχω.

ἐγένετο. Aor mid dep ind 3rd sg γίνομαι.

τοὺς ἀκούοντας. Pres act ptc masc acc pl ἀκούω (substantival).

5:6 ἀναστάντες δὲ οἱ νεώτεροι συνέστειλαν αὐτὸν καὶ ἐξενέγκαντες ἔθαψαν.

ἀναστάντες. Aor act ptc masc nom pl ἀνίστημι (attendant circumstance; see 1:15 on ἀναστὰς). It may be appropriate to render this verse: "The young men immediately wrapped him up, and (then) took him out and buried him" (see v. 17).

νεώτεροι. The substantival adjective is comparative in form.

συνέστειλαν. Aor act ind 3rd pl συστέλλω. The verb means "to wrap up an object, with the implication of getting it ready to remove" (LN 79.119), or more specifically, "to prepare for burial" (Barrett, 261, 268–69).

ἐξενέγκαντες. Aor act ptc masc nom pl ἐκφέρω (attendant circumstance).

ἔθαψαν. Aor act ind 3rd pl θάπτω.

5:7 Ἐγένετο δὲ ὡς ὡρῶν τριῶν διάστημα καὶ ἡ γυνὴ αὐτοῦ μὴ εἰδυῖα τὸ γεγονὸς εἰσῆλθεν.

Ἐγένετο δὲ. Introduces the next stage in this episode (cf. Gault, 393).

Ἐγένετο. Aor mid dep ind 3rd sg γίνομαι.

ὡς. Introduces an approximate measure (cf. Barrett, 269).

διάστημα. Probably a predicate nominative with an impersonal Ἐγένετο.

εἰδυῖα. Prf act ptc fem sg nom οἶδα (attendant circumstance).

τὸ γεγονὸς. Prf act ptc neut acc sg γίνομαι (substantival).

εἰσῆλθεν. Aor act ind 3rd sg εἰσέρχομαι.

5:8 ἀπεκρίθη δὲ πρὸς αὐτὴν Πέτρος, Εἰπέ μοι, εἰ τοσούτου τὸ χωρίον ἀπέδοσθε; ἡ δὲ εἶπεν, Ναί, τοσούτου.

ἀπεκρίθη. Aor pass dep ind 3rd sg ἀποκρίνομαι. The use of the verb (lit. "answered") may indicate that Peter is responding to Sapphira's willingness to continue the deception.

Εἰπέ. Aor act impv 2nd sg λέγω.

εἰ. It is unclear whether εἰ introduces a direct (cf. 1:6) or indirect question ("Tell me whether you sold a field for such an amount"). Given the verb ἀπεκρίθη and the direct discourse that follows, the former is more likely.

τοσούτου. Genitive of price.

ἀπέδοσθε. Aor mid ind 2nd pl ἀποδίδωμι. In the middle voice, this verb means "to sell" (BAGD, 90; cf. 7:9).

ἡ. The article functions like a personal pronoun here (cf. 3:5).

εἶπεν. Aor act ind 3rd sg λέγω.

5:9 ὁ δὲ Πέτρος πρὸς αὐτήν, Τί ὅτι συνεφωνήθη ὑμῖν πειράσαι τὸ πνεῦμα κυρίου; ἰδοὺ οἱ πόδες τῶν θαψάντων τὸν ἄνδρα σου ἐπὶ τῇ θύρᾳ καὶ ἐξοίσουσίν σε.

Τί ὅτι. See 5:4.

συνεφωνήθη. Aor pass ind 3rd sg συμφωνέω. The verb is used in an impersonal construction here (more lit. "Why was it agreed by you . . .").

πειράσαι. Aor act inf πειράζω (complementary; see 1:16 on πληρωθῆναι). The sense of the verb here is "to provoke, by seeing how far you can go" (Barrett, 270).

ἰδοὺ. See 1:10.

οἱ πόδες. Synecdoche (see 1:22 on τοῦ βαπτίσματος Ἰωάννου) for "people."

τῶν θαψάντων. Aor act ptc masc gen pl θάπτω (substantival).

ἐξοίσουσίν. Fut act ind 3rd pl ἐκφέρω. The second accent comes from the enclitic σε (see 1:4 on ἠκούσατέ).

5:10 ἔπεσεν δὲ παραχρῆμα πρὸς τοὺς πόδας αὐτοῦ καὶ ἐξέψυξεν· εἰσελθόντες δὲ οἱ νεανίσκοι εὗρον αὐτὴν νεκράν καὶ ἐξενέγκαντες ἔθαψαν πρὸς τὸν ἄνδρα αὐτῆς,

ἔπεσεν. Aor act ind 3rd sg πίπτω.

ἐξέψυξεν. Aor act ind 3rd sg ἐκψύχω.

εἰσελθόντες. Aor act ptc masc nom pl εἰσέρχομαι (temporal).

οἱ νεανίσκοι. This noun and the substantival comparative adjective νεώτεροι (v. 6) were apparently interchangeable.

εὗρον. Aor act ind 3rd pl εὑρίσκω.

νεκράν. The accusative adjective functions as a complement in an object-complement double accusative construction (see 1:3 on ζῶντα).

ἐξενέγκαντες. Aor act ptc masc nom pl ἐκφέρω (attendant circumstance).

ἔθαψαν. Aor act ind 3rd pl θάπτω.

5:11 καὶ ἐγένετο φόβος μέγας ἐφ' ὅλην τὴν ἐκκλησίαν καὶ ἐπὶ πάντας τοὺς ἀκούοντας ταῦτα.

καὶ ἐγένετο φόβος μέγας ἐφ' ὅλην τὴν ἐκκλησίαν. Cf. the similar expression in 4:33: χάρις τε μεγάλη ἦν ἐπὶ πάντας αὐτούς.

ἐγένετο. Aor mid dep ind 3rd sg γίνομαι.

τοὺς ἀκούοντας. Pres act ptc masc acc pl ἀκούω (substantival).

Acts 5:12–16

[12]Many signs and wonders were being performed through the hands of the apostles among the people, and all of them were (meeting) together in the Porch of Solomon. [13]None of the rest (of the people there) dared to join them, but the people spoke well of them. [14]More than that, those who believed in the Lord were (regularly) being added, large

groups of both men and women. [15]The result of all this was that (people) were even carrying the sick into the streets and placing (them) on mattresses or cots so that when Peter passed by (his) shadow might at least fall on some of them. [16]Crowd(s) from the cities surrounding Jerusalem were also coming together and bringing sick people and those afflicted by unclean spirits; and all were being healed.

5:12 Διὰ δὲ τῶν χειρῶν τῶν ἀποστόλων ἐγίνετο σημεῖα καὶ τέρατα πολλὰ ἐν τῷ λαῷ· καὶ ἦσαν ὁμοθυμαδὸν ἅπαντες ἐν τῇ Στοᾷ Σολομῶντος,

Διὰ . . . τῶν χειρῶν τῶν ἀποστόλων. Instrumental/intermediate agent.

τῶν χειρῶν τῶν ἀποστόλων. Synecdoche (see 1:22 on τοῦ βαπτίσματος Ἰωάννου) for "the apostles."

ἐγίνετο. Impf dep ind 3rd sg γίνομαι.

σημεῖα καὶ τέρατα. See 2:43 on τέρατα καὶ σημεῖα.

ἦσαν. Impf ind 3rd pl εἰμί.

ὁμοθυμαδὸν. Here the adverb is clearly used in a locative expression (see 1:14).

Σολομῶντος. Genitive of identification.

5:13 τῶν δὲ λοιπῶν οὐδεὶς ἐτόλμα κολλᾶσθαι αὐτοῖς, ἀλλ' ἐμεγάλυνεν αὐτοὺς ὁ λαός.

τῶν . . . λοιπῶν. Partitive genitive. This expression is referentially equivalent to ὁ λαός later in this verse. The fact that great crowds of people were indeed converting (v. 14) suggests that τῶν λοιπῶν οὐδεὶς refers to people who were in and around the Porch of Solomon and aware of the Christians' activities there.

ἐτόλμα. Impf act ind 3rd sg τολμάω.

κολλᾶσθαι Pres pass inf κολλάω (complementary). Barrett (274) notes that "the verse suggests that the assembled Christians . . . formed a distinctive group on their own [within Judaism], separate from those who moved about in the Portico, and that to join the group was understood to be virtually equivalent to becoming a Christian."

αὐτοῖς. Dative complement of κολλᾶσθαι.

ἐμεγάλυνεν. Impf act ind 3rd sg μεγαλύνω.

5:14 μᾶλλον δὲ προσετίθεντο πιστεύοντες τῷ κυρίῳ, πλήθη ἀνδρῶν τε καὶ γυναικῶν,

μᾶλλον. Although the adverb could be taken with προσετίθεντο ("were increasingly added"), more likely it introduces a proposition that supplements and clarifies what has preceded (cf. BAGD, 489).

προσετίθεντο. Impf pass ind 3rd pl προστίθημι.

πιστεύοντες. Pres act ptc masc nom pl πιστεύω (substantival subject of προσετίθεντο). It may be possible to take the anarthrous (see 3:3 on Πέτρον καὶ ᾿ Ιωάννου) participle temporally, with πλήθη ἀνδρῶν τε καὶ γυναικῶν being the subject of προσετίθεντο: "Large groups of both men and women, as they believed in the Lord, were being added."

πλήθη. The plural form of this term occurs only in the neuter (here possibly in apposition to a masculine participle; see above).

ἀνδρῶν τε καὶ γυναικῶν. Genitive of content.

5:15 ὥστε καὶ εἰς τὰς πλατείας ἐκφέρειν τοὺς ἀσθενεῖς καὶ τιθέναι ἐπὶ κλιναρίων, καὶ κραβάττων, ἵνα ἐρχομένου Πέτρου κἂν ἡ σκιὰ ἐπισκιάσῃ τινὶ αὐτῶν.

ὥστε. Used with the infinitive to introduce result. The result clause may pick up (1) what immediately precedes (all the new converts were bringing sick friends and relatives for healing), or (2) what has been described in vv. 12–14, particularly v. 12 (cf. 19:11–12).

πλατείας. Probably a reference to "*wide/main* streets" (cf. BAGD, 666).

ἐκφέρειν. Pres act inf ἐκφέρω (result; see ὥστε above).

τιθέναι. Pres act inf τίθημι (result; see ὥστε above).

ἐρχομένου. Pres dep ptc masc gen sg ἔρχομαι. Genitive absolute (see 1:8 on ἐπελθόντος), temporal or conditional.

Πέτρου. Genitive subject (see 1:8 on ἐπελθόντος).

κἂν. A shortened form (crasis) of καὶ ἄν. Here, the καί may be labelled ascensive ("even," "at least"). This same construction (ἵνα κἂν) occurs in an analogous context in Mark 6:56 and is used to express an action that is less likely to bring about the desired results than some other action (in this case direct intervention by the apostles; cf. other passages such as Matt. 9:21).

ἐπισκιάσῃ. Aor act subj 3rd sg ἐπισκιάζω. Used with ἵνα to introduce the purpose of the preceding actions.

τινί. The indefinite pronoun bears an accent (a rare phenomenon) on the ultima here because the preceding word is accented on the penult (Hewitt, 112).

αὐτῶν. Partitive genitive.

5:16 συνήρχετο δὲ καὶ τὸ πλῆθος τῶν πέριξ πόλεων Ἰερουσαλὴμ φέροντες ἀσθενεῖς καὶ ὀχλουμένους ὑπὸ πνευμάτων ἀκαθάρτων, οἵτινες ἐθεραπεύοντο ἅπαντες.

συνήρχετο. Impf dep ind 3rd sg συνέρχομαι.

πόλεων. Genitive of source.

φέροντες. Pres act ptc masc nom pl φέρω (attendant circumstance).

ὀχλουμένους. Pres pass ptc masc acc pl ὀχλέω (substantival).

ὑπὸ. Introduces the agent of the passive participle.

ἀκαθάρτων. Attributive genitive.

οἵτινες . . . ἅπαντες. An emphatic construction (cf. 3:22 on πάντα ὅσα).

ἐθεραπεύοντο. Impf pass ind 3rd pl θεραπεύω.

Acts 5:17–32

17The high priest and all those with him—the local party of the Sadducees—stood up, filled with jealousy. 18They arrested the apostles and put them in the public prison. 19But during the night an angel of the Lord opened the doors of the prison, led them out and said, 20"Go and stand in the temple (courts) and speak to the people all the words of this life." 21When they heard (this) they went, at daybreak, into the temple (courts) and began teaching.

Now when the high priest and those with him arrived, they summoned the Council—that is all the elders of the sons of Israel—and sent (subordinates) to the prison to have them brought. 22But when the subordinates arrived, they could not find them in the prison, so they returned and reported, 23saying, "We found the prison securely locked and the guards standing at the doors, but when we opened (the doors) we found no one inside." 24When the captain of the temple and the chief priests heard these words they were baffled (and wondered) what this could possibly mean. 25But (then) someone arrived and reported to them, "The men you put in prison are standing in the temple (courts) and teaching the people!"

[26]Then the captain went with (his) subordinates and brought them, but not by force since they were afraid of being stoned by the people. [27]They brought them in and made them stand before the Council. And the high priest questioned them, [28]saying, "Didn't we solemnly command you not to teach in this name? But you have filled Jerusalem with your teaching and you intend to bring this man's blood upon us!" [29]Peter and the apostles answered and said, "It is necessary to obey God rather than men. [30]The God of our ancestors raised up Jesus whom you had seized and murdered by crucifying him. [31]This is the one whom God exalted to his right hand, to be ruler and savior, in order to give repentance and forgiveness of sins to Israel. [32]We are witnesses of these things and so is the Holy Spirit whom God gave to those who obey him."

5:17 Ἀναστὰς δὲ ὁ ἀρχιερεὺς καὶ πάντες οἱ σὺν αὐτῷ, ἡ οὖσα αἵρεσις τῶν Σαδδουκαίων, ἐπλήσθησαν ζήλου

Ἀναστὰς. Aor act ptc masc nom sg ἀνίστημι (attendant circumstance; see 1:15 on ἀναστὰς). When ἀνίστημι is used in this manner (with another verb that provides a response to a preceding event), it may at times carry connotative rather than denotative meaning (cf. the Hebrew קוּם in passages such as Jonah 1:2). Rather than indicating that the Sadducees literally "stood up," Ἀναστὰς may connote that the main verb (ἐπλήσθησαν) was a necessary or immediate response to what precedes (see 8:26; cf. 5:6; 6:9; 8:27; 9:6, 11, 39; 10:20, 23; 22:10; and perhaps 10:13; 11:7; 22:16; 23:9). Note also that the singular participle is used with a compound subject (and plural main verb), perhaps to direct the reader's attention to the high priest (see v. 29; cf. v. 21).

οἱ σὺν αὐτῷ. The article functions as a nominalizer (see 1:3 on τὰ).

οὖσα. Pres act ptc fem nom sg εἰμί (attributive modifying the feminine αἵρεσις). On the rendering "local" see Barrett, 283; cf. 13:1; 28:17.

αἵρεσις. This noun stands in apposition to ὁ ἀρχιερεὺς καὶ πάντες οἱ σὺν αὐτῷ or πάντες οἱ σὺν αὐτῷ.

Σαδδουκαίων. Genitive of identification.

ἐπλήσθησαν. Aor pass ind 3rd pl πίμπλημι.

ζήλου. Genitive of content.

5:18 καὶ ἐπέβαλον τὰς χεῖρας ἐπὶ τοὺς ἀποστόλους καὶ ἔθεντο αὐτοὺς ἐν τηρήσει δημοσίᾳ.

ἐπέβαλον . . . ἀποστόλους. Lit. "They laid hands on the apostles"; cf. 4:3.

ἐπέβαλον. Aor act ind 3rd pl ἐπιβάλλω.

ἔθεντο. Aor mid ind 3rd pl τίθημι.

δημοσίᾳ. This term could be either an adjective ("public prison"; presumably a more severe form of imprisonment; Rogers and Rogers, 239) or an adverb ("put them in prison publicly"; so Barrett, 283). The latter view implies public shaming of the apostles.

5:19 ἄγγελος δὲ κυρίου διὰ νυκτὸς ἀνοίξας τὰς θύρας τῆς φυλακῆς ἐξαγαγών τε αὐτοὺς εἶπεν,

ἄγγελος . . . κυρίου. The phrase could also be translated "*the* angel of the Lord" (so Wallace 1996, 252) in which case the genitive κυρίου could denote source ("the angel from the Lord"). The expression, "the angel of the Lord," however, appears to be used frequently in the OT as a periphrastic expression for "the Lord" (see Gen 16:7–14; 21:14–19; 22:11-18; 31:10–13; 32:22–32~Hos 12:3–4; 48:15–16; Exod 3; 14:19~13:21; Judg 2:1–4; 6:11–24; 13:2-23; Zech 3:1–6).

διὰ. Temporal (with the genitive).

ἀνοίξας. Aor act ptc masc nom sg ἀνοίγω (attendant circumstance).

ἐξαγαγών. Aor act ptc masc nom sg ἐξάγω (attendant circumstance).

εἶπεν. Aor act ind 3rd sg λέγω.

5:20 Πορεύεσθε καὶ σταθέντες λαλεῖτε ἐν τῷ ἱερῷ τῷ λαῷ πάντα τὰ ῥήματα τῆς ζωῆς ταύτης.

Πορεύεσθε. Pres dep impv 2nd pl πορεύομαι.

σταθέντες. Aor pass ptc masc nom pl ἵστημι (with an imperative main verb an attendant circumstance participle carries imperatival force). The addition of the participle probably adds the connotation of speaking "in public."

λαλεῖτε. Pres act impv 2nd pl λαλέω.

τὰ ῥήματα τῆς ζωῆς ταύτης. This obscure saying (the feminine singular ταύτης modifies τῆς ζωῆς, not τὰ ῥήματα) may refer to "the words about this *way* of life," or "the words about this life *they are* *being offered*' (cf. 13:26; Barrett, 284).

τῆς ζωῆς ταύτης. Genitive of respect.

5:21 ἀκούσαντες δὲ εἰσῆλθον ὑπὸ τὸν ὄρθρον εἰς τὸ ἱερὸν καὶ ἐδίδασκον. Παραγενόμενος δὲ ὁ ἀρχιερεὺς καὶ οἱ σὺν αὐτῷ συνεκάλεσαν τὸ συνέδριον καὶ πᾶσαν τὴν γερουσίαν τῶν υἱῶν Ἰσραὴλ καὶ ἀπέστειλαν εἰς τὸ δεσμωτήριον ἀχθῆναι αὐτούς.

ἀκούσαντες. Aor act ptc masc nom pl ἀκούω (temporal).

εἰσῆλθον. Aor act ind 3rd pl εἰσέρχομαι.

ὑπὸ τὸν ὄρθρον. The rare use of ὑπό in a temporal expression (only here in the NT; Porter 1994, 178) may suggest stealth.

εἰς. See 1:8 on ἐφ' ὑμᾶς.

ἐδίδασκον. Impf act ind 3rd pl διδάσκω.

Παραγενόμενος. Aor mid dep ptc masc nom sg παραγίνομαι (temporal). The singular participle is used with a compound subject (and plural main verb), perhaps to direct the reader's attention to the high priest (see v. 29; cf. v. 17).

οἱ σὺν αὐτῷ. See v. 17.

συνεκάλεσαν. Aor act ind 3rd pl συγκαλέω.

καὶ. Epexegetical.

ἀπέστειλαν. Aor act ind 3rd pl ἀποστέλλω.

εἰς τὸ. The preposition is locative and the article goes with δεσμωτήριον. This should not be mistaken for an εἰς τὸ plus infinitive construction.

ἀχθῆναι. Aor pass inf ἄγω (purpose).

5:22 οἱ δὲ παραγενόμενοι ὑπηρέται οὐχ εὗρον αὐτοὺς ἐν τῇ φυλακῇ· ἀναστρέψαντες δὲ ἀπήγγειλαν

οἱ . . . ὑπηρέται. The noun ὑπήρετης is masculine.

παραγενόμενοι. Aor mid dep ptc masc nom pl παραγίνομαι. In terms of syntax, the participle is attributive ("the arriving subordinates"). The expression, however, is best rendered in English, "*When* the subordinates arrived . . ."

εὗρον. Aor act ind 3rd pl εὑρίσκω.

ἀναστρέψαντες. Aor act ptc masc nom pl ἀναστρέφω (attendant circumstance).

ἀπήγγειλαν. Aor act ind 3rd pl ἀπαγγέλλω.

5:23 λέγοντες ὅτι Τὸ δεσμωτήριον εὕρομεν κεκλεισμένον ἐν πάσῃ ἀσφαλείᾳ καὶ τοὺς φύλακας ἑστῶτας ἐπὶ τῶν θυρῶν, ἀνοίξαντες δὲ ἔσω οὐδένα εὕρομεν.

λέγοντες. Pres act ptc masc nom pl λέγω (attendant circumstance).

ὅτι. Introduces direct discourse.

εὕρομεν. Aor act ind 1st pl εὑρίσκω.

κεκλεισμένον. Prf pass ptc neut acc sg κλείω. The participle functions as the complement in an object-complement double accusative construction (see 1:3 on ζῶντα).

ἐν πάσῃ ἀσφαλείᾳ. Lit. "in all security," the manner in which the prison was locked.

ἑστῶτας. Prf act ptc masc acc pl ἵστημι. The participle functions as the complement in an object-complement double accusative construction (see 1:3 on ζῶντα).

ἀνοίξαντες. Aor act ptc masc nom pl ἀνοίγω (temporal).

εὕρομεν. Aor act ind 1st pl εὑρίσκω.

5:24 ὡς δὲ ἤκουσαν τοὺς λόγους τούτους ὅ τε στρατηγὸς τοῦ ἱεροῦ καὶ οἱ ἀρχιερεῖς, διηπόρουν περὶ αὐτῶν τί ἂν γένοιτο τοῦτο.

ὡς. Temporal (see 18:5).

ἤκουσαν. Aor act ind 3rd pl ἀκούω.

ὅ. The article should not be mistaken for a relative pronoun. The accent comes from the enclitic τε (see 1:4 on ἠκούσατέ).

στρατηγὸς τοῦ ἱεροῦ. This official was apparently in charge of the Jewish soldiers who guarded the temple.

διηπόρουν περὶ αὐτῶν. Lit. "they were baffled concerning them."

διηπόρουν . . . τί. This construction is analogous to what is found in 2:12 and 10:17. In this case, something like (ἄλλος πρὸς ἄλλον) λέγοντες is left implicit before τί ἂν γένοιτο τοῦτο.

διηπόρουν Impf act ind 3rd pl διαπορέω.

τί ἂν γένοιτο τοῦτο. In this "potential optative" (lit. "What can this be?"), the optative verb is used with the particle ἂν in the apodosis of an incomplete fourth class condition (Wallace 1996, 483). Although we have used indirect discourse in the translation, the context does not rule out a direct quotation (cf. Porter 1989, 176).

γένοιτο. Aor mid dep opt 3rd sg γίνομαι. "The optative, when compared with the subjunctive, appears to be very similar but slightly remoter, vaguer, less assured, or more contigent" (Porter 1994, 59).

τοῦτο. Nominative subject of γένοιτο.

5:25 παραγενόμενος δέ τις ἀπήγγειλεν αὐτοῖς ὅτι Ἰδοὺ οἱ ἄνδρες οὓς ἔθεσθε ἐν τῇ φυλακῇ εἰσὶν ἐν τῷ ἱερῷ ἑστῶτες καὶ διδάσκοντες τὸν λαόν.

παραγενόμενος. Aor mid dep ptc masc nom sg παραγίνομαι (attendant circumstance; see 1:15 on ἀναστὰς). Strictly speaking, the participle should not be considered temporal ("but when someone arrived he reported . . ."; contra most scholars).

ἀπήγγειλεν. Aor act ind 3rd sg ἀπαγγέλλω.

ὅτι. Introduces direct discourse.

Ἰδοὺ. See 1:10.

ἔθεσθε. Aor mid ind 2nd pl τίθημι.

εἰσὶν. Pres act ind 3rd pl εἰμί. The retention of the accent here (see 1:7 on ἐστιν) may indicate emphasis (cf. 2:13 on εἰσίν).

ἑστῶτες. Prf act ptc masc nom pl ἵστημι (perfect periphrastic; see 2:13 on μεμεστωμένοι).

διδάσκοντες. Pres act ptc masc nom pl διδάσκω (present periphrastic; see 4:36 on μεμεστωμένοι).

5:26 τότε ἀπελθὼν ὁ στρατηγὸς σὺν τοῖς ὑπηρέταις ἦγεν αὐτούς οὐ μετὰ βίας, ἐφοβοῦντο γὰρ τὸν λαόν μὴ λιθασθῶσιν.

τότε. The adverb indicates a prompt response (see 1:12).

ἀπελθὼν. Aor act ptc masc nom sg ἀπέρχομαι (temporal).

ἦγεν. Impf act ind 3rd sg ἄγω. On the use of the singular, see 5:1 on ἐπώλησεν.

οὐ μετὰ βίας. The preposition with the genitive noun (from βία) introduces the manner in which the apostles were brought. The phrase may be an example of litotes (see 1:5 on οὐ μετὰ πολλὰς ταύτας ἡμέρας) and thus indicate that the authorities were very careful, cautious, or gentle in the way they treated the apostles in front of the people.

ἐφοβοῦντο. Impf dep ind 3rd pl φοβέομαι.

μὴ λιθασθῶσιν. This reading, supported by א B D E 33 *al*, is much smoother in many manuscripts (A Ψ *Byz*): ἵνα μὴ λιθασθῶσιν.

λιθασθῶσιν. Aor pass subj 3rd pl λιθάζω. The subjunctive with μή is commonly used after verbs of warning or fearing (Wallace 1996,

477) and indicates concern regarding a potential outcome (lit. "For they feared the people lest they should be stoned"; cf. 23:10 on διασπασθῇ).

5:27 Ἀγαγόντες δὲ αὐτοὺς ἔστησαν ἐν τῷ συνεδρίῳ. καὶ ἐπηρώτησεν αὐτοὺς ὁ ἀρχιερεὺς

Ἀγαγόντες . . . συνεδρίῳ. Lit. "bringing them, they stood them in the Council."

Ἀγαγόντες. Aor act ptc masc nom pl ἄγω (attendant circumstance or temporal; see 1:15 on ἀναστὰς).

ἔστησαν. Aor act ind 3rd pl ἵστημι.

ἐπηρώτησεν. Aor act ind 3rd sg ἐπερωτάω.

5:28 λέγων, [Οὐ] παραγγελίᾳ παρηγγείλαμεν ὑμῖν μὴ διδάσκειν ἐπὶ τῷ ὀνόματι τούτῳ, καὶ ἰδοὺ πεπληρώκατε τὴν Ἰερουσαλὴμ τῆς διδαχῆς ὑμῶν καὶ βούλεσθε ἐπαγαγεῖν ἐφ' ἡμᾶς τὸ αἷμα τοῦ ἀνθρώπου τούτου.

λέγων. Pres act ptc masc nom sg λέγω (attendant circumstance, redundant; see 1:6 on λέγοντες).

[Οὐ]. The negativizer introduces a rhetorical question expecting a positive answer. The strongly supported textual variant that omits the negativizer ($\mathfrak{P}^{74}$ א A B *al*), producing a strong positive statement, is functionally equivalent to the rhetorical question found in $א^{c}$ D E (Ψ) *Byz al*.

παραγγελίᾳ. Cognate dative. A noun that is a cognate of the verb it modifies is sometimes added (in the dative case) to strengthen the idea of the verb (lit. "Didn't we command you *with a command*").

παρηγγείλαμεν. Aor act ind 1st pl παραγγέλλω.

ὑμῖν. Dative indirect object of παρηγγείλαμεν. (The infinitive clause is the syntactic direct object of the verb.)

διδάσκειν. Pres act inf διδάσκω (indirect discourse).

ἐπὶ τῷ ὀνόματι. See 4:18.

ὀνόματι. Possibly a metonym (see 1:9 on τῶν ὀφθαλμῶν αὐτῶν) for "person" as in 1:15.

ἰδού. See 1:10.

πεπληρώκατε. Prf act ind 2nd pl πληρόω. The ("extensive") perfect here may emphasize (hyperbolically) the culpability of the apostles (cf. Wallace 1996, 577). The fact that the aorist is also strongly supported in the textual tradition (𝔓[74] א A *al*), however, suggests that ancient readers may have seen little if any difference between the two tenses in this context.

τῆς διδαχῆς. Genitive of content.

βούλεσθε. Pres dep ind 2nd pl βούλομαι.

ἐπαγαγεῖν. Aor act inf ἐπάγω (complementary).

τὸ αἷμα. Metonymy (see 1:9 on τῶν ὀφθαλμῶν αὐτῶν) for "death."

τοῦ ἀνθρώπου τούτου. The indirect reference to Jesus may carry a disparaging tone (cf. Barrett, 288).

5:29 ἀποκριθεὶς δὲ Πέτρος καὶ οἱ ἀπόστολοι εἶπαν, Πειθαρχεῖν δεῖ θεῷ μᾶλλον ἢ ἀνθρώποις.

ἀποκριθεὶς. Aor pass dep ptc masc nom sg ἀποκρίνομαι (attendant circumstance). The singular participle is used with a compound subject (and plural main verb) here, perhaps highlighting the fact that Peter (the first one mentioned in the construction) was the actual speaker (cf. Wallace 1996, 401–2).

εἶπαν. Aor act ind 3rd pl λέγω.

Πειθαρχεῖν. Pres act inf πειθαρχέω (complementary; see 1:16 on ἔδει and πληρωθῆναι).

δεῖ. Pres act ind 3rd sg δεῖ (impersonal).

θεῷ . . . ἀνθρώποις. Dative complements of Πειθαρχεῖν.

5:30 ὁ θεὸς τῶν πατέρων ἡμῶν ἤγειρεν Ἰησοῦν ὃν ὑμεῖς διεχειρίσασθε κρεμάσαντες ἐπὶ ξύλου·

τῶν πατέρων. Genitive of relationship.

ἤγειρεν. Aor act ind 3rd sg ἐγείρω. This verb is typically used of "raising from the dead," even when not part of a phrase like ἤγειρεν ἐκ νεκρῶν (see esp. 10:39–40; 13:22). If this is the sense here (so Barrett, 289), then the aorist verb in the relative clause should be rendered like a pluperfect: "you had murdered." It is less likely that the verb is being used as ἀναστήσει is used in 3:22 ("to bring on the scene"). In this view, the relative clause would present something that the Jewish leaders did after God had "raised up" a Messiah for them.

ὑμεῖς. The explicit fronted (see 3:13 on ὑμεῖς) subject pronoun is emphatic.

διεχειρίσασθε. Aor mid ind 2nd pl διαχειρίζω. Louw and Nida

(20.62) list the following meaning for this verb: "to lay hands on someone and kill." It is possible, however, that the verb is simply used as a figure of speech for "to kill."

κρεμάσαντες ἐπὶ ξύλου. The use of the idiom, κρεμάννυμι ἐπὶ ξύλου ("to hang on a tree"), rather than the verb σταυρόω, links the death of Jesus to the curse mentioned in Deut 21:22–23: "anyone hung on a tree is under God's curse" (Cotterell and Turner, 91–92).

κρεμάσαντες. Aor act ptc masc nom pl κρεμάννυμι (means).

5:31 τοῦτον ὁ θεὸς ἀρχηγὸν καὶ σωτῆρα ὕψωσεν τῇ δεξιᾷ αὐτοῦ [τοῦ] δοῦναι μετάνοιαν τῷ Ἰσραὴλ καὶ ἄφεσιν ἁμαρτιῶν.

τοῦτον. The fronted demonstrative pronoun shifts the focus to Jesus.

ἀρχηγὸν καὶ σωτῆρα. This construction may be viewed as a double accusative ("to exalt someone as something"; so Rogers and Rogers, 240) or the compound accusative noun phrase may be predicative ("to exalt someone to be something"; so Barrett, 290).

ἀρχηγὸν. Though this term generally is used to denote "one who causes something to begin" (LN 68.2), without a genitive modifier, such as τῆς ζωῆς, the expression means "leader or prince" (Barrett, 290). The latter sense is more appropriate in this context.

ὕψωσεν. Aor act ind 3rd sg ὑψόω.

τῇ δεξιᾷ. See 2:33. In this case, the textual variant found in D* gig p sa (δόξῃ) lends some support to taking the phrase as a dative of location.

[τοῦ] δοῦναι. Aor act inf δίδωμι. Purpose, with or without the genitive article (cf. 3:2 on τοῦ αἰτεῖν).

μετάνοιαν . . . ἄφεσιν. Accusative direct objects of δοῦναι.

τῷ Ἰσραὴλ. Dative indirect object of δοῦναι.

ἁμαρτιῶν. Objective genitive.

5:32 καὶ ἡμεῖς ἐσμεν μάρτυρες τῶν ῥημάτων τούτων καὶ τὸ πνεῦμα τὸ ἅγιον ὃ ἔδωκεν ὁ θεὸς τοῖς πειθαρχοῦσιν αὐτῷ.

ἡμεῖς. The explicit fronted (see 3:13 on ὑμεῖς) subject pronoun shifts the focus (see 2:15 on ὑμεῖς) to the apostles.

ἐσμεν. Pres act ind 1st pl εἰμί. On the loss of accent, see 1:7 on ἐστιν.

μάρτυρες. Predicate nominative.

τῶν ῥημάτων. Objective genitive or genitive of reference. The term ῥῆμα is sometimes used, as here, to refer to "a happening to which one may refer" (LN 13.115).

τὸ πνεῦμα τὸ ἅγιον. Predicate nominative.

ἔδωκεν. Aor act ind 3rd sg δίδωμι.

τοῖς πειθαρχοῦσιν αὐτῷ. This expression functions as an implicit jab at the Jewish leaders (who by implication do not obey God). It is no wonder that they have a strong negative response to Peter's speech (v. 33).

τοῖς πειθαρχοῦσιν. Pres act ptc masc dat pl πειθαρχέω (substantival).

αὐτῷ. Dative complement of πειθαρχοῦσιν.

Acts 5:33–42

33When they heard this they were furious and wanted to kill them.
34But a certain man stood up in the Council—a Pharisee named Gamaliel,
a teacher of the law who was respected by all the people—and commanded that the men be put outside for a short time. 35Then he said to
them, "Israelites, be careful about what you are about to do to these
men. 36For not long ago Theudas came along claiming to be someone,
to whom were joined a number of men, about 400. He was killed and
all those who followed him were dispersed and came to nothing. 37After
that, Judas the Galilean came along, at the time of the census, and drew
people after him. He too perished and all those who had followed him
were scattered. 38And now I say to you, stay away from these men and
leave them alone. For if this plan or this deed is of human origin it will
be destroyed. 39But if (on the other hand) it is from God, you will not be
able to destroy them, and you might even find yourselves to be fighting
God!" They were persuaded by him, 40so after summoning the apostles
and having them beaten, they ordered them not to speak in the name of
Jesus and (then) released (them).

41So they went out from the presence of the Council rejoicing because they had been considered worthy to suffer shame for the sake of
the name. 42And every day in the temple and from house to house they
did not stop teaching and preaching the good news that Jesus was the
Christ.

5:33 Οἱ δὲ ἀκούσαντες διεπρίοντο καὶ ἐβούλοντο ἀνελεῖν αὐτούς.

Οἱ . . . ἀκούσαντες. Aor act ptc masc nom pl ἀκούω (substantival). Strictly speaking this participle should probably be viewed as substantival (lit. "those hearing this"), though it could conceivably be temporal (with Οἱ functioning like a pronoun; see 12:15). Either way, however, it will be most natural in English to render the expression temporally.

διεπρίοντο. Impf pass ind 3rd pl διαπρίω. The passive voice is necessitated by the idiomatic use of this verb: lit. "to saw through."

ἐβούλοντο. Impf dep ind 3rd pl βούλομαι. The well-supported variant reading ἐβουλεύοντο ("they planned"; ℵ D *Byz al*) introduces a more active sense to their response.

ἀνελεῖν. Aor act inf ἀναιρέω (complementary).

5:34 ἀναστὰς δέ τις ἐν τῷ συνεδρίῳ Φαρισαῖος ὀνόματι Γαμαλιήλ, νομοδιδάσκαλος τίμιος παντὶ τῷ λαῷ, ἐκέλευσεν ἔξω βραχὺ-τοὺς ἀνθρώπους ποιῆσαι

ἀναστὰς. Aor act ptc masc nom sg ἀνίστημι (attendant circumstance; see 1:15 on ἀναστὰς).

τις ἐν τῷ συνεδρίῳ Φαρισαῖος. It is unclear whether τις should be viewed as a substantive (with Φαρισαῖος then being appositional: "A certain man in the Council, a Pharisee") or as part of a noun phrase in which it modifies Φαρισαῖος: "a certain Pharisee in the Council."

ὀνόματι. Dative of reference.

Γαμαλιήλ . . . νομοδιδάσκαλος. Nominatives in apposition to τις or Φαρισαῖος.

παντὶ τῷ λαῷ. Dative of agency or ethical dative.

ἐκέλευσεν. Aor act ind 3rd sg κελεύω.

ποιῆσαι. Aor act inf ποιέω (indirect discourse). The unusual use of the verb ποιέω here may be explained as a causative construction (see 2:4 on ἐδίδου and 3:12 on πεποιηκόσιν): "cause the men (to be) outside for awhile."

5:35 εἶπέν τε πρὸς αὐτούς, Ἄνδρες Ἰσραηλῖται, προσέχετε ἑαυτοῖς ἐπὶ τοῖς ἀνθρώποις τούτοις τί μέλλετε πράσσειν.

εἶπέν. Aor act ind 3rd sg λέγω. The second accent comes from the enclitic τε (see 1:4 on ἠκούσατέ).

Ἄνδρες. See 1:11.

Ἰσραηλῖται. Vocative.

προσέχετε ἑαυτοῖς. This idiomatic expression (lit. "take heed to yourselves") occurs only in Luke's writings in the NT (Luke 12:1; 17:3; 21:34; Acts 20:28) but is fairly common in the LXX. At times it is used to respond to an unworthy idea (Gen 24:6) or simply to warn against a particular course of action (Exod 34:12).

προσέχετε. Pres act impv 2nd pl προσέχω.

ἐπὶ. Reference. It is less likely that the prepositional phrase ἐπὶ τοῖς ἀνθρώποις τούτοις has been preposed from the interrogatory clause (τί μέλλετε πράσσειν; thus, "think carefully about what you are about to do to these men"), though such a rendering is demanded by English syntax.

τί. Introduces an indirect question here (cf. v. 24).

μέλλετε. Pres act ind 2nd pl μέλλω. On the force of μέλλω plus an infinitive, see 3:3 on μέλλοντας.

πράσσειν. Pres act inf πράσσω (complementary).

5:36 πρὸ γὰρ τούτων τῶν ἡμερῶν ἀνέστη Θευδᾶς λέγων εἶναί τινα ἑαυτόν, ᾧ προσεκλίθη ἀνδρῶν ἀριθμὸς ὡς τετρακοσίων· ὃς ἀνῃρέθη, καὶ πάντες ὅσοι ἐπείθοντο αὐτῷ διελύθησαν καὶ ἐγένοντο εἰς οὐδέν.

πρὸ . . . τούτων τῶν ἡμερῶν. Lit. "before these days."

ἀνέστη. Aor act ind 3rd sg ἀνίστημι.

λέγων. Pres act ptc masc nom sg λέγω (manner).

εἶναί. Pres act inf εἰμί (indirect discourse). The second accent comes from the enclitic τινα (see 1:4 on ἠκούσατέ).

τινα. Predicate accusative (see 1:22 on μάρτυρα).

ἑαυτόν. Accusative subject of the infinitive (see 1:3 on αὐτὸν).

προσεκλίθη. Aor pass ind 3rd sg προσκλίνω.

ἀνδρῶν. Partitive genitive.

ἀριθμὸς. Nominative subject of προσεκλίθη.

ἀνῃρέθη. Aor pass ind 3rd sg ἀναιρέω.

ἐπείθοντο. Impf pass ind 3rd pl πείθω.

αὐτῷ. On the use of the dative case with the passive form of πείθω, see 27:11.

διελύθησαν. Aor pass ind 3rd pl διαλύω.

ἐγένοντο εἰς οὐδέν. This idiomatic expression, which identifies the subject as insignificant (cf. LXX Jer 3:9), substitutes εἰς with an accusative noun for a predicate nominative (see 4:11 on εἰς κεφαλὴν γωνίας).

ἐγένοντο. Aor mid dep ind 3rd pl γίνομαι.

5:37 μετὰ τοῦτον ἀνέστη Ἰούδας ὁ Γαλιλαῖος ἐν ταῖς ἡμέραις τῆς ἀπογραφῆς καὶ ἀπέστησεν λαὸν ὀπίσω αὐτοῦ· κἀκεῖνος ἀπώλετο καὶ πάντες ὅσοι ἐπείθοντο αὐτῷ διεσκορπίσθησαν.

ἀνέστη. Aor act ind 3rd sg ἀνίστημι.

ὁ Γαλιλαῖος. Nominative in apposition to Ἰούδας.

τῆς ἀπογραφῆς. Descriptive genitive.

ἀπέστησεν. Aor act ind 3rd sg ἀφίστημι.

κἀκεῖνος. A shortened form (crasis) of καὶ ἐκεῖνος.

ἀπώλετο. Aor mid ind 3rd sg ἀπόλλυμι.

ἐπείθοντο. Impf pass ind 3rd pl πείθω.

αὐτῷ. On the use of the dative case with the passive form of πείθω, see 27:11.

διεσκορπίσθησαν. Aor pass ind 3rd pl διασκορπίζω.

5:38 καὶ τὰ νῦν λέγω ὑμῖν, ἀπόστητε ἀπὸ τῶν ἀνθρώπων τούτων καὶ ἄφετε αὐτούς· ὅτι ἐὰν ᾖ ἐξ ἀνθρώπων ἡ βουλὴ αὕτη ἢ τὸ ἔργον τοῦτο, καταλυθήσεται,

καὶ τὰ νῦν. See 4:29.

λέγω. Pres act ind 1st sg λέγω.

ἀπόστητε. Aor act impv 2nd pl ἀφίστημι.

ἄφετε. Aor act impv 2nd pl ἀφίημι.

ἐὰν. The use of ἐάν plus a subjunctive verb in the protasis introduces a third class condition. There has been some debate regarding the shift to a first class condition in the following sentence (which contrasts with this one). For some, the third class condition indicates a proposition that Gamaliel views as highly unlikely, while the first class condition (v. 39) states his opinion: "If this plan is of human origin it will be destroyed, but if, *as appears to be the case*, it is of God . . ." (Moule, 150; cf. Porter 1989, 310). Others maintain that no such distinction is intended. BDF (§372) renders the two clauses: "if, as one may suppose, it be . . ., but if (as these persons claim) it really is." It is possible that rather than pointing to Gamaliel's view that the first class condition is the more likely option, the shift in construction is a rhetorical device that simply lends force (like an English exclamation point) to Gamaliel's injunction to leave the men alone.

ᾖ. Pres act subj 3rd sg εἰμί.

καταλυθήσεται. Fut pass ind 3rd sg καταλύω.

5:39 εἰ δὲ ἐκ θεοῦ ἐστιν, οὐ δυνήσεσθε καταλῦσαι αὐτούς μή ποτε καὶ θεομάχοι εὑρεθῆτε. ἐπείσθησαν δὲ αὐτῷ

εἰ. Introduces a first class condition. On the significance of the shift from the third class condition in the previous clause, see v. 38.

ἐστιν. Pres act ind 3rd sg εἰμί. On the loss of accent, see 1:7 on ἐστιν.

δυνήσεσθε. Fut mid dep ind 2nd pl δύναμαι.

καταλῦσαι. Aor act inf καταλύω (complementary).

μήποτε. This adverb (placed, as is normal, in the clause initial position) with the subjunctive verb expresses a potential outcome that is to be avoided.

θεομάχοι. Complement in a subject-complement double nominative construction with the passive εὑρεθῆτε (cf. 4:36 on υἱὸς and 1:12 on Ἐλαιῶνος).

εὑρεθῆτε. Aor pass subj 2nd pl εὑρίσκω.

ἐπείσθησαν. Aor pass ind 3rd pl πείθω.

αὐτῷ. On the use of the dative case with the passive form of πείθω, see 27:11.

5:40 καὶ προσκαλεσάμενοι τοὺς ἀποστόλους δείραντες παρήγγειλαν μὴ λαλεῖν ἐπὶ τῷ ὀνόματι τοῦ Ἰησοῦ καὶ ἀπέλυσαν.

προσκαλεσάμενοι. Aor mid dep ptc masc nom pl προσκαλέομαι (temporal).

δείραντες. Aor act ptc masc nom pl δέρω (temporal). The agent who actually carried out the beating is left implicit.

παρήγγειλαν. Aor act ind 3rd pl παραγγέλλω.

λαλεῖν. Pres act inf λαλέω (indirect discourse).

ἐπὶ τῷ ὀνόματι. See 4:18.

ἀπέλυσαν. Aor act ind 3rd pl ἀπολύω.

5:41 Οἱ μὲν οὖν ἐπορεύοντο χαίροντες ἀπὸ προσώπου τοῦ συνεδρίου ὅτι κατηξιώθησαν ὑπὲρ τοῦ ὀνόματος ἀτιμασθῆναι,

Οἱ. The article is used like a pronoun (cf. 3:5) here.

μὲν οὖν. Here, the conjunction indicates a response that follows naturally not from the immediately preceding statement (the authorities' mistreatment of the apostles) but from the apostles' resolution to obey God rather than people (vv. 29–32; Levinsohn 1987, 142).

ἐπορεύοντο. Impf dep ind 3rd pl πορεύομαι.

χαίροντες. Pres act ptc masc nom pl **χαίρω** (manner).

κατηξιώθησαν . . . ἀτιμασθῆναι. In a society where honor and shame were so important, the irony of this statement ("worthy to be dishonored") would have been striking.

κατηξιώθησαν. Aor pass ind 3rd pl καταξιόω.

τοῦ ὀνόματος. Probably metonymy (see 1:9 on τῶν ὀφθαλμῶν αὐτῶν) for Jesus.

ἀτιμασθῆναι. Aor pass inf ἀτιμάζω (complementary; cf. the similar construction, εἰμὶ ἄξιος plus an epexegetical infinitive, in Luke 15:19).

5:42 πᾶσάν τε ἡμέραν ἐν τῷ ἱερῷ καὶ κατ' οἶκον οὐκ ἐπαύοντο διδάσκοντες καὶ εὐαγγελιζόμενοι τὸν Χριστόν Ἰησοῦν.

πᾶσάν τε ἡμέραν. Accusative marking duration of time. On the fronting of this expression see note on ἱκανὸν χρόνον at 14:3.

κατ' οἶκον. See 2:46 on καθ' ἡμέραν.

ἐπαύοντο. Impf mid ind 3rd pl παύω.

διδάσκοντες. Pres act ptc masc nom pl διδάσκω (complementary; see Wallace 1996, 646).

εὐαγγελιζόμενοι. Pres mid ptc masc nom pl εὐαγγελίζω (complementary; see Wallace 1996, 646).

τὸν Χριστόν Ἰησοῦν. This construction may be viewed as a noun phrase ("Christ Jesus"), or the proper noun Ἰησοῦν may be the subject (so Wallace 1996, 184) or predicate constituent of a double accusative construction (or a construction where εἶναι is implied; cf. 18:5): "preaching that Jesus was the Christ."

Acts 6:1–7

[1]In those days, when the number of disciples was increasing, there was a complaint among the Hellenists against the Hebrews because

their widows were being overlooked in the daily distribution. [2]So the Twelve summoned the group of disciples and said, "It would not be right for us to neglect the Word of God and (instead) distribute food. [3]So, brothers, look for seven respected men among yourselves who are full of the Spirit and wisdom, and we will put them in charge of this task. [4]And we will devote ourselves to prayer and the ministry of the word."

[5]The entire group was pleased with this plan, so they chose Stephen, a man full of faith and the Holy Spirit, and Philip, Prochorus, Nicanor, Timon, Parmenas, and Nicolaus, a proselyte from Antioch. [6]They brought them to the apostles and then laid their hands on them and prayed.

[7]So the message of God spread, the number of disciples in Jerusalem increased greatly, and a large group of priests became obedient to the faith.

6:1 Ἐν δὲ ταῖς ἡμέραις ταύταις πληθυνόντων τῶν μαθητῶν ἐγένετο γογγυσμὸς τῶν Ἑλληνιστῶν πρὸς τοὺς Ἑβραίους, ὅτι παρεθεωροῦντο ἐν τῇ διακονίᾳ τῇ καθημερινῇ αἱ χῆραι αὐτῶν.

Ἐν δὲ ταῖς ἡμέραις ταύταις. See 1:15.

πληθυνόντων. Pres act ptc masc gen pl πληθύνω. Genitive absolute (see 1:8 on ἐπελθόντος), temporal.

ἐγένετο. Aor mid dep ind 3rd sg γίνομαι.

Ἑλληνιστῶν. It is unclear whether this term, which also occurs in 9:29 and 11:20, refers primarily to language, culture, or both (see Brehm, 199).

Ἑβραίους. Although this term may simply refer to Jews who spoke Hebrew/Aramaic as well as Greek, Brehm (199) has suggested that it may be used in Acts to distinguish believing Jews from the Ἰουδαῖοι who did not believe.

ὅτι. The ὅτι is either causal or it could introduce the content of the "grumbling" (Omanson). Given the distance between ἐγένετο γογγυσμὸς and the lack of an explicit verb of speaking, the former is more likely.

παρεθεωροῦντο. Impf pass ind 3rd pl παραθεωρέω.

τῇ διακονίᾳ. It is unclear whether this term refers to "a [general] procedure for taking care of the needs of people" (LN 35.38) or, more specifically, to "money given to help someone in need" (LN 57.119). The context, which points to a concern for unmet needs rather than a concern that every one get their "fair share," favors the more general usage.

6:2 προσκαλεσάμενοι δὲ οἱ δώδεκα τὸ πλῆθος τῶν μαθητῶν εἶπαν, Οὐκ ἀρεστόν ἐστιν ἡμᾶς καταλείψαντας τὸν λόγον τοῦ θεοῦ διακονεῖν τραπέζαις.

προσκαλεσάμενοι. Aor mid dep ptc masc nom pl προσκαλέομαι (attendant circumstance or temporal; see 1:15 on ἀναστὰς).

εἶπαν. Aor act ind 3rd pl λέγω.

ἀρεστόν. Predicate adjective.

ἐστιν. Pres act ind 3rd sg εἰμί. On the loss of accent, see 1:7 on ἐστιν.

ἡμᾶς. Accusative subject of the infinitive διακονεῖν (see 1:3 on αὐτὸν). The impersonal construction with ἀρεστός takes an accusative noun plus an infinitive (BAGD 105; BDF §408).

καταλείψαντας. Aor act ptc masc acc pl καταλείπω. It is unclear whether the participle indicates (1) a condition (presumably "It *would* not be right if we . . ."; Rogers and Rogers, 241), (2) the means by which the action of the infinitive is accomplished ("It is not appropriate for us (to make time) to wait tables by neglecting the Word of God"), (3) the result of the action of the infinitive ("It is not appropriate for us to wait tables and consequently neglect the Word of God"), or (4) simply an attendant circumstance of the infinitive. Option (4) is to be preferred since (a) the syntactic structure does not support the conditional view ("It would not be right for us, if we neglect the word of God, to wait tables"); (b) participles indicating result are typically present tense and follow the verb they modify (Wallace 1996, 638), and (c) participles indicating means also typically follow the verb they modify (Wallace 1996, 629).

διακονεῖν τραπέζαις. Lit. "to wait tables."

διακονεῖν. Pres act inf διακονέω. The infinitival clause, ἡμᾶς καταλείψαντας τὸν λόγον τοῦ θεοῦ διακονεῖν τραπέζαις, serves as the subject of ἐστιν (cf. 9:32 on κατελθεῖν). The infinitive cannot introduce a purpose clause (contra Barrett, 311) since it is modified by the participle rather than vice versa.

6:3 ἐπισκέψασθε δέ, ἀδελφοί, ἄνδρας ἐξ ὑμῶν μαρτυρουμένους ἑπτά, πλήρεις πνεύματος καὶ σοφίας, οὓς καταστήσομεν ἐπὶ τῆς χρείας ταύτης,

ἐπισκέψασθε. Aor mid dep impv 2nd pl ἐπισκέπτομαι.

ἄνδρας. Accusative direct object of ἐπισκέψασθε.

μαρτυρουμένους. Pres pass ptc masc acc pl μαρτυρέω (attributive).

ἑπτά. Modifies ἄνδρας.

πλήρεις. Accusative in apposition to ἄνδρας.

πνεύματος καὶ σοφίας. Genitive of content.

καταστήσομεν. Fut act ind 1st pl καθίστημι.

6:4 ἡμεῖς δὲ τῇ προσευχῇ καὶ τῇ διακονίᾳ τοῦ λόγου προσκαρτερήσομεν.

ἡμεῖς δὲ τῇ προσευχῇ καὶ τῇ διακονίᾳ τοῦ λόγου. The fronting (see 3:13 on ὑμεῖς) of both the explicit subject pronoun and the dative complement of προσκαρτερήσομεν (cf. 1:14 on τῇ προσευχῇ) highlights the contrast between "waiting tables" and "prayer and the ministry of the word."

τοῦ λόγου. Objective genitive.

προσκαρτερήσομεν. Fut act ind 1st pl προσκαρτερέω.

6:5 καὶ ἤρεσεν ὁ λόγος ἐνώπιον παντὸς τοῦ πλήθους καὶ ἐξελέξαντο Στέφανον, ἄνδρα πλήρης πίστεως καὶ πνεύματος ἁγίου, καὶ Φίλιππον καὶ Πρόχορον καὶ Νικάνορα καὶ Τίμωνα καὶ Παρμενᾶν καὶ Νικόλαον προσήλυτον Ἀντιοχέα,

καὶ . . . πλήθους. Lit. "the plan was pleasing before all the group."

ἤρεσεν. Aor act ind 3rd sg ἀρέσκω.

ἐξελέξαντο. Aor mid dep ind 3rd pl ἐκλέγομαι.

ἄνδρα. Accusative in apposition to Στέφανον.

πίστεως . . . πνεύματος ἁγίου. Genitive of content.

προσήλυτον. Accusative in apposition to Νικόλαον.

Ἀντιοχέα. Lit. "an Antiochean."

6:6 οὓς ἔστησαν ἐνώπιον τῶν ἀποστόλων, καὶ προσευξάμενοι ἐπέθηκαν αὐτοῖς τὰς χεῖρας.

ἔστησαν . . . ἀποστόλων. Lit. "they placed (them) before the apostles."

ἔστησαν. Aor act ind 3rd pl ἵστημι.

προσευξάμενοι. Aor mid dep ptc masc pl προσεύχομαι (attendant circumstance).

ἐπέθηκαν. Aor act ind 3rd pl ἐπιτίθημι. While it is possible that the actions of the participle and main verb should be attributed to the apostles alone (Fitzmyer 1998, 351), without an explicit change of subject it is difficult to argue for this position from the syntax (cf. Barrett, 315–16).

6:7 Καὶ ὁ λόγος τοῦ θεοῦ ηὔξανεν καὶ ἐπληθύνετο ὁ ἀριθμὸς τῶν μαθητῶν ἐν Ἰερουσαλὴμ σφόδρα, πολύς τε ὄχλος τῶν ἱερέων ὑπήκουον τῇ πίστει.

ηὔξανεν. Impf act ind 3rd sg αὐξάνω.

ἐπληθύνετο. Impf pass ind 3rd sg πληθύνω.

καὶ . . . τε. The grouping of events by καί and τε in vv. 5–7 indicates that they are part of a larger incident and thus "preliminary . . . to the confrontation which ends with the martyrdom of the deacon Stephen" (Levinsohn 1987, 116). This verse should thus not be viewed as the end of the first major section of the book of Acts.

ὑπήκουον. Impf act ind 3rd pl ὑπακούω. The plural verb is used with the collective singular subject ὄχλος (Wallace 1996, 401).

Acts 6:8–15

[8]Now Stephen, full of grace and power, was performing great wonders and signs among the people. [9]But certain men from the so-called "Synagogue of the Freedmen"—Cyrenians, Alexandrians, and those from Cilicia and Asia—came forward to debate with Stephen, [10]but they were not able to overcome the spiritual wisdom with which he spoke.

[11]Then they bribed men to say, "We have heard him speak blasphemous words against Moses and God." [12]They stirred up the people, the elders, and the scribes and then went and seized (Stephen) and brought him to the Council. [13]Then they put forward false witnesses who said, "This man never stops saying things against the holy place and the law. [14]For we have heard him saying that this Jesus, the Nazarene, will tear down this place and change the customs that Moses handed down to us."

[15]All those sitting in the Council watched (Stephen) closely and saw that his face looked like the face of an angel.

6:8 Στέφανος δὲ πλήρης χάριτος καὶ δυνάμεως ἐποίει τέρατα καὶ σημεῖα μεγάλα ἐν τῷ λαῷ.

χάριτος καὶ δυνάμεως. Genitive of content.

ἐποίει. Impf act ind 3rd sg ποιέω.

τέρατα καὶ σημεῖα. The near synonyms probably function as a doublet (see 2:43) emphasizing the miraculous nature of the actions. They also highlight the continuity between Stephen and Moses, Jesus, the Twelve, and later, Paul and Barnabas, all of whom performed "signs and wonders."

6:9 ἀνέστησαν δέ τινες τῶν ἐκ τῆς συναγωγῆς τῆς λεγομένης Λιβερτίνων καὶ Κυρηναίων καὶ Ἀλεξανδρέων καὶ τῶν ἀπὸ Κιλικίας καὶ Ἀσίας συζητοῦντες τῷ Στεφάνῳ,

ἀνέστησαν. Aor act ind 3rd pl ἀνίστημι. When used intransitively this verb means "to come forward" (Fitzmyer 1998, 358).

τῶν. Partitive genitive. The article functions as a nominalizer (see 1:3 on τὰ): "some of the ones from . . ."

λεγομένης. Pres pass ptc fem gen sg λέγω (attributive).

καὶ Κυρηναίων. The conjunction is epexegetical and thus introduces various groups that are part of a single synagogue (cf. Bruce, 187; Fitzmyer 1998, 358). Although Barrett (323) argues for two groups based on the repetition of the article τῶν, the article is necessary in order to make the following prepositional phrase a substantive: "those from Cilicia and Asia."

τῶν ἀπὸ Κιλικίας. The article functions as a nominalizer (see 1:3 on τὰ).

συζητοῦντες. Pres act ptc masc nom pl συζητέω (purpose).

6:10 καὶ οὐκ ἴσχυον ἀντιστῆναι τῇ σοφίᾳ καὶ τῷ πνεύματι ᾧ ἐλάλει.

καὶ. Adversative.

ἴσχυον. Impf act ind 3rd pl ἰσχύω.

ἀντιστῆναι. Aor act inf ἀνθίστημι (complementary).

τῇ σοφίᾳ καὶ τῷ πνεύματι. Dative complement of ἀντιστῆναι. Although most scholars render this phrase (which does not occur elsewhere in the NT) "the wisdom and the S/spirit," it may be better to treat it as a hendiadys ("spiritual wisdom"; see 1:25 on τῆς διακονίας καὶ ἀποστολῆς) highlighting the nature of Stephen's wisdom.

ᾧ. Dative of manner.

ἐλάλει. Impf act ind 3rd sg λαλέω.

6:11 τότε ὑπέβαλον ἄνδρας λέγοντας ὅτι Ἀκηκόαμεν αὐτοῦ λαλοῦντος ῥήματα βλάσφημα εἰς Μωϋσῆν καὶ τὸν θεόν·

τότε. The adverb indicates that Stephen's enemies took prompt action (see 1:12).

ὑπέβαλον ἄνδρας λέγοντας. Lit. "they suborned men who said."

ὑπέβαλον. Aor act ind 3rd pl ὑποβάλλω.

λέγοντας. Pres act ptc masc acc pl λέγω (attributive).

ὅτι. Introduces direct discourse.

Ἀκηκόαμεν. Prf act ind 1st pl ἀκούω.

αὐτοῦ. Genitive object of Ἀκηκόαμεν.

λαλοῦντος. Pres act ptc masc gen sg λαλέω (genitive complement of ἀκούω in an object-complement "double genitive" construction; see 2:6 on λαλούντων).

ῥήματα βλάσφημα. Accusative direct object of λαλοῦντος.

εἰς. Disadvantage.

6:12 συνεκίνησάν τε τὸν λαὸν καὶ τοὺς πρεσβυτέρους καὶ τοὺς γραμματεῖς, καὶ ἐπιστάντες συνήρπασαν αὐτὸν καὶ ἤγαγον εἰς τὸ συνέδριον,

συνεκίνησάν. Aor act ind 3rd pl συγκινέω. The second accent comes from the enclitic τε (see 1:4 on ἠκούσατέ).

ἐπιστάντες. Aor act ptc masc nom pl ἐφίστημι (attendant circumstance). The verb may indicate that they took him by surprise (Barrett, 327).

συνήρπασαν. Aor act ind 3rd pl συναρπάζω. Syntactically, it appears that those who incited the people were also the ones who seized Stephen and brought him to the Council.

ἤγαγον. Aor act ind 3rd pl ἄγω.

6:13 ἔστησάν τε μάρτυρας ψευδεῖς λέγοντας, Ὁ ἄνθρωπος οὗτος οὐ παύεται λαλῶν ῥήματα κατὰ τοῦ τόπου τοῦ ἁγίου [τούτου] καὶ τοῦ νόμου·

ἔστησάν. Aor act ind 3rd pl ἵστημι. The second accent comes from the enclitic τε (see 1:4 on ἠκούσατέ).

λέγοντας. Pres act ptc masc acc pl λέγω (attributive).

οὗτος. The demonstrative may carry a pejorative connotation here (Barrett, 327; Fitzmyer 1998, 359; cf. 19:26).

παύεται. Pres mid ind 3rd sg παύω.

λαλῶν. Pres act ptc masc nom sg λαλέω (complementary; see Wallace 1996, 646).

[τούτου]. External evidence favors its omission (Bruce, 188). Its presence in some manuscripts (B C 1739 *al*) can be explained as certain scribes intuitively including information that is implicit in the text.

6:14 ἀκηκόαμεν γὰρ αὐτοῦ λέγοντος ὅτι Ἰησοῦς ὁ Ναζωραῖος οὗτος καταλύσει τὸν τόπον τοῦτον καὶ ἀλλάξει τὰ ἔθη ἃ παρέδωκεν ἡμῖν Μωϋσῆς.

ἀκηκόαμεν. Prf act ind 1st pl ἀκούω.

αὐτοῦ. Genitive object of ἀκηκόαμεν.

λέγοντος. Pres act ptc masc gen sg λέγω (genitive complement of ἀκούω in an object-complement "double genitive" construction; see 2:6 on λαλούντων).

ὅτι. Introduces indirect discourse (the clausal complement of λέγοντος).

οὗτος. The demonstrative probably lends a contemptuous or derogatory tone to the statement (Bruce, 188; Barrett, 328; cf. 19:26).

καταλύσει. Fut act ind 3rd sg καταλύω.

ἀλλάξει. Fut act ind 3rd sg ἀλλάσσω.

τὰ ἔθη. Accusative direct object of ἀλλάξει.

παρέδωκεν. Aor act ind 3rd sg παραδίδωμι.

ἡμῖν. Dative indirect object of παρέδωκεν.

6:15 καὶ ἀτενίσαντες εἰς αὐτὸν πάντες οἱ καθεζόμενοι ἐν τῷ συνεδρίῳ εἶδον τὸ πρόσωπον αὐτοῦ ὡσεὶ πρόσωπον ἀγγέλου.

ἀτενίσαντες. Aor act ptc masc nom pl ἀτενίζω (attendant circumstance).

οἱ καθεζόμενοι. Pres dep ptc masc nom pl καθέζομαι (substantival).

εἶδον . . . ἀγγέλου. Lit. "they saw his face like the face of an angel."

εἶδον. Aor act ind 3rd pl ὁράω.

Acts 7:1–8

[1]Then the high priest said, “Are these things true?” [2]And he replied, “Brothers and fathers, listen! The glorious God appeared to our ancestor Abraham while he was in Mesopotamia before he settled in Haran. [3]He said to him, ‘Leave your country and your relatives and come to the land I will show you.’

[4]Then (Abraham) left the land of the Chaldeans and settled in Haran; and from there, after his father died, God resettled him in this land in which you now live. [5]But (God) did not give him a portion of it, not even a foot of space. Yet although he still did not have children, (God) promised to give it to him and to his descendents after him as a possession.

[6]God spoke in this way because his descendants would be temporary residents in a foreign land and (the citizens of that land) would enslave them and mistreat them for four hundred years. [7]But God said, ‘I will punish the nation to whom they will be enslaved; and after these things they will come out and worship me in this place.’ [8]And he gave the covenant of circumcision to him; and consequently he had a son, Isaac, and circumcised him on the eighth day, and Isaac did the same to Jacob, and Jacob to the twelve patriarchs.”

7:1 **Εἶπεν δὲ ὁ ἀρχιερεύς, Εἰ ταῦτα οὕτως ἔχει;**

Εἶπεν. Aor act ind 3rd sg λέγω.

Εἰ. Introduces a direct question (cf. 1:6; 4:19).

ταῦτα. Nominative subject of ἔχει.

οὕτως ἔχει. The verb ἔχω plus an adverb (a common idiomatic construction in Acts; Barrett, 340) denotes a state, and is thus comparable to εἰμί (BAGD, 334; cf. 17:11).

ἔχει. Pres act ind 3rd sg ἔχω.

7:2 **ὁ δὲ ἔφη, Ἄνδρες ἀδελφοὶ καὶ πατέρες, ἀκούσατε. Ὁ θεὸς τῆς δόξης ὤφθη τῷ πατρὶ ἡμῶν Ἀβραὰμ ὄντι ἐν τῇ Μεσοποταμίᾳ πρὶν ἢ κατοικῆσαι αὐτὸν ἐν Χαρρὰν**

ὁ. The article functions like a personal pronoun here (cf. 3:5).

ἔφη. Aor/Impf act ind 3rd sg φημί. On the question of whether the form is aorist or imperfect, see Porter (1989, 443–46) who concludes that the form is aspectually ambiguous.

Ἄνδρες. See 1:11.

ἀδελφοὶ καὶ πατέρες. The use of relational terms may help the speaker establish rapport with the audience. Here, as in 13:15; 22:1, 5; 23:1, 5, 6; and 28:17, 21, ἀδελφοὶ is used to refer to fellow Jews rather than as a technical term for "believers" (cf. 1:15). Witherington (1998, 264–65) notes that Stephen does not "distinguish himself from his audience until after the speech becomes overtly polemical."

ἀκούσατε. Aor act impv 2nd pl ἀκούω.

τῆς δόξης. Attributive genitive (Wallace 1996, 87; Bruce, 192).

ὤφθη. Aor pass ind 3rd sg ὁράω. In the passive, this verb means "to appear" (see Wallace 1996, 165, n. 72).

ὄντι. Pres act ptc masc dat sg εἰμί. Strictly speaking, the participle is attributive, since it has a different subject than the main verb, though the most natural rendering in English will be temporal (see Culy 2004).

πρὶν ἢ κατοικῆσαι. Aor act inf κατοικέω. Used with πρὶν ἢ (or πρὶν) the infinitive denotes subsequent time (see 2:20 on πρὶν ἐλθεῖν).

αὐτὸν. Accusative subject of the infinitive (see 1:3 on αὐτὸν).

7:3 καὶ εἶπεν πρὸς αὐτόν, Ἔξελθε ἐκ τῆς γῆς σου καὶ [ἐκ] τῆς συγγενείας σου, καὶ δεῦρο εἰς τὴν γῆν ἣν ἄν σοι δείξω.

εἶπεν. Aor act ind 3rd sg λέγω.

Ἔξελθε ἐκ τῆς γῆς σου. Lit. "come out from your land."

Ἔξελθε. Aor act impv 2nd sg ἐξέρχομαι.

ἐκ τῆς γῆς σου. It is unclear whether the genitive pronoun σου denotes possession ("the land you own") or identification ("the land/country where you live"). The next verse (γῆς Χαλδαίων) makes the latter more likely.

δεῦρο. This directional adverb, meaning "here," was often used like an imperative verb, "Come here!"

ἄν σοι δείξω. The construction ἄν plus a subjunctive verb is analogous to a future indicative verb (see 8:31 on ὁδηγήσει).

δείξω. Aor act subj 1st sg δείκνυμι. Presumably, the subjunctive is used here because the "showing" is contingent upon Abraham's response to the command.

7:4 τότε ἐξελθὼν ἐκ γῆς Χαλδαίων κατῴκησεν ἐν Χαρράν. κἀκεῖθεν μετὰ τὸ ἀποθανεῖν τὸν πατέρα αὐτοῦ μετῴκισεν αὐτὸν εἰς τὴν γῆν ταύτην εἰς ἣν ὑμεῖς νῦν κατοικεῖτε,

ἐξελθὼν. Aor act ptc masc nom sg ἐξέρχομαι. Although the participle could be functioning temporally, given the presence of τότε it is preferable to view it as denoting an attendant circumstance.

κατῴκησεν. Aor act ind 3rd sg κατοικέω.

κἀκεῖθεν. A shortened form (crasis) of καὶ ἐκεῖθεν.

ἀποθανεῖν. Aor act inf ἀποθνῄσκω. Used with μετὰ τό to indicate antecedent time (see 1:3 on μετὰ τὸ παθεῖν).

τὸν πατέρα. Accusative subject of the infinitive (see 1:3 on αὐτὸν).

μετῴκισεν. Aor act ind 3rd sg μετοικίζω. Given the semantics of μετοικίζω ("to cause someone to change a place of habitation"; LN 85.83), "God" must be the unexpressed subject. If the writer had meant to say that Abraham (subject of the verb) "moved" his father's bones or corpse (with αὐτὸν referring to his deceased father), he would have had to use a different verb (such as συναναφέρω; see LXX Gen 50:25; Exod 13:19).

κατοικεῖτε. Pres act ind 2nd pl κατοικέω.

7:5 καὶ οὐκ ἔδωκεν αὐτῷ κληρονομίαν ἐν αὐτῇ οὐδὲ βῆμα ποδός καὶ ἐπηγγείλατο δοῦναι αὐτῷ εἰς κατάσχεσιν αὐτὴν καὶ τῷ σπέρματι αὐτοῦ μετ' αὐτόν, οὐκ ὄντος αὐτῷ τέκνου.

καὶ. Adversative.

οὐκ . . . αὐτῇ. Lit. "he did not give property in it to him."

ἔδωκεν. Aor act ind 3rd sg δίδωμι.

κληρονομίαν. Accusative direct object of ἔδωκεν.

βῆμα ποδός. An idiom for a very small space: "not even a square foot!" (lit. "a step of a foot"; cf. LXX Deut 2:5).

ἐπηγγείλατο. Aor mid dep ind 3rd sg ἐπαγγέλλομαι.

δοῦναι. Aor act inf δίδωμι (indirect discourse or complementary).

εἰς κατάσχεσιν. The preposition εἰς with an accusative noun functions like a predicate modifier of αὐτὴν (see 4:11 on εἰς κεφαλὴν γωνίας).

αὐτὴν. Accusative direct object of δοῦναι.

τῷ σπέρματι. Dative indirect object of δοῦναι (along with αὐτῷ).

οὐκ ὄντος αὐτῷ τέκνου. The position of this clause at the end of the sentence suggests that it should be understood as emphatic.

ὄντος. Pres act ptc neut gen sg εἰμί. Genitive absolute (see 1:8 on ἐπελθόντος). The participle is best viewed as concessive (Rogers and Rogers, 242; BDF §423.5), rather than temporal.

αὐτῷ. Dative of possession (with εἰμί).

τέκνου. Genitive subject (see 1:8 on ἐπελθόντος).

7:6 ἐλάλησεν δὲ οὕτως ὁ θεὸς ὅτι ἔσται τὸ σπέρμα αὐτοῦ πάροικον ἐν γῇ ἀλλοτρίᾳ καὶ δουλώσουσιν αὐτὸ καὶ κακώσουσιν ἔτη τετρακόσια·

ἐλάλησεν. Aor act ind 3rd sg λαλέω.

οὕτως. The function of this adverb is difficult to determine in this context. Most scholars and translations take it (cataphorically) as introducing the quotation that follows (e.g., NIV: "God spoke to him in this way: 'Your descendants will be strangers in a country not their own.'"). If the adverb were used in this way, one would expect a direct quotation as in the NIV (cf. 13:34, 47). The Greek quotation, however, is clearly indirect given the use of the pronoun αὐτοῦ rather than σου. This incongruity appears to have led to several alterations in the text: some manuscripts substitute αὐτῷ for οὕτως (𝔓[74] א Ψ 104 *al*), while others read ἐλάλησεν δὲ οὕτως ὁ θεὸς πρὸς αὐτὸν ὅτι (D). It may be better, then, to take the adverb (anaphorically) as a reference to what precedes with the ὅτι introducing a causal clause rather than indirect discourse.

ἔσται. Fut ind 3rd sg εἰμί.

πάροικον. Predicate nominative.

δουλώσουσιν. Fut act ind 3rd pl δουλόω. The subject, apparently the inhabitants of the foreign land, is unexpressed.

αὐτό. Neuter accusative direct object of δουλώσουσιν. The antecedent is τὸ σπέρμα.

κακώσουσιν. Fut act ind 3rd pl κακόω.

ἔτη. Accusative indicating extent of time (see v. 20 on μῆνας).

7:7 καὶ τὸ ἔθνος ᾧ ἐὰν δουλεύσουσιν κρινῶ ἐγώ, ὁ θεὸς εἶπεν, καὶ μετὰ ταῦτα ἐξελεύσονται καὶ λατρεύσουσίν μοι ἐν τῷ τόπῳ τούτῳ.

τὸ ἔθνος. Accusative direct object of κρινῶ. The fronting (see 3:13 on ὑμεῖς) of the direct object places it in focus (see 2:15 on ὑμεῖς).

δουλεύσουσιν. Fut act ind 3rd pl δουλεύω.

κρινῶ. Fut act ind 1st sg κρίνω.

εἶπεν. Aor act ind 3rd sg λέγω.

ταῦτα. Refers to the events mentioned in v. 6.

ἐξελεύσονται. Fut mid dep ind 3rd pl ἐξέρχομαι.

λατρεύσουσίν. Fut act ind 3rd pl λατρεύω. The second accent comes from the enclitic μοι (see 1:4 on ἠκούσατέ).

μοι. Dative complement of λατρεύσουσιν.

7:8 καὶ ἔδωκεν αὐτῷ διαθήκην περιτομῆς· καὶ οὕτως ἐγέννησεν τὸν Ἰσαὰκ καὶ περιέτεμεν αὐτὸν τῇ ἡμέρᾳ τῇ ὀγδόῃ, καὶ Ἰσαὰκ τὸν Ἰακώβ, καὶ Ἰακὼβ τοὺς δώδεκα πατριάρχας.

ἔδωκεν. Aor act ind 3rd sg δίδωμι.

διαθήκην. Accusative direct object of ἔδωκεν.

περιτομῆς. It may be appropriate to describe this as an "epexegetical genitive" and render διαθήκην περιτομῆς, "a covenant consisting of circumcision" (so Barrett, 346; cf. Gen 17:10-13) or "a covenant characterized by circumcision" (since circumcision was the sign or ratification symbol of the covenant; so Witherington 1998, 266).

οὕτως. The adverb introduces material that summarizes the implications of the preceding statement (cf. BAGD, 597).

ἐγέννησεν. Aor act ind 3rd sg γεννάω.

περιέτεμεν. Aor act ind 3rd sg περιτέμνω.

καὶ Ἰσαὰκ τὸν Ἰακώβ. The *focal* implicit event in this and the following clause is περιέτεμεν rather than ἐγέννησεν (so TEV; NCV; CEV; NJB; REB; God's Word; contra Fitzmyer 1998, 372; Witherington 1998, 267; NIV; NRSV; NLT). The οὕτως (see above) makes it clear that the point of what follows is the continuation of the covenant of circumcision.

Acts 7:9–16

9"(Later,) The patriarchs were jealous of Joseph so they sold him into (slavery in) Egypt; but God was with him. 10He rescued him from all his troubles and gave him favor and wisdom before Pharaoh, king of Egypt. He had him appointed ruler over Egypt and over Pharaoh's entire household. 11Then a famine came over the whole (land) of Egypt and Canaan, (indeed) great suffering, and our ancestors were unable to find food.

[12]When Jacob heard that there was grain in Egypt, he sent our ancestors on their first trip. [13]On their second trip, Joseph allowed himself to be recognized by his brothers and Joseph's racial background became known to Pharaoh. [14]Then Joseph sent (someone) and summoned his father Jacob and all his relatives—seventy-five people in all.

[15]So Jacob went down to Egypt, and both he and our other ancestors died there. [16]Their bodies were (later) moved to Shechem and placed in the tomb that Abraham had bought for a sum of silver from the sons of Hamor in Shechem."

7:9 Καὶ οἱ πατριάρχαι ζηλώσαντες τὸν Ἰωσὴφ ἀπέδοντο εἰς Αἴγυπτον· καὶ ἦν ὁ θεὸς μετ' αὐτοῦ

ζηλώσαντες. Aor act ptc masc nom pl ζηλόω (causal).

τὸν Ἰωσήφ. Accusative direct object of ζηλώσαντες, or less likely the object of ἀπέδοντο, given the word order (cf. BAGD, 338).

ἀπέδοντο. Aor mid ind 3rd pl ἀποδίδωμι. In the middle voice, this verb means "to sell" (BAGD, 90; cf. 5:8).

καί. Adversative.

ἦν. Impf ind 3rd sg εἰμί.

7:10 καὶ ἐξείλατο αὐτὸν ἐκ πασῶν τῶν θλίψεων αὐτοῦ καὶ ἔδωκεν αὐτῷ χάριν καὶ σοφίαν ἐναντίον Φαραὼ βασιλέως Αἰγύπτου καὶ κατέστησεν αὐτὸν ἡγούμενον ἐπ' Αἴγυπτον καὶ [ἐφ'] ὅλον τὸν οἶκον αὐτοῦ.

ἐξείλατο. Aor mid ind 3rd sg ἐξαιρέω.

ἔδωκεν. Aor act ind 3rd sg δίδωμι.

χάριν. The sense here is that God caused Joseph to appear "pleasing" and wise to Pharaoh (cf. Newman and Nida, 148).

βασιλέως. Genitive in apposition to Φαραώ.

Αἰγύπτου. Genitive of subordination.

κατέστησεν. Aor act ind 3rd sg καθίστημι. The subject of κατέστησεν could be either God or Pharaoh. While the reference to τὸν οἶκον αὐτοῦ at the end of the clause superficially makes the latter more attractive ("Pharaoh appointed him ruler over *his* entire household"), given the fact that no change of subject is indicated, Luke appears to have intended the former. Such a reading fits well with the focus on the agency of God in the preceding clauses, where each action is expressed with a finite verb and linked with a καί: God rescued, God granted, God appointed.

ἡγούμενον. Pres dep ptc masc acc sg ἡγέομαι. This accusative substantival participle is the complement in an object-complement double accusative construction (see 1:3 on ζῶντα).

ἐπ'. Subordination.

7:11 ἦλθεν δὲ λιμὸς ἐφ' ὅλην τὴν Αἴγυπτον καὶ Χανάαν καὶ θλῖψις μεγάλη, καὶ οὐχ ηὕρισκον χορτάσματα οἱ πατέρες ἡμῶν.

ἦλθεν. Aor act ind 3rd sg ἔρχομαι. The use of this verb with an inanimate object (λιμὸς) and the preposition ἐπί is unusual and makes the narrative more vivid.

θλῖψις μεγάλη. This nominative noun phrase could be viewed as part of a conjoined clause with an implicit ἦν ("and there was great suffering") or an elided ἦλθεν ἐφ' ὅλην τὴν Αἴγυπτον καὶ Χανάαν ("and great suffering came upon all of Egypt and Canaan"), as a displaced part of the subject of ἦλθεν (λιμὸς καὶ θλῖψις μεγάλη; "a famine and great suffering came upon the land"), or as an absolute expression (see Porter 1994, 85).

οὐχ ηὕρισκον. Impf act ind 3rd pl εὑρίσκω. The use of the imperfect with the negative denotes "could not find" (Bruce, 195).

7:12 ἀκούσας δὲ Ἰακὼβ ὄντα σιτία εἰς Αἴγυπτον ἐξαπέστειλεν τοὺς πατέρας ἡμῶν πρῶτον.

ἀκούσας. Aor act ptc masc nom sg ἀκούω (temporal or causal; Rogers and Rogers, 242).

ὄντα Pres act ptc neut acc pl εἰμί. Wallace labels this use of the participle, "indirect discourse" and notes that "An anarthrous participle in the accusative case, in conjunction with an accusative noun or pronoun, sometimes indicates indirect discourse after a verb of perception or communication" (Wallace 1996, 645; on anarthrous see 3:3 on Πέτρον καὶ' Ιωάννη). In terms of syntax, however, it is more appropriate simply to maintain that the participle functions as the complement of an object-complement double accusative construction (see 1:3 on ζῶντα).

ἐξαπέστειλεν. Aor act ind 3rd sg ἐξαποστέλλω.

πρῶτον. Cf. 1:1.

7:13 καὶ ἐν τῷ δευτέρῳ ἀνεγνωρίσθη Ἰωσὴφ τοῖς ἀδελφοῖς αὐτοῦ καὶ φανερὸν ἐγένετο τῷ Φαραὼ τὸ γένος [τοῦ] Ἰωσήφ.

ἀνεγνωρίσθη. Aor pass ind 3rd sg ἀναγνωρίζω (permissive passive; Fitzmyer [1998, 373] calls it a "middle sense").

τοῖς ἀδελφοῖς. While "Joseph allowed himself to be recognized *by* his brothers" is a good idiomatic translation of ἀνεγνωρίσθη Ἰωσὴφ τοῖς ἀδελφοῖς, τοῖς ἀδελφοῖς should not be viewed as a dative of agent (contra Barrett, 349). Syntactically, τοῖς ἀδελφοῖς is an indirect object: a literal rendering would be "Joseph was made known *to* his brothers."

φανερὸν. Predicate adjective. Although translations of this term often imply relational "knowing" (NRSV: " Joseph's family became known to Pharaoh"), such a nuance is inconsistent with the term φανερὸν. The focus of 7:13 is most likely on Joseph's revelation of his identity to his brothers, and his racial background (τὸ γένος; see below) to Pharaoh.

ἐγένετο. Aor mid dep ind 3rd sg γίνομαι.

τὸ γένος. This term may refer to either "racial background" or "family." The use of φανερὸν (see above) suggests the former (contra Barrett, 350).

7:14 ἀποστείλας δὲ Ἰωσὴφ μετεκαλέσατο Ἰακὼβ τὸν πατέρα αὐτοῦ καὶ πᾶσαν τὴν συγγένειαν ἐν ψυχαῖς ἑβδομήκοντα πέντε.

ἀποστείλας. Aor act ptc masc nom sg ἀποστέλλω (attendant circumstance).

μετεκαλέσατο. Aor mid ind 3rd sg μετακαλέω.

Ἰακὼβ. Accusative direct object of μετεκαλέσατο.

τὸν πατέρα. Accusative in apposition to Ἰακὼβ.

τὴν συγγένειαν. Accusative direct object of μετεκαλέσατο.

ἐν ψυχαῖς ἑβδομήκοντα πέντε. Lit. "in souls, seventy-five."

ἐν. Although many have suggested that ἐν here means "amounting to" (Barrett, 350; Bruce, 195; Fitzmyer 1998, 374; BDF §198.1), it is better to simply understand the preposition as denoting reference: "*with reference to* souls, seventy-five." The construction is not analogous to LXX Deut 10:22 where ἐν denotes association, "with" (contra Bruce, 195).

ψυχαῖς. Synecdoche (see 1:22 on τοῦ βαπτίσματος Ἰωάννου) for "people."

7:15 καὶ κατέβη Ἰακὼβ εἰς Αἴγυπτον καὶ ἐτελεύτησεν αὐτὸς καὶ οἱ πατέρες ἡμῶν

κατέβη. Aor act ind 3rd sg καταβαίνω.

ἐτελεύτησεν. Aor act ind 3rd sg τελευτάω. The use of the singular verb with a compound subject probably keeps the focus on Jacob (αὐτὸς; see Wallace 1996, 401; cf. 11:14; 16:31, 33; 26:30).

7:16 καὶ μετετέθησαν εἰς Συχὲμ καὶ ἐτέθησαν ἐν τῷ μνήματι ᾧ ὠνήσατο Ἀβραὰμ τιμῆς ἀργυρίου παρὰ τῶν υἱῶν Ἑμμὼρ ἐν Συχέμ.

μετετέθησαν. Aor pass ind 3rd pl μετατίθημι.

ἐτέθησαν. Aor pass ind 3rd pl τίθημι.

ᾧ. Dative by attraction (see 1:1 on ὧν) to τῷ μνήματι (it normally would have been accusative as the direct object of ὠνήσατο).

ὠνήσατο. Aor mid dep ind 3rd sg ὠνέομαι.

τιμῆς. Genitive of price.

ἐν Συχέμ. Although the UBS[4]/NA[27] text is well-attested (א* B C 36 181), there is also strong support (𝔓[74] D Ψ *Byz*) for the reading τοῦ Συχέμ ("son of Shechem," or perhaps, "from Shechem"). A third reading, τοῦ ἐν Συχέμ, has weaker support (א[2] A E 1409).

Acts 7:17–22

[17]"As the time related to the promise that God had declared to Abraham drew near, the people multiplied and increased in Egypt [18]until another king came to power over Egypt who did not know Joseph. [19]This man cunningly exploited our people and treated our ancestors cruelly, forcing them to abandon their babies so that they would die. [20]At that very time, Moses was born and he was very pleasing to God. For three months he was raised in his father's house. [21]But when he was abandoned, Pharaoh's daughter picked him up and raised him as her own son. [22]And Moses was trained in all the wisdom of Egypt, and his words and deeds were powerful."

7:17 Καθὼς δὲ ἤγγιζεν ὁ χρόνος τῆς ἐπαγγελίας ἧς ὡμολόγησεν ὁ θεὸς τῷ Ἀβραάμ, ηὔξησεν ὁ λαὸς καὶ ἐπληθύνθη ἐν Αἰγύπτῳ

Καθὼς. Most scholars argue that καθὼς carries a temporal sense in this passage (Barrett, 352; Fitzmyer 1998, 374; Robertson 1934, 968). If so, it would be the only time it is used this way in the NT (cf. Barrett, 352). There is no doubt that the clause itself has a temporal component, given the verb ἤγγιζεν and the noun χρόνος. These temporal terms, however, do not necessarily force καθὼς to function temporally. Instead, the term may be functioning (as it often does) as a "marker of similarity in events and states, with the possible implication of something being in accordance with something else" (LN 64.14). If this interpretation is correct, the point of the verse is that the increase in population was in accord with the imminent fulfilment of the promise.

ἤγγιζεν. Impf act ind 3rd sg ἐγγίζω.

τῆς ἐπαγγελίας. Genitive of respect.

ἧς. Genitive by attraction (see 1:1 on ὧν) to τῆς ἐπαγγελίας (it normally would have been accusative as the direct object of ὡμολόγησεν).

ὡμολόγησεν. Aor act ind 3rd sg ὁμολογέω.

ηὔξησεν . . . καὶ ἐπληθύνθη. The two verbs function like a doublet (see 2:43 on τέρατα καὶ σημεῖα) emphasizing the extent of the Israelites' numerical growth: "the number of people in Egypt grew and grew."

ηὔξησεν. Aor act ind 3rd sg αὐξάνω.

ἐπληθύνθη. Aor pass ind 3rd sg πληθύνω.

7:18 ἄχρι οὗ ἀνέστη βασιλεὺς ἕτερος [ἐπ' Αἴγυπτον] ὃς οὐκ ᾔδει τὸν Ἰωσήφ.

ἄχρι οὗ. This lexicalized phrase (a phrase that has come to function as a single lexical unit) probably derived from the phrase, ἄχρι τοῦ χρόνου ἐν ᾧ (cf. 27:33; Luke 21:24; Rom 11:25; 1 Cor 11:26; 15:25; Gal 3:19; Heb 3:13; Rev 2:25; Moule, 82; see also Culy 1989, 43). It typically carries the sense of "until." When the expression is in the clause initial position, however, it may mean "when." One must thus question the segmentation of the present passage. If we follow the UBS⁴/NA²⁷ text, ἄχρι οὗ should be rendered "until." If, however, v. 18 begins a new sentence, then vv. 17–19 should probably be rendered, ". . . the people in Egypt grew and grew. When another king came to power over Egypt, who did not know Joseph, this man exploited our people . . ."

ἀνέστη. Aor act ind 3rd sg ἀνίστημι.

ᾔδει. Plprf act ind 3rd sg οἶδα. In the NT, the pluperfect form of this verb is deponent and functions like a past tense verb.

7:19 οὗτος κατασοφισάμενος τὸ γένος ἡμῶν ἐκάκωσεν τοὺς πατέρας [ἡμῶν] τοῦ ποιεῖν τὰ βρέφη ἔκθετα αὐτῶν εἰς τὸ μὴ ζῳογονεῖσθαι.

κατασοφισάμενος. Aor mid dep ptc masc nom sg κατασοφίζομαι (attendant circumstance or perhaps means: "by deceiving our people he mistreated our ancestors"). Only here in the NT ("to exploit by means of craftiness and cunning, implying false arguments"; LN 88.147).

ἐκάκωσεν. Aor act ind 3rd pl κακόω.

τοὺς πατέρας. Although this noun phrase could be taken as the accusative subject of the infinitive (so Wallace 1996, 195), its position makes it more likely that it is the direct object of ἐκάκωσεν.

τοῦ ποιεῖν τὰ βρέφη ἔκθετα αὐτῶν. The difficulties posed by the word order of this infinitival clause, supported by 𝔓[74] א A B C *al* (lit. "making the infants exposed of them"), apparently led many scribes to adjust the order: τοῦ ποιεῖν ἔκθετα τὰ βρέφη αὐτῶν (𝔓[45] D E Ψ *Byz*; Bruce, 197, inadvertantly smooths out the order as well!). The unusual word order reflected in UBS[4]/NA[27] is best explained as a focus construction. In a finite clause, focus involves placing a constituent in front of the verb (see 3:13 on ὑμεῖς). In the present case, it appears that part of the noun phrase τὰ βρέφη αὐτῶν has been moved up in the infinitival clause, probably to highlight the heinous nature of the Egyptians' actions. It is not uncommon for one part of a noun phrase to be fronted leaving another part behind.

ποιεῖν. Pres act inf ποιέω (epexegetical). Although Wallace (1996, 592) suggests that the infinitive indicates purpose or result, this would only be possible if τοὺς πατέρας were the subject of the infinitive (see above) or if a passive infinitive were used and τὰ βρέφη was the subject of the infinitive ("so that their infants was forced to be exposed"). Since the subject of the infinitive is most likely the same as the subject of the main verb (οὗτος/Pharaoh), and neither the purpose nor result of Pharaoh's actions was that *he* expose their infants, it is better to take the infinitive as epexegetical (so Rogers and Rogers, 243).

τὰ βρέφη. Accusative direct object of ποιεῖν.

ἔκθετα. Accusative second complement in an object-complement double accusative construction (see 1:3 on ζῶντα).

εἰς τὸ μὴ ζῳογονεῖσθαι. Pres pass inf ζῳογονέω. The construction, εἰς τό plus an infinitive, denotes purpose here.

7:20 ἐν ᾧ καιρῷ ἐγεννήθη Μωϋσῆς, καὶ ἦν ἀστεῖος τῷ θεῷ· ὃς ἀνετράφη μῆνας τρεῖς ἐν τῷ οἴκῳ τοῦ πατρός,

ἐν ᾧ καιρῷ. The internally headed relative clause (see 1:2 on ἄχρι ἧς ἡμέρας) probably intensifies this adverbial idiom, "at that *very* time."

ἐγεννήθη. Aor pass ind 3rd sg γεννάω.

ἦν. Impf ind 3rd sg εἰμί.

ἀστεῖος. The meaning of this distinctive term (it occurs only here and in Heb 11:23 in the NT), which is taken from LXX Exod 2:2, is unclear. It could be used to refer specifically to physical beauty, or as a general term of approval (Ellingworth 609–10). In the present case, it is likely that the author is following a well-established Jewish tradition that linked Moses' extraordinary appearance to his parents' decision to preserve his life (see Philo, *Moses* 1.2; 1.9; Josephus *Ant*. 2.230–32; Lane 369–70). If the phrase ἀστεῖος τῷ θεῷ is taken as an idiomatic (Semitic) construction denoting degree (see below), this interpretation is strengthened.

τῷ θεῷ. Dative of opinion (ethical dative). The dative noun phrase, τῷ θεῷ, may reflect an idiomatic way of expressing an emphatic (almost superlative) quality in Hebrew (cf. Bruce 197; Witherington 1998, 269, n. 298). A good example of this construction is found in Jonah 3:3 where the phrase עִיר־גְּדוֹלָה לֵאלֹהִים, lit. "a great city to God," should almost certainly be understood as a figurative expression denoting "an extremely large city" (so most scholars).

ἀνετράφη. Aor pass ind 3rd sg ἀνατρέφω.

μῆνας. Accusative indicating extent of time (cf. 7:6, 36, 42; 9:9, 19b, 43; 10:48; 11:26; 13:18, 21; 14:3, 28; 16:12; 18:11; 20:6, 31; 21:4, 7, 20; 25:6, 14; 26:7; 27:33; 28:7, 12, 14, 30).

τοῦ. The article functions like a possessive pronoun.

7:21 ἐκτεθέντος δὲ αὐτοῦ ἀνείλατο αὐτὸν ἡ θυγάτηρ Φαραὼ καὶ ἀνεθρέψατο αὐτὸν ἑαυτῇ εἰς υἱόν.

The precise meaning of this verse is difficult to determine, though the overall sense is readily apparent. ἀνείλατο αὐτὸν could mean either "she took him up (from the water)" as in LXX Exod 2:5, or "she adopted him." Bruce (197–98) seems to argue that Stephen has used LXX vocabulary in a different sense; that is, although in Exod 2:5 the verb means "took up (out of the water)," here it means "adopted." BAGD

(55) and Barrett (355) both cite extra-biblical sources in support of the meaning "adopted." While ἀνεθρέψατο αὐτὸν ἑαυτῇ εἰς υἱόν is clearly a reference to adoption, however, it is probably better to read ἀνείλατο αὐτὸν in its primary sense, "she took him up" (as in the LXX allusion), as a reaction to ἐκτεθέντος. Finally, since the καί marks a clause boundary, ἑαυτῇ εἰς υἱόν must modify ἀνεθρέψατο αὐτὸν rather than ἀνείλατο αὐτὸν.

ἐκτεθέντος. Aor pass ptc masc gen sg ἐκτίθημι. Genitive absolute (see 1:8 on ἐπελθόντος), temporal. This is a good example of the rule that genitive absolute constructions are used when the subject of the participle is different from the subject of the main verb. That the subject of the participle is a direct object in the main clause (αὐτὸν) is irrelevant (*pace* Bruce, 197).

αὐτοῦ. Genitive subject (see 1:8 on ἐπελθόντος).

ἀνείλατο. Aor mid ind 3rd sg ἀναιρέω. On the meaning of this verb see below.

ἀνεθρέψατο. Aor mid ind 3rd sg ἀνατρέφω.

εἰς υἱόν. The prepositional phrase functions like a predicate modifier (see 4:11 on εἰς κεφαλὴν γωνίας; Bruce, 198; Robertson 1934, 481).

ἑαυτῇ. Dative of advantage or dative of possession. The latter should probably be excluded since ἑαυτῇ is outside the prepositional phrase, though there is little difference in meaning between the two.

7:22 καὶ ἐπαιδεύθη Μωϋσῆς [ἐν] πάσῃ σοφίᾳ Αἰγυπτίων, ἦν δὲ δυνατὸς ἐν λόγοις καὶ ἔργοις αὐτοῦ.

ἐπαιδεύθη. Aor pass ind 3rd sg παιδεύω.

ἦν. Impf ind 3rd sg εἰμί.

δυνατὸς. Predicate adjective.

ἐν. Denotes reference.

Acts 7:23–29

[23]"When he was forty years old, an idea formed in his mind to visit his countrymen, the Israelites. [24]When he saw one of them being mistreated, he came to his aid and took revenge for the person who was mistreated by killing the Egyptian. [25]Now, he was thinking that his countrymen would see that God was bringing salvation to them through his efforts; but they did not see it that way. [26]On the following day, he

unexpectedly came upon them—men who were fighting!—and he tried to make peace between them by saying, 'Men! You are brothers! Why are you mistreating one another?' [27]But the one who was mistreating his neighbor refused to listen and said, 'Who appointed you as ruler and judge over us? [28]Surely you're not planning to do away with me in the same way that you did away with the Egyptian yesterday?' [29]When he heard this, Moses fled and became a temporary resident in the land of Midian, where he had two sons."

7:23 Ὡς δὲ ἐπληροῦτο αὐτῷ τεσσερακονταετὴς χρόνος, ἀνέβη ἐπὶ τὴν καρδίαν αὐτοῦ ἐπισκέψασθαι τοὺς ἀδελφοὺς αὐτοῦ τοὺς υἱοὺς Ἰσραήλ.

Ὡς. Temporal (see 18:5).

ἐπληροῦτο αὐτῷ τεσσερακονταετὴς χρόνος. An idiomatic expression denoting a person's age (lit. "forty years time was completed to him"; cf. 9:23; see also 13:25 on ἐπλήρου). The rare phrase τεσσερακονταετὴς χρόνος is also used in 13:18.

ἐπληροῦτο. Impf pass ind 3rd sg πληρόω.

ἀνέβη. Aor act ind 3rd sg ἀναβαίνω.

ἐπισκέψασθαι. Aor mid dep inf ἐπισκέπτομαι (subject). Barrett (357) argues that the term ἐπισκέψασθαι denotes more than a simple "visit" here. While it is true that Moses intended to come to the aid of his people, however, such a meaning is derived from the context or the readers' knowledge of the story, rather than from the semantics of the verb.

τοὺς ἀδελφοὺς. Accusative direct object of the infinitive.

τοὺς υἱοὺς. Accusative in apposition to τοὺς ἀδελφοὺς αὐτοῦ.

7:24 καὶ ἰδών τινα ἀδικούμενον ἠμύνατο καὶ ἐποίησεν ἐκδίκησιν τῷ καταπονουμένῳ πατάξας τὸν Αἰγύπτιον.

ἰδών. Aor act ptc masc nom sg ὁράω (temporal).

τινα. Accusative substantival object of ἰδών.

ἀδικούμενον. Pres pass ptc masc acc sg ἀδικέω. The participle could either be taken attributively or as the complement in an object-complement double accusative construction (see 1:3 on ζῶντα). The fact that the focus is on the event Moses witnessed, rather than on seeing a particular person, makes the latter more likely.

ἠμύνατο. Aor mid dep ind 3rd sg ἀμύνομαι. Barrett (357) understands the verb to mean something like "defend" here, with the middle form being deponent. While the form is probably deponent, the sense may be "ward off, repel" rather than defend (cf. LXX Psalm 117 (118): 10, 11, 12; Joshua 10:13).

ἐποίησεν. Aor act ind 3rd sg ποιέω. ποιέω ἐκδίκησιν means "to take revenge."

τῷ καταπονουμένῳ. Pres pass ptc masc dat sg καταπονέω (substantival). Dative of advantage (Rogers and Rogers, 243).

πατάξας. Aor act ptc masc nom sg πατάσσω (means; not manner, contra Rogers and Rogers, 243). Lit. "striking."

7:25 ἐνόμιζεν δὲ συνιέναι τοὺς ἀδελφοὺς [αὐτοῦ] ὅτι ὁ θεὸς διὰ χειρὸς αὐτοῦ δίδωσιν σωτηρίαν αὐτοῖς· οἱ δὲ οὐ συνῆκαν.

ἐνόμιζεν. Impf act ind 3rd sg νομίζω.

συνιέναι. Pres act inf συνίημι (indirect discourse; Rogers and Rogers, 243). Lit. "understand." The fine distinction that Barrett (357) makes based on the present tense of the infinitive (something like, "they *already* understood") is unwarranted.

τοὺς ἀδελφοὺς. Accusative subject of the infinitive.

ὅτι. Introduces the clausal complement of συνιέναι (perhaps indirect discourse).

διὰ. Means.

χειρὸς αὐτοῦ. Metonymy for "his effort." The antecedent of αὐτοῦ is Moses.

δίδωσιν. Pres act ind 3rd sg δίδωμι.

οἱ. The article functions like a personal pronoun here (cf. 3:5).

συνῆκαν. Aor act ind 3rd pl συνίημι.

7:26 τῇ τε ἐπιούσῃ ἡμέρᾳ ὤφθη αὐτοῖς μαχομένοις καὶ συνήλλασσεν αὐτοὺς εἰς εἰρήνην εἰπών, Ἄνδρες, ἀδελφοί ἐστε· ἱνατί ἀδικεῖτε ἀλλήλους;

τε. Used here as a marker of a close relationship between sequential events or states (LN 89.88).

ἐπιούσῃ. Pres act ptc fem dat sg ἔπειμι (attributive).

ἡμέρᾳ. Dative of time.

ὤφθη. Aor pass ind 3rd sg ὁράω. In the passive voice, this verb means "to appear" (see Wallace 1996, 165, n. 72). The expression probably implies an unexpected meeting (cf. Rogers and Rogers, 243).

αὐτοῖς. The cataphoric pronoun draws attention to the inappropriate nature of the event. It is possible that the pronoun is anaphoric with τοὺς ἀδελφοὺς in v. 25 being the antecedent.

μαχομένοις. Pres dep ptc masc dat pl μάχομαι (substantival). The participle stands in apposition to αὐτοῖς. It may be possible to take this participle as part of a dative construction that takes two complements (see the discussion of participles that function as the complement in an object-complement double accusative construction; 1:3 on ζῶντα). The sense would be something like, "The next day he came upon/encountered them fighting."

συνήλλασσεν . . . εἰρήνην. Lit. "he was reconciling them into peace."

συνήλλασσεν. Impf act ind 3rd sg συναλλάσσω. Given the context, a conative translation is appropriate: "He attempted to . . ." (Wallace 1996, 551).

εἰπών. Aor act ptc masc nom sg λέγω (means; not manner, contra Rogers and Rogers, 243).

Ἄνδρες. In this case, the vocative is not further qualified and should therefore be rendered "Men!" (cf. 1:11).

ἀδελφοί. Predicate nominative.

ἐστε. Pres act ind 2nd pl εἰμί. On the loss of accent, see 1:7 on **ἐστιν.**

ἱνατί. Interrogative adverb; a shortened, lexicalized form of ἵνα τί γένηται, "in order that what might happen?" (BAGD, 378).

ἀδικεῖτε. Pres act ind 2nd pl ἀδικέω.

7:27 ὁ δὲ ἀδικῶν τὸν πλησίον ἀπώσατο αὐτὸν εἰπών, Τίς σε κατέστησεν ἄρχοντα καὶ δικαστὴν ἐφ' ἡμῶν;

ὁ . . . ἀδικῶν. Pres act ptc masc nom sg ἀδικέω (substantival).

δὲ. In this case, the conjunction introduces a series of clauses that run against the expectations of both Moses and the reader.

τὸν. The article functions like a possessive pronoun (cf. v. 20).

πλησίον. Direct object of ἀδικῶν.

ἀπώσατο. Aor mid dep ind 3rd sg ἀπωθέομαι. Although this verb may be used of physically pushing someone away (LN 15.46 prefer this sense here), it always appears to be used metaphorically elsewhere in the NT (Acts 7:39; 13:46; Rom 11:1, 2; 1 Tim 1:19) to indicate rejection of someone or something. While a physical sense could fit the present context, the well-known story from Exod 2, where there is no indication of a physical response, supports the (usual) metaphorical sense.

εἰπών. Aor act ptc masc nom sg λέγω (attendant circumstance).

Τίς σε κατέστησεν ἄρχοντα καὶ δικαστὴν ἐφ' ἡμῶν; The question is rhetorical (Barrett, 359) and functions like an emphatic statement.

κατέστησεν. Aor act ind 3rd sg καθίστημι.

ἄρχοντα καὶ δικαστὴν. The complement in an object-complement double accusative construction (see 1:3 on ζῶντα) with καθίστημι, "to appoint someone (to be) *something*" (σε is the object).

7:28 μὴ ἀνελεῖν με σὺ θέλεις ὃν τρόπον ἀνεῖλες ἐχθὲς τὸν Αἰγύπτιον;

This second rhetorical question is equivalent to an emphatic negative statement (with μή), and carries a taunting tone.

ἀνελεῖν. Aor act inf ἀναιρέω (complementary).

με. Accusative direct object of the infinitive.

θέλεις. Pres act ind 2nd sg θέλω.

ὃν τρόπον. Another idiomatic expression using an internally headed relative clause (see 1:2 on ἄχρι ἧς ἡμέρας) to intensify the expression: "in the *same* way."

ἀνεῖλες. Aor act ind 2nd sg ἀναιρέω.

7:29 ἔφυγεν δὲ Μωϋσῆς ἐν τῷ λόγῳ τούτῳ καὶ ἐγένετο πάροικος ἐν γῇ Μαδιάμ, οὗ ἐγέννησεν υἱοὺς δύο.

ἔφυγεν. Aor act ind 3rd sg φεύγω.

ἐν τῷ λόγῳ τούτῳ. Lit. "at this remark." Strictly speaking, the preposition should probably be described as causal, indicating that Moses fled in response to what he had heard (cf. Bruce 199; BDF §219.2).

ἐγένετο. Aor mid dep ind 3rd sg γίνομαι.

πάροικος. Predicate nominative with impersonal ἐγένετο.

οὗ. See 1:13.

ἐγέννησεν. Aor act ind 3rd sg γεννάω.

υἱοὺς. Accusative direct object of ἐγέννησεν.

Acts 7:30–43

[30]"After forty years had passed, an angel in the flame of a burning bush appeared to him in the desert of Mt. Sinai. [31]When Moses saw this, he was amazed at the sight, and when he approached it to get a closer look, (he heard) the voice of the Lord: [32]'I am the God of your ancestors, the God of Abraham, Isaac, and Jacob.' Moses began to tremble and did not dare look any closer. [33]Then the Lord said to him, 'Take off your sandals, for the place where you are standing is holy ground. [34]I have surely seen the mistreatment of my people in Egypt and I have heard their groaning, and I have come down to take them away (from there). Now come, let me send you to Egypt.'

[35]This Moses—whom they had rejected by saying, 'Who appointed you as ruler and judge?'—this is the one God sent as both ruler and deliverer with the help of the angel who appeared to him in the bush. [36]This man led them out and he did wonders and signs in the land of Egypt, at the Red Sea, and for forty years in the wilderness. [37]This is the Moses who said to the people of Israel, 'God will raise up for you a prophet like me from your brothers. [38]This is the man who was in the assembly in the wilderness with the angel who spoke to him on Mount Sinai—and with our fathers—who (also) received living oracles to give to us.

[39]Our ancestors were unwilling to obey him, but rejected (him) and, in their hearts, returned to Egypt. [40]They said to Aaron, 'Make us gods who will go before us, for this Moses, who led us out of the land of Egypt, we don't know what has happened to him.' [41]They made a calf at that time, and offered a sacrifice to the idol, and began to celebrate what they had made.

[42]So God rejected (them) and handed them over to worship the stars of the sky, as it is written in the Book of the Prophets, 'Did you bring offerings and sacrifices to me for forty years in the wilderness, people of Israel? (No!) [43]But you took along the tent of Molech and the star of [your] God Rephan, the images you made to worship, so I will deport you beyond Babylon.'"

7:30 Καὶ πληρωθέντων ἐτῶν τεσσεράκοντα ὤφθη αὐτῷ ἐν τῇ ἐρήμῳ τοῦ ὄρους Σινᾶ ἄγγελος ἐν φλογὶ πυρὸς βάτου.

πληρωθέντων. Aor pass ptc neut gen pl πληρόω. Genitive absolute (see 1:8 on ἐπελθόντος), temporal. A comparison of this verse (Καὶ πληρωθέντων ἐτῶν τεσσεράκοντα) with v. 23 (Ὡς δὲ ἐπληροῦτο αὐτῷ τεσσερακονταετὴς χρόνος) provides a good example of when Greek writers needed to utilize temporal genitive absolute constructions rather than an adverbial temporal expression. In this verse, the genitive absolute indicates that there is topic continuity between what precedes and what follows, in spite of the fact that the temporal setting changes. In contrast, the use of the adverbial expression in v. 23 indicates a major shift in scene (see Levinsohn 1992, 214).

ἐτῶν τεσσεράκοντα. Genitive subject (see 1:8 on ἐπελθόντος).

ὤφθη. Aor pass ind 3rd sg ὁράω. In the passive voice, this verb means "to appear" (see Wallace 1996, 165, n. 72). On its connotation see v. 26.

Σινᾶ. Genitive in apposition to τοῦ ὄρους.

ἄγγελος. Nominative subject of ὤφθη.

ἐν. See 1:10.

πυρὸς. Attributive genitive modifying βάτου.

7:31 ὁ δὲ Μωϋσῆς ἰδὼν ἐθαύμαζεν τὸ ὅραμα, προσερχομένου δὲ αὐτοῦ κατανοῆσαι ἐγένετο φωνὴ κυρίου,

ἰδὼν. Aor act ptc masc nom sg ὁράω (temporal).

ἐθαύμαζεν. Impf act ind 3rd sg θαυμάζω. This verb can be used transitively (i.e., take a direct object) in Greek, meaning "to marvel at."

τὸ ὅραμα. Accusative object of θαυμάζω.

προσερχομένου. Pres dep ptc masc gen sg προσέρχομαι. This participle should be viewed as a genitive absolute functioning temporally, rather than simply as a temporal participle (contra Rogers and Rogers, 243), since the main verb (ἐγένετο) has a different subject (see 1:8 on ἐπελθόντος).

αὐτοῦ. Genitive subject (see 1:8 on ἐπελθόντος).

κατανοῆσαι Aor act inf κατανοέω. The infinitive supplies the purpose of προσερχομένου αὐτοῦ.

ἐγένετο φωνὴ κυρίου. Lit. "the voice of the Lord happened."

ἐγένετο. Aor mid dep ind 3rd sg γίνομαι.

7:32 Ἐγὼ ὁ θεὸς τῶν πατέρων σου, ὁ θεὸς Ἀβραὰμ καὶ Ἰσαὰκ καὶ Ἰακώβ. ἔντρομος δὲ γενόμενος Μωϋσῆς οὐκ ἐτόλμα κατανοῆσαι.

'Εγὼ ὁ θεὸς. The verb εἰμί is implied.

ὁ θεὸς 'Αβραὰμ καὶ 'Ισαὰκ καὶ 'Ιακώβ. This noun phrase stands in apposition to ὁ θεὸς τῶν πατέρων σου and is thus epexegetical.

ἔντρομος. Predicate adjective.

γενόμενος. Aor mid dep ptc masc nom sg γίνομαι. The participle probably denotes attendant circumstance (Rogers and Rogers, 244, call it causal). Less likely, it could be viewed as attributive: "Moses, who was trembling . . ."

ἐτόλμα. Impf act ind 3rd sg τολμάω.

κατανοῆσαι. Aor act inf κατανοέω (complementary). In this context the verb probably indicates that Moses did not "look too closely" (cf. LN 30.4).

7:33 εἶπεν δὲ αὐτῷ ὁ κύριος, Λῦσον τὸ ὑπόδημα τῶν ποδῶν σου, ὁ γὰρ τόπος ἐφ' ᾧ ἕστηκας γῆ ἁγία ἐστίν.

εἶπεν. Aor act ind 3rd sg λέγω.

Λῦσον. Aor act impv 2nd sg λύω.

Λῦσον . . . σου. Lit. "loose the sandal of your feet."

ἕστηκας. Prf act ind 2nd sg ἵστημι. On the use of the perfect, see 1:11 on ἑστήκατε.

γῆ. Predicate nominative.

ἐστίν. Pres act ind 3rd sg εἰμί. On the retention of the accent, see 2:13 on εἰσίν.

7:34 ἰδὼν εἶδον τὴν κάκωσιν τοῦ λαοῦ μου τοῦ ἐν Αἰγύπτῳ καὶ τοῦ στεναγμοῦ αὐτῶν ἤκουσα, καὶ κατέβην ἐξελέσθαι αὐτούς· καὶ νῦν δεῦρο ἀποστείλω σε εἰς Αἴγυπτον.

ἰδὼν. Aor act ptc masc nom sg ὁράω. The use of the cognate participle with εἶδον (lit. "seeing, I saw) reflects a Semitic idiom (the infinitive absolute plus finite verb) that intensifies the sense of the main verb (cf. 28:26 on ἀκοῇ ἀκούσετε).

εἶδον. Aor act ind 1st sg ὁράω.

τοῦ λαοῦ. Objective genitive.

τοῦ ἐν Αἰγύπτῳ. The article functions as an adjectivizer (see 2:5 on τῶν ὑπὸ τὸν οὐρανόν), changing the prepositional phrase to an attributive modifier.

τοῦ στεναγμοῦ. Genitive object of ἤκουσα.

ἤκουσα. Aor act ind 1st sg ἀκούω.

κατέβην. Aor act ind 1st sg καταβαίνω.

ἐξελέσθαι. Aor mid inf ἐξαιρέω (purpose). The middle voice probably indicates that God was acting in his own interest (indirect middle; Rogers and Rogers, 244).

καὶ νῦν. See 4:29.

δεῦρο. See v. 3.

ἀποστείλω. Aor act subj 1st sg ἀποστέλλω (hortatory). The relatively rare singular hortatory subjunctive is always preceded by δεῦρο or ἄφες in the NT (Robertson 1934, 931; Wallace 1996, 464).

7:35 Τοῦτον τὸν Μωϋσῆν, ὃν ἠρνήσαντο εἰπόντες, Τίς σε κατέστησεν ἄρχοντα καὶ δικαστήν; τοῦτον ὁ θεὸς [καὶ] ἄρχοντα καὶ λυτρωτὴν ἀπέσταλκεν σὺν χειρὶ ἀγγέλου τοῦ ὀφθέντος αὐτῷ ἐν τῇ βάτῳ.

Τοῦτον τὸν Μωϋσῆν. The fronting (see 3:13 on ὑμεῖς) of this constituent and the use of τοῦτον places the focus (see 2:15 on ὑμεῖς) securely on Moses and indicates that Stephen's argument is about to become more pointed (cf. Fitzmyer 1998, 378; Witherington 1998, 270).

ἠρνήσαντο. Aor mid dep ind 3rd pl ἀρνέομαι. Here, the sense is "to refuse to follow someone as a leader" (LN 36.43).

εἰπόντες. Aor act ptc masc nom pl λέγω (means; or temporal, "when they said").

κατέστησεν. Aor act ind 3rd sg καθίστημι.

ἄρχοντα καὶ δικαστήν. See v. 27.

τοῦτον. In this position, the (resumptive) demonstrative pronoun reestablishes the focus on Moses.

ἄρχοντα καὶ λυτρωτήν. The complement in an object-complement double accusative construction ("God sent him as ruler and deliverer"; see 1:3 on ζῶντα).

ἀπέσταλκεν. Prf act ind 3rd sg ἀποστέλλω. The use of the perfect rather than the aorist may emphasize the significance of God's action in sending Moses. Wallace (1996, 578) calls it a dramatic perfect. Moule (14–15) refers to it as a "perfect of allegory," a usage that focuses on the present paradigmatic significance of an OT event.

σὺν χειρὶ. Metonymy (see 1:9 on τῶν ὀφθαλμῶν αὐτῶν) for "aid" or "power" (lit. "with the hand"). The preposition indicates accompaniment.

ὀφθέντος. Aor pass ptc masc gen sg ὁράω (attributive). See v. 30 on ὤφθη.

7:36 οὗτος ἐξήγαγεν αὐτοὺς ποιήσας τέρατα καὶ σημεῖα ἐν γῇ Αἰγύπτῳ καὶ ἐν Ἐρυθρᾷ Θαλάσσῃ καὶ ἐν τῇ ἐρήμῳ ἔτη τεσσεράκοντα.

οὗτος. The recurrent (resumptive) use of the demonstrative pronoun (vv. 35, 36, 37, 38) makes for powerful rhetoric.

ἐξήγαγεν. Aor act ind 3rd sg ἐξάγω.

ποιήσας. Aor act ptc masc nom sg ποιέω. The participle could be taken as means and explain how Moses led the Israelites out of Egypt. In this case, the final statement (or perhaps the final two statements) would be something of an afterthought: "This man led them out by doing wonders and signs in the land of Egypt and at the Red Sea—and in the desert for forty years." Given the inclusion of the last statement, however, it may be better to take it as attendant circumstance.

τέρατα καὶ σημεῖα. See 2:43.

ἐν γῇ Αἰγύπτῳ. Lit. "in Egypt land." Some scribes changed Αἰγύπτῳ to the expected Αἰγύπτου.

ἔτη. Accusative indicating extent of time (see v. 20 on μῆνας).

7:37 οὗτός ἐστιν ὁ Μωϋσῆς ὁ εἴπας τοῖς υἱοῖς Ἰσραήλ, Προφήτην ὑμῖν ἀναστήσει ὁ θεὸς ἐκ τῶν ἀδελφῶν ὑμῶν ὡς ἐμέ.

οὗτός. See v. 36. The second accent comes from the enclitic ἐστιν (see 1:4 on ἠκούσατέ).

ἐστιν. Pres act ind 3rd sg εἰμί. On the loss of accent, see 1:7 on ἐστιν.

ὁ Μωϋσῆς. Predicate nominative.

εἴπας. Aor act ptc masc nom sg λέγω (attributive).

Προφήτην. Accusative direct object of ἀναστήσει.

ὑμῖν. Dative of advantage.

ἀναστήσει. Fut act ind 3rd sg ἀνίστημι. On the meaning of the verb, see 3:26 on ἀναστήσας.

ὡς ἐμε. The comparison, "like me," could be either with Προφήτην, "a prophet like me," or with ἀναστήσει, "like he raised me up." The former is more likely (see 3:22; contra Barrett, 332).

7:38 οὗτός ἐστιν ὁ γενόμενος ἐν τῇ ἐκκλησίᾳ ἐν τῇ ἐρήμῳ μετὰ τοῦ ἀγγέλου τοῦ λαλοῦντος αὐτῷ ἐν τῷ ὄρει Σινᾶ καὶ τῶν πατέρων ἡμῶν, ὃς ἐδέξατο λόγια ζῶντα δοῦναι ἡμῖν,

οὗτός. See v. 36. The second accent comes from the enclitic ἐστιν (see 1:4 on ἠκούσατέ).

ἐστιν. Pres act ind 3rd sg εἰμί. On the loss of accent, see 1:7 on ἐστιν.

ὁ γενόμενος. Aor mid dep ptc masc nom sg γίνομαι (substantival; predicate nominative).

μετὰ. Accompaniment.

λαλοῦντος. Pres act ptc masc gen sg λαλέω (attributive).

τῶν πατέρων. Genitive governed by μετὰ.

ὃς. The (singular) antecedent is Moses not τῶν πατέρων ἡμῶν.

ἐδέξατο. Aor mid dep ind 3rd sg δέχομαι.

ζῶντα. Pres act ptc neut acc pl ζάω (attributive).

δοῦναι. Aor act inf δίδωμι (purpose).

ἡμῖν. There is also strong manuscript support for ὑμῖν. Since the two forms were pronounced the same, the matter must be decided by determining whether Stephen would have associated himself with his hearers (using ἡμῖν) or not. Since he closely links himself with his hearers until v. 51, ἡμῖν is to be preferred (so Barrett, Metzger, Omanson).

7:39 ᾧ οὐκ ἠθέλησαν ὑπήκοοι γενέσθαι οἱ πατέρες ἡμῶν, ἀλλὰ ἀπώσαντο καὶ ἐστράφησαν ἐν ταῖς καρδίαις αὐτῶν εἰς Αἴγυπτον

ᾧ οὐκ . . . ἡμῶν. Lit. "to whom our fathers were not willing to be obedient."

ᾧ. The antecedent is still Moses.

ἠθέλησαν. Aor act ind 3rd pl θέλω.

ὑπήκοοι. Predicate adjective.

γενέσθαι. Aor mid dep inf γίνωμαι (complementary).

οἱ πατέρες. Nominative subject of ἠθέλησαν.

ἀπώσαντο. Aor mid dep ind 3rd pl ἀπωθέομαι. Moses is the unexpressed object of the verb. On the sense of this term, see v. 27 on ἀπώσατο.

ἐστράφησαν ἐν ταῖς καρδίαις αὐτῶν εἰς Αἴγυπτον. It is unclear whether this expression indicates a decision to return to Egypt (which would be consistent with Num 14:3–4, but an unusual way of expressing it; cf. Barrett, 366), or simply "they began thinking about/longing for Egypt" (cf. Witherington 1998, 271).

ἐστράφησαν. Aor pass ind 3rd pl στρέφω.

7:40 εἰπόντες τῷ Ἀαρών, Ποίησον ἡμῖν θεοὺς οἳ προπορεύσονται ἡμῶν· ὁ γὰρ Μωϋσῆς οὗτος, ὃς ἐξήγαγεν ἡμᾶς ἐκ γῆς Αἰγύπτου, οὐκ οἴδαμεν τί ἐγένετο αὐτῷ.

εἰπόντες. Aor act ptc masc nom pl λέγω (attendant circumstance).

Ποίησον. Aor act impv 2nd sg ποιέω.

προπορεύσονται. Fut mid dep ind 3rd pl προπορεύομαι. Rogers and Rogers (244) describe this as an example of a future tense verb used with a relative pronoun to express purpose. It is probably better, however, simply to say that the future, in accord with its usual semantic value, conveys expectation (cf. Porter 1989, 415).

ἡμῶν. Genitive complement of προπορεύομαι.

ὁ . . . Μωϋσῆς οὗτος. The *nominativus pendens* ("hanging nominative," sometimes called the nominative absolute) introduces the topic (cf. 2:22 on Ἰησοῦν τὸν Ναζωραῖον) of the sentence, though it will not be the syntactic subject of the sentence. Here, it is modified by a relative clause.

οὗτος. The use of the demonstrative with a name probably implies a dismissive tone here (cf. 6:14).

ἐξήγαγεν. Aor act ind 3rd sg ἐξάγω.

ἐκ. See 1:8 on ἐφ᾽ ὑμᾶς.

οἴδαμεν. Prf act ind 1st pl οἶδα.

ἐγένετο. Aor mid dep ind 3rd sg γίνομαι.

7:41 καὶ ἐμοσχοποίησαν ἐν ταῖς ἡμέραις ἐκείναις καὶ ἀνήγαγον θυσίαν τῷ εἰδώλῳ καὶ εὐφραίνοντο ἐν τοῖς ἔργοις τῶν χειρῶν αὐτῶν.

ἐμοσχοποίησαν. Aor act ind 3rd pl μοσχοποιέω (μόσχος = "calf"). Apparently, a Lukan neologism.

ἀνήγαγον. Aor act ind 3rd pl ἀνάγω.

εὐφραίνοντο . . . αὐτῶν. Lit. "celebrated in the works of their hands."

εὐφραίνοντο. Impf pass ind 3rd pl εὐφραίνω.

ἐν. The preposition may indicate cause or reference, though the whole expression, εὐφραίνοντο ἐν, is probably idiomatic.

7:42 ἔστρεψεν δὲ ὁ θεὸς καὶ παρέδωκεν αὐτοὺς λατρεύειν τῇ στρατιᾷ τοῦ οὐρανοῦ καθὼς γέγραπται ἐν βίβλῳ τῶν προφητῶν, Μὴ σφάγια καὶ θυσίας προσηνέγκατέ μοι ἔτη τεσσεράκοντα ἐν τῇ ἐρήμῳ, οἶκος Ἰσραήλ;

ἔστρεψεν. Aor act ind 3rd sg στρέφω. Lit. "turned." The sense here may either be (a) transitive— "God turned (them)," with αὐτοὺς serving as the understood object of both verbs; or (b) intransitive—"God changed (his attitude toward them)." In favor of the latter, which Barrett (368) and Bruce (203) prefer, is the use of στρέφω to denote attitude in v. 39, though there the sense is made clear by ἐν ταῖς καρδίαις αὐτῶν. If the former sense is correct (so Johnson, 131), then the expression is essentially synonymous with παρέδωκεν αὐτοὺς λατρεύειν.

παρέδωκεν. Aor act ind 3rd sg παραδίδωμι.

λατρεύειν. Pres act inf λατρεύω. The use of παραδίδωμι with the infinitive suggests purpose (though result is also possible). Any theological problems associated with such a view are already inherent in the expression ὁ θεὸς παρέδωκεν αὐτοὺς.

τῇ στρατιᾷ τοῦ οὐρανοῦ. Lit. "the army of heaven."

τῇ στρατιᾳ. Dative complement of λατρεύω. Barrett (368) argues that this expression refers to "heavenly bodies, worshipped as deities."

γέγραπται. Prf pass ind 3rd sg γράφω.

Μή. The negativizer introduces a question that expects a negative answer. The negated question does not imply that the Israelites failed to offer any sacrifices, but rather that God was not the one to whom they were offered (cf. Witherington 1998, 272; Finley, 257).

προσηνέγκατέ. Aor act ind 2nd pl προσφέρω.

ἔτη. Accusative indicating extent of time (see v. 20 on μῆνας).

οἶκος Ἰσραήλ. Vocative. Lit. "house of Israel."

7:43 καὶ ἀνελάβετε τὴν σκηνὴν τοῦ Μολὸχ καὶ τὸ ἄστρον τοῦ θεοῦ [ὑμῶν] Ῥαιφάν, τοὺς τύπους οὓς ἐποιήσατε προσκυνεῖν αὐτοῖς, καὶ μετοικιῶ ὑμᾶς ἐπέκεινα Βαβυλῶνος.

ἀνελάβετε. Aor act ind 2nd pl ἀναλαμβάνω.

τὴν σκηνὴν τοῦ Μολὸχ. This expression is clearly meant to contrast with ἡ σκηνὴ τοῦ μαρτυρίου mentioned in the following verse.

"To take along the tent of Molech," then, is a figurative reference to worshipping Molech.

'Ραιφάν. Genitive in apposition to τοῦ θεοῦ.

τοὺς τύπους. Accusative plural in apposition to the compound noun phrase τὴν σκηνὴν . . . καὶ τὸ ἄστρον.

ἐποιήσατε. Aor act ind 2nd pl ποιέω.

προσκυνεῖν. Pres act inf προσκυνέω (purpose).

αὐτοῖς. Dative complement of προσκυνέω.

καί. Introduces God's pronouncement upon Israel, which is a response to what was mentioned in the preceding clauses (cf. Niehaus's comments on the Hebrew text of Amos 5:27 [434]).

μετοικιῶ. Fut act ind 1st sg μετοικίζω.

Acts 7:44–53

[44]"Our ancestors had the tent of testimony in the wilderness, just as he who spoke to Moses commanded (him) to make it according to the pattern he had seen. [45]Our ancestors inherited it and brought it with Joshua when they took possession of the nations that God drove out from the presence of our ancestors until the days of David. [46]David found favor before God and asked to find a dwelling place for the descendants of Jacob, [47]but Solomon built a house for him. [48]Yet the Most High certainly does not live in something made by human hands, as the prophet says, [49]'"Heaven is my throne, and the earth my footstool. What sort of house will you build for me?" says the Lord. "Or what will be my place of rest? [50]Didn't my hand make all of these things?"'

[51]You stiff-necked people! Uncircumcised in heart and in ears! You always resist the Holy Spirit; as your ancestors did, so do you! [52]Which of the prophets did your ancestors not persecute? They killed those who foretold the coming of the Righteous One, whose betrayers and murderers you have now become—[53]you people who received the law through decrees given by angels, but did not keep it!"

7:44 'Η σκηνὴ τοῦ μαρτυρίου ἦν τοῖς πατράσιν ἡμῶν ἐν τῇ ἐρήμῳ καθὼς διετάξατο ὁ λαλῶν τῷ Μωϋσῇ ποιῆσαι αὐτὴν κατὰ τὸν τύπον ὃν ἑωράκει·

'Η σκηνὴ τοῦ μαρτυρίου. This common LXX expression for the tabernacle/tent used by the Jews as a central place of worship prior to the building of the temple, stands in stark contrast to τὴν σκηνὴν τοῦ Μολὸχ in v. 43.

τοῦ μαρτυρίου. Although the phrase ἡ σκηνὴ τοῦ μαρτυρίου is itself another name for the tabernacle, τοῦ μαρτυρίου probably referred to the ten commandments, which were kept in the "ark of the testimony" (Exod 25:16) inside the "tent of the testimony" (Exod 38:21; see Bruce, 205).

ἦν. Impf ind 3rd sg εἰμί.

τοῖς πατράσιν. Dative of possession (with εἰμί).

διετάξατο. Aor mid ind 3rd sg διατάσσω. The unexpressed object, the recipient of the command, should be understood as Moses in light of the singular ἑωράκει.

ὁ λαλῶν. Pres act ptc masc nom sg λαλέω (substantival subject of διετάξατο).

ποιῆσαι. Aor act inf ποιέω (indirect discourse modifying διετάξατο).

κατὰ. Standard (i.e., in accord with a particular standard).

τὸν τύπον. The use of this term here may be intended to add further contrast with the idolatrous τύπους in v. 43 (Bruce, 205).

ἑωράκει. Plprf act ind 3rd sg ὁράω.

7:45 ἣν καὶ εἰσήγαγον διαδεξάμενοι οἱ πατέρες ἡμῶν μετὰ Ἰησοῦ ἐν τῇ κατασχέσει τῶν ἐθνῶν, ὧν ἐξῶσεν ὁ θεὸς ἀπὸ προσώπου τῶν πατέρων ἡμῶν ἕως τῶν ἡμερῶν Δαυίδ,

ἣν. The antecedent is ἡ σκηνὴ τοῦ μαρτυρίου in v. 44.

εἰσήγαγον. Aor act ind 3rd pl εἰσάγω.

διαδεξάμενοι. Aor mid dep ptc masc nom pl διαδέχομαι (temporal; Wallace 1996, 627). Barrett (371) suggests that the term may be an adverbial expression meaning "in their turn."

ἐν. Temporal.

κατασχέσει. "The act of taking possession of something" (LN 57.57).

Ἰησοῦ. Here, "Joshua" (the same Greek form is used for "Jesus").

ὧν. Genitive by attraction (see 1:1 on ὧν) to τῶν ἐθνῶν (it normally would have been accusative as the direct object of ἐξῶσεν).

ἐξῶσεν. Aor act ind 3rd sg ἐξωθέω.

ἕως τῶν ἡμερῶν Δαυίδ. Syntactically this temporal phrase goes more naturally with ἐξωθέω than with διαδεξάμενοι (contra Bruce, 206). It may be better, however, to view it as loosely connected to the entire verse and indicative of the "life-span" of the "tent of meeting" (see Barrett, 372).

7:46 ὃς εὗρεν χάριν ἐνώπιον τοῦ θεοῦ καὶ ᾐτήσατο εὑρεῖν σκήνωμα τῷ οἴκῳ Ἰακώβ.

ὅς. The antecedent is Δαυίδ.

εὗρεν. Aor act ind 3rd sg εὑρίσκω.

ᾐτήσατο. Aor mid ind 3rd sg αἰτέω. The middle denotes personal benefit to the one asking (cf. 9:2).

εὑρεῖν σκήνωμα τῷ οἴκῳ Ἰακώβ. According to most scholars (cf. Barrett, 372), this unusual expression (found in 𝔓[74] א* B D H) apparently led some scribes to change the text to εὑρεῖν σκήνωμα τῷ θεῷ Ἰακώβ (which is consistent with LXX Ps 131:5; see א[c] A C E Ψ 33 *Byz*). The resolution of this difficult textual problem affects how v. 47 is read as well (see below on αὐτῷ). On the whole, we prefer the UBS[4]/NA[27] text, which adopts the harder reading.

εὑρεῖν. Aor act inf εὑρίσκω (indirect discourse modifying ᾐτήσατο).

τῷ οἴκῳ Ἰακώβ. Dative of advantage. Lit. "for the house of Jacob."

7:47 Σολομῶν δὲ οἰκοδόμησεν αὐτῷ οἶκον.

οἰκοδόμησεν. Aor act ind 3rd sg οἰκοδομέω.

αὐτῷ. Dative of advantage. Here, the antecedent depends on which variant reading in v. 46 is followed: either "Solomon built a house for him (τῷ θεῷ)" or "Solomon built a house for it (τῷ οἴκῳ Ἰακώβ)." Superficially, τῷ οἴκῷ is an unlikely antecedent for αὐτῷ. In the LXX, and in the one example in the NT, a plural pronoun is consistently used when οἶκος Ἰσραήλ is the antecedent (see Heb 8:10; Judg 2:1; Ps 113:17; Isa 63:7; Ezek 3:4; 12:23; 36:17, 37; 37:11; 39:22; 43:7; 45:8; Hos 1:6). It is possible, however, that the expression σκήνωμα τῷ οἴκῳ Ἰακώβ would have itself been understood as a reference to the temple (cf. Barrett, 372). In that case, the question of the antecedent of αὐτῷ would become moot.

7:48 ἀλλ' οὐχ ὁ ὕψιστος ἐν χειροποιήτοις κατοικεῖ, καθὼς ὁ προφήτης λέγει,

ἀλλ'. The conjunction intensifies the negative statement.

οὐχ. The placement of the negativer here, rather than preceding the verb, focuses attention on ὁ ὕψιστος.

ὁ ὕψιστος. This expression was a common title for God in both Jewish and Greco-Roman literature (see Fitzmyer 1998, 384).

χειροποιήτοις. Substantival.

κατοικεῖ. Pres act ind 3rd sg κατοικέω.

λέγει. Pres act ind 3rd sg λέγω.

7:49 Ὁ οὐρανός μοι θρόνος, ἡ δὲ γῆ ὑποπόδιον τῶν ποδῶν μου· ποῖον οἶκον οἰκοδομήσετέ μοι, λέγει κύριος, ἢ τίς τόπος τῆς καταπαύσεώς μου;

μοι. Dative of advantage or possession.

θρόνος . . . ὑποπόδιον. Predicate nominatives (with ἐστιν implicit).

ποῖον . . . τίς . . . The two rhetorical questions imply that no "house" could be suitable for God.

οἶκον. Accusative object of οἰκοδομήσετε.

οἰκοδομήσετέ. Fut act ind 2nd pl οἰκοδομέω. The second accent comes from the enclitic μοι (see 1:4 on ἠκούσατέ).

μοι. Dative of advantage.

λέγει. Pres act ind 3rd sg λέγω.

τόπος. Predicate nominative (with ἐστιν or ἔσται implicit).

7:50 οὐχὶ ἡ χείρ μου ἐποίησεν ταῦτα πάντα;

οὐχι. A strengthened form of οὐ that, here, introduces a question expecting an emphatic positive answer: "Of course!" (Rogers and Rogers, 245).

ἡ χείρ μου. Synecdoche (see 1:22 on τοῦ βαπτίσματος Ἰωάννου) for "I."

ἐποίησεν. Aor act ind 3rd sg ποιέω.

ταῦτα πάντα. The antecedents are ὁ οὐρανός and ἡ γῆ of v. 49.

7:51 Σκληροτράχηλοι καὶ ἀπερίτμητοι καρδίαις καὶ τοῖς ὠσίν, ὑμεῖς ἀεὶ τῷ πνεύματι τῷ ἁγίῳ ἀντιπίπτετε ὡς οἱ πατέρες ὑμῶν καὶ ὑμεῖς.

Σκληροτράχηλοι καὶ ἀπερίτμητοι. The two highly inflamatory vocatives mark a sharp shift in Stephen's rhetorical approach.

Σκληροτράχηλοι. "Stubborn in the extreme, obstinant."

ἀπερίτμητοι καρδίαις καὶ τοῖς ὠσίν. The rhetorical significance of this label should not be overlooked. The Jews were "the circumcised." To be "uncircumcised in heart" is to be placed spiritually outside the ranks of God's people. To be "uncircumcised in the ears" is likely a reference to being "unwilling to listen to the truth" (Witherington 1998, 274, 266–67).

καρδίαις καὶ τοῖς ὠσίν. Dative of respect.

τῷ πνεύματι τῷ ἁγίῳ. Dative complement of ἀντιπίπτετε.

ὑμεῖς. The fronted (see 3:13 on ὑμεῖς) subject pronoun pointedly directs the accusation at Stephen's listeners.

ἀεὶ. Rhetorically effective hyperbole (cf. 1:18 on πάντα).

ἀντιπίπτετε. Pres act ind 2nd pl ἀντιπίπτω. The use of the adverb ἀεὶ requires the use of a present tense verb (Porter 1989, 187).

ὡς οἱ πατέρες ὑμῶν καὶ ὑμεῖς. The comparison clause is elliptical (lit. "as your fathers, so also you") with ἐποίησαν implied.

πατέρες ὑμῶν. The fact that Stephen is no longer referring to "*our* fathers" (πατέρες ἡμῶν) further strengthens the polemical tone.

7:52 **τίνα τῶν προφητῶν οὐκ ἐδίωξαν οἱ πατέρες ὑμῶν; καὶ ἀπέκτειναν τοὺς προκαταγγείλαντας περὶ τῆς ἐλεύσεως τοῦ δικαίου, οὗ νῦν ὑμεῖς προδόται καὶ φονεῖς ἐγένεσθε,**

τίνα. Accusative object of ἐδίωξαν.

τῶν προφητῶν. Partitive genitive.

οὐκ. The question here is both rhetorical and hyperbolic (cf. 1:18 on πάντα).

ἐδίωξαν. Aor act ind 3rd pl διώκω.

ἀπέκτειναν. Aor act ind 3rd pl ἀποκτείνω.

τοὺς προκαταγγείλαντας περὶ. Lit. "those who made announcements long ago concerning."

τοὺς προκαταγγείλαντας. Aor act ptc masc acc pl προκαταγγέλλω (substantival).

ἐλεύσεως. In other early Christian literature, ἔλευσις was used as a technical term for either Christ's first or second advent. Some scholars suggest that by the first century, Jews were using the term to refer to the advent of Messiah (see Bruce, 208).

ὑμεῖς. The explicit subject pronoun is emphatic.

προδόται καὶ φονεῖς. Predicate nominative.

ἐγένεσθε. Aor mid dep ind 2nd pl γίνομαι.

7:53 οἵτινες ἐλάβετε τὸν νόμον εἰς διαταγὰς ἀγγέλων καὶ οὐκ ἐφυλάξατε.

ἐλάβετε. Aor act ind 2nd pl λαμβάνω.

εἰς. This is probably another example where the preposition εἰς with an accusative noun functions like a predicate modifier (see 4:11 on εἰς κεφαλὴν γωνίας; so Dana and Mantey, 103). The emphasis is then on the fact that although they viewed the law in such exalted terms (lit. "as decrees of angels") they still failed to keep it. Or, it could be taken instrumentally.

ἀγγέλων. Subjective genitive (the angels gave the instructions; cf. Gal 3:19; Heb 2:2). Fitzmyer (1998, 386) takes the genitive ἀγγέλων to denote the recipient of the instructions (from God) and thus interprets the prepositional phrase, "by God's directing of angels to transmit it."

καὶ. Adversative.

ἐφυλάξατε. Aor act ind 2nd pl φυλάσσω.

Acts 7:54–8:1a

[54]When they heard these things, they were enraged and ground their teeth at him. [55]But since he was full of the Holy Spirit, he gazed into heaven and saw God's glory and Jesus standing at the right hand of God. [56]He exclaimed, "I see the heavens standing open, and the Son of Man standing at the right hand of God!" [57] Then they shouted with a loud voice, covered their ears, and together rushed at him." [58]When they had thrown him out of the city, they began to stone him. The witnesses placed their outer garments at the feet of a young man named Saul. [59]They continued stoning Stephen, who called upon (the Lord) and said, "Lord Jesus, receive my spirit." [60]As he fell to his knees, he cried out in a loud voice, "Lord, do not count this sin against them." When he had said this, he died. [8:1a]Now, Saul approved of his murder.

7:54 Ἀκούοντες δὲ ταῦτα διεπρίοντο ταῖς καρδίαις αὐτῶν καὶ ἔβρυχον τοὺς ὀδόντας ἐπ' αὐτόν.

Ἀκούοντες. Pres act ptc masc nom pl ἀκούω (temporal).

διεπρίοντο ταῖς καρδίαις. A vivid idiom denoting intense inner anger (lit. "they were sawn through in/to their hearts").

διεπρίοντο. Impf pass ind 3rd pl διαπρίω.

ἔβρυχον τοὺς ὀδόντας ἐπ' αὐτόν. Another idiom denoting intense anger (lit. "they ground their teeth at him"). In this case, there is an outward (apparent) demonstration of the anger toward the one causing the anger.

ἔβρυχον. Impf act ind 3rd pl βρύχω.

7:55 ὑπάρχων δὲ πλήρης πνεύματος ἁγίου ἀτενίσας εἰς τὸν οὐρανὸν εἶδεν δόξαν θεοῦ καὶ Ἰησοῦν ἑστῶτα ἐκ δεξιῶν τοῦ θεοῦ

ὑπάρχων. Pres act ptc masc nom sg ὑπάρχω (causal).

πνεύματος. See 2:4.

ἀτενίσας. Aor act ptc masc nom sg ἀτενίζω (attendant circumstance or temporal).

εἶδεν. Aor act ind 3rd sg ὁράω.

θεοῦ. Genitive of possession, or perhaps "attributed genitive" ("glorious God"; see Wallace 1996, 89).

Ἰησοῦν. Accusative object (conjoined with δόξαν θεοῦ) of εἶδεν.

ἑστῶτα. Prf act ptc masc acc sg ἵστημι. Although the participle could be taken as attributive, it is better to view it as the complement in an object-complement double accusative construction (see 1:3 on ζῶντα). The latter places the emphasis not on the person who is seen, but on what that person is doing (cf. 7:24 on ἀδικούμενον).

ἐκ δεξιῶν τοῦ θεοῦ. Locative expression refers to the preeminent position of power (see 2:25).

7:56 καὶ εἶπεν, Ἰδοὺ θεωρῶ τοὺς οὐρανοὺς διηνοιγμένους καὶ τὸν υἱὸν τοῦ ἀνθρώπου ἐκ δεξιῶν ἑστῶτα τοῦ θεοῦ.

εἶπεν. Aor act ind 3rd sg λέγω.

Ἰδοὺ. See 1:10.

θεωρῶ. Pres act ind 1st sg θεωρέω. "To observe something with continuity and attention, often with the implication that what is observed is something unusual" (LN 24.14).

διηνοιγμένους. Prf pass ptc masc acc pl διανοίγω. Stephen's statement contains two (conjoined) direct objects, each of which is modified by an accusative participle. διηνοιγμένους functions as the complement in an object-complement double accusative construction (see 1:3 on ζῶντα) describing τοὺς οὐρανοὺς, while ἑστῶτα functions as the complement in an object-complement double accusative construction describing τὸν υἱὸν τοῦ ἀνθρώπου.

τὸν υἱὸν τοῦ ἀνθρώπου. In the Gospels and in other early Jewish literature (cf. 1 Enoch 70–71; 4 Ezra 13; 4Q286) this expression is used as a messianic title (drawn from Dan 7:13–14). The present passage is the only example of the title in the NT outside of the Gospels.

ἐκ δεξιῶν ἑστῶτα τοῦ θεου. See v. 55.

ἑστῶτα. Prf act ptc masc acc sg ἵστημι (see v. 55).

7:57 κράξαντες δὲ φωνῇ μεγάλῃ συνέσχον τὰ ὦτα αὐτῶν καὶ ὥρμησαν ὁμοθυμαδὸν ἐπ' αὐτὸν

κράξαντες. Aor act ptc masc nom pl κράζω (attendant circumstance).

φωνῇ μεγάλῃ. In terms of syntax, dative of instrument. In terms of semantics, the manner in which they shouted.

μεγάλῃ. Used with sounds, the adjective denotes "loud."

συνέσχον τὰ ὦτα αὐτῶν. This (symbolic) reaction to what they perceived to be a blasphemous statement would protect their ears from further defilement.

συνέσχον. Aor act ind 3rd pl συνέχω.

ὥρμησαν. Aor act ind 3rd pl ὁρμάω.

ὁμοθυμαδὸν. See 1:14.

7:58 καὶ ἐκβαλόντες ἔξω τῆς πόλεως ἐλιθοβόλουν. καὶ οἱ μάρτυρες ἀπέθεντο τὰ ἱμάτια αὐτῶν παρὰ τοὺς πόδας νεανίου καλουμένου Σαύλου,

ἐκβαλόντες. Aor act ptc masc nom pl ἐκβάλλω (attendant circumstance or temporal).

ἐλιθοβόλουν. Impf act ind 3rd pl λιθοβολέω.

ἀπέθεντο. Aor mid ind 3rd pl ἀποτίθημι.

νεανίου. This term could refer to anyone from 24 to 40 years old (Fitzmyer 1998, 394).

καλουμένου. Pres pass ptc masc gen sg καλέω (attributive).

Σαύλου. The genitive noun serves as a complement in a passive object-complement double case construction (cf. 1:12 on' Ελαιῶνος).

7:59 καὶ ἐλιθοβόλουν τὸν Στέφανον ἐπικαλούμενον καὶ λέγοντα, Κύριε 'Ιησοῦ, δέξαι τὸ πνεῦμά μου.

ἐλιθοβόλουν. Impf act ind 3rd pl λιθοβολέω.

ἐπικαλούμενον. Pres mid ptc masc acc sg ἐπικαλέω (attributive). The object of the verb, "the Lord," is left implicit. Most scholars treat ἐπικαλούμενον as a temporal participle (cf. Rogers and Rogers, 245). Since the subject of the participle is different from the subject of the main verb, however, one would expect a genitive absolute construction (see 1:8 on ἐπελθόντος), if the participle were being used adverbially (see Culy 2004). (The label "accusative absolute" does not fit here either since the participle modifies the direct object of the main verb and its usage is thus not "absolute.") On occasion, anarthrous (see 3:3 on Πέτρον καὶ Ἰωαννην) attributive participles may modify an articular noun as here.

λέγοντα. Pres act ptc masc acc sg λέγω (attributive; see above).

Κύριε Ἰησοῦ. Vocative.

δέξαι. Aor mid dep impv 2nd sg δέχομαι.

7:60 θεὶς δὲ τὰ γόνατα ἔκραξεν φωνῇ μεγάλῃ, Κύριε, μὴ στήσῃς αὐτοῖς ταύτην τὴν ἁμαρτίαν. καὶ τοῦτο εἰπὼν ἐκοιμήθη.

θεὶς τὰ γόνατα. Lit. "having placed the knees" = "having knelt" or "having fallen to his knees."

θεὶς. Aor act ptc masc nom sg τίθημι (temporal or attendant circumstance).

ἔκραξεν. Aor act ind 3rd sg κράζω.

φωνῇ μεγάλῃ. See v. 57.

Κύριε. Vocative.

μὴ στήσῃς. Aor act subj 2nd sg ἵστημι (prohibitive subjunctive). Second person negative commands always use the subjunctive rather than the imperative in the NT (cf. 9:38; 18:9). On the choice of tense in a negative command, see 20:10 on Μὴ θορυβεῖσθε.

αὐτοῖς. Dative of disadvantage.

τοῦτο. Used with a conceptual antecedent here (see Wallace 1996, 333–35).

εἰπὼν. Aor act ptc masc nom sg λέγω (temporal).

ἐκοιμήθη. Aor pass dep ind 3rd sg κοιμάομαι. Here, a euphemism for death (lit. "he fell asleep").

8:1a Σαῦλος δὲ ἦν συνευδοκῶν τῇ ἀναιρέσει αὐτοῦ.

Σαῦλος. The fronted (see 3:13 on ὑμεῖς) subject shifts the focus (see 2:15 on ὑμεῖς) to Saul.

ἦν. Impf ind 3rd sg εἰμί.

συνευδοκῶν. Pres act ptc masc nom sg συνευδοκέω (imperfect periphrastic; see 1:10 on ἀτενίζοντες). According to Porter (1989, 46), "the periphrastic construction pushes the narrative forward, foreshadowing the importance of this new figure." The verb συνευδοκέω means "to decide with someone else that something is preferable or good" (LN 31.17).

τῇ ἀναιρέσει. Dative complement of συνευδοκῶν (Rogers and Rogers, 245).

Acts 8:1b–3

[1b]On that day, a severe persecution broke out against the Jerusalem church, and all except the apostles were scattered throughout the regions of Judea and Samaria. [2](Some) Devout men buried Stephen and mourned loudly for him. [3]But Saul was devastating the church; he was going from house to house, dragging off both men and women, and delivering them to prison.

8:1b Ἐγένετο δὲ ἐν ἐκείνῃ τῇ ἡμέρᾳ διωγμὸς μέγας ἐπὶ τὴν ἐκκλησίαν τὴν ἐν Ἱεροσολύμοις, πάντες δὲ διεσπάρησαν κατὰ τὰς χώρας τῆς Ἰουδαίας καὶ Σαμαρείας πλὴν τῶν ἀποστόλων.

Ἐγένετο. Aor mid dep ind 3rd sg γίνομαι.

διωγμὸς. Nominative subject of Ἐγένετο.

ἐπὶ τὴν ἐκκλησίαν. The preposition with the accusative noun indicates opposition.

τὴν ἐν Ἱεροσολύμοις. The article functions as an adjectivizer (see 2:5 on τῶν ὑπὸ τὸν οὐρανόν), changing the prepositional phrase into an attributive modifier.

πάντες δὲ. In light of passages such as 9:26; 11:22; and 15:4, πάντες is clearly hyperbolic. The conjunction, in this case, introduces a clause that supplies the result of the previous proposition.

διεσπάρησαν. Aor pass ind 3rd pl διασπείρω.

κατὰ. Distributive.

πλὴν τῶν ἀποστόλων. This prepositional phrase modifies πάντες.

8:2 συνεκόμισαν δὲ τὸν Στέφανον ἄνδρες εὐλαβεῖς καὶ ἐποίησαν κοπετὸν μέγαν ἐπ' αὐτῷ.

συνεκόμισαν. Aor act ind 3rd pl συγκομίζω. Lit. "to bring together, collect (a harvest)." This term occurs only here in the NT and is used as a euphemism meaning "to carry out arrangements for burial" (LN 52.5).

εὐλαβεῖς. "Pertaining to being reverent toward God" (LN 53.8).

ἐποίησαν κοπετὸν μέγαν ἐπ' αὐτῷ. Lit. "they made loud lamentation upon/over him."

ἐποίησαν. Aor act ind 3rd pl ποιέω.

μέγαν. See v. 57.

ἐπ' αὐτῷ. Although the prepositional phrase could be viewed as causal, "because of him," it is probable that the entire expression, "to make lamentation upon/over someone," is idiomatic.

8:3 Σαῦλος δὲ ἐλυμαίνετο τὴν ἐκκλησίαν κατὰ τοὺς οἴκους εἰσπορευόμενος, σύρων τε ἄνδρας καὶ γυναῖκας παρεδίδου εἰς φυλακήν.

ἐλυμαίνετο. Impf mid ind 3rd sg λυμαίνομαι. Lit. "he was destroying." The expression may be hyperbolic and mean "he was causing great harm to" (cf. LN 20.24), or the sense could be: "he was trying to destroy." It is unclear how the participles that follow relate to the rest of the verse. Since the final verb παρεδίδου is not linked to the rest of the sentence with a conjunction, it must be modified by at least the second participle (σύρων). The main question, then, is whether εἰσπορευόμενος modifies παρεδίδου or ἐλυμαίνετο. On the whole, it seems best to take it with παρεδίδου and understand κατὰ τοὺς οἴκους εἰσπορευόμενος, σύρων τε ἄνδρας καὶ γυναῖκας παρεδίδου εἰς φυλακήν as epexegetical, explaining how Saul was trying to destroy the church.

κατὰ. Distributive.

εἰσπορευόμενος. Pres dep ptc masc nom sg εἰσπορεύομαι. The participle probably introduces an attendant circumstance of παρεδίδου, though it may supply the means of ἐλυμαίνετο (see above).

σύρων. Pres act ptc masc nom sg σύρω (attendant circumstance of παρεδίδου).

παρεδίδου. Impf act ind 3rd sg παραδίδωμι.

Acts 8:4–8

[4]Those who had been scattered traveled around preaching the word. [5]After going down to a city in Samaria, Philip preached to them about

the Christ. [6]When they heard and saw the signs that he was doing, the crowds, without exception, paid close attention to the things that Philip was saying. [7](In the case of) Many of those who had them, unclean spirits were screaming in a loud voice and coming out; and many who had been paralyzed or lame were healed. [8]So there was great joy in that city.

8:4 Οἱ μὲν οὖν διασπαρέντες διῆλθον εὐαγγελιζόμενοι τὸν λόγον.

Οἱ. The article modifies the participle (cf. 1:6) as a nominalizer (see 1:3 on τὰ).

μὲν οὖν. The use of μὲν οὖν (see 1:6) "implies that the information of v. 4 forms the background to that described in v. 5" (Levinsohn 1992, 167). The story that follows develops specifically from the events of v. 5 rather than v. 4.

Οἱ διασπαρέντες. Aor pass ptc masc nom pl διασπείρω (substantival).

διῆλθον. Aor act ind 3rd pl διέρχομαι.

εὐαγγελιζόμενοι. Pres mid ptc masc nom pl εὐαγγελίζω (manner).

8:5 Φίλιππος δὲ κατελθὼν εἰς [τὴν] πόλιν τῆς Σαμαρείας ἐκήρυσσεν αὐτοῖς τὸν Χριστόν.

Φίλιππος. Philip should be identified with the deacon (6:5) and evangelist (21:8) of the same name rather than the apostle Philip, since the apostles remained in Jerusalem (8:1b).

κατελθὼν. Aor act ptc masc nom sg κατέρχομαι (temporal).

[τὴν]. The textual tradition leaves it uncertain whether the reference is to an unspecified city in Samaria (C D E Ψ 33 *Byz al*) or a known [τὴν] city of Samaria (𝔓[74] ℵ A B *pc*).

Σαμαρείας. Depending on how the textual problem is resolved, this noun could function either as a genitive of location ("a city *which is in* Samaria"; cf. John 4:5; Luke 1:26; 4:31) or a genitive of identification ("the city *which is known as* Samaria" = genitive of apposition; see Wallace 1996, 95–100).

ἐκήρυσσεν. Impf act ind 3rd sg κηρύσσω. The imperfect form should not be mistaken for the third singular aorist active indicative: ἐκήρυξεν.

8:6 προσεῖχον δὲ οἱ ὄχλοι τοῖς λεγομένοις ὑπὸ τοῦ Φιλίππου ὁμοθυμαδὸν ἐν τῷ ἀκούειν αὐτοὺς καὶ βλέπειν τὰ σημεῖα ἃ ἐποίει.

προσεῖχον. Impf act ind 3rd pl προσέχω.

τοῖς λεγομένοις. Pres pass ptc neut dat pl λέγω (substantival). Dative complement of προσεῖχον.

ὑπὸ. Introduces the agent of the passive participle.

ὁμοθυμαδὸν. Here, the term appears to indicate unanimity (thus, "without exception").

ἀκούειν. Pres act inf ἀκούω. Used with ἐν τῷ to denote contemporaneous time (cf. 2:1 on συμπληροῦσθαι).

αὐτοὺς. Accusative subject of the infinitives (see 1:3 on αὐτὸν). Verse 7 suggests that the object of this infinitive is also τὰ σημεῖα rather than an implicit "him."

βλέπειν. Pres act inf βλέπω. Used with ἐν τῷ to denote contemporaneous time (cf. 2:1 on συμπληροῦσθαι).

ἐποίει. Impf act ind 3rd sg ποιέω.

8:7 πολλοὶ γὰρ τῶν ἐχόντων πνεύματα ἀκάθαρτα βοῶντα φωνῇ μεγάλῃ ἐξήρχοντο, πολλοὶ δὲ παραλελυμένοι καὶ χωλοὶ ἐθεραπεύθησαν·

The syntax of the first half this verse (the UBS[4]/NA[27] text is supported by 𝔓[74] ℵ A B C D E 33 *al*) is extremely difficult. The textual tradition contains a number of attempts to mend the sentence. It appears, at first glance, that the subject of the only finite verb (ἐξήρχοντο) is πολλοὶ: "Many of those who had unclean spirits which cried out with a loud voice were coming out (of the city)." One expects, however, the verb ἐξήρχοντο to refer to the exorcism of unclean spirits, particularly when used with βοῶντα φωνῇ μεγάλῃ. One possible way to resolve the syntax is to read πολλοὶ τῶν ἐχόντων as a *nominativus pendens* (see 7:40 on ὁ Μωϋσῆς οὗτος), with the direct object of the participle remaining implicit. We could then take πνεύματα ἀκάθαρτα as a neuter *nominative* subject of the sentence, modified by a neuter nominative participle βοῶντα: "(In the case of) Many of those who had (them), unclean spirits were shouting in a loud voice and coming out."

πολλοὶ. Substantival.

τῶν ἐχόντων. Pres act ptc masc pl ἔχω (substantival). Partitive genitive.

πνεύματα. Nominative subject of ἐξήρχοντο (see above), or accusative direct object of ἐχόντων.

βοῶντα. Pres act ptc neut nom/acc pl βοάω (attendant circumstance or attributive).

φωνῇ μεγάλῃ. See 7:57.

ἐξήρχοντο. Impf dep ind 3rd pl ἔρχομαι.

πολλοὶ. Attributive.

παραλελυμένοι. Prf pass ptc masc nom pl παραλύω. The participle should be viewed as substantival since it is linked (καὶ) to what must be a substantival adjective χωλοὶ.

ἐθεραπεύθησαν. Aor pass ind 3rd pl θεραπεύω.

8:8 ἐγένετο δὲ πολλὴ χαρὰ ἐν τῇ πόλει ἐκείνῃ.

ἐγένετο. Aor mid dep ind 3rd sg γίνομαι.

χαρὰ. Predicate nominative with impersonal ἐγένετο.

Acts 8:9–13

9Now, a certain man named Simon had lived in the city for some time, practicing magic and amazing the nation of Samaria, and claiming to be someone great. 10Everyone, from the least to the greatest, was paying attention to him and saying, "This (man) is the power of God which is called "Great." 11They paid close attention to him because he had amazed them with his magic for a long time. 12But when they believed Philip, who was preaching about the kingdom of God and the name of Jesus Christ, both men and women were baptized. 13Even Simon himself believed, and after being baptized he stayed close to Philip. As he observed the signs and great miracles that were occurring, he was amazed.

8:9 Ἀνὴρ δέ τις ὀνόματι Σίμων προϋπῆρχεν ἐν τῇ πόλει μαγεύων καὶ ἐξιστάνων τὸ ἔθνος τῆς Σαμαρείας, λέγων εἶναί τινα ἑαυτὸν μέγαν,

τις. The pronoun may be used like an indefinite article here (cf. Porter 1994, 103, n. 2; see also 9:10).

ὀνόματι. Dative of reference.

Σίμων. Nominative in apposition to Ἀνὴρ ("a man, Simon by name").

προϋπῆρχεν. Impf act ind 3rd sg προϋπάρχω. On the diaeresis over the *upsilon*, see 2:31 on προϊδὼν.

μαγεύων. Pres act ptc masc nom sg μαγεύω. The participle may introduce an attendant circumstance, but the only other use of προϋπάρχω in the NT (Luke 23:12) suggests that it may be used with a participle in a periphrastic construction: "Now a man named Simon had been practicing sorcery and amazing the people of Samaria." Both Robertson (1934, 1121) and BDF (§414) argue that the participle is periphrastic in Luke 23:12, but circumstantial here.

ἐξιστάνων. Pres act ptc masc nom sg ἐξίστημι (see μαγεύων above).

λέγων. Pres act ptc masc nom sg λέγω (attendant circumstance).

εἶναί. Pres act inf εἰμί (indirect discourse). The second accent comes from the enclitic τινα (see 1:4 on ἠκούσατέ).

τινα . . . μέγαν. The two adjectives could be construed as (1) predicate substantival appositional adjectives, or (2) an adjective (τινα) modifying a substantival predicate adjective (μέγαν). The fact that they are not contiguous supports the former option. The unusual word order (cf. Codex D's reading of 5:36) may highlight the presumptuous nature of Simon's claim.

ἑαυτὸν. Accusative subject of the infinitive (see 1:3 on αὑτὸν).

8:10 ᾧ προσεῖχον πάντες ἀπὸ μικροῦ ἕως μεγάλου λέγοντες, Οὗτός ἐστιν ἡ δύναμις τοῦ θεοῦ ἡ καλουμένη Μεγάλη.

ᾧ. Dative complement of προσεῖχον.

προσεῖχον. Impf act ind 3rd pl προσέχω.

πάντες. Substantival; hyperbole (cf. 1:18 on πάντα).

ἀπὸ μικροῦ ἕως μεγάλου. This expression (lit. "from small to great") intensifies the hyperbolic πάντες.

λέγοντες. Pres act ptc masc nom pl λέγω (attendant circumstance).

Οὗτός. Nominative substantival subject of ἐστιν. The second accent comes from the enclitic ἐστιν (see 1:4 on ἠκούσατέ).

ἐστιν. Pres act ind 3rd sg εἰμί.

ἡ δύναμις. Predicate nominative.

τοῦ θεοῦ. Probably genitive of source.

καλουμένη. Pres pass ptc fem nom sg καλέω (attributive).

Μεγάλη. Complement in a subject-complement double nominative construction with the passive καλουμένη (cf. 4:36 on υἱὸς and 1:12 on Ἐλαιῶνος).

8:11 προσεῖχον δὲ αὐτῷ διὰ τὸ ἱκανῷ χρόνῳ ταῖς μαγείαις ἐξεστακέναι αὐτούς.

προσεῖχον. Impf act ind 3rd pl προσέχω.

αὐτῷ. Dative complement of προσεῖχον.

διὰ τὸ. See below on ἐξεστακέναι.

χρόνῳ. Dative of time (the adjective ἱκανῷ makes it clear that duration of time is in view).

ταῖς μαγείαις. Dative of instrument.

ἐξεστακέναι. Prf act inf ἐξίστημι. Used with διὰ τὸ to indicate cause.

αὐτούς. Accusative direct object of ἐξεστακέναι.

8:12 ὅτε δὲ ἐπίστευσαν τῷ Φιλίππῳ εὐαγγελιζομένῳ περὶ τῆς βασιλείας τοῦ θεοῦ καὶ τοῦ ὀνόματος Ἰησοῦ Χριστοῦ, ἐβαπτίζοντο ἄνδρες τε καὶ γυναῖκες.

ἐπίστευσαν. Aor act ind 3rd pl πιστεύω.

τῷ Φιλίππῳ. Dative complement of ἐπίστευσαν.

εὐαγγελιζομένῳ. Pres mid ptc masc dat sg εὐαγγελίζω (attributive).

τῆς βασιλείας τοῦ θεοῦ. See 1:3 on τῆς βασιλείας τοῦ θεοῦ.

ἐβαπτίζοντο. Impf pass ind 3rd pl βαπτίζω.

8:13 ὁ δὲ Σίμων καὶ αὐτὸς ἐπίστευσεν καὶ βαπτισθεὶς ἦν προσκαρτερῶν τῷ Φιλίππῳ, θεωρῶν τε σημεῖα καὶ δυνάμεις μεγάλας γινομένας ἐξίστατο.

αὐτὸς. Intensive.

ἐπίστευσεν. Aor act ind 3rd sg πιστεύω.

βαπτισθεὶς. Aor pass ptc masc nom sg βαπτίζω. Although Porter (1994, 49) lists this verse as one of three possible examples of a periphrastic construction with an aorist participle, it is probably better to take βαπτισθεὶς as a temporal participle that modifies the periphrastic construction that follows.

ἦν. Impf ind 3rd sg εἰμί.

προσκαρτερῶν. Pres act ptc masc nom sg προσκαρτερέω (imperfect periphrastic; see 1:10 on ἀτενίζοντες).

τῷ Φιλίππῳ. Dative complement of προσκαρτερῶν.

θεωρῶν. Pres act ptc masc nom sg θεωρέω (temporal).
γινομένας. Pres dep ptc fem acc pl γίνομαι (attributive).
ἐξίστατο. Impf mid ind 3rd sg ἐξίστημι.

Acts 8:14–25

14When the apostles in Jerusalem heard that the people of Samaria
had received the message of God, they sent them Peter and John, 15who
went down and prayed for them that they might receive the Holy Spirit.
16For (the Holy Spirit) had not yet fallen on any of them. They had only
been baptized in the name of the Lord Jesus. 17Then they laid (their)
hands on them and they received the Holy Spirit.

18When Simon saw that the Spirit was given through the laying on of
the apostles' hands, he offered them money 19and said, "Give me this
power also so that whomever I lay (my) hands on will receive the Holy
Spirit." 20But Peter said to him, "May your silver be destroyed with
you, because you thought you could obtain God's gift with money!
21You have absolutely no part or share in this matter, for your heart is
not right before God! 22Therefore, repent of this wickedness of yours,
and pray to the Lord that he might perhaps forgive the intention of your
heart. 23For I can see that you are full of bitterness and bound by (your)
evil ways." 24Simon answered and said, "You must pray to the Lord on
my behalf so that none of what you have said will come upon me!"

25So then, (Peter and John) who had testified and spoken the message of the Lord, returned to Jerusalem, preaching the gospel in many Samaritan villages (as they went).

8:14 Ἀκούσαντες δὲ οἱ ἐν Ἱεροσολύμοις ἀπόστολοι ὅτι δέδεκται ἡ Σαμάρεια τὸν λόγον τοῦ θεοῦ, ἀπέστειλαν πρὸς αὐτοὺς Πέτρον καὶ Ἰωάννην,

Ἀκούσαντες. Aor act ptc masc nom pl ἀκούω (temporal).
ὅτι. Introduces indirect discourse.
δέδεκται. Prf dep ind 3rd sg δέχομαι. The perfect is retained in indirect discourse.
ἡ Σαμάρεια. Metonymy (see 1:9 on τῶν ὀφθαλμῶν αὐτῶν) for "the people of Samaria."
ἀπέστειλαν. Aor act ind 3rd pl ἀποστέλλω.

8:15 οἵτινες καταβάντες προσηύξαντο περὶ αὐτῶν ὅπως λάβωσιν πνεῦμα ἅγιον·

καταβάντες. Aor act ptc masc nom pl καταβαίνω (attendant circumstance or temporal).

προσηύξαντο. Aor mid dep ind 3rd pl προσεύχομαι.

λάβωσιν. Aor act subj 3rd pl λαμβάνω. The subjunctive is used with ὅπως to introduce a purpose clause.

8:16 οὐδέπω γὰρ ἦν ἐπ' οὐδενὶ αὐτῶν ἐπιπεπτωκός, μόνον δὲ βεβαπτισμένοι ὑπῆρχον εἰς τὸ ὄνομα τοῦ κυρίου Ἰησοῦ.

ἦν. Impf ind 3rd sg εἰμί.

ἐπ'. See 1:8 on ἐφ' ὑμᾶς.

ἐπιπεπτωκός. Prf act ptc neut nom sg ἐπιπίπτω (pluperfect periphrastic; see 1:17 on κατηριθμημένος).

βεβαπτισμένοι. Prf pass ptc masc nom pl βαπτίζω (used with ὑπῆρχον to form a pluperfect periphrastic construction; see 1:17 on κατηριθμημένος).

ὑπῆρχον. Impf act ind 3rd pl ὑπάρχω.

8:17 τότε ἐπετίθεσαν τὰς χεῖρας ἐπ' αὐτοὺς καὶ ἐλάμβανον πνεῦμα ἅγιον.

ἐπετίθεσαν. Impf act ind 3rd pl ἐπιτίθημι. Although the imperfect tense may indicate that the apostles moved from person to person, it is probably better to explain the shift from aorist (vv. 14–15) to imperfect as indicative of a shift from background to foreground material.

ἐλάμβανον. Impf act ind 3rd pl λαμβάνω. On the use of the imperfect see above. The aorist form would be ἔλαβον.

8:18 ἰδὼν δὲ ὁ Σίμων ὅτι διὰ τῆς ἐπιθέσεως τῶν χειρῶν τῶν ἀποστόλων δίδοται τὸ πνεῦμα, προσήνεγκεν αὐτοῖς χρήματα

ἰδὼν. Aor act ptc masc nom sg ὁράω (temporal).

ὅτι. Introduces the clausal complement of ἰδών.

διὰ. Means.

τῶν χειρῶν. Objective genitive.

δίδοται. Pres pass ind 3rd sg δίδωμι.

τὸ πνεῦμα. Nominative subject of the passive verb.
προσήνεγκεν. Aor act ind 3rd sg προσφέρω.

8:19 λέγων, Δότε κἀμοὶ τὴν ἐξουσίαν ταύτην ἵνα ᾧ ἐὰν ἐπιθῶ τὰς χεῖρας λαμβάνῃ πνεῦμα ἅγιον.

λέγων. Pres act ptc masc nom sg λέγω (attendant circumstance).
Δότε. Aor act impv 2nd pl δίδωμι (request).
κἀμοὶ. A shortened form (crasis) of καὶ ἐμοί.
ᾧ. The relative pronoun introduces a headless relative clause (see 3:6 on ὃ): lit. "on *the one* whom I place . . ."
ἐὰν. Used with a subjunctive verb to form the protasis of a third class condition.
ἐπιθῶ. Aor act subj 1st sg ἐπιτίθημι.
λαμβάνῃ. Pres act subj 3rd sg λαμβάνω.
πνεῦμα ἅγιον. Accusative direct object of λαμβάνῃ.

8:20 Πέτρος δὲ εἶπεν πρὸς αὐτόν, Τὸ ἀργύριόν σου σὺν σοὶ εἴη εἰς ἀπώλειαν ὅτι τὴν δωρεὰν τοῦ θεοῦ ἐνόμισας διὰ χρημάτων κτᾶσθαι·

εἶπεν. Aor act ind 3rd sg λέγω.
Τὸ ἀργύριόν. Nominative subject of εἴη. The second accent comes from the enclitic σου (see 1:4 on ἠκούσατέ).
εἴη. Pres act opt 3rd sg εἰμί. The optative is used to express a wish, or in this case, a "curse" (see also 5:24 on τί ἂν γένοιτο τοῦτο; cf. the use of the aorist optative in Mark 11:14 and Jude 9).
εἰς ἀπώλειαν. This phrase (lit. "to destruction") is used with the verb εἰμί to form a periphrastic expression meaning, "to be destroyed" (cf. LXX Dan 2:5). Syntactically, εἰς ἀπώλειαν should probably be viewed as a substitute for a predicate nominative (see 4:11 on εἰς κεφαλὴν γωνίας).
ὅτι. Causal.
τὴν δωρεὰν. The accusative direct object of the infinitive (with its genitive modifier τοῦ θεοῦ) is fronted (see 3:13 on ὑμεῖς) in order to place it in focus (see 2:15 on ὑμεῖς).
τοῦ θεοῦ. Subjective genitive.
ἐνόμισας. Aor act ind 2nd sg νομίζω.
διὰ. Means.

κτᾶσθαι. Pres dep inf κτάομαι (indirect discourse with a verb of cognition).

8:21 οὐκ ἔστιν σοι μερὶς οὐδὲ κλῆρος ἐν τῷ λόγῳ τούτῳ, ἡ γὰρ καρδία σου οὐκ ἔστιν εὐθεῖα ἔναντι τοῦ θεοῦ.

ἔστιν. Pres act ind 3rd sg εἰμί. On the accent, see 4:12.

σοι. Dative of possession (with εἰμί).

μερὶς οὐδὲ κλῆρος. Lit. "portion nor share." The conjoined nominative nouns (which function as the syntactic subject of ἔστιν and the semantic patient (= object) of the idiom: "You do not have μερὶς οὐδὲ κλῆρος") should probably be viewed as a doublet (see 2:43 on τέρατα καὶ σημεῖα) used for emphasis: "You have absolutely no share . . ."

κλῆρος. Nominative subject of ἔστιν.

τῷ λόγῳ. Here, the term λόγος refers to "the topic of discussion" (cf. LN 13.115).

ἔστιν. Pres act ind 3rd sg εἰμί.

εὐθεῖα. Predicate adjective.

8:22 μετανόησον οὖν ἀπὸ τῆς κακίας σου ταύτης καὶ δεήθητι τοῦ κυρίου εἰ ἄρα ἀφεθήσεταί σοι ἡ ἐπίνοια τῆς καρδίας σου,

μετανόησον. Aor act impv 2nd sg μετανοέω.

ἀπὸ. Separation.

δεήθητι. Aor pass dep impv 2nd sg δέομαι.

τοῦ κυρίου. Genitive object of δεήθητι.

εἰ. Strictly speaking, εἰ introduces an elliptical first class condition. Functionally, it introduces the complement of δεήθητι (cf. Robertson 1934, 430). In contrast to complements introduced by ὅτι ("that"), a complement introduced by εἰ may carry a connotation of uncertainty: "that perhaps" (cf. 1024).

ἄρα. Used with εἰ to intensify the sense of uncertainty. Such an emphasis in the present context has the rhetorical effect of further stressing the heinous nature of Simon's actions.

ἀφεθήσεταί . . . σου. Lit. "that the intention of your heart will be forgiven to you."

ἀφεθήσεταί. Fut pass ind 3rd sg ἀφίημι. The second accent comes from the enclitic σοι (see 1:4 on ἠκούσατέ).

ἡ ἐπίνοια. Nominative subject of the passive verb.

8:23 εἰς γὰρ χολὴν πικρίας καὶ σύνδεσμον ἀδικίας ὁρῶ σε ὄντα.

εἰς χολὴν πικρίας καὶ σύνδεσμον ἀδικίας. The prepositional phrase functions as a predicate of ὄντα (see 4:11 on εἰς κεφαλὴν γωνίας). Louw and Nida (88.166) suggest that this idiom (εἰς χολὴν πικρίας εἰμί, lit. "to be in the gall of bitterness") means "to be particularly envious or resentful of someone."

πικρίας. Attributive genitive.

εἰς . . . σύνδεσμον ἀδικίας. Lit. "in a bond of wrongdoing."

ὁρῶ. Pres act ind 1st sg ὁράω.

σε. Accusative direct object of ὁρῶ.

ὄντα. Pres act ptc masc acc sg εἰμί. The participle functions as the complement in an object-complement double accusative construction (see 1:3 on ζῶντα).

8:24 ἀποκριθεὶς δὲ ὁ Σίμων εἶπεν, Δεήθητε ὑμεῖς ὑπὲρ ἐμοῦ πρὸς τὸν κύριον ὅπως μηδὲν ἐπέλθῃ ἐπ' ἐμὲ ὧν εἰρήκατε.

ἀποκριθεὶς. Aor pass dep ptc masc nom sg ἀποκρίνομαι (attendant circumstance).

εἶπεν. Aor act ind 3rd sg λέγω.

Δεήθητε. Aor pass dep impv 2nd pl δέομαι (request).

ὑμεῖς. The explicit subject pronoun with the imperative verb emphasizes Simon's sense of desperation.

μηδὲν. The substantival adjective is fronted (see 3:13 on ὑμεῖς) to intensify or emphasize the idea. The whole expression μηδὲν . . . ὧν εἰρήκατε serves as the subject of ἐπέλθῃ.

ἐπέλθῃ. Aor act subj 3rd sg ἐπέρχομαι. The subjunctive is used with ὅπως to introduce the purpose behind Simon's plea to the apostles to pray for him.

ἐπ'. See 1:8 on ἐφ' ὑμᾶς.

ὧν. Although it would be possible to argue that the relative pronoun introduces a headless relative clause (see 3:6 on ὅ) and the case stems from attraction to an unexpressed antecedent (τουτῶν—partitive genitive; for how this can take place, see 22:15 on ὧν), it is far less cumbersome to treat the case as a genitive of reference.

εἰρήκατε. Prf act ind 2nd pl λέγω.

8:25 Οἱ μὲν οὖν διαμαρτυράμενοι καὶ λαλήσαντες τὸν λόγον τοῦ κυρίου ὑπέστρεφον εἰς Ἱεροσόλυμα, πολλάς τε κώμας τῶν Σαμαριτῶν εὐηγγελίζοντο.

Οἱ. The article modifies the participles διαμαρτυράμενοι καὶ λαλήσαντες (cf. 1:6) as a nominalizer (see 1:3 on τὰ).

μὲν οὖν. This verse should not be taken simply as a conclusion to the preceding narrative, but rather as a transition (introduced by μὲν οὖν) that removes Peter and John from the scene and unites the two incidents involving Philip (Levinsohn 1992, 192; 1987, 146; see also 1:6).

Οἱ διαμαρτυράμενοι. Aor mid dep ptc masc nom pl διαμαρτύρομαι (substantival). The referents of the two participles are Peter and John (v. 14).

λαλήσαντες. Aor act ptc masc nom pl λαλέω (substantival).

ὑπέστρεφον. Impf act ind 3rd pl ὑποστρέφω.

πολλάς κώμας. This noun phrase could be taken as an accusative of location (see 1:19 on Ἰερουσαλήμ), accusative of extent of space, or an accusative addressee (by metonymy: "people in many villages"; see 1:9 on τῶν ὀφθαλμῶν αὐτῶν) of εὐηγγελίζοντο. A good example of the latter is found in 13:32 where the addressee of εὐαγγελίζω is the accusative ὑμᾶς. Many linguists would argue that in such cases the indirect object has "advanced" to the direct object position and thus bears the accusative case. Such advancements are common in English (cf. "I gave the ball to the boy" with "I gave the boy the ball") and serve to draw more attention to the indirect object. (Note: In passive constructions, the direct object "advances" to the subject position.)

εὐηγγελίζοντο. Impf mid ind 3rd pl εὐαγγελίζω.

Acts 8:26–40

[26]Then an angel of the Lord spoke to Philip and said, "Go south at once, on the road that goes down from Jerusalem to Gaza"—this is a desert (road). [27]So he immediately set out. (Meanwhile,) An Ethiopian man, a eunuch and minister of Candace, queen of the Ethiopians, who was in charge of all her treasury and had come to Jerusalem to worship, [28]was returning (home), sitting in his chariot, and reading the prophet Isaiah.

[29]The Spirit said to Philip, "Go over and join (the man in) this chariot." [30]So Philip ran up to it and heard him reading Isaiah the prophet. He

asked him, "Do you really understand what you are reading?" [31]He replied, "How can I possibly (understand), unless someone guides me?" So he invited Philip to come up and sit with him.

[32]Now the passage of Scripture that he was reading was this: "Like a sheep led to the slaughter, and like a lamb before its shearer is silent, so he does not open his mouth. [33]In [his] humiliation, justice was withheld from him. Who can list his descendants? For his life was taken up from the earth."

[34]Then the eunuch said to Philip, "Please tell me, about whom does the prophet say this, about himself or about someone else?" [35]So Philip began to speak, and starting with this (passage of) Scripture, he preached the good news about Jesus to him.

[36]As they were going along the road, they came upon some water, and the eunuch said, "Look, water! What is preventing me from being baptized?" [38]He commanded the chariot to stop, and they went down together into the water, both Philip and the eunuch, and he baptized him. [39]When they came up out of the water, the Spirit of the Lord snatched Philip away. The eunuch did not see him anymore, since he went on his way rejoicing [40]but Philip ended up at Azotus. As he traveled through (that region) he preached the good news to all the cities until he came to Caesarea.

8:26 Ἄγγελος δὲ κυρίου ἐλάλησεν πρὸς Φίλιππον λέγων, Ἀνάστηθι καὶ πορεύου κατὰ μεσημβρίαν ἐπὶ τὴν ὁδὸν τὴν καταβαίνουσαν ἀπὸ Ἰερουσαλὴμ εἰς Γάζαν, αὕτη ἐστὶν ἔρημος.

Ἄγγελος . . . κυρίου. See 5:19.

δὲ. The conjunction shifts the focus from Peter and John to Philip (see Levinsohn 1987, 26).

ἐλάλησεν. Aor act ind 3rd sg λαλέω.

λέγων. Pres act ptc masc nom sg λέγω (attendant circumstance, redundant; see 1:6 on λέγοντες).

Ἀνάστηθι πορεύου. The use of these two verbs together probably reflects a common Semitic construction. The Hebrew verb קוּם (lit. "arise"; Greek, ἀνάστηθι) was sometimes used as a helping verb. In the phrase קוּם לֵךְ (lit. "arise, go!") in Jonah 1:2, for example, קוּם appears to carry functional rather than semantic value, adding a connotation of urgency to the second verb (cf. Andersen, 57). The sense then is "Go at once!" or simply "Go!"

'Ανάστηθι. Aor act impv 2nd sg ἀνίστημι.

πορεύου. Pres dep impv 2nd sg πορεύομαι.

κατὰ μεσημβρίαν. This expression could refer to either time ("at noon") or direction ("toward the south"). In favor of the former is the resulting temporal ("at noon") and directional ("on the road that goes down from Jerusalem to Gaza") adverbial expressions, rather than two directional expressions. In favor of the latter, however, is (1) in the only other occurrence of μεσημβρία in the NT, where the usage is clearly temporal, περί is used rather than κατά; (2) Luke uses κατά elsewhere with a directional term (also occurs in 27:12); and most important, (3) if the analysis of 'Ανάστηθι πορεύου argued above is correct ("Go immediately!"), the temporal interpretation of κατὰ μεσημβρίαν ("at noon") is ruled out.

καταβαίνουσαν. Pres act ptc fem acc sg καταβαίνω (attributive).

αὕτη ἐστὶν ἔρημος. The use of asyndeton plus an anaphoric demonstrative is a typical strategy for introducing a parenthetical comment (cf. Levinsohn 1992, 52).

ἐστὶν. Pres act ind 3rd sg εἰμί.

ἔρημος. Predicate adjective.

8:27 **καὶ ἀναστὰς ἐπορεύθη· καὶ ἰδοὺ ἀνὴρ Αἰθίοψ εὐνοῦχος δυνάστης Κανδάκης βασιλίσσης Αἰθιόπων, ὃς ἦν ἐπὶ πάσης τῆς γάζης αὐτῆς, ὃς ἐληλύθει προσκυνήσων εἰς 'Ιερουσαλήμ,**

ἀναστὰς. Aor act ptc masc nom sg ἀνίστημι (attendant circumstance; on its pragmatic function, see v. 26 on 'Ανάστηθι πορεύου).

ἐπορεύθη. Aor pass dep ind 3rd sg πορεύομαι.

ἰδοὺ. See 1:10.

ἀνὴρ. This word, along with the remainder of v. 27, serves as the subject of ἦν ὑποστρέφων (v. 28).

Αἰθίοψ. Nominative in apposition to ἀνὴρ.

εὐνοῦχος. Nominative in apposition to ἀνὴρ.

δυνάστης. Nominative in apposition to ἀνὴρ.

Κανδάκης. In contrast to the genitive of subordination (see Αἰθιόπων below), here the genitive indicates the person to whom the head noun (δυνάστης) is subordinate.

βασιλίσσης. Genitive in apposition to Κανδάκης.

Αἰθιόπων. Genitive of subordination.

ἦν. Impf ind 3rd sg εἰμί.

ἐληλύθει. Plpf act ind 3rd sg ἔρχομαι.

προσκυνήσων. Fut act ptc masc nom sg προσκυνέω (purpose). The use of the future active participle to express purpose was a common idiom in ancient Greek, but is rare in the NT (Robertson 1934, 1128).

8:28 ἦν τε ὑποστρέφων καὶ καθήμενος ἐπὶ τοῦ ἅρματος αὐτοῦ καὶ ἀνεγίνωσκεν τὸν προφήτην Ἠσαΐαν.

ἦν. Impf ind 3rd sg εἰμί.

ὑποστρέφων. Pres act ptc masc nom sg ὑποστέφω (imperfect periphrastic; see 1:10 on ἀτενίζοντες).

καθήμενος. Pres dep ptc masc nom sg κάθημαι (imperfect periphrastic; see 1:10 on ἀτενίζοντες).

ἀνεγίνωσκεν. Impf act ind 3rd sg ἀναγινώσκω.

τὸν προφήτην Ἠσαΐαν. Metonymy (see 1:9 on τῶν ὀφθαλμῶν αὐτῶν) for "the book that Isaiah wrote."

Ἠσαΐαν. Accusative in apposition to τὸν προφήτην. On the diaeresis over the *iota*, see 2:31 on προϊδὼν.

8:29 εἶπεν δὲ τὸ πνεῦμα τῷ Φιλίππῳ, Πρόσελθε καὶ κολλήθητι τῷ ἅρματι τούτῳ.

εἶπεν. Aor act ind 3rd sg λέγω.

Πρόσελθε. Aor act impv 2nd sg προσέρχομαι.

κολλήθητι. Aor pass impv 2nd sg κολλάω.

τῷ ἅρματι. Dative complement of Πρόσελθε and κολλήθητι.

8:30 προσδραμὼν δὲ ὁ Φίλιππος ἤκουσεν αὐτοῦ ἀναγινώσκοντος Ἠσαΐαν τὸν προφήτην καὶ εἶπεν, Ἆρά γε γινώσκεις ἃ ἀναγινώσκεις;

προσδραμὼν. Aor act ptc masc nom sg προστρέχω (attendant circumstance).

ἤκουσεν. Aor act ind 3rd sg ἀκούω.

αὐτοῦ. Genitive object of ἤκουσεν.

ἀναγινώσκοντος. Pres act ptc masc gen sg ἀναγινώσκω (genitive complement of ἀκούω in an object-complement "double genitive" construction; see 2:6 on λαλούντων).

Ἠσαΐαν τὸν προφήτην. See v. 28. In this case τὸν προφήτην is in apposition to Ἠσαΐαν.

εἶπεν. Aor act ind 3rd sg λέγω.

Ἆρά γε. It is probably appropriate to take the presence of γε as indicating a sense of doubt (Moule, 158). The second accent on Ἆρά comes from the enclitic γε (see 1:4 on ἠκούσατέ).

γινώσκεις. Pres act ind 2nd sg γινώσκω.

ἅ. The relative pronoun introduces a headless relative clause (see 3:6 on ὅ): "*that* which you are reading."

ἀναγινώσκεις. Pres act ind 2nd sg ἀναγινώσκω.

8:31 ὁ δὲ εἶπεν, Πῶς γὰρ ἂν δυναίμην ἐὰν μή τις ὁδηγήσει με; παρεκάλεσέν τε τὸν Φίλιππον ἀναβάντα καθίσαι σὺν αὐτῷ.

ὁ. The article functions like a personal pronoun here (cf. 3:5).

εἶπεν. Aor act ind 3rd sg λέγω.

γὰρ. According to Barrett (428), the γάρ adds weight to the negative reply. It may be more precise, however, to take it as an explanation of an implicit negative response: "Of course not! For how can I . . ."

ἂν. Introduces the apodosis (which in this case precedes the protasis) of a mixed condition.

δυναίμην. Pres dep opt 1st sg δύναμαι. The optative with ἄν is usually used to form the apodosis of a fourth class condition (cf. 5:24 on τί ἂν γένοιτο τοῦτο).

ἐὰν. Introduces the protasis of a mixed condition.

ὁδηγήσει. Fut act ind 3rd sg ὁδηγέω. The subjunctive with ἐάν is usually used to form the protasis of a third class condition. Here, the future indicative is used in place of the subjunctive (cf. 7:3 on ἄν σοι δείξω). "The future form seems to carry with it a higher degree of expectation for fulfilment regarding the action" than the subjunctive (Porter 1994, 45).

παρεκάλεσέν. Aor act ind 3rd sg παρακαλέω. The second accent comes from the enclitic τε (see 1:4 on ἠκούσατέ).

τὸν Φίλιππον. Either the accusative subject of the infinitive καθίσαι (see 1:3 on αὐτὸν) or the accusative noun in a participle of indirect discourse construction.

ἀναβάντα. Aor act ptc masc acc sg ἀναβαίνω. The participle may be viewed as introducing indirect discourse itself (see 7:12 on ὄντα) or as introducing an attendant circumstance of καθίσαι.

καθίσαι. Aor act inf καθίζω (indirect discourse).

8:32 ἡ δὲ περιοχὴ τῆς γραφῆς ἣν ἀνεγίνωσκεν ἦν αὕτη· Ὡς πρόβατον ἐπὶ σφαγὴν ἤχθη καὶ ὡς ἀμνὸς ἐναντίον τοῦ κείραντος αὐτὸν ἄφωνος, οὕτως οὐκ ἀνοίγει τὸ στόμα αὐτοῦ.

ἡ . . . περιοχὴ. Nominative subject of ἦν.

ἀνεγίνωσκεν. Impf act ind 3rd sg ἀναγινώσκω.

ἦν. Impf ind 3rd sg εἰμί.

αὕτη. Predicate nominative.

Ὡς. The first comparison clause may be taken in two ways: (1) "Like a sheep led to slaughter," or (2) "He was led to slaughter like a sheep." The first view treats Ὡς πρόβατον ἐπὶ σφαγὴν ἤχθη as part of a compound clause ("Like a sheep led to slaughter and like a lamb before its shearer is silent . . ."). The second view treats Ὡς πρόβατον ἐπὶ σφαγὴν ἤχθη as a complete comparison on its own.

ἤχθη. Aor pass ind 3rd sg ἄγω.

τοῦ κείραντος. Aor act ptc masc gen sg κείρω (substantival).

αὐτὸν. Accusative direct object of κείραντος.

ἄφωνος. Predicate adjective with an implicit verb. Porter (1994, 85), however, argues that a nominative by itself can be used to form a "nominal clause" (cf. 26:14 on σκληρόν).

ἀνοίγει. Pres act ind 3rd sg ἀνοίγω.

8:33 Ἐν τῇ ταπεινώσει [αὐτοῦ] ἡ κρίσις αὐτοῦ ἤρθη· τὴν γενεὰν αὐτοῦ τίς διηγήσεται; ὅτι αἴρεται ἀπὸ τῆς γῆς ἡ ζωὴ αὐτοῦ.

ἡ κρίσις αὐτοῦ ἤρθη. Lit. "his justice was taken away."

ἤρθη. Aor pass ind 3rd sg αἴρω.

τὴν . . . διηγήσεται; Lit. "Who will relate his generation?" The rhetorical question functions as a powerful lament for a life cut short before procreation.

τὴν γενεὰν. Here, "posterity, descendants" (LN 10.28).

διηγήσεται. Fut mid dep ind 3rd sg διηγέομαι.

ὅτι. Introduces the reason for the implied negative response.

αἴρεται. Pres pass ind 3rd sg αἴρω. The use of the present tense results in a vivid expression of loss.

ἡ ζωὴ. Nominative subject of the passive verb.

8:34 Ἀποκριθεὶς δὲ ὁ εὐνοῦχος τῷ Φιλίππῳ εἶπεν, Δέομαί σου, περὶ τίνος ὁ προφήτης λέγει τοῦτο; περὶ ἑαυτοῦ ἢ περὶ ἑτέρου τινός;

Ἀποκριθεὶς. Aor pass dep ptc masc nom sg ἀποκρίνομαι (attendant circumstance).

τῷ Φιλίππῳ. Dative indirect object of εἶπεν.

εἶπεν. Aor act ind 3rd sg λέγω.

Δέομαί σου. Lit. "I ask you."

Δέομαί. Pres dep ind 1st sg δέομαι. The second accent comes from the enclitic σου (see 1:4 on ἠκούσατέ).

λέγει. Pres act ind 3rd sg λέγω.

τοῦτο. Accusative direct object of λέγει.

περὶ ἑαυτοῦ ἢ περὶ ἑτέρου τινός. The phrase λέγει τοῦτο is implicit.

8:35 ἀνοίξας δὲ ὁ Φίλιππος τὸ στόμα αὐτοῦ καὶ ἀρξάμενος ἀπὸ τῆς γραφῆς ταύτης εὐηγγελίσατο αὐτῷ τὸν Ἰησοῦν.

ἀνοίξας ὁ Φίλιππος τὸ στόμα αὐτοῦ. Lit. "Philip opened his mouth."

ἀνοίξας. Aor act ptc masc nom sg ἀνοίγω (attendant circumstance).

ἀρξάμενος. Aor mid ptc masc nom sg ἄρχω. The participle may indicate manner or an attendant circumstance. Alternatively, ἀρξάμενος ἀπό may represent a set idiomatic expression (see 10:37; cf. Luke 24:27).

εὐηγγελίσατο. Aor mid ind 3rd sg εὐαγγελίζω.

8:36 ὡς δὲ ἐπορεύοντο κατὰ τὴν ὁδόν, ἦλθον ἐπί τι ὕδωρ, καί φησιν ὁ εὐνοῦχος, Ἰδοὺ ὕδωρ· τί κωλύει με βαπτισθῆναι;

ὡς. Temporal (see 18:5).

ἐπορεύοντο. Impf dep ind 3rd pl πορεύομαι.

ἦλθον. Aor act ind 3rd pl ἔρχομαι.

φησιν. Pres act ind 3rd sg φημι.

Ἰδοὺ. See 1:10.

ὕδωρ. Nominative absolute.

κωλύει. Pres act ind 3rd sg κωλύω.

με. The accusative pronoun is most likely the subject of the infinitive (see 1:3 on αὐτὸν) rather than the direct object of κωλύει (for an analogous example, see 24:23 on μηδένα).

βαπτισθῆναι. Aor pass inf βαπτίζω. The infinitive should probably be viewed as complementary (assuming με is the subject of the infinitive). The construction, κωλύω + infinitive, means "to prevent someone from doing something."

8:37 This verse, which is omitted by 𝔓[45, 74] א A B C Ψ *Byz al*, is found in many miniscules: εἶπε δὲ αὐτῷ, Εἰ πιστεύεις ἐξ ὅλης τῆς καρδίας σου, ἔξεστιν· ἀποκριθεὶς δὲ εἶπε, Πιστεύω τὸν υἱὸν τοῦ θεοῦ εἶναι ᾿Ιησοῦν Χριστὸν (He said to him, "If you believe with your whole heart, it is permissible." He answered and said, "I believe that Jesus Christ is the Son of God."). Codex E *al* add εἶπε δὲ αὐτῷ ὁ Φίλιππος, ᾿Εὰν πιστεύεις ἐξ ὅλης τῆς καρδίας σου, σωθήσει· ἀποκριθεὶς δὲ εἶπε, Πιστεύω εἰς τὸν Χριστὸν τὸν υἱὸν τοῦ θεοῦ (Philip said to him, "If you believe with your whole heart, you will be saved. He answered and said, "I believe in Christ, the Son of God."). Metzger (359) points out that there is no reason why scribes should have omitted the material if it had originally stood in the text.

8:38 καὶ ἐκέλευσεν στῆναι τὸ ἅρμα, καὶ κατέβησαν ἀμφότεροι εἰς τὸ ὕδωρ, ὅ τε Φίλιππος καὶ ὁ εὐνοῦχος, καὶ ἐβάπτισεν αὐτόν.

ἐκέλευσεν. Aor act ind 3rd sg κελεύω.

στῆναι. Aor act inf ἵστημι (indirect discourse).

τὸ ἅρμα. Accusative subject of the infinitive (see 1:3 on αὐτὸν).

κατέβησαν. Aor act ind 3rd pl καταβαίνω.

ὅ. The article, which modifies Φίλιππος, should not be mistaken for a relative pronoun. The accent comes from the enclitic τε (see 1:4 on ἠκούσατέ).

ἐβάπτισεν. Aor act ind 3rd sg βαπτίζω.

8:39 ὅτε δὲ ἀνέβησαν ἐκ τοῦ ὕδατος, πνεῦμα κυρίου ἥρπασεν τὸν Φίλιππον καὶ οὐκ εἶδεν αὐτὸν οὐκέτι ὁ εὐνοῦχος, ἐπορεύετο γὰρ τὴν ὁδὸν αὐτοῦ χαίρων.

ἀνέβησαν. Aor act ind 3rd pl ἀναβαίνω.

πνεῦμα κυρίου ἥρπασεν. This reading is supported by 𝔓[45, 74] א* A B C E Ψ *al*. A fuller reading is found in A[c] 36 307 453 *al*: πνεῦμα ἅγιον ἐπέπεσεν ἐπὶ τὸν εὐνοῦχον, ἄγγελος δὲ κυρίου ἥρπασεν ("the Holy Spirit fell upon the eunuch and an angel of the Lord snatched").

ἥρπασεν. Aor act ind 3rd sg ἁρπάζω.

εἶδεν. Aor act ind 3rd sg ὁράω.

ἐπορεύετο. Impf dep ind 3rd sg πορεύομαι.

γάρ. According to BAGD (152), under certain circumstances γάρ can be used in place of δέ. It is not clear, however, what function of δέ could be in view here, nor is it clear what would motivate such a usage. Barrett's attempt (434) to explain the problem by positing an elliptical construction ("The eunuch saw no more of Philip, for he, unlike Philip, was not supernaturally removed but simply continued his journey") is not convincing. It may be best to (1) take γάρ as a transition marker that highlights the significance of the clause it introduces (cf. 4:27; 9:16; LN 91.1), or (2) take γάρ as introducing a compound sentence that includes Φίλιππος δὲ εὑρέθη εἰς Ἄζωτον (v. 40): "The eunuch did not see him anymore, since he went on his way rejoicing but Philip ended up at Azotus."

χαίρων. Pres act ptc masc nom sg χαίρω (manner).

8:40 Φίλιππος δὲ εὑρέθη εἰς Ἄζωτον· καὶ διερχόμενος εὐηγγελίζετο τὰς πόλεις πάσας ἕως τοῦ ἐλθεῖν αὐτὸν εἰς Καισάρειαν.

εὑρέθη. Aor pass ind 3rd sg εὑρίσκω. Lit. "was found."

Ἄζωτον. A coastal city (OT Ashdod) about 20 miles north of Gaza.

διερχόμενος. Pres dep ptc masc nom sg διέρχομαι (temporal or attendant circumstance).

εὐηγγελίζετο. Impf mid ind 3rd sg εὐαγγελίζω. On the use of the imperfect, see 8:17.

τὰς πόλεις. Accusative of location (see 1:19 on Ἰερουσαλήμ).

ἐλθεῖν. Aor act inf ἔρχομαι (temporal with ἕως τοῦ).

αὐτὸν. Accusative subject of the infinitive (see 1:3 on αὐτὸν).

Acts 9:1–19a

[1]Meanwhile, Saul, who was still voicing murderous threats against the Lord's disciples, went to the high priest [2]and requested letters from him (addressed) to the synagogues in Damascus, so that if he found anyone who belonged to the Way, he might bring (them) in chains—both men and women—to Jerusalem.

[3]As he journeyed he came near to Damascus; and suddenly, a light from the sky flashed around him. [4]He fell to the ground and heard a voice saying to him, "Saul, Saul, why are you persecuting me?" [5]So he asked, "Who are you, Lord?" And he (replied), "I am Jesus whom you are persecuting. [6]Now, get up and go into the city; and you will be told what you must do."

[7]The men who were traveling with him stood (there) speechless, because they heard the voice but did not see anyone. [8]Saul got up from the ground; but when he opened his eyes he could not see anything. So, leading him by the hand, they brought him into Damascus. [9]For three days he could not see; and he neither ate nor drank.

[10]Now, there was a disciple in Damascus named Ananias. The Lord said to him in a vision, "Ananias!" And he replied, "Yes, Lord." [11]Then the Lord (said) to him, "Go at once to the street called Straight, and at the house of Judah look for a Tarsian named Saul. For, he is praying [12]and he has seen [in a vision] a man named Ananias coming in and laying hands on him so that he may see again." [13]But Ananias answered, "Lord, I have heard a lot of people talk about the many terrible things this man has done to your people in Jerusalem; [14]and he has authority here from the chief priests to arrest all who call on your name." [15]Then the Lord said to him, "Go, for I have chosen this man as an instrument to carry my name before the Gentiles, kings, and the people of Israel. [16]I will show him how much he must suffer for the sake of my name."

[17]So Ananias left (his house), went into the house (of Judah), and as he laid (his) hands on Saul he said, "Brother Saul, the Lord—Jesus, who appeared to you on the road you traveled—has sent me so that you may see again and be filled with the Holy Spirit." [18]Immediately, things like scales fell from his eyes; and he not only was able to see again, but also got up and was baptized. [19a]Then, after having (some) food, he regained his strength.

9:1 Ὁ δὲ Σαῦλος ἔτι ἐμπνέων ἀπειλῆς καὶ φόνου εἰς τοὺς μαθητὰς τοῦ κυρίου, προσελθὼν τῷ ἀρχιερεῖ

Ὁ . . . Σαῦλος. The article is used with the name to reintroduce Saul into the narrative (cf. 18:18).

ἐμπνέων. Pres act ptc masc nom sg ἐμπνέω (attributive). Lit. "breathing."

ἀπειλῆς καὶ φόνου. Genitive object of ἐμπνέων; hendiadys (lit.

"threats and murder"; see 1:25 on τῆς διακονίας καὶ ἀποστολῆς).

εἰς. Disadvantage.

προσελθὼν. Aor act ptc masc nom sg προσέρχομαι (attendant circumstance).

9:2 ᾐτήσατο παρ' αὐτοῦ ἐπιστολὰς εἰς Δαμασκὸν πρὸς τὰς συναγωγάς, ὅπως ἐάν τινας εὕρῃ τῆς ὁδοῦ ὄντας, ἄνδρας τε καὶ γυναῖκας, δεδεμένους ἀγάγῃ εἰς Ἰερουσαλήμ.

ᾐτήσατο. Aor mid ind 3rd sg αἰτέω. The middle denotes personal benefit to the one asking (cf. 7:46).

παρ'. Source.

τινας. Accusative direct object of εὕρῃ. The fronting (see 3:13 on ὑμεῖς) of this substantival adjective probably intensifies the idea: "any at all."

ἐάν. Used with a subjunctive verb to form a third class condition.

εὕρῃ. Aor act subj 3rd sg εὑρίσκω.

τῆς ὁδοῦ. Predicate partitive genitive. The Christian movement is also referred to as "the Way" in 19:9, 23; 24:14, 22.

ὄντας. Pres act ptc masc acc pl εἰμί. The participle should probably be viewed as an attributive modifier of the substantival τινας.

δεδεμένους. Prf pass ptc masc acc pl δέω. The participle should probably be viewed as a complement in an object-complement double accusative construction (see 1:3 on ζῶντα), with ἄνδρας τε καὶ γυναῖκας serving as the object. It cannot be adverbial since it has a different subject than ἀγάγῃ (see Culy 2004). Thus, the clause literally reads, "he might bring both men and women bound to Jerusalem."

ἀγάγῃ. Aor act subj 3rd sg ἄγω. The subjunctive is used with ὅπως to introduce Saul's purpose in obtaining the letters.

9:3 ἐν δὲ τῷ πορεύεσθαι ἐγένετο αὐτὸν ἐγγίζειν τῇ Δαμασκῷ, ἐξαίφνης τε αὐτὸν περιήστραψεν φῶς ἐκ τοῦ οὐρανοῦ

πορεύεσθαι. Pres dep inf πορεύομαι. Used with ἐν τῷ to denote contemporaneous time (cf. 2:1).

ἐγένετο. Aor mid dep ind 3rd sg γίνομαι. Here, ἐγένετο δὲ introduces the event line of the narrative following the setting of vv. 1–2 (Gault, 392).

τε. The conjunction introduces "the specific lead-in to the exchange" (Levinsohn 1987, 133).

αὐτὸν. Accusative subject of the infinitive (see 1:3 on αὐτὸν).

ἐγγίζειν. Pres act inf ἐγγίζω. The infinitival clause, αὐτὸν ἐγγίζειν τῇ Δαμασκῷ, functions as the subject of ἐγένετο (see also v. 32 on κατελθεῖν).

περιήστραψεν. Aor act ind 3rd sg περιαστράπτω.

9:4 καὶ πεσὼν ἐπὶ τὴν γῆν ἤκουσεν φωνὴν λέγουσαν αὐτῷ, Σαοὺλ Σαούλ, τί με διώκεις;

πεσὼν. Aor act ptc masc nom sg πίπτω (attendant circumstance).

ἤκουσεν. Aor act ind 3rd sg ἀκούω.

φωνὴν. On the significance of the shift from accusative (also at 26:14) to genitive at 22:7, see v. 7 on φωνῆς and Wallace 1996, 133–34.

λέγουσαν. Pres act ptc acc fem sg λέγω. Although the participle could be viewed as attributive, since verbs of perception commonly take double accusatives it is better to take it as the complement in an object-complement double accusative construction (see 1:3 on ζῶντα).

Σαοὺλ Σαούλ. The use of the vocative doublet (here, a repetition of the same word; cf. 2:43 on τέρατα καὶ σημεῖα) intensifies the address.

διώκεις. Pres act ind 2nd sg διώκω.

9:5 εἶπεν δέ, Τίς εἶ, κύριε; ὁ δέ, Ἐγώ εἰμι Ἰησοῦς ὃν σὺ διώκεις·

εἶπεν δέ. On the use of this construction, see 19:4.

εἶπεν. Aor act ind 3rd sg λέγω.

εἶ. Pres act ind 2nd sg εἰμί.

κύριε. On the position of the vocative, see 10:13 on Πέτρε.

ὁ δέ. See 12:15 on οἱ δέ . . . ἡ δέ . . . οἱ δὲ.

εἰμι. Pres act ind 1st sg εἰμί.

Ἰησοῦς. Predicate nominative.

διώκεις. Pres act ind 2nd sg διώκω.

9:6 ἀλλὰ ἀνάστηθι καὶ εἴσελθε εἰς τὴν πόλιν, καὶ λαληθήσεταί σοι ὅ τί σε δεῖ ποιεῖν.

ἀλλὰ. The conjunction probably indicates that what follows will be contra Saul's expectations.

ἀνάστηθι. Aor act impv 2nd sg ἀνίστημι. Here, the verb should probably be taken literally, though it is possible that it serves to lend a sense of urgency to εἴσελθε (cf. 8:26).

εἴσελθε. Aor act impv 2nd sg εἰσέρχομαι.

λαληθήσεταί. Fut pass ind 3rd sg λαλέω. The second accent comes from the enclitic σοι (see 1:4 on ἠκούσατέ).

ὅ τί. This form may be an indefinite accusative relative pronoun that serves as the direct object of the infinitive. Robertson (1934, 731) lists this verse as the only example in the NT of ὅ τι used in an indirect question, a position rejected by Blass (cited in Robertson) as inconsistent with general usage. Robertson's idiosyncratic view may, however, be avoided if ὅ τί σε δεῖ ποιεῖν is taken as a substantival clause that functions as the subject of the passive verb λαληθήσεταί. The ὅ would then be a nominative singular article that functions as a nominalizer (see 1:3 on τὰ) rather than an accusative singular relative pronoun. The accent on the article would come from the enclitic τι (see 1:4 on ἠκού σατέ), which in this case has itself received an accent from the enclitic σε that follows. The unusual construction may have led to the easier reading that has τί rather than ὅ τί (E Ψ *Byz*).

σε. Accusative subject of the infinitive (see 1:3 on αὐτὸν).

δεῖ. Pres act ind 3rd sg δεῖ (impersonal).

ποιεῖν. Pres act inf ποιέω (complementary; see 1:16 on ἔδει).

9:7 οἱ δὲ ἄνδρες οἱ συνοδεύοντες αὐτῷ εἱστήκεισαν ἐνεοί, ἀκούοντες μὲν τῆς φωνῆς μηδένα δὲ θεωροῦντες.

συνοδεύοντες. Pres act ptc masc nom pl συνοδεύω (attributive).

αὐτῷ. Verbs with a συν- prefix take a dative complement.

εἱστήκεισαν. Plprf act ind 3rd pl ἵστημι.

ἐνεοί. Predicate adjective.

ἀκούοντες. Pres act ptc masc nom pl ἀκούω (causal). The participle cannot be concessive (contra Rogers and Rogers, 248) since it modifies the finite verb εἱστήκεισαν not the participle θεωροῦντες.

φωνῆς. Genitive object of ἀκούοντες. Commenting on the apparent contradiction between this verse (they heard the voice) and 22:9 (they *did not* hear the voice), Robertson (1934, 506) notes that the objects are in different cases and argues that "it is perfectly proper to appeal to the distinction in the cases in the apparent contradiction between ἀκού-οντες μὲν τῆς φωνῆς (Acts 9:7) and τὴν δὲ φωνὴν οὐκ ἤκουσαν (22:9). The accusative case (case of extent) accents the intellectual apprehension of the sound, while the genitive (specifying case) calls attention to the sound of the voice. . . . The word ἀκούω itself has two senses . . . , one 'to hear,' the other 'to understand'." Wallace (1996, 133–34), however, points out that the distinction that Robertson draws between the two cases is not consistent with NT usage. (It is not even in accord with Lukan usage; Bratcher, 243–45.) He, therefore, argues that "regardless of how one works through the accounts of Paul's conversion, an appeal to different cases probably ought *not* form any part of the solution." Chrysostom attempted to resolve the apparent contradiction by suggesting that it was Saul's voice that the fellow travelers heard (*Hom. on Acts*, 19; cited by Bruce, 236).

θεωροῦντες. Pres act ptc masc nom pl θεωρέω (causal).

9:8 ἠγέρθη δὲ Σαῦλος ἀπὸ τῆς γῆς, ἀνεῳγμένων δὲ τῶν ὀφθαλμῶν αὐτοῦ οὐδὲν ἔβλεπεν· χειραγωγοῦντες δὲ αὐτὸν εἰσήγαγον εἰς Δαμασκόν.

ἠγέρθη. Aor pass ind 3rd sg ἐγείρω. Perhaps, "was helped up."

ἀνεῳγμένων. Prf pass ptc masc gen pl ἀνοίγω. Genitive absolute (see 1:8 on ἐπελθόντος), temporal. The genitive absolute is used because technically the subject of the participle (the genitive τῶν ὀφθαλμῶν) is different than the subject of the main verb.

ἔβλεπεν. Impf act ind 3rd sg βλέπω.

χειραγωγοῦντες. Pres act ptc masc nom pl χειραγωγέω (means).

εἰσήγαγον. Aor act ind 3rd pl εἰσάγω.

9:9 καὶ ἦν ἡμέρας τρεῖς μὴ βλέπων, καὶ οὐκ ἔφαγεν οὐδὲ ἔπιεν.

ἦν. Impf ind 3rd sg εἰμί.

ἡμέρας. Accusative indicating extent of time (see 7:20 on μῆνας).

βλέπων. Pres act ptc masc nom sg βλέπω (imperfect periphrastic; see 1:10 on ἀτενίζοντες).

ἔφαγεν. Aor act ind 3rd sg ἐσθίω.

ἔπιεν. Aor act ind 3rd sg πίνω.

9:10 Ἦν δέ τις μαθητὴς ἐν Δαμασκῷ ὀνόματι Ἁνανίας, καὶ εἶπεν πρὸς αὐτὸν ἐν ὁράματι ὁ κύριος, Ἁνανία. ὁ δὲ εἶπεν, Ἰδοὺ ἐγώ, κύριε.

Ἦν. Impf ind 3rd sg εἰμί.

τις. When major participants are introduced in a non-event clause, τις plus a noun is often used (Levinsohn 1992, 114). See also 8:9.

ὀνόματι. Dative of reference.

Ἁνανίας. Nominative in apposition to μαθητὴς.

εἶπεν . . . εἶπεν. Aor act ind 3rd sg λέγω.

ὁ δὲ. See 12:15 on οἱ δέ . . . ἡ δέ . . . οἱ δε (cf. v. 5).

Ἰδοὺ ἐγώ. An idiomatic expression, equivalent to the Hebrew הִנֵּנִי, used to answer a summons (cf. 1 Sam 3:1–9); see also 1:10.

ἐγώ. Nominative absolute.

κύριε. Vocative.

9:11 ὁ δὲ κύριος πρὸς αὐτόν, Ἀναστὰς πορεύθητι ἐπὶ τὴν ῥύμην τὴν καλουμένην Εὐθεῖαν καὶ ζήτησον ἐν οἰκίᾳ Ἰούδα Σαῦλον ὀνόματι Ταρσέα· ἰδοὺ γὰρ προσεύχεται

Ἀναστὰς. Aor act ptc masc nom sg ἀνίστημι (with an imperative main verb an attendant circumstance participle carries imperatival force). On the pragmatic force of this verb, see 8:26 on Ἀνάστηθι πορεύου. That the Lord wanted Ananias to go immediately is clear from the statement that Saul was praying at that moment (cf. the analogous construction and context at 22:16).

πορεύθητι. Aor pass dep impv 2nd sg πορεύομαι.

καλουμένην. Pres pass ptc fem acc sg καλέω (attributive).

Εὐθεῖαν. The accusative noun serves as a complement in a passive object-complement double case construction (cf. 1:12 on Ελαιῶνος).

ζήτησον. Aor act impv 2nd sg ζητέω.

Σαῦλον. Accusative in apposition to Ταρσέα (or vice versa).

ὀνόματι. Dative of reference.

ἰδοὺ. See 1:10.

προσεύχεται. Pres dep ind 3rd sg προσεύχομαι.

9:12 καὶ εἶδεν ἄνδρα [ἐν ὁράματι] Ἁνανίαν ὀνόματι εἰσελθόντα καὶ ἐπιθέντα αὐτῷ [τὰς] χεῖρας ὅπως ἀναβλέψῃ.

εἶδεν. Aor act ind 3rd sg ὁράω.

[ἐν ὁράματι]. The variety of readings that include the bracketed phrase (see B C E 33 Ψ *Byz al*) may reflect the natural (intuitive) scribal inclusion of information that is implicit in the text. On the other hand, scribes listening to the dictation of the text could just as easily have omitted what was already implicit (see 𝔓[74] א A 81 *al*).

᾿Ανανίαν. Accusative in apposition to ἄνδρα.

ὀνόματι. Dative of reference.

εἰσελθόντα. Aor act ptc masc acc sg εἰσέρχομαι. The participle functions as the complement in an object-complement double accusative construction (see 1:3 on ζῶντα).

ἐπιθέντα. Aor act ptc masc acc sg ἐπιτίθημι. The participle functions as the complement in an object-complement double accusative construction (see 1:3 on ζῶντα).

ἀναβλέψῃ. Aor act subj 3rd sg ἀναβλέπω. The subjunctive is used with ὅπως to form a purpose clause.

9:13 ἀπεκρίθη δὲ ᾿Ανανίας, Κύριε, ἤκουσα ἀπὸ πολλῶν περὶ τοῦ ἀνδρὸς τούτου ὅσα κακὰ τοῖς ἁγίοις σου ἐποίησεν ἐν ᾿Ιερουσαλήμ·

ἀπεκρίθη. Aor pass dep ind 3rd sg ἀποκρίνομαι. The use of ἀποκρίνομαι here introduces an objection or counter-assertion that shifts the conversation in a new direction (Levinsohn 1987, 36; 1992, 135).

Κύριε. Vocative.

ἤκουσα . . . ἐποίησεν. Lit. "I have heard from many people about this man, how many terrible things . . . he did."

ἤκουσα. Aor act ind 1st sg ἀκούω.

ὅσα. The relative pronoun introduces an internally headed relative clause (see 1:2 on ἄχρι ἧς ἡμέρας; κακά is the accusative direct object of ἤκουσα) that probably emphasizes the extent of Saul's mistreatment of God's people (cf. the similar construction and sense in Luke 3:19).

τοῖς ἁγίοις. Dative of disadvantage. Used in the plural as a substantive, this expression usually refers to "God's people."

ἐποίησεν. Aor act ind 3rd sg ποιέω.

9:14 καὶ ὧδε ἔχει ἐξουσίαν παρὰ τῶν ἀρχιερέων δῆσαι πάντας τοὺς ἐπικαλουμένους τὸ ὄνομά σου.

ἔχει. Pres act ind 3rd sg ἔχω.

δῆσαι. Aor act inf δέω (epexegetical).

τοὺς ἐπικαλουμένους. Pres mid ptc masc acc pl ἐπικαλέω (substantival).

9:15 εἶπεν δὲ πρὸς αὐτὸν ὁ κύριος, Πορεύου, ὅτι σκεῦος ἐκλογῆς ἐστίν μοι οὗτος τοῦ βαστάσαι τὸ ὄνομά μου ἐνώπιον ἐθνῶν τε καὶ βασιλέων υἱῶν τε Ἰσραήλ·

εἶπεν. Aor act ind 3rd sg λέγω. The use of the verb-initial construction marks v. 15 as the "resolving utterance" of the exchange (see 19:4 on εἶπεν δὲ).

Πορεύου. Pres dep impv 2nd sg πορεύομαι.

ὅτι. Causal.

σκεῦος . . . οὗτος. Lit. "this man is a chosen vessel for me."

σκεῦος. Predicate nominative.

ἐκλογῆς. Attributive genitive.

ἐστίν. Pres act ind 3rd sg εἰμί. The unexpected accent (see 1:7 on ἐστιν) comes from the enclitic μοι (see 1:4 on ἠκούσατέ). It does not indicate emphasis (cf. 2:13 on εἰσίν).

μοι. The dative may indicate possession (though this is unlikely when ἐστιν has a predicate nominative), advantage, or agency (the agent of the implicit action in ἐκλογῆς). The third option is supported by the presence of the infinitival purpose clause (see below).

τοῦ βαστάσαι τὸ ὄνομά μου. According to Louw and Nida (33.210), βαστάζω ὄνομα (lit. "to carry a name") is an idiom meaning "to spread information extensively about a person."

βαστάσαι. Aor act inf βαστάζω. Rather than taking the infinitive as epexegetical (Rogers and Rogers, 249) or appositional (Wallace 1996, 607), it is probably better to say that the infinitive introduces the purpose (see 3:2 on τοῦ αἰτεῖν; cf. 15:20 on ἀπέχεσθαι) of the implicit action expressed in the noun ἐκλογῆς (Barrett [456] calls it consecutive): "I chose this man that he might bear. . . ."

ὄνομά. Accusative object of βαστάσαι. The second accent comes from the enclitic μου (see 1:4 on ἠκούσατέ).

βασιλέων υἱῶν. These two words should not be viewed as a single noun phrase. Rather, υἱῶν is linked to ἐθνῶν and βασιλέων by the conjunction τε, which always follows the item being conjoined.

9:16 ἐγὼ γὰρ ὑποδείξω αὐτῷ ὅσα δεῖ αὐτὸν ὑπὲρ τοῦ ὀνόματός μου παθεῖν.

ἐγὼ. The explicit fronted (see 3:13 on ὑμεῖς) subject pronoun shifts the focus (see 2:15 on ὑμεῖς) to God.

ὑποδείξω. Fut act ind 1st sg ὑποδείκνυμι.

γὰρ. The conjunction could be taken as supplying a second reason why Ananias is being commanded to visit the despised Saul of Tarsus. It may be better, however, simply to view the conjunction as a transition marker that highlights the significance of the clause it introduces (cf. 4:27; 8:39; LN 91.1).

αὐτῷ. Dative indirect object of ὑποδείξω.

ὅσα. The relative pronoun introduces a headless relative clause (see 3:6 on ὃ): "how many things he must suffer." It is the accusative direct object of παθεῖν. Its unexpressed antecedent is the direct object of ὑποδείξω.

δεῖ. Pres act ind 3rd sg δεῖ (impersonal).

αὐτὸν. Accusative subject of the infinitive (see 1:3 on αὐτὸν).

παθεῖν. Aor act inf πάσχω (complementary; see 1:16 on ἔδει).

9:17 Ἀπῆλθεν δὲ Ἁνανίας καὶ εἰσῆλθεν εἰς τὴν οἰκίαν καὶ ἐπιθεὶς ἐπ' αὐτὸν τὰς χεῖρας εἶπεν, Σαοὺλ ἀδελφέ, ὁ κύριος ἀπέσταλκέν με, Ἰησοῦς ὁ ὀφθείς σοι ἐν τῇ ὁδῷ ᾗ ἤρχου, ὅπως ἀναβλέψῃς καὶ πλησθῇς πνεύματος ἁγίου.

Ἀπῆλθεν. Aor act ind 3rd sg ἀπέρχομαι.

εἰσῆλθεν. Aor act ind 3rd sg εἰσέρχομαι.

εἰς. See 1:8 on ἐφ' ὑμᾶς.

ἐπιθεὶς. Aor act ptc masc nom sg ἐπιτίθημι (attendant circumstance or temporal).

ἐπ'. See 1:8 on ἐφ' ὑμᾶς.

εἶπεν. Aor act ind 3rd sg λέγω.

Σαοὺλ ἀδελφέ. Vocative.

ἀπέσταλκέν. Prf act ind 3rd sg ἀποστέλλω. The second accent comes from the enclitic με (see 1:4 on ἠκούσατέ).

Ἰησοῦς. Nominative in apposition to ὁ κύριος.

ὀφθείς. Aor pass ptc masc nom sg ὁράω (attributive). See 7:2, 26.

ἤρχου. Impf dep ind 2nd sg ἔρχομαι.

ἀναβλέψῃς. Aor act subj 2nd sg ἀναβλέπω. The subjunctive is used with ὅπως to form a purpose clause.

πλησθῇς. Aor pass subj 2nd sg πίμπλημι. The subjunctive is used with ὅπως to form a purpose clause.

πνεύματος. See 2:4.

9:18 καὶ εὐθέως ἀπέπεσαν αὐτοῦ ἀπὸ τῶν ὀφθαλμῶν ὡς λεπίδες, ἀνέβλεψέν τε καὶ ἀναστὰς ἐβαπτίσθη

ἀπέπεσαν. Aor act ind 3rd pl ἀποπίπτω.

αὐτοῦ ἀπὸ τῶν ὀφθαλμῶν. The unusual word order (αὐτοῦ is typically treated as a possessor of τῶν ὀφθαλμῶν: "his eyes") is found only in 𝔓[45vid] A B 1175 *pc.* The whole phrase is omitted by 𝔓[74] ℵ C E Ψ *Byz.* It is possible that the laconic εὐθέως ἀπέπεσαν ὡς λεπίδες of most manuscripts was filled out by a few scribes. What remains unclear, however, is why they would have placed αὐτοῦ where they did. Given the word order and the textual variant, it is possible that αὐτοῦ is the genitive complement of ἀπέπεσαν and stands in apposition to ἀπὸ τῶν ὀφθαλμῶν: "they fell away from him, that is, from his eyes, like scales." The nature of the comparison is also ambiguous. The clause could either mean "things like scales fell away from his eyes," or perhaps, "things fell away from his eyes like scales are peeled away."

ἀπὸ. See 1:8 on ἐφ' ὑμᾶς.

λεπίδες. This nominative noun is the second component of a comparative construction. The topic of the construction is unexpressed ("*things* like scales").

ἀνέβλεψέν. Aor act ind 3rd sg ἀναβλέπω.

ἀναστὰς. Aor act ptc masc nom sg ἀνίστημι (attendant circumstance).

ἐβαπτίσθη. Aor pass ind 3rd sg βαπτίζω.

9:19a καὶ λαβὼν τροφὴν ἐνίσχυσεν.

λαβὼν. Aor act ptc masc nom sg λαμβάνω (temporal).

ἐνίσχυσεν. Aor act ind 3rd sg ἐνισχύω.

Acts 9:19b–31

19b Saul was with the disciples in Damascus for several days. 20 Right away, he began to proclaim Jesus in the synagogues, (saying), "This man is the Son of God." 21 All who heard (him) were amazed and were saying, "Isn't this the one who in Jerusalem tried to destroy those who called on this name? Hadn't he come here for this (very) purpose—that he might bring them in chains before the chief priests?" 22 But Saul was becoming more powerful and confounding the Jews who lived in Damascus by proving that Jesus is the Messiah.

[23]When many days had passed, the Jews made plans to kill him. [24]Their plot, however, became known to Saul. Now, they were watching the gates day and night in order that they might kill him, [25]so his disciples took him at night and let him down through (an opening in) the wall by lowering (him) in a basket.

[26]When he arrived in Jerusalem, he tried to join the disciples, but they were all afraid of him because they did not believe that he was a disciple. [27]But Barnabas helped him. He brought him to the apostles and described to them how he had seen the Lord on the road, that he had spoken to him, and how in Damascus he had spoken boldly in the name of Jesus. [28](After that) he went around with them in Jerusalem, speaking boldly in the name of the Lord. [29]He was both speaking and debating against the Hellenists; but they were trying to kill him. [30]When the believers learned (of this), they brought him down to Caesarea and sent him away to Tarsus.

[31]So the church throughout all of Judea, Galilee, and Samaria had peace. And as the church was strengthened, and lived in the fear of the Lord and (experienced) the Holy Spirit's encouragement, it kept growing in number.

9:19b Ἐγένετο δὲ μετὰ τῶν ἐν Δαμασκῷ μαθητῶν ἡμέρας τινάς

Ἐγένετο. Aor mid dep ind 3rd sg γίνομαι. Levinsohn (1992, 210; cf. Barrett, 463) argues that "the absence of overt reference to the subject in v. 19b implies that Luke did not consider v. 19b to be the beginning of a new narrative unit (unless the variant ὁ Σαῦλος is read)."

ἡμέρας. Accusative indicating extent of time (see 7:20 on μῆνας).

9:20 καὶ εὐθέως ἐν ταῖς συναγωγαῖς ἐκήρυσσεν τὸν Ἰησοῦν ὅτι οὗτός ἐστιν ὁ υἱὸς τοῦ θεοῦ.

ἐκήρυσσεν. Impf act ind 3rd sg κηρύσσω. See also 8:5.

ὅτι. The ὅτι clause stands in apposition to τὸν Ἰησοῦν and introduces a clausal complement (indirect discourse) of ἐκήρυσσεν.

οὗτός. The second accent comes from the enclitic ἐστιν (see 1:4 on ἠκούσατέ).

ἐστιν. Pres act ind 3rd sg εἰμί.

ὁ υἱός. Predicate nominative.

9:21 ἐξίσταντο δὲ πάντες οἱ ἀκούοντες καὶ ἔλεγον, Οὐχ οὗτός ἐστιν ὁ πορθήσας εἰς Ἰερουσαλὴμ τοὺς ἐπικαλουμένους τὸ ὄνομα τοῦτο, καὶ ὧδε εἰς τοῦτο ἐληλύθει ἵνα δεδεμένους αὐτοὺς ἀγάγῃ ἐπὶ τοὺς ἀρχιερεῖς;

ἐξίσταντο. Impf mid ind 3rd pl ἐξίστημι.

οἱ ἀκούοντες. Pres act ptc masc nom pl ἀκούω (substantival).

ἔλεγον. Impf act ind 3rd pl λέγω.

οὗτός. The second accent comes from the enclitic ἐστιν (see 1:4 on ἠκούσατέ).

ἐστιν. Pres act ind 3rd sg εἰμί.

ὁ πορθήσας. Aor act ptc masc nom sg πορθέω (substantival). Predicate nominative.

τοὺς ἐπικαλουμένους. Pres mid ptc masc acc pl ἐπικαλέω (substantival).

εἰς τοῦτο. "For this (reason)," or, in apposition to ὧδε, "to this (place)."

ἐληλύθει. Plpf act ind 3rd sg ἔρχομαι.

δεδεμένους. Prf pass ptc masc acc pl δέω. The participle should probably be viewed as a complement in an object-complement double accusative construction (see v. 2).

ἀγάγῃ. Aor act subj 3rd sg ἄγω. The subjunctive is used with ἵνα to indicate the purpose for Paul's visit to Damascus.

9:22 Σαῦλος δὲ μᾶλλον ἐνεδυναμοῦτο καὶ συνέχυννεν [τοὺς] Ἰουδαίους τοὺς κατοικοῦντας ἐν Δαμασκῷ συμβιβάζων ὅτι οὗτός ἐστιν ὁ Χριστός.

ἐνεδυναμοῦτο. Impf pass ind 3rd sg ἐνδυναμόω.

συνέχυννεν. Impf act ind 3rd sg συγχέω.

κατοικοῦντας. Pres act ptc masc acc pl κατοικέω (attributive).

συμβιβάζων. Pres act ptc masc nom sg συμβιβάζω (means).

ὅτι. Introduces the clausal complement of συμβιβάζων.

οὗτός. The second accent comes from the enclitic ἐστιν (see 1:4 on ἠκούσατέ).

ἐστιν. Pres act ind 3rd sg εἰμί.

ὁ Χριστός. Predicate nominative.

9:23 Ὡς δὲ ἐπληροῦντο ἡμέραι ἱκαναί, συνεβουλεύσαντο οἱ

'Ιουδαῖοι ἀνελεῖν αὐτόν·

'Ως. Temporal (see 18:5).

ἐπληροῦντο. Impf pass ind 3rd pl πληρόω. The use of the imperfect may suggest that "as time went on" the situation was becoming increasingly intolerable (Lake and Cadbury, 105; cf. 7:23; see also 13:25 on ἐπλήρου).

ἡμέραι. Nominative subject of ἐπληροῦντο.

συνεβουλεύσαντο. Aor mid ind 3rd pl συμβουλεύω. In the middle voice this verb means "to engage in joint planning so as to devise a course of common action, often one with a harmful or evil purpose" (LN 30.74).

ἀνελεῖν. Aor act inf ἀναιρέω (complementary).

9:24 ἐγνώσθη δὲ τῷ Σαύλῳ ἡ ἐπιβουλὴ αὐτῶν. παρετηροῦντο δὲ καὶ τὰς πύλας ἡμέρας τε καὶ νυκτὸς ὅπως αὐτὸν ἀνέλωσιν·

ἐγνώσθη. Aor pass ind 3rd sg γινώσκω.

παρετηροῦντο. Impf mid ind 3rd pl παρατηρέω.

ἡμέρας τε καὶ νυκτὸς. Genitive of time. Here, "all the time."

ἀνέλωσιν. Aor act subj 3rd pl ἀναιρέω. The subjunctive is used with ὅπως to form a purpose clause.

9:25 λαβόντες δὲ οἱ μαθηταὶ αὐτοῦ νυκτὸς διὰ τοῦ τείχους καθῆκαν αὐτὸν χαλάσαντες ἐν σπυρίδι.

λαβόντες. Aor act ptc masc nom pl λαμβάνω (attendant circumstance).

νυκτὸς. Genitive of time.

διὰ τοῦ τείχους. The specific nature of Paul's escape (through a *window* in the wall; see 2 Cor 11:33) is left implicit.

καθῆκαν. Aor act ind 3rd pl καθίημι.

χαλάσαντες. Aor act ptc masc nom pl χαλάω (means).

9:26 Παραγενόμενος δὲ εἰς 'Ιερουσαλὴμ ἐπείραζεν κολλᾶσθαι τοῖς μαθηταῖς, καὶ πάντες ἐφοβοῦντο αὐτόν μὴ πιστεύοντες ὅτι ἐστὶν μαθητής.

Παραγενόμενος. Aor mid dep ptc masc nom sg παραγίνομαι (temporal).

ἐπείραζεν. Impf act ind 3rd sg πειράζω.

κολλᾶσθαι. Pres pass inf κολλάω (complementary).

τοῖς μαθηταῖς. Dative complement of κολλᾶσθαι.

καὶ. Adversative.

ἐφοβοῦντο. Impf dep ind 3rd pl φοβέομαι.

πιστεύοντες. Pres act ptc masc nom pl πιστεύω (causal).

ὅτι. Introduces the causal complement of πιστεύοντες.

ἐστὶν. Pres act ind 3rd sg εἰμί. The enclitic ἐστιν (see 1:7) retains its accent following ὅτι. The present tense is retained in indirect discourse.

μαθητής. Predicate nominative.

9:27 Βαρναβᾶς δὲ ἐπιλαβόμενος αὐτὸν ἤγαγεν πρὸς τοὺς ἀποστόλους καὶ διηγήσατο αὐτοῖς πῶς ἐν τῇ ὁδῷ εἶδεν τὸν κύριον καὶ ὅτι ἐλάλησεν αὐτῷ, καὶ πῶς ἐν Δαμασκῷ ἐπαρρησιάσατο ἐν τῷ ὀνόματι τοῦ Ἰησοῦ.

ἐπιλαβόμενος. Aor mid dep ptc masc nom sg ἐπιλαμβάνομαι (attendant circumstance).

αὐτὸν. Accusative direct object of ἐπιλαβόμενος. According to BAGD (295), where ἐπιλαμβάνομαι appears to take an accusative object, the accusative substantive is actually the object of the finite verb that ἐπιλαβόμενος modifies (here ἤγαγεν). While it would be possible to take αὐτὸν with ἤγαγεν, however, it more likely modifies ἐπιλαβόμενος. First, direct objects usually follow the verb they modify. Second, there are unambiguous examples where ἐπιλαμβάνομαι takes an accusative object. In Luke 9:47, παιδίον must modify ἐπιλαβόμενος since the main verb has a pronominal direct object (αὐτὸ). Similarly, in Luke 23:26, the accusative Σίμωνά must be the direct object of ἐπιλαβόμενοι since the main verb ἐπέθηκαν already has an object (τὸν σταυρὸν). Many scribes were apparently uncomfortable with the accusative παιδίον in Luke 9:47 ($\mathfrak{P}^{75}$ B C D *al*) and the accusative Σίμωνα in Luke 23:26 (found in $\mathfrak{P}^{75}$ ℵ B 33 *al*) and thus changed them to genitives (9:47—ℵ A L W Q C Ψ *Byz al*; 23:36—A W Q Ψ *Byz al*). It is unclear whether the use of different cases affected the semantics or was simply the result of stylistic or dialectal variation.

ἤγαγεν. Aor act ind 3rd sg ἄγω.

διηγήσατο. Aor mid dep ind 3rd sg διηγέομαι.

πῶς . . . πῶς. Introduces two of the three conjoined clausal complements of διηγήσατο, which Porter (1994, 272) describes as indirect questions. In contrast to ὅτι, when used to introduce a clausal complement πῶς appears to indicate that the speaker is providing more general details about the subject. He is "talking about something" rather than "telling something" to someone (cf. 11:13; 12:17; 15:36).

εἶδεν. Aor act ind 3rd sg ὁράω.

ὅτι. Introduces the second complement of διηγήσατο.

ἐλάλησεν. Aor act ind 3rd sg λαλέω.

ἐπαρρησιάσατο. Aor mid dep ind 3rd sg παρρησιάζομαι.

ἐν τῷ ὀνόματι. The expression probably does not refer to speaking with Jesus' authority here (cf. 3:6), though that sense is certainly possible with ἐπαρρησιάσατο. The phrase probably simply indicates that Paul was now speaking positively about Jesus and thus highlights an unexpected change of events: the person who once sought to destroy Jesus' followers was now speaking *in favor* of Jesus.

9:28 καὶ ἦν μετ' αὐτῶν εἰσπορευόμενος καὶ ἐκπορευόμενος εἰς Ἰερουσαλήμ, παρρησιαζόμενος ἐν τῷ ὀνόματι τοῦ κυρίου,

ἦν. Impf ind 3rd sg εἰμί.

μετ' . . . εἰσπορευόμενος καὶ ἐκπορευόμενος. Although this phrase may be taken as an idiom meaning, "to live or to conduct oneself in relationship to some community or group" (LN 41.24; cf. 1:22 on εἰσῆλθεν καὶ ἐξῆλθεν ἐφ'), in light of the following participle it may be better to take it more literally as indicating movement around Jerusalem.

εἰσπορευόμενος. Pres dep ptc masc nom sg εἰσπορεύομαι (imperfect periphrastic; see 1:10 on ἀτενίζοντες).

ἐκπορευόμενος. Pres dep ptc masc nom sg ἐκπορεύομαι (imperfect periphrastic; see 1:10 on ἀτενίζοντες).

παρρησιαζόμενος. Pres dep ptc masc nom sg παρρησιάζομαι (imperfect periphrastic; see 1:10 on ἀτενίζοντες).

9:29 ἐλάλει τε καὶ συνεζήτει πρὸς τοὺς Ἑλληνιστάς, οἱ δὲ ἐπεχείρουν ἀνελεῖν αὐτόν.

ἐλάλει. Impf act ind 3rd sg λαλέω.

συνεζήτει. Impf act ind 3rd sg συζητέω.

Ἑλληνιστάς. See 6:1.

οἱ. The article is used like a personal pronoun here (cf. 3:5).

ἐπεχείρουν. Impf act ind 3rd pl ἐπιχειρέω.
ἀνελεῖν. Aor act inf ἀναιρέω (complementary).

9:30 ἐπιγνόντες δὲ οἱ ἀδελφοὶ κατήγαγον αὐτὸν εἰς Καισάρειαν καὶ ἐξαπέστειλαν αὐτὸν εἰς Ταρσόν.

ἐπιγνόντες. Aor act ptc masc nom pl ἐπιγινώσκω (temporal).
ἀδελφοὶ. See 1:15.
κατήγαγον. Aor act ind 3rd pl κατάγω.
ἐξαπέστειλαν. Aor act ind 3rd pl ἐξαποστέλλω.

9:31 Ἡ μὲν οὖν ἐκκλησία καθ' ὅλης τῆς Ἰουδαίας καὶ Γαλιλαίας καὶ Σαμαρείας εἶχεν εἰρήνην οἰκοδομουμένη καὶ πορευομένη τῷ φόβῳ τοῦ κυρίου καὶ τῇ παρακλήσει τοῦ ἁγίου πνεύματος ἐπληθύνετο.

οὖν. The conjunction introduces "a state which results naturally from the outcome of the previous incident as a whole" (Levinsohn 1987, 142).

καθ'. Distributive.

εἶχεν. Aor act ind 3rd sg ἔχω.

οἰκοδομουμένη. Pres pass ptc fem nom sg οἰκοδομέω. It is not clear how the participles relate to the finite verbs in this verse (cf. Omanson). οἰκοδομουμένη probably modifies ἐπληθύνετο, since it is conjoined with πορευομένη, and should be taken temporally.

πορευομένη. Pres dep ptc fem nom sg πορεύομαι (probably temporal; see above).

τοῦ κυρίου. Objective genitive.

τοῦ ἁγίου πνεύματος. Genitive of source or subjective genitive.

ἐπληθύνετο. Impf pass ind 3rd sg πληθύνω.

Acts 9:32–43

[32]Now, Peter, who was traveling all over, also visited God's people who lived in Lydda. [33]There, he found a certain man named Aeneas, who had been paralyzed and confined to bed for eight years. [34]Peter said to him, "Aeneas, Jesus Christ heals you! Get up and make your bed!" And immediately, he got up. [35]Everyone who lived in Lydda and Sharon saw him, and they turned to the Lord.

[36]Now, in Joppa there was a certain disciple named Tabitha, which translated means Dorcas. She was known for all the good deeds and charitable acts that she did. [37]In those days, she got sick and died; and they washed (her body) and laid her in an upper room.

[38]Now, since Lydda was near Joppa, when the disciples heard that Peter was there, they sent two men to him and urged him, "Come to us without delay." [39]So, Peter got up and went with them. When he arrived they brought him up to the upper room. All the widows stood by him, crying and showing the clothes and coats that Dorcas had made when she was with them. [40]After sending them all outside, Peter knelt and prayed. Then, turning to the body he said, "Tabitha, get up!" She opened her eyes, and when she saw Peter, she sat up. [41]Then (Peter) gave her a hand and helped her get up. After calling God's people, including the widows, he showed (them) that she was alive. [42](This) became known throughout all of Joppa, and many people believed in the Lord. [43]Then, he stayed for many days in Joppa with a certain Simon the Tanner.

9:32 Ἐγένετο δὲ Πέτρον διερχόμενον διὰ πάντων κατελθεῖν καὶ πρὸς τοὺς ἁγίους τοὺς κατοικοῦντας Λύδδα.

Ἐγένετο δὲ. Introduces a new episode (cf. Gault, 392).

Ἐγένετο. Aor mid dep ind 3rd sg γίνομαι.

Πέτρον. Accusative subject of the infinitive (see 1:3 on αὐτὸν).

διερχόμενον. Pres mid ptc acc masc sg διέρχομαι (attributive).

διὰ πάντων. Lit. "through all." On the presence of the preposition see 1:8 on ἐφ᾽ ὑμᾶς.

κατελθεῖν. Aor act inf κατέρχομαι (lit. "to go down"). The whole infinitival clause, Πέτρον διερχόμενον διὰ πάντων κατελθεῖν καὶ πρὸς τοὺς ἁγίους τοὺς κατοικοῦντας Λύδδα, serves as the subject of Ἐγένετο (see also 4:5; 9:3, 37, 43; 10:25; 11:26; 14:1; 16:16; 19:1; 20:16; 21:21, 5; 22:6, 16; 27:44; 28:8, 17). "In Acts, the infinitival subject of ἐγένετο typically presents an event which is the specific circumstance for the following foreground events" (Levinsohn 1992, 174; cf. Gault, 393).

τοὺς ἁγίους. See v. 13.

κατοικοῦντας. Pres act ptc masc acc pl κατοικέω (attributive).

Λύδδα. Accusative of location (see 1:19 on Ἱερουσαλήμ).

9:33 εὗρεν δὲ ἐκεῖ ἄνθρωπόν τινα ὀνόματι Αἰνέαν ἐξ ἐτῶν ὀκτὼ κατακείμενον ἐπὶ κραβάττου, ὃς ἦν παραλελυμένος.

εὗρεν. Aor act ind 3rd sg εὑρίσκω.

ἄνθρωπόν. The second accent comes from the enclitic τινα (see 1:4 on ἠκούσατε).

τινα. See v. 10 on τις; 8:9 on τις.

ὀνόματι. Dative of reference.

Αἰνέαν. Accusative in apposition to ἄνθρωπόν.

ἐξ ἐτῶν ὀκτὼ. Probably "for eight years," rather than "from the age of eight" (Barrett, 480), though "with expressions of time ἐκ [usually] gives the point of departure" (Robertson 1934, 597; cf. 24:10).

κατακείμενον. Pres dep ptc masc sg acc κατάκειμαι (attributive).

ἦν. Impf ind 3rd sg εἰμί.

παραλελυμένος. Prf pass ptc masc nom sg παραλύω (pluperfect periphrastic; see 1:17 on κατηριθμημένος).

9:34 καὶ εἶπεν αὐτῷ ὁ Πέτρος, Αἰνέα, ἰᾶταί σε Ἰησοῦς Χριστός· ἀνάστηθι καὶ στρῶσον σεαυτῷ. καὶ εὐθέως ἀνέστη.

εἶπεν. Aor act ind 3rd sg λέγω.

Αἰνέα. Vocative.

ἰᾶταί. Pres dep ind 3rd sg ἰάομαι. The second accent comes from the enclitic σε (see 1:4 on ἠκούσατέ).

ἀνάστηθι. Aor act impv 2nd sg ἀνίστημι.

στρῶσον σεαυτῷ. The meaning of this command is uncertain. Louw and Nida (46.10) suggest that the verb can refer to preparing a bed either for sleeping or making up a bed after using it (see also BDAG, 949). They maintain that "it is possible to argue that στρώννυμι . . . has only the base meaning 'to spread something out' (as in Matt 21.8; see 16.22), but this term seems to be used in an absolute sense in rather highly diverse contexts, and therefore one is justified in setting up more than one distinct meaning." In the only other biblical use of the verb with a dative complement that is coreferential with the subject of the verb (LXX Esth 4:3—σάκκον καὶ σποδὸν ἔστρωσαν ἑαυτοῖς), the sense appears to be "spread out (on the ground)," though the verb could refer to "clothing oneself" in σάκκον ("sackcloth") and "spreading out" σποδὸν ("ashes") on the ground.

στρῶσον. Aor act impv 2nd sg στρωννύω/στρώννυμι.

σεαυτῷ. Dative of advantage. Here, probably part of an idiomatic expression (see above).

ἀνέστη. Aor act ind 3rd sg ἀνίστημι.

9:35 καὶ εἶδαν αὐτὸν πάντες οἱ κατοικοῦντες Λύδδα καὶ τὸν Σαρῶνα, οἵτινες ἐπέστρεψαν ἐπὶ τὸν κύριον.

εἶδαν. Aor act ind 3rd pl ὁράω.

οἱ κατοικοῦντες. Pres act ptc masc nom pl κατοικέω (substantival).

Λύδδα καὶ τὸν Σαρῶνα. Accusative of location (see 1:19 on Ἰερουσαλήμ).

ἐπέστρεψαν. Aor act ind 3rd pl ἐπιστρέφω.

ἐπὶ. See 1:8 on ἐφ᾽ ὑμᾶς.

9:36 Ἐν Ἰόππῃ δέ τις ἦν μαθήτρια ὀνόματι Ταβιθά, ἣ διερμηνευομένη λέγεται Δορκάς· αὕτη ἦν πλήρης ἔργων ἀγαθῶν καὶ ἐλεημοσυνῶν ὧν ἐποίει.

τις. See 9:10; 8:9.

ἦν. Impf ind 3rd sg εἰμί.

ὀνόματι. Dative of reference.

Ταβιθά. Nominative in apposition to μαθήτρια.

ἣ διερμηνευομένη λέγεται. Lit. "which being translated is said." This construction differs from the common "interpretive relative phrase" that uses a neuter nominative relative pronoun (see 4:36 on ὅ).

διερμηνευομένη. Pres pass ptc fem nom sg διερμηνεύω (temporal).

λέγεται. Pres pass ind 3rd sg λέγω.

Δορκάς. Nominative of appellation (see Wallace 1996, 61).

ἦν. Impf ind 3rd sg εἰμί.

πλήρης ἔργων ἀγαθῶν καὶ ἐλεημοσυνῶν. Lit. "full of good works and alms."

πλήρης. Predicate adjective.

ἔργων . . . ἐλεημοσυνῶν. Genitive of content.

ὧν. Genitive by attraction (see 1:1 on ὧν) to ἔργων . . . ἐλεημοσυνῶν (it normally would have been accusative as the object of ἐποίει).

ἐποίει Impf act ind 3rd sg ποιέω.

9:37 ἐγένετο δὲ ἐν ταῖς ἡμέραις ἐκείναις ἀσθενήσασαν αὐτὴν ἀποθανεῖν· λούσαντες δὲ ἔθηκαν [αὐτὴν] ἐν ὑπερῴῳ.

ἐγένετο δὲ. Introduces the event line of the narrative following the setting of v. 36 (cf. Gault, 392).

ἐγένετο. Aor mid ind 3rd sg γίνομαι.

ἐν ταῖς ἡμέραις ἐκείναις. See 1:15.

ἀσθενήσασαν. Aor act ptc fem acc sg ἀσθενέω. As an attendant circumstance of the infinitive, the participle bears the case of the subject of the infinitive.

αὐτὴν. Accusative subject of the infinitive (see 1:3 on αὐτὸν).

ἀποθανεῖν. Aor act inf ἀποθνῄσκω. The infinitival clause, ἀσθενήσασαν αὐτὴν ἀποθανεῖν, serves as the subject of ἐγένετο (see also v. 32 on κατελθεῖν).

λούσαντες. Aor act ptc masc nom pl λούω (attendant circumstance or temporal).

ἔθηκαν. Aor act ind 3rd pl τίθημι.

9:38 ἐγγὺς δὲ οὔσης Λύδδας τῇ Ἰόππῃ οἱ μαθηταὶ ἀκούσαντες ὅτι Πέτρος ἐστὶν ἐν αὐτῇ ἀπέστειλαν δύο ἄνδρας πρὸς αὐτὸν παρακαλοῦντες, Μὴ ὀκνήσῃς διελθεῖν ἕως ἡμῶν.

ἐγγὺς. Predicate adjective. See 27:8.

οὔσης. Pres act ptc fem gen sg εἰμί. Genitive absolute (see 1:8 on ἐπελθόντος), causal (Levinsohn 1987, 75).

Λύδδας. Genitive subject (see 1:8 on ἐπελθόντος).

ἀκούσαντες. Aor act ptc masc nom pl ἀκούω (temporal).

ὅτι. Introduces the clausal complement (indirect discourse) of ἀκούσαντες.

ἐστὶν. Pres act ind 3rd sg εἰμί. The retention of the accent here (see 1:7 on ἐστιν) may indicate emphasis (Robertson 1934, 233–34; cf. 2:13, 29; 5:25): "they heard that Peter was *there*." The present tense is retained in indirect discourse.

ἀπέστειλαν. Aor act ind 3rd pl ἀποστέλλω.

παρακαλοῦντες. Pres act ptc masc nom pl παρακαλέω. The participle must be adverbial, modifying ἀπέστειλαν, since it is nominative. Most likely it introduces a purpose clause.

Μὴ ὀκνήσῃς διελθεῖν ἕως ἡμῶν. Lit. "you should not hesitate to come down to us."

μὴ ὀκνήσῃς. Aor act subj 2nd sg ὀκνέω (prohibitive subjunctive; see 7:60 on μὴ στήσῃς). On the choice of tense in a negative command, see 20:10 on Μὴ θορυβεῖσθε.

διελθεῖν. Aor act inf διέρχομαι (complementary).

9:39 ἀναστὰς δὲ Πέτρος συνῆλθεν αὐτοῖς· ὃν παραγενόμενον ἀνήγαγον εἰς τὸ ὑπερῷον καὶ παρέστησαν αὐτῷ πᾶσαι αἱ χῆραι κλαίουσαι καὶ ἐπιδεικνύμεναι χιτῶνας καὶ ἱμάτια ὅσα ἐποίει μετ᾽ αὐτῶν οὖσα ἡ Δορκάς.

ἀναστὰς. Aor act ptc masc nom sg ἀνίστημι (attendant circumstance). The participle may carry connotative (a sense of urgency) rather than semantic value here: "Peter immediately went away with them" (see 8:26 on ᾽Ανάστηθι πορεύου; cf. 10:23b).

συνῆλθεν. Aor act ind 3rd sg συνέρχομαι.

αὐτοῖς. Verbs with a συν- prefix take a dative complement.

ὃν παραγενόμενον. This construction (an accusative relative pronoun followed by a coreferential accusative participle) is extremely rare (it occurs only here and at 28:4 in the NT). It appears to function like a genitive absolute (παραγενόμενου αὐτοῦ could have been used instead of ὃν παραγενόμενον). Luke, however, wanted to make another statement about Peter that was closely linked to what precedes so he used a relative pronoun. The relative pronoun is in the accusative case as the direct object of ἀνήγαγον. To identify when Peter was led upstairs, the participle was added. Strictly speaking, the participle is attributive ("They led him who had arrived . . ."). It cannot be adverbial since it does not have the same subject as the finite verb (see Culy 2004).

παραγενόμενον. Aor mid dep ptc masc acc sg παραγίνομαι. The participle is attributive, though in English it should be rendered with a temporal expression (see above).

ἀνήγαγον. Aor act ind 3rd pl ἀνάγω.

παρέστησαν. Aor act ind 3rd pl παρίστημι.

κλαίουσαι. Pres act ptc fem nom pl κλαίω (manner).

ἐπιδεικνύμεναι. Pres mid ptc fem nom pl ἐπιδείκνυμι (manner). The middle voice may indicate that they showed Peter clothes that they were wearing (cf. BDF §316) or simply clothes that Dorcas had given them (cf. Barrett, 485).

ἐποίει. Impf act ind 3rd sg ποιέω.

οὖσα. Pres act ptc fem nom sg εἰμί (temporal).

9:40 ἐκβαλὼν δὲ ἔξω πάντας ὁ Πέτρος καὶ θεὶς τὰ γόνατα προσηύξατο καὶ ἐπιστρέψας πρὸς τὸ σῶμα εἶπεν, Ταβιθά, ἀνάστηθι. ἡ δὲ ἤνοιξεν τοὺς ὀφθαλμοὺς αὐτῆς, καὶ ἰδοῦσα τὸν Πέτρον ἀνεκάθισεν.

ἐκβαλὼν. Aor act ptc masc nom sg ἐκβάλλω (temporal).

πάντας. Substantival direct object of ἐκβαλὼν. Barrett (485) argues that the use of the masculine (instead of πάσας) suggests that there was a group of people including men in the upper room when Peter arrived.

θεὶς τὰ γόνατα. See 7:60.

θεὶς. Aor act ptc masc nom sg τίθημι (temporal).

προσηύξατο. Aor mid dep ind 3rd sg προσεύχομαι.

ἐπιστρέψας. Aor act ptc masc nom sg ἐπιστρέφω (attendant circumstance).

εἶπεν. Aor act ind 3rd sg λέγω.

Ταβιθά. Vocative.

ἀνάστηθι. Aor act impv 2nd sg ἀνίστημι.

ἡ. The article functions like a personal pronoun here (cf. 3:5).

ἤνοιξεν. Aor act ind 3rd sg ἀνοίγω.

ἰδοῦσα. Aor act ptc fem nom sg ὁράω (temporal).

ἀνεκάθισεν. Aor act ind 3rd sg ἀνακαθίζω.

9:41 δοὺς δὲ αὐτῇ χεῖρα ἀνέστησεν αὐτήν· φωνήσας δὲ τοὺς ἁγίους καὶ τὰς χήρας παρέστησεν αὐτὴν ζῶσαν.

δοὺς. Aor act ptc masc nom sg δίδωμι (attendant circumstance).

ἀνέστησεν. Aor act ind 3rd sg ἀνίστημι.

φωνήσας. Aor act ptc masc nom sg φωνέω (temporal).

τοὺς ἁγίους. See v. 13.

παρέστησεν. Aor act ind 3rd sg παρίστημι.

ζῶσαν. Pres act ptc fem acc sg ζάω. The participle functions as the complement in an object-complement double accusative construction (see 1:3 on ζῶντα).

9:42 γνωστὸν δὲ ἐγένετο καθ᾽ ὅλης τῆς Ἰόππης, καὶ ἐπίστευσαν πολλοὶ ἐπὶ τὸν κύριον.

γνωστὸν. Predicate adjective.

ἐγένετο. Aor mid dep ind 3rd sg γίνομαι.
καθ᾽. Distributive.
ἐπίστευσαν. Aor act ind 3rd pl πιστεύω.
ἐπὶ. See 1:8 on ἐφ᾽ ὑμᾶς.

9:43 ᾽Εγένετο δὲ ἡμέρας ἱκανὰς μεῖναι ἐν ᾽Ιόππῃ παρά τινι Σίμωνι βυρσεῖ.

᾽Εγένετο δὲ. It is not clear whether this formulaic expression is intended to introduce the setting of a new episode (cf. Gault, 392), or bring closure to the previous episode.

ἡμέρας. Accusative indicating extent of time (see 7:20 on μῆνας).

μεῖναι. Aor act inf μένω. The subject of the infinitive (Peter) is left implicit. The infinitival clause, ἡμέρας ἱκανὰς μεῖναι ἐν᾽ Ιόππῃ παρά τινι Σίμωνι βυρσεῖ, serves as the subject of ἐγένετο (cf. v. 37 on ἀποθανεῖν).

βυρσεῖ. Dative in apposition to Σίμωνι.

Acts 10:1–8

[1]Now, a certain man in Caesarea named Cornelius, a centurion in the Italian Regiment, [2]who was devout and feared God along with all of his household, and who did many charitable acts for his people and prayed to God regularly, [3]saw clearly in a vision—as if it were mid-afternoon—an angel of God approaching him and saying to him, "Cornelius!" [4]He stared at him and was terrified. He said, "What is it, Lord?" The angel said to him, "Your prayers and charitable acts have gone up as a memorial before God. [5]Now, send men to Joppa and summon a certain Simon, who is called Peter. [6]This man is staying with a certain Simon the Tanner, whose house is by the sea.

[7]When the angel who had been speaking to him left, he called two of (his) personal servants and a devout soldier from among those who served him. [8]After explaining everything to them, he sent them to Joppa.

10:1 ᾽Ανὴρ δέ τις ἐν Καισαρείᾳ ὀνόματι Κορνήλιος, ἑκατοντάρχης ἐκ σπείρης τῆς καλουμένης ᾽Ιταλικῆς,

᾽Ανὴρ . . . τις. In this case, reference to the new character is placed at the beginning of the clause rather than the new spatial setting (ἐν Καισαρείᾳ) because the following narrative "is concerned specifically with Cornelius (the first Gentile convert to Christianity [but see Parsons 1994, 1097]), and the location of the incident is of secondary importance" (Levinsohn 1987, 58). All of vv. 1–2 form the subject of εἶδεν (v. 3).

ὀνόματι. Dative of reference.

Κορνήλιος . . . ἑκατοντάρχης. Nominatives in apposition to ʼΑνήρ.

ἐκ . . . ʼΙταλικῆς. Lit. "from the cohort that is called 'Italian'."

σπείρης. "A Roman military unit of about 600 soldiers (LN 55.9).

καλουμένης. Pres pass ptc fem gen sg καλέω (attributive).

ʼΙταλικῆς. The genitive noun serves as a complement in a passive object-complement double case construction (cf. 1:12 on ʼ Ελαιῶνος).

10:2 εὐσεβὴς καὶ φοβούμενος τὸν θεὸν σὺν παντὶ τῷ οἴκῳ αὐτοῦ, ποιῶν ἐλεημοσύνας πολλὰς τῷ λαῷ καὶ δεόμενος τοῦ θεοῦ διὰ παντός,

εὐσεβὴς. Attributive modifier of ἑκατοντάρχης or substantival in apposition to ʼΑνήρ (v. 1).

φοβούμενος τὸν θεὸν. See 13:16 on οἱ φοβούμενοι.

φοβούμενος. Pres dep ptc masc nom sg φοβέομαι. Attributive modifier of ἑκατοντάρχης or substantival in apposition to ʼΑνὴρ (v. 1).

ποιῶν. Pres act ptc masc nom sg ποιέω. Attributive modifier of ἑκατοντάρχης or substantival in apposition to ʼΑνὴρ (v. 1).

τῷ λαῷ. Dative of advantage.

δεόμενος. Pres dep ptc masc nom sg δέομαι. Attributive modifier of ἑκατοντάρχης or substantival in apposition to ʼΑνὴρ (v. 1).

τοῦ θεοῦ. The verb δέομαι takes its addressee in the genitive case.

διὰ παντός. An idiomatic expression meaning "always" (cf. 2:25; 24:16).

10:3 εἶδεν ἐν ὁράματι φανερῶς ὡσεὶ περὶ ὥραν ἐνάτην τῆς ἡμέρας ἄγγελον τοῦ θεοῦ εἰσελθόντα πρὸς αὐτὸν καὶ εἰπόντα αὐτῷ, Κορνήλιε.

εἶδεν. Aor act ind 3rd sg ὁράω.

ὡσεὶ περὶ ὥραν ἐνάτην τῆς ἡμέρας. Lit. "as about the ninth hour of the day." The phrase ὡσεὶ περὶ occurs only here in the NT. It is not clear whether the Byzantine scribes' preference for ὡσεὶ rather than ὡσεὶ περὶ reflects an attempt to alter the meaning (placing the time of the vision at about 3:00 p.m.), or simply an alternative way of expressing the same thing. As it stands, the sense appears to be that Cornelius saw a vision, and in the vision it appeared to be about 3:00 p.m., a time of day when he would be able to see everything very clearly (φανερῶς).

ἄγγελον. Accusative direct object of εἶδεν.

εἰσελθόντα. Aor act ptc masc acc sg εἰσέρχομαι. The participle functions as the complement in an object-complement double accusative construction (see 1:3 on ζῶντα).

εἰπόντα. Aor act ptc masc acc sg λέγω. The participle functions as a second complement in an object-complement double accusative construction.

Κορνήλιε. Vocative.

10:4 ὁ δὲ ἀτενίσας αὐτῷ καὶ ἔμφοβος γενόμενος εἶπεν, Τί ἐστιν, κύριε; εἶπεν δὲ αὐτῷ, Αἱ προσευχαί σου καὶ αἱ ἐλεημοσύναι σου ἀνέβησαν εἰς μνημόσυνον ἔμπροσθεν τοῦ θεοῦ.

ὁ. The article functions like a personal pronoun here (cf. 3:5).

ἀτενίσας. Aor act ptc masc nom sg ἀτενίζω. Though it is best to translate this participle temporally, its function should probably be described as attendant circumstance since conjoined participles typically bear the same relationship to the finite verb they modify, and it is unlikely that γενόμενος could be read temporally.

ἔμφοβος. Predicate adjective of γενόμενος.

γενόμενος. Aor mid dep ptc masc nom sg γίνομαι (attendant circumstance).

εἶπεν . . . εἶπεν. Aor act ind 3rd sg λέγω.

ἐστιν. Pres act ind 3rd sg εἰμί.

κύριε. Vocative.

σου . . . σου. Subjective genitive.

ἀνέβησαν. Aor act ind 3rd pl ἀναβαίνω.

εἰς. Purpose.

10:5 καὶ νῦν πέμψον ἄνδρας εἰς Ἰόππην καὶ μετάπεμψαι Σίμωνά τινα ὃς ἐπικαλεῖται Πέτρος·

καὶ νῦν. See 4:29 on καὶ τὰ νῦν.

πέμψον. Aor act impv 2nd sg πέμπω.

μετάπεμψαι. Aor mid impv 2nd sg μεταπέμπω. The claim that the middle implies personal interest (cf. Rogers and Rogers, 251) may be true. Since, however, this verb never appears in the active voice, and the notion of personal interest is inherent in the verb itself, one should probably not make too much of the middle voice.

Σίμωνά. The second accent comes from the enclitic τινα (see 1:4 on ἠκούσατέ).

ἐπικαλεῖται. Pres pass ind 3rd sg ἐπικαλέω.

Πέτρος. Predicate nominative.

10:6 οὗτος ξενίζεται παρά τινι Σίμωνι βυρσεῖ, ᾧ ἐστιν οἰκία παρὰ θάλασσαν.

ξενίζεται. Pres pass ind 3rd sg ξενίζω.

παρά. The rare use of παρά with the dative should probably not be viewed as equivalent to ἐν (contra Moulton, 273: "in the house of"). When used with ξενίζω, παρά more likely draws attention to the person who serves as the host (cf. 21:16 on παρ' . . . ξενισθῶμεν). The clause literally reads: "This man is being entertained as a guest in the presence of a certain Simon the Tanner."

βυρσεῖ. Dative in apposition to Σίμωνι.

ᾧ. Dative of possession (with εἰμί).

ἐστιν. Pres act ind 3rd sg εἰμί.

οἰκία. Nominative subject of ἐστιν.

10:7 ὡς δὲ ἀπῆλθεν ὁ ἄγγελος ὁ λαλῶν αὐτῷ, φωνήσας δύο τῶν οἰκετῶν καὶ στρατιώτην εὐσεβῆ τῶν προσκαρτερούντων αὐτῷ

ὡς. Temporal (see 18:5).

ἀπῆλθεν. Aor act ind 3rd sg ἀπέρχομαι.

λαλῶν. Pres act ptc masc nom sg λαλέω (attributive).

φωνήσας. Aor act ptc masc nom sg φωνέω. Conjoined with ἐξηγησάμενος (v. 8) this participle should probably be taken as a temporal modifier of ἀπέστειλεν (v. 8).

τῶν οἰκετῶν. Partitive genitive.

προσκαρτερούντων. Pres act ptc masc gen pl προσκαρτερέω (substantival, partitive genitive).

αὐτῷ. Dative complement of προσκαρτερέω (cf. 1:14 on τῇ προσευχῇ).

10:8 καὶ ἐξηγησάμενος ἅπαντα αὐτοῖς ἀπέστειλεν αὐτοὺς εἰς τὴν Ἰόππην.

ἐξηγησάμενος. Aor mid dep ptc masc nom sg ἐξηγέομαι (temporal).
ἀπέστειλεν. Aor act ind 3rd sg ἀποστέλλω.

Acts 10:9–23a

[9]On the next day, at about noon, while they were traveling and getting close to the city, Peter went up on the roof to pray. [10]He became hungry and wanted to eat, but while they were preparing the meal, he went into a trance. [11]He saw the sky standing open and an object, like a large sheet, descending and being lowered to the ground by its four corners. [12]On it were all kinds of four-footed animals and reptiles and birds. [13]Then a voice (said) to him, "Get up, Peter! Slaughter and eat!" [14]But Peter replied, "Certainly not, Lord! For I have never eaten anything that is impure and contaminated!" [15]Then the voice (spoke) to him again, a second time: "That which God has made pure, do not call impure." [16]This happened three times, and then the object was immediately taken (back) up into the sky.

[17]While Peter was wondering what the vision that he had seen could possibly mean, the men sent by Cornelius had learned where Simon's house was and were (now) standing at the gate! [18]They called out and asked, "Is Simon, who is called Peter, staying here?" [19]Now, while Peter was (still) thinking about the vision, the Spirit said [to him], "Three men are looking for you! [20]Go right down and go with them, without hesitation, for I have sent them." [21]So Peter went down and said to the men, "I am the one you are looking for. Why have you come?" [22]They replied, "Cornelius, a centurion who is a just man and who fears God and is respected by the whole nation of Jews, was instructed by a holy angel to summon you to his house and to listen to what you say." [23]So he invited them in to stay with him.

10:9 Τῇ δὲ ἐπαύριον, ὁδοιπορούντων ἐκείνων καὶ τῇ πόλει ἐγγιζόντων ἀνέβη Πέτρος ἐπὶ τὸ δῶμα προσεύξασθαι περὶ ὥραν ἕκτην.

ὁδοιπορούντων. Pres act ptc masc gen pl ὁδοιπορέω. Genitive absolute (see 1:8 on ἐπελθόντος), temporal.
ἐκείνων. Genitive subject (see 1:8 on ἐπελθόντος).
ἐγγιζόντων. Pres act ptc masc gen pl ἐγγίζω. Genitive absolute (see

1:8 on ἐπελθόντος), temporal.

ἀνέβη. Aor act ind 3rd sg ἀναβαίνω.

προσεύξασθαι. Aor mid dep inf προσεύχομαι (purpose).

10:10 ἐγένετο δὲ πρόσπεινος καὶ ἤθελεν γεύσασθαι, παρασκευαζόντων δὲ αὐτῶν ἐγένετο ἐπ' αὐτὸν ἔκστασις

ἐγένετο. Aor mid dep ind 3rd sg γίνομαι.

πρόσπεινος. Predicate adjective.

ἤθελεν. Impf act ind 3rd sg θέλω.

γεύσασθαι. Aor mid dep inf γεύομαι (complementary).

παρασκευαζόντων. Pres act ptc masc gen pl παρασκευάζω. Genitive absolute (see 1:8 on ἐπελθόντος), temporal.

αὐτῶν. Genitive subject (see 1:8 on ἐπελθόντος).

ἐγένετο ἐπ' αὐτὸν ἔκστασις. Lit. "a trance happened upon him." Many scribes apparently attempted to make the sense clearer by changing the verb: ἐπέπεσεν ἐπ' αὐτὸν ἔκστασις (see E Ψ*Byz al*).

ἔκστασις. Nominative subject of ἐγένετο.

10:11 καὶ θεωρεῖ τὸν οὐρανὸν ἀνεῳγμένον καὶ καταβαῖνον σκεῦός τι ὡς ὀθόνην μεγάλην τέσσαρσιν ἀρχαῖς καθιέμενον ἐπὶ τῆς γῆς,

θεωρεῖ. Pres act ind 3rd sg θεωρέω. The shift to the ("historic") present highlights the account of Peter's vision (Porter 1994, 31).

τὸν οὐρανὸν. The first of two accusative direct objects of θεωρεῖ.

ἀνεῳγμένον. Prf pass ptc masc acc sg ἀνοίγω. The participle functions as the complement in an object-complement double accusative construction (see 1:3 on ζῶντα) modifiying τὸν οὐρανὸν.

καταβαῖνον. Pres act ptc neut acc sg καταβαίνω. The participle functions as the complement in an object-complement double accusative construction (see 1:3 on ζῶντα) modifiying σκεῦός.

σκεῦός. The second of two accusative direct objects of θεωρεῖ. The second accent comes from the enclitic τι (see 1:4 on ἠκούσατέ).

τέσσαρσιν ἀρχαῖς. The dative noun phrase provides the means by which the sheet was lowered.

καθιέμενον. Pres pass ptc neut acc sg καθίημι. Unlike in 11:5 where the feminine participle (καθιεμένην) modifies ὀθόνην μεγάλην, here the neuter participle modifies σκεῦός τι. Thus, given the absence of a conjunction, the participle stands in apposition to the previous participle (καταβαῖνον) and functions in the same manner, i.e., as a complement in an object-complement double accusative construction.

10:12 ἐν ᾧ ὑπῆρχεν πάντα τὰ τετράποδα καὶ ἑρπετὰ τῆς γῆς καὶ πετεινὰ τοῦ οὐρανοῦ.

ἐν ᾧ. Lit. "in it."

ὑπῆρχεν. Impf act ind 3rd sg ὑπάρχω. The singular verb is used with a compound subject.

ἑρπετὰ τῆς γῆς. Lit. "reptiles of the earth." Louw and Nida (4.51) note that "though ἑρπετόν is often interpreted as referring only to snakes, it also includes in biblical contexts (as the result of the influence of classifications based on Hebrew terminology, as in Gen 1.25, 26, and 30) a number of small four-footed animals as well as snakes, for example, rats, mice, frogs, toads, salamanders, and lizards. However, in the various NT contexts (e.g., Acts 10.12, 11.6; Rom 1.23; and Jas 3.7 where 'creeping things' are contrasted with birds, animals, and fish) it is probably more satisfactory to use a term which designates primarily snakes."

πετεινὰ τοῦ οὐρανοῦ. Lit. "birds of the sky."

10:13 καὶ ἐγένετο φωνὴ πρὸς αὐτόν, Ἀναστάς, Πέτρε, θῦσον καὶ φάγε.

ἐγένετο. Aor mid dep ind 3rd sg γίνομαι.

φωνὴ. Nominative subject of personal ἐγένετο (lit. "a voice happened toward him").

Ἀναστάς. Aor act ptc masc nom sg ἀνίστημι (with an imperative main verb an attendant circumstance participle carries imperatival force). Once again, it is possible that this imperative carries connotative value (a sense of urgency) rather than semantic value (thus, "Slaughter and eat, right away!" See 8:26 on Ἀνάστηθι . . . πορεύου; cf. 9:6, 11, 18).

Πέτρε. Vocative. In narrative texts, such as Acts, the vocative normally occurs in the sentence-initial position. Two factors may lead to displacement from this position: (1) when another constituent (such as a one-word adverbial phrase or an interjection) must occur in that position; and (2) when there is an "increased social distance between the interlocutors" (Clark 1999, 102). The latter may occur when a superior addresses an inferior (Acts 10:13; 11:7; 18:14; 21:20; 26:24; 27:24), when an inferior addresses a superior (Acts 24:3; 26:2, 25, 27; 27:25; and possibly 1:24 and 23:5), or when a rebuke is involved (23:3; and possibly 10:14; 11:8; 27:21; see Clark 1999, 101–4).

θῦσον. Aor act impv 2nd sg θύω.

φάγε. Aor act impv 2nd sg ἐσθίω.

10:14 ὁ δὲ Πέτρος εἶπεν, Μηδαμῶς, κύριε, ὅτι οὐδέποτε ἔφαγον πᾶν κοινὸν καὶ ἀκάθαρτον.

εἶπεν. Aor act ind 3rd sg λέγω.

Μηδαμῶς. This adverb, here functioning as an interjection, marks a strongly emphatic negation: "by no means, most certainly not, not a chance!" (LN 69.6).

κύριε. The placement of the vocative may indicate a rebuke (see v. 13 on Πέτρε).

ὅτι. Causal.

ἔφαγον. Aor act ind 1st sg ἐσθίω.

πᾶν. With the negative οὐδέποτε: "any."

κοινὸν καὶ ἀκάθαρτον. The conjoined substantival adjectives probably function as a doublet emphasizing Peter's abhorence at the idea. Both terms refer to being impure or contaminated from a religious point of view.

10:15 καὶ φωνὴ πάλιν ἐκ δευτέρου πρὸς αὐτόν, Ἃ ὁ θεὸς ἐκαθάρισεν σὺ μὴ κοίνου.

φωνὴ. Nominative subject of an implicit verb (ἐγένετο) or nominative absolute (see Porter 1994, 85).

πάλιν ἐκ δευτέρου. BDF (§484) notes that strictly speaking this expression is not redundant since the second element is more specific than the first.

ἐκ δευτέρου. A rare temporal use of ἐκ (cf. 9:33 on ἐξ ἐτῶν ὀκτώ).

Ἃ. The relative pronoun introduces a headless relative clause (see 3:6 on ὅ): "*that* which . . . ."

ἐκαθάρισεν. Aor act ind 3rd sg καθαρίζω.

σὺ. The use of the explicit fronted (see 3:13 on ὑμεῖς) subject pronoun makes the statement more emphatic.

κοίνου. Pres act impv 2nd sg κοινόω. "To call or to regard something as common or defiled" (LN 53.40).

10:16 τοῦτο δὲ ἐγένετο ἐπὶ τρὶς καὶ εὐθὺς ἀνελήμφθη τὸ σκεῦος εἰς τὸν οὐρανόν.

τοῦτο. The antecedent is the interchange between Peter and the voice.
ἐγένετο. Aor mid dep ind 3rd sg γίνομαι.
ἐπὶ τρίς. "Three times."
ἀνελήμφθη. Aor pass ind 3rd sg ἀναλαμβάνω.

10:17 Ὡς δὲ ἐν ἑαυτῷ διηπόρει ὁ Πέτρος τί ἂν εἴη τὸ ὅραμα ὃ εἶδεν, ἰδοὺ οἱ ἄνδρες οἱ ἀπεσταλμένοι ὑπὸ τοῦ Κορνηλίου διερωτήσαντες τὴν οἰκίαν τοῦ Σίμωνος ἐπέστησαν ἐπὶ τὸν πυλῶνα,

Ὡς. Temporal (see 18:5).
ἐν ἑαυτῷ διηπόρει. Lit. "was perplexed in himself."
διηπόρει. Impf act ind 3rd sg διαπορέω.
τί ἂν εἴη τὸ ὅραμα. See 5:24 on τί ἂν γένοιτο τοῦτο.
εἴη. Pres act opt 3rd sg εἰμί. On the use of the optative, see 5:24.
τὸ ὅραμα Nominative subject of εἴη.
εἶδεν. Aor act ind 3rd sg ὁράω.
ἰδοὺ. See 1:10.
ἀπεσταλμένοι. Prf pass ptc masc nom pl ἀποστέλλω (attributive).
διερωτήσαντες. Aor act ptc masc nom pl διερωτάω (temporal). "To acquire information by questioning" (LN 27.11).
ἐπέστησαν. Aor act ind 3rd pl ἐφίστημι.
ἐπί. See 1:8 on ἐφ᾽ ὑμᾶς.

10:18 καὶ φωνήσαντες ἐπυνθάνοντο εἰ Σίμων ὁ ἐπικαλούμενος Πέτρος ἐνθάδε ξενίζεται.

φωνήσαντες. Aor act ptc masc nom pl φωνέω. The participle should probably be taken as indicating a redundant attendant circumstance of ἐπυνθάνοντο: "they called out and asked." It could, however, indicate the means of their asking ("they asked by shouting out"), or a separate temporal event that preceded their inquiry ("after calling out—to make their presence known—they asked").
ἐπυνθάνοντο. Impf dep ind 3rd pl πυνθάνομαι.
εἰ. Probably introduces a direct question here since ἐνθάδε is used rather than ἐκεί (see Moule, 154).
ἐπικαλούμενος. Pres pass ptc masc nom sg ἐπικαλέω (attributive).

Πέτρος. Complement in a subject-complement double nominative construction with the passive ἐπικαλούμενος (cf. 4:36 on υἱὸς and 1:12 on 'Ελαιῶνος).

ξενίζεται. Pres pass ind 3rd sg ξενίζω.

10:19 τοῦ δὲ Πέτρου διενθυμουμένου περὶ τοῦ ὁράματος εἶπεν [αὐτῷ] τὸ πνεῦμα, 'Ιδοὺ ἄνδρες τρεῖς ζητοῦντές σε,

Πέτρου. Genitive subject (see 1:8 on ἐπελθόντος).

διενθυμουμένου. Pres dep ptc masc gen sg διενθυμέομαι. Genitive absolute (see 1:8 on ἐπελθόντος), temporal.

εἶπεν. Aor act ind 3rd sg λέγω.

[αὐτῷ]. The use of brackets in UBS[4]/NA[27] to indicate that the enclosed text is disputed, implies far more uncertainty than the data indicates. The omission of the pronoun by one witness (Codex B) can easily be explained as a natural (accidental) omission of information that is already implicit in the text. Similarly, the variation in the placement of the pronoun should probably be viewed as an intuitive change by scribes who accidentally placed αὐτῷ in its more typical position following the subject: εἶπεν τὸ πνεῦμα αὐτῷ is found in 𝔓[74] ℵ A C *al.* The UBS[4]/NA[27] text is supported by 𝔓[45] D E Ψ *Byz al.*

'Ιδοὺ. See 1:10.

ἄνδρες. Nominative absolute (there is no finite verb in UBS[4]/NA[27]).

τρεῖς. The UBS[4]/NA[27] text is supported by 𝔓[74] ℵ A C E 33 81 *al.* Codex B reads δύο, while D Ψ *Byz al* omit the number altogether. Metzger (373) suggests that an accidental omission could have occurred as a result of the similar endings of τρεῖς and ἄνδρες. Omanson suggests that the reading of Codex B may indicate that the scribe (or perhaps Luke) viewed the two servants of v. 7 as the messengers.

ζητοῦντές. Pres act ptc masc nom pl ζητέω. Since 'Ιδοὺ does not require that a complete sentence follow, the participle should be viewed as attributive (lit. "Behold, three men who are seeking you!"). Many scribes were apparently uncomfortable with the lack of a finite verb (the harder reading) and changed the participle (found in 𝔓[74] ℵ B 81 *pc*) to ζητοῦσιν (𝔓[45] A C D E Ψ *Byz*). The second accent comes from the enclitic σε (see 1:4 on ἠκούσατέ).

10:20 ἀλλὰ ἀναστὰς κατάβηθι καὶ πορεύου σὺν αὐτοῖς μηδὲν διακρινόμενος ὅτι ἐγὼ ἀπέσταλκα αὐτούς.

ἀλλὰ. The use of this conjunction suggests that the directions that follow are going to go against Peter's expectations. Smyth (2784c) argues that when used in a command, as here, ἀλλά often implies an impatient tone.

ἀναστὰς. Aor act ptc masc nom sg ἀνίστημι (with an imperative main verb an attendant circumstance participle carries imperatival force). On the pragmatic force of the participle, see v. 13.

κατάβηθι. Aor act impv 2nd sg καταβαίνω.

πορεύου. Pres dep impv 2nd sg πορεύομαι.

μηδὲν διακρινόμενος. Lit. "doubting nothing."

μηδὲν. Accusative direct object of διακρινόμενος.

διακρινόμενος. Pres mid ptc masc nom sg διακρίνω (manner).

ὅτι. Introduces the reason why Peter should follow these unusual and unexpected instructions.

ἐγὼ. The explicit fronted (see 3:13 on ὑμεῖς) subject pronoun lends an emphatic tone to the command.

ἀπέσταλκα. Prf act ind 1st sg ἀποστέλλω.

10:21 καταβὰς δὲ Πέτρος πρὸς τοὺς ἄνδρας εἶπεν, Ἰδοὺ ἐγώ εἰμι ὃν ζητεῖτε· τίς ἡ αἰτία δι' ἣν πάρεστε;

καταβὰς. Aor act ptc masc nom sg καταβαίνω (attendant circumstance).

πρὸς τοὺς ἄνδρας. The prepositional phrase probably modifies εἶπεν rather than καταβὰς ("went down to them").

εἶπεν. Aor act ind 3rd sg λέγω.

Ἰδοὺ ἐγὼ. See 9:10.

εἰμι. Pres act ind 1st sg εἰμί. On the lack of accent, see 1:7 on ἐστιν.

ὃν. The relative pronoun introduces a headless relative clause (see 3:6 on ὃ). The predicate nominative antecedent is unexpressed.

ζητεῖτε. Pres act ind 2nd pl ζητέω.

τίς ἡ αἰτία δι' ἣν πάρεστε; Lit. "What is the reason for which you are here?"

δι'. Causal.

πάρεστε. Pres act ind 2nd pl πάρειμι.

10:22 οἱ δὲ εἶπαν, Κορνήλιος ἑκατοντάρχης, ἀνὴρ δίκαιος καὶ φοβούμενος τὸν θεὸν μαρτυρούμενός τε ὑπὸ ὅλου τοῦ ἔθνους τῶν Ἰουδαίων, ἐχρηματίσθη ὑπὸ ἀγγέλου ἁγίου μεταπέμψασθαί σε εἰς τὸν οἶκον αὐτοῦ καὶ ἀκοῦσαι ῥήματα παρὰ σοῦ.

οἱ. The article functions like a personal pronoun here (cf. 3:5).

εἶπαν. Aor act ind 3rd pl λέγω.

ἑκατοντάρχης. Nominative in apposition to Κορνήλιος.

ἀνὴρ. Nominative in apposition to Κορνήλιος.

φοβούμενος τὸν θεὸν. See 13:16 on οἱ φοβούμενοι.

φοβούμενος. Pres dep ptc masc nom sg φοβέομαι. The participle should probably be taken as an attributive modifier of ἀνὴρ since it is linked to the attributive adjective δίκαιος by the conjunction καί.

μαρτυρούμενός. Pres pass ptc masc nom sg μαρτυρέω (attributive). The sense of μαρτυρέω here is probably "spoken well of" or "respected" (cf. 16:2; 22:12). The second accent comes from the enclitic τε (see 1:4 on ἠκούσατέ).

ἐχρηματίσθη. Aor pass ind 3rd sg χρηματίζω.

μεταπέμψασθαί. Aor mid inf μεταπέμπω (indirect discourse). The second accent comes from the enclitic σε (see 1:4 on ἠκούσατέ).

ἀκοῦσαι ῥήματα παρὰ σοῦ. Lit. "to hear words from you."

ἀκοῦσαι. Aor act inf ἀκούω (indirect discourse).

10:23a εἰσκαλεσάμενος οὖν αὐτοὺς ἐξένισεν.

εἰσκαλεσάμενος . . . αὐτοὺς ἐξένισεν. Lit. "he invited them in and showed them hospitality."

εἰσκαλεσάμενος. Aor mid dep ptc masc nom sg εἰσκαλέομαι (attendant circumstance).

οὖν. The conjunction "makes the consequential relationship explicit, and tells the reader that Peter is acting in conformity with the divine instruction 'to accompany them' (v 20)" (Levinsohn 1987, 139).

ἐξένισεν. Aor act ind 3rd sg ξενίζω.

Acts 10:23b–33

[23b]The next day he got up and went with them, and some of the believers from Joppa went along with him. [24]On the following day, they entered Caesarea. Now, Cornelius was expecting them so he had called together his relatives and close friends. [25]When Peter arrived, Cornelius

met him, fell at his feet and began to worship him. [26]But Peter helped him up, saying, "Get up! I myself am also (just) a man." [27]Then, as he talked with him, he went in and found many people had gathered. [28]He said to them, "You yourselves know how it is forbidden for a Jewish man to associate with or visit a foreigner; but God has shown me that no one should call a person impure or contaminated. [29]That is why I came without any objection when I was summoned. May I ask, then, why you sent for me?"

[30]Then Cornelius said, "Four days ago, at this very hour, I was praying the ninth hour prayer in my house. Suddenly, a man in shining clothing stood before me!" [31]He said, 'Cornelius, God has listened to your prayer and he is aware of your charitable acts. [32]So send (someone) to Joppa and summon Simon, who is called Peter. He is staying in the house of Simon the Tanner by the sea.' [33]Therefore, I immediately sent (someone) to you, and you have done well by coming. So, all of us are now here in God's presence to hear all that the Lord has instructed you (to say)."

10:23b Τῇ δὲ ἐπαύριον ἀναστὰς ἐξῆλθεν σὺν αὐτοῖς καί τινες τῶν ἀδελφῶν τῶν ἀπὸ Ἰόππης συνῆλθον αὐτῷ.

ἀναστὰς. Aor act ptc masc nom sg ἀνίστημι (attendant circumstance). The participle may carry connotative (a sense of urgency) rather than semantic value here: "Peter immediately went away with them" (see 8:26 on Ἀνάστηθι . . . πορεύου; cf. 9:39).

ἐξῆλθεν. Aor act ind 3rd sg ἐξέρχομαι.

τῶν ἀδελφῶν. Partitive genitive. On the sense of ἀδελφῶν, see 1:15.

τῶν ἀπὸ Ἰόππης. The article functions as an adjectivizer (see 2:5 on τῶν ὑπὸ τὸν οὐρανόν), changing the prepositional phrase into an attributive modifier.

συνῆλθον. Aor act ind 3rd pl συνέρχομαι.

αὐτῷ. Verbs with a συν- prefix take a dative complement.

10:24 τῇ δὲ ἐπαύριον εἰσῆλθεν εἰς τὴν Καισάρειαν· ὁ δὲ Κορνήλιος ἦν προσδοκῶν αὐτούς συγκαλεσάμενος τοὺς συγγενεῖς αὐτοῦ καὶ τοὺς ἀναγκαίους φίλους.

εἰσῆλθεν. Aor act ind 3rd sg εἰσέρχομαι. Many manuscripts have the plural εἰσῆλθον (𝔓[74] א A C E Byz *al*) rather than the singular form attested by B D Ψ *al*. The plural form is most likely the original (contra Metzger, 374; Omanson), given the preceding reference to a group with Peter and the following clause that refers to the entire group (αὐτούς). A change to the singular may have been introduced to focus more attention on Peter.

εἰς. See 1:8 on ἐφ᾽ ὑμᾶς.

ἦν. Impf ind 3rd sg εἰμί.

προσδοκῶν. Pres act ptc masc nom sg προσδοκάω (imperfect periphrastic; see 1:10 on ἀτενίζοντες).

συγκαλεσάμενος. Aor mid ptc masc nom sg συγκαλέω (result or attendant circumstance).

10:25 ὡς δὲ ἐγένετο τοῦ εἰσελθεῖν τὸν Πέτρον, συναντήσας αὐτῷ ὁ Κορνήλιος πεσὼν ἐπὶ τοὺς πόδας προσεκύνησεν.

ὡς δὲ ἐγένετο. This phrase, which takes an infinitival subject, occurs only in Acts in the NT (see also 14:5; 21:1; cf. 2 Macc 1:22). It may emphasize the close temporal link between this event and the ones that follow.

ὡς. Temporal (see 18:5).

ἐγένετο. Aor mid dep ind 3rd sg γίνομαι.

εἰσελθεῖν. Aor act inf εἰσέρχομαι. The infinitival clause, τοῦ εἰσελθεῖν τὸν Πέτρον, serves as the subject of ἐγένετο (see also 9:32 on κατελθεῖν).

τὸν Πέτρον. Accusative subject of the infinitive (see 1:3 on αὐτὸν).

συναντήσας. Aor act ptc masc nom sg συναντάω (attendant circumstance).

αὐτῷ. Verbs with a συν- prefix take a dative complement.

πεσὼν. Aor act ptc masc nom sg πίπτω (attendant circumstance).

προσεκύνησεν. Aor act ind 3rd sg προσκυνέω. Although the verb can simply mean "to prostrate oneself before someone as an act of reverence, fear, or supplication" (LN 17.21), given Peter's response in the following verse, the more specific sense of "worship" is probably intended.

10:26 ὁ δὲ Πέτρος ἤγειρεν αὐτὸν λέγων, Ἀνάστηθι· καὶ ἐγὼ αὐτὸς ἄνθρωπός εἰμι.

ἤγειρεν. Aor act ind 3rd sg ἐγείρω.

λέγων. Pres act ptc masc nom sg λέγω (attendant circumstance).

᾿Ανάστηθι. Aor act impv 2nd sg ἀνίστημι.

ἐγὼ αὐτὸς ἄνθρωπός. The fronted (see 3:13 on ὑμεῖς) subject and predicate, combined with an intensive subject pronoun αὐτὸς, form a highly emphatic statement.

ἄνθρωπός. Predicate nominative. The second accent comes from the enclitic εἰμι (see 1:4 on ἠκούσατέ).

εἰμι. Pres act ind 1st sg εἰμί.

10:27 καὶ συνομιλῶν αὐτῷ εἰσῆλθεν καὶ εὑρίσκει συνεληλυθότας πολλούς,

συνομιλῶν. Pres act ptc masc nom sg συνομιλέω (manner).

αὐτῷ. Verbs with a συν- prefix take a dative complement.

εἰσῆλθεν. Aor act ind 3rd sg εἰσέρχομαι.

εὑρίσκει. Pres act ind 3rd sg εὑρίσκω. The shift to the present tense may indicate a sense of surprise on Peter's part.

συνεληλυθότας. Prf act ptc masc acc pl συνέρχομαι. Typically, in object-complement double accusative constructions (see 1:3 on ζῶντα), the participle follows the direct object and functions as the complement. Here it precedes πολλούς, the substantival direct object.

10:28 ἔφη τε πρὸς αὐτούς, ῾Υμεῖς ἐπίστασθε ὡς ἀθέμιτόν ἐστιν ἀνδρὶ ᾿Ιουδαίῳ κολλᾶσθαι ἢ προσέρχεσθαι ἀλλοφύλῳ· κἀμοὶ ὁ θεὸς ἔδειξεν μηδένα κοινὸν ἢ ἀκάθαρτον λέγειν ἄνθρωπον·

ἔφη. Aor/Impf act ind 3rd sg φημί. On the tense, see 7:2.

῾Υμεῖς. The explicit subject pronoun should probably be taken as intensive.

ἐπίστασθε. Pres dep ind 2nd pl ἐπίσταμαι.

ὡς. Introduces a clausal complement of ἐπίστασθε. On the use of this term as a complementizer, see v. 38.

ἀθέμιτόν. Predicate adjective. The second accent comes from the enclitic ἐστιν (see 1:4 on ἠκούσατέ).

ἐστιν. Pres act ind 3rd sg εἰμί.

ἀνδρὶ. Dative of respect.

κολλᾶσθαι. Pres pass inf κολλάω (subject of ἐστιν; lit. "to associate with or visit a foreigner is unlawful for a Jewish man").

προσέρχεσθαι. Pres dep inf προσέρχομαι (subject of ἐστιν).

ἀλλοφύλῳ. Dative complement of κολλᾶσθαι and προσέρχεσθαι.

κἀμοὶ. A shortened form (crasis) of καὶ ἐμοί (καί = adversative; ἐμοί = dative indirect object of ἔδειξεν).

ἔδειξεν. Aor act ind 3rd sg δείκνυμι.

μηδένα. Most scholars take this accusative adjective as an emphatic attributive modifier of ἄνθρωπον (because it is placed in front of the infinitive; see 3:13 on ὑμεῖς), with the subject of λέγειν remaining unexpressed ("God has shown me that I should not call *any* person impure or contaminated"). Given the distance between μηδένα and ἄνθρωπον, however, it would also be possible to take μηδένα as the accusative subject of the infinitive (see 1:3 on αὐτὸν): "no one should call a person impure or contaminated."

κοινὸν ἢ ἀκάθαρτον. The adjectival complement in an object-complement double accusative construction (cf. 1:3 on ζῶντα) with λέγω.

λέγειν. Pres act inf λέγω. The whole infinitival clause, μηδένα κοινὸν ἢ ἀκάθαρτον λέγειν ἄνθρωπον, serves as the direct object of ἔδειξεν.

ἄνθρωπον. Accusative direct object of λέγειν (in an object-complement double accusative construction; cf. 1:3 on ζῶντα).

10:29 διὸ καὶ ἀναντιρρήτως ἦλθον μεταπεμφθείς. πυνθάνομαι οὖν τίνι λόγῳ μετεπέμψασθέ με;

διὸ καὶ. "That is why" (O'Brien, 233).

ἀναντιρρήτως. Only here in the NT ("pertaining to what cannot be spoken against or objected to"; LN 33.458).

ἦλθον. Aor act ind 1st sg ἔρχομαι.

μεταπεμφθείς. Aor pass ptc masc nom sg μεταπέμπω (temporal).

πυνθάνομαι. Pres dep ind 1st sg πυνθάνομαι.

τίνι λόγῳ. Lit. "for what reason." This noun phrase should probably be taken as a dative of reference/respect. The notion of cause is inherent in the term λόγῳ.

μετεπέμψασθέ. Aor mid ind 2nd pl μεταπέμπω. The second accent comes from the enclitic με (see 1:4 on ἠκούσατέ).

10:30 καὶ ὁ Κορνήλιος ἔφη, Ἀπὸ τετάρτης ἡμέρας μέχρι ταύτης τῆς ὥρας ἤμην τὴν ἐνάτην προσευχόμενος ἐν τῷ οἴκῳ μου, καὶ ἰδοὺ ἀνὴρ ἔστη ἐνώπιόν μου ἐν ἐσθῆτι λαμπρᾷ

ἔφη. Aor/Impf act ind 3rd sg φημι. On the tense, see 7:2.

᾽Απὸ . . . ὥρας. The meaning of this temporal expression (lit. "from the fourth day until this hour") is difficult to determine. Perhaps the confusion stems from Cornelius' attempt to reckon the time of the vision with reference to the time of his current conversation. The reference to four days rather than three suggests a different approach to counting days in which the day of the vision is viewed as the first day. Some English translations consequently use "three days."

ἤμην. Impf ind 1st sg εἰμί.

τὴν ἐνάτην. This expression is probably short for "the prayer that is said at the ninth hour."

προσευχόμενος. Pres mid ptc masc nom sg προσεύχομαι (imperfect periphrastic; see 1:10 on ἀτενίζοντες).

ἰδοὺ. See 1:10.

ἔστη. Aor act ind 3rd sg ἵστημι.

ἐν ἐσθῆτι λαμπρᾷ. See 1:10 on ἐν ἐσθήσεσι λευκαῖς.

10:31 καὶ φησίν, Κορνήλιε, εἰσηκούσθη σου ἡ προσευχὴ καὶ αἱ ἐλεημοσύναι σου ἐμνήσθησαν ἐνώπιον τοῦ θεοῦ.

φησίν. Pres act ind 3rd sg φημί.

Κορνήλιε. Vocative.

εἰσηκούσθη . . . θεοῦ. Lit. "Your prayer has been listened to and your charitable acts have been remembered before God." This type of language is commonly used in the LXX to indicate that God had decided to deliver his people or a particular person from a serious problem (see, e.g., Gen 30:22—ἐμνήσθη δὲ ὁ θεὸς τῆς Ραχηλ καὶ ἐπήκουσεν αὐτῆς ὁ θεὸς καὶ ἀνέῳξεν αὐτῆς τὴν μήτραν).

εἰσηκούσθη. Aor pass ind 3rd sg εἰσακούω.

ἐμνήσθησαν ἐνώπιον τοῦ θεοῦ. This construction is equivalent to the common LXX construction that uses the passive verb with God as the nominative subject and the person remembered in the genitive case (e.g., Gen 8:1—ἐμνήσθη ὁ θεὸς τοῦ Νωε). The focus is less on God recalling something than on his responding to a situation of which he is aware (see above). Sometimes that situation demands judgment (see Rev 16:19, the only other NT use of ἐμνήσθησαν ἐνώπιον τοῦ θεοῦ).

ἐμνήσθησαν. Aor pass ind 3rd pl μιμνῄσκομαι.

10:32 πέμψον οὖν εἰς Ἰόππην καὶ μετακάλεσαι Σίμωνα ὃς ἐπικαλεῖται Πέτρος, οὗτος ξενίζεται ἐν οἰκίᾳ Σίμωνος βυρσέως παρὰ θάλασσαν.

πέμψον. Aor act impv 2nd sg πέμπω.

μετακάλεσαι. Aor mid impv 2nd sg μετακαλέω.

ἐπικαλεῖται. Pres pass ind 3rd sg ἐπικαλέω.

Πέτρος. Complement in a subject-complement double nominative construction with the passive ἐπικαλεῖται (cf. 4:36 on ὑιος and 1:12 on' Ελαιῶνος).

ξενίζεται. Pres pass ind 3rd sg ξενίζω.

βυρσέως. Genitive in apposition to Σίμωνος.

10:33 ἐξαυτῆς οὖν ἔπεμψα πρὸς σέ, σύ τε καλῶς ἐποίησας παραγενόμενος. νῦν οὖν πάντες ἡμεῖς ἐνώπιον τοῦ θεοῦ πάρεσμεν ἀκοῦσαι πάντα τὰ προστεταγμένα σοι ὑπὸ τοῦ κυρίου.

ἐξαυτῆς. "Immediately."

ἔπεμψα. Aor act ind 1st sg πέμπω.

ἐποίησας. Aor act ind 2nd sg ποιέω.

παραγενόμενος. Aor mid dep ptc masc nom sg παραγίνομαι. The participle explains the way in which Peter did well. Thus, it could be considered epexegetical, or it may indicate the means or cause of his "doing well" (cf. Phil 4:14 and 3 John 1:6 where the same construction occurs).

πάρεσμεν. Pres act ind 1st pl πάρειμι.

ἀκοῦσαι. Aor act inf ἀκούω (purpose).

τὰ προστεταγμένα. Prf pass ptc neut acc pl προστάσσω (substantival; see above).

τὰ. The article functions as a nominalizer (see 1:3 on τὰ) that changes the participial clause into a substantive.

Acts 10:34–43

[34]Then Peter opened (his) mouth and said, "I have truly come to understand that God does not show favoritism. [35]Rather, in every nation, the one who fears him and does what is right is acceptable to him. [36](You know) the message that he sent to the people of Israel preaching the good news of peace through Jesus Christ—he is Lord of all. [37]You know what happened throughout all of Judea, beginning in Galilee with

the baptism that John proclaimed. [38](You know about) Jesus of Nazareth—how God annointed him with the Holy Spirit and with power—who went around doing good and healing all who were oppressed by the devil, because God was with him. [39]And we are witnesses of all the things he did both in the Jew's region and in Jerusalem. He whom they killed by crucifixion, [40]this is the one whom God raised on the third day and caused to be revealed, [41]not to all the people, but only to the witnesses who had been chosen in advance by God—to us, who ate and drank with him after he rose from the dead. [42]He commanded us to proclaim to the people and testify that he is the one who was appointed by God as the judge of the living and the dead. [43]About this man, all the prophets testify that everyone who believes in him receives forgiveness of sins through his name."

10:34 ᾿Ανοίξας δὲ Πέτρος τὸ στόμα εἶπεν, ᾿Επ᾿ ἀληθείας καταλαμβάνομαι ὅτι οὐκ ἔστιν προσωπολήμπτης ὁ θεός,

᾿Ανοίξας. Aor act ptc masc nom sg ἀνοίγω (attendant circumstance).

Πέτρος. The use of the anarthrous (see 3:3 on Πέτρον καὶ ᾿Ιωάννου) proper name (contrast vv. 25, 26, 30) indicates that the following speech is the key speech of this incident (Levinsohn 1992, 104).

εἶπεν. Aor act ind 3rd sg λέγω.

᾿Επ᾿ ἀληθείας. See 4:27.

καταλαμβάνομαι. Pres mid ind 1st sg καταλαμβάνω. Here, the verb means "to come to understand something which was not understood or perceived previously" (LN 32.18).

ὅτι. Introduces the clausal complement of καταλαμβάνομαι.

ἔστιν. Pres act ind 3rd sg εἰμί. The enclitic ἐστιν (see 1:7) retains its accent following οὐκ.

προσωπολήμπτης. Predicate nominative.

10:35 ἀλλ᾿ ἐν παντὶ ἔθνει ὁ φοβούμενος αὐτὸν καὶ ἐργαζόμενος δικαιοσύνην δεκτὸς αὐτῷ ἐστιν.

ὁ φοβούμενος. Pres dep ptc masc nom sg φοβέομαι (substantival; subject of ἐστιν).

ἐργαζόμενος. Pres mid ptc masc nom sg ἐργάζομαι (substantival; subject of ἐστιν).

δεκτὸς. Predicate adjective.

ἐστιν. Pres act ind 3rd sg εἰμί.

10:36 τὸν λόγον [ὃν] ἀπέστειλεν τοῖς υἱοῖς Ἰσραὴλ εὐαγγελιζόμενος εἰρήνην διὰ Ἰησοῦ Χριστοῦ, οὗτός ἐστιν πάντων κύριος,

τὸν λόγον [ὃν]. Barrett (521) describes the language of this verse, and the verses that follow, as "so difficult as to be untranslatable," while Witherington (1998, 356) sees it as "yet another hint of the unrevised state of this document." The difficulty lies primarily in determining how τὸν λόγον functions if ὃν is part of the text. The relative pronoun is found in the vast majority of manuscripts (𝔓[74] ℵ C D E Ψ *Byz*). It is omitted, however, by a few important manuscripts (ℵ[1] A B 81 *al*). Given the fact that the pronoun could have easily been accidentally omitted since it repeats the final two letters of the preceding word, and the fact that it is the harder reading (though an accidental repetition of the final letters of λόγον would make the harder reading principle irrelevant), the inclusion of the relative pronoun is preferred. τὸν λόγον should then be taken as the topicalized (see 2:22 on Ἰησοῦν τὸν Ναζωραῖον) direct object of οἴδατε (v. 37; cf. Fitzmyer 1998, 463; contra Barrett, 522). It should not be mistaken as "a statement in apposition to what has been said before" (contra Witherington 1998, 356). Furthermore, its role as a direct object accounts for its accusative case. There is no need to posit inverse attraction (contra Fitzmyer 1998, 463). Inverse attraction occurs when an antecedent takes on the case of the relative pronoun that follows it. This rare phenomenon appears to be limited to antecedents that serve as the subject of their clause (see Culy 1989, 129–46; Robertson [1934, 715] claims that classical Greek allowed non-subjects to attract to the case of their antecedent but supplies no examples). Other examples in the NT include Matt 21:42//Mark 12:10//Luke 20:17 (cf. the parallel text in 1 Pet 2:7 where no attraction occurs); 1 Cor 10:16 (see also LXX Gen 31:16; Num 19:22; Shepherd of Hermas, *Sim.* 9.13.3). In Luke 12:48, παντὶ should probably be treated as a dative of reference rather than inverse attraction (correcting Culy 1989, 132–33). Like attraction (see 1:1 on ὧν) inverse attraction appears to be strictly stylistic in nature.

ἀπέστειλεν. Aor act ind 3rd sg ἀποστέλλω.

εὐαγγελιζόμενος. Pres mid ptc masc nom sg εὐαγγελίζω (temporal).

οὗτός ἐστιν πάντων κύριος. A parenthetical statement (see 8:26 on αὕτη ἐστὶν ἔρημος).

οὗτός. The second accent comes from the enclitic ἐστιν (see 1:4 on ἠκούσατέ).

πάντων. Genitive of subordination.

κύριος. Predicate nominative.

10:37 ὑμεῖς οἴδατε τὸ γενόμενον ῥῆμα καθ' ὅλης τῆς 'Ιουδαίας, ἀρξάμενος ἀπὸ τῆς Γαλιλαίας μετὰ τὸ βάπτισμα ὃ ἐκήρυξεν 'Ιωάννης,

οἴδατε. Prf act ind 2nd pl οἶδα.

τὸ γενόμενον ῥῆμα. Lit. "the thing that happened." This appositional expression functions much like a resumptive demonstrative pronoun and picks up the topic introduced in v. 36 (τὸν λόγον) which is followed by a long relative clause and parenthetical statement.

γενόμενον. Aor mid dep ptc neut acc sg γίνομαι (attributive).

καθ'. Distributive.

ἀρξάμενος. Aor mid ptc masc nom sg ἄρχω. Barrett (523) notes that there is no constituent in this sentence from which the participle can get its nominative case marking and again sees a sign of sloppy editing. In light of the other occurrences of ἀρξάμενος ἀπὸ in the NT, however, it appears that the construction is a set idiom with the participle always occurring in the nominative case (cf. 1:22; 8:35). That it was an unusual idiom is suggested by the textual history of the present verse ($\mathfrak{P}^{45}$ *Byz* change the participle to an accusative), Luke 23:5 (where many witnesses drop the participle to leave a more common expression) and Luke 24:47 (where the textual variants include three different cases for the participle as well as a change from the plural to the singular in some witnesses).

ἐκήρυξεν. Aor act ind 3rd sg κηρύσσω.

10:38 'Ιησοῦν τὸν ἀπὸ Ναζαρέθ, ὡς ἔχρισεν αὐτὸν ὁ θεὸς πνεύματι ἁγίῳ καὶ δυνάμει, ὃς διῆλθεν εὐεργετῶν καὶ ἰώμενος πάντας τοὺς καταδυναστευομένους ὑπὸ τοῦ διαβόλου, ὅτι ὁ θεὸς ἦν μετ' αὐτοῦ.

'Ιησοῦν τὸν ἀπὸ Ναζαρέθ. Another topic construction (see 2:22 on 'Ιησοῦν τὸν Ναζωραῖον).

τὸν. The article functions as an adjectivizer (see 2:5 on τῶν ὑπὸ τὸν οὐρανόν), changing the prepositional phrase into an attributive modifier.

ὡς. Introduces another complement of οἴδατε (v. 37). As in v. 28, the use of ὡς rather than ὅτι (see 15:7) may suggest a focus on manner: "(you know) the degree to which God annointed him," or point to general rather than specific knowledge: "you know about God annointing him."

ἔχρισεν. Aor act ind 3rd sg χρίω.

πνεύματι ἁγίῳ καὶ δυνάμει. Dative of instrument.

διῆλθεν. Aor act ind 3rd sg διέρχομαι. Porter (1989, 184) cites this as a good example of the fact that the aorist does not indicate once-for-all action.

εὐεργετῶν. Pres act ptc masc nom sg εὐεργετέω (manner).

ἰώμενος. Pres mid ptc masc nom sg ἰάομαι (manner).

τοὺς. The article functions as a nominalizer (see 1:3 on τὰ) that changes the participial clause into a substantive.

τοὺς καταδυναστευομένους. Pres pass ptc masc acc pl καταδυναστεύω (substantival).

ἦν. Impf ind 3rd sg εἰμί.

10:39 καὶ ἡμεῖς μάρτυρες πάντων ὧν ἐποίησεν ἔν τε τῇ χώρᾳ τῶν Ἰουδαίων καὶ [ἐν] Ἰερουσαλήμ. ὃν καὶ ἀνεῖλαν κρεμάσαντες ἐπὶ ξύλου,

μάρτυρες. Predicate nominative. The verb (ἐσμεν) is left implicit (but see Porter 1994, 85).

πάντων. Genitive of reference.

ὧν. Genitive by attraction (see 1:1) to πάντων (it normally would have been accusative as the object of ἐποίησεν).

ἐποίησεν. Aor act ind 3rd sg ποιέω.

ἔν. The accent on the preposition comes from the enclitic τε (see 1:4 on ἠκούσατέ).

ὃν. The relative pronoun introduces a topicalized (see 2:22 on Ἰησοῦν τὸν Ναζωραῖον) headless relative clause (see 3:6 on ὃ): lit. "he whom they also killed."

ἀνεῖλαν. Aor act ind 3rd pl ἀναιρέω.

κρεμάσαντες ἐπὶ ξύλου. An idiom for crucifixion (lit. "by hanging on a tree").

κρεμάσαντες. Aor act ptc masc nom pl κρεμάννυμι (means).

10:40 τοῦτον ὁ θεὸς ἤγειρεν [ἐν] τῇ τρίτῃ ἡμέρᾳ καὶ ἔδωκεν

αὐτὸν ἐμφανῆ γενέσθαι,

τοῦτον. The topicalized (see 2:22 on Ἰησοῦν τὸν Ναζωραῖον) demonstrative is resumptive, picking up the topic of v. 38: Ἰησοῦν τὸν ἀπὸ Ναζαρέθ.

ἤγειρεν. Aor act ind 3rd sg ἐγείρω.

ἔδωκεν. Aor act ind 3rd sg δίδωμι. Here δίδωμι is used in a causative construction (see 2:4 on ἐδίδου).

αὐτὸν. Accusative subject of the infinitive (see 1:3 on αὐτὸν). If the pronoun were the indirect object of ἔδωκεν, it would be in the dative case.

ἐμφανῆ. Predicate adjective.

γενέσθαι. Aor mid dep inf γίνομαι. The infinitival clause functions as the clausal direct object of ἔδωκεν.

10:41 οὐ παντὶ τῷ λαῷ ἀλλὰ μάρτυσιν τοῖς προκεχειροτονημένοις ὑπὸ τοῦ θεοῦ, ἡμῖν, οἵτινες συνεφάγομεν καὶ συνεπίομεν αὐτῷ μετὰ τὸ ἀναστῆναι αὐτὸν ἐκ νεκρῶν·

τῷ λαῷ . . . μάρτυσιν. Dative indirect objects of ἔδωκεν.

προκεχειροτονημένοις. Prf pass ptc masc dat pl προχειροτονέω (attributive).

ἡμῖν. Dative in apposition to μάρτυσιν.

συνεφάγομεν. Aor act ind 1st pl συνεσθίω.

συνεπίομεν. Aor act ind 1st pl συμπίνω.

αὐτῷ. Verbs with a συν- prefix take a dative complement.

ἀναστῆναι. Aor act inf ἀνίστημι. Used with μετὰ τό to indicate antecedent time (see 1:3 on μετὰ τὸ παθεῖν).

αὐτὸν. Accusative subject of the infinitive (see 1:3 on αὐτὸν).

10:42 καὶ παρήγγειλεν ἡμῖν κηρύξαι τῷ λαῷ καὶ διαμαρτύρασθαι ὅτι οὗτός ἐστιν ὁ ὡρισμένος ὑπὸ τοῦ θεοῦ κριτὴς ζώντων καὶ νεκρῶν.

παρήγγειλεν. Aor act ind 3rd sg παραγγέλλω.

ἡμῖν. Dative indirect object of παρήγγειλεν.

κηρύξαι. Aor act inf κηρύσσω (indirect discourse).

διαμαρτύρασθαι. Aor mid dep inf διαμαρτύρομαι (indirect discourse).

οὗτός. The second accent comes from the enclitic ἐστιν (see 1:4 on ἠκούσατέ).

ὁ ὡρισμένος. Prf pass ptc masc nom sg ὁρίζω (substantival; predicate nominative).

κριτὴς. Complement in a subject-complement double nominative construction with the passive ὡρισμένος (cf. 4:36 on υἱὸς and 1:12 on Ἐλαιῶνος).

ζώντων καὶ νεκρῶν. Objective genitive.

ζώντων. Pres act ptc masc gen pl ζάω (substantival).

10:43 τούτῳ πάντες οἱ προφῆται μαρτυροῦσιν ἄφεσιν ἁμαρτιῶν λαβεῖν διὰ τοῦ ὀνόματος αὐτοῦ πάντα τὸν πιστεύοντα εἰς αὐτόν.

τούτῳ. Dative of reference. The antecedent could be Jesus (οὗτός, v. 42), or a general reference to the conversation as a whole (so Barrett, 528). The proximity of οὗτός makes the former more likely.

μαρτυροῦσιν. Pres act ind 3rd pl μαρτυρέω.

ἄφεσιν. Accusative direct object of λαβεῖν.

ἁμαρτιῶν. Objective genitive.

λαβεῖν. Aor act inf λαμβάνω (indirect discourse).

διὰ. Means.

τὸν. The article functions as a nominalizer (see 1:3 on τὰ) that changes the participial phrase into a substantive.

τὸν πιστεύοντα. Pres act ptc masc acc sg πιστεύω (substantival; see above). Accusative subject of the infinitive (see 1:3 on αὐτὸν).

Acts 10:44–48

[44]While Peter was still speaking these words, the Holy Spirit fell upon all those who heard the message. [45]The circumcised believers who had come with Peter were amazed because the gift of the Holy Spirit had even been poured out upon the Gentiles. [46]For they heard them speaking in tongues and magnifying God. Then Peter responded, [47]"Surely no one is going to withhold water in an effort to keep these people, who have received the Holy Spirit like us, from being baptized!" [48]So he commanded them to be baptized in the name of Jesus Christ. Then they asked him to stay for several days.

10:44 Ἔτι λαλοῦντος τοῦ Πέτρου τὰ ῥήματα ταῦτα ἐπέπεσεν τὸ

πνεῦμα τὸ ἅγιον ἐπὶ πάντας τοὺς ἀκούοντας τὸν λόγον.

λαλοῦντος. Pres act ptc masc gen sg λαλέω. Genitive absolute (see 1:8 on ἐπελθόντος), temporal.

Πέτρου. Genitive subject (see 1:8 on ἐπελθόντος).

ἐπέπεσεν. Aor act ind 3rd sg ἐπιπίπτω.

ἐπὶ. See 1:8 on ἐφ' ὑμᾶς.

τοὺς. The article functions as a nominalizer (see 1:3 on τὰ) that changes the participial phrase into a substantive.

τοὺς ἀκούοντας. Pres act ptc masc acc pl ἀκούω (substantival).

10:45 καὶ ἐξέστησαν οἱ ἐκ περιτομῆς πιστοὶ ὅσοι συνῆλθαν τῷ Πέτρῳ, ὅτι καὶ ἐπὶ τὰ ἔθνη ἡ δωρεὰ τοῦ ἁγίου πνεύματος ἐκκέχυται·

ἐξέστησαν. Aor act ind 3rd pl ἐξίστημι.

οἱ ἐκ περιτομῆς πιστοὶ. A rare idiom for "Jewish believers" (lit. "the faithful from the circumcision").

ἐκ περιτομῆς. A prepositional phrase is frequently incorporated into a noun phrase, as here, and functions as an attributive modifier (cf. ἐξ αὐτῶν in 11:20).

συνῆλθαν. Aor act ind 3rd pl συνέρχομαι.

Πέτρῳ. Verbs with a συν- prefix take a dative complement.

ὅτι. Causal.

τοῦ ἁγίου πνεύματος. Epexegetical genitive.

ἐκκέχυται. Prf pass ind 3rd sg ἐκχέω.

10:46 ἤκουον γὰρ αὐτῶν λαλούντων γλώσσαις καὶ μεγαλυνόντων τὸν θεόν. τότε ἀπεκρίθη Πέτρος,

ἤκουον. Impf act ind 3rd pl ἀκούω.

αὐτῶν. Genitive object of ἤκουον.

λαλούντων. Pres act ptc masc gen pl λαλέω (genitive complement of ἀκούω in an object-complement "double genitive" construction; see 2:6 on λαλούντων).

γλώσσαις. Dative of instrument (cf. 2:4, 11; 19:6).

μεγαλυνόντων. Pres act ptc masc gen pl μεγαλύνω. The participle functions as the genitive complement of ἀκούω in an object-complement "double genitive" construction (see 2:6 on λαλούντων).

ἀπεκρίθη. Aor pass dep ind 3rd sg ἀποκρίνομαι.

10:47 Μήτι τὸ ὕδωρ δύναται κωλῦσαί τις τοῦ μὴ βαπτισθῆναι τούτους, οἵτινες τὸ πνεῦμα τὸ ἅγιον ἔλαβον ὡς καὶ ἡμεῖς;

Μήτι τὸ ὕδωρ δύναται κωλῦσαί τις τοῦ μὴ βαπτισθῆναι τούτους. Lit. "Surely someone is not able to withold water in order that these people not be baptized?"

Μήτι. Introduces a question that expects a negative answer.

δύναται. Pres dep ind 3rd sg δύναμαι.

κωλῦσαί. Aor act inf κωλύω (complementary). The second accent comes from the enclitic τις (see 1:4 on ἠκούσατέ).

τοῦ μὴ βαπτισθῆναι. Aor pass inf βαπτίζω (purpose; see 3:2 on τοῦ αἰτεῖν).

τούτους. Accusative subject of the passive infinitive (see 1:3 on αὐτὸν).

ἔλαβον. Aor act ind 3rd pl λαμβάνω.

10:48 προσέταξεν δὲ αὐτοὺς ἐν τῷ ὀνόματι Ἰησοῦ Χριστοῦ βαπτισθῆναι. τότε ἠρώτησαν αὐτὸν ἐπιμεῖναι ἡμέρας τινάς.

προσέταξεν. Aor act ind 3rd sg προστάσσω.

αὐτοὺς. Accusative subject of the infinitive (see 1:3 on αὐτὸν). The pronoun cannot be the object of προστάσσω since the recipient of the command takes the dative case with this verb.

ἐν τῷ ὀνόματι Ἰησοῦ Χριστοῦ. On the surface, the prepositional phrase could modify either προσέταξεν or βαπτισθῆναι. Since, however, αὐτοὺς is part of the infinitival clause (see above) and precedes the prepositional phrase, ἐν τῷ ὀνόματι Ἰησοῦ Χριστοῦ most likely modifies the infinitive.

βαπτισθῆναι. Aor pass inf βαπτίζω (indirect discourse).

ἠρώτησαν. Aor act ind 3rd pl ἐρωτάω.

αὐτὸν. Accusative subject of the infinitive (see 1:3 on αὐτὸν).

ἐπιμεῖναι. Aor act inf ἐπιμένω (indirect discourse).

ἡμέρας τινάς. Accusative indicating extent of time (see 7:20 on μῆνας).

Acts 11:1–18

[1]Now, the apostles and other believers throughout Judea heard that

the Gentiles had also accepted the message of God. [2]So when Peter went up to Jerusalem, (some of) those (believers) who were circumcised started arguing with him, [3]saying, "You visited men who were uncircumcised and ate with them!" [4]Peter began (speaking) and explained (everything) to them in an orderly manner. He said, [5]"I was praying in the city of Joppa and saw a vision while in a trance, an object descending, like a large sheet that was being lowered from the sky by its four corners; and it came right down to me. [6]As I stared at it, I began to look carefully and saw four-footed animals, wild animals, reptiles, and birds. [7]Then I heard a voice saying to me, 'Get up, Peter! Slaughter and eat!' [8]But I said, 'Certainly not, Lord! For nothing impure or contaminated has ever entered my mouth!' [9]Then the voice spoke from heaven a second time: 'That which God has made pure, do not call impure.' [10]This happened three times, and then everything was drawn back up into the sky again.

[11]Then, at that moment, three men, who had been sent from Caesarea to me, were standing (outside) the house where we were staying! [12]The Spirit told me to go with them without any questions. These six believers also went with me and we entered the man's house. [13]He informed us of how he had seen an angel standing in his house and saying, 'Send (someone) to Joppa and summon Simon, who is called Peter. [14]He will tell you how you, along with your whole household, can be saved.'

[15]Then, just as I was starting to speak (to them), the Holy Spirit fell upon them just as (he fell) upon us at the beginning. [16]And I remembered the words of the Lord, how he had said, 'John baptized with water, but you will be baptized with the Holy Spirit.'

[17]If, then, God gave the same gift to them as to us, who have believed in the Lord Jesus Christ, who was I to try to stop God?" [18]When they heard these things, they stopped (arguing) and glorified God, and said, "Perhaps God has also given the repentance that leads to life to the Gentiles."

11:1 Ἤκουσαν δὲ οἱ ἀπόστολοι καὶ οἱ ἀδελφοὶ οἱ ὄντες κατὰ τὴν Ἰουδαίαν ὅτι καὶ τὰ ἔθνη ἐδέξαντο τὸν λόγον τοῦ θεοῦ.

Ἤκουσαν. Aor act ind 3rd pl ἀκούω.
ἀδελφοὶ. See 1:15.
ὄντες. Pres act ptc masc nom pl εἰμί (attributive).
κατὰ. Distributive.

ὅτι. Introduces a clausal complement (indirect discourse) of Ἤκουσαν.

ἐδέξαντο. Aor mid dep ind 3rd pl δέχομαι. Here, "to readily receive information and to regard it as true" (LN 31.51).

11:2 ὅτε δὲ ἀνέβη Πέτρος εἰς Ἰερουσαλήμ, διεκρίνοντο πρὸς αὐτὸν οἱ ἐκ περιτομῆς

ἀνέβη. Aor act ind 3rd sg ἀναβαίνω.

διεκρίνοντο. Impf mid ind 3rd pl διακρίνω.

οἱ ἐκ περιτομῆς. The article functions as a nominalizer (see 1:3 on τὰ), changing the prepositional phrase into a substantive.

11:3 λέγοντες ὅτι Εἰσῆλθες πρὸς ἄνδρας ἀκροβυστίαν ἔχοντας καὶ συνέφαγες αὐτοῖς.

λέγοντες. Pres act ptc masc nom pl λέγω (attendant circumstance).

ὅτι. Introduces direct discourse.

Εἰσῆλθες. Aor act ind 2nd sg εἰσέρχομαι.

ἄνδρας ἀκροβυστίαν ἔχοντας. Lit. "men having uncircumcision."

ἀκροβυστίαν. Accusative direct object of the participle.

ἔχοντας. Pres act ptc masc acc pl ἔχω (attributive).

συνέφαγες. Aor act ind 2nd sg συνεσθίω.

11:4 ἀρξάμενος δὲ Πέτρος ἐξετίθετο αὐτοῖς καθεξῆς λέγων,

ἀρξάμενος. Aor mid ptc masc nom sg ἄρχω. Although some view the participle as redundant (see BDF §419), the participle probably indicates that Peter began at the beginning of the story. As such it would either provide an attendant circumstance (Rogers and Rogers, 254), or perhaps indicate the manner in which Peter related the story ("starting at the beginning"; cf. 10:37).

ἐξετίθετο. Impf mid ind 3rd sg ἐκτίθημι/ἐκτίθεμαι.

καθεξῆς. "A sequence of one after another in time, space, or logic" (LN 61.1).

λέγων. Pres act ptc masc nom sg λέγω (attendant circumstance, redundant; see 1:6 on λέγοντες).

11:5 Ἐγὼ ἤμην ἐν πόλει Ἰόππῃ προσευχόμενος καὶ εἶδον ἐν ἐκστάσει ὅραμα, καταβαῖνον σκεῦός τι ὡς ὀθόνην μεγάλην τέσσαρσιν ἀρχαῖς καθιεμένην ἐκ τοῦ οὐρανοῦ, καὶ ἦλθεν ἄχρι ἐμοῦ.

ἤμην. Impf ind 1st sg εἰμί.

προσευχόμενος. Pres dep ptc masc nom sg προσεύχομαι (imperfect periphrastic; see 1:10 on ἀτενίζοντες).

εἶδον. Aor act ind 1st sg ὁράω.

ἐν ἐκστάσει. Temporal.

ὅραμα. Accusative direct object of εἶδον.

καταβαῖνον. Pres act ptc neut acc sg καταβαίνω. The participle functions as the complement in an object-complement double accusative construction (see 1:3 on ζῶντα) with σκεῦός as the object. This construction stands in apposition to ὅραμα.

σκεῦός. Neuter accusative direct object of εἶδον in apposition to ὅραμα. The second accent comes from the enclitic τι (see 1:4 on ἠκούσατέ).

τέσσαρσιν ἀρχαῖς. Means.

καθιεμένην. Pres pass ptc fem acc sg καθίημι. Unlike in 10:11 where the neuter participle (καθιεμένον) modifies σκεῦός τι, here the feminine participle modifies ὀθόνην μεγάλην.

ἦλθεν. Aor act ind 3rd sg ἔρχομαι.

11:6 εἰς ἣν ἀτενίσας κατενόουν καὶ εἶδον τὰ τετράποδα τῆς γῆς καὶ τὰ θηρία καὶ τὰ ἑρπετὰ καὶ τὰ πετεινὰ τοῦ οὐρανοῦ.

εἰς ἥν. The prepositional phrase could modify either ἀτενίσας or κατενόουν. Since, however, κατανοέω does not occur with εἰς in the NT, while ἀτενίζω frequently does, it is better to take the prepositional phrase with the participle. The preposition probably indicates general direction ("at") rather than "into" (cf. the use of ἀτενίζω with εἰς in 3:14; 6:15). The antecedent of the relative pronoun is ὀθόνην μεγάλην.

ἀτενίσας. Aor act ptc masc nom sg ἀτενίζω (attendant circumstance).

κατενόουν. Impf act ind 1st sg κατανοέω.

εἶδον. Aor act ind 1st sg ὁράω.

τὰ . . . γῆς. Lit. "four-footed animals of the earth." Here, the reference appears to be to domestic animals.

τὰ . . . οὐρανοῦ. Lit. "birds of the sky."

11:7 ἤκουσα δὲ καὶ φωνῆς λεγούσης μοι, Ἀναστάς, Πέτρε, θῦσον καὶ φάγε.

ἤκουσα. Aor act ind 1st sg ἀκούω.

φωνῆς. Genitive object of ἤκουσα.

λεγούσης. Pres act ptc fem gen sg λέγω. The participle functions as the complement of φωνῆς in an object-complement "double genitive" construction (see 2:6 on λαλούντων).

Ἀναστάς. Aor act ptc masc nom sg ἀνίστημι (with an imperative main verb an attendant circumstance participle carries imperatival force). Once again, it is possible that this term carries connotative value (a sense of urgency) rather than semantic value (thus, "Slaughter and eat, right away!" See 8:26 on Ἀνάστηθι πορεύου; cf. 9:6, 11, 18), though such a usage may require the imperatival rather than participial form.

Πέτρε. Vocative. On the placement of the vocative, see 10:13.

θῦσον. Aor act impv 2nd sg θύω.

φάγε. Aor act impv 2nd sg ἐσθίω.

11:8 εἶπον δέ, Μηδαμῶς, κύριε, ὅτι κοινὸν ἢ ἀκάθαρτον οὐδέποτε εἰσῆλθεν εἰς τὸ στόμα μου.

εἶπον. Aor act ind 1st sg λέγω.

Μηδαμῶς. See 10:14.

κύριε. See 10:14.

ὅτι. Causal.

κοινὸν ἢ ἀκάθαρτον. Unlike in 10:14, where the two substantival adjectives are conjoined to form a doublet, here the conjunction distinguishes between the two. The word κοίνος refers to that which is defiled by association, while ἀκάθαρτος denotes that which is unclean by its very nature (cf. Parsons 2001).

εἰσῆλθεν. Aor act ind 3rd sg εἰσέρχομαι. This verb is more forceful than ἐσθίω ("never touched my lips!").

εἰς. See 1:8 on ἐφ' ὑμᾶς.

11:9 ἀπεκρίθη δὲ φωνὴ ἐκ δευτέρου ἐκ τοῦ οὐρανοῦ, Ἃ ὁ θεὸς ἐκαθάρισεν σὺ μὴ κοίνου.

ἀπεκρίθη. Aor pass dep ind 3rd sg ἀποκρίνομαι.

ἐκ δευτέρου. See 10:15.

Ἅ. See 10:15.

ἐκαθάρισεν. Aor act ind 3rd sg καθαρίζω.

σὺ. See 10:15.

κοίνου. Pres act impv 2nd sg κοινόω. "To call or to regard something as common or defiled" (LN 53.40).

11:10 τοῦτο δὲ ἐγένετο ἐπὶ τρίς, καὶ ἀνεσπάσθη πάλιν ἅπαντα εἰς τὸν οὐρανόν.

τοῦτο. See 10:16.

ἐγένετο. Aor mid dep ind 3rd sg γίνομαι.

ἐπὶ τρίς. See 10:16.

ἀνεσπάσθη. Aor pass ind 3rd sg ἀνασπάω.

11:11 καὶ ἰδοὺ ἐξαυτῆς τρεῖς ἄνδρες ἐπέστησαν ἐπὶ τὴν οἰκίαν ἐν ᾗ ἦμεν, ἀπεσταλμένοι ἀπὸ Καισαρείας πρός με.

ἰδοὺ. See 1:10.

ἐξαυτῆς. "Immediately."

ἐπέστησαν. Aor act ind 3rd pl ἐφίστημι.

ἦμεν. Impf ind 1st pl εἰμί. Many manuscripts (𝔓[45] E Ψ 33 *Byz al*) have the singular form (ἤμην), referring to Peter, rather than the plural (𝔓[74] ℵ A B D *al*), which is the harder reading. An accidental change due to the similar sound of the two forms, however, would invalidate the application of the harder reading principle in this case.

ἀπεσταλμένοι. Prf pass ptc masc nom pl ἀποστέλλω (attributive modifying ἄνδρες).

ἀπὸ. See 1:8 on ἐφ᾽ ὑμᾶς.

11:12 εἶπεν δὲ τὸ πνεῦμά μοι συνελθεῖν αὐτοῖς μηδὲν διακρίναντα. ἦλθον δὲ σὺν ἐμοὶ καὶ οἱ ἓξ ἀδελφοὶ οὗτοι καὶ εἰσήλθομεν εἰς τὸν οἶκον τοῦ ἀνδρός.

εἶπεν. Aor act ind 3rd sg λέγω.

συνελθεῖν. Aor act inf συνέρχομαι (indirect discourse).

αὐτοῖς. Verbs with a συν- prefix take a dative complement.

μηδὲν διακρίναντα. See 10:20.

μηδὲν. Accusative direct object of διακρίναντα.

διακρίναντα. Aor act ptc masc acc sg διακρίνω (manner). The accusative case agrees with the unexpressed accusative subject of the infinitive (see 1:3 on αὐτὸν).

ἦλθον. Aor act ind 3rd pl ἔρχομαι.

οἱ ἓξ ἀδελφοὶ οὗτοι. Nominative subject of ἦλθον.

εἰσήλθομεν. Aor act ind 1st pl εἰσέρχομαι.

εἰς. See 1:8 on ἐφ᾽ ὑμᾶς.

11:13 ἀπήγγειλεν δὲ ἡμῖν πῶς εἶδεν [τὸν] ἄγγελον ἐν τῷ οἴκῳ αὐτοῦ σταθέντα καὶ εἰπόντα, Ἀπόστειλον εἰς Ἰόππην καὶ μετάπεμψαι Σίμωνα τὸν ἐπικαλούμενον Πέτρον,

ἀπήγγειλεν. Aor act ind 3rd sg ἀπαγγέλλω.

ἡμῖν. Dative indirect object of ἀπήγγειλεν.

πῶς. See 9:27.

εἶδεν. Aor act ind 3rd sg ὁράω.

σταθέντα. Aor pass ptc masc acc sg ἵστημι. The participle functions as the complement in an object-complement double accusative construction (see 1:3 on ζῶντα).

εἰπόντα. Aor act ptc masc acc sg λέγω. The participle functions as a conjoined complement in an object-complement double accusative construction (see 1:3 on ζῶντα).

Ἀπόστειλον. Aor act impv 2nd sg ἀποστέλλω.

μετάπεμψαι. Aor mid impv 2nd sg μεταπέμπω. On the use of the middle voice, see 10:5.

ἐπικαλούμενον. Pres pass ptc masc acc sg ἐπικαλέω (attributive).

Πέτρον. The accusative noun serves as a complement in a passive object-complement double case construction (cf. 1:12 on' Ελαιῶνος).

11:14 ὃς λαλήσει ῥήματα πρὸς σὲ ἐν οἷς σωθήσῃ σὺ καὶ πᾶς ὁ οἶκός σου.

ὃς . . . σου. Lit. "who will speak words to you by which you and your entire household will be saved."

λαλήσει. Fut act ind 3rd sg λαλέω.

ἐν. Means.

σωθήσῃ. Fut pass ind 2nd sg σῴζω. The singular verb is used with a compound subject, probably because the focus remains on Cornelius (cf. 7:15; 26:30).

οἶκός. The second accent comes from the enclitic σου (see 1:4 on ἠκούσατέ).

11:15 ἐν δὲ τῷ ἄρξασθαί με λαλεῖν ἐπέπεσεν τὸ πνεῦμα τὸ ἅγιον ἐπ' αὐτοὺς ὥσπερ καὶ ἐφ' ἡμᾶς ἐν ἀρχῇ.

ἄρξασθαί. Aor mid inf ἄρχω. Used with ἐν τῷ to denote contemporaneous time (Wallace 1996, 595). The second accent comes from the enclitic με (see 1:4 on ἠκούσατέ).

με. Accusative subject of the infinitive (see 1:3 on αὐτὸν).

λαλεῖν. Pres act inf λαλέω (complementary).

ἐπέπεσεν. Aor act ind 3rd sg ἐπιπίπτω.

ἐπ'. See 1:8 on ἐφ' ὑμᾶς.

ὥσπερ. See 2:2.

11:16 ἐμνήσθην δὲ τοῦ ῥήματος τοῦ κυρίου ὡς ἔλεγεν, 'Ιωάννης μὲν ἐβάπτισεν ὕδατι, ὑμεῖς δὲ βαπτισθήσεσθε ἐν πνεύματι ἁγίῳ.

ἐμνήσθην. Aor pass dep ind 1st sg μιμνῄσκομαι.

τοῦ ῥήματος. Genitive object of ἐμνήσθην.

τοῦ κυρίου. Subjective genitive.

ὡς. Temporal (see 18:5).

ἔλεγεν. Impf act ind 3rd sg λέγω.

ἐβάπτισεν. Aor act ind 3rd sg βαπτίζω.

ὕδατι. See 1:5.

βαπτισθήσεσθε. Fut pass ind 2nd pl βαπτίζω.

ἐν πνεύματι ἁγίῳ. See 1:5.

11:17 εἰ οὖν τὴν ἴσην δωρεὰν ἔδωκεν αὐτοῖς ὁ θεὸς ὡς καὶ ἡμῖν πιστεύσασιν ἐπὶ τὸν κύριον 'Ιησοῦν Χριστόν, ἐγὼ τίς ἤμην δυνατὸς κωλῦσαι τὸν θεόν;

εἰ. Introduces a first class condition. Here, the apodosis is in the form of a question.

ἔδωκεν. Aor act ind 3rd sg δίδωμι.

ἡμῖν. Dative indirect object of an implicit ἔδωκεν.

πιστεύσασιν. Aor act ptc masc dat pl πιστεύω (attributive). The participle should be taken with the contiguous ἡμῖν, not αὐτοῖς.

ἐγὼ τίς ἤμην δυνατὸς κωλῦσαι τὸν θεόν; Since one sentence cannot have both a predicate nominative (τίς) and a predicate adjective (δυνατὸς), in terms of syntax, it is best to take this construction as two questions, with the first having an implicit verb: "Who am I? Am I able to hinder God?" (cf. Page, 151).

τίς. Predicate nominative ("I am who?") of an implied verb (ἤμην probably goes with what follows).

ἤμην. Impf ind 1st sg εἰμί.

δυνατὸς. Predicate adjective of ἤμην.

κωλῦσαι. Aor act inf κωλύω (epexegetical).

11:18 ἀκούσαντες δὲ ταῦτα ἡσύχασαν καὶ ἐδόξασαν τὸν θεὸν λέγοντες, Ἄρα καὶ τοῖς ἔθνεσιν ὁ θεὸς τὴν μετάνοιαν εἰς ζωὴν ἔδωκεν.

ἀκούσαντες. Aor act ptc masc nom pl ἀκούω (temporal).

ἡσύχασαν. Aor act ind 3rd pl ἡσυχάζω.

ἐδόξασαν. Aor act ind 3rd pl δοξάζω.

λέγοντες. Pres act ptc masc nom pl λέγω (attendant circumstance).

εἰς ζωὴν. Purpose.

ἔδωκεν. Aor act ind 3rd sg δίδωμι.

Acts 11:19–26

[19]Then, those who had been scattered as a result of the trouble that had happened because of Stephen traveled as far as Phoenicia, Cyprus, and Antioch, telling the message to no one but Jews. [20]But there were certain men among them, who were from Cyprus and Cyrene, who went to Antioch and began speaking to the Greeks as well, preaching the good news of the Lord Jesus. [21]The hand of the Lord was with them and a large number, who had believed, turned to the Lord.

[22]The news about them reached the church in Jerusalem, and they sent Barnabas to Antioch. [23]When he arrived and saw the grace of God, he rejoiced and began urging them all to remain loyal to the Lord with determination. [24]For he was a good man, full of the Holy Spirit and faith. And a substantial crowd turned to the Lord.

[25]Then, Barnabas left for Tarsus to look for Saul. [26]When he found him he brought him to Antioch. For an entire year they met with (the believers) in the assembly and taught a substantial crowd. Now, it was in Antioch that the disciples were first called "Christians."

11:19 Οἱ μὲν οὖν διασπαρέντες ἀπὸ τῆς θλίψεως τῆς γενομένης ἐπὶ Στεφάνῳ διῆλθον ἕως Φοινίκης καὶ Κύπρου καὶ Ἀντιοχείας μηδενὶ λαλοῦντες τὸν λόγον εἰ μὴ μόνον Ἰουδαίοις.

Οἱ. The article modifies the participle (cf. 1:6).

μὲν οὖν. Here, μὲν οὖν "occurs in connection with the reintroduction [see 8:4] of a participant" (Levinsohn 1987, 143; cf. 1:6).

διασπαρέντες. Aor pass ptc masc nom pl διασπείρω (substantival).

ἀπὸ. Cause/result.

γενομένης. Aor mid dep ptc fem gen sg γίνομαι (attributive).

ἐπὶ. Cause.

διῆλθον. Aor act ind 3rd pl διέρχομαι.

μηδενὶ. Dative indirect object of λαλοῦντες.

λαλοῦντες. Pres act ptc masc nom pl λαλέω (manner).

Ἰουδαίοις. Dative indirect object of λαλοῦντες.

11:20 ἦσαν δέ τινες ἐξ αὐτῶν ἄνδρες Κύπριοι καὶ Κυρηναῖοι, οἵτινες ἐλθόντες εἰς Ἀντιόχειαν ἐλάλουν καὶ πρὸς τοὺς Ἑλληνιστάς εὐαγγελιζόμενοι τὸν κύριον Ἰησοῦν.

ἦσαν. Impf ind 3rd pl εἰμί.

ἐξ αὐτῶν. See 10:45 on ἐκ περιτομῆς.

Κύπριοι καὶ Κυρηναῖοι. Nominative in apposition to ἄνδρες.

ἐλθόντες. Aor act ptc masc nom pl ἔρχομαι (temporal).

ἐλάλουν. Impf act ind 3rd pl λαλέω.

Ἑλληνιστάς. The sense in this verse appears to be more general than in 6:1 where the term refers to Greek-speaking *Jews*. Given v. 19, these Ἑλληνιστάς were clearly not Jews. The ambiguity apparently led to some variation in the textual tradition: 𝔓[74] ℵ[c] A D* all have the more generic Ἕλληνας, "Greeks."

εὐαγγελιζόμενοι. Pres mid ptc masc nom pl εὐαγγελίζω (manner).

11:21 καὶ ἦν χεὶρ κυρίου μετ' αὐτῶν, πολύς τε ἀριθμὸς ὁ πιστεύσας ἐπέστρεψεν ἐπὶ τὸν κύριον.

ἦν. Impf ind 3rd sg εἰμί.

χεὶρ κυρίου. Synecdoche (see 1:22 on τοῦ βαπτίσματος Ἰωάννου; cf. 4:28; 12:11; 13:11) for "the Lord."

πολύς ἀριθμὸς ὁ πιστεύσας. The fronted (see 3:13 on ὑμεῖς) subject of the clause emphasizes the size of the group (Levinsohn 1987, 9).

ὁ πιστεύσας. Aor act ptc masc nom sg πιστεύω (attributive). The articular singular participle modifies πολύς ἀριθμὸς.

πολύς ἀριθμὸς ὁ πιστεύσας. This expression does not denote "a great number *of believers*," which would require a genitive plural participle (cf. 4:4; 6:7).

ἐπέστρεψεν. Aor act ind 3rd sg ἐπιστρέφω.

ἐπὶ. See 1:8 on ἐφ' ὑμᾶς.

11:22 ἠκούσθη δὲ ὁ λόγος εἰς τὰ ὦτα τῆς ἐκκλησίας τῆς οὔσης ἐν Ἰερουσαλὴμ περὶ αὐτῶν καὶ ἐξαπέστειλαν Βαρναβᾶν [διελθεῖν] ἕως Ἀντιοχείας.

ἠκούσθη . . . εἰς τὰ ὦτα. This unusual expression (lit. "was heard in the ears") seems to be an idiom referring to information coming to the attention of someone. It is used twice in the LXX (Isa 5:9; Odes of Solomon 10:9—ἠκούσθη γὰρ ταῦτα πάντα εἰς τὰ ὦτα κυρίου σαβαώθ) with the Lord being the one who "hears." The expression seems to carry the connotation that a response to the news is imminent.

ἠκούσθη. Aor pass ind 3rd sg ἀκούω.

οὔσης. Pres act ptc fem gen sg εἰμί (attributive).

περὶ αὐτῶν. Reference (modifying ὁ λόγος).

ἐξαπέστειλαν. Aor act ind 3rd pl ἐξαποστέλλω.

[διελθεῖν]. Aor act inf διέρχομαι (purpose). While there is some support for the inclusion of this term (D E Ψ *Byz al*), there are many early manuscripts that omit it ($\mathfrak{P}^{74}$ ℵ A B 81 *al*). The expression, ἐξαπέστειλαν διελθεῖν ἕως, is consistent with Luke's style (see 17:14) but does not occur elsewhere in the NT; nor are there any (other) examples of ἐξαπέστειλαν ἕως.

11:23 ὃς παραγενόμενος καὶ ἰδὼν τὴν χάριν [τὴν] τοῦ θεοῦ, ἐχάρη καὶ παρεκάλει πάντας τῇ προθέσει τῆς καρδίας προσμένειν τῷ κυρίῳ,

παραγενόμενος. Aor mid dep ptc masc nom sg παραγίνομαι (temporal).

ἰδὼν. Aor act ptc masc nom sg ὁράω (temporal).

[τὴν] τοῦ θεου. On the use of the seemingly superfluous first article as an adjectivizer (see 2:5 on τῶν ὑπὸ τὸν οὐρανόν), see 26:12 on τῆς τῶν ἀρχιερέων.

ἐχάρη. Aor pass dep ind 3rd sg χαίρω.

παρεκάλει. Impf act ind 3rd sg παρακαλέω.

τῇ προθέσει τῆς καρδίας. Dative of manner (lit. "with purpose of heart" = "with determination"; Lake and Cadbury, 129). Given its position in the sentence, following πάντας, it should probably be taken as a modifier of προσμένειν rather than παρεκάλει.

πάντας. Accusative subject of the infinitive (see 1:3 on αὐτὸν).

προσμένειν. Pres act inf προσμένω (indirect discourse).

11:24 ὅτι ἦν ἀνὴρ ἀγαθὸς καὶ πλήρης πνεύματος ἁγίου καὶ πίστεως. καὶ προσετέθη ὄχλος ἱκανὸς τῷ κυρίῳ.

ὅτι. Introduces a reason for why Barnabas acted as he did (v. 23).

ἦν. Impf ind 3rd sg εἰμί.

ἀνὴρ. Predicate nominative.

πλήρης. Predicate adjective.

πνεύματος . . . πίστεως. Genitives of content.

προσετέθη . . . κυρίῳ. Lit. "a significant crowd was added to the Lord." It is probably best to take the whole expression, προσετέθη τῷ κυρίῳ, as an idiomatic way of stating the conversion of a group of people, and avoid taking τῷ κυρίῳ as a dative of agency (contra Schneider, 2.91).

προσετέθη. Aor pass ind 3rd sg προστίθημι.

11:25 ἐξῆλθεν δὲ εἰς Ταρσὸν ἀναζητῆσαι Σαῦλον,

ἐξῆλθεν. Aor act ind 3rd sg ἐξέρχομαι.

ἀναζητῆσαι. Aor act inf ἀναζητέω (purpose).

11:26 καὶ εὑρὼν ἤγαγεν εἰς Ἀντιόχειαν. ἐγένετο δὲ αὐτοῖς καὶ ἐνιαυτὸν ὅλον συναχθῆναι ἐν τῇ ἐκκλησίᾳ καὶ διδάξαι ὄχλον ἱκανόν, χρηματίσαι τε πρώτως ἐν Ἀντιοχείᾳ τοὺς μαθητὰς Χριστιανούς.

εὑρὼν. Aor act ptc masc nom sg εὑρίσκω (temporal).

ἤγαγεν. Aor act ind 3rd sg ἄγω.

ἐγένετο. Aor mid dep ind 3rd sg γίνομαι.

αὐτοῖς. Dative of association.

ἐνιαυτὸν ὅλον. Accusative indicating extent of time (see 7:20 on μῆνας).

συναχθῆναι. Aor pass inf συνάγω. The subject of the infinitive (presumably both Barnabas and Saul) is left implicit. The compound infinitival clause, ἐνιαυτὸν ὅλον συναχθῆναι ἐν τῇ ἐκκλησίᾳ καὶ διδάξαι ὄχλον ἱκανόν, serves as the subject of ἐγένετο (see also 9:32 on κατελθεῖν).

ἐν τῇ ἐκκλησίᾳ. Locative. The point here is not that Barnabas and Saul met with the members of the *ekklesia*, which would require the simple dative (τῇ ἐκκλησίᾳ) following συναχθῆναι, but that they met with them as part of the communal worship experience.

διδάξαι. Aor act inf διδάσκω.

χρηματίσαι. Aor act inf χρηματίζω. This infinitive also functions as a subject of ἐγένετο (see above).

μαθητὰς. Accusative subject of the infinitive (see 1:3 on αὐτὸν).

Χριστιανούς. Accusative direct object of χρηματίσαι.

Acts 11:27–30

[27]In those days, prophets went down to Antioch from Jerusalem. [28]One of them, named Agabus, stood up and indicated through the Spirit that a severe famine was about to occur throughout the entire world—it happened during Claudius' reign. [29]Now, each of the disciples, in accordance with his financial ability, decided to send (something) as a contribution to the believers living in Judea. [30]They did this by sending (the contribution) to the elders through Barnabas and Saul.

11:27 **Ἐν ταύταις δὲ ταῖς ἡμέραις κατῆλθον ἀπὸ Ἱεροσολύμων προφῆται εἰς Ἀντιόχειαν.**

Ἐν ταύταις δὲ ταῖς ἡμέραις. See 1:15.

κατῆλθον. Aor act ind 3rd pl κατέρχομαι.

11:28 **ἀναστὰς δὲ εἷς ἐξ αὐτῶν ὀνόματι Ἄγαβος ἐσήμανεν διὰ τοῦ πνεύματος λιμὸν μεγάλην μέλλειν ἔσεσθαι ἐφ᾽ ὅλην τὴν οἰκουμένην, ἥτις ἐγένετο ἐπὶ Κλαυδίου.**

ἀναστὰς. Aor act ptc masc nom sg ἀνίστημι (attendant circumstance).

ὀνόματι. Dative of reference.

Ἄγαβος. Nominative in apposition to the substantival εἷς.

ἐσήμανεν. Aor act ind 3rd sg σημαίνω.

λιμὸν. Accusative subject of the infinitive (see 1:3 on αὐτὸν).

μέλλειν. Pres act inf μέλλω (indirect discourse). On the force of μέλλω plus an infinitive, see 3:3 on μέλλοντας.

ἔσεσθαι. Fut mid dep inf εἰμί (complementary). The use of the future infinitive is very rare (in the NT only here and 23:30; 24:15; 27:10; Heb 3:18). Used with μέλλω, the infinitive of εἰμί is always in the future tense in the NT (cf. 24:15; 27:10; and the reading of *Byz* at 23:30). See also 3:3 on μέλλοντας.

ἥτις. The antecedent is λιμὸν μεγάλην.

ἐγένετο. Aor mid dep ind 3rd sg γίνομαι.

ἐπὶ. Temporal (with genitive).

11:29 **τῶν δὲ μαθητῶν, καθὼς εὐπορεῖτό τις ὥρισαν ἕκαστος αὐτῶν εἰς διακονίαν πέμψαι τοῖς κατοικοῦσιν ἐν τῇ Ἰουδαίᾳ ἀδελφοῖς·**

τῶν . . . αὐτῶν. Lit. "of the disciples, just as any were well-off, each of them decided."

μαθητῶν. Partitive genitive in a topic construction (see 2:22 on Ἰησοῦν τὸν Ναζωραῖον).

καθὼς εὐπορεῖτό τις. According to Barrett (565), "καθὼς is used in the sense of measure: *in proportion as any prospered.*" On the translation, "in accordance with his financial ability," see NET Bible, 431; BAGD, 324.

εὐπορεῖτό. Impf mid ind 3rd sg εὐπορέω. The second accent comes from the enclitic τις (see 1:4 on ἠκούσατέ).

τις. Nominative subject of εὐπορεῖτό.

ὥρισαν. Aor act ind 3rd pl ὁρίζω.

ἕκαστος. Nominative subject of ὥρισαν.

αὐτῶν. Resumptive (picks up τῶν μαθητῶν).

εἰς διακονίαν. The preposition εἰς with an accusative noun probably functions like a predicate modifier (see 4:11 on εἰς κεφαλὴν γωνίας).

πέμψαι. Aor act inf πέμπω (complementary).

κατοικοῦσιν. Pres act ptc mac dat pl κατοικέω (attributive).

ἀδελφοῖς. See 1:15.

11:30 ὃ καὶ ἐποίησαν ἀποστείλαντες πρὸς τοὺς πρεσβυτέρους διὰ χειρὸς Βαρναβᾶ καὶ Σαύλου.

ὅ. The antecedent of the neuter singular relative pronoun is the general content of v. 29.

ἐποίησαν. Aor act ind 3rd pl ποιέω.

ἀποστείλαντες. Aor act ptc masc nom pl ἀποστέλλω (means).

διὰ. Instrumental/intermediate agent.

χειρὸς. Synecdoche (see 1:22 on τοῦ βαπτίσματος 'Ιωάννου).

Acts 12:1–17

[1]About that time, King Herod arrested some members of the church
in order to mistreat them. [2]He had James, the brother of John, executed
by the sword. [3]And when he saw that it pleased the Jews, he proceeded
to also seize Peter—this happened during the feast of Unleavened Bread.
[4]He arrested him and put him in prison, where he was guarded by four
squads of four soldiers, because he was planning to present him to the
people (for execution) after the Passover. [5]So Peter was kept in prison,
but prayers were fervently being offered to God on his behalf by the
church.

[6]Now on the night before Herod was going to bring him before (the
people for execution), Peter was sleeping between two soldiers. He had
been bound with two chains and there were guards in front of the (prison)
gate guarding the prison. [7]Suddenly, an angel of the Lord appeared and
a light shone in the prison cell. He tapped Peter on the side and woke
him up, saying, "Get up quickly," and his chains fell off of his hands.
[8]The angel said to him, "Get dressed and put on your sandals." And he
did so. Then he said to him, "Put on your coat and follow me." [9]So he
went out (of the cell) and followed him. He did not know that what was
happening through the angel was real, but thought he was seeing a
vision.

[10]After passing through the first and second guard post, they came to
the iron gate that led into the city, and it opened for them by itself. They
went out and had walked down (just) one street when the angel suddenly left him. [11]When Peter came to himself, he said, "Now I know for
certain that the Lord sent his angel and rescued me from Herod's hands
and from everything that the Jewish people were anticipating." [12]Realizing this, he went to the house of Mary the mother of John, who was
called Mark, where a substantial number of people had gathered

together and were praying. [13]When he knocked on the door at the outer gate, a servant girl named Rhoda came to answer it. [14]But when she recognized Peter's voice, she was so excited that she did not open the gate. Instead, she ran inside and told (them) that Peter was standing at the gate. [15]They told her, "You're crazy!" But she kept insisting that it was true. They, however, kept saying, "It must be his angel!"

[16]Meanwhile, Peter continued knocking. When they opened the door, they saw him and were amazed. [17]He motioned to them with his hand to quiet down and (then) related to them how the Lord had brought him out of the prison and said, "Report these things to James and the other believers." Then he left and went somewhere else.

12:1 Κατ' ἐκεῖνον δὲ τὸν καιρὸν ἐπέβαλεν Ἡρῴδης ὁ βασιλεὺς τὰς χεῖρας κακῶσαί τινας τῶν ἀπὸ τῆς ἐκκλησίας.

Κατ'. Used with an accusative noun to indicate approximate time.
ἐπέβαλεν . . . τὰς χεῖρας. See 4:3 on ἐπέβαλον αὐτοῖς τὰς χεῖρας.
ἐπέβαλεν. Aor act ind 3rd sg ἐπιβάλλω.
ὁ βασιλεὺς. Nominative in apposition to Ἡρῴδης. The reference is to Herod Agrippa I.
κακῶσαί. Aor act inf κακόω (purpose; Barrett [574] has epexegetical). The second accent comes from the enclitic τινας (see 1:4 on ἠκούσατέ).
τῶν. Partitive genitive. The article functions as a nominalizer (see 1:3 on τὰ).

12:2 ἀνεῖλεν δὲ Ἰάκωβον τὸν ἀδελφὸν Ἰωάννου μαχαίρῃ.

ἀνεῖλεν. Aor act ind 3rd sg ἀναιρέω.
τὸν ἀδελφὸν. Accusative in apposition to Ἰάκωβον.
μαχαίρῃ. Dative of instrument.

12:3 ἰδὼν δὲ ὅτι ἀρεστόν ἐστιν τοῖς Ἰουδαίοις, προσέθετο συλλαβεῖν καὶ Πέτρον—ἦσαν δὲ [αἱ] ἡμέραι τῶν ἀζύμων—

ἰδὼν. Aor act ptc masc nom sg ὁράω (temporal or causal).
ὅτι. Introduces a clausal complement of ἰδὼν.
ἀρεστόν. Predicate adjective.
ἐστιν. Pres act ind 3rd sg εἰμί.

προσέθετο συλλαβεῖν. This construction, προστίθημι plus an infinitive, indicates that the action of the infinitive was done in addition to some other action (cf. Luke 20:11, 12//Mark 12:4; see also Porter 1989, 120).

προσέθετο. Aor mid ind 3rd sg προστίθημι.

συλλαβεῖν. Aor act inf συλλαμβάνω (direct object).

Πέτρον. Accusative direct object of συλλαβεῖν. "When a participant is first mentioned, reference to him or her by name typically is *anarthrous*. However, once (s)he has been introduced, subsequent references to him or her by name within the same incident are *arthrous*" (Levinsohn 1992, 100; see 3:3 on Πέτρον καὶ ' Ιωάννην). This principle is illustrated in this verse, where Peter is reintroduced into the narrative without an article and then referred to with an article in subsequent references in vv. 5–16.

ἦσαν. Impf ind 3rd pl εἰμί.

ἡμέραι. Predicate nominative.

12:4 ὃν καὶ πιάσας ἔθετο εἰς φυλακήν, παραδοὺς τέσσαρσιν τετραδίοις στρατιωτῶν φυλάσσειν αὐτόν, βουλόμενος μετὰ τὸ πάσχα ἀναγαγεῖν αὐτὸν τῷ λαῷ.

πιάσας. Aor act ptc masc nom sg πιάζω (attendant circumstance).

ἔθετο. Aor mid ind 3rd sg τίθημι.

παραδοὺς . . . αὐτόν. Lit. "handing (him) over to four squads of four soldiers in order to guard him."

παραδοὺς. Aor act ptc masc nom sg παραδίδωμι (attendant circumstance).

τετραδίοις. "A detachment of four soldiers" (LN 55.11).

φυλάσσειν. Pres act inf φυλάσσω (purpose).

βουλόμενος. Pres mid dep ptc masc nom sg βούλομαι (causal).

ἀναγαγεῖν αὐτὸν τῷ λαῷ. Though the expression may refer to a public trial (LN 15.176), Barrett (577) is probably correct in reading a reference to public execution given the context (see v. 2).

ἀναγαγεῖν. Aor act inf ἀνάγω (complementary).

αὐτὸν. Accusative direct object of ἀναγαγεῖν.

12:5 ὁ μὲν οὖν Πέτρος ἐτηρεῖτο ἐν τῇ φυλακῇ· προσευχὴ δὲ ἦν ἐκτενῶς γινομένη ὑπὸ τῆς ἐκκλησίας πρὸς τὸν θεὸν περὶ αὐτοῦ.

μὲν οὖν. See 1:6.

ἐτηρεῖτο. Impf pass ind 3rd sg τηρέω.

ἦν. Impf ind 3rd sg εἰμί.

γινομένη ὑπὸ. On the significance of this construction, see 26:6 on γενομένης ὑπὸ.

γινομένη. Pres mid dep ptc fem nom sg γίνομαι (imperfect periphrastic; see 1:10 on ἀτενίζοντες).

12:6 Ὅτε δὲ ἤμελλεν προαγαγεῖν αὐτὸν ὁ Ἡρῴδης, τῇ νυκτὶ ἐκείνῃ ἦν ὁ Πέτρος κοιμώμενος μεταξὺ δύο στρατιωτῶν δεδεμένος ἁλύσεσιν δυσίν φύλακές τε πρὸ τῆς θύρας ἐτήρουν τὴν φυλακήν.

ἤμελλεν. Impf act ind 3rd sg μέλλω. On the force of μέλλω plus an infinitive, see 3:3 on μέλλοντας.

προαγαγεῖν. Aor act inf προάγω (complementary).

ὁ Ἡρῴδης. Nominative subject of ἤμελλεν.

τῇ νυκτὶ ἐκείνῃ. Dative of time (lit. "on that night").

ἦν. Impf ind 3rd sg εἰμί.

κοιμώμενος. Pres mid dep ptc masc nom sg κοιμάομαι (imperfect periphrastic; see 1:10 on ἀτενίζοντες).

δεδεμένος. Prf pass ptc masc nom sg δέω (manner). For the participle to be part of a pluperfect periphrastic construction, a καί would be required (cf. v. 12).

ἁλύσεσιν. Dative of instrument.

φύλακές. The second accent comes from the enclitic τε (see 1:4 on ἠκούσατέ).

πρὸ. This preposition is used to describe a place only four times in the NT (12:14; 14:13; Jas 5:9; Robertson 1934, 621).

ἐτήρουν. Impf act ind 3rd pl τηρέω.

12:7 καὶ ἰδοὺ ἄγγελος κυρίου ἐπέστη καὶ φῶς ἔλαμψεν ἐν τῷ οἰκήματι· πατάξας δὲ τὴν πλευρὰν τοῦ Πέτρου ἤγειρεν αὐτὸν λέγων, Ἀνάστα ἐν τάχει. καὶ ἐξέπεσαν αὐτοῦ αἱ ἁλύσεις ἐκ τῶν χειρῶν.

ἰδοὺ. See 1:10.

ἄγγελος κυρίου. See 5:19.

ἐπέστη. Aor act ind 3rd sg ἐφίστημι.

ἔλαμψεν. Aor act ind 3rd sg λάμπω.

πατάξας. Aor act ptc masc nom sg πατάσσω (attendant circumstance). Although this term normally carries a negative connotation (see v. 23; cf. 7:24; Louw and Nida define it "to strike a heavy blow" [19.3]), here the connotation is clearly benevolent.

ἤγειρεν. Aor act ind 3rd sg ἐγείρω.

λέγων. Pres act ptc masc nom sg λέγω (attendant circumstance).

᾿Ανάστα. Aor act impv 2nd sg ἀνίστημι.

ἐν τάχει. "Quickly" (lit. "with speed").

ἐξέπεσαν. Aor act ind 3rd pl ἐκπίπτω.

12:8 εἶπεν δὲ ὁ ἄγγελος πρὸς αὐτόν, Ζῶσαι καὶ ὑπόδησαι τὰ σανδάλιά σου. ἐποίησεν δὲ οὕτως. καὶ λέγει αὐτῷ, Περιβαλοῦ τὸ ἱμάτιόν σου καὶ ἀκολούθει μοι.

εἶπεν. Aor act ind 3rd sg λέγω.

Ζῶσαι. Aor mid impv 2nd sg ζωννύω/ζώννυμι. This verb may also be taken as "to gird, to fasten one's belt, to wear a narrow band of cloth around the waist" (LN 49.14).

ὑπόδησαι. Aor mid impv 2nd sg ὑποδέω.

ἐποίησεν. Aor act ind 3rd sg ποιέω.

λέγει. Pres act ind 3rd sg λέγω.

Περιβαλοῦ. Aor mid impv 2nd sg περιβάλλω.

ἀκολούθει. Pres act impv 2nd pl ἀκολουθέω.

12:9 καὶ ἐξελθὼν ἠκολούθει καὶ οὐκ ᾔδει ὅτι ἀληθές ἐστιν τὸ γινόμενον διὰ τοῦ ἀγγέλου· ἐδόκει δὲ ὅραμα βλέπειν.

ἐξελθὼν. Aor act ptc masc nom sg ἐξέρχομαι (attendant circumstance).

ἠκολούθει. Impf act ind 3rd sg ἀκολουθέω.

ᾔδει. Plprf act ind 3rd sg οἶδα. On the use of the pluperfect, see 7:18.

ἀληθές. Predicate adjective.

ἐστιν. Pres act ind 3rd sg εἰμί.

τὸ γινόμενον. Pres dep ptc neut nom sg γίνομαι (substantival subject of ἐστιν).

ἐδόκει. Impf act ind 3rd sg δοκέω.

βλέπειν. Pres act inf βλέπω (indirect discourse with a verb of cognition).

12:10 διελθόντες δὲ πρώτην φυλακὴν καὶ δευτέραν ἦλθαν ἐπὶ τὴν πύλην τὴν σιδηρᾶν τὴν φέρουσαν εἰς τὴν πόλιν, ἥτις αὐτομάτη ἠνοίγη αὐτοῖς καὶ ἐξελθόντες προῆλθον ῥύμην μίαν, καὶ εὐθέως ἀπέστη ὁ ἄγγελος ἀπ' αὐτοῦ.

διελθόντες. Aor act ptc masc nom pl διέρχομαι (temporal).

φυλακὴν. Here probably "a place or post for guarding" (LN 37.173).

ἦλθαν. Aor act ind 3rd pl ἔρχομαι.

φέρουσαν. Pres act ptc fem acc sg φέρω (attributive).

αὐτομάτη. Unlike adverbial accusatives (see Wallace 1996, 293), when the adjective αὐτόματος is used adverbially, as here, it appears in the nominative case and agrees in number and gender with the subject of the verb (cf. Mark 4:28; Job 24:24).

ἠνοίγη. Aor pass ind 3rd sg ἀνοίγω.

αὐτοῖς. Dative of advantage.

ἐξελθόντες. Aor act ptc masc nom pl ἐξέρχομαι (attendant circumstance).

προῆλθον. Aor act ind 3rd pl προσέρχομαι.

ἀπέστη. Aor act ind 3rd sg ἀφίστημι.

ἀπ'. See 1:8 on ἐφ' ὑμᾶς.

12:11 καὶ ὁ Πέτρος ἐν ἑαυτῷ γενόμενος εἶπεν, Νῦν οἶδα ἀληθῶς ὅτι ἐξαπέστειλεν [ὁ] κύριος τὸν ἄγγελον αὐτοῦ καὶ ἐξείλατό με ἐκ χειρὸς Ἡρῴδου καὶ πάσης τῆς προσδοκίας τοῦ λαοῦ τῶν Ἰουδαίων.

ἐν ἑαυτῷ γενόμενος. According to Barrett (582), this unusual expression means "to come to one's right mind."

γενόμενος. Aor mid dep ptc masc nom sg γίνομαι (temporal).

εἶπεν. Aor act ind 3rd sg λέγω.

οἶδα. Prf act ind 1st sg οἶδα.

ἐξαπέστειλεν. Aor act ind 3rd sg ἐξαποστέλλω.

ἐξείλατό. Aor mid ind 3rd sg ἐξαιρέω. The second accent comes from the enclitic με (see 1:4 on ἠκούσατέ).

χειρὸς Ἡρῴδου. Synecdoche (see 1:21–22 on τοῦ βαπτίσματος Ἰωάννου; cf. 4:28; 11:21; 13:11) for "from Herod" or metonymy (see 1:9 on τῶν ὀφθαλμῶν αὐτῶν) for "from Herod's *power*."

τῆς προσδοκίας. Their anticipation no doubt related to what Herod had already done to James (v. 2).

τοῦ λαοῦ. Subjective genitive.

τοῦ λαοῦ τῶν Ἰουδαίων. Only here in the NT or LXX is τοῦ λαοῦ, which usually refers to "the Jewish people" by itself, modified by τῶν Ἰουδαίων to highlight the identity of Peter's adversaries (cf. Barrett, 582–83).

12:12 συνιδών τε ἦλθεν ἐπὶ τὴν οἰκίαν τῆς Μαρίας τῆς μητρὸς Ἰωάννου τοῦ ἐπικαλουμένου Μάρκου, οὗ ἦσαν ἱκανοὶ συνηθροισμένοι καὶ προσευχόμενοι.

συνιδών. Aor act ptc masc nom sg συνοράω (temporal).

τε. In this passage, following the clauses introduced by καί, "the τέ clause introduces the *specific lead-in* to the next development in the storyline" (Levinsohn 1992, 55).

ἦλθεν. Aor act ind 3rd sg ἔρχομαι.

τῆς μητρὸς. Genitive in apposition to τῆς Μαρίας.

ἐπικαλουμένου. Pres pass ptc masc gen sg ἐπικαλέω (attributive).

Μάρκου. The genitive noun serves as a complement in a passive object-complement double case construction (cf. 1:12 on Ἐλαιῶνος).

οὗ. See 1:13.

ἦσαν. Impf ind 3rd pl εἰμί.

συνηθροισμένοι. Prf pass ptc masc nom pl συναθροίζω (pluperfect periphrastic; see 1:17 on κατηριθμημένος).

προσευχόμενοι. Pres mid ptc masc nom pl προσεύχομαι (imperfect periphrastic; see 1:10 on ἀτενίζοντες).

12:13 κρούσαντος δὲ αὐτοῦ τὴν θύραν τοῦ πυλῶνος προσῆλθεν παιδίσκη ὑπακοῦσαι ὀνόματι Ῥόδη,

κρούσαντος. Aor act ptc masc gen sg κρούω. Genitive absolute (see 1:8 on ἐπελθόντος), temporal.

αὐτοῦ. Genitive subject (see 1:8 on ἐπελθόντος).

προσῆλθεν. Aor act ind 3rd sg προσέρχομαι.

παιδίσκη. Barrett (584) suggests that this term does not necessarily indicate that the young woman was a servant. Witherington (1998, 387), on the other hand, maintains that the term is always used of slaves in the NT, and Louw and Nida (87.83, n. 2) suggest that a παιδίσκη is probably simply a young δουλή.

ὑπακοῦσαι. Aor act inf ὑπακούω (purpose). In this passage, the verb means, "to respond to someone knocking or calling at a door" (LN 46.11).

ὀνόματι. Dative of reference.

'Ρόδη. Nominative in apposition to παιδίσκη.

12:14 καὶ ἐπιγνοῦσα τὴν φωνὴν τοῦ Πέτρου ἀπὸ τῆς χαρᾶς οὐκ ἤνοιξεν τὸν πυλῶνα, εἰσδραμοῦσα δὲ ἀπήγγειλεν ἑστάναι τὸν Πέτρον πρὸ τοῦ πυλῶνος.

ἐπιγνοῦσα. Aor act ptc fem nom sg ἐπιγινώσκω (temporal, or perhaps concessive).

ἀπὸ. Causal.

ἤνοιξεν. Aor act ind 3rd sg ἀνοίγω.

εἰσδραμοῦσα. Aor act ptc fem nom sg εἰστρέχω (attendant circumstance).

ἀπήγγειλεν. Aor act ind 3rd sg ἀπαγγέλλω.

ἑστάναι. Prf act inf ἵστημι (indirect discourse).

τὸν Πέτρον. Accusative subject of the infinitive (see 1:3 on αὐτὸν).

πρὸ. See v. 6.

12:15 οἱ δὲ πρὸς αὐτὴν εἶπαν, Μαίνῃ. ἡ δὲ διϊσχυρίζετο οὕτως ἔχειν. οἱ δὲ ἔλεγον, 'Ο ἄγγελός ἐστιν αὐτοῦ.

οἱ δέ . . . ἡ δέ . . . οἱ δὲ. The articles function like personal pronouns here (cf. 3:5). Levinsohn (1992, 128) notes that "except in John's Gospel, the most common way for non-initial speeches of tight-knit, closed conversations to be introduced in Koine Greek is with an articular pronoun and δέ."

εἶπαν. Aor act ind 3rd pl λέγω.

Μαίνῃ. Pres dep ind 2nd sg μαίνομαι.

διϊσχυρίζετο. Impf dep ind 3rd sg διϊσχυρίζομαι. On the diaeresis over the second *iota*, see 2:31 on προϊδὼν.

οὕτως ἔχειν. See 7:1.

ἔχειν. Pres act inf ἔχω (indirect discourse).

ἔλεγον. Impf act ind 3rd pl λέγω.

'Ο ἄγγελός. Predicate nominative. The second accent comes from the enclitic ἐστιν (see 1:4 on ἠκούσατέ). Moving the predicate noun to the front (see 3:13 on ὑμεῖς) of the sentence, away from its genitive modifier, lends a note of emphasis to the statement.

12:16 ὁ δὲ Πέτρος ἐπέμενεν κρούων· ἀνοίξαντες δὲ εἶδαν αὐτὸν καὶ ἐξέστησαν.

ἐπέμενεν. Impf act ind 3rd sg ἐπιμένω.

κρούων. Pres act ptc masc nom sg κρούω. When used in the sense of "to continue," ἐπιμένω takes a complementary participle (cf. Wallace 1996, 646).

ἀνοίξαντες. Aor act ptc masc nom pl ἀνοίγω (temporal).

εἶδαν. Aor act ind 3rd pl ὁράω.

ἐξέστησαν. Aor act ind 3rd pl ἐξίστημι.

12:17 κατασείσας δὲ αὐτοῖς τῇ χειρὶ σιγᾶν διηγήσατο [αὐτοῖς] πῶς ὁ κύριος αὐτὸν ἐξήγαγεν ἐκ τῆς φυλακῆς εἶπέν τε, Ἀπαγγείλατε Ἰακώβῳ καὶ τοῖς ἀδελφοῖς ταῦτα. καὶ ἐξελθὼν ἐπορεύθη εἰς ἕτερον τόπον.

κατασείσας. Aor act ptc masc nom sg κατασείω (attendant circumstance or temporal).

τῇ χειρὶ. Dative of instrument.

σιγᾶν. Pres act inf σιγάω (epexegetical or indirect discourse with a gesture rather than speech). The use of the infinitive in this construction is analogous to infinitives in indirect discourse.

διηγήσατο. Aor mid dep ind 3rd sg διηγέομαι.

πῶς. See 9:27.

ἐξήγαγεν. Aor act ind 3rd sg ἐξάγω.

ἐκ. See 1:8 on ἐφ' ὑμᾶς.

εἶπέν. Aor act ind 3rd sg λέγω. The second accent comes from the enclitic τε (see 1:4 on ἠκούσατέ).

Ἀπαγγείλατε. Aor act impv 2nd pl ἀπαγγέλλω.

ἀδελφοῖς. See 1:15.

ἐξελθὼν. Aor act ptc masc nom sg ἐξέρχομαι (attendant circumstance).

ἐπορεύθη. Aor pass dep ind 3rd sg πορεύομαι.

Acts 12:18–25

[18]Now as the day was dawning, there was great anxiety among the soldiers regarding what could have become of Peter. [19]Herod, after searching for him and not finding him, questioned the guards and then ordered them to be taken away (for execution). Then he left Judea and

stayed in Caesarea.

[20]Now Herod was furious with the people of Tyre and Sidon, so they went to him together and by persuading Blastus, the king's personal assistant, (to let them speak to the king) they began asking for peace because their countries got their food (supply) from the king. [21]On the appointed day, after Herod had dressed in his royal clothing and sat down on the judgment seat, he began to deliver a speech to them. [22]But the citizens started shouting, "This is the voice of a god, not of a man!" [23]Immediately, an angel of the Lord struck him down because he did not give the glory to God; and he was eaten by worms and died.

[24]So the message of God spread widely. [25]Meanwhile, Barnabas and Saul returned from Jerusalem, after completing their ministry, and took John, who was called Mark, along.

12:18 Γενομένης δὲ ἡμέρας ἦν τάραχος οὐκ ὀλίγος ἐν τοῖς στρατιώταις τί ἄρα ὁ Πέτρος ἐγένετο.

Γενομένης. Aor mid dep ptc fem gen sg γίνομαι. Genitive absolute (see 1:8 on ἐπελθόντος), temporal.

ἡμέρας. Genitive subject (see 1:8 on ἐπελθόντος).

ἦν. Impf ind 3rd sg εἰμί.

τάραχος οὐκ ὀλίγος. Litotes (see 1:5 on οὐ μετὰ πολλὰς ταύτας ἡμέρας).

τάραχος. Predicate adjective.

τί . . . ἐγένετο. Lit. " what then Peter had become."

τί. Introduces an indirect question. Accusative of reference. The interrogative pronoun could also be taken as a predicate nominative.

ἄρα. Probably emphasizes the sense of uncertainty (cf. 8:22).

ὁ Πέτρος. Nominative subject of ἐγένετο.

ἐγένετο. Aor mid dep ind 3rd sg γίνομαι.

12:19 Ἡρῴδης δὲ ἐπιζητήσας αὐτὸν καὶ μὴ εὑρών, ἀνακρίνας τοὺς φύλακας ἐκέλευσεν ἀπαχθῆναι, καὶ κατελθὼν ἀπὸ τῆς Ἰουδαίας εἰς Καισάρειαν διέτριβεν.

Ἡρῴδης. On the absence of the article see v. 3 on Πέτρον.

ἐπιζητήσας. Aor act ptc masc nom sg ἐπιζητέω (temporal). Given the conjunction that links the participles, ἐπιζητήσας should not be taken as concessive; contra Rogers and Rogers, 258.

εὑρὼν. Aor act ptc masc nom sg εὑρίσκω (temporal).

ἀνακρίνας. Aor act ptc masc nom sg ἀνακρίνω (temporal).

ἐκέλευσεν. Aor act ind 3rd sg κελεύω.

ἀπαχθῆναι. Aor pass inf ἀπάγω (indirect discourse). Barrett (588) argues that "for execution" is implicit in this context (cf. LN 20.65 and 56.38).

κατελθὼν. Aor act ptc masc nom sg κατέρχομαι (attendant circumstance).

διέτριβεν. Impf act ind 3rd sg διατρίβω.

12:20 Ἦν δὲ θυμομαχῶν Τυρίοις καὶ Σιδωνίοις· ὁμοθυμαδὸν δὲ παρῆσαν πρὸς αὐτόν καὶ πείσαντες Βλάστον, τὸν ἐπὶ τοῦ κοιτῶνος τοῦ βασιλέως, ᾐτοῦντο εἰρήνην διὰ τὸ τρέφεσθαι αὐτῶν τὴν χώραν ἀπὸ τῆς βασιλικῆς.

Ἦν. Impf ind 3rd sg εἰμί.

θυμομαχῶν. Pres act ptc masc nom sg θυμομαχέω (imperfect periphrastic; see 1:10 on ἀτενίζοντες).

Τυρίοις καὶ Σιδωνίοις. Dative of disadvantage.

παρῆσαν. Impf act ind 3rd pl πάρειμι.

πείσαντες. Aor act ptc masc nom pl πείθω (means or temporal). The use of this verb here implies that the delegation had to deal with Blastus if they were going to gain an audience with the king.

τὸν . . . βασιλέως. Lit. "the one over the bedroom of the king." As Louw and Nida (7.29) point out, this person would have been "a highly respected person with considerable responsibility for the king's living quarters and personal affairs." The article τὸν functions as an adjectivizer (see 2:5 on τῶν ὑπὸ τὸν οὐρανόν), changing the prepositional phrase into a modifier of Βλάστον.

ᾐτοῦντο. Impf mid ind 3rd pl αἰτέω. Although the verb may indicate that the delegates began their discussion with Herod at this point, in light of the following verse, it may be better to posit that the present dialogue did not directly involve the king. Such a face-to-face meeting was scheduled for a later time (v. 21).

τρέφεσθαι. Pres pass inf τρέφω. Used with διὰ τὸ to indicate cause.

τὴν χώραν. Accusative subject of the passive infinitive (see 1:3 on αὐτὸν).

12:21 τακτῇ δὲ ἡμέρᾳ ὁ Ἡρῴδης ἐνδυσάμενος ἐσθῆτα βασιλικὴν [καὶ] καθίσας ἐπὶ τοῦ βήματος ἐδημηγόρει πρὸς αὐτούς,

τακτῇ . . . ἡμέρᾳ. Dative of time. It is difficult to see how v. 20 would be relevant if the "appointed day" does not refer to a scheduled meeting between Herod and the delegates from Tyre and Sidon. Though it may be that a public speech, in which the citizen body was addressed (v. 22), coincided with the meeting.

ὁ Ἡρῴδης On the presence of the article, see v. 3.

ἐνδυσάμενος. Aor mid ptc masc nom sg ἐνδύω (temporal).

καθίσας. Aor act ptc masc nom sg καθίζω (temporal).

ἐδημηγόρει. Impf act ind 3rd sg δημηγορέω. Only here in the NT ("to speak in a somewhat formal setting"; LN 33.26).

αὐτούς. The antecedent is the joint delegation from Tyre and Sidon (v. 20), but probably included others (the δῆμος; v. 22) as well.

12:22 ὁ δὲ δῆμος ἐπεφώνει, Θεοῦ φωνὴ καὶ οὐκ ἀνθρώπου.

ὁ . . . δῆμος. See 19:30.

ἐπεφώνει. Impf act ind 3rd sg ἐπιφωνέω.

φωνή. Nominative absolute.

12:23 παραχρῆμα δὲ ἐπάταξεν αὐτὸν ἄγγελος κυρίου ἀνθ' ὧν οὐκ ἔδωκεν τὴν δόξαν τῷ θεῷ, καὶ γενόμενος σκωληκόβρωτος ἐξέψυξεν.

ἐπάταξεν. Aor act ind 3rd sg πατάσσω.

ἄγγελος κυρίου. See 5:19.

ἀνθ' ὧν. The preposition ἀντί with a genitive plural relative pronoun forms a causal idiomatic expression (cf. Luke 1:20; 12:3; 19:44; 2 Thess 2:10; Culy 1989, 39–40, 160).

ἔδωκεν. Aor act ind 3rd sg δίδωμι.

καὶ γενόμενος σκωληκόβρωτος ἐξέψυξεν. It is not clear whether the two events in this clause followed the separate action of the angel or are a description of how the angel struck Herod. According to Josephus (*Antiquities* 19.8.2), Herod's death occurred five days after he was struck with pain in his abdomen.

γενόμενος. Aor mid dep ptc masc nom sg γίνομαι (attendant circumstance).

σκωληκόβρωτος. Predicate adjective.

ἐξέψυξεν. Aor act ind 3rd sg ἐκψύχω.

12:24 Ὁ δὲ λόγος τοῦ θεοῦ ηὔξανεν καὶ ἐπληθύνετο.

ηὔξανεν καὶ ἐπληθύνετο. The conjoined verbs probably represent a doublet (see 2:43 on τέρατα καὶ σημεῖα) used to emphasize the degree to which God's message spread, though it is possible that ἐπληθύνετο points to a growing number of people who responded to the spreading message (cf. 6:7).

ηὔξανεν. Impf act ind 3rd sg αὐξάνω.

ἐπληθύνετο. Impf pass ind 3rd sg πληθύνω.

12:25 Βαρναβᾶς δὲ καὶ Σαῦλος ὑπέστρεψαν εἰς Ἰερουσαλὴμ πληρώσαντες τὴν διακονίαν, συμπαραλαβόντες Ἰωάννην τὸν ἐπικληθέντα Μᾶρκον.

δὲ καὶ. This verse illustrates how conjunctions can function not only at the sentence or phrase level (the καί links Βαρναβᾶς and Σαῦλος) but also at the discourse level (the δέ introduces the next development in the narrative).

Βαρναβᾶς . . . Σαῦλος. The two names are anarthrous (see 3:3 on Πέτρον καὶ Ἰωάννην) since the apostles are being reintroduced into the narrative (Levinsohn 1992, 101; see also comments on v. 3).

ὑπέστρεψαν. Aor act ind 3rd pl ὑποστρέφω.

εἰς. The problem of whether the original text read εἰς, ἐξ, or ἀπό can easily lead text critics to despair (see Metzger, 400, n. 22). The UBS[4]/NA[27] text, which the committee found the "least unsatisfactory" reading (Metzger, 400), is supported by א B 81 1409 *Byz pc*. A number of manuscripts (𝔓[74] A 33 2344 *al*) read ἐξ, while others (D E Ψ 36 181 *al*) read ἀπό. While εἰς is clearly the "harder reading," since one would expect to find Barnabas and Saul returning "from" Jerusalem following 11:30ff., the harder reading principle is irrelevant in the case of unintentional scribal changes. It is worth pointing out that ὑποστρέφω εἰς occurs seventeen times in the NT, with sixteen of these being found in Luke-Acts. In contrast, ὑποστρέφω ἐκ occurs only once (2 Pet 2:21), while ὑποστρέφω ἀπό occurs only in Luke 4:1; 24:9; and Heb 7:1. It is possible, that early scribes who encountered ὑπέστρεψαν ἀπό, an expression that does not occur elsewhere in Acts and is otherwise rare, or the even rarer ὑποστρέφω ἐκ, were so accustomed to writing ὑπέστρεψαν εἰς (see 1:12; 8:25; 12:25; and also 13:34; 14:21; 21:6; 22:17; 23:32) that they inadvertently introduced the error. This error was later corrected to either ἐξ or ἀπό. That scribes were not always thinking about the content of what they were writing is readily obvious from the textual history of the NT.

πληρώσαντες. Aor act ptc masc nom pl πληρόω (temporal).

συμπαραλαβόντες. Aor act ptc masc nom pl συμπαραλαμβάνω (attendant circumstance).

ἐπικληθέντα. Aor pass ptc masc acc sg ἐπικαλέω (attributive).

Μᾶρκον. The accusative noun serves as a complement in a passive object-complement double case construction (cf. 1:12 on Ἐλαιῶνος).

Acts 13:1–3

[1]Now there were many prophets and teachers in the local church at Antioch, including Barnabas, Simeon called Niger, Lucius the Cyrenian, Manaen, a childhood friend of Herod the tetrarch, and Saul. [2]While they were serving the Lord and fasting, the Holy Spirit said (to them), "Set apart for me Barnabas and Saul for the work to which I have called them." [3]Then after they had fasted, prayed and laid (their) hands on them, they sent them off.

13:1 Ἦσαν δὲ ἐν Ἀντιοχείᾳ κατὰ τὴν οὖσαν ἐκκλησίαν προφῆται καὶ διδάσκαλοι ὅ τε Βαρναβᾶς καὶ Συμεὼν ὁ καλούμενος Νίγερ, καὶ Λούκιος ὁ Κυρηναῖος, Μαναήν τε Ἡρῴδου τοῦ τετραάρχου σύντροφος καὶ Σαῦλος.

Ἦσαν. Impf ind 3rd pl εἰμί.

κατὰ. The preposition is probably used distributively to indicate something that was characteristic of the church at Antioch: there were prophets and teachers throughout the various house churches in Antioch, or there were many prophets and teachers in the Antioch church.

οὖσαν. Pres act ptc fem acc sg εἰμί (attributive). On the rendering "local," see Barrett, 283; cf. 5:17. It is possible that Luke was looking back on a world that had since changed and that the participle connotes "existing *at that time*."

προφῆται καὶ διδάσκαλοι. Nominative subject or predicate nominative if Ἦσαν is taken impersonally.

ὅ. The article should not be mistaken for a relative pronoun. The accent comes from the enclitic τε (see 1:4 on ἠκούσατέ).

τε . . . καὶ . . . καὶ . . . τε . . . καὶ. The conjunctions probably simply provide variety rather than indicating separate groups (Barrett, 602–3).

Βαρναβᾶς, Συμεὼν, Λούκιος, Μαναήν, Σαῦλος. The five names stand in apposition to προφῆται καὶ διδάσκαλοι.

καλούμενος. Pres pass ptc masc nom sg καλέω (attributive).

Νίγερ. Complement in a subject-complement double nominative construction with the passive καλούμενος (cf. 4:36 on υἱὸς and 1:12 on Ἐλαιῶνος).

ὁ Κυρηναῖος. Nominative in apposition to Λούκιος.

Ἡρῴδου. Genitive of relationship modifying σύντροφος.

τοῦ τετραάρχου. Genitive in apposition to Ἡρῴδου.

σύντροφος. Nominative in apposition to Μαναήν. It is unclear whether this term refers to a "close friend, intimate friend, friend since childhood" (LN 34.15) or a "foster brother" (LN 10.51). Rogers and Rogers (259) suggest that "Manean was a close friend of Herod Antipas and was probably brought up w. him in the court of Jerusalem."

13:2 λειτουργούντων δὲ αὐτῶν τῷ κυρίῳ καὶ νηστευόντων εἶπεν τὸ πνεῦμα τὸ ἅγιον, Ἀφορίσατε δή μοι τὸν Βαρναβᾶν καὶ Σαῦλον εἰς τὸ ἔργον ὃ προσκέκλημαι αὐτούς.

λειτουργούντων. Pres act ptc masc gen pl λειτουργέω. Genitive absolute (see 1:8 on ἐπελθόντος), temporal. This word, which was commonly used to denote duties performed by priests and Levites in the temple, probably refers to religious duties here as well.

αὐτῶν. Genitive subject (see 1:8 on ἐπελθόντος). The antecedent is the prophets and teachers of v. 1.

νηστευόντων. Pres act ptc masc gen pl νηστεύω. Genitive absolute (see 1:8 on ἐπελθόντος), temporal.

εἶπεν. Aor act ind 3rd sg λέγω.

Ἀφορίσατε. Aor act impv 2nd pl ἀφορίζω.

δή. This particle, which is related to δέ, is typically used with the imperative or the hortatory subjunctive (Porter 1994, 208) and indicates relatively weak emphasis (LN 91.6).

μοι. Dative of advantage.

εἰς. Purpose.

ὃ. Accusative of reference.

προσκέκλημαι. Prf dep ind 1st sg προσκαλέομαι.

13:3 τότε νηστεύσαντες καὶ προσευξάμενοι καὶ ἐπιθέντες τὰς χεῖρας αὐτοῖς ἀπέλυσαν.

νηστεύσαντες. Aor act ptc masc nom pl νηστεύω (temporal).

προσευξάμενοι. Aor mid dep ptc masc nom pl προσεύχομαι (temporal).

ἐπιθέντες. Aor act ptc masc nom pl ἐπιτίθημι (temporal).

ἀπέλυσαν. Aor act ind 3rd pl ἀπολύω.

Acts 13:4–12

[4]So they, after being sent out by the Holy Spirit, went down to Seleucia and from there sailed to Cyprus. [5]While they were in Salamis, they proclaimed the message of God in the Jewish synagogues—and they had John as their assistant. [6]After traveling throughout the island, up to Paphos, they found a man, a magician and Jewish false prophet, who went by the name Bar-Jesus. [7]He was associated with the proconsul Sergius Paulus, an intelligent man.

The proconsul summoned Barnabas and Saul and sought to hear the message of God, [8]but the magician Elymas—yes, that is how his name is translated—opposed them by trying to turn the proconsul away from the faith. [9]Saul, who was also (known as) Paul, and who was filled with the Holy Spirit, looked right at him [10]and said, "You are full of all deceit and every kind of wrongdoing, you son of the devil! You are an enemy of every kind of righteousness! Will you never stop making the straight paths of the Lord crooked? [11]Now, the hand of the Lord is against you! You will be blind, unable to (even) see the sun for a time!"

Immediately, a dark mist fell upon him and he walked around trying to find someone to lead him by the hand. [12]Then, when the proconsul saw what had happened, he believed because he was completely astounded at the teaching about the Lord.

13:4 Αὐτοὶ μὲν οὖν ἐκπεμφθέντες ὑπὸ τοῦ ἁγίου πνεύματος κατῆλθον εἰς Σελεύκειαν, ἐκεῖθέν τε ἀπέπλευσαν εἰς Κύπρον

μὲν οὖν. See 1:6.

ἐκπεμφθέντες. Aor pass ptc masc nom pl ἐκπέμπω (temporal).

κατῆλθον. Aor act ind 3rd pl κατέρχομαι.

ἐκεῖθέν. The second accent comes from the enclitic τε (see 1:4 on ἠκούσατέ).

ἀπέπλευσαν. Aor act ind 3rd pl ἀποπλέω.

13:5 καὶ γενόμενοι ἐν Σαλαμῖνι κατήγγελλον τὸν λόγον τοῦ θεοῦ ἐν ταῖς συναγωγαῖς τῶν Ἰουδαίων. εἶχον δὲ καὶ Ἰωάννην ὑπηρέτην.

γενόμενοι. Aor mid dep ptc masc nom pl γίνομαι (temporal).
Σαλαμῖνι. A city on the island of Cyprus.
κατήγγελλον. Impf act ind 3rd pl καταγγέλλω.
εἶχον. Impf act ind 3rd pl ἔχω.
ὑπηρέτην. The complement in an object-complement double accusative construction (see 1:3 on ζῶντα).

13:6 διελθόντες δὲ ὅλην τὴν νῆσον ἄχρι Πάφου εὗρον ἄνδρα τινὰ μάγον ψευδοπροφήτην Ἰουδαῖον ᾧ ὄνομα Βαριησοῦ

διελθόντες. Aor act ptc masc nom pl διέρχομαι (temporal).
εὗρον. Aor act ind 3rd pl εὑρίσκω.
μάγον. Accusative in apposition to ἄνδρα.
ψευδοπροφήτην. Accusative in apposition to ἄνδρα.
ᾧ ὄνομα Βαριησοῦ. The original form of this phrase is difficult to determine. The UBS[4]/NA[27] text, with the genitive Βαριησοῦ, is found only in 𝔓[74] א *pc* vg. Some witnesses (B C 33 *al*) read the nominative Βαριησους, others (A D[2] *Byz*) have the accusative form Βαριησουν (Ψ has Βαριησουμ), and yet others have a different form of ὄνομα (𝔓[45vid] 36, 453 *pc* read ὀνόματι Βαριησουν, and D* reads ὀνόματι καλούμενον Βαριησουαν. The UBS[4]/NA[27] text clearly reflects the harder reading, and it is difficult to imagine a scribe inadvertantly changing the text to ᾧ ὄνομα Βαριησοῦ.
ᾧ. Dative of possession.
ὄνομα. Nominative subject in a dative of possession construction.
Βαριησοῦ. Assuming the originality of this reading, and assuming that the form is in fact genitive, the case should probably be taken as an epexegetical genitive modifying ὄνομα ("the name of Bar-Jesus to him" = "whose name was Bar-Jesus"). It is possible that the unusual expression means something like "went by the name Bar-Jesus." This would help clarify why a different name for the same person is introduced in v. 8 without explaining why two names are used.

13:7 ὃς ἦν σὺν τῷ ἀνθυπάτῳ Σεργίῳ Παύλῳ, ἀνδρὶ συνετῷ. οὗτος προσκαλεσάμενος Βαρναβᾶν καὶ Σαῦλον ἐπεζήτησεν ἀκοῦσαι τὸν λόγον τοῦ θεοῦ.

ἦν. Impf ind 3rd sg εἰμί.

ἀνθυπάτῳ. This term serves as the Greek equivalent of the Latin proconsul and refers to "an official ruling over a province traditionally under the control of the Roman senate" (LN 37.82).

Σεργίῳ Παύλῳ. Dative in apposition to τῷ ἀνθυπάτῳ.

ἀνδρί. Dative in apposition to τῷ ἀνθυπάτῳ.

προσκαλεσάμενος. Aor mid dep ptc masc nom sg προσκαλέομαι (attendant circumstance).

ἐπεζήτησεν. Aor act ind 3rd sg ἐπιζητέω. Here, the sense is "to desire to have or experience something" (LN 25.9).

ἀκοῦσαι Aor act inf ἀκούω. Since the verb ἐπιζητέω is transitive, it is better to treat the infinitive as a direct object or as complementary rather than epexegetical (contra Rogers and Rogers, 259).

13:8 ἀνθίστατο δὲ αὐτοῖς Ἐλύμας ὁ μάγος, οὕτως γὰρ μεθερμηνεύεται τὸ ὄνομα αὐτοῦ, ζητῶν διαστρέψαι τὸν ἀνθύπατον ἀπὸ τῆς πίστεως.

ἀνθίστατο. Impf mid ind 3rd sg ἀνθίστημι.

αὐτοῖς. Dative complement of ἀνθίστατο.

Ἐλύμας. The use of the appositional noun phrase ὁ μάγος makes it clear that Ἐλύμας is another name for Βαριησοῦ (see v. 6).

ὁ μάγος. Nominative in apposition to Ἐλύμας.

μεθερμηνεύεται. Pres pass ind 3rd sg μεθερμηνεύω.

ζητῶν. Pres act ptc masc nom sg ζητέω (attendant circumstance).

διαστρέψαι. Aor act inf διαστρέφω (complementary; see v. 7 on ἀκοῦσαι).

τὸν ἀνθύπατον. Since διαστρέφω is transitive, ἀνθύπατον must be the accusative direct object of διαστρέψαι rather than its accusative subject.

13:9 Σαῦλος δέ, ὁ καὶ Παῦλος, πλησθεὶς πνεύματος ἁγίου ἀτενίσας εἰς αὐτὸν

ὁ καὶ Παῦλος. This nominative noun phrase stands in apposition to

Σαῦλος. The article functions as a nominalizer (see 1:3 on τὰ) in an idiomatic expression (lit. "the also Paul") that would be equivalent to ὁ καλούμενος καὶ Παῦλος (cf. Barrett, 616).

πλησθεὶς. Aor pass ptc masc nom sg πίμπλημι. The participle should probably be taken as an attributive modifier of the anarthrous Σαῦλος (see 3:3 on Πέτρον καὶ ᾿Ιωάννην), though it could indicate an attendant circumstance (cf. 4:8).

πνεύματος. See 2:4.

ἀτενίσας. Aor act ptc masc nom sg ἀτενίζω (attendant circumstance).

13:10 εἶπεν, Ὦ πλήρης παντὸς δόλου καὶ πάσης ῥᾳδιουργίας, υἱὲ διαβόλου, ἐχθρὲ πάσης δικαιοσύνης, οὐ παύσῃ διαστρέφων τὰς ὁδοὺς [τοῦ] κυρίου τὰς εὐθείας;

εἶπεν. Aor act ind 3rd sg λέγω.

Ὦ πλήρης. The particle ὦ is often used with the vocative to convey deep emotion (Wallace 1996, 68–69). The adjective should probably be viewed as substantival, though it could be taken as an attributive modifier of υἱὲ.

δόλου . . . ῥᾳδιουργίας. Strictly speaking, genitive of content; but the genitive nouns are actually part of an idiom ("to be full of X" means "to be characterized by X").

υἱὲ. Vocative in apposition to πλήρης (but see note on πλήρης).

διαβόλου. Most scholars take this as a genitive of relationship ("son of the devil"). Wallace (1996, 249) notes that this term occurs without an article because it is a monadic (one-of-a-kind) noun. It is also possible, however, given the common Semitic idiom, to take διαβόλου as an attributive genitive (cf. 4:36 on παρακλήσεως): "slanderous/demonic person."

ἐχθρὲ. Vocative in apposition to πλήρης or υἱὲ (see above).

δικαιοσύνης. Genitive of relationship or reference.

οὐ παύσῃ διαστρέφων τὰς ὁδοὺς [τοῦ] κυρίου τὰς εὐθείας; The rhetorical question functions as a powerful indictment against and warning to Elymas.

παύσῃ. Fut mid dep ind 2nd sg παύομαι. The verb is deponent only in the future tense, which here is used in a rhetorical question (see above) to convey implicitly that failure to stop such action will have dire consequences (Wallace [1996, 465, n. 51] lists this clause as an example of a deliberative question).

διαστρέφων. Pres act ptc masc nom sg διαστρέφω (complementary; see Wallace 1996, 646).

13:11 καὶ νῦν ἰδοὺ χεὶρ κυρίου ἐπὶ σέ καὶ ἔσῃ τυφλὸς μὴ βλέπων τὸν ἥλιον ἄχρι καιροῦ. παραχρῆμά τε ἔπεσεν ἐπ' αὐτὸν ἀχλὺς καὶ σκότος καὶ περιάγων ἐζήτει χειραγωγούς.

καὶ νῦν. See 4:29 on καὶ τὰ νῦν.

ἰδοὺ. See 1:10.

χεὶρ κυρίου. See 11:21.

ἔσῃ. Fut ind 2nd sg εἰμί.

τυφλὸς. Predicate adjective.

βλέπων. Pres act ptc masc nom sg βλέπω. The participle is adjectival in nature and probably should be viewed as standing in apposition to τυφλὸς, though it would also be possible to view it as part of a future periphrastic construction (cf. Turner 1963, 89).

παραχρῆμά. The second accent comes from the enclitic τε (see 1:4 on ἠκούσατέ).

ἔπεσεν. Aor act ind 3rd sg πίπτω. Although Louw and Nida (13.122) suggest that this verb can imply a sudden event, such a connotation probably comes strictly from the adverb παραχρῆμά.

ἐπ'. See 1:8 on ἐφ' ὑμᾶς.

ἀχλὺς καὶ σκότος. Hendiadys (lit. "mist and darkness"; see 1:25 on τῆς διακονίας καὶ ἀποστολῆς).

περιάγων. Pres act ptc masc nom sg περιάγω (attendant circumstance).

ἐζήτει. Impf act ind 3rd sg ζητέω.

13:12 τότε ἰδὼν ὁ ἀνθύπατος τὸ γεγονὸς ἐπίστευσεν ἐκπλησσόμενος ἐπὶ τῇ διδαχῇ τοῦ κυρίου.

ἰδὼν. Aor act ptc masc nom sg ὁράω (temporal).

τὸ γεγονὸς. Prf act ptc neut acc sg γίνομαι (substantival).

ἐπίστευσεν. Aor act ind 3rd sg πιστεύω.

ἐκπλησσόμενος. Pres dep ptc masc nom sg ἐκπλήσσομαι (causal). "To be so amazed as to be practically overwhelmed" (LN 25.219).

ἐπὶ. Reference. Bruce (299) notes that this preposition is commonly used with verbs of emotion in Hellenistic Greek.

τοῦ κυρίου. Objective genitive.

Acts 13:13–25

[13]After sailing from Paphos, Paul and his companions came to Perga in Pamphilia, but John deserted them and returned to Jerusalem. [14]Traveling on from Perga, they arrived in Pisidian Antioch and went into the synagogue on the sabbath day and sat down. [15]After the reading of the Law and the Prophets, the leaders of the synagogue sent (a message) to them, saying, "Brothers, if you have a word of encouragement for the people, please share it."

[16]Paul stood up, motioned with his hand, and said, "Israelites and God-fearers, listen (to me)! [17]The God of this people Israel chose our ancestors and made them a great people during the time they lived as foreigners in the land of Egypt. In a powerful way he led them out of Egypt, [18]and he put up with them for about forty years in the wilderness. [19]He overthrew seven nations in the land of Canaan and gave their land (to our ancestors)—[20](all this took place over) about 450 years. After these things, he provided judges until (the time) of Samuel the prophet.

[21]After that, they asked for a king and God gave them Saul son of Kish, a man of the tribe of Benjamin, (who ruled) for forty years. [22]Then, after removing him, he raised up David to be their king. He said, as a testimony, 'I have found David son of Jesse (to be) a man after my heart who will carry out all my plans.' [23]From the descendants of this man, God brought a savior to Israel, Jesus, in accord with (his) promise, [24]after John had preached, prior to his coming, a baptism of repentance to all the people of Israel. [25]But when John was about to complete his mission, he had said, 'What do you think I am? I am not that. But a person is coming after me whose sandals I am not worthy to untie!' "

13:13 Ἀναχθέντες δὲ ἀπὸ τῆς Πάφου οἱ περὶ Παῦλον ἦλθον εἰς Πέργην τῆς Παμφυλίας, Ἰωάννης δὲ ἀποχωρήσας ἀπ᾽ αὐτῶν ὑπέστρεψεν εἰς Ἱεροσόλυμα.

Ἀναχθέντες. Aor pass ptc masc nom pl ἀνάγω (temporal). In the middle or passive this verb means "to set sail."

οἱ περὶ Παῦλον. Lit. "those with Paul." The article functions as a nominalizer (see 1:3 on τὰ). The reference clearly includes Paul, the leader of the group (Bruce, 300).

ἦλθον. Aor act ind 3rd pl ἔρχομαι.

Παμφυλίας. Genitive of place.

ἀποχωρήσας. Aor act ptc masc nom sg ἀποχωρέω (attendant circumstance). Used with ἀπό + a person this verb means "to desert."

ἀπ'. See 1:8 on ἐφ' ὑμᾶς.

ὑπέστρεψεν. Aor act ind 3rd sg ὑποστρέφω.

13:14 αὐτοὶ δὲ διελθόντες ἀπὸ τῆς Πέργης παρεγένοντο εἰς Ἀντιόχειαν τὴν Πισιδίαν, καὶ [εἰσ]ελθόντες εἰς τὴν συναγωγὴν τῇ ἡμέρᾳ τῶν σαββάτων ἐκάθισαν.

διελθόντες. Aor act ptc masc nom pl διέρχομαι (temporal or attendant circumstance).

παρεγένοντο. Aor mid dep ind 3rd pl παραγίνομαι.

[εἰσ]ελθόντες. Aor act ptc masc nom pl [εἰσ]έρχομαι (attendant circumstance).

ἡμέρᾳ. Dative of time.

τῶν σαββάτων. Genitive of identification. There does not appear to be any difference in meaning between the plural (also at 16:13; Luke 4:16) and the singular (Luke 13:14, 16; 14:5) form of σάββατον in this construction (cf. BAGD, 739).

ἐκάθισαν. Aor act ind 3rd pl καθίζω.

13:15 μετὰ δὲ τὴν ἀνάγνωσιν τοῦ νόμου καὶ τῶν προφητῶν ἀπέστειλαν οἱ ἀρχισυνάγωγοι πρὸς αὐτοὺς λέγοντες, ⸀Ἄνδρες ἀδελφοί, εἴ τίς ἐστιν ἐν ὑμῖν λόγος παρακλήσεως πρὸς τὸν λαόν, λέγετε.

τοῦ νόμου . . . τῶν προφητῶν. Objective genitives.

ἀπέστειλαν. Aor act ind 3rd pl ἀποστέλλω.

πρὸς αὐτοὺς. The prepositional phrase modifies ἀπέστειλαν rather than λέγοντες.

λέγοντες. Pres act ptc masc nom pl λέγω (attendant circumstance or means, e.g., "sent word by saying").

⸀Ἄνδρες. See 1:11. In NA[27], the asterisk preceding ⸀Ἄνδρες indicates the beginning of a section in the Eusebian system (see NA[27], 79).

ἀδελφοί. Here, as in vv. 26, 38; 7:2; 22:1, 5; 23:1, 5, 6, this vocative expression is used to refer to fellow Jews rather than as a technical term for "believers" (cf. 1:15).

εἴ τίς ἐστιν ἐν ὑμῖν λόγος παρακλήσεως. Lit. "if there is any word of encouragement among you."

εἴ. Used with an indicative verb to introduce a first class condition.

τίς. The indefinite adjective should not be mistaken for an interrogative pronoun. The accent comes from the enclitic ἐστιν (see 1:4 on ἠκούσατέ). Moving the adjective to the front of the clause, away from the noun it modifies, probably intensifies the expression: "any word at all" (cf. 3:13 on ὑμεῖς).

ἐστιν. Pres act ind 3rd sg εἰμί.

λόγος παρακλήσεως. This phrase may be taken as the nominative subject, or as a predicate nominative if ἐστιν is taken impersonally.

πρὸς τὸν λαόν. The prepositional phrase modifies λόγος παρακλήσεως rather than λέγετε (so UBS[4]/NA[27]).

λέγετε. Pres act impv 2nd pl λέγω. In this case, an imperative verb alone serves as the apodosis of the first class condition.

13:16 ἀναστὰς δὲ Παῦλος καὶ κατασείσας τῇ χειρὶ εἶπεν· Ἄνδρες Ἰσραηλῖται καὶ οἱ φοβούμενοι τὸν θεόν, ἀκούσατε.

ἀναστὰς. Aor act ptc masc nom sg ἀνίστημι (attendant circumstance).

κατασείσας. Aor act ptc masc nom sg κατασείω (attendant circumstance).

τῇ χειρὶ. Dative of instrument.

εἶπεν. Aor act ind 3rd sg λέγω.

Ἄνδρες. See 1:11.

Ἰσραηλῖται. Vocative.

οἱ φοβούμενοι. Pres dep ptc masc nom pl φοβέομαι (substantival). This expression should probably be taken as a reference to a separate group of Jewish proselytes (cf. Barrett, 631), perhaps known by the technical label "God-fearers" (cf. 10:2; 13:26), rather than as a description of the Ἰσραηλῖται (with an epexegetical καί). This reading is supported by the presence of the prepositional phrase within the expression at v. 26: καὶ οἱ *ἐν ὑμῖν* φοβούμενοι τὸν θεόν.

ἀκούσατε. Aor act impv 2nd pl ἀκούω.

13:17 ὁ θεὸς τοῦ λαοῦ τούτου Ἰσραὴλ ἐξελέξατο τοὺς πατέρας ἡμῶν καὶ τὸν λαὸν ὕψωσεν ἐν τῇ παροικίᾳ ἐν γῇ Αἰγύπτου καὶ μετὰ βραχίονος ὑψηλοῦ ἐξήγαγεν αὐτοὺς ἐξ αὐτῆς,

τοῦ λαοῦ. The genitive could indicate either relationship or subordination (so Wallace 1996, 104).

᾿Ισραήλ. Genitive in apposition to λαοῦ.

ἐξελέξατο. Aor mid ind 3rd sg ἐκλέγω.

ὕψωσεν. Aor act ind 3rd sg ὑψόω.

ἐν τῇ παροικίᾳ. Temporal.

Αἰγύπτου. Genitive of identification.

μετὰ βραχίονος ὑψηλοῦ. In terms of syntax, μετά with the genitive indicates that the Israelites "were accompanied by an uplifted arm." In terms of semantics, however, the idiom probably indicates the manner in which God freed the Israelites from slavery rather than the means. This view is supported by both the shift from the more common expression ἐν βραχίονι ὑψηλῷ, which indicates instrument/means (see, e.g., LXX Exod 6:1, 6; Deut 4:34; 5:15), and the use of the same expression in LXX Prov 9:3 to denote manner.

ἐξήγαγεν. Aor act ind 3rd sg ἐξάγω.

ἐξ αὐτῆς. See 1:8 on ἐφ᾽ ὑμᾶς.

13:18 καὶ ὡς τεσσερακονταετῆ χρόνον ἐτροποφόρησεν αὐτοὺς ἐν τῇ ἐρήμῳ

τεσσερακονταετῆ χρόνον. Accusative indicating extent of time (see 7:20 on μῆνας). This rare expression (lit. "forty years time") is also used in 7:23 and may highlight the length of time (cf. the use of the dative in v. 20).

ἐτροποφόρησεν. Aor act ind 3rd sg τροποφορέω. As Metzger (405) notes, the evidence for the two variant readings, ἐτροποφόρησεν (א A*vid B C² D 36 81 *Byz al*) and ἐτροφοφόρησεν (𝔓⁷⁴ Aᶜ C* E Ψ 33vid *al*), is "singularly evenly balanced." The problem is compounded by the textual history of the passage to which Luke alludes, LXX Deut 1:31. It is quite possible that the original version of the LXX passage contained *both* verbs. The same two variants as Acts 13:18 are found in the first part of the verse (according to Metzger, B and 28 other manuscripts have ἐτροφοφόρησεν, while ten other manuscripts have ἐτροποφόρησεν). Later in the verse, there is variation between τροφοφορήσει (Bᶜ *al*) and τροποφορήσει (B* N 75 Origen3/6). It is worth highlighting the fact that the corrector of codex B left a text that had both verbs. In Acts 13:18, ἐτροποφόρησεν should probably be viewed as the harder reading since (1) a reference to God's care for the Israelites (ἐτροφοφόρησεν) is more appropriate in the context, and (2) some scribes may have thought it unseemly to use the verb τροποφορέω ("to put up with someone or something, implying extensive patience"; LN 25.173) with God as the subject. The harder reading principle, however, does not provide decisive evidence since either reading could have been accidentally introduced due to faulty hearing.

13:19 καὶ καθελὼν ἔθνη ἑπτὰ ἐν γῇ Χανάαν κατεκληρονόμησεν τὴν γῆν αὐτῶν

καθελὼν. Aor act ptc masc nom sg καθαιρέω (attendant circumstance or temporal).

κατεκληρονόμησεν. Aor act ind 3rd sg κατακληρονομέω.

13:20 ὡς ἔτεσιν τετρακοσίοις καὶ πεντήκοντα. καὶ μετὰ ταῦτα ἔδωκεν κριτὰς ἕως Σαμουὴλ [τοῦ] προφήτου.

ἔτεσιν τετρακοσίοις καὶ πεντήκοντα. It is unclear why there is a shift from the accusative temporal expression in v. 18 to the dative case here (cf. 8:11). It may be that the latter was more appropriate for a parenthetical statement summarizing the period of time described in vv. 17–19: four hundred years in Egypt, forty years in the wilderness, and about a decade during which the land was being distributed among the various tribes of Israel.

ἔδωκεν. Aor act ind 3rd sg δίδωμι.

προφήτου. Genitive in apposition to Σαμουήλ.

13:21 κἀκεῖθεν ᾐτήσαντο βασιλέα καὶ ἔδωκεν αὐτοῖς ὁ θεὸς τὸν Σαοὺλ υἱὸν Κίς, ἄνδρα ἐκ φυλῆς Βενιαμίν, ἔτη τεσσεράκοντα,

κἀκεῖθεν. A shortened form (crasis) of καὶ ἐκεῖθεν.

ᾐτήσαντο. Aor mid ind 3rd pl αἰτέω. Barrett (635) points out that petitions to God were typically placed in the active voice, and argues that the middle voice therefore suggests a petition to Samuel rather than God. Since, however, the middle voice is used elsewhere in Acts to petition God (7:46) and Luke does not use this verb in the active indicative elsewhere, except for three cases where the future tense is used (Luke 11:11, 12; 12:48), it is probably best not to build an argument for who the addressee was based on the voice of the verb. More likely, the middle voice is used to indicate personal benefit to the ones asking (cf. 7:46).

ἔδωκεν. Aor act ind 3rd sg δίδωμι.

υἱὸν. Accusative in apposition to τὸν Σαοὺλ.

ἄνδρα. Accusative in apposition to τὸν Σαοὺλ.

ἔτη τεσσεράκοντα. Accusative indicating extent of time (see 7:20 on μῆνας).

13:22 καὶ μεταστήσας αὐτὸν ἤγειρεν τὸν Δαυὶδ αὐτοῖς εἰς βασιλέα ᾧ καὶ εἶπεν μαρτυρήσας, Εὗρον Δαυὶδ τὸν τοῦ Ἰεσσαί, ἄνδρα κατὰ τὴν καρδίαν μου, ὃς ποιήσει πάντα τὰ θελήματά μου.

μεταστήσας. Aor act ptc masc nom sg μεθίστημι (temporal).

ἤγειρεν. Aor act ind 3rd sg ἐγείρω.

αὐτοῖς. Dative of advantage.

εἰς βασιλέα. The preposition εἰς with an accusative noun functions like a predicate modifier of τὸν Δαυὶδ (see 4:11 on εἰς κεφαλὴν γωνίας).

εἶπεν. Aor act ind 3rd sg λέγω.

μαρτυρήσας. Aor act ptc masc nom sg μαρτυρέω (attendant circumstance).

Εὗρον. Aor act ind 1st sg εὑρίσκω.

τὸν τοῦ Ἰεσσαί. Accusative in apposition to Δαυὶδ. The accusative article functions as a nominalizer (see 1:3 on τὰ).

κατὰ. Standard (see 7:44).

ποιήσει. Fut act ind 3rd sg ποιέω.

θελήματά. The second accent comes from the enclitic μου (see 1:4 on ἠκούσατέ).

13:23 τούτου ὁ θεὸς ἀπὸ τοῦ σπέρματος κατ᾽ ἐπαγγελίαν ἤγαγεν τῷ Ἰσραὴλ σωτῆρα Ἰησοῦν,

τούτου. The genitive modifier of τοῦ σπέρματος is fronted (see 3:13 on ὑμεῖς) as the topic of the construction (cf. 2:22 on Ἰησοῦν τὸν Ναζωραῖον).

κατ᾽. Standard (see 7:44).

ἤγαγεν. Aor act ind 3rd sg ἄγω.

τῷ Ἰσραήλ. Dative indirect object.

᾿Ιησοῦν. Accusative in apposition to σωτῆρα.

13:24 προκηρύξαντος ᾿Ιωάννου πρὸ προσώπου τῆς εἰσόδου αὐτοῦ βάπτισμα μετανοίας παντὶ τῷ λαῷ ᾿Ισραήλ.

προκηρύξαντος. Aor act ptc masc gen sg προκηρύσσω. Genitive absolute (see 1:8 on ἐπελθόντος), temporal. Although genitive absolute constructions normally occur at the beginning of the sentence, this one is placed at the end of the sentence to allow for the topic construction (see v. 23 on τούτου; cf. 4:37).

᾿Ιωάννου. Genitive subject (see 1:8 on ἐπελθόντος).

πρὸ προσώπου τῆς εἰσόδου αὐτοῦ. In this unusual expression (lit. "before the face of his coming"), πρὸ προσώπου indicates antecedent time (cf. Luke 10:1).

πρὸ. See 1:8 on ἐφ᾿ ὑμᾶς.

μετανοίας. Genitive of description. As Wallace notes (1996, 80), although "there are various *possible* interpretations of this phrase . . . . it may well be best to be non-committal: 'baptism that is somehow related to repentance.'"

13:25 ὡς δὲ ἐπλήρου ᾿Ιωάννης τὸν δρόμον, ἔλεγεν, Τί ἐμὲ ὑπονοεῖτε εἶναι; οὐκ εἰμὶ ἐγώ· ἀλλ᾿ ἰδοὺ ἔρχεται μετ᾿ ἐμὲ οὗ οὐκ εἰμὶ ἄξιος τὸ ὑπόδημα τῶν ποδῶν λῦσαι.

ὡς. Temporal (see 18:5).

ἐπλήρου. Impf act ind 3rd sg πληρόω. The use of the imperfect with this particular verb (the only other NT occurrences are at 7:23; 9:23; 13:52) probably indicates that John had nearly finished the task he had been given.

δρόμον. The figurative use of this term (meaning "a task or function involving continuity, serious effort, and possibly obligation"; LN 42.26) is rare (Barrett, 638).

ἔλεγεν. Impf act ind 3rd sg λέγω. This may be a rare example where it is appropriate to translate the imperfect like a pluperfect (cf. Wallace 1996, 549).

Τί ἐμὲ. In addition to the neuter interrogative pronoun found in UBS[4]/NA[27] and supported by 𝔓[74] ℵ A B E (33 81 με) 1175 *pc*, the masculine form is found in 𝔓[45] C D Ψ 36 181 *Byz al*. Scribes probably would have more naturally changed a neuter form to masculine than vice versa.

Τί. Predicate accusative (see 1:22 on μάρτυρα) of εἶναι.

ἐμὲ. Accusative subject of the infinitive (see 1:3 on αὐτὸν). The pronoun is moved to the front of the sentence (outside the infinitival clause) to put the focus (see 2:15 on ὑμεῖς) on John.

ὑπονοεῖτε. Pres act ind 2nd pl ὑπονοέω.

οὐκ εἰμὶ ἐγώ. In this context, this statement is equivalent to "You're wrong!"

εἰμὶ . . . εἰμὶ. Pres act ind 1st sg εἰμί.

εἶναι. Pres act inf εἰμί (indirect discourse).

ἰδοὺ. See 1:10.

ἔρχεται. Pres dep ind 3rd sg ἔρχομαι.

οὗ. Genitive of possession modifying τῶν ποδῶν. The relative pronoun introduces a headless relative clause (see 3:6 on ὃ). The unexpressed antecedent is the subject of ἔρχεται.

ἄξιος. Predicate adjective.

τὸ ὑπόδημα τῶν ποδῶν. Accusative direct object of λῦσαι (lit. "the sandals of his feet").

λῦσαι. Aor act inf λύω (epexegetical).

Acts 13:26–41

[26]"Brothers, descendants of Abraham's race and others among you
who fear God, the message of this salvation has been sent to us. [27]For
those living in Jerusalem and their rulers, since they lacked understanding concerning (the Messiah) and the voices of the prophets which are
read each and every sabbath day, they fulfilled (the prophecies) by con-
demning (him). [28]And though they found no reason to impose the death
sentence, they (still) asked Pilate to have him executed.

[29]When they had carried out everything that had been written about
him, they took (his body) from the cross and placed (it) in a tomb. [30]But
God raised him from the dead, [31]and he appeared over the course of
many many days to those who had traveled with him from Galilee to
Jerusalem. These people are now his witnesses to the people. [32]And we
preach good news to you about the promise to our ancestors, [33](preaching) that God has fulfilled this (promise) for our children by raising
Jesus, just as it is also written in the second psalm, 'You are my son.
Today I have fathered you.'

[34]Now, that he raised him from the dead to no longer be on the verge
of decay (is proven by the fact that) he spoke in this way: 'I will give
you the divine and trustworthy promises (made to) David.' [35]Therefore,

it also says in another (psalm), 'You will not allow your holy one to experience decay.' [36]For David, after serving his own generation in accord with God's purpose, died, was buried with his ancestors, and experienced decay. [37]But the one whom God raised did not experience decay.

[38a]So, let it be known to you, brothers, that through this (man) forgiveness of sins is proclaimed to you; [38b-39]and by this man all who believe will be justified from all the things you could not be justified from by the Law of Moses. [40]Be careful, then, so that what was said in the Prophets does not happen to you: [41]'Look, you scoffers! Marvel and be destroyed! For I am doing something in your days, a work that you will never believe (even) if someone explains (it) to you!'"

13:26 Ἄνδρες ἀδελφοί, υἱοὶ γένους Ἀβραὰμ καὶ οἱ ἐν ὑμῖν φοβούμενοι τὸν θεόν, ἡμῖν ὁ λόγος τῆς σωτηρίας ταύτης ἐξαπεστάλη.

Ἄνδρες. See 1:11.

ἀδελφοί. See v. 15. The reintroduction of the vocative ἀδελφοί marks a turning point in Paul's speech.

υἱοί. Vocative in apposition to Ἄνδρες ἀδελφοί.

γένους. Genitive of source.

οἱ. The article functions as a nominalizer (see 1:3 on τὰ), making the participle a substantive.

καὶ οἱ ἐν ὑμῖν φοβούμενοι τὸν θεόν. The omission of the conjunction in two early manuscripts (𝔓[45] B) suggests that some scribes may have taken the following expression as another appositional noun phrase, even though the prepositional phrase ἐν ὑμῖν makes it clear that a separate group is intended. On οἱ φοβούμενοι τὸν θεὸν, see 13:16.

οἱ φοβούμενοι. Pres dep ptc masc voc pl φοβέομαι (substantival).

ἐξαπεστάλη. Aor pass ind 3rd sg ἐξαποστέλλω.

13:27 οἱ γὰρ κατοικοῦντες ἐν Ἰερουσαλὴμ καὶ οἱ ἄρχοντες αὐτῶν τοῦτον ἀγνοήσαντες καὶ τὰς φωνὰς τῶν προφητῶν τὰς κατὰ πᾶν σάββατον ἀναγινωσκομένας κρίναντες ἐπλήρωσαν,

οἱ . . . κατοικοῦντες. Pres act ptc masc nom pl κατοικέω (substantival).

τοῦτον. Accusative direct object of ἀγνοήσαντες. The unexpressed antecedent is Jesus.

ἀγνοήσαντες. Aor act ptc masc nom pl ἀγνοέω (causal).

καὶ τὰς φωνὰς. The conjunction suggests that this accusative noun phrase is a second direct object of ἀγνοήσαντες rather than the object of ἐπλήρωσαν.

κατὰ πᾶν σάββατον. The distributive preposition used with πᾶν is probably emphatic (cf. 15:21; 17:17; 18:4; 26:11).

ἀναγινωσκομένας. Pres pass ptc fem acc pl ἀναγινώσκω (attributive, with τὰς).

κρίναντες. Aor act ptc masc nom pl κρίνω (means).

ἐπλήρωσαν. Aor act ind 3rd pl πληρόω.

13:28 καὶ μηδεμίαν αἰτίαν θανάτου εὑρόντες ᾐτήσαντο Πιλᾶτον ἀναιρεθῆναι αὐτόν.

εὑρόντες. Aor act ptc masc nom pl εὑρίσκω (concessive).

ᾐτήσαντο. Aor mid ind 3rd pl αἰτέω.

Πιλᾶτον. Accusative direct object of ᾐτήσαντο, not the subject of the *passive* infinitive (contra Turner 1963, 149) since Pilate was not the one they wanted executed.

ἀναιρεθῆναι. Aor pass inf ἀναιρέω (indirect discourse).

αὐτόν. Accusative subject of the passive infinitive (see 1:3 on αὐτὸν).

13:29 ὡς δὲ ἐτέλεσαν πάντα τὰ περὶ αὐτοῦ γεγραμμένα, καθελόντες ἀπὸ τοῦ ξύλου ἔθηκαν εἰς μνημεῖον.

ὡς. Temporal (see 18:5).

ἐτέλεσαν. Aor act ind 3rd pl τελέω.

τὰ γεγραμμένα. Prf pass ptc neut nom pl γράφω (substantival).

καθελόντες. Aor act ptc masc nom pl καθαιρέω (attendant circumstance).

ἔθηκαν. Aor act ind 3rd pl τίθημι.

13:30 ὁ δὲ θεὸς ἤγειρεν αὐτὸν ἐκ νεκρῶν,

ἤγειρεν. Aor act ind 3rd sg ἐγείρω.

13:31 ὃς ὤφθη ἐπὶ ἡμέρας πλείους τοῖς συναναβᾶσιν αὐτῷ ἀπὸ τῆς Γαλιλαίας εἰς Ἰερουσαλήμ, οἵτινες [νῦν] εἰσιν μάρτυρες αὐτοῦ πρὸς τὸν λαόν.

ὃς. The antecedent is αὐτὸν in the previous verse.

ὤφθη. Aor pass ind 3rd sg ὁράω. See 7:30.

ἐπὶ ἡμέρας πλείους. The preposition (when used with an accusative time noun that has a modifier, like πολύς, that implies duration) introduces extent of time (Moule, 49; see also 16:18; 18:20; 19:8, 10, 34; and perhaps 17:2).

πλείους. Comparative with an elative sense: "very many days" (Wallace 1996, 300). When superlative or comparative adjectives are not part of a comparitive construction they will typically carry elative force.

τοῖς συναναβᾶσιν. Aor act ptc masc dat pl συναναβαίνω (substantival).

αὐτῷ. Verbs with a συν- prefix take a dative complement.

εἰσιν. Pres act ind 3rd pl εἰμί.

μάρτυρες. Predicate nominative.

13:32 καὶ ἡμεῖς ὑμᾶς εὐαγγελιζόμεθα τὴν πρὸς τοὺς πατέρας ἐπαγγελίαν γενομένην,

ἡμεῖς. The fronted (see 3:13 on ὑμεῖς) explicit pronoun shifts the focus (see 2:15 on ὑμεῖς) to the apostles.

ὑμᾶς. The fronted (see 3:13 on ὑμεῖς) object pronoun is also in focus (see 2:15 on ὑμεῖς). Barrett (645; cf. Bruce, 309; BDF §152.2) takes the pronoun as one of two objects in a double accusative construction. It is better, however, to maintain a distinction between double accusative constructions and constructions such as this where the indirect object (ὑμᾶς) has "advanced" to the direct object position (and thus bears the accusative case) in order to highlight the indirect object (cf. 8:25 on πολλάς κώμας). Where such advancement occurs, the semantic patient, i.e., the referent that is affected by the action of the verb (τὴν . . . ἐπαγγελίαν), which has been displaced, is syntactically no longer a direct object (though it still appears in the accusative case).

εὐαγγελιζόμεθα. Pres mid ind 1st pl εὐαγγελίζω. Porter (1994, 21) argues that the shift from the aorist to the present tense implies that this clause is of greater significance within the discourse.

γενομένην. Aor mid dep ptc fem acc sg γίνομαι. This is the only example in Acts where an apparently anarthrous participle (see 3:3 on Πέτρον καὶ ᾿Ιωάννην) appears to serve as an attributive modifier of an articular noun (see also Matt 6:30; 27:37; Mark 6:2; Luke 11:21; 12:28, 28; 16:14; John 2:9; 4:39; 8:9; 14:10; Rom 2:27; 1 Cor 8:12; 2 Cor 4:15; Eph 2:4; 5:27; Heb 3:2; 1 Pet 3:20; 4:12; Boyer 1984, 166, n. 4; Porter 1989, 366).

13:33 ὅτι ταύτην ὁ θεὸς ἐκπεπλήρωκεν τοῖς τέκνοις [αὐτῶν] ἡμῖν ἀναστήσας ᾿Ιησοῦν ὡς καὶ ἐν τῷ ψαλμῷ γέγραπται τῷ δευτέρῳ, Υἱός μου εἶ σύ, ἐγὼ σήμερον γεγέννηκά σε.

ὅτι. Introduces a clausal complement (indirect discourse) that stands in apposition to τὴν ἐπαγγελίαν.

ταύτην. The fronted (see 3:13 on ὑμεῖς) demonstrative pronoun is in focus (see 2:15 on ὑμεῖς).

ἐκπεπλήρωκεν. Prf act ind 3rd sg ἐκπληρόω. It is quite possible that this prefixed form of πληρόω intensifies the sense of the verb (cf. Porter 1994, 140–41; Barrett, 645).

τέκνοις. Dative of advantage.

[αὐτῶν] ἡμῖν. Support for the UBS[4]/NA[27] text is limited to late manuscripts (C[3] E 33 36 81 181 *Byz pm*). In contrast, there is strong early support ($\mathfrak{P}^{74}$ ℵ C* D *pc*) for the variant reading ἡμῶν. Barrett (645) explains the textual history by positing an original mistake by Luke (ἡμῶν instead of ἡμῖν) that was later corrected by scribes. Most scholars reject ἡμῶν, claiming that it gives a "most improbable sense" (Metzger, 410), in spite of the strong manuscript support for this reading. While this reading might superficially appear improbable, it is not nonsensical. Appealing to the fulfillment of a promise for the benefit of "our children" would have been both culturally appropriate and rhetorically powerful. The fact that this reading is superficially the "harder reading" could explain how the other readings arose. If the UBS[4]/NA[27] text is followed, ἡμῖν stands in apposition to τέκνοις.

ἀναστήσας. Aor act ptc masc nom sg ἀνιστήμι (means).

γέγραπται. Prf pass ind 3rd sg γράφω.

δευτέρῳ. The variant reading, πρώτῳ (D most early fathers) may reflect an early tradition in which the first two psalms were viewed as a single psalm (Metzger, 412–14).

Υἱός. Predicate nominative.

εἶ. Pres act ind 2nd sg εἰμί.

γεγέννηκα. Prf act ind 1st sg γεννάω. The second accent comes from the enclitic σε (see 1:4 on ἠκούσατέ).

13:34 ὅτι δὲ ἀνέστησεν αὐτὸν ἐκ νεκρῶν μηκέτι μέλλοντα ὑποστρέφειν εἰς διαφθοράν, οὕτως εἴρηκεν ὅτι Δώσω ὑμῖν τὰ ὅσια Δαυὶδ τὰ πιστά.

ὅτι δὲ. This construction seems to be used in arguments in the NT to introduce a disputed claim that will be followed by a statement designed to substantiate the claim (cf. Luke 20:37 and Gal 3:11).

ἀνέστησεν. Aor act ind 3rd sg ἀνίστημι.

μέλλοντα. Pres act ptc masc acc sg μέλλω. The participle functions as the complement in an object-complement double accusative construction (see 1:3 on ζῶντα). See also 3:3 on μελλοντας.

ὑποστρέφειν. Pres act inf ὑποστρέφω (complementary).

εἴρηκεν. Prf act ind 3rd sg λέγω.

Δώσω. Fut act ind 1st sg δίδωμι.

ὑμῖν. Dative indirect object.

τὰ ὅσια. On the translation of this neuter plural expression, see LN 33.290.

Δαυὶδ. Probably genitive.

τὰ πιστά. Accusative in apposition to τὰ ὅσια (cf. LN 33.290).

13:35 διότι καὶ ἐν ἑτέρῳ λέγει, Οὐ δώσεις τὸν ὅσιόν σου ἰδεῖν διαφθοράν.

λέγει. Pres act ind 3rd sg λέγω. Bruce (310) notes that since the words are addressed to God, the understood subject of λέγει must be ἡ γραφή.

δώσεις. Fut act ind 2nd sg δίδωμι. The verb is used as part of a causative construction (see 2:4 on ἐδίδου) with the infinitive: "You will not *allow* . . . to."

τὸν ὅσιόν. Accusative subject of the infinitive (see 1:3 on αὐτὸν). The second accent comes from the enclitic σου (see 1:4 on ἠκούσατε).

ἰδεῖν διαφθοράν. See 2:27.

ἰδεῖν. Aor act inf ὁράω (complementary; the infinitival clause functions as the clausal direct object of δώσεις).

13:36 Δαυὶδ μὲν γὰρ ἰδίᾳ γενεᾷ ὑπηρετήσας τῇ τοῦ θεοῦ βουλῇ ἐκοιμήθη καὶ προσετέθη πρὸς τοὺς πατέρας αὐτοῦ καὶ εἶδεν διαφθοράν·

ἰδίᾳ γενεᾷ. Dative of time ("during his generation"; so BDF §200) or dative complement of ὑπηρετήσας.

ὑπηρετήσας. Aor act ptc masc nom sg ὑπηρετέω (temporal or attendant circumstance).

τῇ βουλῇ. Dative of rule (see 2:23 on βουλῇ καὶ προγνώσει) or perhaps dative complement of ὑπηρετήσας (if ἰδίᾳ γενεᾷ is dative of time).

ἐκοιμήθη. Aor pass ind 3rd sg κοιμάω. See 7:60.

προσετέθη . . . αὐτοῦ. Lit. "was added to his fathers" (another euphemism).

προσετέθη. Aor pass ind 3rd sg προστίθημι.

εἶδεν διαφθοράν. See 2:27 on ἰδεῖν διαφθοράν.

εἶδεν. Aor act ind 3rd sg ὁράω.

13:37 ὃν δὲ ὁ θεὸς ἤγειρεν, οὐκ εἶδεν διαφθοράν.

ὃν. The relative pronoun introduces a headless relative clause (see 3:6 on ὃ), which functions as the subject of εἶδεν, with Christ as the referent.

δὲ. The conjunction is adversative (to the μέν in v. 36) and contrasts what happened to Christ with what happened to David (Bruce, 311).

ἤγειρεν. Aor act ind 3rd sg ἐγείρω.

εἶδεν διαφθοράν. See 2:27 on ἰδεῖν διαφθοράν.

εἶδεν. Aor act ind 3rd sg ὁράω.

13:38 γνωστὸν οὖν ἔστω ὑμῖν, ἄνδρες ἀδελφοί, ὅτι διὰ τούτου ὑμῖν ἄφεσις ἁμαρτιῶν καταγγέλλεται, [καὶ] ἀπὸ πάντων ὧν οὐκ ἠδυνήθητε ἐν νόμῳ Μωϋσέως δικαιωθῆναι,

γνωστὸν ἔστω. This phrase is unique to Luke in the NT (Barrett, 649).

γνωστὸν. Predicate (neuter nominative) adjective.

ἔστω. Pres act impv 3rd sg εἰμί.

ἄνδρες. Vocative; see 1:11.

ἀδελφοί. See v. 15.

ὅτι. See 28:22.

διὰ τούτου. Instrumental/intermediate agent. The fronted (see 3:13 on ὑμεῖς) prepositional phrase is in focus (see 2:15 on ὑμεῖς).

ὑμῖν. Dative of advantage or dative indirect object.

ἄφεσις. Neuter nominative subject of the passive verb.

καταγγέλλεται. Pres pass ind 3rd sg καταγγέλλω.

ἀπὸ πάντων. The fronted (see 3:13 on ὑμεῖς) prepositional phrase, which one would expect at the end of v. 39, is in focus (see 2:15 on ὑμεῖς).

ὧν. The genitive case could be the result of attraction to πάντων, or it could be taken as a genitive of reference or separation.

ἠδυνήθητε. Aor pass dep ind 2nd pl δύναμαι.

ἐν νόμῳ. Given the contrast in the following verse (ἐν τούτῳ), the prepositional phrase should probably be taken as instrumental/means (cf. Bruce, 312; but see note below on ἐν τούτῳ).

δικαιωθῆναι. Aor pass inf δικαιόω. Used with ἀπό in this context, δικαιόω probably refers to "the act of clearing someone of transgression" (so LN 56.34).

13:39 ἐν τούτῳ πᾶς ὁ πιστεύων δικαιοῦται.

ἐν τούτῳ. This prepositional phrase could be taken with δικαιοῦται as indicating instrument/agent, or with ὁ πιστεύων ("everyone who believes in him is justified"). The frequent use of topic constructions (see 2:22 on Ἰησοῦν τὸν Ναζωραῖον) in this discourse makes either reading possible. Evidence from usage (ἐν appears to always follow πιστεύω elsewhere in the NT when it introduces the object of trust/belief) and the apparent contrast between ἐν τούτῳ and ἐν νόμῳ (v. 38) makes the former more likely (contra Barrett, 651).

ὁ πιστεύων. Pres act ptc masc nom sg πιστεύω (substantival). The present tense should not be pressed to emphasize the continual nature of the belief (contra Wallace 1996, 621).

δικαιοῦται. Pres pass ind 3rd sg δικαιόω. Again, it is inappropriate to suggest that the present tense indicates that "every time someone believes he is justified" (contra Rogers and Rogers, 262).

13:40 βλέπετε οὖν μὴ ἐπέλθῃ τὸ εἰρημένον ἐν τοῖς προφήταις,

βλέπετε. Pres act impv 2nd pl βλέπω.

ἐπέλθῃ. Aor act subj 3rd sg ἐπέρχομαι. In this case, the verb indicates "to happen to someone or something, with the implication of an event which is undesirable" (LN 13.119). The subjunctive with μή is commonly used after verbs of warning or fearing (Wallace 1996, 477) and indicates concern regarding a potential outcome (lit. "Watch out lest what was said in the prophets should happen"; cf. 23:10 on διασπασθῇ).

τὸ εἰρημένον. Prf pass ptc neut nom sg λέγω (substantival). The expression, τὸ εἰρημένον ἐν τοῖς προφήταις, serves as the subject of ἐπέλθῃ.

ἐν τοῖς προφήταις. The prepositional phrase could be locative ("in the prophets"), or less likely, instrumental/agent. The use of the plural (probably as a reference to the twelve "minor" prophets; cf. Bruce, 312) rather than the singular (the quote is from Habakkuk) lends support to the former.

13:41 Ἴδετε, οἱ καταφρονηταί, καὶ θαυμάσατε καὶ ἀφανίσθητε, ὅτι ἔργον ἐργάζομαι ἐγὼ ἐν ταῖς ἡμέραις ὑμῶν, ἔργον ὃ οὐ μὴ πιστεύσητε ἐάν τις ἐκδιηγῆται ὑμῖν.

Ἴδετε. Aor act impv 2nd pl ὁράω. Unlike βλέπετε, which introduces a warning, this imperative verb is used to draw the listeners' attention.

θαυμάσατε. Aor act impv 2nd pl θαυμάζω.

ἀφανίσθητε. Aor pass imp 2nd pl ἀφανίζω.

ὅτι. Causal.

ἔργον. Cognate accusative.

ἐργάζομαι. Pres dep ind 1st sg ἐργάζομαι.

ἔργον. Resumptive in apposition to the earlier ἔργον.

οὐ μὴ πιστεύσητε. Aor act subj 2nd pl πιστεύω. The aorist subjunctive is used with οὐ μὴ to express emphatic negation (cf. 28:26).

ἐκδιηγῆται. Pres dep subj 3rd sg ἐκδιηγέομαι. Used with ἐάν in a third class condition.

Acts 13:42–47

[42]As they were leaving (the synagogue), (the people) urged them to speak to them (again) about these matters on the next sabbath. [43]When the synagogue meeting had ended, many of the Jews and devout proselytes followed Paul and Barnabas, who spoke to them and urged them to continue living in a manner that pleases God.

[44]On the following sabbath, nearly the entire city gathered to hear the message of the Lord. [45]When the Jews saw the crowd, they were filled with jealousy and began speaking (out) in a slanderous manner against what Paul was saying. [46]But both Paul and Barnabas replied boldly, "It was necessary for you to be told God's message first. Since you reject it and do not consider yourselves worthy of eternal life, we are turning (our attention) to the Gentiles!" [47]For this is the command the Lord has given to us: 'I have appointed you as a light for the Gentiles, so that you might bring salvation to the end(s) of the earth.'"

13:42 Ἐξιόντων δὲ αὐτῶν παρεκάλουν εἰς τὸ μεταξὺ σάββατον λαληθῆναι αὐτοῖς τὰ ῥήματα ταῦτα.

Ἐξιόντων. Pres act ptc masc gen pl ἔξειμι. Genitive absolute (see 1:8 on ἐπελθόντος), temporal.

αὐτῶν. Genitive subject (see 1:8 on ἐπελθόντος). The referents are Paul and Barnabas. Many manuscripts (*Byz*[pt]) add the implicit ἐκ τῆς συναγωγῆς τῶν' Ιουδαίων, while others (*Byz*[pt]) also specify that it was the Jews who were leaving and the Gentiles (παρεκάλουν τὰ ἔθνη; *Byz*) who urged the apostles to speak again.

παρεκάλουν. Impf act ind 3rd pl παρακαλέω.

μεταξὺ. Here, as an adjective, μεταξὺ refers to "a point of time which is subsequent in order to a previous point of time" (LN 67.54).

λαληθῆναι. Aor pass inf λαλέω (indirect discourse).

τὰ ῥήματα ταῦτα. Accusative subject of the passive infinitive (lit. "that these words be spoken").

13:43 λυθείσης δὲ τῆς συναγωγῆς ἠκολούθησαν πολλοὶ τῶν Ἰουδαίων καὶ τῶν σεβομένων προσηλύτων τῷ Παύλῳ καὶ τῷ Βαρναβᾷ, οἵτινες προσλαλοῦντες αὐτοῖς ἔπειθον αὐτοὺς προσμένειν τῇ χάριτι τοῦ θεοῦ.

λυθείσης. Aor pass ptc fem gen sg λύω. Genitive absolute (see 1:8 on ἐπελθόντος), temporal.

συναγωγῆς. Genitive subject of the passive participle (see 1:8 on ἐπελθόντος).

ἠκολούθησαν. Aor act ind 3rd pl ἀκολουθέω.

Ἰουδαίων καὶ προσηλύτων. Partitive genitive.

σεβομένων. Pres dep ptc masc gen pl σέβομαι (attributive). See

17:17 on τοῖς σεβομένοις.

τῷ Παύλῳ καὶ τῷ Βαρναβᾷ. Dative complement of ἠκολούθησαν.

προσλαλοῦντες. Pres act ptc masc nom pl προσλαλέω (attendant circumstance).

αὐτοῖς. Dative complement of προσλαλοῦντες.

ἔπειθον. Impf act ind 3rd pl πείθω.

αὐτοὺς. Accusative subject of the infinitive (see 1:3 on αὐτὸν).

προσμένειν τῇ χάριτι τοῦ θεοῦ. The precise meaning of this phrase is difficult to determine. The verb implies that they are already "in the grace of God." The whole expression, then, would serve as the apostles' exhortation to the new converts to remain firm in their faith (cf. Barrett, 654). It is also possible, however, that τῇ χάριτι τοῦ θεοῦ could be applied to pious Jews and proselytes. If so, the expression serves as a more general exhortation to continue living pious lives, lives that bring God's favor.

προσμένειν. Pres act inf προσμένω (indirect discourse).

13:44 Τῷ δὲ ἐρχομένῳ σαββάτῳ σχεδὸν πᾶσα ἡ πόλις συνήχθη ἀκοῦσαι τὸν λόγον τοῦ κυρίου.

ἐρχομένῳ. Pres dep ptc neut dat sg ἔρχομαι (attributive).

σχεδὸν πᾶσα ἡ πόλις. The fronting (see 3:13 on ὑμεῖς) of the subject further emphasizes the size of the group (Levinsohn 1992, 85). Elsewhere, Levinsohn (1987, 41) notes that the emphasized element often "highlights information which is 'of particular . . . significance' for a subsequent development" (cf. 23:10). Here, it is the size of the crowd that arouses the Jews' jealousy (v. 45).

συνήχθη. Aor pass ind 3rd sg συνάγω.

ἀκοῦσαι. Aor act inf ἀκούω. It is better to take the infinitive as denoting purpose rather than being complementary (contra Wallace 1996, 599), since it is not clear that συνάγω ever takes a "helping verb."

τὸν λόγον. Accusative object of the infinitive.

13:45 ἰδόντες δὲ οἱ Ἰουδαῖοι τοὺς ὄχλους ἐπλήσθησαν ζήλου καὶ ἀντέλεγον τοῖς ὑπὸ Παύλου λαλουμένοις βλασφημοῦντες.

ἰδόντες. Aor act ptc masc nom pl ὁράω (temporal).

ἐπλήσθησαν. Aor pass ind 3rd pl πίμπλημι.

ἀντέλεγον. Impf act ind 3rd pl ἀντιλέγω.

ὑπὸ. Introduces the agent of the passive participle λαλουμένοις.

τοῖς λαλουμένοις. Pres pass ptc neut dat pl λαλέω (substantival). Dative complement of ἀντέλεγον.

βλασφημοῦντες. Pres act ptc masc nom pl βλασφημέω. The participle should probably be taken as the manner in which the Jews spoke against Paul, or the means by which they did so ("began speaking (out) against what Paul was saying by slandering him").

13:46 παρρησιασάμενοί τε ὁ Παῦλος καὶ ὁ Βαρναβᾶς εἶπαν, Ὑμῖν ἦν ἀναγκαῖον πρῶτον λαληθῆναι τὸν λόγον τοῦ θεοῦ· ἐπειδὴ ἀπωθεῖσθε αὐτὸν καὶ οὐκ ἀξίους κρίνετε ἑαυτοὺς τῆς αἰωνίου ζωῆς, ἰδοὺ στρεφόμεθα εἰς τὰ ἔθνη.

παρρησιασάμενοί. Aor mid dep ptc masc nom pl παρρησιάζομαι. Strictly speaking, the participle describes an attendant circumstance of the main verb. Since both are verbs of speaking, however, the effect of the participle is to specify the manner in which the apostles spoke. The second accent comes from the enclitic τε (see 1:4 on ἠκούσατέ).

τε. The conjunction τε is sometimes used, as here, to introduce a response to a previous event (see Levinsohn 1987, 135–36; cf. 21:30; 24:10). Here, Paul and Barnabas respond to the Jews' slander by announcing their decision to turn to the Gentiles.

εἶπαν. Aor act ind 3rd pl λέγω.

Ὑμῖν. The fronting (see 3:13 on ὑμεῖς) of the indirect object of λαληθῆναι places it in focus (see 2:15 on ὑμεῖς).

ἦν. Impf ind 3rd sg εἰμί.

ἀναγκαῖον. Predicate adjective.

λαληθῆναι. Aor pass inf λαλέω. The infinitival clause, πρῶτον λαληθῆναι τὸν λόγον τοῦ θεοῦ, serves as the subject of ἦν. This construction commonly occurs with ἐγένετο (see 9:32 on κατελθεῖν).

τὸν λόγον. Accusative subject of the passive infinitive (see 1:3 on αὐτὸν; lit.: "it was necessary for the word of God to be spoken to you first").

ἀπωθεῖσθε. Pres dep ind 2nd pl ἀπωθέομαι.

οὐκ ἀξίους. The fronting (see 3:13 on ὑμεῖς) of the adjectival complement (in an object-complement double accusative construction; see 1:3 on ζῶντα) along with the use of the verb κρίνω in a negative statement makes this clause drip with sarcasm.

κρίνετε. Pres act ind 2nd pl κρίνω.

ἰδοὺ. See 1:10.

στρεφόμεθα. Pres dep ind 1st pl στρέφω.

13:47 οὕτως γὰρ ἐντέταλται ἡμῖν ὁ κύριος, Τέθεικά σε εἰς φῶς ἐθνῶν τοῦ εἶναί σε εἰς σωτηρίαν ἕως ἐσχάτου τῆς γῆς.

ἐντέταλται. Prf dep ind 3rd sg ἐντέλλομαι.

ἡμῖν. Dative indirect object of ἐντέταλται.

Τέθεικά. Prf act ind 1st sg τίθημι. The second accent comes from the enclitic σε (see 1:4 on ἠκούσατέ).

εἰς φῶς. The preposition εἰς with an accusative noun functions like a predicate modifier (see 4:11 on εἰς κεφαλὴν γωνίας).

ἐθνῶν. Objective genitive.

τοῦ . . . σωτηρίαν. Lit. "that you might be for salvation."

εἶναί. Pres act inf εἰμί (purpose; see 3:2 on τοῦ αἰτεῖν). The second accent comes from the enclitic σε (see 1:4 on ἠκούσατέ).

σε. Accusative subject of the infinitive (see 1:3 on αὐτὸν).

εἰς σωτηρίαν. Purpose.

Acts 13:48–52

48When the Gentiles heard (this) they rejoiced and spoke highly of
the Lord's message, and all those who had been appointed to eternal
life believed. 49So the message of the Lord spread through the entire
region. 50But the Jews incited (some) respected pious women and the
leaders of the city. They stirred up persecution against Paul and Barnabas
and drove them from their territory. 51So they shook the dust from their
feet against them and went to Iconium. 52And the disciples were filled
with joy and the Holy Spirit.

13:48 ἀκούοντα δὲ τὰ ἔθνη ἔχαιρον καὶ ἐδόξαζον τὸν λόγον τοῦ κυρίου καὶ ἐπίστευσαν ὅσοι ἦσαν τεταγμένοι εἰς ζωὴν αἰώνιον·

ἀκούοντα. Pres act ptc neut nom pl ἀκούω (temporal).

ἔχαιρον. Impf act ind 3rd pl χαίρω.

ἐδόξαζον. Impf act ind 3rd pl δοξάζω.

ἐπίστευσαν. Aor act ind 3rd pl πιστεύω.

ὅσοι. The relative pronoun introduces a headless relative clause (see 3:6 on ὃ) that serves as the subject of ἐπίστευσαν.

ἦσαν. Impf ind 3rd pl εἰμί.

τεταγμένοι. Prf pass ptc masc nom pl τάσσω (pluperfect periphrastic; see 1:17 on κατηριθμημένος). Louw and Nida (37.96) note that although "τάσσω in Ac 13.48 has sometimes been interpreted as meaning 'to choose,' there seems to be far more involved than merely a matter of selection, since a relationship is specifically assigned."

13:49 διεφέρετο δὲ ὁ λόγος τοῦ κυρίου δι' ὅλης τῆς χώρας.

διεφέρετο. Impf pass inf 3rd sg διαφέρω.

13:50 οἱ δὲ Ἰουδαῖοι παρώτρυναν τὰς σεβομένας γυναῖκας τὰς εὐσχήμονας καὶ τοὺς πρώτους τῆς πόλεως καὶ ἐπήγειραν διωγμὸν ἐπὶ τὸν Παῦλον καὶ Βαρναβᾶν καὶ ἐξέβαλον αὐτοὺς ἀπὸ τῶν ὁρίων αὐτῶν.

παρώτρυναν. Aor act ind 3rd pl παροτρύνω.

σεβομένας. Pres dep ptc fem acc pl σέβομαι (attributive). See 17:17 on τοῖς σεβομένοις.

ἐπήγειραν. Aor act ind 3rd pl ἐπεγείρω. The subject of this verb may be the Jews, those they incited, or both (Barrett, 660).

ἐπὶ. See 1:8 on ἐφ' ὑμᾶς.

ἐξέβαλον. Aor act ind 3rd pl ἐκβάλλω.

13:51 οἱ δὲ ἐκτιναξάμενοι τὸν κονιορτὸν τῶν ποδῶν ἐπ' αὐτοὺς ἦλθον εἰς Ἰκόνιον,

ἐκτιναξάμενοι τὸν κονιορτὸν τῶν ποδῶν ἐπ' αὐτοὺς. This idiom referred to a symbolic action (lit. "shaking the dust from [their] feet against them") that served as a public demonstration "of the breaking off of communion and the forfeiting of responsibility" (Davies and Allison, 178; cf. LN 16.8). The action may well have been somewhat inflammatory in this context. Carson (246) notes that it was a Jewish custom to shake the dust from their feet that had been acquired while traveling abroad to avoid Gentile contamination. Such an action directed at fellow Jews would implicitly place them on the same level as unclean Gentiles.

ἐκτιναξάμενοι. Aor mid dep ptc masc nom pl ἐκτινάσσομαι. Strictly speaking, the participle should probably be viewed as substantival with the postpositive δέ separating it from the nominalizer (see 1:3 on τὰ) οἱ. When articles function like personal pronouns they are typically used either to indicate a change of speaker within a dialogue, or with a finite verb. In rendering this verse in English, however, it will be necessary to treat the participle as if it denotes an attendant circumstance or an action that precedes the action of the main verb.

ἦλθον. Aor act ind 3rd pl ἔρχομαι.

13:52 οἵ τε μαθηταὶ ἐπληροῦντο χαρᾶς καὶ πνεύματος ἁγίου.

οἵ. The second accent on the article comes from the enclitic τε (see 1:4 on ἠκούσατέ).

ἐπληροῦντο. Impf pass ind 3rd pl πληρόω.

χαρᾶς καὶ πνεύματος ἁγίου. Genitive of content.

Acts 14:1–7

[1]In Iconium, they entered the synagogue of the Jews as usual and spoke in such a way that a large number of both Jews and Gentiles believed. [2]But the Jews who did not believe stirred up (trouble) and turned the hearts of the Gentiles against the believers. [3]So they stayed for a considerable amount of time and spoke boldly about the Lord who confirmed the message about his grace by causing signs and wonders to be performed through them.

[4]Now the population of the city was divided, some siding with the Jews and others with the apostles. [5]When both the Gentiles and Jews, along with their rulers, decided to mistreat and stone them, [6]they learned about it and fled to the cities of Lyconia—Lystra and Derbe—and the surrounding region. [7]There they continued to preach the good news.

14:1 Ἐγένετο δὲ ἐν Ἰκονίῳ κατὰ τὸ αὐτὸ εἰσελθεῖν αὐτοὺς εἰς τὴν συναγωγὴν τῶν Ἰουδαίων καὶ λαλῆσαι οὕτως ὥστε πιστεῦσαι Ἰουδαίων τε καὶ Ἑλλήνων πολὺ πλῆθος.

Ἐγένετο. Aor mid dep ind 3rd sg γίνομαι.

κατὰ τὸ αὐτὸ. This prepositional phrase probably indicates that the apostles used the same approach that they had used when they arrived in Salamis (13:5) and Pisidian Antioch (13:14; cf. Barrett, 667) rather than that the apostles entered the synagogue "together" (contra Rogers and Rogers, 263). The construction should also not be taken as in the NET Bible where the rendering seems to imply that κατὰ τὸ αὐτὸ is a predicate adverbial modifier of an impersonal ᾿Εγένετο, with the compound infinitival clause being temporal: "The *same thing happened* in Iconium *when* . . . " "Temporal infinitives" occur only when they are articular and used with a preposition. It may be possible to take κατὰ τὸ αὐτὸ in this manner, however, if the infinitival construction is viewed as epexegetical to the prepositional phrase (cf. TEV: "The same thing happened in Iconium: Paul and Barnabas went . . . ").

εἰσελθεῖν. Aor act inf εἰσέρχομαι. The whole compound infinitival clause, κατὰ τὸ αὐτὸ εἰσελθεῖν αὐτοὺς . . . πολὺ πλῆθος, serves as the subject of ἐγένετο (see also 9:32 on κατελθεῖν).

αὐτοὺς. Accusative subject of the infinitive (see 1:3 on αὐτὸν).

εἰς. See 1:8 on ἐφ᾽ ὑμᾶς.

λαλῆσαι. Aor act inf λαλέω. See above on εἰσελθεῖν.

οὕτως ὥστε. This construction, which was also used in classical Greek, occurs only here and in John 3:16 in the NT (Barrett, 667). It is unclear whether the adverb is anaphoric (referring back to κατὰ τὸ αὐτὸ and indicating that they spoke in "that same way"; so Barrett, 668; cf. also CEV) or generic ("they spoke in such a way"; so NET Bible). The parallel construction in John 3:16 suggests the latter.

πιστεῦσαι. Aor act inf πιστεύω. Used with ὥστε to indicate result.

πλῆθος. Accusative (neuter singular) subject of the infinitive (see 1:3 on αὐτὸν).

14:2 οἱ δὲ ἀπειθήσαντες ᾿Ιουδαῖοι ἐπήγειραν καὶ ἐκάκωσαν τὰς ψυχὰς τῶν ἐθνῶν κατὰ τῶν ἀδελφῶν.

ἀπειθήσαντες. Aor act ptc masc nom pl ἀπειθέω (attributive). Here, the verb means "to refuse to believe the Christian message" (LN 31.107).

ἐπήγειραν. Aor act ind 3rd pl ἐπεγείρω. According to Louw and Nida (68.9), this verb means "to cause to begin and to intensify an activity." Although this meaning works in the one other NT occurrence (Acts 13:50), it is not clear how the verb is used here. The conjoined verbs (ἐπήγειραν καὶ ἐκάκωσαν) may be a perisphrastic construction meaning something like "to begin to mistreat," ἐπήγειραν may be a shortened form of ἐπήγειραν διωγμὸν (the scribes of E 614 *pc* gig sy[h] supplied διωγμὸν), or τὰς ψυχὰς could be viewed as the direct object of ἐπήγειραν as well as ἐκάκωσαν (so Barrett, 668).

ἐκάκωσαν τὰς ψυχὰς τῶν ἐθνῶν κατὰ. The expression κακόω τὴν ψυχὴν κατά (lit. "to harm a soul against") is an idiom that means "to cause someone to have hostile feelings toward someone else" (LN 88.200).

ἐκάκωσαν. Aor act ind 3rd pl κακόω.

ἀδελφῶν. See 1:15.

14:3 ἱκανὸν μὲν οὖν χρόνον διέτριψαν παρρησιαζόμενοι ἐπὶ τῷ κυρίῳ τῷ μαρτυροῦντι [ἐπὶ] τῷ λόγῳ τῆς χάριτος αὐτοῦ, διδόντι σημεῖα καὶ τέρατα γίνεσθαι διὰ τῶν χειρῶν αὐτῶν.

ἱκανὸν χρόνον. Accusative indicating extent of time (see 7:20 on μῆνας).

μὲν οὖν. See 1:6.

διέτριψαν. Aor act ind 3rd pl διατρίβω.

παρρησιαζόμενοι. Pres dep ptc masc nom pl παρρησιάζομαι (manner).

ἐπὶ τῷ κυρίῳ. The preposition could denote "reference" to the content of the apostles' speech, though Barrett (670) argues against this view (cf. the translation of Fitzmyer 1998, 521; see also 4:18 on ἐπὶ τῷ ὀνόματι), or it could be taken as causal (cf. Barrett who describes the prepositional phrase as the "ground" of their bold speech).

μαρτυροῦντι. Pres act ptc masc dat sg μαρτυρέω (attributive).

[ἐπὶ]. The possibility that the preposition reflects an Aramaic original (proposed by Ropes; cited in Metzger, 421) does little to strengthen the limited external evidence (א* A syr[p] cop[bo]) for this reading. If the preceding ἐπί denotes reference following a verb of speech, it would not be surprising for a few scribes to make the following construction (another verb of speech in participial form followed by a dative of reference) parallel by adding ἐπί. In short, the brackets in UBS[4]/NA[27] are unwarranted.

τῆς χάριτος. Probably a genitive of reference ("the message about his grace"), rather than attributive genitive ("his gracious message").

διδόντι. Pres act ptc masc dat sg δίδωμι (means). This is a rare example of an adverbial participle modifying an adjectival participle. The adverbial participle must agree with the subject of the adjectival participle in gender, number, and case. δίδωμι is used with the infinitive to form a causative construction (see 2:4 on ἐδίδου).

σημεῖα καὶ τέρατα. Accusative subject of the infinitive (see 1:3 on αὐτὸν). On the meaning, see 2:43 on τέρατα καὶ σημεῖα.

γίνεσθαι. Pres dep inf γίνομαι (direct object in a causative construction).

διὰ. Instrumental/intermediate agent.

τῶν χειρῶν αὐτῶν. Synecdoche (see 1:22 on τοῦ βαπτίσματος Ἰωάννου) for "them."

14:4 ἐσχίσθη δὲ τὸ πλῆθος τῆς πόλεως, καὶ οἱ μὲν ἦσαν σὺν τοῖς Ἰουδαίοις, οἱ δὲ σὺν τοῖς ἀποστόλοις.

ἐσχίσθη. Aor pass ind 3rd sg σχίζω.

οἱ μὲν . . . οἱ δὲ. See 17:32.

ἦσαν. Impf ind 3rd pl εἰμί.

ἀποστόλοις. Although this title (here and in v. 14) is used here to refer to Paul and Barnabas, elsewhere in Acts it is applied exclusively to the Eleven (and Matthias) who traveled with Jesus (Barrett, 671).

14:5 ὡς δὲ ἐγένετο ὁρμὴ τῶν ἐθνῶν τε καὶ Ἰουδαίων σὺν τοῖς ἄρχουσιν αὐτῶν ὑβρίσαι καὶ λιθοβολῆσαι αὐτούς,

ὡς. Temporal (see 18:5).

ἐγένετο ὁρμή. According to Louw and Nida (30.78), ὁρμὴ γίνομαι is an idiom (lit. 'an impulse happens') meaning "to make a decision to carry out some action, but with emphasis upon the impulse involved."

ἐγένετο. Aor mid dep ind 3rd sg γίνομαι. The use of the impersonal ἐγένετο with a predicate nominative and two epexegetical infinitives (lit. "there was a decision to . . .") should not be confused with the more common ἐγένετο plus a subject infinitive construction found elsewhere in Acts (cf. 9:32 on κατελθεῖν).

ὁρμή. Predicate nominative of the impersonal ἐγένετο.

ἄρχουσιν. This term probably refers to both Gentile (see 13:50) and Jewish leaders (14:2; Bruce 319).

ὑβρίσαι. Aor act inf ὑβρίζω (epexegetical).

λιθοβολῆσαι. Aor act inf λιθοβολέω (epexegetical).

14:6 συνιδόντες κατέφυγον εἰς τὰς πόλεις τῆς Λυκαονίας Λύστραν καὶ Δέρβην καὶ τὴν περίχωρον,

συνιδόντες. Aor act ptc masc nom pl συνοράω (attendant circumstance).

κατέφυγον. Aor act ind 3rd pl καταφεύγω.

Λύστραν . . . Δέρβην. Accusative in apposition to τὰς πόλεις. Lystra is typically treated as a second declension neuter plural noun, as in v. 8, but here it is treated as a first declension singular noun (Barrett, 673).

14:7 **κἀκεῖ εὐαγγελιζόμενοι ἦσαν.**

κἀκεῖ. A shortened form (crasis) of καί ἐκεῖ.
εὐαγγελιζόμενοι. Pres mid ptc masc nom pl εὐαγγελίζω (imperfect periphrastic; see 1:10 on ἀτενίζοντες).
ἦσαν. Impf ind 3rd pl εἰμί.

Acts 14:8–20

[8]In Lystra sat a man who could not use his feet. He had been lame since birth and had never walked. [9]He listened to Paul speaking. When Paul looked directly at him and saw that he had faith to be healed, [10]he said in a loud voice, "Stand upright on your feet!" And he jumped up and began walking.

[11]When the crowds saw what Paul had done, they shouted in the Lycaonian language, "The gods have taken on human form and come down to us!" [12]They began calling Barnabas 'Zeus' and Paul 'Hermes,' since he was the main speaker. [13]Moreover, the priest of (the temple of) Zeus, which was located in front of the city, together with the crowds, brought bulls and garlands to the city gates and were wanting to offer sacrifices (to them).

[14]But when the apostles, Barnabas and Paul, heard (about this) they tore their garments and rushed out to the crowd shouting, [15]"Men! Why are you doing these things? We too are men, with the same natures as you, who preach the good news to you to turn from these useless things to the living God who made the sky, the earth, the sea, and all that is in them. [16]In past generations he allowed all the nations to go their own way. [17]And yet, he did not leave himself without a witness. For he did good things (for you). He gave you rain from heaven and fruitful seasons, and he satisfied (your bodies) with food and your hearts with gladness." [18]Even by saying these things, they barely prevented the crowd from sacrificing to them.

[19]Then, (some) Jews came from Antioch and Iconium. After winning over the crowd and stoning Paul, they dragged him outside the city because they thought he was dead. [20]But when the disciples gathered around him, he got up and went into the city. On the next day, he went away with Barnabas to Derbe.

14:8 Καί τις ἀνὴρ ἀδύνατος ἐν Λύστροις τοῖς ποσὶν ἐκάθητο, χωλὸς ἐκ κοιλίας μητρὸς αὐτοῦ, ὃς οὐδέποτε περιεπάτησεν.

τις. See 8:9.

ἀδύνατος. "Pertaining to not being able to do or experience something" (LN 74.22). The expression, ἀδύνατος τοῖς ποσὶν (lit. "unable in the feet"), refers to the inability to use one's feet. The fronting of the adjective, along with the appositional phrase and relative clause that follow, serves to emphasize the extent of the man's plight and thus highlight the miraculous nature of the subsequent cure.

ἐκάθητο. Impf dep ind 3rd sg κάθημαι. Although Louw and Nida (85.63) note that this verb may simply indicate "to remain for some time in a place, often with the implication of a settled situation" and cite this verse as an example of such a usage (74.22), the context favors a more literal rendering.

χωλὸς. Nominative in apposition to ἀνὴρ.

ἐκ κοιλίας μητρὸς αὐτοῦ. Metonymy (see 1:9 on τῶν ὀφθαλμῶν αὐτῶν) for "from birth."

περιεπάτησεν. Aor act ind 3rd sg περιπατέω.

14:9 οὗτος ἤκουσεν τοῦ Παύλου λαλοῦντος· ὃς ἀτενίσας αὐτῷ καὶ ἰδὼν ὅτι ἔχει πίστιν τοῦ σωθῆναι,

ἤκουσεν. Aor act ind 3rd sg ἀκούω.

Παύλου. Genitive object of ἤκουσεν.

λαλοῦντος. Pres act ptc masc gen sg λαλέω (genitive complement of ἀκούω in an object-complement "double genitive" construction; see 2:6 on λαλούντων; contra Rogers and Rogers, 263, who call it substantival).

ἀτενίσας. Aor act ptc masc nom sg ἀτενίζω (attendant circumstance or temporal).

ἰδὼν. Aor act ptc masc nom sg ὁράω (attendant circumstance or temporal).

ἔχει. Pres act ind 3rd sg ἔχω.

τοῦ σωθῆναι. Aor pass inf σῴζω (probably epexegetical; so Porter 1994, 198).

14:10 εἶπεν μεγάλῃ φωνῇ, Ἀνάστηθι ἐπὶ τοὺς πόδας σου ὀρθός. καὶ ἥλατο καὶ περιεπάτει.

εἶπεν. Aor act ind 3rd sg λέγω.
μεγάλῃ φωνῇ. See 7:57 on φωνῇ μεγάλῃ.
Ἀνάστηθι. Aor act impv 2nd sg ἀνίστημι.
ὀρθός. The nominative adjective is used adverbially.
ἥλατο. Aor mid dep ind 3rd sg ἅλλομαι.
περιεπάτει. Impf act ind 3rd sg περιπατέω.

14:11 οἵ τε ὄχλοι ἰδόντες ὃ ἐποίησεν Παῦλος ἐπῆραν τὴν φωνὴν αὐτῶν Λυκαονιστὶ λέγοντες, Οἱ θεοὶ ὁμοιωθέντες ἀνθρώποις κατέβησαν πρὸς ἡμᾶς,

οἵ. The article should not be mistaken for a relative pronoun. The accent comes from the enclitic τε (see 1:4 on ἠκούσατε).
ἰδόντες. Aor act ptc masc nom pl ὁράω (temporal).
ὃ. The relative pronoun introduces a headless relative clause (see 3:6).
ἐποίησεν. Aor act ind 3rd sg ποιέω.
ἐπῆραν . . . λέγοντες. Lit. "they raised their voice, saying."
ἐπῆραν. Aor act ind 3rd pl ἐπαίρω.
λέγοντες. Pres act ptc masc nom pl λέγω (attendant circumstance).
ὁμοιωθέντες. Aor pass ptc masc nom pl ὁμοιόω (attendant circumstance).
ἀνθρώποις. Dative complement of ὁμοιωθέντες.
κατέβησαν. Aor act ind 3rd pl καταβαίνω.

14:12 ἐκάλουν τε τὸν Βαρναβᾶν Δία, τὸν δὲ Παῦλον Ἑρμῆν, ἐπειδὴ αὐτὸς ἦν ὁ ἡγούμενος τοῦ λόγου.

ἐκάλουν. Impf act ind 3rd pl καλέω.
Δία . . . Ἑρμῆν. The complements in object-complement double accusative constructions (see 1:3 on ζῶντα).
ἦν. Impf ind 3rd sg εἰμί.
ὁ ἡγούμενος τοῦ λόγου. Lit. "leader of the message."
ὁ ἡγούμενος. Pres dep ptc masc nom sg ἡγέομαι (substantival; predicate nominative).

14:13 ὅ τε ἱερεὺς τοῦ Διὸς τοῦ ὄντος πρὸ τῆς πόλεως ταύρους καὶ στέμματα ἐπὶ τοὺς πυλῶνας ἐνέγκας σὺν τοῖς ὄχλοις ἤθελεν θύειν.

ὅ. See v. 11 on ὅ.

ὄντος. Pres act ptc masc gen sg εἰμί (attributive).

πρὸ. See 12:6.

στέμματα. Wreaths "of wool to which leaves and flowers might be added and either wound around a staff or woven into a garland to be worn on the head" (LN 6.193).

πυλῶνας. It is unclear whether the gates were the city gates, the temple gates, or gates of the house where the apostles were staying (Bruce, 322; cf. LN 7.48).

ἐνέγκας. Aor act ptc masc nom sg φέρω (attendant circumstance).

ἤθελεν. Impf act ind 3rd sg θέλω.

θύειν. Pres act inf θύω (complementary).

14:14 ἀκούσαντες δὲ οἱ ἀπόστολοι Βαρναβᾶς καὶ Παῦλος, διαρρήξαντες τὰ ἱμάτια αὐτῶν ἐξεπήδησαν εἰς τὸν ὄχλον κράζοντες

ἀκούσαντες. Aor act ptc masc nom pl ἀκούω (temporal).

Βαρναβᾶς καὶ Παῦλος. Nominative in apposition to ἀπόστολοι.

διαρρήξαντες. Aor act ptc masc nom pl διαρρήγνυμι (attendant circumstance).

ἐξεπήδησαν. Aor act ind 3rd pl ἐκπηδάω.

κράζοντες. Pres act ptc masc nom pl κράζω (manner).

14:15 καὶ λέγοντες, Ἄνδρες, τί ταῦτα ποιεῖτε; καὶ ἡμεῖς ὁμοιοπαθεῖς ἐσμεν ὑμῖν ἄνθρωποι εὐαγγελιζόμενοι ὑμᾶς ἀπὸ τούτων τῶν ματαίων ἐπιστρέφειν ἐπὶ θεὸν ζῶντα, ὃς ἐποίησεν τὸν οὐρανὸν καὶ τὴν γῆν καὶ τὴν θάλασσαν καὶ πάντα τὰ ἐν αὐτοῖς·

λέγοντες. Pres act ptc masc nom pl λέγω (manner).

Ἄνδρες. In this case, the vocative is not further qualified and should therefore be rendered "Men!" (cf. 1:11).

ποιεῖτε. Pres act ind 2nd pl ποιέω.

ἡμεῖς. The overt fronted (see 3:13 on ὑμεῖς) subject pronoun places the apostles in focus (see 2:15 on ὑμεῖς).

ὁμοιοπαθεῖς. Predicate adjective.

ἐσμεν. Pres act ind 1st pl εἰμί.

ἄνθρωποι. Predicate nominative (in apposition to ὁμοιοπαθεῖς).

εὐαγγελιζόμενοι. Pres dep ptc masc nom pl εὐαγγελίζομαι (attributive).

ὑμᾶς. The pronoun could be viewed as either the accusative subject of the infinitive (see 1:3 on αὐτὸν) or as the indirect object (addressee) that has "advanced" (see 13:32).

ἐπιστρέφειν. Pres act inf ἐπιστρέφω (indirect discourse).

ζῶντα. Pres act ptc masc act sg ζάω (attributive).

ἐποίησεν. Aor act ind 3rd sg ποιέω.

τὰ. The article functions as a nominalizer (see 1:3 on τὰ), changing the prepositional phrase into a substantive.

14:16 ὃς ἐν ταῖς παρῳχημέναις γενεαῖς εἴασεν πάντα τὰ ἔθνη πορεύεσθαι ταῖς ὁδοῖς αὐτῶν·

παρῳχημέναις. Prf dep ptc fem dat pl παροίχομαι (attributive).

εἴασεν. Aor act ind 3rd sg ἐάω.

τὰ ἔθνη. Accusative subject of the infinitive (see 1:3 on αὐτὸν).

πορεύεσθαι. Pres dep inf πορεύομαι (complementary).

ὁδοῖς. Dative of rule (see 2:23 on βουλῇ καὶ προγνώσει).

14:17 καίτοι οὐκ ἀμάρτυρον αὐτὸν ἀφῆκεν ἀγαθουργῶν, οὐρανόθεν ὑμῖν ὑετοὺς διδοὺς καὶ καιροὺς καρποφόρους, ἐμπιπλῶν τροφῆς καὶ εὐφροσύνης τὰς καρδίας ὑμῶν.

οὐκ ἀμάρτυρον αὐτὸν ἀφῆκεν ἀγαθουργῶν. This clause could be viewed as a litotes (see 1:5 on οὐ μετὰ πολλὰς ταύτας ἡμέρας; so Fitzmyer 1998, 532), presumably meaning something like "he certainly left himself a witness by doing good things."

ἀφῆκεν. Aor act ind 3rd sg ἀφίημι.

ἀμάρτυρον. The adjectival complement of the direct object (αὐτὸν) in a double accusative construction (see 1:3 on ζῶντα).

αὐτὸν. The personal pronoun is used as a reflexive pronoun here.

ἀγαθουργῶν. Pres act ptc masc nom sg ἀγαθοεργέω (causal or means).

οὐρανόθεν. The adverb could refer either to the place the rain comes from ("the sky") or the place from which God gives the rain ("heaven").

διδοὺς. Pres act ptc masc nom sg δίδωμι (epexegetical to ἀγαθουργῶν and thus causal or means).

καιροὺς. It is better to take this noun as part of a compound direct object ("rain and seasons") rather than as part of a hendiadys (see 1:25 on τῆς διακονίας καὶ ἀποστολῆς; contra BDF §442) given the position of the participle which splits the putative hendiadys.

ἐμπιπλῶν. Pres act ptc masc nom sg ἐμπίπλημι (epexegetical to ἀγαθουργῶν and thus causal or means).

τροφῆς καὶ εὐφροσύνης. Genitive of content. BDF (§442) may be correct in taking this conjoined noun phrase as a hendiadys, though the sense would probably then be "joyous food" rather than "joy for food." Against this reading is the presence of τὰς καρδίας ὑμῶν, which implies that the "satisfaction" involves emotional well-being. It is probably better to take the construction as elliptical as our translation suggests (cf. Witherington, 427, Fitzmyer 1998, 532).

14:18 **καὶ ταῦτα λέγοντες μόλις κατέπαυσαν τοὺς ὄχλους τοῦ μὴ θύειν αὐτοῖς.**

λέγοντες. Pres act ptc masc nom pl λέγω (means or concessive: "although they said these things").

κατέπαυσαν. Aor act ind 3rd pl καταπαύω. Ellingworth (249) argues that καταπαύω means "to pacify" here.

τοὺς ὄχλους τοῦ μὴ θύειν. The accusative noun phrase could be viewed as either the direct object of κατέπαυσαν or as the subject of the infinitive (see 1:3 on αὐτὸν). In the latter case, the infinitival clause would serve as the direct object of κατέπαυσαν. In the former case, which is more likely given the negative infinitive, the infinitive indicates result (it is not epexegetical; contra Rogers and Rogers, 264).

τοῦ μὴ θύειν. Pres act inf θύω (see above).

14:19 **᾿Επῆλθαν δὲ ἀπὸ ᾿Αντιοχείας καὶ ᾿Ικονίου ᾿Ιουδαῖοι καὶ πείσαντες τοὺς ὄχλους καὶ λιθάσαντες τὸν Παῦλον ἔσυρον ἔξω τῆς πόλεως, νομίζοντες αὐτὸν τεθνηκέναι.**

᾿Επῆλθαν. Aor act ind 3rd pl ἐπέρχομαι.

πείσαντες. Aor act ptc masc nom pl πείθω (temporal).

λιθάσαντες. Aor act ptc masc nom pl λιθάζω (temporal).

ἔσυρον. Impf act ind 3rd pl σύρω. Although some find the use of the imperfect here surprising (Barrett, 684) and less appropriate than the aorist ἔσυραν (BDF §327), it is not suprising that Luke would portray dragging Paul out of the city as a process and thus use the imperfect (σύρω can be used with the aorist as well; see, e.g., 4 Macc 6:1).

νομίζοντες. Pres act ptc masc nom pl νομίζω (causal).

αὐτὸν. Accusative subject of the infinitive (see 1:3 on αὐτὸν).

τεθνηκέναι. Prf act inf θνῄσκω (indirect discourse).

14:20 κυκλωσάντων δὲ τῶν μαθητῶν αὐτὸν ἀναστὰς εἰσῆλθεν εἰς τὴν πόλιν. καὶ τῇ ἐπαύριον ἐξῆλθεν σὺν τῷ Βαρναβᾷ εἰς Δέρβην.

κυκλωσάντων. Aor act ptc masc gen pl κυκλόω. Genitive absolute (see 1:8 on ἐπελθόντος), temporal.

τῶν μαθητῶν. Genitive subject (see 1:8 on ἐπελθόντος).

ἀναστὰς. Aor act ptc masc nom sg ἀνίστημι (attendant circumstance).

εἰσῆλθεν. Aor act ind 3rd sg εἰσέρχομαι.

εἰς. See 1:8 on ἐφ' ὑμᾶς.

ἐξῆλθεν. Aor act ind 3rd sg ἐξέρχομαι.

Acts 14:21–28

[21]After preaching the good news in that city and making a substantial number of disciples they returned to Lystra, Iconium, and Antioch [22]in order to strengthen the disciples, encourage them to remain in the faith, and (remind them) that we will inevitably pass through many trials prior to entering the kingdom of God. [23]After appointing elders for them in each church, they prayed and fasted and committed them to the Lord in whom they had come to believe. [24]Then after passing through Pisidia, they came into (the province of) Pamphilia. [25]And after speaking the message in Perga they went down to Attalia. [26]From there they sailed back to Antioch, where they had been commended to the grace of God for the work which they had (now) completed. [27]After they arrived and had gathered the church together, they reported all that God had done with them and that he had opened a door of faith among the Gentiles. [28]And they stayed for a considerable amount of time with the disciples.

14:21 Εὐαγγελισάμενοί τε τὴν πόλιν ἐκείνην καὶ μαθητεύσαντες ἱκανοὺς ὑπέστρεψαν εἰς τὴν Λύστραν καὶ εἰς Ἰκόνιον καὶ εἰς Ἀντιόχειαν

Εὐαγγελισάμενοί. Aor mid dep ptc masc nom pl εὐαγγελιζόμαι (temporal). The second accent comes from the enclitic τε (see 1:4 on ἠκούσατέ).

πόλιν. On the use of the accusative case with the indirect object, see 8:25 on πολλάς κώμας.

μαθητεύσαντες. Aor act ptc masc nom pl μαθητεύω (temporal).

ὑπέστρεψαν. Aor act ind 3rd pl ὑποστρέφω.

14:22 ἐπιστηρίζοντες τὰς ψυχὰς τῶν μαθητῶν, παρακαλοῦντες ἐμμένειν τῇ πίστει καὶ ὅτι διὰ πολλῶν θλίψεων δεῖ ἡμᾶς εἰσελθεῖν εἰς τὴν βασιλείαν τοῦ θεοῦ.

ἐπιστηρίζοντες. Pres act ptc masc nom pl ἐπιστηρίζω. Present participles are frequently used to express purpose (Wallace 1996, 636; contra Barrett, 685).

τὰς ψυχὰς τῶν μαθητῶν. Synecdoche (see 1:22 on τοῦ βαπτίσματος Ἰωάννου; lit. "the souls of the disciples") for "the disciples."

παρακαλοῦντες. Pres act ptc masc nom pl παρακαλέω (purpose; see above).

ἐμμένειν. Pres act inf ἐμμένω (indirect discourse).

ὅτι. If there were no καί, the ὅτι could be taken causally. As it stands, the ὅτι introduces indirect discourse following an elided παρακαλοῦντες or an implicit verb of speaking (cf. Barrett, 686).

διὰ πολλῶν θλίψεων δεῖ ἡμᾶς εἰσελθεῖν εἰς τὴν βασιλείαν τοῦ θεοῦ. Lit. "it is necessary for us to enter the kingdom of God through many trials." Strictly speaking, διὰ πολλῶν θλίψεων, which is fronted (see 3:13 on ὑμεῖς) to highlight it, could indicate the necessary (δεῖ) means of entering the kingdom of God. It is better (theologically and otherwise), however, to view the infinitive as indicating that believers will *inevitably* pass through (διά in a spatial sense) trials.

δεῖ. Pres act ind 3rd sg δεῖ.

ἡμᾶς. Accusative subject of εἰσελθεῖν (see 1:3 on αὐτὸν).

εἰσελθεῖν. Aor act inf εἰσέρχομαι (complementary; see 1:16 on ἔδει).

εἰς. See 1:8 on ἐφ᾽ ὑμᾶς.

τὴν βασιλείαν τοῦ θεοῦ. See 1:3.

14:23 χειροτονήσαντες δὲ αὐτοῖς κατ' ἐκκλησίαν πρεσβυτέ ρους, προσευξάμενοι μετὰ νηστειῶν παρέθεντο αὐτοὺς τῷ κυρίῳ εἰς ὃν πεπιστεύκεισαν.

χειροτονήσαντες. Aor act ptc masc nom pl χειροτονέω (temporal). Louw and Nida point out that this verb may indicate "to formally appoint or assign someone to a particular task" (37.103) or "to choose or select, presumably by a group and possibly by the actual raising of the hand" (30.101). The fact that the subject of the participle is the same as the subject of the main verb (Paul and Barnabas) supports the former sense.

αὐτοῖς. Dative of advantage.

κατ' ἐκκλησίαν. Distributive (lit. "throughout the church").

προσευξάμενοι. Aor mid dep ptc masc nom pl προσεύχομαι (attendant circumstance).

παρέθεντο. Aor mid dep ind 3rd pl παρατίθημι.

αὐτοὺς. The antecedent is most likely the same as the antecedent of αὐτοῖς (the disciples of v. 22), rather than the πρεσβυτέρους.

πεπιστεύκεισαν. Plprf act ind 3rd pl πιστεύω. On the form, see 4:22 on γεγόνει.

14:24 καὶ διελθόντες τὴν Πισιδίαν ἦλθον εἰς τὴν Παμφυλίαν

διελθόντες. Aor act ptc masc nom pl διέρχομαι (temporal).

ἦλθον. Aor act ind 3rd pl ἔρχομαι.

14:25 καὶ λαλήσαντες ἐν Πέργῃ τὸν λόγον κατέβησαν εἰς 'Αττάλειαν

λαλήσαντες. Aor act ptc masc nom pl λαλέω (temporal).

κατέβησαν. Aor act ind 3rd pl καταβαίνω.

14:26 κἀκεῖθεν ἀπέπλευσαν εἰς 'Αντιόχειαν, ὅθεν ἦσαν παραδεδομένοι τῇ χάριτι τοῦ θεοῦ εἰς τὸ ἔργον ὃ ἐπλήρωσαν.

κἀκεῖθεν. A shortened form (crasis) of καὶ ἐκεῖθεν.

ἀπέπλευσαν. Aor act ind 3rd pl ἀποπλέω.

ἦσαν. Impf ind 3rd pl εἰμί.

παραδεδομένοι τῇ χάριτι τοῦ θεοῦ. This expression probably indicates a formal occasion on which the believers entrusted Paul and Silas to the Lord's care (cf. 15:40).

παραδεδομένοι. Prf pass ptc masc nom pl παραδίδωμι (pluperfect periphrastic; see 1:17 on κατηριθμημένος).

εἰς τὸ ἔργον. Purpose.

ἐπλήρωσαν. Aor act ind 3rd pl πληρόω.

14:27 παραγενόμενοι δὲ καὶ συναγαγόντες τὴν ἐκκλησίαν ἀνήγγελλον ὅσα ἐποίησεν ὁ θεὸς μετ' αὐτῶν καὶ ὅτι ἤνοιξεν τοῖς ἔθνεσιν θύραν πίστεως.

παραγενόμενοι. Aor mid dep ptc masc nom pl παραγίνομαι (temporal).

συναγαγόντες. Aor act ptc masc nom pl συνάγω (temporal).

ἀνήγγελλον. Impf act ind 3rd pl ἀναγγέλλω.

ὅσα. Introduces a headless relative clause (see 3:6 on ὃ) that functions as the direct object of ἀνήγγελλον.

ἐποίησεν. Aor act ind 3rd sg ποιέω.

μετ' αὐτῶν. The prepositional phrase most likely denotes association, making the passage theologically analogous to some variants of 1 Thessalonians 3:2 that describe Timothy as a συνεργὸν τοῦ θεοῦ.

ὅτι. Introduces a clausal complement (indirect discourse) of ἀνήγγελλον that stands in apposition to the relative clause.

ἤνοιξεν. Aor act ind 3rd sg ἀνοίγω.

θύραν πίστεως. Although Barrett (692) states that the genitive could be objective ("a door leading to faith"), subjective ("a door where faith enters"), or appositional ("the door [into salvation] which consists of faith), he also notes the danger of seeking a precise function in this case. Indeed, this phrase provides a good example of the importance of not seeking to identify the function of the various components of an idiom. Here, the whole expression ἤνοιξεν θύραν πίστεως means something like, "to provide an opportunity for evangelism" (cf. Col 4:3; 2 Cor 2:12).

14:28 διέτριβον δὲ χρόνον οὐκ ὀλίγον σὺν τοῖς μαθηταῖς.

διέτριβον. Impf act ind 3rd pl διατρίβω.

χρόνον οὐκ ὀλίγον. Litotes (see 1:5 on οὐ μετὰ πολλὰς ταύτας ἡμέρας). Accusative indicating extent of time (see 7:20 on μῆνας).

Acts 15:1–5

[1]Now some people came down from Judea and began teaching the believers, "Unless you are circumcised in accord with the Mosaic custom, you cannot be saved." [2]When Paul and Barnabas had a very serious argument with them, (the church) instructed Paul, Barnabas, and some others of their own people to go up (and meet with) the apostles and elders in Jerusalem concerning this point of disagreement. [3]So then, those who were sent on their way by the church passed through both Phoenicia and Samaria, relating the conversion of the Gentiles (as they went), and brought great joy to all the believers. [4]When they arrived in Jerusalem, they were welcomed by the church, the apostles, and the elders and they reported all that God had done with them. [5]But some from the sect of the Pharisees, who were believers, stood up and said, "It is necessary to circumcise them and to order (them) to keep the Law of Moses."

15:1 Καί τινες κατελθόντες ἀπὸ τῆς Ἰουδαίας ἐδίδασκον τοὺς ἀδελφοὺς ὅτι, Ἐὰν μὴ περιτμηθῆτε τῷ ἔθει τῷ Μωϋσέως, οὐ δύνασθε σωθῆναι.

κατελθόντες. Aor act ptc masc nom pl κατέρχομαι. The participle could be either substantival (modified by τινες) or temporal.

ἐδίδασκον. Impf act ind 3rd pl διδάσκω.

ἀδελφοὺς. See 1:15.

ὅτι. Introduces direct discourse.

Ἐὰν. This particle is used with a subjunctive verb to introduce a third class condition (a contigency).

περιτμηθῆτε. Aor pass subj 2nd pl περιτέμνω.

τῷ ἔθει. Dative of rule (see 2:23 on βουλῇ καὶ προγνώσει).

τῷ Μωϋσέως. The article functions as an adjectivizer (see 2:5 on τῶν ὑπὸ τὸν οὐρανόν), changing the genitive noun into an attributive modifier of τῷ ἔθει.

δύνασθε. Pres dep ind 2nd pl δύναμαι.

σωθῆναι. Aor pass inf σῴζω (complementary).

15:2 γενομένης δὲ στάσεως καὶ ζητήσεως οὐκ ὀλίγης τῷ Παύλῳ καὶ τῷ Βαρναβᾷ πρὸς αὐτοὺς ἔταξαν ἀναβαίνειν Παῦλον καὶ Βαρναβᾶν καί τινας ἄλλους ἐξ αὐτῶν πρὸς τοὺς ἀποστόλους καὶ πρεσβυτέρους εἰς Ἰερουσαλὴμ περὶ τοῦ ζητήματος τούτου.

γενομένης. Aor mid dep ptc fem gen sg γίνομαι. Genitive absolute (see 1:8 on ἐπελθόντος), temporal.

στάσεως καὶ ζητήσεως οὐκ ὀλίγης. Probably genitive subject (see 1:8 on ἐπελθόντος) rather than predicate genitive of an impersonal γενομένης. It is difficult to account for the dative τῷ Παύλῳ καὶ τῷ Βαρναβᾷ followed by πρὸς αὐτοὺς otherwise. Taken together, the use of a doublet (στάσεως καὶ ζητήσεως; see 2:43 on τέρατα καὶ σημεῖα) and litotes (οὐκ ὀλίγης; see 1:5 on οὐ μετὰ πολλὰς ταύτας ἡμέρας) strongly emphasize the serious nature of the dispute.

τῷ Παύλῳ καὶ τῷ Βαρναβᾷ. While using the genitive case for the two conflicting parties would have identified the dispute as something that arose "between" them (cf. 23:7: ἐγένετο στάσις τῶν Φαρισαίων καὶ Σαδδουκαίων), the use of the dative (of respect) with Paul and Barnabas and πρός with their opponents emphasizes that it was the apostles who took exception to the teaching of the Judaizers.

ἔταξαν. Aor act ind 3rd pl τάσσω.

ἀναβαίνειν. Pres act inf ἀναβαίνω. The infinitive should probably be viewed as introducing indirect discourse with τάσσω being a verb of speaking (rather than as a direct object or epexegetical infinitive; contra Rogers and Rogers, 265).

Παῦλον καὶ Βαρναβᾶν καί τινας ἄλλους. Accusative subject of the infinitive (see 1:3 on αὐτὸν).

15:3 Οἱ μὲν οὖν προπεμφθέντες ὑπὸ τῆς ἐκκλησίας διήρχοντο τήν τε Φοινίκην καὶ Σαμάρειαν ἐκδιηγούμενοι τὴν ἐπιστροφὴν τῶν ἐθνῶν καὶ ἐποίουν χαρὰν μεγάλην πᾶσιν τοῖς ἀδελφοῖς.

Οἱ. The article functions as a nominalizer (see 1:3 on τὰ), rather than a personal pronoun (contra Wallace 1996, 212; see also 1:6 on οἱ . . . συνελθόντες and Οἱ). Wallace's analysis appears to be dictated by concerns relating to translation rather than syntax (an adverbial rendering may sound better in English).

μὲν οὖν. The conjunction indicates that the events of this verse (passing through Phoenicia and Samaria) were a natural outcome of the events of the previous verse (being appointed to go up to Jerusalem; cf. Levinsohn 1987, 144).

προπεμφθέντες. Aor pass ptc masc nom pl προπέμπω (substantival; see above).

διήρχοντο. Impf dep ind 3rd pl διέρχομαι.

ἐκδιηγούμενοι. Pres dep ptc masc nom pl ἐκδιηγέομαι (attendant circumstance).

τῶν ἐθνῶν. Subjective genitive.

ἐποίουν. Impf act ind 3rd pl ποιέω.

15:4 παραγενόμενοι δὲ εἰς Ἰερουσαλὴμ παρεδέχθησαν ἀπὸ τῆς ἐκκλησίας καὶ τῶν ἀποστόλων καὶ τῶν πρεσβυτέρων, ἀνήγγειλάν τε ὅσα ὁ θεὸς ἐποίησεν μετ' αὐτῶν.

παραγενόμενοι. Aor mid dep ptc masc nom pl παραγίνομαι (temporal).

παρεδέχθησαν. Aor pass ind 3rd pl παραδέχομαι.

ἀνήγγειλάν. Aor act ind 3rd pl ἀναγγέλλω. The second accent comes from the enclitic τε (see 1:4 on ἠκούσατέ).

ἐποίησεν. Aor act ind 3rd sg ποιέω.

μετ' αὐτῶν. See 14:27.

15:5 ἐξανέστησαν δέ τινες τῶν ἀπὸ τῆς αἱρέσεως τῶν Φαρισαίων πεπιστευκότες λέγοντες ὅτι δεῖ περιτέμνειν αὐτοὺς παραγγέλλειν τε τηρεῖν τὸν νόμον Μωϋσέως.

ἐξανέστησαν. Aor act ind 3rd pl ἐξανίστημι.

τῶν. The article functions as a nominalizer (see 1:3 on τὰ), changing the prepositional phrase into a (partitive) gentitive noun phrase.

πεπιστευκότες. Prf act ptc masc nom pl πιστεύω. Since τινες is modified by a long nominalized construction, τῶν ἀπὸ τῆς αἱρέσεως τῶν Φαρισαίων, the participle should probably be viewed as an attributive modifier of a substantival τινες, rather than as a substantival participle with τινες as an attributive modifier.

λέγοντες. Pres act ptc masc nom pl λέγω (attendant circumstance).

ὅτι. The complement clause introduced by ὅτι could be taken as either direct or indirect discourse.

δεῖ. Pres act ind 3rd sg δεῖ (impersonal).

περιτέμνειν. Pres act inf περιτέμνω (complementary; see 1:16 on ἔδει).

αὐτοὺς. Direct object of περιτέμνειν.

παραγγέλλειν. Pres act inf παραγγέλλω (complementary; see 1:16 on ἔδει).

τηρεῖν. Pres act inf τηρέω (indirect discourse).

Acts 15:6–11

[6]Both the apostles and elders gathered to deal with this matter. [7]After much debate, Peter stood up and said to them, "Fellow believers, you know that long ago God chose me from among you so that through my mouth the Gentiles would hear the message of the Gospel and believe. [8]And God, who knows the heart, has provided evidence for them by giving (them) the Holy Spirit just as (he gave him) to us. [9]He made no distinction between them and us regarding our faith, but cleansed their hearts (as well as ours). [10]So then, why are you now putting God to the test by placing a yoke on the disciples' necks that neither our ancestors nor we ourselves have been able to bear? [11]On the contrary, we believe that we are saved through the grace of our Lord Jesus in the very same manner as these people!"

15:6 Συνήχθησάν τε οἱ ἀπόστολοι καὶ οἱ πρεσβύτεροι ἰδεῖν περὶ τοῦ λόγου τούτου.

Συνήχθησάν. Aor pass ind 3rd pl συνάγω. The second accent comes from the enclitic τε (see 1:4 on ἠκούσατε).

ἰδεῖν. Aor act inf ὁράω (purpose). The use of ἰδεῖν περὶ is analogous to the English expression, "to see to (something)," which indicates "to take care of (business), to deal with (some circumstance)." The verb can also be used alone in the imperative to convey this idea (see 18:15 on ὄψεσθε).

15:7 πολλῆς δὲ ζητήσεως γενομένης ἀναστὰς Πέτρος εἶπεν πρὸς αὐτούς, Ἄνδρες ἀδελφοί, ὑμεῖς ἐπίστασθε ὅτι ἀφ' ἡμερῶν ἀρχαίων ἐν ὑμῖν ἐξελέξατο ὁ θεὸς διὰ τοῦ στόματός μου ἀκοῦσαι τὰ ἔθνη τὸν λόγον τοῦ εὐαγγελίου καὶ πιστεῦσαι.

ζητήσεως. Genitive subject (see 1:8 on ἐπελθόντος) or predicate genitive of an impersonal γενομένης.

γενομένης. Aor mid dep ptc fem gen sg γίνομαι. Genitive absolute (see 1:8 on ἐπελθόντος), temporal.

ἀναστὰς. Aor act ptc masc nom sg ἀνίστημι (attendant circumstance).

εἶπεν. Aor act ind 3rd sg λέγω.

Ἄνδρες. See 1:11.

ἀδελφοί. See 1:15.

ἐπίστασθε. Pres dep ind 2nd pl ἐπίσταμαι.

ἀφ' ἡμερῶν ἀρχαίων. This idiom (lit. "from ancient days") could (1) simply emphasize that Peter's call to share the good news with the Gentiles (Cornelius) took place some time ago, or (2) indicate that Peter's call to share the good news with the Gentiles was established "in ancient times" (cf. v. 21) by God, thus pointing to God's foreknowledge and/or sovereign plan. Given the context, and the fact that there are many clearer ways to emphasize God's eternal plans, the former view is more likely.

ἐξελέξατο. Aor mid ind 3rd sg ἐκλέγω.

ἀκοῦσαι. Aor act inf ἀκούω. The infinitival clause, διὰ τοῦ στόματός μου ἀκοῦσαι τὰ ἔθνη τὸν λόγον τοῦ εὐαγγελίου καὶ πιστεῦσαι, serves as the direct object of ἐξελέξατο.

τὰ ἔθνη. Accusative subject of the infinitives (see 1:3 on αὐτὸν).

πιστεῦσαι. Aor act inf πιστεύω (direct object; see above).

15:8 καὶ ὁ καρδιογνώστης θεὸς ἐμαρτύρησεν αὐτοῖς δοὺς τὸ πνεῦμα τὸ ἅγιον καθὼς καὶ ἡμῖν

ἐμαρτύρησεν. Aor act ind 3rd sg μαρτυρέω.

αὐτοῖς. Indirect object of ἐμαρτύρησεν.

δοὺς. Aor act ptc masc nom sg δίδωμι (means).

15:9 καὶ οὐθὲν διέκρινεν μεταξὺ ἡμῶν τε καὶ αὐτῶν τῇ πίστει καθαρίσας τὰς καρδίας αὐτῶν.

οὐθὲν. A variant form of οὐδὲν.

διέκρινεν. Aor act ind 3rd sg διακρίνω.

τῇ πίστει. Although τῇ πίστει could go with the following participle and indicate the instrument/means by which their hearts were cleansed ("He made no distinction between them and us but cleansed their hearts through their faith"), given its position and the context it makes better sense to take τῇ πίστει with what precedes as a dative of reference that highlights the fact that the quality of the Gentile's faith was the same as the Jews' faith.

καθαρίσας. Aor act ptc masc nom sg καθαρίζω. The attendant circumstance indicated by the participle is appropriately introduced into the translation by "but" following the negative idea in the main clause.

15:10 νῦν οὖν τί πειράζετε τὸν θεόν ἐπιθεῖναι ζυγὸν ἐπὶ τὸν τράχηλον τῶν μαθητῶν ὃν οὔτε οἱ πατέρες ἡμῶν οὔτε ἡμεῖς ἰσχύσαμεν βαστάσαι;

πειράζετε. Pres act ind 2nd pl πειράζω.

ἐπιθεῖναι. Aor act inf ἐπιτίθημι. Strictly speaking, the infinitival clause is epexegetical, referring to the same action as πειράζετε τὸν θεόν, although an appropriate translation may imply that it denotes means (for which we would have expected ἐν τῷ + infinitive).

ἰσχύσαμεν. Aor act ind 1st pl ἰσχύω.

βαστάσαι. Aor act inf βαστάζω (complementary).

15:11 ἀλλὰ διὰ τῆς χάριτος τοῦ κυρίου Ἰησοῦ πιστεύομεν σωθῆναι καθ' ὃν τρόπον κἀκεῖνοι.

διὰ τῆς χάριτος τοῦ κυρίου Ἰησοῦ. The interpretation of this verse rests upon how this prepositional phrase is understood. It could either modify πιστεύομεν or σωθῆναι. If it modifies πιστεύομεν, then the focus of the statement is on the Lord Jesus' role in allowing belief to occur, which in turn leads to or results in salvation (with σωθῆναι functioning as an infinitive of result): "On the contrary, it is through the grace of our Lord Jesus that we believe and are thus saved in the very same manner as these people!" One strength of this view is the similar construction in 18:27, where διὰ τῆς χάριτος almost certainly modifies πιστεύω. The primary weakness of this view is that it makes the presence of καθ' ὃν τρόπον κἀκεῖνοι difficult to explain. The more likely view takes the prepositional phrase as a modifier of σωθῆναι that has been fronted (see 3:13 on ὑμεῖς) for emphasis. The construction, πιστεύω plus an infinitive, is taken as a periphrastic expression that probably means "to believe that, to feel confident that" (LSJ 1408), with the infinitive introducing indirect discourse. The only other occurrence of this construction in the NT (Rom 14:2) carries the same ambiguity but is probably best taken as Liddell and Scott suggest.

πιστεύομεν. Pres act ind 1st pl πιστεύω.

σωθῆναι. Aor pass inf σῴζω (see above).

καθ' ὃν τρόπον. The internally headed relative clause (see 1:2 on ἄχρι ἧς ἡμέρας) combined with the distributive preposition produces a strong intensive expression: "in the *very* same manner" (cf. 1:11).

κἀκεῖνοι. A shortened form (crasis) of καὶ ἐκεῖνοι.

Acts 15:12–21

[12]Then the whole group became quiet and listened as Barnabas and
Paul explained all the many signs and wonders that God had done
through them among the Gentiles. [13]After they had finished speaking,
James replied, "Fellow believers, listen to me. [14]Simeon has explained
how God first acted and took a people from among the Gentiles for
himself. [15]And the words of the prophets agree with this, just as it is
written, [16]'After these things I will return, and I will restore the tent of
David, which had fallen. I will rebuild its ruins and restore it [17]in order
that the rest of humankind may seek the Lord, even all the nations whom
I have called by my name, says the Lord who made these things [18]known
long ago.' [19]Therefore, I have concluded that we should not trouble
those among the Gentiles who turn to God. [20]Instead, (we should simply) write them a letter in order that they might abstain from things
defiled by idols, from sexual immorality, from (eating the meat of animals that have been) strangled, and from (eating/drinking) blood. [21]For
since ancient times, the Law of Moses has been proclaimed from city to
city as it is read in the synagogues each and every sabbath day."

15:12 Ἐσίγησεν δὲ πᾶν τὸ πλῆθος, καὶ ἤκουον Βαρναβᾶ καὶ Παύλου ἐξηγουμένων ὅσα ἐποίησεν ὁ θεὸς σημεῖα καὶ τέρατα ἐν τοῖς ἔθνεσιν δι' αὐτῶν.

Ἐσίγησεν. Aor act ind 3rd sg σιγάω.

ἤκουον. Impf act ind 3rd pl ἀκούω.

Βαρναβᾶ . . . Παύλου. Genitive objects of ἤκουον.

ἐξηγουμένων. Pres dep ptc masc gen pl ἐξηγέομαι (genitive complement of ἀκούω in an object-complement "double genitive" construction; see 2:6 on λαλούντων).

ὅσα. This relative pronoun, which typically introduces a headless relative clause (see 3:6 on ὃ), here introduces an internally headed relative clause (the antecedent, σημεῖα καὶ τέρατα, is inside the relative clause; see 1:2 on ἄχρι ἧς ἡμέρας) that intensifies the statement.

ἐποίησεν. Aor act ind 3rd sg ποιέω.

σημεῖα καὶ τέρατα. See 2:43 on τέρατα καὶ σημεῖα.

15:13 Μετὰ δὲ τὸ σιγῆσαι αὐτοὺς ἀπεκρίθη Ἰάκωβος λέγων, Ἄνδρες ἀδελφοί, ἀκούσατέ μου.

σιγῆσαι. Aor act inf σιγάω. Used with μετά τό to indicate antecedent time (see 1:3 on μετὰ τὸ παθεῖν). Given the context and the antecedent of αὐτοὺς (see below), the sense of the verb here must be something like "to stop speaking."

αὐτοὺς. Accusative subject of the infinitive (see 1:3 on αὐτὸν). The antecedent is Paul and Barnabas.

ἀπεκρίθη. Aor pass dep ind 3rd sg ἀποκρίνομαι.

λέγων. Pres act ptc masc nom sg λέγω (attendant circumstance, redundant; see 1:6 on λέγοντες).

Ἄνδρες. See 1:11.

ἀδελφοί. See 1:15.

ἀκούσατέ. Aor act impv 2nd pl ἀκούω. The second accent comes from the enclitic μου (see 1:4 on ἠκούσατέ).

μου. Genitive object of ἀκούσατέ.

15:14 Συμεὼν ἐξηγήσατο καθὼς πρῶτον ὁ θεὸς ἐπεσκέψατο λαβεῖν ἐξ ἐθνῶν λαὸν τῷ ὀνόματι αὐτοῦ.

ἐξηγήσατο. Aor mid ind 3rd sg ἐξηγέομαι.

καθὼς. Introduces a clausal complement of ἐξηγήσατο (indirect discourse; BAGD 391).

ἐπεσκέψατο. Aor mid dep ind 3rd sg ἐπισκέπτομαι.

λαβεῖν. Aor act inf λαμβάνω. Although the literal function of the infinitive in relation to the main verb is probably purpose, the expression, ἐπισκέπτομαι λαβεῖν (lit. "visit to take") should probably be viewed as an idiom that carries a connotation of beneficent intervention: perhaps, "was willing to take."

λαὸν. The application of this term (commonly referring to Israel) to refer to Gentiles reveals the realization of a significant theological shift in what constitutes the people of God (cf. Tannehill, 186-87).

τῷ ὀνόματι αὐτοῦ. Dative of advantage. The expression ὀνόματι αὐτοῦ is a metonym (see 1:9 on τῶν ὀφθαλμῶν αὐτῶν) for "himself."

15:15 καὶ τούτῳ συμφωνοῦσιν οἱ λόγοι τῶν προφητῶν, καθὼς γέγραπται,

τούτῳ. Verbs with a συν- prefix take a dative complement.
συμφωνοῦσιν. Pres act ind 3rd pl συνφωνέω.
γέγραπται. Prf pass ind 3rd sg γράφω.

15:16 Μετὰ ταῦτα ἀναστρέψω καὶ ἀνοικοδομήσω τὴν σκηνὴν Δαυὶδ τὴν πεπτωκυῖαν καὶ τὰ κατεσκαμμένα αὐτῆς ἀνοικοδομήσω καὶ ἀνορθώσω αὐτήν,

ἀναστρέψω. Fut act ind 1st sg ἀναστρέφω.
ἀνοικοδομήσω. Fut act ind 1st sg ἀνοικοδομέω.
πεπτωκυῖαν. Prf act ptc fem acc sg πίπτω (attributive).
τὰ κατεσκαμμένα. Prf pass ptc neut acc pl καταστρέφω (substantival).
ἀνοικοδομήσω. Fut act ind 1st sg ἀνοικοδομέω.
ἀνορθώσω. Fut act ind 1st sg ἀνορθόω.

15:17-18 ὅπως ἂν ἐκζητήσωσιν οἱ κατάλοιποι τῶν ἀνθρώπων τὸν κύριον καὶ πάντα τὰ ἔθνη ἐφ' οὓς ἐπικέκληται τὸ ὄνομά μου ἐπ' αὐτούς, λέγει κύριος ποιῶν ταῦτα γνωστὰ ἀπ' αἰῶνος.

ἐκζητήσωσιν. Aor act subj 3rd pl ἐκζητέω. The subjunctive is used with ὅπως to introduce a purpose clause.

πάντα τὰ ἔθνη. Nominative subject (with οἱ κατάλοιποι) of ἐκζητήσωσιν.

ἐπικέκληται. Prf pass ind 3rd sg ἐπικαλέω.

ἐπ' αὐτούς. The pronoun, which has the same referent as the relative pronoun, is redundant. This construction "was attested, but rare, in classical Greek. Its more frequent usage in the NT (although it is still used sparingly . . .) may be related to the frequency of use in the LXX. . . . In the LXX, this is clearly due to a literal following of the Hebrew text, where pleonastic pronouns are common" (Culy 1989, 34–35; see, e.g., Gen 1:11; Exod 6:26; Num 13:33; 35:25).

λέγει. Pres act ind 3rd sg λέγω.

ποιῶν. Pres act ptc masc nom sg ποιέω (attributive).

γνωστὰ ἀπ' αἰῶνος. Omanson points out that the text of Amos 9:12 ends with ταῦτα and "it is not clear whether the concluding words γνωστὰ ἀπ' αἰῶνος are intended to be part of the quotation (as in most translations) or whether they are meant to be a comment by James following the quotation. Because some copyists understood γνωστὰ απ' αἰῶνος to be a comment by James, they made various attempts to reword the phrase, rounding it out as an independent sentence such as 'Known to God from of old are all his works' (NIV footnote)." It is helpful to point out, however, that Amos 9:12 ends with κύριος ποιῶν πάντα ταῦτα, "the Lord who does all these things," rather than κύριος ποιῶν ταῦτα (though the Byzantine tradition adds πάντα). Thus, James has altered the end of the verse in order to make a different point through a different syntactic construction. If we take the actual Scripture quotation as ending with αὐτούς, (1) the adjective γνωστὰ should then be viewed as a complement in a double accusative (object-complement) construction (see 1:3 on ζῶντα), or (2) the whole participial clause, ποιῶν ταῦτα γνωστὰ, could perhaps be viewed as a causative construction in which γνωστὰ is a predicate adjective of an implicit εἶναι.

15:19 διὸ ἐγὼ κρίνω μὴ παρενοχλεῖν τοῖς ἀπὸ τῶν ἐθνῶν ἐπιστρέφουσιν ἐπὶ τὸν θεόν,

κρίνω. Pres act ind 1st sg κρίνω. It is unclear whether κρίνω in this context indicates that James is about to (1) express what he has personally decided should be done (cf. LN 30.75), (2) express his personal preference in the matter (cf. LN 30.99), or (3) issue a legal ruling (cf. LN 56.20). The apparently formal nature of the meeting and the explicit fronted subject pronoun ἐγώ tend to support the view that James was voicing more than his personal preference.

παρενοχλεῖν. Pres act inf παρενοχλέω (indirect discourse).

τοῖς ἐπιστρέφουσιν. Pres act ptc masc dat pl ἐπιστρέφω (substantival).

15:20 ἀλλὰ ἐπιστεῖλαι αὐτοῖς τοῦ ἀπέχεσθαι τῶν ἀλισγημάτων τῶν εἰδώλων καὶ τῆς πορνείας καὶ τοῦ πνικτοῦ καὶ τοῦ αἵματος.

ἐπιστεῖλαι. Aor act inf ἐπιστέλλω (indirect discourse).

ἀπέχεσθαι. Pres mid inf ἀπέχω. The articular infinitive could be viewed as the clausal complement (direct object) of the verb ἐπιστεῖλαι, used to introduce indirect discourse (cf. Rogers and Rogers, 266). It may be better, however, in light of the use of the genitive article, which is not typically used with infinitives that introduce indirect discourse (apparently leading Barrett [730] to label it pleonastic), to take the genitive articular infinitive as indicating purpose (cf. 9:15 on βαστάσαι). The infinitive cannot be viewed as appositional (contra Wallace 1996, 607) since it is not in apposition to any noun (αὐτοῖς is the indirect object or recipient of ἐπιστεῖλαι).

τῶν ἀλισγημάτων . . . αἵματος. When ἀπέχω is used intransitively (in the middle voice) the thing that is abstained from is placed in the genitive case. There is some variation in the textual tradition of the "apostolic decree," which is repeated in v. 29 and 21:25 (for an extended discussion, see Strange 87–105).

πορνείας. The term πορνεία may be used to refer to various kinds of sexual immorality. Given the nature of the other kinds of behavior that are proscribed in the apostolic decree, some have argued that here πορνεία refers specifically to marriages that Jews would view as incestuous and therefore outside the will of God. Witherington (460–64), on the other hand, has suggested that all four of the activities listed were typical events at pagan temples. The advantage of this view is that (1) it makes good sense of why these four particular activities are mentioned, (2) it allows us to take πορνεία in its common sense of "prostitution," and (3) it removes the apparent redundancy between the last two members of the list (one who ate strangled animals would obviously be eating blood), allowing them to be understood as the ritual strangulation of animals and the ritual drinking or tasting of the animals' blood.

τοῦ πνικτοῦ. The singular is used as a class noun (cf. v. 29).

15:21 Μωϋσῆς γὰρ ἐκ γενεῶν ἀρχαίων κατὰ πόλιν τοὺς κηρύσσοντας αὐτὸν ἔχει ἐν ταῖς συναγωγαῖς κατὰ πᾶν σάββατον ἀναγινωσκόμενος.

Μωϋσῆς . . . τοὺς κηρύσσοντας αὐτὸν ἔχει. Lit. "Moses . . . has those who preach him."

Μωϋσῆς. A metonym (see 1:9 on τῶν ὀφθαλμῶν αὐτῶν) for "the Law of Moses," as is made clear by the modifying participle ἀναγινωσκόμενος.

κατὰ πόλιν. Distributive.

τοὺς κηρύσσοντας. Pres act ptc masc acc pl κηρύσσω (substantival).

ἔχει. Pres act ind 3rd sg ἔχω.

ἐν ταῖς συναγωγαῖς. This prepositional phrase could be taken either with τοὺς κηρύσσοντας ("those who proclaim him in the synagogues") or ἀναγινωσκόμενος ("read in the synagogues"). The word order, in which the verb ἔχει separates the prepositional phrase from τοὺς κηρύσσοντας, may provide some support for the latter reading.

κατὰ πᾶν σάββατον. The distributive preposition used with πᾶν is probably emphatic (cf. 13:27 on τὰς κατὰ πᾶν σάββατον).

ἀναγινωσκόμενος. Pres pass ptc masc nom sg ἀναγινώσκω. The singular participle agrees with Μωϋσῆς rather than τοὺς κηρύσσοντας and probably functions temporally, though it may indicate the means of the proclamation.

Acts 15:22–29

[22]Then the apostles and elders, along with the whole church, decided to send (some) chosen men to Antioch with Paul and Barnabas—Judas, who was called Barsabbas, and Silas, men who were leaders among the believers. [23]They sent (this) letter with them:

> *The apostles and elders, (your) fellow believers, to the believers among the Gentiles, in Antioch, Syria, and Cilicia. Greetings. [24] Since we have heard that some people have gone out from among us, whom we did not send, and upset you with (their) message and troubled your hearts, [25]we decided, after unanimously choosing (certain) men, to send (them) to you along with our beloved Barnabas and Paul—[26]men who have risked their lives for the name of our Lord Jesus Christ. [27]So we are sending Judas and Silas, who will orally inform you of these same things (which we have written). [28]It seemed best to the Holy Spirit and to us to lay no greater burden on you than these necessary (things): [29] to abstain from (eating) meat offered to idols, from blood, from (the meat of animals that have been) strangled, and from sexual immorality. If you keep yourselves from these things, you will do well. Farewell.*

15:22 Τότε ἔδοξε τοῖς ἀποστόλοις καὶ τοῖς πρεσβυτέροις σὺν ὅλῃ τῇ ἐκκλησίᾳ ἐκλεξαμένους ἄνδρας ἐξ αὐτῶν πέμψαι εἰς Ἀντιόχειαν σὺν τῷ Παύλῳ καὶ Βαρναβᾷ, Ἰούδαν τὸν καλού-

μενον Βαρσαββᾶν καὶ Σιλᾶν, ἄνδρας ἡγουμένους ἐν τοῖς ἀδελφοῖς,

ἔδοξε τοῖς ἀποστόλοις καὶ τοῖς πρεσβυτέροις. This impersonal construction (lit. "it seemed good to the apostles and elders") is an idiomatic way of expressing, "the apostles and elders decided."

ἔδοξε. Aor act ind 3rd sg δοκέω (impersonal).

ἐκλεξαμένους. Aor mid ptc masc acc pl ἐκλέγω (attributive).

ἄνδρας. Accusative object of πέμψαι.

πέμψαι. Act act inf πέμπω (complementary; see 1:16 on ἔδει).

'Ιούδαν τὸν καλούμενον Βαρσαββᾶν . . . Σιλᾶν. Accusatives in apposition to the first ἄνδρας.

καλούμενον. Pres pass ptc masc acc sg καλέω (attributive).

ἄνδρας. Resumptive.

ἡγουμένους. Pres dep ptc masc acc pl ἡγέομαι (attributive).

ἀδελφοῖς. See 1:15 on ἀδελφοί.

15:23 **γράψαντες διὰ χειρὸς αὐτῶν, Οἱ ἀπόστολοι καὶ οἱ πρεσβύτεροι ἀδελφοὶ τοῖς κατὰ τὴν 'Αντιόχειαν καὶ Συρίαν καὶ Κιλικίαν ἀδελφοῖς τοῖς ἐξ ἐθνῶν χαίρειν.**

γράψαντες διὰ χειρὸς αὐτῶν. In this expression (lit. "writing through their hand"), the direct object and an intervening event is left implicit: "writing *a letter to be delivered* by their hand."

γράψαντες. Aor act ptc masc nom pl γράφω. Rogers and Rogers (267) call the participle a nominative absolute since there does not appear to be a nominative subject with which it can agree. Wallace (1996, 654), however, notes that nominative absolute participles are always substantival (unlike here). It may be best to take the participle as attributive agreeing with the logical "subject" of ἔδοξε τοῖς ἀποστόλοις καὶ τοῖς πρεσβυτέροις (v. 22), i.e., the apostles and elders, in gender and number.

διὰ χειρὸς αὐτῶν. Instrumental/means; synecdoche (see 1:22 on τοῦ βαπτίσματος 'Ιωάννου) for "through them."

ἀδελφοί. See 1:15. Many scribes apparently added καὶ οἱ before ἀδελφοί, creating a third group in agreement with v. 22. The simple nominative ἀδελφοὶ of the the UBS[4]/NA[27] text, however, which stands in apposition to Οἱ ἀπόστολοι καὶ οἱ πρεσβύτεροι, provides a rhetorically powerful reminder that the Jerusalem "pillars" (Gal 2:9) are addressing the Gentile believers as "brothers."

τοῖς ἐξ ἐθνῶν. The article functions as an adjectivizer (see 2:5 on τῶν ὑπὸ τὸν οὐρανόν), changing the prepositional phrase into an attributive modifier of τοῖς . . . ἀδελφοῖς.

χαίρειν. Pres act inf χαίρω (infinitive absolute). The customary greeting in ancient Greek letters (cf. 23:26).

15:24 Ἐπειδὴ ἠκούσαμεν ὅτι τινὲς ἐξ ἡμῶν [ἐξελθόντες] ἐτάραξαν ὑμᾶς λόγοις ἀνασκευάζοντες τὰς ψυχὰς ὑμῶν οἷς οὐ διεστειλάμεθα,

ἠκούσαμεν. Aor act ind 1st pl ἀκούω.

ὅτι. Introduces indirect discourse.

[ἐξελθόντες]. Aor act ptc masc nom pl ἐξέρχομαι (attendant circumstance). Although the manuscript evidence heavily favors the inclusion of ἐξελθόντες, UBS[4]/NA[27] place it in brackets since it is omitted by א* and B and could have been implicit information that was accidentally added by other scribes, information that was added intentionally or unintentionally in conformity with Gal 2:12, or information that was intentionally added to avoid the possibility that these individuals were associated with the senders of the letter (Metzger, 436). On the whole, it seems best to argue that the scribes of א* and B accidentally omitted the participle since the information it conveys is already implicit.

ἐτάραξαν. Aor act ind 3rd pl ταράσσω.

λόγοις. Dative of instrument/means.

ἀνασκευάζοντες. Pres act ptc masc nom pl ἀνασκευάζω (attendant circumstance or result; so Healey and Healey, 219).

διεστειλάμεθα. Aor mid ind 1st pl διαστέλλω.

15:25 ἔδοξεν ἡμῖν γενομένοις ὁμοθυμαδὸν ἐκλεξαμένοις ἄνδρας πέμψαι πρὸς ὑμᾶς σὺν τοῖς ἀγαπητοῖς ἡμῶν Βαρναβᾷ καὶ Παύλῳ,

ἔδοξεν. Aor act ind 3rd sg δοκέω (impersonal). On the sense of the whole expression, ἔδοξεν ἡμῖν, see v. 22.

γενομένοις. Aor mid dep ptc masc dat pl γίνομαι (attributive; but see below).

ὁμοθυμαδὸν. The participial clause, γενομένοις ὁμοθυμαδὸν, could point to a gathering or indicate unanimity (see 1:14).

ἐκλεξαμένοις. Aor mid ptc masc dat pl ἐκλέγω. Although many manuscripts (א C D E 36 181 *Byz*[pt] *al*) have the accusative form, ἐκλεξαμένους (as an attributive modifier of ἄνδρας), the dative form (A B Ψ 33 81 *Byz*[pt] *al*) is the conceptually harder reading while the accusative brings this verse into line with v. 22. Even if the dative reading is accepted as original, however, the function of the participle is difficult to determine. Having two attributive participles in apposition to each other would be unusual at best. It may be possible to take the entire phrase, γενομένοις ὁμοθυμαδὸν ἐκλεξαμένοις, as an attributive periphrastic expression ("It seemed good to us, who had unanimously chosen men . . ."), though a temporal expression makes for a better English translation.

ἄνδρας. The accusative noun could be taken as the direct object of either ἐκλεξαμένοις or πέμψαι.

πέμψαι. Aor act inf πέμπω (complementary; see 1:16 on ἔδει).

15:26 ἀνθρώποις παραδεδωκόσι τὰς ψυχὰς αὐτῶν ὑπὲρ τοῦ ὀνόματος τοῦ κυρίου ἡμῶν Ἰησοῦ Χριστοῦ.

ἀνθρώποις. Dative in apposition to Βαρναβᾷ καὶ Παύλῳ (v. 25).

παραδεδωκόσι τὰς ψυχὰς αὐτῶν. An idiom (lit. "who have handed over their souls").

παραδεδωκόσι. Prf act ptc masc dat pl παραδίδωμι (attributive).

15:27 ἀπεστάλκαμεν οὖν Ἰούδαν καὶ Σιλᾶν καὶ αὐτοὺς διὰ λόγου ἀπαγγέλλοντας τὰ αὐτά.

ἀπεστάλκαμεν. Prf act ind 1st pl ἀποστέλλω.

καὶ αὐτοὺς. This epexegetical expression draws attention to the activity, state, or role of the referent(s) (cf. v. 32; Mark 1:19; Luke 1:36).

διὰ λόγου. An idiomatic expression meaning "orally."

ἀπαγγέλλοντας. Pres act ptc masc acc pl ἀπαγέλλω (attributive). The accusative participle cannot function adverbially (contra Rogers and Rogers, 267) since the case indicates that its referent is different than the subject of the main verb (see Culy 2004).

15:28 ἔδοξεν γὰρ τῷ πνεύματι τῷ ἁγίῳ καὶ ἡμῖν μηδὲν πλέον ἐπιτίθεσθαι ὑμῖν βάρος πλὴν τούτων τῶν ἐπάναγκες,

ἔδοξεν. Aor act ind 3rd sg δοκέω (impersonal). On the sense of the whole expression, ἔδοξεν . . . ἡμῖν, see v. 22.

μηδὲν πλέον βάρος. Accusative (neuter singular) direct object of ἐπιτίθεσθαι.

ἐπιτίθεσθαι. Pres mid inf ἐπιτίθημι (complementary; see 1:16 on ἔδει).

τῶν ἐπάναγκες. The article functions as a nominalizer (see 1:3 on τά), changing the adverb into a substantive.

15:29 ἀπέχεσθαι εἰδωλοθύτων καὶ αἵματος καὶ πνικτῶν καὶ πορνείας, ἐξ ὧν διατηροῦντες ἑαυτοὺς εὖ πράξετε. Ἔρρωσθε.

ἀπέχεσθαι. Pres mid inf ἀπέχω. The (anarthrous; see 3:3 on Πέτρον καὶ Ἰωάννην) infinitive is epexegetical (cf. v. 20).

εἰδωλοθύτων . . . πορνείας. When ἀπέχω is used intransitively (in the middle voice) the thing that is abstained from is placed in the genitive case. D and a few other witnesses omit καὶ τῶν πνικτῶν and add a negative version of the Golden Rule at the end of the verse (cf. v. 20), while many manuscripts have the singular τοῦ πνικτοῦ (as in v. 20) rather than the plural form.

πορνείας. On the meaning of this term, see verse 20.

διατηροῦντες. Pres act ptc masc nom pl διατηρέω (conditional or perhaps means; Wallace 1996, 632–33).

πράξετε. Fut act ind 2nd pl πράσσω.

Ἔρρωσθε. Prf dep impv 2nd pl ῥύομαι. The imperative expression is used formally to close a letter.

Acts 15:30–35

[30]So those who had been sent arrived in Antioch and, after gathering the group together, they delivered the letter. [31]When they had read it, they rejoiced because of its encouragement. [32]Both Judas and Silas, who were also prophets themselves, spoke for a long time and encouraged and strengthened the believers. [33]After spending (some) time (there), they were sent off in peace by the believers (to return) to those who had sent them. [35]But Paul and Barnabas remained in Antioch and, along with many others, taught and preached the message of the Lord.

15:30 Οἱ μὲν οὖν ἀπολυθέντες κατῆλθον εἰς Ἀντιόχειαν, καὶ συναγαγόντες τὸ πλῆθος ἐπέδωκαν τὴν ἐπιστολήν.

Οἱ. The article functions as a nominalizer (see v. 3 on Οἱ).
μὲν οὖν. See 1:6.
ἀπολυθέντες. Aor pass ptc masc nom pl ἀπολύω (substantival).
κατῆλθον. Aor act ind 3rd pl κατέρχομαι.
συναγαγόντες. Aor act ptc masc nom pl συνάγω (temporal).
τὸ πλῆθος. Accusative direct object of συναγαγόντες.
ἐπέδωκαν. Aor act ind 3rd pl ἐπιδίδωμι.

15:31 ἀναγνόντες δὲ ἐχάρησαν ἐπὶ τῇ παρακλήσει.

ἀναγνόντες. Aor act ptc masc nom pl ἀναγινώσκω (temporal).
ἐχάρησαν. Aor pass dep ind 3rd pl χαίρω.
ἐπὶ. Causal (with dative).

15:32 Ἰούδας τε καὶ Σιλᾶς καὶ αὐτοὶ προφῆται ὄντες διὰ λόγου πολλοῦ παρεκάλεσαν τοὺς ἀδελφοὺς καὶ ἐπεστήριξαν,

καὶ αὐτοὶ. See v. 27 on καὶ αὐτοὺς.
αὐτοὶ. Nominative subject of ὄντες.
προφῆται. Predicate nominative of ὄντες.
ὄντες. Pres act ptc masc nom pl εἰμί (attributive modifier of Ἰούδας τε καὶ Σιλᾶς).
διὰ λόγου πολλοῦ. Lit. "through many a word." For an analogous use of this singular expression, see 20:2.
παρεκάλεσαν. Aor act ind 3rd pl παρακαλέω.
ἀδελφοὺς. See 1:15 on ἀδελφοὶ.
ἐπεστήριξαν. Aor act ind 3rd pl ἐπιστηρίζω.

15:33 ποιήσαντες δὲ χρόνον ἀπελύθησαν μετ' εἰρήνης ἀπὸ τῶν ἀδελφῶν πρὸς τοὺς ἀποστείλαντας αὐτούς.

ποιήσαντες χρόνον. This expression (lit. "making time") is equivalent to the English expression "to spend time" (cf. 18:23; 20:3).
ποιήσαντες. Aor act ptc masc nom pl ποιέω (temporal).
ἀπελύθησαν. Aor pass ind 3rd pl ἀπολύω.
ἀπὸ. The preposition could either indicate source ("from the brothers") or agency ("by the brothers"). Since the latter is a rare use of

ἀπό and the preposition is used with πρός here, the former is to be preferred, though English usage requires the latter translation.

τοὺς ἀποστείλαντας. Aor act ptc masc acc pl ἀποστέλλω (substantival).

[15:34] This entire verse is omitted by 𝔓[74] א A B E Ψ 049 056 0142 81 104 330 451 629 1241 1505 1877 2127 2492 *Byz* vg[st] syr[p] cop[bo] *al*. A number of manuscripts (33 36 307 453 610 614 1175 1409 1678 1739 *al*) read ἔδοξε δὲ τῷ Σιλᾷ ἐπιμεῖναι αὐτοῦ ("But it seemed good to Silas to remain there"; C changes αὐτοῦ to αὐτούς ["But it seemed good to Silas that *they* should remain"], while 181 changes ἐπιμεῖναι to ἐπιμένειν), while D[1] and it[d] read ἔδοξε δὲ τῷ Σιλᾷ ἐπιμεῖναι πρὸς αὐτοὺς, μόνος δὲ ᾿Ιούδας ἐπορεύθη ("But it seemed good to Silas to remain there, so Judas traveled alone"; D* has Σιλεᾷ and omits πρὸς, while a number of versions read αὐτοῦ in place of πρὸς αὐτοὺς). "The insertion, whether in the longer or the shorter version, was no doubt made by copyists to account for the presence of Silas at Antioch in ver. 40" (Metzger, 439).

ἔδοξεν. Aor act ind 3rd sg δοκέω (impersonal). On the sense of the whole expression, ἔδοξεν . . . τῷ Σιλᾷ, see v. 22.

ἐπιμεῖναι. Aor act inf ἐπιμένω (complementary; see 1:16 on ἔδει).

αὐτοῦ. See 18:19.

ἐπορεύθη. Aor pass dep ind 3rd sg πορεύομαι.

15:35 **Παῦλος δὲ καὶ Βαρναβᾶς διέτριβον ἐν ᾿Αντιοχείᾳ διδάσκοντες καὶ εὐαγγελιζόμενοι μετὰ καὶ ἑτέρων πολλῶν τὸν λόγον τοῦ κυρίου.**

διέτριβον. Impf act ind 3rd pl διατρίβω.

διδάσκοντες. Pres act ptc masc nom pl διδάσκω (attendant circumstance).

εὐαγγελιζόμενοι. Pres mid ptc masc nom pl εὐαγγελίζω (attendant circumstance).

Acts 15:36–41

After some days (had passed), Paul said to Barnabas, "Let's go back and visit the believers in each and every city where we proclaimed the message of the Lord (to see) how they are." [37]Now, Barnabas wanted to take along John, who was called Mark, [38]but Paul thought it best not to take someone who had deserted them in Pamphylia and not accompanied them in their work. [39]They had such a strong disagreement that they separated from each other and Barnabas took Mark and sailed for Cyprus. [40]Paul, however, chose Silas and departed after being commended to the grace of the Lord by the believers. [41]He traveled through Syria and Cilicia and strengthened the churches.

15:36 Μετὰ δέ τινας ἡμέρας εἶπεν πρὸς Βαρναβᾶν Παῦλος, Ἐπιστρέψαντες δὴ ἐπισκεψώμεθα τοὺς ἀδελφοὺς κατὰ πόλιν πᾶσαν ἐν αἷς κατηγγείλαμεν τὸν λόγον τοῦ κυρίου πῶς ἔχουσιν.

εἶπεν. Aor act ind 3rd sg λέγω.

Ἐπιστρέψαντες. Aor act ptc masc nom pl ἐπιστρέφω (attendant circumstance).

δή. See 13:2.

ἐπισκεψώμεθα. Aor mid dep subj 1st pl ἐπισκέπτομαι (hortatory).

ἀδελφούς. See 1:15 on ἀδελφοί.

κατὰ πόλιν πᾶσαν. The distributive preposition used with πᾶσαν is probably emphatic (cf. 13:27 on κατὰ πᾶν σάββατον).

αἷς. The plural relative pronoun agrees with the sense of its syntactically singular antecedent, πόλιν πᾶσαν.

κατηγγείλαμεν. Aor act ind 1st pl καταγγέλλω.

πῶς ἔχουσιν. This independent interrogative clause supplies the reason for the visit. See also 7:1 on οὕτως ἔχει.

ἔχουσιν. Pres act ind 3rd pl ἔχω.

15:37 Βαρναβᾶς δὲ ἐβούλετο συμπαραλαβεῖν καὶ τὸν Ἰωάννην τὸν καλούμενον Μᾶρκον·

ἐβούλετο. Impf dep ind 3rd sg βούλομαι. Although Wallace (1996, 544) cites this verb form as an example of a "progressive (descriptive) imperfect," the fact that βούλομαι is not used in the aorist indicative (in the NT) suggests that the choice of tense is probably governed by the lexical features of the verb.

συμπαραλαβεῖν. Aor act inf συμπαραλαμβάνω (complementary).

καλούμενον. Pres pass ptc masc acc sg καλέω (attributive).

15:38 Παῦλος δὲ ἠξίου, τὸν ἀποστάντα ἀπ' αὐτῶν ἀπὸ Παμφυλίας καὶ μὴ συνελθόντα αὐτοῖς εἰς τὸ ἔργον μὴ συμπαραλαμβάνειν τοῦτον.

ἠξίου. Impf act ind 3rd sg ἀξιόω. Again, the function of the imperfect should not be pressed. When the verb is used in the indicative with this sense ("to think something best") it is always in the imperfect.

τὸν ἀποστάντα ἀπ' αὐτῶν ἀπὸ Παμφυλίας καὶ μὴ συνελθόντα αὐτοῖς εἰς τὸ ἔργον. This accusative noun phrase is fronted (see 3:13 on ὑμεῖς) in a topic construction (see 2:22 on' Ἰησοῦν τὸν Ναζωραῖον).

τὸν ἀποστάντα. Aor act ptc masc acc sg ἀφίστημι (substantival).

(τὸν) συνελθόντα. Aor act ptc masc acc sg συνέρχομαι (substantival).

αὐτοῖς. Verbs with a συν- prefix take a dative complement.

συμπαραλαμβάνειν. Pres act inf συμπαραλαμβάνω. The infinitive could be viewed as (1) complementary, with ἠξίου; (2) objective (ἀξιόω appears to take a direct object at times: "to deem/think *something* best/worthy"; see Luke 7:7); or perhaps (3) as introducing indirect discourse with a verb of cognition (cf. 28:22 on ἀκοῦσαι).

τοῦτον. Resumptive.

15:39 ἐγένετο δὲ παροξυσμὸς ὥστε ἀποχωρισθῆναι αὐτοὺς ἀπ' ἀλλήλων, τόν τε Βαρναβᾶν παραλαβόντα τὸν Μᾶρκον ἐκπλεῦσαι εἰς Κύπρον,

ἐγένετο. Aor mid dep ind 3rd sg γίνομαι.

παροξυσμὸς. Predicate nominative in an impersonal construction.

ἀποχωρισθῆναι. Aor pass inf ἀποχωρίζω. Used with ὥστε to indicate result.

ἀπ'. See 1:8 on ἐφ' ὑμᾶς.

αὐτοὺς. Accusative subject of the infinitive (see 1:3 on αὐτὸν).

τόν Βαρναβᾶν. Accusative subject of the infinitive ἐκπλεῦσαι (see 1:3 on αὐτὸν). Levinsohn (1987, 103) argues that the use of the article with the proper name here indicates that the reader's attention is being directed away from Barnabas as he leaves the scene. Indeed, Luke does not mention Barnabas again at all.

παραλαβόντα. Aor act ptc masc acc sg παραλαμβάνω (attendant circumstance of ἐκπλεῦσαι).

ἐκπλεῦσαι. Aor act inf ἐκπλέω. Used with ὥστε to indicate result.

15:40 Παῦλος δὲ ἐπιλεξάμενος Σιλᾶν ἐξῆλθεν παραδοθεὶς τῇ χάριτι τοῦ κυρίου ὑπὸ τῶν ἀδελφῶν.

ἐπιλεξάμενος. Aor mid ptc masc nom sg ἐπιλέγω (attendant circumstance).

ἐξῆλθεν. Aor act ind 3rd sg ἐξέρχομαι.

παραδοθεὶς τῇ χάριτι τοῦ κυρίου. See 14:26.

παραδοθεὶς. Aor pass ptc masc nom sg παραδίδωμι (temporal).

ἀδελφῶν. See 1:15 on ἀδελφοί.

15:41 διήρχετο δὲ τὴν Συρίαν καὶ [τὴν] Κιλικίαν ἐπιστηρίζων τὰς ἐκκλησίας.

διήρχετο. Impf mid ind 3rd sg διέρχομαι.

ἐπιστηρίζων. Pres act ptc masc nom sg ἐπιστηρίζω (attendant circumstance). Codex D describes how they strengthened the churches: παραδιδοὺς τὰς ἐντολὰς τῶν πρεσβυτέρων ("delivering the commands of the elders").

Acts 16:1–5

[1]He (eventually) reached Derbe and (then) Lystra, where there was a disciple named Timothy, the son of a believing Jewish woman and a Greek father. [2]He was respected by the believers in (both) Lystra and Iconium. [3]Paul wanted him to go with him, so he took him and had him circumcised because of the Jews who were in that place. For they all knew that his father was a Greek. [4]As they went through the towns, they passed on to them the rules that the apostles and elders in Jerusalem had decided on so that they could follow them. [5]So the churches were strengthened in the faith and grew in number every day.

16:1–5 Porter has argued that the three aspects of Greek—perfective (= aorist tense), imperfective (= present and imperfect tense), and stative (= perfect and pluperfect tense)—function, on the discourse level, to mark background, foreground, and frontground material respectively. His comments on 16:1–5 (1989, 93) provide a helpful illustration of the value of his analysis: "In Acts 16:1–5, the author uses the Aorist to establish the basic framework of events: he (Paul) arrived (κατήντησεν) in Derbe and Lystra, where there was a disciple named Timothy. The (defined) foreground aspect (Imperfect) is then used to highlight a significant feature about this new character, Timothy: he was commended (ἐμαρτυρεῖτο) by the brethren. The background line then continues with the Aorist (ἠθέλησεν [want]; ἐξελθεῖν [go away]; λαβών [take]; περιέτεμεν [circumcise]). The reason for his circumcision is then given with the frontground aspect, reinforced by the (defined) foreground aspect: for all knew (ᾔδεισαν [stative]) that his father was (ὑπῆρχεν [imperfective]) Greek. Doctrine is obviously important in this passage, thus when the narrative continues, since the mission of Paul and his companions is related to teaching and building up churches, the (defined) foreground aspect is used (διεπορεύοντο [pass through]; παρεδίδοσαν [entrust]; φυλάσσειν [guard]), with the frontground aspect again employed to describe the dogma being guarded: the one determined (τὰ κεκριμένα) by the apostles and elders in Jerusalem. The successful result, again in the (defined) foreground aspect, is church growth (ἐστερεοῦντο [grow]; ἐπερίσσευον [grow rich]). The next narrative incident (16:6) continues with the background aspect (διῆλθον [pass through])."

16:1 Κατήντησεν δὲ [καὶ] εἰς Δέρβην καὶ εἰς Λύστραν. καὶ ἰδοὺ μαθητής τις ἦν ἐκεῖ ὀνόματι Τιμόθεος, υἱὸς γυναικὸς Ἰουδαίας πιστῆς, πατρὸς δὲ Ἕλληνος,

Κατήντησεν. Aor act ind 3rd sg καταντάω.
καὶ ἰδοὺ. See 1:10 on ἰδού.
τις. See 8:9.
ἦν. Impf ind 3rd sg εἰμί.
ὀνόματι. Dative of reference.
Τιμόθεος. Nominative in apposition to μαθητής.
υἱὸς. Nominative in apposition to μαθητής.

16:2 ὃς ἐμαρτυρεῖτο ὑπὸ τῶν ἐν Λύστροις καὶ Ἰκονίῳ ἀδελφῶν.

ἐμαρτυρεῖτο. Impf pass ind 3rd sg μαρτυρέω. The sense of μαρτυρέω here is probably "spoken well of" or "respected" (cf. 10:22).

16:3 τοῦτον ἠθέλησεν ὁ Παῦλος σὺν αὐτῷ ἐξελθεῖν, καὶ λαβὼν περιέτεμεν αὐτὸν διὰ τοὺς Ἰουδαίους τοὺς ὄντας ἐν τοῖς τόποις ἐκείνοις· ᾔδεισαν γὰρ ἅπαντες ὅτι Ἕλλην ὁ πατὴρ αὐτοῦ ὑπῆρχεν.

τοῦτον. The fronted (see 3:13 on ὑμεῖς) demonstrative pronoun introduces the topic (see 2:22 on Ἰησοῦν τὸν Ναζωραῖον) of the sentence. Syntactically, it is the accusative subject of the infinitive (see 1:3 on αὐτὸν).

ἠθέλησεν. Aor act ind 3rd sg θέλω.

ἐξελθεῖν. Aor act inf ἐξέρχομαι (object of ἠθέλησεν).

λαβὼν. Aor act ptc masc nom sg λαμβάνω (attendant circumstance).

περιέτεμεν. Aor act ind 3rd sg περιτέμνω. Wallace (1996, 411–12) is correct in noting that Paul was not the actual agent here. The fact that the "executive agent" (i.e., the one actually performing the action; see Deibler) is left implicit, however, does not warrant a new syntactic category (contra Wallace, who calls it the "causative active").

ὄντας. Pres act ptc masc acc pl εἰμί (attributive).

ᾔδεισαν. Plprf act ind 3rd pl οἶδα.

ὅτι. Introduces the clausal complement of ᾔδεισαν.

Ἕλλην. Predicate nominative.

ὑπῆρχεν. Impf act ind 3rd sg ὑπάρχω.

16:4 ὡς δὲ διεπορεύοντο τὰς πόλεις, παρεδίδοσαν αὐτοῖς φυλάσσειν τὰ δόγματα τὰ κεκριμένα ὑπὸ τῶν ἀποστόλων καὶ πρεσβυτέρων τῶν ἐν Ἱεροσολύμοις.

ὡς. Temporal (see 18:5).

διεπορεύοντο. Impf dep ind 3rd pl διαπορεύομαι.

παρεδίδοσαν. Impf act ind 3rd pl παραδίδωμι.

φυλάσσειν. Pres act inf φυλάσσω (purpose).

τὰ δόγματα. Accusative direct object of παρεδίδοσαν.

κεκριμένα. Prf pass ptc neut acc pl κρίνω (attributive).

τῶν ἐν Ἱεροσολύμοις. The article functions as an adjectivizer (see 2:5 on τῶν ὑπὸ τὸν οὐρανόν), changing the prepositional phrase into an attributive modifier of τῶν ἀποστόλων καὶ πρεσβυτέρων.

16:5 αἱ μὲν οὖν ἐκκλησίαι ἐστερεοῦντο τῇ πίστει καὶ ἐπερίσσευον τῷ ἀριθμῷ καθ' ἡμέραν.

μὲν οὖν. See 1:6.

ἐστερεοῦντο. Impf pass ind 3rd pl στερεόω.

τῇ πίστει. Dative of reference.

ἐπερίσσευον. Impf act ind 3rd pl περισσεύω.

καθ' ἡμέραν. Distributive (see 2:46).

Acts 16:6–10

[6]They went through the region of Phrygia and Galatia because the Holy Spirit prevented them from speaking the message in (the province of) Asia. [7]When they had come as far as (the province of) Mysia, they tried to enter (the province of) Bithynia but the Spirit of Jesus would not allow them. [8]So having arrived at Mysia they went down to Troas. [9](There) Paul saw a vision during the night in which a Macedonia man was standing and calling him, saying, "Come over to Macedonia and help us!" [10]When he saw the vision, we immediately sought to go into Macedonia because we concluded that God had called us to preach the good news to them.

16:6 Διῆλθον δὲ τὴν Φρυγίαν καὶ Γαλατικὴν χώραν κωλυθέντες ὑπὸ τοῦ ἁγίου πνεύματος λαλῆσαι τὸν λόγον ἐν τῇ Ἀσίᾳ·

Διῆλθον. Aor act ind 3rd pl διέρχομαι.

τὴν Φρυγίαν καὶ Γαλατικὴν χώραν. Witherington (1998, 478) argues that this phrase refers to a single region, Phrygian Galatia, that *included* the cities that Paul visited on his first missionary journey. If he is correct, this verse indicates that Paul continued on his way visiting the cities where churches had earlier been established (cf. 15:36), but was not able to continue westward into Asia. Such a reading would strike a fatal blow to the "North Galatian hypothesis." The weakness of Witherington's view, however, is the fact that Luke already stated in v. 4 that Paul visited the churches he had established earlier. The traditional view that Paul turned north when the Holy Spirit would not let him enter Asia makes better sense of the syntax and the reference to Mysia (northwest of Asia) in the following verse. Paul thus went *around* Asia to get to Mysia.

κωλυθέντες. Aor pass ptc masc nom pl κωλύω (probably causal).

λαλῆσαι. Aor act inf λαλέω (complementary; see 8:36 on βαπτισθῆναι).

16:7 ἐλθόντες δὲ κατὰ τὴν Μυσίαν ἐπείραζον εἰς τὴν Βιθυνίαν πορευθῆναι, καὶ οὐκ εἴασεν αὐτοὺς τὸ πνεῦμα Ἰησοῦ·

ἐλθόντες. Aor act ptc masc nom pl ἔρχομαι (temporal).

ἐπείραζον. Impf act ind 3rd pl πειράζω.

πορευθῆναι. Aor pass inf πορεύομαι (complementary).

καὶ. Adversative.

εἴασεν. Aor act ind 3rd sg ἐάω.

τὸ πνεῦμα ’Ιησοῦ. This rare expression (only here in the NT) apparently led many scribes either to replace ’Ιησοῦ with κυρίου (C* it[dem, gig] cop[bo mss] geo) or omit the entire phrase (81[c] 945 1891 *Byz al*).

16:8 παρελθόντες δὲ τὴν Μυσίαν κατέβησαν εἰς Τρῳάδα.

παρελθόντες. Aor act ptc masc nom pl παρέρχομαι (temporal). It is unclear how παρέρχομαι should be understood in this context. (1) Luke may have used it as a synonym for διέρχομαι (Codex D reads διελθόντες and this meaning is attested in extrabiblical material; see BAGD, 626). (2) It may carry the sense "to come to or arrive" and thus indicate that since they had come as far as Mysia they decided to make the short trip down to Troas. (3) It could carry its more typical sense of "to pass by" and indicate that they did not stop to preach the Gospel in this region as they went.

κατέβησαν. Aor act ind 3rd pl καταβαίνω.

16:9 καὶ ὅραμα διὰ [τῆς] νυκτὸς τῷ Παύλῳ ὤφθη, ἀνήρ Μακεδών τις ἦν ἑστὼς καὶ παρακαλῶν αὐτὸν καὶ λέγων, Διαβὰς εἰς Μακεδονίαν βοήθησον ἡμῖν.

ὅραμα. Nominative subject of the passive verb (lit. "a vision appeared to Paul").

ὤφθη. Aor pass ind 3rd sg ὁράω.

ἀνήρ . . . ἡμῖν. The entire clause stands in apposition to ὅραμα.

τις. See 8:9.

ἦν. Impf ind 3rd sg εἰμί.

ἑστὼς. Prf act ptc masc nom sg ἵστημι. Strictly speaking, the use of the perfect participle with the imperfect ἦν forms a pluperfect periphrastic construction (see 1:17 on κατηριθμημένος). Since, however, ἵστημι is not used in the present tense in this sense, it is better to view the perfect participle as functionally equivalent to the present participles that follow.

παρακαλῶν. Pres act ptc masc nom sg παρακαλέω (imperfect periphrastic; see 1:10 on ἀτενίζοντες).

λέγων. Pres act ptc masc nom sg λέγω (imperfect periphrastic; see 1:10 on ἀτενίζοντες).

Διαβὰς. Aor act ptc masc nom sg διαβαίνω (attendant circumstance).

βοήθησον. Aor act impv 2nd sg βοηθέω.

ἡμῖν. Dative complement of βοηθέω.

16:10 ὡς δὲ τὸ ὅραμα εἶδεν, εὐθέως ἐζητήσαμεν ἐξελθεῖν εἰς Μακεδονίαν συμβιβάζοντες ὅτι προσκέκληται ἡμᾶς ὁ θεὸς εὐαγγελίσασθαι αὐτούς.

ὡς. Temporal (see 18:5).

εἶδεν. Aor act ind 3rd sg ὁράω.

ἐζητήσαμεν. Aor act ind 1st pl ζητέω. The abrupt change from third person to first person plural marks the beginning of the first so-called "we" section in Acts (16:10–17; 20:5–15; 21:1–18; 27:1–29; 28:1–16). Scholars generally account for the "we" sections in one of three ways: (1) they represent the author's eyewitness accounts; (2) the author used a source from one of Paul's traveling companions; or (3) the author used a literary device common in ancient travel narratives (see, e.g., Witherington 1998, 480–86).

ἐξελθεῖν. Aor act inf ἐξέρχομαι (complementary).

συμβιβάζοντες. Pres act ptc masc nom pl συμβιβάζω (causal).

ὅτι. Introduces the clausal complement (indirect discourse with a verb of cognition) of συμβιβάζοντες.

προσκέκληται. Prf dep ind 3rd sg προσκαλέομαι.

εὐαγγελίσασθαι. Aor mid inf εὐαγγελίζω. Used with προσκαλέομαι in the sense of "to urgently invite someone to accept responsibilities for a particular task" (LN 33.312), the infinitive should probably be viewed as complementary or epexegetical, though it could perhaps indicate purpose (so Rogers and Rogers, 269).

αὐτούς. On the use of the accusative case with an indirect object, see 8:25 on πολλάς κώμας and 13:32 on ὑμᾶς.

Acts 16:11–15

[11]We set sail from Troas and sailed a straight course to Samothrace. On the next day, (we went on to) Neapolis. [12]From there (we continued on) to Philippi, which is a main city in that district of Macedonia and a (Roman) colony. We stayed in that city for several days.

[13]On the sabbath day we went outside the city to a river where we

thought there would be (a place for) prayer. After sitting down, we began speaking to the women who had gathered (there). [14]A woman named Lydia, a dealer in purple cloth from the city of Thyatira, who worshipped God, was listening to us, and the Lord opened her heart so that she paid close attention to what Paul was saying. [15]After she and her household had been baptized, she invited us (to her home). She said, "If you have concluded that I am faithful to the Lord, come and stay in my house." And she persuaded us.

16:11 Ἀναχθέντες δὲ ἀπὸ Τρῳάδος εὐθυδρομήσαμεν εἰς Σαμοθρᾴκην, τῇ δὲ ἐπιούσῃ εἰς Νέαν Πόλιν

Ἀναχθέντες. Aor pass ptc masc nom pl ἀνάγω (attendant circumstance or temporal). On the meaning, see 13:13.

εὐθυδρομήσαμεν. Aor act ind 1st pl εὐθυδρομέω.

16:12 κἀκεῖθεν εἰς Φιλίππους, ἥτις ἐστὶν πρώτη[ς] μερίδος τῆς Μακεδονίας πόλις, κολωνία. ἦμεν δὲ ἐν ταύτῃ τῇ πόλει διατρίβοντες ἡμέρας τινάς.

κἀκεῖθεν. A shortened form (crasis) of καὶ ἐκεῖθεν.

ἥτις. The antecedent of this feminine relative pronoun is an implicit πόλιν.

ἐστὶν. Pres act ind 3rd sg εἰμί.

πρώτη[ς]. Omanson notes that "the original text is most uncertain, and Hort thought that the original reading no longer existed in the surviving manuscripts. The oldest form of the text in the existing Greek witnesses [𝔓[74] א A C Ψ 33 81 *al*] appears to be πρώτη μερίδος τῆς Μακεδονίας πόλις" (B *Byz al* read πρώτη (τῆς) μερίδος τῆς Μακεδονίας πόλις). The difficulty of this reading lies in determining the sense of πρώτη. Thessalonica, rather than Philippi, was the "chief city" of Macedonia and Amphipolis was the chief city of the Macedonian district in which Philippi was located. Although some have suggested that the text indicates that Philippi was the first Macedonian city that Paul visited in that district, it appears that Neapolis, which he had already visited, is in the same district. These problems led the UBS committee to take the drastic step of positing a conjectural reading (πρώτης μερίδος τῆς Μακεδονίας πόλις: "a city of the first district of Macedonia") that is supported by only three late Latin manuscripts (see

Omanson; Metzger, 444–46). We have followed the UBS Committee minority opinion, which many translations have also followed (NRSV, NIV, REB), and prefer the well-attested reading πρώτη μερίδος τῆς Μακεδονίας πόλις.

κολωνία. Nominative in apposition to πόλις.

ἦμεν. Impf ind 1st pl εἰμί.

διατρίβοντες. Pres act ptc masc nom pl διατρίβω (imperfect periphrastic; see 1:10 on ἀτενίζοντες).

ἡμέρας. Accusative indicating extent of time (see 7:20 on μῆνας).

16:13 τῇ τε ἡμέρᾳ τῶν σαββάτων ἐξήλθομεν ἔξω τῆς πύλης παρὰ ποταμὸν οὗ ἐνομίζομεν προσευχὴν εἶναι, καὶ καθίσαντες ἐλαλοῦμεν ταῖς συνελθούσαις γυναιξίν.

ἡμέρᾳ. Dative of time.

τῶν σαββάτων. See 13:14.

ἐξήλθομεν. Aor act ind 1st pl ἐξέρχομαι.

ἔξω τῆς πύλης. Lit. "outside the gate."

οὗ. See 1:13.

ἐνομίζομεν προσευχὴν. Although the sense of the text is clear enough, the textual tradition is extremely diverse. The UBS[4]/NA[27] text is supported by A[2] C Ψ 33 81 2344 cop[sa, bo]. Other readings include the passive impersonal form ἐνομίζετο προσευχήν εἶναι (36 307 610 1678: "it was thought there was a place of prayer" or "it was the custom for there to be prayer"), the same form with the noun in the nominative case, ἐνομίζετο προσευχή εἶναι (E 453 614 *Byz al*), the singular active form with the noun in the nominative case, ἐνόμιζεν προσευχή εἶναι (𝔓[74]), the same reading with the noun in the accusative case, ἐνόμιζεν προσευχηύ εἶναι (א), and a reading with a different verb altogether, ἐδόκει προσευχή εἶναι (D *pc*).

ἐνομίζομεν. Impf act ind 1st pl νομίζω.

προσευχὴν. Accusative subject of the infinitive (see 1:3 on αὐτὸν). If one of the nominative readings is followed, προσευχή must be taken as the subject of the main verb.

εἶναι. Pres act inf εἰμί (indirect discourse).

καθίσαντες. Aor act ptc masc nom pl καθίζω (temporal).

ἐλαλοῦμεν. Impf act ind 1st pl λαλέω.

συνελθούσαις. Aor act ptc fem dat pl συνέρχομαι (attributive).

16:14 καί τις γυνὴ ὀνόματι Λυδία, πορφυρόπωλις πόλεως Θυατείρων σεβομένη τὸν θεόν, ἤκουεν, ἧς ὁ κύριος διήνοιξεν τὴν καρδίαν προσέχειν τοῖς λαλουμένοις ὑπὸ τοῦ Παύλου.

τις. See 8:9.
ὀνόματι. Dative of reference.
Λυδία. Nominative in apposition to γυνὴ.
πορφυρόπωλις. Nominative in apposition to γυνὴ.
σεβομένη. Pres mid ptc fem nom sg σέβομαι. Substantival (nominative) in apposition to γυνὴ or attributive. See also 17:17 on τοῖς σεβομένοις.
ἤκουεν. Impf act ind 3rd sg ἀκούω.
ἧς . . . τὴν καρδίαν. Lit. "whose heart."
διήνοιξεν. Aor act ind 3rd sg διανοίγω.
προσέχειν. Pres act inf προσέχω (result).
τοῖς λαλουμένοις. Pres pass ptc neut dat pl λαλέω (substantival).

16:15 ὡς δὲ ἐβαπτίσθη καὶ ὁ οἶκος αὐτῆς, παρεκάλεσεν λέγουσα, Εἰ κεκρίκατέ με πιστὴν τῷ κυρίῳ εἶναι, εἰσελθόντες εἰς τὸν οἶκόν μου μένετε· καὶ παρεβιάσατο ἡμᾶς.

ὡς. Temporal (see 18:5).
ἐβαπτίσθη. Aor pass ind 3rd sg βαπτίζω.
παρεκάλεσεν. Aor act ind 3rd sg παρακαλέω.
λέγουσα. Pres act ptc fem nom sg λέγω (attendant circumstance, redundant; see 1:6 on λέγοντες).
Εἰ. Introduces a first class condition.
κεκρίκατέ. Prf act ind 2nd pl κρίνω. The second accent comes from the enclitic με (see 1:4 on ἠκούσατέ).
με. Accusative subject of the infinitive (see 1:3 on αὐτὸν).
πιστὴν. The accusative adjective, which agrees with the subject με, could be taken as either as a predicate adjective ("faithful") or a substantival predicate accusative ("believer").
εἶναι. Pres act inf εἰμί (indirect discourse with a verb of cognition).
εἰσελθόντες. Aor act ptc masc nom pl εἰσέρχομαι (attendant circumstance).
οἶκόν. The second accent comes from the enclitic μου (see 1:4 on ἠκούσατέ).
μένετε. Pres act impv 2nd pl μένω.
παρεβιάσατο. Aor mid dep ind 3rd sg παραβιάζομαι.

Acts 16:16–24

[16]Now as we were going to (the place of) prayer, a slave girl met us who was possessed by a "Python spirit." She made a lot of money for her owners by telling fortunes. [17]She followed Paul and (the rest of) us, shouting, "These men are servants of the Most High God, who are proclaiming to you the way of salvation!" [18]She went on doing this for many days. (Finally,) Paul became really annoyed and turned around and said to the spirit, "I command you in the name of Jesus Christ to come out of her!" And it came out of her at that very moment.

[19]Now, when her masters saw that their hope of making money was gone, they grabbed Paul and Silas and dragged them before the authorities in the public square. [20]After bringing them before the magistrates, they said, "These men, who are Jews, are stirring up trouble in our city [21]and are advocating customs that are unlawful for us either to accept or practice, since we are Romans."

[22]The crowd joined the attack against them, and after the magistrates had had the clothes torn off them they gave orders to beat them. [23]After severely beating them, they threw them into prison and ordered the jailer to guard them carefully. [24]Having received such an order, he took them into the inner part of the prison and fastened their feet in stocks.

16:16 Ἐγένετο δὲ πορευομένων ἡμῶν εἰς τὴν προσευχὴν παιδίσκην τινὰ ἔχουσαν πνεῦμα πύθωνα ὑπαντῆσαι ἡμῖν, ἥτις ἐργασίαν πολλὴν παρεῖχεν τοῖς κυρίοις αὐτῆς μαντευομένη.

Ἐγένετο . . . ὑπαντῆσαι. This construction (ἐγένετο plus an infinitive) is used to indicate that the incident described in verse 16 supplies the general background for the following events (Levinsohn 1992, 213).

Ἐγένετο. Aor mid dep ind 3rd sg γίνομαι.

πορευομένων. Pres dep ptc masc gen pl πορεύομαι. Genitive absolute (see 1:8 on ἐπελθόντος), temporal.

ἡμῶν. Genitive subject (see 1:8 on ἐπελθόντος).

παιδίσκην. Accusative subject of the infinitive (see 1:3 on αὐτὸν). On the meaning, see 12:13.

ἔχουσαν. Pres act ptc fem acc sg ἔχω (attributive).

πνεῦμα πύθωνα. The sense here is probably, "a spirit of divination." The unusual combination of the two accusative nouns ($\mathfrak{P}^{74}$ א A B C* D* 81 326 1837 vg arm) led many scribes ($\mathfrak{P}^{45}$ C^3 D^2 E H L P *al*) to substitute the genitive form πύθωνος. Barrett (785) notes that in the harder reading, πύθωνα may be taken as appositional ("a spirit, a python") or as an adjectival use of the substantive ("a pythonic spirit").

ὑπαντῆσαι. Aor act inf ὑπαντάω. The infinitival clause, παιδίσκην τινὰ ἔχουσαν πνεῦμα πύθωνα ὑπαντῆσαι ἡμῖν, serves as the subject of ἐγένετο (see also 9:32 on κατελθεῖν).

παρεῖχεν. Impf act ind 3rd sg παρέχω.

κυρίοις. Dative of advantage.

μαντευομένη. Pres mid ptc fem nom sg μαντεύομαι (means).

16:17 αὕτη κατακολουθοῦσα τῷ Παύλῳ καὶ ἡμῖν ἔκραζεν λέγουσα, Οὗτοι οἱ ἄνθρωποι δοῦλοι τοῦ θεοῦ τοῦ ὑψίστου εἰσίν, οἵτινες καταγγέλλουσιν ὑμῖν ὁδὸν σωτηρίας.

κατακολουθοῦσα. Pres act ptc fem nom sg κατακολουθέω (attendant circumstance).

τῷ Παύλῳ καὶ ἡμῖν. Dative complement of κατακολουθοῦσα.

ἔκραζεν. Impf act ind 3rd sg κράζω.

λέγουσα. Pres act ptc fem nom sg λέγω (attendant circumstance, redundant; see 1:6 on λέγοντες).

δοῦλοι. Predicate nominative.

εἰσίν. Pres act ind 3rd pl εἰμί.

καταγγέλλουσιν. Pres act ind 3rd pl καταγγέλλω.

σωτηρίας. It is not particularly helpful to label the genitive "genitive of destination" (Wallace 1996, 101). The idiomatic expression ὁδὸν σωτηρίας denotes, "how you can be saved."

16:18 τοῦτο δὲ ἐποίει ἐπὶ πολλὰς ἡμέρας. διαπονηθεὶς δὲ Παῦλος καὶ ἐπιστρέψας τῷ πνεύματι εἶπεν, Παραγγέλλω σοι ἐν ὀνόματι Ἰησοῦ Χριστοῦ ἐξελθεῖν ἀπ' αὐτῆς· καὶ ἐξῆλθεν αὐτῇ τῇ ὥρᾳ.

ἐποίει. Impf act ind 3rd sg ποιέω.

ἐπὶ πολλὰς ἡμέρας. See 13:31 on ἐπὶ ἡμέρας πλείους.

διαπονηθείς. Aor pass ptc masc nom sg διαπονέομαι (attendant circumstance). Given the fact that conjoined participles must share the same function, διαπονηθεὶς cannot be causal since it is conjoined to ἐπιστρέψας, which is clearly not causal.

ἐπιστρέψας. Aor act ptc masc nom sg ἐπιστρέφω (attendant circumstance).

εἶπεν. Aor act ind 3rd sg λέγω.

Παραγγέλλω. Pres act ind 1st sg παραγγέλλω.

ἐξελθεῖν. Aor act inf ἐξέρχομαι (indirect discourse).

ἐξῆλθεν. Aor act ind 3rd sg ἐξέρχομαι.

αὐτῇ τῇ ὥρᾳ. Lit. "at that very hour."

16:19 ἰδόντες δὲ οἱ κύριοι αὐτῆς ὅτι ἐξῆλθεν ἡ ἐλπὶς τῆς ἐργασίας αὐτῶν, ἐπιλαβόμενοι τὸν Παῦλον καὶ τὸν Σιλᾶν εἵλκυσαν εἰς τὴν ἀγορὰν ἐπὶ τοὺς ἄρχοντας

ἰδόντες. Aor act ptc masc nom pl ὁράω (temporal).

ὅτι. Introduces the clausal complement of ἰδόντες.

ἐξῆλθεν. Aor act ind 3rd sg ἐξέρχομαι.

ἐπιλαβόμενοι. Aor mid dep ptc masc nom pl ἐπιλαμβάνομαι (attendant circumstance).

εἵλκυσαν. Aor act ind 3rd pl ἕλκω.

ἀγορὰν. Since the ἀγορά "was used for all kinds of public purposes, including judicial purposes" (Barrett, 788), the TEV's "public square" or the CEV's "court" is more appropriate than "marketplace."

16:20 καὶ προσαγαγόντες αὐτοὺς τοῖς στρατηγοῖς εἶπαν, Οὗτοι οἱ ἄνθρωποι ἐκταράσσουσιν ἡμῶν τὴν πόλιν, Ἰουδαῖοι ὑπάρχοντες,

προσαγαγόντες. Aor act ptc masc nom pl προσάγω (temporal).

εἶπαν. Aor act ind 3rd pl λέγω.

ἐκταράσσουσιν. Pres act ind 3rd pl ἐκταράσσω.

Ἰουδαῖοι. Predicate nominative.

ὑπάρχοντες. Pres act ptc masc nom pl ὑπάρχω. The participle could be taken as an attributive modifier of ἄνθρωποι or as an adverbial (attendant circumstance) modifier of καταγγέλλουσιν (v. 21). On the whole, the parallel construction at the end of v. 21 and the presence of the conjunction at the beginning of v. 21 make the latter less likely since adverbial participles are not typically linked to the main verb with a conjunction.

16:21 καὶ καταγγέλλουσιν ἔθη ἃ οὐκ ἔξεστιν ἡμῖν παραδέχεσθαι οὐδὲ ποιεῖν Ῥωμαίοις οὖσιν.

καταγγέλλουσιν. Pres act ind 3rd pl καταγγέλλω.

ἅ. The relative pronoun is the accusative object of the infinitives rather than the nominative subject of the impersonal ἔξεστιν.

ἔξεστιν. Pres act ind 3rd sg ἔξεστι (impersonal).

παραδέχεσθαι. Pres mid inf παραδέχομαι (complementary; see 1:16 on ἔδει).

ποιεῖν. Pres act inf ποιέω (complementary; see 1:16 on ἔδει).

Ῥωμαίοις. Predicate dative. As the predicate of the attributive participle οὖσιν, Ῥωμαίοις must agree in gender, number, and case with the referent it describes (ἡμῖν; cf. 1:16 on ὁδηγοῦ).

οὖσιν. Pres act ptc masc dat pl εἰμί (attributive modifier of ἡμῖν).

16:22 καὶ συνεπέστη ὁ ὄχλος κατ᾽ αὐτῶν καὶ οἱ στρατηγοὶ περιρήξαντες αὐτῶν τὰ ἱμάτια ἐκέλευον ῥαβδίζειν,

συνεπέστη. Aor act ind 3rd sg συνεφίστημι.

περιρήξαντες. Aor act ptc masc nom pl περιρήγνυμι (temporal).

ἐκέλευον. Impf act ind 3rd pl κελεύω.

ῥαβδίζειν. Pres act inf ῥαβδίζω (indirect discourse).

16:23 πολλάς τε ἐπιθέντες αὐτοῖς πληγὰς ἔβαλον εἰς φυλακὴν παραγγείλαντες τῷ δεσμοφύλακι ἀσφαλῶς τηρεῖν αὐτούς.

πολλάς . . . πληγὰς. Lit. "laying many blows on them."

ἐπιθέντες. Aor act ptc masc nom pl ἐπιτίθημι (temporal).

ἔβαλον. Aor act ind 3rd pl βάλλω.

παραγγείλαντες. Aor act ptc masc nom pl παραγγέλλω (attendant circumstance).

δεσμοφύλακι. Dative indirect object of παραγγείλαντες.

τηρεῖν. Pres act inf τηρέω (indirect discourse).

16:24 ὃς παραγγελίαν τοιαύτην λαβὼν ἔβαλεν αὐτοὺς εἰς τὴν ἐσωτέραν φυλακὴν καὶ τοὺς πόδας ἠσφαλίσατο αὐτῶν εἰς τὸ ξύλον.

ὃς. The antecedent is τῷ δεσμοφύλακι (v. 23).

λαβὼν. Aor act ptc masc nom sg λαμβάνω (temporal).

ἔβαλεν. Aor act ind 3rd sg βάλλω.

τὴν ἐσωτέραν φυλακὴν. The comparative ἐσωτέραν may carry superlative force: "innermost (cell of the) prison," "dungeon" (Bruce, 363).

ἠσφαλίσατο. Aor mid ind 3rd sg ἀσφαλίζω.

Acts 16:25–34

[25]Now at midnight Paul and Silas were praying and singing hymns to God and the other prisoners were listening to them. [26]Suddenly, there was an earthquake that was so strong that it shook the foundations of the prison. Right away, all of the doors opened and the chains of all (the prisoners) came loose.

[27]When the jailer woke up and saw the prison doors standing open, he drew his sword and was about to kill himself because he thought that the prisoners had escaped. [28]But Paul shouted loudly, "Don't harm yourself! We're all here!" [29]After asking for (some) lights, he rushed in and fell down before Paul and Silas trembling. [30]Then he took them outside and said, "Sirs, what must I do to be saved?" [31]They replied, "Believe in the Lord Jesus and you will be saved—you and your household." [32]Then they told him, along with all those in his household, the message of the Lord.

[33](The jailer) took them, at that very hour of the night, and cleaned their wounds. Then he and his whole family were immediately baptized. [34](After that,) He brought them into (his) house and fed them; and he was full of joy because he, with his entire household, had come to believe in God.

16:25 Κατὰ δὲ τὸ μεσονύκτιον Παῦλος καὶ Σιλᾶς προσευχόμενοι ὕμνουν τὸν θεόν, ἐπηκροῶντο δὲ αὐτῶν οἱ δέσμιοι.

προσευχόμενοι. Pres dep ptc masc nom pl προσεύχομαι (attendant circumstance).

ὕμνουν. Impf act ind 3rd pl ὑμνέω.

ἐπηκροῶντο. Impf dep ind 3rd pl ἐπακροάομαι.

αὐτῶν. Genitive object of ἐπηκροῶντο.

16:26 ἄφνω δὲ σεισμὸς ἐγένετο μέγας ὥστε σαλευθῆναι τὰ θεμέλια τοῦ δεσμωτηρίου· ἠνεῴχθησαν δὲ παραχρῆμα αἱ θύραι πᾶσαι καὶ πάντων τὰ δεσμὰ ἀνέθη.

σεισμὸς. Predicate nominative of an impersonal ἐγένετο.

ἐγένετο. Aor mid dep ind 3rd sg γίνομαι.

σαλευθῆναι. Aor pass inf σαλεύω. Used with ὥστε to indicate result.

ἠνεῴχθησαν. Aor pass ind 3rd pl ἀνοίγω.

παραχρῆμα. It is possible that in the present context παραχρῆμα draws attention to the unexpected nature of the events rather than their temporal proximity to the preceding event. Louw and Nida (67.113), however, point out that "in a number of contexts there is the implication of unexpectedness, but this seems to be a derivative of the context as a whole and not a part of the meaning of the lexical items."

πάντων τὰ δεσμὰ. According to Levinsohn (1987, 41), the fronting of the subject (see 3:13 on ὑμεῖς) highlights information that will be surprising to the readers: it was not just the apostles' chains that fell off.

πάντων. Substantival.

δεσμὰ. The masculine noun δεσμός frequently appears as a neuter in the plural (cf. 20:23; Luke 8:29; contrast Phil 1:13).

ἀνέθη. Aor pass ind 3rd sg ἀνίημι.

16:27 ἔξυπνος δὲ γενόμενος ὁ δεσμοφύλαξ καὶ ἰδὼν ἀνεῳγμένας τὰς θύρας τῆς φυλακῆς, σπασάμενος [τὴν] μάχαιραν ἤμελλεν ἑαυτὸν ἀναιρεῖν νομίζων ἐκπεφευγέναι τοὺς δεσμίους.

ἔξυπνος. Predicate adjective.

γενόμενος. Aor mid dep ptc masc nom sg γίνομαι (temporal).

ἰδὼν. Aor act ptc masc nom sg ὁράω (temporal).

ἀνεῳγμένας. Prf pass ptc fem acc pl ἀνοίγω. The participle functions as the complement in an object-complement double accusative construction (see 1:3 on ζῶντα).

σπασάμενος. Aor mid ptc masc nom sg σπάω (attendant circumstance). The unusual use of an *aorist* participle introducing an attendant circumstance of an *imperfect* main verb (see above, p. xvii) may be explained by the fact that μέλλω is never used in the aorist tense.

ἤμελλεν. Impf act ind 3rd sg μέλλω. See 3:3 on μέλλοντας.

ἀναιρεῖν. Pres act inf ἀναιρέω (complementary).

νομίζων. Pres act ptc masc nom sg νομίζω (causal).

ἐκπεφευγέναι. Prf act inf ἐκφεύγω (indirect discourse).

τοὺς δεσμίους. Accusative subject of the infinitive (see 1:3 on αὐτὸν).

16:28 ἐφώνησεν δὲ μεγάλῃ φωνῇ [ὁ] Παῦλος λέγων, Μηδὲν πράξῃς σεαυτῷ κακόν, ἅπαντες γάρ ἐσμεν ἐνθάδε.

ἐφώνησεν. Aor act ind 3rd sg φωνέω.

μεγάλῃ φωνῇ. Strictly speaking, dative of instrument ("using a loud voice"), but the effect of the phrase is to indicate the manner in which Paul called out ("loudly"). There is great diversity among extant manuscripts regarding the word order of the phrase μεγάλῃ φωνῇ [ὁ] Παῦλος. The UBS[4]/NA[27] reading is reflected in a single manuscript (A).

λέγων. Pres act ptc masc nom sg λέγω (attendant circumstance, redundant; see 1:6 on λέγοντες).

Μηδὲν. The adjective modifies the substantival κακόν.

πράξῃς. Aor act subj 2nd sg πράσσω (prohibitive subjunctive).

ἐσμεν. Pres act ind 1st pl εἰμί.

16:29 αἰτήσας δὲ φῶτα εἰσεπήδησεν καὶ ἔντρομος γενόμενος προσέπεσεν τῷ Παύλῳ καὶ [τῷ] Σιλᾷ

αἰτήσας. Aor act ptc masc nom sg αἰτέω (temporal).

εἰσεπήδησεν. Aor act ind 3rd sg εἰσπηδάω.

ἔντρομος. Predicate adjective.

γενόμενος. Aor mid ptc masc nom sg γίνομαι (attendant circumstance).

προσέπεσεν. Aor act ind 3rd sg προσπίπτω.

τῷ Παύλῳ . . . [τῷ] Σιλᾷ. Dative complements of προσέπεσεν.

16:30 καὶ προαγαγὼν αὐτοὺς ἔξω ἔφη, Κύριοι, τί με δεῖ ποιεῖν ἵνα σωθῶ;

προαγαγὼν. Aor act ptc masc nom sg προάγω (attendant circumstance).

ἔφη. Aor/Impf act ind 3rd sg φημί. On the tense, see 7:2.

με. Accusative subject of the infinitive (see 1:3 on αὐτὸν).

δεῖ. Pres act ind 3rd sg δεῖ (impersonal).

ποιεῖν. Pres act inf ποιέω (complementary; see 1:16 on ἔδει).

σωθῶ. Aor pass subj 1st sg σῴζω. The subjunctive is used with ἵνα to indicate purpose.

16:31 οἱ δὲ εἶπαν, Πίστευσον ἐπὶ τὸν κύριον Ἰησοῦν καὶ σωθήσῃ σὺ καὶ ὁ οἶκός σου.

οἱ. The article functions like a personal pronoun here (cf. 3:5).

εἶπαν. Aor act ind 3rd pl λέγω.

Πίστευσον. Aor act impv 2nd sg πιστεύω.

σωθήσῃ. Fut pass ind 2nd sg σῴζω. The use of the singular verb with the compound subject keeps the focus on the jailer (cf. v. 33; 7:15; 11:14; 26:30).

οἶκός. The second accent comes from the enclitic σου (see 1:4 on ἠκούσατέ).

16:32 καὶ ἐλάλησαν αὐτῷ τὸν λόγον τοῦ κυρίου σὺν πᾶσιν τοῖς ἐν τῇ οἰκίᾳ αὐτοῦ.

ἐλάλησαν. Aor act ind 3rd pl λαλέω.

16:33 καὶ παραλαβὼν αὐτοὺς ἐν ἐκείνῃ τῇ ὥρᾳ τῆς νυκτὸς ἔλουσεν ἀπὸ τῶν πληγῶν, καὶ ἐβαπτίσθη αὐτὸς καὶ οἱ αὐτοῦ πάντες παραχρῆμα,

παραλαβὼν. Aor act ptc masc nom sg παραλαμβάνω (attendant circumstance).

ἔλουσεν ἀπὸ τῶν πληγῶν. This expression (lit. "bathed from the wounds") is probably simply an idiom for "to clean wounds" (contra BAGD, 480).

ἔλουσεν. Aor act ind 3rd sg λούω.

ἐβαπτίσθη. Aor pass ind 3rd sg βαπτίζω. The use of the singular verb with the compound subject keeps the focus on the jailer (cf. v. 31).

16:34 ἀναγαγών τε αὐτοὺς εἰς τὸν οἶκον παρέθηκεν τράπεζαν, καὶ ἠγαλλιάσατο πανοικεὶ πεπιστευκὼς τῷ θεῷ.

ἀναγαγών. Aor act ptc masc nom sg ἀνάγω (attendant circumstance).

παρέθηκεν τράπεζαν. Lit. "placed on the table."

παρέθηκεν. Aor act ind 3rd sg παρατίθημι.

ἠγαλλιάσατο. Aor mid ind 3rd sg ἀγαλλιάω.

πανοικεὶ. An adverb meaning "with one's whole household."

πεπιστευκὼς. Prf act ptc masc nom sg πιστεύω (causal).

Acts 16:35–40

[35]When daylight had come, the magistrates sent (a message to the jailer with some) police officers, saying, "Release those men." [36]The jailer reported these words to Paul (saying), "The magistrates have sent

(word) to release you. So (you can) leave now and go in peace." [37]But Paul replied to (the police officers), "They beat us publicly without a trial, even though we are Roman citizens, and threw us into prison. And now they want to send us away secretly? Certainly not! They themselves must come and let us out!" [38]So the police officers reported these words to the magistrates.

When they heard that Paul and Silas were Roman citizens, they were afraid, [39]so they went and apologized to them. Then, after bringing them out, they asked (them) to leave the city. [40]After leaving the prison, they went to (the home of) Lydia. When they saw the believers (there), they encouraged them and then left.

16:35 Ἡμέρας δὲ γενομένης ἀπέστειλαν οἱ στρατηγοὶ τοὺς ῥαβδούχους λέγοντες, Ἀπόλυσον τοὺς ἀνθρώπους ἐκείνους.

Ἡμέρας. Genitive subject (see 1:8 on ἐπελθόντος) or predicate genitive with an impersonal γενομένης.

γενομένης. Aor mid dep ptc fem gen sg γίνομαι. Genitive absolute (see 1:8 on ἐπελθόντος), temporal.

ἀπέστειλαν. Aor act ind 3rd pl ἀποστέλλω.

λέγοντες. Pres act ptc masc nom pl λέγω (attendant circumstance). The participle, which introduces an action of οἱ στρατηγοὶ rather than τοὺς ῥαβδούχους, is used as part of a construction (ἀπέστειλαν . . . λέγοντες) that means "to send a message" (cf. 13:15) though syntactically τοὺς ῥαβδούχους is the direct object of ἀπέστειλαν. That the command is directed at the jailer rather than τοὺς ῥαβδούχους is made clear by the use of the imperative singular verb that follows.

Ἀπόλυσον. Aor act impv 2nd sg ἀπολύω.

16:36 ἀπήγγειλεν δὲ ὁ δεσμοφύλαξ τοὺς λόγους [τούτους] πρὸς τὸν Παῦλον ὅτι Ἀπέσταλκαν οἱ στρατηγοὶ ἵνα ἀπολυθῆτε· νῦν οὖν ἐξελθόντες πορεύεσθε ἐν εἰρήνῃ.

ἀπήγγειλεν. Aor act ind 3rd sg ἀπαγέλλω.

Ἀπέσταλκαν. Prf act ind 3rd pl ἀποστέλλω. The aorist active ending –αν was sometimes used in place of the normal perfect active ending –ασι (BDF §83).

ἀπολυθῆτε. Aor pass subj 2nd pl ἀπολύω. The subjunctive is used with ἵνα to indicate the purpose of the message, though a good English translation will not use a purpose clause here.

ἐξελθόντες. Aor act ptc masc nom pl ἐξέρχομαι (attendant circumstance).

πορεύεσθε. Pres mid impv 2nd pl πορεύομαι.

ἐν εἰρήνῃ. Manner.

16:37 ὁ δὲ Παῦλος ἔφη πρὸς αὐτούς, δείραντες ἡμᾶς δημοσίᾳ ἀκατακρίτους, ἀνθρώπους Ῥωμαίους ὑπάρχοντας, ἔβαλαν εἰς φυλακήν, καὶ νῦν λάθρᾳ ἡμᾶς ἐκβάλλουσιν; οὐ γάρ, ἀλλὰ ἐλθόντες αὐτοὶ ἡμᾶς ἐξαγαγέτωσαν.

ἔφη. Aor/Impf act ind 3rd sg φημί. On the tense, see 7:2.

δείραντες. Aor act ptc masc nom pl δέρω (attendant circumstance).

δημοσίᾳ. Dative of manner.

ἀνθρώπους. Accusative in apposition to ἡμᾶς.

Ῥωμαίους. Predicate accusative (see 1:22 on μάρτυρα).

ὑπάρχοντας. Pres act ptc masc acc pl ὑπάρχω. Given the presence of ἀνθρώπους, the participle must be understood as attributive (lit. "men who are Romans") rather than concessive (contra Rogers and Rogers, 272), though an English translation that uses a concessive clause is appropriate.

ἔβαλαν. Aor act ind 3rd pl βάλλω.

λάθρᾳ. Dative of manner.

ἐκβάλλουσιν Pres act ind 3rd pl ἐκβάλλω.

οὐ γάρ. An emphatic way of rejecting a proposition.

ἐλθόντες. Aor act ptc masc nom pl ἔρχομαι (attendant circumstance).

ἐξαγαγέτωσαν. Aor act impv 3rd pl ἐξάγω.

16:38 ἀπήγγειλαν δὲ τοῖς στρατηγοῖς οἱ ῥαβδοῦχοι τὰ ῥήματα ταῦτα. ἐφοβήθησαν δὲ ἀκούσαντες ὅτι Ῥωμαῖοί εἰσιν,

ἀπήγγειλαν. Aor act ind 3rd pl ἀπαγγέλλω.

ἐφοβήθησαν. Aor pass ind 3rd pl φοβέω.

ἀκούσαντες. Aor act ptc masc nom pl ἀκούω (temporal).

Ῥωμαῖοί. Predicate nominative. The second accent comes from the enclitic εἰσιν (see 1:4 on ἠκούσατέ).

εἰσιν. Pres act ind 3rd pl εἰμί.

16:39 καὶ ἐλθόντες παρεκάλεσαν αὐτούς καὶ ἐξαγαγόντες ἠρώτων ἀπελθεῖν ἀπὸ τῆς πόλεως.

ἐλθόντες. Aor act ptc masc nom pl ἔρχομαι (attendant circumstance).

παρεκάλεσαν. Aor act ind 3rd pl παρακαλέω. The sense of the verb here is probably something like "to placate" (Fitzmyer 1998, 582), or perhaps "to apologize" (BAGD, 617).

ἐξαγαγόντες. Aor act ptc masc nom pl ἐξάγω (temporal).

ἠρώτων. Impf act ind 3rd pl ἐρωτάω.

ἀπελθεῖν. Aor act inf ἀπέρχομαι (indirect discourse).

16:40 ἐξελθόντες δὲ ἀπὸ τῆς φυλακῆς εἰσῆλθον πρὸς τὴν Λυδίαν καὶ ἰδόντες παρεκάλεσαν τοὺς ἀδελφοὺς καὶ ἐξῆλθαν.

ἐξελθόντες. Aor act ptc masc nom pl ἐξέρχομαι (temporal).

εἰσῆλθον. Aor act ind 3rd pl ἐισέρχομαι.

ἰδόντες. Aor act ptc masc nom pl ὁράω (temporal).

παρεκάλεσαν. Aor act ind 3rd pl παρακαλέω.

ἀδελφοὺς. See 1:15.

ἐξῆλθαν. Aor act ind 3rd pl ἐξέρχομαι. On the use of this spelling rather than ἐξῆλθον, see 28:15 on ἦλθαν.

Acts 17:1–9

[1]After traveling through Amphipolis and Apollonia, they came to Thessalonica, where there was a Jewish synagogue. [2]As was Paul's custom, he went in (to the synagogue) with them and had a discussion with them about the Scriptures on three sabbath days. [3]He explained (the Scriptures) and tried to demonstrate (to them) that it was necessary for the Christ to suffer and to rise from the dead. (He told them,) "This Jesus, whom I am proclaiming to you, is the Christ."

[4]Some of them—a large group of pious Greeks and many prominent women—were persuaded and joined Paul and Silas. [5]But the Jews became jealous, gathered some worthless bums (from the marketplace), formed a mob, and started a riot in the city. Then they showed up at Jason's house and were trying to find (Paul and Silas) and drag them before the assembly of citizens. [6]But when they did not find them (there) they dragged Jason and some other believers before the city officials, shouting, "These men who have caused trouble throughout the world have now come here! [7]Jason has welcomed them, and all of them are

violating the decrees of Caesar by saying there is another king, (called) Jesus." [8]So they stirred up the crowd and the city officials who had heard what they had said. [9](Then,) After receiving bail from Jason and the others, they released them.

17:1 Διοδεύσαντες δὲ τὴν Ἀμφίπολιν καὶ τὴν Ἀπολλωνίαν ἦλθον εἰς Θεσσαλονίκην ὅπου ἦν συναγωγὴ τῶν Ἰουδαίων.

Διοδεύσαντες. Aor act ptc masc nom pl διοδεύω (temporal).

ἦλθον. Aor act ind 3rd pl ἔρχομαι.

ἦν. Impf ind 3rd sg εἰμί.

συναγωγή. Nominative subject or predicate nominative of an impersonal ἦν.

17:2 κατὰ δὲ τὸ εἰωθὸς τῷ Παύλῳ εἰσῆλθεν πρὸς αὐτοὺς καὶ ἐπὶ σάββατα τρία διελέξατο αὐτοῖς ἀπὸ τῶν γραφῶν,

τὸ εἰωθὸς. Prf act ptc neut acc sg εἴωθάἔθω (substantival).

Παύλῳ. Dative of possession (Barrett, 809).

εἰσῆλθεν. Aor act ind 3rd sg εἰσέρχομαι.

ἐπὶ σάββατα τρία. There is some uncertainty whether this phrase refers to a period of time ("for three weeks"; see 13:31 on ἐπὶ ἡμέρας πλείους) or a number occasions ("on three [consecutive?] sabbaths"). Many scholars point to Phil 4:16 and Paul's first letter to the Thessalonians as evidence that he stayed in Thessalonica for more than three weeks (cf. Barrett, 809).

διελέξατο. Aor mid dep ind 3rd sg διαλέγομαι.

ἀπὸ τῶν γραφῶν. Lit. "from the Scriptures."

17:3 διανοίγων καὶ παρατιθέμενος ὅτι τὸν Χριστὸν ἔδει παθεῖν καὶ ἀναστῆναι ἐκ νεκρῶν καὶ ὅτι οὗτός ἐστιν ὁ Χριστός [ὁ] Ἰησοῦς ὃν ἐγὼ καταγγέλλω ὑμῖν.

διανοίγων καὶ παρατιθέμενος. In this context, the two participles could be viewed as near synonyms that form a doublet (see 2:43 on τέρατα καὶ σημεῖα) emphasizing the nature of Paul's efforts: "systematically demonstrating."

διανοίγων. Pres act ptc masc nom sg διανοίγω. The two participles probably indicate the manner in which Paul "debated" with the synagogue members.

παρατιθέμενος. Pres mid ptc masc nom sg παρατίθημι (see above).

ὅτι. Introduces indirect discourse.

Χριστὸν. Accusative subject of the infinitives (see 1:3 on αὐτὸν).

ἔδει. Impf act ind 3rd sg δεῖ (impersonal).

παθεῖν. Aor act inf πάσχω (complementary; see 1:16 on ἔδει).

ἀναστῆναι. Aor act inf ἀνίστημι (complementary; see 1:16 on ἔδει).

οὗτός. The demonstrative could be taken as either substantival, with Ἰησοῦς being in apposition to it, or as a modifier of Ἰησοῦς that has been fronted (see 3:13 on ὑμεῖς) for emphasis. The second accent comes from the enclitic ἐστιν (see 1:4 on ἠκούσατέ).

ἐστιν. Pres act ind 3rd sg εἰμί.

Χριστός. Predicate nominative.

καταγγέλλω. Pres act ind 1st sg καταγγέλλω.

17:4 καί τινες ἐξ αὐτῶν ἐπείσθησαν καὶ προσεκληρώθησαν τῷ Παύλῳ καὶ τῷ Σιλᾷ, τῶν τε σεβομένων Ἑλλήνων πλῆθος πολὺ, γυναικῶν τε τῶν πρώτων οὐκ ὀλίγαι.

ἐπείσθησαν. Aor pass ind 3rd pl πείθω.

προσεκληρώθησαν. Aor pass ind 3rd pl προσκληρόω.

σεβομένων. Pres dep ptc masc gen pl σέβομαι (attributive). See v. 17 on σεβομένοις.

Ἑλλήνων. Partitive genitive modifying πλῆθος.

πλῆθος . . . ὀλίγαι. Nominatives in apposition to τινες. Unlike many English translations, the syntax (appositional nominatives with τε . . . τε) suggests that the τινες were predominately "devout Greeks and prominent women."

γυναικῶν. Partitive genitive modifying ὀλίγαι. Some scribes (D lat) made their view clear that the women were "*wives* of the leading men" by omitting the τε and using the nominative form (γυναῖκες) after a καὶ (cf. v. 12).

οὐκ ὀλίγαι. Litotes (lit. "not a few"; see 1:5 on ου) μετὰ πολλὰς ταύτας ἡμέρας). See above on πλῆθος . . . ὀλίγαι also.

17:5 Ζηλώσαντες δὲ οἱ Ἰουδαῖοι καὶ προσλαβόμενοι τῶν ἀγοραίων ἄνδρας τινὰς πονηροὺς καὶ ὀχλοποιήσαντες ἐθορύβουν τὴν πόλιν καὶ ἐπιστάντες τῇ οἰκίᾳ Ἰάσονος ἐζήτουν αὐτοὺς προαγαγεῖν εἰς τὸν δῆμον·

Ζηλώσαντες. Aor act ptc masc nom pl ζηλόω (attendant circumstance). The unusual use of an *aorist* participle introducing an attendant circumstance of an *imperfect* main verb (see above, p. xvii) may be explained by the fact that in the NT θορυβέω is never used in the aorist tense (cf. 16:27 on σπασάμενος).

προσλαβόμενοι. Aor mid ptc masc nom pl προσλαμβάνω (attendant circumstance).

ἀγοραίων. Witherington (1998, 507) notes that this term, which referred to a person who habitually loitered in the marketplace, carried a negative connotation like the English "malcontent," "agitator," "loafer," or even "lowlife." Here, the nature of these men is made clear by the adjective πονηροὺς.

ὀχλοποιήσαντες. Aor act ptc masc nom pl ὀχλοποιέω (attendant circumstance).

ἐθορύβουν. Impf act ind 3rd pl θορυβέω.

ἐπιστάντες. Aor act ptc masc nom pl ἐφίστημι (temporal). Louw and Nida (39.47) argue that in this context ἐφίστημι means, "to use sudden physical force against someone as the outgrowth of a hostile attitude—'to attack, to assault.'" While the context indicates an attack, however, it is not clear that the verb itself carries such a sense.

ἐζήτουν. Impf act ind 3rd pl ζητέω.

προαγαγεῖν. Aor act inf προάγω (complementary).

τὸν δῆμον. See 19:30.

17:6 μὴ εὑρόντες δὲ αὐτοὺς ἔσυρον Ἰάσονα καί τινας ἀδελφοὺς ἐπὶ τοὺς πολιτάρχας βοῶντες ὅτι Οἱ τὴν οἰκουμένην ἀναστατώσαντες οὗτοι καὶ ἐνθάδε πάρεισιν,

εὑρόντες. Aor act ptc masc nom pl εὑρίσκω (temporal).

ἔσυρον. Impf act ind 3rd pl σύρω.

ἀδελφοὺς. See 1:15.

βοῶντες. Pres act ptc masc nom pl βοάω (attendant circumstance).

Οἱ . . . πάρεισιν. Lit. "these inciters of the world have also come here."

Οἱ . . . ἀναστατώσαντες. Aor act ptc masc nom pl ἀναστατόω (substantival).

πάρεισιν. Pres act ind 3rd pl πάρειμι.

17:7 οὓς ὑποδέδεκται Ἰάσων· καὶ οὗτοι πάντες ἀπέναντι τῶν δογμάτων Καίσαρος πράσσουσι, βασιλέα ἕτερον λέγοντες εἶναι Ἰησοῦν.

ὑποδέδεκται. Prf dep ind 3rd sg ὑποδέχομαι.

ἀπέναντι . . . πράσσουσι. Lit. "acting against."

πράσσουσι. Pres act ind 3rd pl πράσσω.

βασιλέα. Predicate accusative of the impersonal infinitive εἶναι, fronted (see 3:13 on ὑμεῖς) for emphasis.

λέγοντες. Pres act ptc masc nom pl λέγω (means).

εἶναι. Pres act inf εἰμί (indirect discourse).

Ἰησοῦν. Accusative in apposition to βασιλέα.

17:8 ἐτάραξαν δὲ τὸν ὄχλον καὶ τοὺς πολιτάρχας ἀκούοντας ταῦτα,

ἐτάραξαν. Aor act ind 3rd pl ταράσσω.

ἀκούοντας. Pres act ptc masc acc pl ἀκούω (attributive).

17:9 καὶ λαβόντες τὸ ἱκανὸν παρὰ τοῦ Ἰάσονος καὶ τῶν λοιπῶν ἀπέλυσαν αὐτούς.

λαβόντες. Aor act ptc masc nom pl λαμβάνω (temporal). Louw and Nida (57.169) define ἱκανὸν as "the amount of money required to release someone who has been held in custody."

ἀπέλυσαν. Aor act ind 3rd pl ἀπολύω.

Acts 17:10–15

10The believers immediately sent Paul and Barnabas away to Berea
during the night. When they arrived, they went to the Jewish synagogue.
11The people there were more willing to learn than those in
Thessalonica. They were extremely eager to receive the message and each day would carefully examine the Scriptures (to determine) whether the things (the apostles were saying) were true.
12And so, many of them
believed—in particular, quite a few respected Greek women and men.

13When the Jews from Thessalonica learned that Paul had also proclaimed God's message in Berea, they went there too to stir up the
crowds.
14Without delay, the believers sent Paul away to the seacoast,

and both Silas and Timothy remained there. [15]Those who escorted Paul took him as far as Athens. Then, after receiving a message to Silas and Timothy that they should come to him as quickly as possible, they left.

17:10 Οἱ δὲ ἀδελφοὶ εὐθέως διὰ νυκτὸς ἐξέπεμψαν τόν τε Παῦλον καὶ τὸν Σιλᾶν εἰς Βέροιαν, οἵτινες παραγενόμενοι εἰς τὴν συναγωγὴν τῶν Ἰουδαίων ἀπῄεσαν.

ἀδελφοί. See 1:15.

ἐξέπεμψαν. Aor act ind 3rd pl ἐκπέμπω.

παραγενόμενοι. Aor mid dep ptc masc nom pl παραγίνομαι (temporal).

ἀπῄεσαν. Impf act ind 3rd pl ἄπειμι.

17:11 οὗτοι δὲ ἦσαν εὐγενέστεροι τῶν ἐν Θεσσαλονίκῃ, οἵτινες ἐδέξαντο τὸν λόγον μετὰ πάσης προθυμίας καθ' ἡμέραν ἀνακρίνοντες τὰς γραφὰς εἰ ἔχοι ταῦτα οὕτως.

ἦσαν. Impf ind 3rd pl εἰμί.

εὐγενέστεροι. According to Louw and Nida (27.48), this (predicate comparative) adjective indicates "a willingness to learn and evaluate something fairly."

τῶν. Genitive of comparison. The article functions as a nominalizer (see 1:3 on τὰ).

ἐδέξαντο. Aor mid dep ind 3rd pl δέχομαι.

μετὰ πάσης προθυμίας. The preposition literally indicates what accompanied τὸν λόγον. Functionally, however, the whole prepositional phrase indicates the manner in which τὸν λόγον was received.

καθ' ἡμέραν. Distributive (see 2:46).

ἀνακρίνοντες. Pres act ptc masc nom pl ἀνακρίνω. The participial clause provides a specific example of the Bereans' eagerness. Functionally, it probably indicates the manner in which the Bereans received the message.

ἔχοι ταῦτα οὕτως. See 7:1 on οὕτως ἔχει.

εἰ. Introduces an indirect question.

ἔχοι. Pres act opt 3rd sg ἔχω. The optative is probably used in place of the subjunctive of the direct question (cf. Wallace 1996, 483; Porter 1994, 61).

17:12 πολλοὶ μὲν οὖν ἐξ αὐτῶν ἐπίστευσαν καὶ τῶν Ἑλληνίδων γυναικῶν τῶν εὐσχημόνων καὶ ἀνδρῶν οὐκ ὀλίγοι.

μὲν οὖν. The use of μὲν οὖν implies that widespread conversion was a natural result of the Bereans' devotion to spiritual things (see 1:6; Levinsohn 1987, 141–50).

ἐπίστευσαν . . . γυναικῶν τῶν εὐσχημόνων. The scribe of Codex D appears determined, once again, to downplay the role of the women in the narrative: καὶ τῶν Ἑλλήνων καὶ τῶν εὐσχημόνων ἄνδρες καὶ γυναῖκες ἱκανοὶ ἐπίστευσαν.

ἐπίστευσαν. Aor act ind 3rd pl πιστεύω.

οὐκ ὀλίγοι. Litotes (lit. "not a few"; see 1:5 on οὐ μετὰ πολλὰς ταύτας ἡμέρας).

17:13 Ὡς δὲ ἔγνωσαν οἱ ἀπὸ τῆς Θεσσαλονίκης Ἰουδαῖοι ὅτι καὶ ἐν τῇ Βεροίᾳ κατηγγέλη ὑπὸ τοῦ Παύλου ὁ λόγος τοῦ θεοῦ, ἦλθον κἀκεῖ σαλεύοντες καὶ ταράσσοντες τοὺς ὄχλους.

Ὡς. Temporal (see 18:5).

ἔγνωσαν. Aor act ind 3rd pl γινώσκω.

ὅτι. Introduces a clausal complement of ἔγνωσαν.

κατηγγέλη. Aor pass ind 3rd sg καταγγέλλω.

ἦλθον. Aor act ind 3rd pl ἔρχομαι.

κἀκεῖ. A shortened form (crasis) of καί ἐκεῖ.

σαλεύοντες καὶ ταράσσοντες. The conjoined near synonyms should probably be viewed as a doublet (see 2:43 on τέρατα καὶ σημεῖα) that emphasizes the vigor of their actions, though this is difficult to capture in English (perhaps, "thoroughly stir up"). Some scribes (𝔓[45] E 0120 *Byz*), however, appear to have felt that καὶ ταράσσοντες was superfluous, and thus omitted it.

σαλεύοντες. Pres act ptc masc nom pl σαλεύω (purpose).

ταράσσοντες. Pres act ptc masc nom ταράσσω (purpose).

17:14 εὐθέως δὲ τότε τὸν Παῦλον ἐξαπέστειλαν οἱ ἀδελφοὶ πορεύεσθαι ἕως ἐπὶ τὴν θάλασσαν, ὑπέμεινάν τε ὅ τε Σιλᾶς καὶ ὁ Τιμόθεος ἐκεῖ.

τότε. The use of τότε with εὐθέως emphasizes the believers' quick unequivocal response to the situation (see 1:12).

ἐξαπέστειλαν. Aor act ind 3rd pl ἐξαποστέλλω.

οἱ ἀδελφοὶ. See 1:15.

πορεύεσθαι. Pres dep inf πορεύομαι (purpose).

ἕως. Assuming this reading (the variant ὡς is found in 0120 *Byz* syr[h]: "towards the sea"), the preposition used with the verb ἐξαποστέλλω probably indicates that the believers escorted Paul "as far as the sea" (v. 15; see Barrett, 819–20).

ὑπέμεινάν τε ὅ τε Σιλᾶς καὶ ὁ Τιμόθεος ἐκεῖ. "The use of *te*, rather than *de*, indicates that the statement is not in contrast with v 14a. . . . The failure to place the subject before the verb confirms this, and suggests that v 14b is a result of . . . v 14a" (Levinsohn 1987, 14), and is of less importance to the overall narrative (129).

ὑπέμεινάν. Aor act ind 3rd pl ὑπομένω. The second accent comes from the enclitic τε (see 1:4 on ἠκούσατέ).

ὅ. The article should not be mistaken for a relative pronoun. The accent comes from the enclitic τε (see 1:4 on ἠκούσατε).

17:15 οἱ δὲ καθιστάνοντες τὸν Παῦλον ἤγαγον ἕως Ἀθηνῶν, καὶ λαβόντες ἐντολὴν πρὸς τὸν Σιλᾶν καὶ τὸν Τιμόθεον ἵνα ὡς τάχιστα ἔλθωσιν πρὸς αὐτὸν ἐξῄεσαν.

οἱ καθιστάνοντες. Pres act ptc masc nom pl καθίστημι (substantival).

ἤγαγον. Aor act ind 3rd pl ἄγω.

λαβόντες. Aor act ptc masc nom pl λαμβάνω (temporal).

ἐντολὴν. Lit. "an order."

ἔλθωσιν. Aor act subj 3rd pl ἔρχομαι. The subjunctive is used with ἵνα to form a purpose clause.

ἐξῄεσαν. Impf act ind 3rd pl ἔξειμι.

Acts 17:16–34

16While Paul was waiting for them in Athens, he became very troubled when he saw that the city was full of idols. 17So he debated in the synagogue with the Jews and (other) worshippers, and also in the marketplace each and every day with whomever happened to be there. 18Some of the Epicureans and Stoic philosophers debated with him, and some were saying, "What is this foolish babbler trying to say?" Others (said), "He seems to be a herald of foreign deities." (They said this) because he was preaching about Jesus and the resurrection. 19Then they grabbed him and brought him to the Areopagus, saying, "We would like to know, what is this new teaching that you have been talking about? [20]For you are bringing some strange things to our ears, and we want to know what these things mean."

[21]Now, all the Athenians and the foreigners living among them spent their time in nothing other than (trying) either to say or to hear something novel. [22]Paul stood up in front of the Areopagus (Council) and said, "Athenians! I see that you are very religious in every way. [23]For as I walked around and carefully observed your objects of worship, I even discovered an altar upon which had been inscribed, 'To an unknown god.' Therefore, that which you worship in ignorance, this is what I am proclaiming to you. [24]The God who made the universe and all that is in it, the one who is Lord of heaven and earth, he does not live in temples made by human hands, [25]nor is he tended to by human hands as if he needs something, since he himself gives life and breath and everything else to all (people). [26]From a single person he made every race of people to live throughout the world, having established orderly seasons and boundaries within which to live, [27]and to seek God. If only they might really search hard for him and find (the one) who is not far from any one of us. [28]For in him we live and move and exist, as even some of your own poets have said, 'For we too are his offspring.' [29]Therefore, since we are God's offspring, we should not think that the divine one is like gold or silver or stone, (like) an image (made) by a person's skill and creativity."

[30]"So then, although God overlooked the times of (their) ignorance, he is now commanding people—everyone, everywhere—to repent. [31]For he has set the day on which he is going to judge the world according to the standard of righteousness by the man he has appointed, and he has provided proof (of this) for all by raising him from the dead."

[32]When they heard about the resurrection from the dead some started laughing, but others said, "We would like to hear you (speak) about this matter again!" [33]So, Paul left them. [34]But some men joined him and believed, among whom was Dionysius the Areopagite. There was also a woman named Damaris, and others with them.

17:16 Ἐν δὲ ταῖς Ἀθήναις ἐκδεχομένου αὐτοὺς τοῦ Παύλου παρωξύνετο τὸ πνεῦμα αὐτοῦ ἐν αὐτῷ θεωροῦντος κατείδωλον οὖσαν τὴν πόλιν.

ἐκδεχομένου. Pres dep ptc masc gen sg ἐκδέχομαι. Genitive absolute (see 1:8 on ἐπελθόντος), temporal.

τοῦ Παύλου. Genitive subject (see 1:8 on ἐπελθόντος).

παρωξύνετο . . . αὐτῷ. Lit. "his spirit became greatly upset within him."

παρωξύνετο. Impf pass ind 3rd sg παροξύνω. Bruce (376) calls this a "strong word" and notes the cognate noun in 15:39.

θεωροῦντος. Pres act ptc masc gen sg θεωρέω. Genitive absolute (see 1:8 on ἐπελθόντος), temporal or causal. The use of the genitive absolute is necessitated by the syntactic shift in subject from "his spirit" to "him."

κατείδωλον. Predicate accusative. The adjective functions as the predicate of the following participle and therefore must agree in case with the subject of the participial clause (τὴν πόλιν).

οὖσαν. Pres act ptc fem acc sg εἰμί. Although Wallace (1996, 646) has "indirect discourse" as the function of the participle, it is probably better to treat it as the complement in an object-complement double accusative construction (see 1:3 on ζῶντα).

17:17 **διελέγετο μὲν οὖν ἐν τῇ συναγωγῇ τοῖς Ἰουδαίοις καὶ τοῖς σεβομένοις καὶ ἐν τῇ ἀγορᾷ κατὰ πᾶσαν ἡμέραν πρὸς τοὺς παρατυγχάνοντας.**

διελέγετο. Impf dep ind 3rd sg διαλέγομαι.

τοῖς Ἰουδαίοις καὶ τοῖς σεβομένοις. Dative of association (equivalent to πρός plus an accusative noun). **σεβομένοις.** Pres mid ptc masc dat pl σέβω (substantival). Luke appears to use this verb to refer to piety or worship of the true God by non-Jews as here, where the participle is used substantivally in conjunction with τοῖς Ἰουδαίοις, suggesting that the "worshippers" were non-Jews. In v. 4, the reference to non-Jews is explicit ("pious *Greeks*"), as it is in 13:43, where the reference is to "pious *proselytes*."

κατὰ πᾶσαν ἡμέραν. Elsewhere the author has used the preposition alone to function distributively (καθ' ἡμέραν = "every day" in 2:47). Here, the addition of πᾶσαν probably makes the expression more emphatic: "every single day" (cf. 13:27; 15:21; 18:4; 26:11).

τοὺς παρατυγχάνοντας. Pres act ptc masc acc pl παρατυγχάνω (substantival).

17:18 τινὲς δὲ καὶ τῶν Ἐπικουρείων καὶ Στοϊκῶν φιλοσόφων συνέβαλλον αὐτῷ, καί τινες ἔλεγον, Τί ἂν θέλοι ὁ σπερμολόγος οὗτος λέγειν; οἱ δέ, Ξένων δαιμονίων δοκεῖ καταγγελεὺς εἶναι, ὅτι τὸν Ἰησοῦν καὶ τὴν ἀνάστασιν εὐηγγελίζετο.

συνέβαλλον. Impf act ind 3rd pl συμβάλλω. Although this verb may carry a neutral ("to meet with") or confrontational sense ("to debate"), the present context points to the latter.

ἔλεγον. Impf act ind 3rd pl λέγω.

Τί ἂν θέλοι ὁ σπερμολόγος οὗτος λέγειν. Potential optative; see 5:24. Wallace (1996, 484) suggests that the implicit protasis in this incomplete fourth class condition is something like: "If he could say anything that made sense!"

θέλοι. Pres act opt 3rd sg θέλω. The optative makes it very clear that the philosophers did not think it was likely that Paul could say anything of value (Wallace 1996, 701).

σπερμολόγος. According to Louw and Nida (27.19; 33.381), this term may refer either to (1) a person "who acquires bits and pieces of relatively extraneous information and proceeds to pass them on with pretense and show" (thus, "ignorant show-off, charlatan"), or (2) a person "who is not able to say anything worthwhile in view of his miscellaneous collection of tidbits of information" (thus, "foolish babbler"). Barrett (930) suggests that the expression refers to a person who has stolen ideas from others and used them as his own (cf. Bruce, 377).

οὗτος. When the demonstrative is used to refer to someone who is present, it often carries a disparaging or contemptuous connotation (see 19:26; BDF §290.6.1; cf. also 6:13, 14). Here, however, the disparagement comes more from the adjective than the demonstrative.

λέγειν. Pres act inf λέγω (complementary).

οἱ δέ. The plural article is often used with δέ to denote "others," usually in contrast to οἱ μέν (cf. 17:32 where both occur).

δαιμονίων. Objective genitive.

δοκεῖ. Pres act ind 3rd sg δοκέω.

καταγγελεὺς. Predicate nominative (of the infinitive εἶναι). Although we would normally expect the predicate of an infinitive to be in the accusative case, the verb δοκεῖ is idiosyncratic in that it takes its infinitival predicate in the nominative case (cf. 1 Cor 14:37; Gal 2:9).

εἶναι. Pres act inf εἰμί (complementary; contra Rogers and Rogers, 274, who for some reason say it introduces indirect discourse).

τὴν ἀνάστασιν. As Fitzmyer notes (1998, 605), the Athenians may have misunderstood ἀνάστασιν as the name of the consort of a foreign deity ("Jesus and Anastasis").

εὐηγγελίζετο. Impf mid ind 3rd sg εὐαγγελίζω.

17:19 ἐπιλαβόμενοί τε αὐτοῦ ἐπὶ τὸν Ἄρειον Πάγον ἤγαγον λέγοντες, Δυνάμεθα γνῶναι τίς ἡ καινὴ αὕτη ἡ ὑπὸ σοῦ λαλουμένη διδαχή;

ἐπιλαβόμενοί. Aor mid dep ptc masc nom pl ἐπιλαμβάνομαι (attendant circumstance). The second accent comes from the enclitic τε (see 1:4 on ἠκούσατέ).

αὐτοῦ. Genitive object of ἐπιλαβόμενοί.

Ἄρειον Πάγον. See v. 22.

ἤγαγον. Aor act ind 3rd pl ἄγω.

λέγοντες. Pres act ptc masc nom pl λέγω (attendant circumstance).

Δυνάμεθα. Pres dep ind 1st pl δύναμαι. Here, the verb is used to introduce a polite request.

γνῶναι. Aor act inf γινώσκω (complementary).

αὕτη. Feminine nominative singular of οὗτος.

λαλουμένη. Pres pass ptc fem nom sg λαλέω (attributive modifier of διδαχή).

17:20 ξενίζοντα γάρ τινα εἰσφέρεις εἰς τὰς ἀκοὰς ἡμῶν· βουλόμεθα οὖν γνῶναι τίνα θέλει ταῦτα εἶναι.

ξενίζοντα. Pres act ptc neut acc pl ξενίζω (substantival).

εἰσφέρεις. Pres act ind 2nd sg εἰσφέρω.

βουλόμεθα. Pres dep ind 1st pl βούλομαι.

γνῶναι. Aor act inf γινώσκω (complementary).

τίνα θέλει ταῦτα εἶναι. See 2:12 on Τί θέλει τοῦτο εἶναι.

τίνα. Predicate nominative of εἶναι rather than the more typical predicate accusative (see 18:15 on κριτής).

θέλει. Pres act ind 3rd sg θέλω.

ταῦτα. The demonstrative pronoun should be viewed as the nominative subject of the main verb θέλει rather than the accusative subject of the infinitive (see 1:3 on αὐτὸν).

εἶναι. Pres act inf εἰμί (complementary).

17:21 Ἀθηναῖοι δὲ πάντες καὶ οἱ ἐπιδημοῦντες ξένοι εἰς οὐδὲν ἕτερον ηὐκαίρουν ἢ λέγειν τι ἢ ἀκούειν τι καινότερον.

οἱ ἐπιδημοῦντες. Pres act ptc masc nom pl ἐπιδημέω (attributive, modifying the substantival adjective ξένοι, or vice versa).

εἰς. The preposition introduces the purpose or goal for which they were using their time.

οὐδὲν ἕτερον. This phrase makes it clear that the narrator does not approve of how the inhabitants of Athens used their time.

ηὐκαίρουν. Impf act ind 3rd pl εὐκαιρέω.

λέγειν. Pres act inf λέγω (substantival in a comparative construction).

ἀκούειν. Pres act inf ἀκούω (substantival in a comparative construction).

17:22 Σταθεὶς δὲ [ὁ] Παῦλος ἐν μέσῳ τοῦ Ἀρείου Πάγου ἔφη, Ἄνδρες Ἀθηναῖοι, κατὰ πάντα ὡς δεισιδαιμονεστέρους ὑμᾶς θεωρῶ.

Σταθεὶς. Aor pass ptc masc nom sg ἵστημι (attendant circumstance).

Ἀρείου Πάγου. The Areopagus (lit. "hill of Mars,") could refer to "the location of an Athenian court, traditionally associated with a rocky hill close to the Acropolis, though probably located in the marketplace at the foot of the hill" (LN 93.412), or to the Council of the Areopagus—the advisory council of Athens that dealt with ethical, cultural, and religious matters (LN 11.81). The prepositional phrase ἐν μέσῳ, however, suggests that the latter is in focus here (cf. Bruce, 379).

ἔφη. Aor/Impf act ind 3rd sg φημί. On the tense, see 7:2.

Ἄνδρες. See 1:11.

Ἀθηναῖοι. Vocative.

ὡς. Although ὡς could introduce the complement of θεωρῶ ("I see *that* . . ."; cf. 10:28), it more likely functions here as an intensifier of the comparative adjective ("I see how religious . . .").

δεισιδαιμονεστέρους. The comparative adjective is emphatic in nature ("elative"; Wallace 1996, 300). It may be viewed as either a complement in an object-complement double accusative construction (see 1:3 on ζῶντα) or as a predicate accusative adjective with an implicit εἶναι (see 1:22 on μάρτυρα).

θεωρῶ. Pres act ind 1st sg θεωρέω.

17:23 διερχόμενος γὰρ καὶ ἀναθεωρῶν τὰ σεβάσματα ὑμῶν εὗρον καὶ βωμὸν ἐν ᾧ ἐπεγέγραπτο, Ἀγνώστῳ θεῷ. ὃ οὖν ἀγνοοῦντες εὐσεβεῖτε, τοῦτο ἐγὼ καταγγέλλω ὑμῖν.

διερχόμενος. Pres dep ptc masc nom sg διέρχομαι (temporal).

ἀναθεωρῶν. Pres act ptc masc nom sg ἀναθεωρέω (temporal).

εὗρον. Aor act ind 1st sg εὑρίσκω.

ἐπεγέγραπτο. Plprf pass ind 3rd sg ἐπιγράφω.

Ἀγνώστῳ θεῷ. Dative of advantage.

ὃ οὖν ἀγνοοῦντες εὐσεβεῖτε. The relative pronoun introduces a headless relative clause (see 3:6 on ὃ). ὃ οὖν ἀγνοοῦντες cannot function as the direct object of εὐσεβεῖτε ("you worship that which you do not know") since it would leave the relative clause without a finite verb. Instead, εὐσεβεῖτε must be part of the relative clause ("that which you worship in ignorance"), which itself is part of a larger topic construction (see 2:22 on Ἰησοῦν τὸν Ναζωραῖον): the accusative relative clause introduces the topic (picked up by τοῦτο) of what follows.

ἀγνοοῦντες. Pres act ptc masc nom pl ἀγνοέω (manner).

εὐσεβεῖτε. Pres act ind 2nd pl εὐσεβέω.

καταγγέλλω. Pres act ind 1st sg καταγγέλλω.

17:24 ὁ θεὸς ὁ ποιήσας τὸν κόσμον καὶ πάντα τὰ ἐν αὐτῷ, οὗτος οὐρανοῦ καὶ γῆς ὑπάρχων κύριος οὐκ ἐν χειροποιήτοις ναοῖς κατοικεῖ

ὁ θεὸς ὁ ποιήσας τὸν κόσμον καὶ πάντα τὰ ἐν αὐτῷ. The whole nominative construction introduces the topic (see 2:22 on Ἰησοῦν τὸν Ναζωραῖον) of the sentence, which is picked up with the resumptive οὗτος.

ποιήσας. Aor act ptc masc nom sg ποιέω (attributive).

τὰ. The article functions as a nominalizer (see 1:3 on τὰ).

ὑπάρχων. Pres act ptc masc nom sg ὑπάρχω. The participle could be either attributive (lit. "this one, who is Lord of heaven and earth") or causal ("this one, since he is Lord of heaven and earth").

κύριος. Predicate nominative.

κατοικεῖ. Pres act ind 3rd sg κατοικέω.

17:25 οὐδὲ ὑπὸ χειρῶν ἀνθρωπίνων θεραπεύεται προσδεόμενός τινος, αὐτὸς διδοὺς πᾶσι ζωὴν καὶ πνοὴν καὶ τὰ πάντα·

ὑπὸ χειρῶν ἀνθρωπίνων. The prepositional phrase introduces the agent of the passive verb, with χειρῶν ἀνθρωπίνων being a synecdoche (see 1:22 on τοῦ βαπτίσματος Ἰωάννου) for "human being."

θεραπεύεται. Pres pass ind 3rd sg θεραπεύω. Louw and Nida (35.19) and BAGD (359) both list this passage as the only place in the NT where this verb means "to serve." Such a sense for the term would make Paul's statement here play to "the Epicurean doctrine that God needs nothing from human beings," while the following statement would play to "the Stoic belief that he is the source of all life" (Bruce, 382). Although this meaning is attested outside the NT, however, taking the verb in its usual sense of "to heal" or "to take care of" would make the proposition that much more ridiculous and, thus, appropriate to the context (cf. Barrett, 840).

προσδεόμενός. Pres dep ptc masc nom sg προσδέομαι (causal). The second accent comes from the enclitic τινος (see 1:4 on ἠκούσατέ). While the translation "as if he had need of anyone" may be an appropriate rendering of a causal participle, such a translation does not derive from a conditional function of the participle (contra Rogers and Rogers, 275).

αὐτὸς. The subject pronoun is emphatic.

διδοὺς. Pres act ptc masc nom sg δίδωμι (causal). It would also be possible to take the participle as attributive with the entire expression, αὐτὸς διδοὺς πᾶσι ζωὴν καὶ πνοὴν καὶ τὰ πάντα, serving as the subject of θεραπεύεται.

17:26 ἐποίησέν τε ἐξ ἑνὸς πᾶν ἔθνος ἀνθρώπων κατοικεῖν ἐπὶ παντὸς προσώπου τῆς γῆς, ὁρίσας προστεταγμένους καιροὺς καὶ τὰς ὁροθεσίας τῆς κατοικίας αὐτῶν

ἐποίησέν. Aor act ind 3rd sg ποιέω. The second accent comes from the enclitic τε (see 1:4 on ἠκούσατέ).

ἐξ ἑνὸς. The preposition denotes source.

κατοικεῖν . . . γῆς. Lit. "to live upon the whole face of the earth."

κατοικεῖν. Pres act inf κατοικέω. The infinitive probably should be taken as denoting purpose, though Bruce (383) and Barrett (842) call it epexegetical. It cannot be an object infinitive (contra Rogers and Rogers, 275) since the main verb already has a direct object: πᾶν ἔθνος. Although the infinitive could be complementary to ἐποίησέν and part of a causative construction ("He caused all the races . . . to live"), such a reading does not make good sense with ἐξ ἑνός.

ὁρίσας. Aor act ptc masc nom sg ὁρίζω (temporal). The participial clause serves as a parenthetical statement between the two appositional infinitival clauses in vv. 26–27.

προστεταγμένους. Prf pass ptc masc acc pl προστάσσω (attributive).

καιροὺς. There is some debate over whether this term should be taken literally ("seasons of the year") or figuratively ("periods of history"). If the genitive noun phrase that follows (τῆς κατοικίας αὐτῶν) modifies both καιροὺς and τὰς ὁροθεσίας, then καιροὺς should be understood as a reference to periods of people's existence. Since, however, καιροὺς has its own modifier (προστεταγμένους probably modifies the anarthrous καιροὺς [see 3:3 on Πέτρον καὶ Ἰωάννην] but not τὰς ὁροθεσίας, since the latter is articular), it is more likely that the genitive noun phrase modifies τὰς ὁροθεσίας only and that καιροὺς should be taken literally.

17:27 ζητεῖν τὸν θεόν, εἰ ἄρα γε ψηλαφήσειαν αὐτὸν καὶ εὕροιεν, καί γε οὐ μακρὰν ἀπὸ ἑνὸς ἑκάστου ἡμῶν ὑπάρχοντα.

ζητεῖν. Pres act inf ζητέω (a second purpose of ἐποίησέν in apposition to κατοικεῖν ἐπὶ παντὸς προσώπου τῆς γῆς [v. 26]; but see above on κατοικεῖν).

εἰ ἄρα γε ψηλαφήσειαν αὐτὸν καὶ εὕροιεν. The use of εἰ with two optative verbs forms a (double) fourth class condition (always incomplete in the NT), which is normally used to express something that has only a remote possibility of happening in the future. The use of ἄρα and γε further emphasizes the sense of uncertainty (cf. 8:22). Fitzmyer (1998, 609) renders this clause: "perhaps even grope for him, and eventually find him." It is probably better, however, to interpret the construction as a parenthetical statement that expresses the hopeful reason behind humankind's pursuit of God (cf. 27:12).

ψηλαφήσειαν. Aor act opt 3rd pl ψηλαφάω. This verb (lit. "to touch, to feel") is used figuratively to refer to making "an effort, despite difficulties, to come to know something, when the chances of success in such an enterprise are not particularly great—'to feel around for, to grope for, to try to find'" (LN 27.40).

εὕροιεν. Aor act opt 3rd pl εὑρίσκω.

ὑπάρχοντα. Pres act ptc masc acc sg ὑπάρχω. While a concessive translation may make good sense in the context, strictly speaking the participle, which is accusative, cannot be adverbial but must be an attributive modifier of τὸν θεὸν (cf. 3:26 on εὐλογοῦντα; see Culy 2004), lit.: "to seek God, who is really not far from any one of us—if they might only search hard for him and find him!"

17:28 Ἐν αὐτῷ γὰρ ζῶμεν καὶ κινούμεθα καὶ ἐσμέν, ὥς καί τινες τῶν καθ' ὑμᾶς ποιητῶν εἰρήκασιν, Τοῦ γὰρ καὶ γένος ἐσμέν.

Ἐν αὐτῷ. This expression appears to indicate sphere of influence. Thus to live "in him" is to live under his control (cf. Porter 1994, 157, 159).

ζῶμεν καὶ κινούμεθα καὶ ἐσμέν. These three verbs form a triad, all referring to the same essential reality. The use of three terms makes the expression particularly emphatic (cf. 2:43 on τέρατα καὶ σημεῖα): "Our entire existence is utterly dependent upon our relationship with him" (cf. Barrett, 846).

ζῶμεν. Pres act ind 1st pl ζάω.

κινούμεθα. Pres mid/pass ind 1st pl κινέω.

ἐσμέν. Pres act ind 1st pl εἰμί.

καθ' ὑμᾶς. This expression is probably a bit more emphatic than a possessive pronoun (cf. Barrett, 848).

εἰρήκασιν. Prf act ind 3rd pl λέγω.

Τοῦ. According to Barrett (849; cf. Porter 1994, 107), this is the only place in the NT where the article functions like a demonstrative pronoun. It may be better, however, rather than positing a new usage, to say that the article functions as a personal pronoun with the genitive case indicating possession or source.

γένος. Predicate nominative.

ἐσμέν. Pres act ind 1st pl εἰμί.

17:29 γένος οὖν ὑπάρχοντες τοῦ θεοῦ οὐκ ὀφείλομεν νομίζειν χρυσῷ ἢ ἀργύρῳ ἢ λίθῳ, χαράγματι τέχνης καὶ ἐνθυμήσεως ἀνθρώπου, τὸ θεῖον εἶναι ὅμοιον.

γένος. Predicate nominative.

ὑπάρχοντες. Pres act ptc masc nom pl ὑπάρχω (causal).

ὀφείλομεν. Pres act ind 1st pl ὀφείλω.

νομίζειν. Pres act inf νομίζω (complementary).

χρυσῷ . . . ἀργύρῳ . . . λίθῳ, χαράγματι. The four nouns are in the dative case as complements of ὅμοιον.

χαράγματι. Stands in apposition to χρυσῷ . . . ἀργύρῳ . . . λίθῳ.

τέχνης καὶ ἐνθυμήσεως ἀνθρώπου. The first two genitives (τέχνης and ἐνθυμήσεως) denote the means of the implicit verbal idea ("made"; contra Barrett, 849, who calls the genitives subjective).

τὸ θεῖον. Accusative subject of the infinitive (see 1:3 on αὐτὸν).

εἶναι. Pres act inf εἰμί (indirect discourse).

ὅμοιον. Predicate accusative (see 1:22 on μάρτυρα).

17:30 **τοὺς μὲν οὖν χρόνους τῆς ἀγνοίας ὑπεριδὼν ὁ θεὸς, τὰ νῦν παραγγέλλει τοῖς ἀνθρώποις πάντας πανταχοῦ μετανοεῖν,**

τῆς ἀγνοίας. Genitive of description.

ὑπεριδὼν. Aor act ptc masc nom sg ὑπεροράω (concessive).

τὰ νῦν. The use of the neuter accusative plural article (as a nominalizer; see 1:3) with the adverb νῦν may make the shift in time more emphatic (cf. 4:29 on καὶ τὰ νῦν).

παραγγέλλει. Pres act inf 3rd sg παραγγέλλω.

τοῖς ἀνθρώποις. Dative indirect object of παραγγέλλει.

πάντας. Accusative subject of the infinitive (see 1:3 on αὐτὸν).

μετανοεῖν. Pres act inf μετανοέω (indirect discourse).

17:31 **καθότι ἔστησεν ἡμέραν ἐν ᾗ μέλλει κρίνειν τὴν οἰκουμένην ἐν δικαιοσύνῃ ἐν ἀνδρὶ ᾧ ὥρισεν, πίστιν παρασχὼν πᾶσιν ἀναστήσας αὐτὸν ἐκ νεκρῶν.**

ἔστησεν. Aor act ind 3rd sg ἵστημι.

μέλλει. Pres act ind 3rd sg μέλλω. On the force of μέλλω plus an infinitive, see 3:3 on μέλλοντας.

κρίνειν. Pres act inf κρίνω (complementary).

ἐν δικαιοσύνῃ. The prepositional phrase could indicate the manner in which God is going to judge the world (cf. Barrett, 852), or, more likely, the standard against which the world will be judged.

ἐν ἀνδρι. The prepositional phrase could indicate association ("with the man"), but more likely indicates the intermediate agent ("by the man") given the relative clause that follows.

ᾧ. Dative by attraction (see 1:1 on ὧν) to ἀνδρὶ (it normally would have been accusative as the object of ὥρισεν).

ὥρισεν. Aor act ind 3rd sg ὁρίζω.

πίστιν παρασχὼν. When πίστις and παρέχω are used together, they appear to function as a technical expression meaning "to provide proof" (cf. Josephus, *A.J.* 15.260; Vettius Valens 277.29f.; Bruce, 386).

παρασχὼν. Aor act ptc masc nom sg παρέχω (attendant circumstance of ἔστησεν).

ἀναστήσας. Aor act ptc masc nom sg ἀνίστημι (means).

17:32 Ἀκούσαντες δὲ ἀνάστασιν νεκρῶν οἱ μὲν ἐχλεύαζον, οἱ δὲ εἶπαν, Ἀκουσόμεθά σου περὶ τούτου καὶ πάλιν.

Ἀκούσαντες. Aor act ptc masc nom pl ἀκούω (temporal).

νεκρῶν. Objective genitive.

οἱ μὲν. The plural article is often used with μέν to denote "some," in contrast to οἱ δέ "others."

ἐχλεύαζον. Impf act ind 3rd pl χλευάζω.

οἱ δὲ. See above.

εἶπαν. Aor act ind 3rd pl λέγω.

Ἀκουσόμεθά. Fut mid ind 1st pl ἀκούω. The second accent comes from the enclitic σου (see 1:4 on ἠκούσατέ).

σου. Genitive object of Ἀκουσόμεθα.

καὶ. The intensive conjunction makes the statement more emphatic.

17:33 οὕτως ὁ Παῦλος ἐξῆλθεν ἐκ μέσου αὐτῶν.

ἐξῆλθεν. Aor act ind 3rd sg ἐξέρχομαι.

17:34 τινὲς δὲ ἄνδρες κολληθέντες αὐτῷ ἐπίστευσαν, ἐν οἷς καὶ Διονύσιος ὁ Ἀρεοπαγίτης καὶ γυνὴ ὀνόματι Δάμαρις καὶ ἕτεροι σὺν αὐτοῖς.

κολληθέντες. Aor pass ptc masc nom pl κολλάω (attendant circumstance).

αὐτῷ. Dative complement of κολληθέντες.

ἐπίστευσαν. Aor act ind 3rd pl πιστεύω.

ὁ Ἀρεοπαγίτης. Nominative in apposition to Διονύσιος. A member of the Areopagus (see v. 22 on Ἀρείου πάγον).

ὀνόματι. Dative of reference.

Δάμαρις. Nominative in apposition to γυνή.

Acts 18:1–11

[1]After this Paul left Athens and went to Corinth. [2](There,) He found a Jew named Aquila—a native of Pontus who had recently come from Italy, along with Priscilla his wife, because Claudius had ordered all Jews to leave Rome—and he approached them. [3]Since he practiced the same trade (as them), he stayed with them and worked—for they were tentmakers by trade. [4]He debated in the synagogue every sabbath, and tried to persuade both Jews and Greeks. [5]But when Silas and Timothy came down from Macedonia, Paul became completely absorbed with the message and testified to the Jews that the Christ was Jesus. [6]When they opposed (him) and slandered (him), he shook out his clothes and said to them, "Your blood is on your (own) head(s); I am clean. From now on, I will go to the Gentiles."

[7]So he left there and went into the house of a certain man named Titus Justus who worshiped God (and) whose house was next door to the synagogue. [8]And Crispus, the leader of the synagogue, believed in the Lord along with his whole household, and many of the Corinthians who heard believed and were baptized.

[9]One night in a vision, the Lord said to Paul, "Do not be afraid, but speak and do not keep silent. [10]For I am with you and no one will attack you or harm you, because I have many people in this city." [11]So he stayed and taught the word of God among them for one year and six months.

18:1 Μετὰ ταῦτα χωρισθεὶς ἐκ τῶν Ἀθηνῶν ἦλθεν εἰς Κόρινθον.

Μετὰ ταῦτα. The use of this prepositional phrase (lit "after these things") with asyndeton (no conjunction) indicates that "there is no direct connection between the events which follow and those that precede" (Levinsohn 1992, 59).

χωρισθεὶς. Aor pass ptc masc nom sg χωρίζω (attendant circumstance). The participle should probably not be viewed as temporal (contra Rogers and Rogers, 276), since the sentence is already introduced with a temporal expression: μετὰ ταῦτα.

ἦλθεν. Aor act ind 3rd sg ἔρχομαι.

18:2 καὶ εὑρών τινα Ἰουδαῖον ὀνόματι Ἀκύλαν, Ποντικὸν τῷ γένει, προσφάτως ἐληλυθότα ἀπὸ τῆς Ἰταλίας καὶ Πρίσκιλλαν γυναῖκα αὐτοῦ διὰ τὸ διατεταχέναι Κλαύδιον χωρίζεσθαι πάντας τοὺς Ἰουδαίους ἀπὸ τῆς Ῥώμης, προσῆλθεν αὐτοῖς

εὑρών. Aor act ptc masc nom sg εὑρίσκω (attendant circumstance or temporal).

τινα. See 8:9 on τις.

ὀνόματι. Dative of reference.

Ἀκύλαν. Accusative in apposition to Ἰουδαῖον.

Ποντικὸν. Accusative in apposition to Ἰουδαῖον.

τῷ γένει. Dative of reference.

ἐληλυθότα. Prf act ptc masc acc sg ἔρχομαι (attributive).

διατεταχέναι. Prf act inf διατάσσω. Used with διά τὸ to indicate cause.

Κλαύδιον. Accusative subject of the infinitive (see 1:3 on αὐτὸν).

χωρίζεσθαι. Pres pass inf χωρίζω (indirect discourse).

τοὺς Ἰουδαίους. Accusative subject of the infinitive (see 1:3 on αὐτὸν).

προσῆλθεν. Aor act ind 3rd sg προσέρχομαι.

αὐτοῖς. Dative complement of προσῆλθεν.

18:3 καὶ διὰ τὸ ὁμότεχνον εἶναι ἔμενεν παρ᾽ αὐτοῖς καὶ ἠργάζετο· ἦσαν γὰρ σκηνοποιοὶ τῇ τέχνῃ.

ὁμότεχνον. Predicate accusative (see 1:22 on μάρτυρα) in agreement with the unspecified subject of the infinitive (lit. "[he] was of the same trade").

εἶναι. Pres act inf εἰμί. Used with διὰ τὸ to indicate cause.

ἔμενεν. Impf act ind 3rd sg μένω.

ἠργάζετο. Impf dep ind 3rd sg ἐργάζομαι.

ἦσαν. Impf ind 3rd pl εἰμί. Although the plural subject could be Paul and Aquila (Barrett, 863), it more likely refers to the same referent as αὐτοῖς: Priscilla and Aquila.

σκηνοποιοὶ. Predicate nominative. "While the etymological sense of σκηνοποιός is 'tent-maker,' this term was often used in the wider sense of 'leather-worker'" (Bruce, 392).

τῇ τέχνῃ. Dative of reference.

18:4 διελέγετο δὲ ἐν τῇ συναγωγῇ κατὰ πᾶν σάββατον, ἔπειθέν τε Ἰουδαίους καὶ Ἕλληνας.

διελέγετο. Impf dep ind 3rd sg διαλέγομαι.

κατὰ πᾶν. The combination of the distributive preposition and the adjective πᾶς may be emphatic: "every sabbath without fail" (cf. 17:17).

ἔπειθέν. Impf act ind 3rd sg πείθω. The second accent comes from the enclitic τε (see 1:4 on ἠκούσατέ).

18:5 Ὡς δὲ κατῆλθον ἀπὸ τῆς Μακεδονίας ὅ τε Σιλᾶς καὶ ὁ Τιμόθεος, συνείχετο τῷ λόγῳ ὁ Παῦλος, διαμαρτυρόμενος τοῖς Ἰουδαίοις εἶναι τὸν Χριστόν Ἰησοῦν.

Ὡς. The temporal use of ὡς is characteristic of Acts (Barrett, 864; see 1:10; 5:24; 7:23; 8:36; 9:23; 10:7, 17, 25; 11:16; 13:25, 29; 14:5; 16:4, 10, 15; 17:13; 19:9, 21, 34; 20:14, 18; 21:1, 12, 27; 22:25; 25:14; 28:4).

κατῆλθον. Aor act ind 3rd pl κατέρχομαι.

ὅ. The article should not be mistaken for a relative pronoun. The accent comes from the enclitic τε (see 1:4 on ἠκούσατέ).

συνείχετο. Impf mid/pass ind 3rd sg συνέχω. The verb should probably be viewed as middle rather than passive. The expression implies that although Paul had previously spent most of his time making tents, when Silas and Timothy returned he focused his attention on evangelism (cf. Barrett, 866).

τῷ λόγῳ. The majority text replaces τῷ λόγῳ with τῷ πνεύματι (dative of agency, with a passive συνείχετο).

διαμαρτυρόμενος. Pres dep ptc masc nom sg διαμαρτύρομαι (attendant circumstance).

εἶναι. Pres act inf εἰμί (indirect discourse).

τὸν Χριστόν. Accusative subject of the infinitive (see 1:3 on αὐτὸν).

Ἰησοῦν. Predicate accusative (see 1:22 on μάρτυρα). Theoretically, τὸν Χριστόν could be viewed as the predicate and Ἰησοῦν as the subject, with no essential difference in meaning, since one is articular and the other is a proper name (see Wallace 1996, 194). The proximity of τὸν Χριστόν to the infinitive, however, makes it more likely that it is the subject of the infinitive clause (cf. Wallace's note on Phil 1:7; p. 197), though in English it may be more natural to make Jesus the subject: "that Jesus was the Christ."

18:6 ἀντιτασσομένων δὲ αὐτῶν καὶ βλασφημούντων ἐκτιναξάμενος τὰ ἱμάτια εἶπεν πρὸς αὐτούς, Τὸ αἷμα ὑμῶν ἐπὶ τὴν κεφαλὴν ὑμῶν· καθαρὸς ἐγώ· ἀπὸ τοῦ νῦν εἰς τὰ ἔθνη πορεύσομαι.

ἀντιτασσομένων. Pres mid ptc masc gen pl ἀντιτάσσω. Genitive absolute (see 1:8 on ἐπελθόντος), temporal.

βλασφημούντων. Pres act ptc masc gen pl βλασφημέω. Genitive absolute (see 1:8 on ἐπελθόντος), temporal.

ἐκτιναξάμενος τὰ ἱμάτια. This expression (lit. "shook out his clothes" or "shook the dust from his clothes") referred to a symbolic way of showing displeasure with a state of affairs.

ἐκτιναξάμενος. Aor mid ptc masc nom sg ἐκτινάσσω (attendant circumstance).

εἶπεν. Aor act ind 3rd sg λέγω.

Τὸ αἷμα ὑμῶν ἐπὶ τὴν κεφαλὴν ὑμῶν. A formal (and rather graphic) expression used to abdicate responsibility for the addressees' impending fate (cf. Matt 23:35). In both this stative clause ("X is Y") and the following one (καθαρὸς ἐγώ), the verb (ἐστιν) must be supplied.

τοῦ νῦν. The article functions as a nominalizer (see 1:3).

πορεύσομαι. Fut mid dep ind 1st sg πορεύομαι.

18:7 καὶ μεταβὰς ἐκεῖθεν εἰσῆλθεν εἰς οἰκίαν τινὸς ὀνόματι Τιτίου Ἰούστου σεβομένου τὸν θεόν, οὗ ἡ οἰκία ἦν συνομοροῦσα τῇ συναγωγῇ.

μεταβὰς. Aor act ptc masc nom sg μεταβαίνω (attendant circumstance).

εἰσῆλθεν. Aor act ind 3rd sg εἰσέρχομαι.

εἰς. See 1:8 on ἐφ᾽ ὑμᾶς.

τινὸς. Substantival.

ὀνόματι. Dative of reference.

Τιτίου Ἰούστου. Genitive in apposition to τινὸς.

σεβομένου. Pres mid ptc masc gen sg σέβω (attributive). See also 17:17.

ἦν. Impf ind 3rd sg εἰμί.

συνομοροῦσα. Pres act ptc fem nom sg συνομορέω (imperfect periphrastic; see 1:10 on ἀτενίζοντες).

18:8 Κρίσπος δὲ ὁ ἀρχισυνάγωγος ἐπίστευσεν τῷ κυρίῳ σὺν

ὅλῳ τῷ οἴκῳ αὐτοῦ, καὶ πολλοὶ τῶν Κορινθίων ἀκούοντες ἐπίστευον καὶ ἐβαπτίζοντο.

ἀρχισυνάγωγος. See 13:15.

ἐπίστευσεν. Aor act ind 3rd sg πιστεύω.

ἀκούοντες. Pres act ptc masc nom pl ἀκούω (attributive or temporal). It is unclear whether the unspecified direct object is Paul's preaching or, more likely, the report of Crispus' conversion.

ἐπίστευον. Impf act ind 3rd pl πιστεύω.

ἐβαπτίζοντο. Impf pass ind 3rd pl βαπτίζω.

18:9 εἶπεν δὲ ὁ κύριος ἐν νυκτὶ δι' ὁράματος τῷ Παύλῳ, Μὴ φοβοῦ, ἀλλὰ λάλει καὶ μὴ σιωπήσῃς,

εἶπεν. Aor act ind 3rd sg λέγω.

δι' ὁράματος. Instrumental.

φοβοῦ. Pres dep impv 2nd sg φοβέομαι. Wallace (1996, 724) argues that this is an example of a present imperative with μή used to call for an end to an act that is already in progress. The sense would then be "Stop being afraid!" While such a notion may be derived from the context, however, Porter (1989, 335–61) and others have provided strong evidence against the common view that the present imperative refers to action already begun and the aorist to action not yet begun (cf. Acts 22:10 where the present imperative indicates a new action). Indeed, Boyer (1987, 40–45) has argued that the negated present imperative in the NT is used only 74 of 174 times to call for the cessation of action that is already in progress.

λάλει. Pres act impv 2nd sg λαλέω.

μὴ σιωπήσῃς. Aor act subj 2nd sg σιωπάω (prohibitive subjunctive; see 7:60 on στήσῃς). On the choice of tense in a negative command, see 20:10 on Μὴ θορυβεῖσθε.

18:10 διότι ἐγώ εἰμι μετὰ σοῦ καὶ οὐδεὶς ἐπιθήσεταί σοι τοῦ κακῶσαί σε, διότι λαός ἐστί μοι πολὺς ἐν τῇ πόλει ταύτῃ.

εἰμι. Pres act ind 1st sg εἰμί.

ἐπιθήσεται. Fut mid ind 3rd sg ἐπιτίθημι. The second accent comes from the enclitic σοι (see 1:4 on ἠκούσατέ). In the middle voice followed by a dative complement this verb can mean, "to attack" (BAGD, 303).

σοι. Dative complement of ἐπιτίθημι.

κακῶσαί. Aor act inf κακόω. In this passage, the articular (τοῦ) infinitive may either indicate purpose or be epexegetical (so Barrett, 870). The second accent comes from the enclitic σε.

ἐστί. Pres act ind 3rd sg εἰμί. Here, the accent comes from the clitic that follows (see 1:4 on ἠκούσατέ; cf. 2:13 on εἰσίν).

μοι. Dative of possession (used with εἰμί).

18:11 Ἐκάθισεν δὲ ἐνιαυτὸν καὶ μῆνας ἓξ διδάσκων ἐν αὐτοῖς τὸν λόγον τοῦ θεοῦ.

Ἐκάθισεν. Aor act ind 3rd sg καθίζω. This verb appears to mean "to stay" in Luke 24:49 and in several places in the LXX (Plummer, 564). The fact that it is a finite verb followed by a temporal expression denoting extent of time favors this sense here as well (so most scholars).

ἐνιαυτὸν καὶ μῆνας ἕξ. Accusative indicating extent of time (see 7:20 on μῆνας).

διδάσκων. Pres act ptc masc nom sg διδάσκω (attendant circumstance). Although participles denoting an attendant circumstance of an aorist verb are normally aorist (see above, p. xvii), the fact that διδάσκω as a participle never appears in the aorist form in the NT may explain the atypical combination here.

Acts 18:12–17

[12]While Gallio was the proconsul of Achaia, the Jews attacked Paul together and brought him to the judgment seat. [13]They said, "This man is inciting people to worship God in a way that is against the law." [14]When Paul was about to respond, Gallio said to the Jews, "If there were some crime or terrible wrongdoing, I would be patient with you Jews in this matter. [15]But since the disputes are about a statement, names, and your own law, you must deal with it yourselves. I do not care to be a judge of these things." [16]So he drove them away from the judgment seat.

[17]Then, after they had all seized Sosthenes, the leader of the synagogue, they beat him in front of the judgment seat. But none of these things were of any concern to Gallio.

18:12 Γαλλίωνος δὲ ἀνθυπάτου ὄντος τῆς Ἀχαΐας κατεπέστησαν

ὁμοθυμαδὸν οἱ Ἰουδαῖοι τῷ Παύλῳ καὶ ἤγαγον αὐτὸν ἐπὶ τὸ βῆμα

Γαλλίωνος. Genitive subject (see 1:8 on ἐπελθόντος).

ἀνθυπάτου. Predicate genitive in an equative construction (see 1:16 on ὁδηγοῦ). On the meaning of ἀνθυπάτου see 13:7.

ὄντος. Pres act ptc masc gen sg εἰμί. Genitive absolute (see 1:8 on ἐπελθόντος), temporal.

κατεπέστησαν. Aor act ind 3rd pl κατεφίσταμαι/κατεφίστημι.

ὁμοθυμαδὸν. See 1:14.

ἤγαγον. Aor act ind 3rd pl ἄγω.

18:13 λέγοντες ὅτι Παρὰ τὸν νόμον ἀναπείθει οὗτος τοὺς ἀνθρώπους σέβεσθαι τὸν θεόν.

λέγοντες. Pres act ptc masc nom pl λέγω (attendant circumstance).

ὅτι. Introduces direct discourse.

ἀναπείθει. Pres act ind 3rd sg ἀναπείθω.

τοὺς ἀνθρώπους. This noun could be either the direct object of the main verb or the accusative subject of the infinitive. Since ἀναπείθω is transitive, the former is more likely.

σέβεσθαι. Pres mid inf σέβω. The infinitive could be viewed as result/purpose ("he is inciting people so/with the result that they worship . . .") or, more likely, complementary, but not objective (contra Rogers and Rogers, 278) if τοὺς ἀνθρώπους is the direct object.

18:14 μέλλοντος δὲ τοῦ Παύλου ἀνοίγειν τὸ στόμα εἶπεν ὁ Γαλλίων πρὸς τοὺς Ἰουδαίους, Εἰ μὲν ἦν ἀδίκημά τι ἢ ῥᾳδιούργημα πονηρόν, ὦ Ἰουδαῖοι, κατὰ λόγον ἂν ἀνεσχόμην ὑμῶν,

μέλλοντος. Pres act ptc masc gen sg μέλλω. Genitive absolute (see 1:8 on ἐπελθόντος), temporal. See 3:3 on μέλλοντας.

Παύλου. Genitive subject (see 1:8 on ἐπελθόντος).

ἀνοίγειν. Pres act inf ἀνοίγω (complementary).

εἶπεν. Aor act ind 3rd sg λέγω.

Εἰ . . . ἂν . . . The use of εἰ with an indicative verb (ἦν) in the protasis and ἄν with an indicative verb (ἀνεσχόμην) in the apodosis makes this a second class condition (the only one in Acts), a "condition which as a matter of fact has not been met and follows with a statement of what would have been true if it had" (Boyer 1982, 83).

ἦν. Impf ind 3rd sg εἰμί (impersonal).

ἀδίκημα . . . ῥᾳδιούργημα. Predicate nominatives of the impersonal ἦν.

ὦ Ἰουδαῖοι. On the use of the the particle ὦ, see 13:10 on Ὦ πλήρης. On the position of the vocative, see 10:13 on Πέτρε.

κατὰ λόγον. . . ἀνεσχόμην. Louw and Nida (56.10) suggest that κατὰ λόγον ἀνέχομαι was probably an idiom meaning "to accept a complaint in court, to admit a complaint to judgment." They concede, however, that the verb could have carried its usual sense here ("to be patient with"). Since there is no clear evidence to support the former view we have taken ἀνεσχόμην in its usual NT sense. The prepositional phrase, κατὰ λόγον, can then be viewed as indicating reference ("with reference to this matter"), or perhaps as an adverbial expression meaning "reasonably" (thus, "it would be reasonable for me to be patient with you"; cf. Bruce, 396).

ἀνεσχόμην. Aor mid ind 1st sg ἀνέχω.

ὑμῶν. The verb ἀνέχομαι takes its complement (the person one is patient with) in the genitive case.

18:15 εἰ δὲ ζητήματά ἐστιν περὶ λόγου καὶ ὀνομάτων καὶ νόμου τοῦ καθ' ὑμᾶς, ὄψεσθε αὐτοί· κριτὴς ἐγὼ τούτων οὐ βούλομαι εἶναι.

εἰ. This is a good example where a condition (that is left open) is appropriately rendered "since . . ." (contra Wallace 1996, 690, n. 12).

ζητήματά. The second accent comes from the enclitic ἐστιν (see 1:4 on ἠκούσατέ).

ἐστιν. Pres act ind 3rd sg εἰμί. Neuter plural subjects typically take a singular verb as here.

λόγου καὶ ὀνομάτων. The intended meaning of these two nouns (lit. "a word and names") is uncertain. Barrett (874) renders λόγου, "talk," and ὀνομάτων, "words." While the former may be appropriate, Barrett offers no evidence for the latter. It is better either to understand ὀνομάτων literally (cf. Bruce, 396) or perhaps as a metonym (see 1:9 on τῶν ὀφθαλμῶν αὐτῶν) for "people" (it is clearly used this way in Acts 1:15 and Rev 3:4). It may also be possible to take the first καί as epexegetical, so that the second and third nouns describe the "statement" or "matter." Either way, the expression is probably intended as a somewhat derogatory remark.

τοῦ καθ' ὑμᾶς. "Your own law" (cf. 17:28 on καθ' ὑμᾶς) as opposed to Roman law.

ὄψεσθε. Fut mid dep ind 2nd pl ὁράω (imperatival future). David New (125) argues that, in contrast to the imperative mood, the imperatival future is used when an authority figure is imposing his will on the addressee. The use of ὁράω in an imperative expression (cf. also 15:6 on ἰδεῖν) is analogous to the English expression, "to see to (something)," which indicates "to take care of (business), to deal with (some circumstance)."

αὐτοί. The pronoun is intensive.

κριτής. As the predicate of the infinitive we would expect the accusative κριτήν. When (at least some) verbs of wishing are modified by an infinitival construction with εἰμί and an unexpressed subject of the infinitive, the predicate of εἰμί occurs in the nominative rather than accusative case (see also Mark 10:44; Matt 19:21; 20:27//Mark 9:35; for examples with an expressed subject of the infinitive, see Rom 16:19; 1 Cor 7:7, 32).

βούλομαι. Pres dep ind 1st sg βούλομαι.

εἶναι. Pres act inf εἰμί (complementary).

18:16 καὶ ἀπήλασεν αὐτοὺς ἀπὸ τοῦ βήματος.

καὶ . . . βήματος. Or, "Then he had them thrown out of court."

ἀπήλασεν. Aor act ind 3rd sg ἀπελαύνω.

18:17 ἐπιλαβόμενοι δὲ πάντες Σωσθένην τὸν ἀρχισυνάγωγον ἔτυπτον ἔμπροσθεν τοῦ βήματος· καὶ οὐδὲν τούτων τῷ Γαλλίωνι ἔμελεν.

ἐπιλαβόμενοι. Aor mid dep ptc masc nom pl ἐπιλαμβάνομαι (temporal).

πάντες. Substantival. The referent is specified in the Western and Byzantine traditions: οἱ Ἕλληνες.

Σωσθένην. The accusative case presumably comes from the main verb since ἐπιλαμβάνομαι takes a genitive object (Barrett, 876).

ἔτυπτον Impf act ind 3rd pl τύπτω.

οὐδὲν τούτων τῷ Γαλλίωνι ἔμελεν. This clause (lit. "none of these things were of concern to Gallio") could appropriately be rendered, "Gallio could not have cared less about these things!"

τούτων. Substantival demonstrative; partitive genitive.

ἔμελεν. Impf act ind 3rd sg μέλει. Although this verb is typically used in impersonal constructions ("it was of concern"), in this case it has a subject: οὐδὲν τούτων.

Acts 18:18–23

[18]When Paul had stayed for a number of days more with the believers, after saying goodbye, he sailed off to Syria, along with Priscilla and Aquila, having cut his hair at Cenchreae because of a vow he had taken. [19]They landed at Ephesus, and he left them there while he himself went into the synagogue and debated with the Jews. [20]Although they asked him to stay longer, he did not consent. [21]Instead, after saying goodbye and telling them, "I will return to you, if God is willing," he set sail from Ephesus.

[22]When he landed in Caesarea he went up and greeted the church (at Jerusalem), and then went down to Antioch. [23]After staying for a certain time he left and traveled from place to place in the region of Galatia and Phrygia, strengthening all the disciples.

18:18 Ὁ δὲ Παῦλος ἔτι προσμείνας ἡμέρας ἱκανὰς τοῖς ἀδελφοῖς ἀποταξάμενος ἐξέπλει εἰς τὴν Συρίαν, καὶ σὺν αὐτῷ Πρίσκιλλα καὶ Ἀκύλας, κειράμενος ἐν Κεγχρεαῖς τὴν κεφαλήν, εἶχεν γὰρ εὐχήν.

Ὁ . . . Παῦλος. Paul's name appears with the article as he is reintroduced into the narrative since he has been established as the single central character of the second half of Acts (Levinsohn 1992, 101; see also 12:3 on Πέτρον).

προσμείνας. Aor act ptc masc nom sg προσμένω (temporal).

ἡμέρας ἱκανὰς. Accusative (extent) of time.

ἀποταξάμενος. Aor mid ptc masc nom sg ἀποτάσσω (temporal).

ἐξέπλει. Impf act ind 3rd sg ἐκπλέω.

κειράμενος. Aor mid ptc masc nom sg κείρω (temporal). The subject of the participle is most likely Paul, the topic of the verse, rather than Aquila.

Κεγχρεαῖς. Cenchreae, one of two seaports at Corinth, was situated on the Saronic Gulf and "was the natural port of embarkation for eastward voyages" (Barrett, 877–78).

εἶχεν. Impf act ind 3rd sg ἔχω. The expression ἔχω εὐχήν means "to take a vow."

18:19 κατήντησαν δὲ εἰς Ἔφεσον, κἀκείνους κατέλιπεν αὐτοῦ, αὐτὸς δὲ εἰσελθὼν εἰς τὴν συναγωγὴν διελέξατο τοῖς Ἰουδαίοις.

κατήντησαν. Aor act ind 3rd pl καταντάω.

κἀκείνους. A shortened form (crasis) of καί ἐκεῖνος.

κατέλιπεν. Aor act ind 3rd sg καταλείπω.

αὐτοῦ. The genitive singular pronoun apparently could be used as an adverb of place (cf. 15:34; 21:4; BAGD, 124). A large number of early scribes (𝔓[74vid] ℵ A D E 33 104 326 1241 *al*), however, sought to make the verse clearer by changing the pronoun to ἐκεῖ. It is still not completely clear, however, where "there" is. Paul may have parted company with Priscilla and Aquila when they landed in Ephesus and then headed for the synagogue, or αὐτοῦ may refer to Ephesus in a sort of parenthetical proleptic clause ("he would later leave them there" (cf. Newman and Nida).

εἰσελθὼν. Aor act ptc masc nom sg εἰσέρχομαι (attendant circumstance).

εἰς. See 1:8 on ἐφ᾿ ὑμᾶς.

διελέξατο. Aor mid dep ind 3rd sg διαλέγομαι.

18:20 ἐρωτώντων δὲ αὐτῶν ἐπὶ πλείονα χρόνον μεῖναι οὐκ ἐπένευσεν,

ἐρωτώντων. Pres act ptc masc gen pl ἐρωτάω. Genitive absolute (see 1:8 on ἐπελθόντος), concessive.

αὐτῶν. Genitive subject (see 1:8 on ἐπελθόντος).

ἐπὶ πλείονα χρόνον. See 13:31 on ἐπὶ ἡμέρας πλείους.

μεῖναι. Aor act inf μένω (indirect discourse).

ἐπένευσεν. Aor act ind 3rd sg ἐπινεύω.

18:21 ἀλλὰ ἀποταξάμενος καὶ εἰπών, Πάλιν ἀνακάμψω πρὸς ὑμᾶς τοῦ θεοῦ θέλοντος, ἀνήχθη ἀπὸ τῆς Ἐφέσου,

ἀποταξάμενος. Aor mid ptc masc nom sg ἀποτάσσω (temporal).

εἰπών. Aor act ptc masc nom sg λέγω (temporal). After εἰπών, the Western and Byzantine texts add (with several variations): "I must certainly keep the feast day that is coming in Jerusalem."

ἀνακάμψω. Fut act ind 1st sg ἀνακάμπτω.

θέλοντος. Pres act ptc masc gen sg θέλω. The genitive absolute should probably be taken as conditional (so Wallace 1996, 633; Rogers and Rogers, 278). Since, however, this same thought is typically expressed by ἐὰν plus a subjunctive form of θέλω (see 1 Cor 4:19; 16:7; Heb 6:3; Jas 4:15; Barrett, 879), it may be better to treat the expression as idiomatic, with the genitive absolute functioning (literally) in its most common manner, i.e., temporally ("I will return to you when God is willing").

ἀνήχθη. Aor pass ind 3rd sg ἀνάγω. On the meaning, see 13:13 on Ἀναχθέντες.

18:22 καὶ κατελθὼν εἰς Καισάρειαν, ἀναβὰς καὶ ἀσπασάμενος τὴν ἐκκλησίαν, κατέβη εἰς Ἀντιόχειαν.

καὶ. The use of καί here and in the following verse, rather than δέ, reflects the fact that Luke's main concern is detailing the continuing events at Ephesus rather than Paul's travels (Levinsohn 1987, 116–17).

κατελθὼν. Aor act ptc masc nom sg κατέρχομαι (temporal).

ἀναβὰς. Aor act ptc masc nom sg ἀναβαίνω (temporal). Particularly in light of the main clause, "he *went down* to Antioch," Bruce (400; cf. Barrett, 880–81) argues that ἀναβὰς must refer to a visit to the Jerusalem church (one would not "go down" to Antioch from Caesarea, a seaport).

ἀσπασάμενος. Aor mid dep ptc masc nom sg ἀσπάζομαι (temporal).

κατέβη. Aor act ind 3rd sg καταβαίνω.

18:23 καὶ ποιήσας χρόνον τινὰ ἐξῆλθεν, διερχόμενος καθεξῆς τὴν Γαλατικὴν χώραν καὶ Φρυγίαν, ἐπιστηρίζων πάντας τοὺς μαθητάς.

Some scholars (e.g., Fitzmyer 1998, 633, 636) introduce a major division between vv. 22 and 23. Levinsohn (1992, 214), however, points out that (1) the use of καί (implying a continuation of the same series of events), (2) the use of a participial clause with an initial participle to introduce v. 23, and (3) the failure to use a full noun phrase to refer to Paul in v. 23, all indicate that no boundary should be perceived after v. 22.

ποιήσας χρόνον τινα. An idiom meaning, "to stay for an unspecified amount of time" (cf. 15:33; 20:3 on ποιήσας μῆνας τρεῖς).

ποιήσας. Aor act ptc masc nom sg ποιέω (temporal).

ἐξῆλθεν. Aor act ind 3rd sg ἐξέρχομαι.

διερχόμενος. Pres dep ptc masc nom sg διέρχομαι (attendant circumstance).

καθεξῆς. This adverb may emphasize that Paul systematically covered all of Galatia and Phrygia (cf. Barrett, 881; Bruce, 400).

ἐπιστηρίζων. Pres act ptc masc nom sg ἐπιστηρίζω (attendant circumstance or perhaps purpose; so Barrett, 881).

Acts 18:24–28

24Now, a Jew from Alexandria named Apollos arrived in Ephesus. He was an eloquent man who knew the Scriptures well. 25He had been trained in the way of the Lord, and he spoke with great enthusiasm and accurately taught things about Jesus, even though he only knew the baptism of John. 26(On one occasion,) He began to speak boldly in the synagogue. But when Priscilla and Aquila heard him they took him aside and explained the way (of God) to him more accurately.

27(Later,) When he wanted to travel to Achaia, the believers encouraged him and wrote to the disciples so that they would welcome him. After he arrived (in Achaia) he greatly helped those who had believed through grace. 28For he vigorously refuted the Jews in public by demonstrating through the Scriptures that the Christ was Jesus.

18:24 Ἰουδαῖος δέ τις Ἀπολλῶς ὀνόματι, Ἀλεξανδρεὺς τῷ γένει, ἀνὴρ λόγιος, κατήντησεν εἰς Ἔφεσον, δυνατὸς ὢν ἐν ταῖς γραφαῖς.

τις. See 8:9.

Ἀπολλῶς. Nominative in apposition to Ἰουδαῖος.

ὀνόματι. Dative of reference.

Ἀλεξανδρεὺς . . . ἀνὴρ. These nominative nouns are both in apposition to Ἰουδαῖος.

τῷ γένει. Dative of reference.

λόγιος. This term could refer to either knowledge ("learned"; LN 27.20) or skill in speaking ("eloquent"; LN 33.22). The contextual focus on Apollos' speech makes the latter more likely. That Apollos was also "learned" is indicated in the participial clause that follows.

κατήντησεν. Aor act ind 3rd sg καταντάω.

δυνατὸς. Predicate nominative.

ὢν. Pres act ptc masc nom sg εἰμί (attributive).

18:25 οὗτος ἦν κατηχημένος τὴν ὁδὸν τοῦ κυρίου καὶ ζέων τῷ πνεύματι ἐλάλει καὶ ἐδίδασκεν ἀκριβῶς τὰ περὶ τοῦ Ἰησοῦ, ἐπιστάμενος μόνον τὸ βάπτισμα Ἰωάννου·

ἦν. Impf ind 3rd sg εἰμί.

κατηχημένος. Prf pass ptc masc nom sg κατηχέω (pluperfect periphrastic; see 1:17 on κατηριθμημένος).

τὴν ὁδὸν. Accusative of reference. On the expression τὴν ὁδὸν τοῦ κυρίου, cf. 9:2 on τῆς ὁδοῦ.

ζέων τῷ πνεύματι. Barrett (888) argues that this idiom (lit. "to boil in the spirit") has a Christian connotation and cites Rom 12:11 as evidence (cf. Bruce, 402). This could be true if the καί links ζέων τῷ πνεύματι to κατηχημένος as part of a periphrastic construction (cf. Rogers and Rogers, 279). It is more likely, however, that the conjunction links the first clause (οὗτος ἦν κατηχημένος τὴν ὁδὸν τοῦ κυρίου) to the second one, of which ζέων τῷ πνεύματι is a part. (In the periphrastic analysis no link exists between the two main clauses.) In this analysis, the participial clause functions not as a description of Apollos, but rather denotes the manner in which Apollos spoke (ἐλάλει). If this is correct, the expression means "to show great eagerness toward something, to show enthusiasm, to commit oneself completely to" (LN 25.73).

ζέων. Pres act ptc masc nom sg ζέω (manner; see above).

ἐλάλει. Impf act ind 3rd sg λαλέω.

ἐδίδασκεν. Impf act ind 3rd sg διδάσκω (the aorist form would be ἐδίδαξέν).

ἀκριβῶς. The explicit statement that Apollos "accurately taught things about Jesus" appears to contradict the following verse, which indicates that his theological deficiencies were readily apparent. The two verses are best taken as an indication that Apollos accurately taught what he knew (as a follower of John the Baptist), though his knowledge was limited.

τὰ. The article functions as a nominalizer (see 1:3 on τά).

ἐπιστάμενος. Pres dep ptc masc nom sg ἐπίσταμαι (concessive).

18:26 οὗτός τε ἤρξατο παρρησιάζεσθαι ἐν τῇ συναγωγῇ. ἀκού-

σαντες δὲ αὐτοῦ Πρίσκιλλα καὶ Ἀκύλας προσελάβοντο αὐτὸν καὶ ἀκριβέστερον αὐτῷ ἐξέθεντο τὴν ὁδὸν [τοῦ θεοῦ].

ἤρξατο. Aor mid ind 3rd sg ἄρχω.
παρρησιάζεσθαι. Pres dep inf παρρησιάζομαι (complementary).
ἀκούσαντες. Aor act ptc masc nom pl ἀκούω (temporal).
αὐτοῦ. Genitive object of ἀκούσαντες.
προσελάβοντο. Aor mid ind 3rd pl προσλαμβάνω.
ἀκριβέστερον. The comparitive adjective is used adverbially.
ἐξέθεντο. Aor mid ind 3rd pl ἐκτίθημι.
τὴν ὁδὸν [τοῦ θεοῦ]. The textual problem makes no difference in meaning; τὴν ὁδὸν and τὴν ὁδὸν τοῦ θεοῦ are both synonymous with τὴν ὁδὸν τοῦ κυρίου (see v. 25; 9:2).

18:27 βουλομένου δὲ αὐτοῦ διελθεῖν εἰς τὴν Ἀχαΐαν, προτρεψάμενοι οἱ ἀδελφοὶ ἔγραψαν τοῖς μαθηταῖς ἀποδέξασθαι αὐτόν, ὃς παραγενόμενος συνεβάλετο πολὺ τοῖς πεπιστευκόσιν διὰ τῆς χάριτος·

βουλομένου. Pres dep ptc masc gen sg βούλομαι. Genitive absolute (see 1:8 on ἐπελθόντος), temporal.
αὐτοῦ. Genitive subject (see 1:8 on ἐπελθόντος).
διελθεῖν. Aor act inf διέρχομαι (complementary).
Ἀχαΐαν. On the diaeresis over the *iota*, see 2:31 on προϊδὼν.
προτρεψάμενοι. Aor mid ptc masc pl nom προτρέπω (attendant circumstance).
ἀδελφοὶ. See 1:15.
ἔγραψαν. Aor act ind 3rd pl γράφω.
ἀποδέξασθαι. Aor mid dep inf ἀποδέχομαι. The infinitive could be taken as introducing indirect discourse. The textual tradition, however, suggests that some scribes understood the infinitival clause as a somewhat ambiguous expression of purpose (the Western text replaces the infinitive with ὅπως ἀποδέξωνται).
παραγενόμενος. Aor mid dep ptc masc nom sg παραγίνομαι (temporal).
συνεβάλετο. Aor mid ind 3rd sg συμβάλλω. In the middle voice (only here in the NT), this verb means "to help or assist."
πολύ. Here, an adverb modifying συνεβάλετο.
τοῖς πεπιστευκόσιν Prf act ptc masc dat pl πιστεύω (substantival). Verbs with a συν- prefix take a dative complement.

διὰ τῆς χάριτος. Means. The prepositional phrase most likely modifies the closer τοῖς πεπιστευκόσιν ("believed *through [God's] grace*"), rather than συνεβάλετο ("greatly helped them *through [God's] grace*"). Bruce (404), however, argues that the latter makes better sense (cf. 15:11).

18:28 εὐτόνως γὰρ τοῖς Ἰουδαίοις διακατηλέγχετο δημοσίᾳ ἐπιδεικνὺς διὰ τῶν γραφῶν εἶναι τὸν Χριστὸν Ἰησοῦν.

Ἰουδαίοις. Dative complement of διακατηλέγχετο.

διακατηλέγχετο. Impf dep ind 3rd sg διακατελέγχομαι. Luke has used a very rare term here that occurs nowhere else in the NT and elsewhere only in John Chrysostom's commentary on this passage (see *The Homilies of St. John Chrysotom* 60.283, 284). It is unclear whether the term refers to debate in general, or more specifically to successful debate, i.e., refutation.

ἐπιδεικνύς. Pres act ptc masc sg nom ἐπιδείκνυμι. The function of the participle depends on the meaning of διακατηλέγχετο. If it means "to debate," then the participle introduces an attendant circumstance ("and demonstrated"). If, however, the word means "to refute," then the participle could indicate means ("by demonstrating").

εἶναι. Pres act inf εἰμί (objective).

τὸν Χριστὸν. Accusative subject of the infinitive (see 1:3 on αὐτὸν).

Ἰησοῦν. Predicate accusative (see 1:22 on μάρτυρα). On the question of whether τὸν Χριστὸν or Ἰησοῦν should be viewed as the subject, see 18:5.

Acts 19:1–7

[1]While Apollos was in Corinth, Paul, after traveling through the inland regions, came to Ephesus and found some disciples (there). [2]He asked them, "Did you receive the Holy Spirit when you believed?" They told him, "We have not even heard whether there is a Holy Spirit." [3]So he said, "How then were you baptized?" "With John's baptism," they replied. [4]Then Paul said, "John baptized (using) a baptism of repentance and told the people that they should believe in the one who was coming after him—that is, in Jesus." [5]When they heard (this), they were baptized in the name of the Lord Jesus. [6](Then,) When Paul placed his hands on them, the Holy Spirit came on them, and they began speaking in tongues and prophesying. [7]There were about twelve men (there) in all.

19:1 ᾿Εγένετο δὲ ἐν τῷ τὸν ᾿Απολλῶ εἶναι ἐν Κορίνθῳ Παῦλον διελθόντα τὰ ἀνωτερικὰ μέρη [κατ]ελθεῖν εἰς Ἔφεσον καὶ εὑρεῖν τινας μαθητάς

᾿Εγένετο. Aor mid dep ind 3rd sg γίνομαι.

τὸν ᾿Απολλῶ. Accusative subject of the infinitive (see 1:3 on αὐτὸν).

εἶναι. Pres act inf εἰμί. Used with ἐν τῷ to form a temporal expression.

Παῦλον. Accusative subject of the infinitive (both [κατ]ελθεῖν and εὑρεῖν; see 1:3 on αὐτὸν).

διελθόντα. Aor act ptc masc acc sg διέρχομαι (temporal).

ἀνωτερικὰ. According to Louw and Nida (1.65), this adjective refers to land that is located in "an inland or higher area, presumably away from the shoreline."

[κατ]ελθεῖν. Aor act inf [κατ]έρχομαι. The conjoined infinitival clauses, Παῦλον διελθόντα τὰ ἀνωτερικὰ μέρη [κατ]ελθεῖν εἰς Ἔφεσον καὶ εὑρεῖν τινας μαθητάς, serve as the subject of ἐγένετο (see also 9:32 on κατελθεῖν; contra Rogers and Rogers, 279, who link the infinitives with ἐν τῷ).

εὑρεῖν. Aor act inf εὑρίσκω (see above on [κατ]ελθεῖν).

19:2 εἶπέν τε πρὸς αὐτούς, Εἰ πνεῦμα ἅγιον ἐλάβετε πιστεύσαντες; οἱ δὲ πρὸς αὐτόν, ᾿Αλλ᾿ οὐδ᾿ εἰ πνεῦμα ἅγιον ἔστιν ἠκούσαμεν.

εἶπέν. Aor act ind 3rd sg λέγω. The second accent comes from the enclitic τε (see 1:4 on ἠκούσατέ).

Εἰ. Introduces a direct question.

ἐλάβετε. Aor act ind 2nd pl λαμβάνω.

πιστεύσαντες. Aor act ptc masc nom pl πιστεύω (temporal).

οἱ δὲ. The article functions like a personal pronoun here (cf. 3:5).

᾿Αλλ᾿. Practically speaking, the adversative conjunction serves to make the statement emphatic (Dana and Mantey, 241).

εἰ Introduces a conditional clausal complement of ἠκούσαμεν.

πνεῦμα ἅγιον. Predicate nominative of an impersonal ἔστιν.

ἔστιν. Pres act ind 3rd sg εἰμί. According to Robertson (1934, 233–34), when ἔστιν retains its accent it is "emphatic and expresses existence or possibility" (cf. 2:29).

ἠκούσαμεν. Aor act ind 1st pl ἀκούω.

19:3 εἶπέν τε, Εἰς τί οὖν ἐβαπτίσθητε; οἱ δὲ εἶπαν, Εἰς τὸ Ἰωάννου βάπτισμα.

εἶπέν. Aor act ind 3rd sg λέγω. The second accent comes from the enclitic τε (see 1:4 on ἠκούσατέ).

Εἰς τί οὖν ἐβαπτίσθητε. It is unclear whether εἰς τί should be taken literally ("into what") or in its more typical sense ("for what purpose," "why"). The construction was typically used in rhetorical questions to question particular actions or a state of affairs (cf. Matt 14:31; 26:8; Mark 14:4; 15:34) and carried a connotation of incredulity. Here it is used to form a real question that either means "Into what then were you baptized?" or "What then was the point of your baptism?" The former fits more naturally with the answer that follows (Lit. "Into John's baptism"; cf. also v. 5), though it may be possible to take the Ephesians' response as, "To follow John's way of baptism."

ἐβαπτίσθητε. Aor pass ind 2nd pl βαπτίζω.

οἱ δὲ. The article functions like a personal pronoun here (cf. 3:5).

εἶπαν. Aor act ind 3rd pl λέγω.

19:4 εἶπεν δὲ Παῦλος, Ἰωάννης ἐβάπτισεν βάπτισμα μετανοίας τῷ λαῷ λέγων εἰς τὸν ἐρχόμενον μετ᾽ αὐτὸν ἵνα πιστεύσωσιν, τοῦτ᾽ ἔστιν εἰς τὸν Ἰησοῦν.

εἶπεν δὲ. The shift from the articular pronoun plus δέ to introduce the dialogue in verses 2b–3b to the verb-initial construction here marks the utterance in verse 4 as the "resolving utterance," i.e., the utterance that indicates that the goal of one of the participants has been attained (Levinsohn 1992, 132).

εἶπεν. Aor act ind 3rd sg λέγω.

ἐβάπτισεν. Aor act ind 3rd sg βαπτίζω.

βάπτισμα. Cognate accusative (Barrett, 896).

μετανοίας. See 13:24.

τῷ λαῷ. Dative indirect object of λεγων.

λέγων. Pres act ptc masc sg nom λέγω (attendant circumstance).

εἰς. The prepositional phrase should be viewed as a displaced modifier of πιστεύσωσιν. Its position lends prominence to the expression (cf. Bruce, 407).

τὸν ἐρχόμενον. Pres dep ptc masc acc sg ἔρχομαι (substantival).

ἵνα. Introduces the clausal complement (indirect discourse) of λέγων.

πιστεύσωσιν. Aor act subj 3rd pl πιστεύω.

ἔστιν. Pres act ind 3rd sg εἰμί. On the retention of the accent, see 1:19 on τοῦτ᾽ ἔστιν.

19:5 ἀκούσαντες δὲ ἐβαπτίσθησαν εἰς τὸ ὄνομα τοῦ κυρίου Ἰησοῦ,

ἀκούσαντες. Aor act ptc masc nom pl ἀκούω (temporal).

ἐβαπτίσθησαν. Aor pass ind 3rd pl βαπτίζω.

19:6 καὶ ἐπιθέντος αὐτοῖς τοῦ Παύλου [τὰς] χεῖρας ἦλθε τὸ πνεῦμα τὸ ἅγιον ἐπ᾽ αὐτούς, ἐλάλουν τε γλώσσαις καὶ ἐπροφήτευον.

ἐπιθέντος. Aor act ptc masc gen sg ἐπιτίθημι. Genitive absolute (see 1:8 on ἐπελθόντος), temporal.

τοῦ Παύλου. Genitive subject (see 1:8 on ἐπελθόντος).

ἦλθε. Aor act ind 3rd sg ἔρχομαι.

τὸ πνεῦμα. The article should not be viewed as an anaphoric reference back to v. 2 that can be rendered "that very Holy Spirit" (contra Turner, 1965:20; Barrett, 898). Rather, it simply marks "Holy Spirit" as information that is already known (from the discourse) to the readers.

ἐλάλουν. Impf act ind 3rd pl λαλέω.

γλώσσαις. Dative of instrument (cf. 2:4, 11; 10:46).

ἐπροφήτευον. Impf act ind 3rd pl προφητεύω.

19:7 ἦσαν δὲ οἱ πάντες ἄνδρες ὡσεὶ δώδεκα.

ἦσαν. Impf ind 3rd pl εἰμί.

οἱ πάντες. This construction indicates the total number of a group.

ὡσεὶ. Used with οἱ πάντες, the adverb introduces a precise number rather than the usual approximation (cf. Bruce, 407).

Acts 19:8–10

[8]After entering the synagogue, Paul spoke boldly over the course of three months, debating and trying to convince (them) about the kingdom of God. [9]When certain men became stubborn and refused to believe, and (even) denounced the Way in front of the crowd, he left them,

took the disciples, and began speaking daily in the lecture hall of Tyrannus. [10]This went on for two years, so that all those living in Asia, both Jews and Greeks, heard the message of the Lord.

19:8 Εἰσελθὼν δὲ εἰς τὴν συναγωγὴν ἐπαρρησιάζετο ἐπὶ μῆνας τρεῖς διαλεγόμενος καὶ πείθων [τὰ] περὶ τῆς βασιλείας τοῦ θεοῦ.

Εἰσελθὼν. Aor act ptc masc nom sg εἰσέρχομαι (temporal).

ἐπαρρησιάζετο. Impf dep ind 3rd sg παρρησιάζομαι.

ἐπὶ μῆνας τρεῖς. See 13:31 on ἐπὶ ἡμέρας πλείους. This temporal expression modifies ἐπαρρησιάζετο rather than διαλεγόμενος since it customarily follows the verb it modifies.

διαλεγόμενος καὶ πείθων. Although it is possible to take the conjoined participles as a hendiadys (see 1:25 on τῆς διακονίας καὶ ἀποστολῆς), given their use together elsewhere as independent verbs (cf. 18:4) it is more likely that they indicate two distinct processes.

διαλεγόμενος. Pres dep ptc masc nom sg διαλέγομαι. This verb, which probably implies a formal address here (cf. LN 33.26), introduces an attendant circumstance or the means by which Paul spoke boldly.

πείθων. Pres act ptc masc nom sg πείθω (attendant circumstance or means; see above).

[τὰ]. Accusative of respect. The article functions as a nominalizer (see 1:3 on τὰ), changing the prepositional phrase into a substantive (lit. "about the things concerning the kingdom of God"). The textual question has little bearing on the meaning of the clause.

τῆς βασιλείας τοῦ θεοῦ. See 1:3.

19:9 ὡς δέ τινες ἐσκληρύνοντο καὶ ἠπείθουν κακολογοῦντες τὴν ὁδὸν ἐνώπιον τοῦ πλήθους, ἀποστὰς ἀπ' αὐτῶν ἀφώρισεν τοὺς μαθητάς καθ' ἡμέραν διαλεγόμενος ἐν τῇ σχολῇ Τυράννου.

ὡς. Temporal (see 18:5).

ἐσκληρύνοντο. Impf pass ind 3rd pl σκληρύνω.

ἠπείθουν. Impf act ind 3rd pl ἀπειθέω.

κακολογοῦντες. Pres act ptc masc nom pl κακολογέω (attendant circumstance; Rogers and Rogers [280] have manner/means).

τὴν ὁδὸν. See 9:2. Accusative direct object of κακολογοῦντες.

τοῦ πλήθους. Barrett (904) notes that this could be a reference to (1)

Christians in the synagogue, (2) the whole synagogue community, or (3) the general population of the city. He prefers the third option. The context of v. 8 and the fact that he "left them," however, points to option 2.

ἀποστὰς. Aor act ptc masc nom sg ἀφίστημι (attendant circumstance of ἀφώρισεν).

ἀφώρισεν. Aor act ind 3rd sg ἀφορίζω.

καθ' ἡμέραν. Distributive (see 2:46).

διαλεγόμενος. Pres dep ptc masc nom sg διαλέγομαι (attendant circumstance).

Τυράννου. The Western text adds "from the fifth hour to the tenth" (11 a.m. to 4 p.m.), probably indicating that Paul used the lecture hall during the siesta hours, while it was available (Barrett, 905).

19:10 τοῦτο δὲ ἐγένετο ἐπὶ ἔτη δύο, ὥστε πάντας τοὺς κατοικοῦντας τὴν 'Ασίαν ἀκοῦσαι τὸν λόγον τοῦ κυρίου, 'Ιουδαίους τε καὶ Ἕλληνας.

ἐγένετο. Aor mid dep ind 3rd sg γίνομαι.

ἐπὶ ἔτη δύο. See 13:31 on ἐπὶ ἡμέρας πλείους.

τοὺς κατοικοῦντας. Pres act ptc masc acc pl κατοικέω (substantival). Accusative subject of the infinitive (see 1:3 on αὐτὸν).

τὴν 'Ασίαν. On the use of the accusative case with κατοικέω, see 1:19 on 'Ιερουσαλήμ.

ἀκοῦσαι. Aor act inf ἀκούω. Used with ὥστε to indicate result.

'Ιουδαίους τε καὶ Ἕλληνας. Accusative in apposition to τοὺς κατοικοῦντας.

Acts 19:11–20

[11]God performed extraordinary miracles through the hands of Paul
[12]so that even handkerchiefs and aprons (he had used) were taken from
him to the sick and the sickness left them and the evil spirits went away.
[13]Now some of the itinerant Jewish exorcists also attempted to invoke
the name of the Lord Jesus over those who had evil spirits by saying, "I
order you by Jesus whom Paul preaches (to come out)." [14]Seven sons of
Sceva, a Jewish chief priest, were the ones who were doing this. [15]An
evil spirit responded to them, "I know Jesus, and I know about Paul,
but who are you?" [16]Then the man who had the evil spirit in him jumped

on them. He overpowered them all and defeated them so that they ran away from that house naked and wounded.

[17]This (incident) became known to all who lived in Ephesus, both Jews and Greeks. They were all afraid, and the name of the Lord Jesus was greatly honored. [18]And many of those who had believed were coming and openly confessing what they had done. [19]A substantial number of those who had practiced magic gathered (their) books and then burned them before everyone. They added up the value of the books and found (that they had been worth) 50,000 silver coins. [20]In this powerful way, the message of the Lord spread and prevailed.

19:11 Δυνάμεις τε οὐ τὰς τυχούσας ὁ θεὸς ἐποίει διὰ τῶν χειρῶν Παύλου,

τε. The use of τε here suggests that this verse goes with what follows, rather than with what proceeds, and provides the specific lead-in to a new development in the story (see Levinsohn 1987, 129–35).

οὐ τὰς τυχούσας. This idiomatic adjectival expression (another example of litotes; see 1:5 on οὐ μετὰ πολλὰς ταύτας ἡμέρας) means "unusual, extraordinary" (cf. 28:2).

τυχούσας. Aor act ptc fem acc pl τυγχάνω (attributive).

ἐποίει. Impf act ind 3rd sg ποιέω.

τῶν χειρῶν Παύλου. Synecdoche (see 1:22 on τοῦ βαπτίσματος Ἰωάννου) for "Paul" (contra Bruce, 410).

19:12 ὥστε καὶ ἐπὶ τοὺς ἀσθενοῦντας ἀποφέρεσθαι ἀπὸ τοῦ χρωτὸς αὐτοῦ σουδάρια ἢ σιμικίνθια καὶ ἀπαλλάσσεσθαι ἀπ' αὐτῶν τὰς νόσους, τά τε πνεύματα τὰ πονηρὰ ἐκπορεύεσθαι.

τοὺς ἀσθενοῦντας. Pres act ptc masc acc pl ἀσθενέω (substantival).

ἀποφέρεσθαι. Pres pass inf ἀποφέρω. Used with ὥστε to indicate result.

ἀπο. See 1:8 on ἐφ' ὑμᾶς.

τοῦ χρωτὸς. This term (lit. "skin") was commonly used to render the Hebrew word for "flesh/body" (בָּשָׂר) in the LXX (Bruce, 410) and may thus function as a synecdoche (see 1:22 on τοῦ βαπτίσματος Ἰωάννου).

σουδάρια ἢ σιμικίνθια. Accusative subject of the infinitive ἀποφέρεσθαι (see 1:3 on αὐτὸν). Both terms are Latin loan words. The former were apparently "kerchiefs or sweat rags worn on the head" (Witherington 1998, 579), while the latter referred to a workman's apron (LN 6.179).

ἀπαλλάσσεσθαι. Pres pass inf ἀπαλλάσσω. Used with ὥστε to indicate result.

τὰς νόσους . . . πνευμάτα. Accusative subject of the infinitive ἀπαλλάσσεσθαι (see 1:3 on αὐτὸν).

ἐκπορεύεσθαι. Pres dep inf ἐκπορεύομαι. Used with ὥστε to indicate result.

19:13 ἐπεχείρησαν δέ τινες καὶ τῶν περιερχομένων Ἰουδαίων ἐξορκιστῶν ὀνομάζειν ἐπὶ τοὺς ἔχοντας τὰ πνεύματα τὰ πονηρὰ τὸ ὄνομα τοῦ κυρίου Ἰησοῦ λέγοντες, Ὁρκίζω ὑμᾶς τὸν Ἰησοῦν ὃν Παῦλος κηρύσσει.

ἐπεχείρησαν. Aor act ind 3rd pl ἐπιχειρέω.

περιερχομένων. Pres dep ptc masc gen pl περιέρχομαι (attributive).

ὀνομάζειν. Pres act inf ὀνομάζω (complementary). This verb means "to utter a name in a ritual context" (LN 33.133).

τοὺς ἔχοντας. Pres act ptc masc acc pl ἔχω (substantival).

τὸ ὄνομα. Cognate accusative.

λέγοντες. Pres act ptc masc nom pl λέγω (means).

Ὁρκίζω. Pres act ind 1st sg ὁρκίζω. This verb is used in ritual contexts to solemnly command someone to do or to swear something.

τὸν Ἰησοῦν. The one making the solemn command does so based upon the authority of someone greater (usually God). The person or thing by whom or by which one swears is placed in the accusative case (Wallace 1996, 204). This noun phrase is not part of a double accusative construction (contra Bruce, 410; Barrett, 908) since the two accusatives refer to different people.

κηρύσσει. Pres act ind 3rd sg κηρύσσω.

19:14 ἦσαν δέ τινος Σκευᾶ Ἰουδαίου ἀρχιερέως ἑπτὰ υἱοὶ τοῦτο ποιοῦντες.

ἦσαν. Impf ind 3rd pl εἰμί.

τινος. A significant group of important early manuscripts (𝔓[74] ℵ A Ψ *Byz* lat sy[h]) read τινες (modifying υἱοὶ).

'Ιουδαίου ἀρχιερέως. These genitive nouns stand in apposition to Σκευᾶ.

ποιοῦντες. Pres act ptc masc nom pl ποιέω. Although the participle may be taken periphrastically (imperfect periphrastic; see 1:10 on ἀτενίζοντες), it may be preferable to take it as attributive since it is so far removed from the verb (cf. Barrett, 908). The difference in connotation is slight.

19:15 ἀποκριθὲν δὲ τὸ πνεῦμα τὸ πονηρὸν εἶπεν αὐτοῖς, Τὸν [μὲν] 'Ιησοῦν γινώσκω καὶ τὸν Παῦλον ἐπίσταμαι, ὑμεῖς δὲ τίνες ἐστέ;

ἀποκριθὲν. Aor pass dep ptc neut nom sg ἀποκρίνομαι (attendant circumstance).

τὸ πνεῦμα. This is an example of an articular noun that should be viewed as indefinite. The article simply marks the noun phrase as information that has already been introduced.

εἶπεν. Aor act ind 3rd sg λέγω.

γινώσκω. Pres act ind 1st sg γινώσκω.

τὸν Παῦλον. The article is probably used simply to mark the noun as known information not to make the expression anaphoric (contra Robertson 1934, 762; Wallace 1996, 217–19). The first reference to Paul, in v. 13, is anarthrous (see 3:3 on Πέτρον καὶ 'Ιωάννην) because he is new information in the address to the evil spirits.

ἐπίσταμαι. Pres dep ind 1st sg ἐπίσταμαι. Any difference in the meaning of the verbs must be gleaned from the context rather than the terms themselves (cf. Bruce, 411). It may be that γινώσκω here refers to personal knowledge, while ἐπίσταμαι refers to knowledge *about* something (cf. LN 28:3); or, the two verbs may simply be used for stylistic variation (so Barrett, 910).

ὑμεῖς. The explicit subject pronoun is emphatic.

ἐστέ. Pres act ind 2nd pl εἰμί.

19:16 καὶ ἐφαλόμενος ὁ ἄνθρωπος ἐπ' αὐτοὺς ἐν ᾧ ἦν τὸ πνεῦμα τὸ πονηρὸν, κατακυριεύσας ἀμφοτέρων ἴσχυσεν κατ' αὐτῶν ὥστε γυμνοὺς καὶ τετραυματισμένους ἐκφυγεῖν ἐκ τοῦ οἴκου ἐκείνου.

ἐφαλόμενος. Aor mid dep ptc masc nom sg ἐφάλλομαι (attendant circumstance).

ἐπ'. See 1:8 on ἐφ' ὑμᾶς.

ἦν. Impf ind 3rd sg εἰμί.

κατακυριεύσας. Aor act ptc masc nom sg κατακυριεύω (attendant circumstance).

ἀμφοτέρων. Although the adjective ἀμφότεροι usually means "both," here (and at 23:8) it should be taken as "all" (a sense well attested in later Greek literature; Bruce, 411) in reference to the seven sons of Sceva (see Barrett, 911; cf. LN 59.26).

ἴσχυσεν κατ' αὐτῶν. This expression (lit. "he was strong against them") is probably an idiom meaning "he defeated them" (on this use of κατά, see BAGD, 405, 2a).

ἴσχυσεν. Aor act ind 3rd sg ἰσχύω.

γυμνοὺς. Along with the conjoined participle τετραυματισμένους, this adjective is in the accusative case in apposition to the unexpressed accusative subject of the infinitive (see 1:3 on αὐτὸν), and indicates the state the men were in when they fled.

τετραυματισμένους. Prf pass ptc masc acc pl τραυματίζω (manner; the accusative case comes from agreement with the implied subject of the infinitive).

ἐκφυγεῖν. Aor act inf ἐκφεύγω. Used with ὥστε to indicate result.

ἐκείνου. The reference to "that house" is abrupt, since no house has yet been mentioned in the narrative. This need not, however, indicate the incorporation of a fragmentary tradition or poor editorial skills on the part of the writer. Instead, the expression τοῦ οἴκου ἐκείνου should probably be viewed as a shorter equivalent of "the house where they had been."

19:17 τοῦτο δὲ ἐγένετο γνωστὸν πᾶσιν Ἰουδαίοις τε καὶ Ἕλλησιν τοῖς κατοικοῦσιν τὴν Ἔφεσον καὶ ἐπέπεσεν φόβος ἐπὶ πάντας αὐτούς καὶ ἐμεγαλύνετο τὸ ὄνομα τοῦ κυρίου Ἰησοῦ

ἐγένετο. Aor mid dep ind 3rd sg γίνομαι.

γνωστὸν. Predicate nominative.

κατοικοῦσιν. Pres act ptc masc pl dat κατοικέω (attributive).

τὴν Ἔφεσον. On the use of the accusative case with κατοικέω, see 1:19 on Ἰερουσαλήμ.

ἐπέπεσεν. Aor act ind 3rd sg ἐπιπίπτω.

ἐπὶ. See 1:8 on ἐφ' ὑμᾶς.

ἐμεγαλύνετο. Impf pass ind 3rd sg μεγαλύνω.

19:18 πολλοί τε τῶν πεπιστευκότων ἤρχοντο ἐξομολογούμενοι καὶ ἀναγγέλλοντες τὰς πράξεις αὐτῶν.

τῶν πεπιστευκότων. Prf act ptc masc gen pl πιστεύω (substantival; partitive genitive).

ἤρχοντο. Impf dep ind 3rd pl ἔρχομαι.

ἐξομολογούμενοι καὶ ἀναγγέλλοντες. The conjoined verbs could be viewed as a doublet (see 2:43 on τέρατα καὶ σημεῖα) that emphasizes the frank revelation of sinful behavior. Alternatively, the first verb could indicate general confession of sins, while the second refers to more specific disclosure of particular sins.

ἐξομολογούμενοι. Pres mid ptc masc nom pl ἐξομολογέω (attendant circumstance).

ἀναγγέλλοντες. Pres act ptc masc nom pl ἀναγγέλλω (attendant circumstance, or perhaps purpose).

τὰς πράξεις. Accusative direct object of both participles. Although it is possible to take the term πρᾶξις in its technical sense ("magical spells") and view the disclosure of the spells as a means of rendering them powerless (Bruce, 412), the more general sense of "deeds" is more obvious in the context. The specific nature of (some of?) their misdeeds is introduced in the following verse (τῶν τὰ περίεργα πραξάντων).

19:19 ἱκανοὶ δὲ τῶν τὰ περίεργα πραξάντων συνενέγκαντες τὰς βίβλους κατέκαιον ἐνώπιον πάντων, καὶ συνεψήφισαν τὰς τιμὰς αὐτῶν καὶ εὗρον ἀργυρίου μυριάδας πέντε.

τὰ περίεργα. Accusative direct object of πραξάντων.

τῶν πραξάντων. Aor act ptc masc gen pl πράσσω (substantival).

συνενέγκαντες. Aor act ptc masc nom pl συμφέρω (temporal).

κατέκαιον. Impf act ind 3rd pl κατακαίω.

πάντων. Substantival.

συνεψήφισαν. Aor act ind 3rd pl συμψηφίζω.

εὗρον. Aor act ind 3rd pl εὑρίσκω.

ἀργυρίου. Genitive of price.

19:20 Οὕτως κατὰ κράτος τοῦ κυρίου ὁ λόγος ηὔξανεν καὶ ἴσχυεν.

κατὰ κράτος τοῦ κυρίου ὁ λόγος. This is the only place where τοῦ κυρίου precedes ὁ λόγος in the expression "the word of the Lord" (on the possibility of taking τοῦ κυρίου with κράτος: "according to the power of the Lord"; see Barrett, 914).

κατὰ κράτος. This preposition with an accusative noun is frequently used in Acts as an adverbial expression that indicates that the action of the verb was done "in accord with a particular standard" (see also 3:17; 7:44; 22:3; cf. 26:5).

τοῦ κυρίου. In the UBS[4]/NA[27] text (see above), the genitive noun phrase could modify either κατὰ κράτος or ὁ λόγος. The scribal understanding reflected in the variant readings supports the latter interpretation.

ηὔξανεν. Impf act ind 3rd sg αὐξάνω.

ἴσχυεν. Impf act ind 3rd sg ἰσχύω.

Acts 19:21–40

[21]After these things had happened, Paul decided to travel through Macedonia and Achaia and go to Jerusalem. He said (to himself), "After I have been there, I must also see Rome." [22]He sent two of those who helped him—Timothy and Erastus—(ahead) to Macedonia, while he himself stayed for a while longer in Asia.

[23]At that time there was a serious disturbance concerning the Way. [24]For a certain man named Demetrius, a silversmith, by making silver shrines of Artemis provided a substantial profit for his fellow craftsmen. [25]He gathered them together—those of the same trade—and said, "Men! You know that our prosperity comes from this business, [26]and you have seen and heard how this Paul has persuaded and misled a substantial crowd, not only in Ephesus but in nearly all of Asia, by saying that these things that are made by (human) hands are not gods. [27]Now, not only is there a danger for us that this business will be seriously criticized, but also that the temple of the great goddess Artemis will be considered unimportant, and even that the one whom the whole of Asia and the world worship will soon be thrown down from her greatness!"

[28]When they heard (this) they too were filled with rage and began shouting, "Great is Artemis of the Ephesians!" [29]The city was filled with confusion, and (the mob) rushed together into the theater dragging Gaius and Aristarchus, who were Macedonians and traveling companions of Paul. [30]When Paul wanted to go in to (the theater to address) the citizen assembly, the disciples would not let him. [31]Even some of the

Asiarchs, who were his friends, sent (a message) to him and urged him not to venture into the theater. [32]So then, some were shouting one thing, others were shouting something else. For the assembly was confused and most of them did not (even) know why they had come together.

[33]Some people from the crowd gave instructions to Alexander after the Jews had put him forward. So Alexander waved his hand (to show that) he wanted to present a defense to the people. [34]But when they recognized that he was a Jew, one cry arose from all those who were shouting, for about two hours: "Great is Artemis of the Ephesians!" [35](Later,) When the town clerk had settled the crowd, he said, "Ephesians! Is there anyone anywhere who does not know that the city of Ephesus is the keeper of the temple of the great Artemis and the stone from the sky? [36]Since these things are undeniable, you must restrain yourselves and not do anything rash. [37]For you led these men (here) who are neither temple robbers nor blasphemers of our goddess. [38]So then, if Demetrius and the craftsmen with him have a legal complaint against someone, the courts are in session and there are proconsuls (available). Let them bring charges against one another (there). [39]And if you are wanting to deal with anything else, it will have to be resolved in a legal assembly. [40]For we are in danger of being accused of rioting for (what has happened) today, since there is no cause we can offer as an explanation for this commotion." [41]After saying these things, he dismissed the assembly.

19:21 Ὡς δὲ ἐπληρώθη ταῦτα, ἔθετο ὁ Παῦλος ἐν τῷ πνεύματι διελθὼν τὴν Μακεδονίαν καὶ Ἀχαΐαν πορεύεσθαι εἰς Ἱεροσόλυμα εἰπὼν ὅτι Μετὰ τὸ γενέσθαι με ἐκεῖ δεῖ με καὶ Ῥώμην ἰδεῖν.

ἐπληρώθη. Aor pass ind 3rd sg πληρόω. The singular verb is typical with a neuter plural subject (ταῦτα).

ἔθετο. Aor mid ind 3rd sg τίθημι.

ἐν τῷ πνεύματι. Although this expression could be a reference to the Holy Spirit ("led by the Spirit"), it more likely forms an idiom with the middle form of the verb τίθημι that means "to engage in the process of deciding, to make up one's mind, to decide" (LN 30.76; contra Bruce, 413). For related expressions, see Acts 5:4 (ἔθου ἐν τῇ καρδίᾳ σου) and Luke 21:14 (θέτε ἐν ταῖς καρδίαις ὑμῶν).

διελθὼν. Aor act ptc masc nom sg διέρχομαι. It appears that constructions such as this (main verb plus complementary or direct object infinitive) can have a participle that technically refers to action relating to the infinitive but is nevertheless in the nominative rather than accusative case (cf. Luke 19:37). While the idea of a "preaching tour" might be gleaned from the context (cf. 13:6), it should probably not be viewed as a semantic component of the verb itself (contra Barrett, 919).

τὴν Μακεδονίαν . . . 'Ἀχαΐαν. Accusative complements of διελθὼν.

'Ἀχαΐαν. On the diaeresis over the *iota*, see 2:31 on προϊδὼν.

πορεύεσθαι. Pres dep inf πορεύομαι (direct object). The idiom τίθεμαι ἐν τῷ πνεύματι/τῇ καρδίᾳ can take either a noun phrase (as in Acts 5:4 where τὸ πρᾶγμα τοῦτο is the direct object) or an infinitival clause as the direct object (as here).

εἰπὼν. Aor act ptc masc nom sg λέγω (attendant circumstance to the main verb ἔθετο). Barrett (919) is probably correct in taking this participle as a reference to a thought of Paul (and thus to the same event as the main verb) rather than a conversation (subsequent to the action of the main verb).

ὅτι. Introduces direct discourse.

γενέσθαι. Aor mid dep inf γίνομαι. Used with μετὰ τό to indicate antecedent time (see 1:3 on μετὰ τὸ παθεῖν).

με. Accusative subject of the infinitive γενέσθαι (see 1:3 on αὐτὸν).

δεῖ. Pres act ind 3rd sg δεῖ (impersonal).

με. Accusative subject of the infinitive ἰδεῖν (see 1:3 on αὐτὸν).

ἰδεῖν. Aor act inf ὁράω (complementary).

19:22 ἀποστείλας δὲ εἰς τὴν Μακεδονίαν δύο τῶν διακονούντων αὐτῷ, Τιμόθεον καὶ Ἔραστον, αὐτὸς ἐπέσχεν χρόνον εἰς τὴν 'Ἀσίαν.

ἀποστείλας. Aor act ptc masc nom sg ἀποστέλλω (attendant circumstance or temporal).

τῶν διακονούντων. Pres act ptc masc gen pl διακονέω (substantival). Partitive genitive.

αὐτῷ. Dative complement of διακονούντων.

Τιμόθεον καὶ Ἔραστον. The accusative nouns stand in apposition to δύο.

αὐτὸς. The overt subject pronoun is intensive and sharpens the contrast between the itinerary of Paul and that of Timothy and Erastus.

ἐπέσχεν. Aor act ind 3rd sg ἐπέχω.

χρόνον. The accusative noun on its own denotes "for a time, for awhile."

19:23 ᾿Εγένετο δὲ κατὰ τὸν καιρὸν ἐκεῖνον τάραχος οὐκ ὀλίγος περὶ τῆς ὁδοῦ.

᾿Εγένετο. Aor mid dep ind 3rd sg γίνομαι.

τάραχος. Nominative subject or predicate nominative of an impersonal ᾿Εγένετο.

τάραχος οὐκ ὀλίγος. Litotes (see 1:5 on οὐ μετὰ πολλὰς ταύτας ἡμέρας).

τῆς ὁδοῦ. See 9:2.

19:24 Δημήτριος γάρ τις ὀνόματι, ἀργυροκόπος, ποιῶν ναοὺς ἀργυροῦς ᾿Αρτέμιδος παρείχετο τοῖς τεχνίταις οὐκ ὀλίγην ἐργασίαν,

Δημήτριος. Nominative in apposition to τις.

τις. Substantival.

ὀνόματι. Dative of reference.

ἀργυροκόπος. Nominative in apposition to Δημήτριος.

ποιῶν. Pres act ptc masc nom sg ποιέω. The participle could be taken as indicating the means of the main verb, or it could be attributive (this is certainly the case in codex D: Δημήτριος γάρ τις ἦν ἀργυροκόπος ποιῶν).

ναούς. The ναοί were probably miniature shrines that devotees would dedicate in the temple (Bruce, 415).

παρείχετο. Impf mid ind 3rd sg παρέχω.

οὐκ ὀλίγην ἐργασίαν. Litotes (see 1:5 on οὐ μετὰ πολλὰς ταύτας ἡμέρας).

19:25 οὓς συναθροίσας καὶ τοὺς περὶ τὰ τοιαῦτα ἐργάτας εἶπεν, ῎Ανδρες, ἐπίστασθε ὅτι ἐκ ταύτης τῆς ἐργασίας ἡ εὐπορία ἡμῖν ἐστιν

οὓς. The antecedent is τοῖς τεχνίταις (v. 24).

συναθροίσας. Aor act ptc masc nom sg συναθροίζω (attendant circumstance or temporal).

καί. Epexegetical.

τοὺς. The article functions as a nominalizer (see 1:3 on τά), changing the following prepositional phrase (περὶ τὰ τοιαῦτα ἐργάτας) into a, somewhat awkward, noun phrase.

εἶπεν. Aor act ind 3rd sg λέγω.

Ἄνδρες. In this case, the vocative is not further qualified and should therefore be rendered "Men!" (cf. 1:11).

ἐπίστασθε. Pres dep ind 2nd pl ἐπίσταμαι.

ὅτι. Introduces the clausal complement of ἐπίστασθε.

ἡμῖν. Dative of possession (used with εἰμί).

ἐστιν. Pres act ind 3rd sg εἰμί.

19:26 καὶ θεωρεῖτε καὶ ἀκούετε ὅτι οὐ μόνον Ἐφέσου ἀλλὰ σχεδὸν πάσης τῆς Ἀσίας ὁ Παῦλος οὗτος πείσας μετέστησεν ἱκανὸν ὄχλον λέγων ὅτι οὐκ εἰσὶν θεοὶ οἱ διὰ χειρῶν γινόμενοι.

θεωρεῖτε. Pres act ind 2nd pl θεωρέω.

ἀκούετε. Pres act ind 2nd pl ἀκούω.

ὅτι. Introduces the clausal complement of θεωρεῖτε and ἀκούετε.

οὐ μόνον . . . ἀλλα. This construction ("not only X but also Y") also occurs in v. 27; Rom 5:3, 11; 8:23; 9:10; 2 Cor 7:7; 8:19; 1 Tim 5:13; and 2 Tim 4:8.

Ἐφέσου...τῆς Ἀσίας. Genitive of source modifying ἱκανὸν ὄχλον.

οὗτος. When the demonstrative is used to refer to someone who is present, it often carries a disparaging or contemptuous connotation (BDF §290.6.1; cf. 6:13, 14; 17:18).

πείσας. Aor act ptc masc nom sg πείθω (attendant circumstance).

μετέστησεν. Aor act ind 3rd sg μεθίστημι.

λέγων. Pres act ptc masc nom sg λέγω (means).

εἰσὶν. Pres act ind 3rd pl εἰμί.

θεοὶ. Predicate nominative.

οἱ γινόμενοι. Pres dep ptc masc nom pl γίνομαι (substantival nominative subject: οἱ διὰ χειρῶν γινόμενοι = "the created by hands ones").

19:27 οὐ μόνον δὲ τοῦτο κινδυνεύει ἡμῖν τὸ μέρος εἰς ἀπελεγμὸν ἐλθεῖν ἀλλὰ καὶ τὸ τῆς μεγάλης θεᾶς Ἀρτέμιδος ἱερὸν εἰς οὐθὲν λογισθῆναι, μέλλειν τε καὶ καθαιρεῖσθαι τῆς μεγαλειότητος αὐτῆς ἣν ὅλη ἡ Ἀσία καὶ ἡ οἰκουμένη σέβεται.

τοῦτο. It is unclear whether the demonstrative is anaphoric (with οὐ μόνον referring to what has just been stated in v. 26) or a modifier of τὸ μέρος.

κινδυνεύει. Pres act ind 3rd sg κινδυνεύω (impersonal).

ἡμῖν. Dative of (dis)advantage, modifying κινδυνεύει.

τὸ μέρος. Accusative subject of the infinitive (see 1:3 on αὐτὸν). Louw and Nida (57.199; cf. Bruce, 416) list this passage as one example where μέρος refers to "a particular kind of business activity or occupation."

ἀπελεγμὸν. This term refers to serious criticism (LN 33.416). The whole expression, εἰς ἀπελεγμὸν ἐλθεῖν (lit. "to come to serious criticism"), is idiomatic for "to be strongly criticized."

ἐλθεῖν. Aor act inf ἔρχομαι. The entire conjoined infinitival clause (τὸ μέρος εἰς ἀπελεγμὸν ἐλθεῖν . . . λογισθῆναι, μέλλειν . . . σέβεται) serves as the subject of κινδυνεύει.

ἱερὸν. Accusative subject of the infinitive λογισθῆναι (see 1:3 on αὐτὸν).

εἰς οὐθὲν. The prepositional phrase functions like a predicate modifier (see 4:11 on εἰς κεφαλὴν γωνίας; cf. 5:36).

οὐθὲν. A variant form of οὐδὲν (see Barrett's note on 15:9 [716]).

λογισθῆναι. Aor pass inf λογίζομαι (subject of κινδυνεύει; see above).

μέλλειν. Pres act inf μέλλω (subject of κινδυνεύει; see above). See 3:3 on μέλλοντας.

καθαιρεῖσθαι. Pres pass inf καθαιρέω (complementary).

ἣν ὅλη ἡ Ἀσία καὶ ἡ οἰκουμένη σέβεται. This "headless" relative clause ("*she* whom the whole of Asia and the world worship") is the syntactic subject of the infinitive (καθαιρεῖσθαι).

σέβεται. Pres mid ind 3rd sg σέβω. Singular verbs are sometimes used with compound subjects.

19:28 Ἀκούσαντες δὲ καὶ γενόμενοι πλήρεις θυμοῦ ἔκραζον λέγοντες, Μεγάλη ἡ Ἄρτεμις Ἐφεσίων.

Ἀκούσαντες. Aor act ptc masc nom pl ἀκούω (temporal).

γενόμενοι. Aor mid dep ptc masc nom pl γίνομαι. Strictly speaking, this participle must function in the same manner as the one to which it is conjoined (temporal: "After hearing this and becoming enraged, they shouted . . ."), though using an English rendering that implies an attendant circumstance is more natural.

πλήρεις. Predicate nominative.

θυμοῦ. Genitive of content. Codex D adds δραμόντες εἰς τὸ ἄμφοδον ("running into the street").

ἔκραζον. Impf act ind 3rd pl κράζω.

λέγοντες. Pres act ptc masc nom pl λέγω (attendant circumstance; redundant; see 1:6 on λέγοντες).

Μεγάλη. Predicate nominative.

19:29 καὶ ἐπλήσθη ἡ πόλις τῆς συγχύσεως, ὥρμησάν τε ὁμοθυμαδὸν εἰς τὸ θέατρον συναρπάσαντες Γάϊον καὶ Ἀρίσταρχον Μακεδόνας, συνεκδήμους Παύλου.

ἐπλήσθη. Aor pass ind 3rd sg πίμπλημι.

τῆς συγχύσεως. Genitive of content.

ὥρμησάν. Aor act ind 3rd pl ὁρμάω. The second accent comes from the enclitic τε (see 1:4 on ἠκούσατέ).

ὁμοθυμαδὸν. See 1:14.

τὸ θέατρον. The theater at Ephesus—the only one mentioned in the NT—probably held at least 24,000 people (see Barrett, 928).

συναρπάσαντες. Aor act ptc masc nom pl συναρπάζω (attendant circumstance).

Γάϊον. On the diaeresis over the *iota*, see 2:31 on προϊδὼν.

Μακεδόνας συνεκδήμους. The accusative plural nouns stand in apposition to Γάϊον καὶ Ἀρίσταρχον.

Παύλου. Genitive of association (Wallace 1996, 130).

19:30 Παύλου δὲ βουλομένου εἰσελθεῖν εἰς τὸν δῆμον οὐκ εἴων αὐτὸν οἱ μαθηταί·

Παύλου. Genitive subject (see 1:8 on ἐπελθόντος).

βουλομένου. Pres dep ptc masc gen sg βούλομαι. Genitive absolute (see 1:8 on ἐπελθόντος), temporal.

εἰσελθεῖν. Aor act inf εἰσέρχομαι (complementary).

τὸν δῆμον. "The citizen body of a Greek city" (Bruce, 418).

εἴων. Impf act ind 3rd pl ἐάω.

αὐτὸν. This is a good example of the rule that genitive absolute constructions in Koine Greek occur specifically in cases where the subject of the genitive participle is different from the *subject* of the main verb. The fact that Paul is referred to in the main clause with a pronoun (αὐτὸν) is irrelevant and should not be viewed as an indication of poor style (contra Barrett, 930).

19:31 τινὲς δὲ καὶ τῶν Ἀσιαρχῶν, ὄντες αὐτῷ φίλοι, πέμψαντες πρὸς αὐτὸν παρεκάλουν μὴ δοῦναι ἑαυτὸν εἰς τὸ θέατρον.

τινὲς. Substantival.

Ἀσιαρχῶν. Partitive genitive. "The Asiarchs were the leading men of the province of Asia . . . current and former holders of the high office in the league (κοινόν) of the cities of Asia" (Bruce, 418).

ὄντες. Pres act ptc masc nom pl εἰμί (attributive).

αὐτῷ. Dative of possession (used with εἰμί).

φίλοι. Predicate nominative.

πέμψαντες. Aor act ptc masc nom pl πέμπω (attendant circumstance).

παρεκάλουν. Impf act ind 3rd pl παρακαλέω.

μὴ δοῦναι ἑαυτὸν εἰς τὸ θέατρον. Although Barrett (930) argues that this expression does not mean more than "go into the theater," it probably connotes that Paul should not let himself "fall into the hands" of the people in the theater.

δοῦναι. Aor act inf δίδωμι (indirect discourse).

τὸ θέατρον. See v. 29.

19:32 ἄλλοι μὲν οὖν ἄλλο τι ἔκραζον· ἦν γὰρ ἡ ἐκκλησία συγκεχυμένη, καὶ οἱ πλείους οὐκ ᾔδεισαν τίνος ἕνεκα συνεληλύθεισαν.

ἄλλοι . . . ἄλλο. Robertson (1934, 747) notes that ἄλλος . . . ἄλλο was a common classical idiom meaning "one one thing, one another" (cf. 21:34).

ἔκραζον. Impf act ind 3rd pl κράζω.

μὲν οὖν. See 1:6.

ἦν. Impf ind 3rd sg εἰμί.

ἐκκλησία. One of several examples in Acts (also vv. 39, 40; cf. 7:38) where this term is used to refer to a secular gathering.

συγκεχυμένη. Prf pass ptc fem nom sg συγχέω (pluperfect periphrastic; see 1:17 on κατηριθμημένος).

οἱ πλείους οὐκ ᾔδεισαν τίνος ἕνεκα συνεληλύθεισαν. "The humor of this remark is unmistakable" (Bruce, 419).

πλείους. Substantival.
ᾔδεισαν. Plprf act ind 3rd pl οἶδα.
τίνος ἕνεκα. Lit. "on account of what?"
συνεληλύθεισαν. Plprf act ind 3rd pl συνέρχομαι.

19:33 ἐκ δὲ τοῦ ὄχλου συνεβίβασαν Ἀλέξανδρον, προβαλόντων αὐτὸν τῶν Ἰουδαίων· ὁ δὲ Ἀλέξανδρος κατασείσας τὴν χεῖρα ἤθελεν ἀπολογεῖσθαι τῷ δήμῳ.

ἐκ τοῦ ὄχλου. According to BDF (§164.2.6; cf. Bruce, 419) this is an example of a partitive genitive phrase that serves as the subject of the verb, with τινες being implicit. In light of the analogous construction in 21:16, this view is likely correct. Barrett (932), however, notes that the phrase could also be taken adverbially and thus indicate the place from which Alexander was "chosen." Thus, "they instructed Alexander *to come forward* out of the crowd."

συνεβίβασαν. Aor act ind 3rd pl συμβιβάζω. This verb generally means (1) "to cause something to be known as certain" (LN 28.46), (2) "to come to a solution or a decision, implying a process of putting together different aspects of related information" (30.82), (3) "to bring together into a unit, to unite" (63.5), or (4) "to advise by giving instructions" (33.298). While the first (9:22) and second (16:10) senses occur elsewhere in Acts, in the only other passage in the NT where the verb is used with a direct object, the fourth sense is in view (as here).

προβαλόντων. Aor act ptc masc gen pl προβάλλω. Genitive absolute (see 1:8 on ἐπελθόντος), temporal or purpose.

τῶν Ἰουδαίων. Genitive subject (see 1:8 on ἐπελθόντος).

κατασείσας. Aor act ptc masc nom sg κατασείω (result). Since the main verb (ἤθελεν) provides the cause for which the participle is the effect it may be appropriate to label the participle "result," even though it does not follow Wallace's criteria of being present tense and following the verb (1996, 638).

τὴν χεῖρα. Elsewhere, the verb κατασείω is used with a dative (instrumental) noun (see 12:17; 13:16; 21:40). The accusative direct object may indicate a slight difference in sense: "he waved his hand" rather than "he gestured/motioned with his hand."

ἤθελεν. Impf act ind 3rd sg θέλω.

ἀπολογεῖσθαι. Pres dep inf ἀπολογέομαι (complementary).

19:34 ἐπιγνόντες δὲ ὅτι Ἰουδαῖός ἐστιν φωνὴ ἐγένετο μία ἐκ πάντων ὡς ἐπὶ ὥρας δύο κραζόντων, Μεγάλη ἡ Ἄρτεμις Ἐφεσίων.

ἐπιγνόντες. Aor act ptc masc nom pl ἐπιγινώσκω (temporal). Strictly speaking, the participle is part of a nominative absolute clause since the actual subject of the participle is different than the subject of the main verb (ἐγένετο). The conceptual link between those who "knew" and those who shouted may account for the use of the nominative rather than the genitive absolute.

Ἰουδαῖός. Predicate nominative (of ἐστιν) with an unexpressed subject. The second accent comes from the enclitic ἐστιν (see 1:4 on ἠκούσατέ).

ἐστιν. Pres act ind 3rd sg εἰμί.

φωνὴ. Nominative subject or predicate nominative of an impersonal ἐγένετο.

ἐγένετο. Aor mid dep ind 3rd sg γίνομαι.

μία ἐκ πάντων. Although Fitzmyer (1998, 654) implies that μία ἐκ πάντων is an idiomatic expression meaning something like, "in unison," such a claim cannot account for the genitive case of κραζόντων. The numeral, therefore, must modify φωνὴ (so Barrett, 933), with πάντων being substantival and modified by κραζόντων.

ὡς ἐπὶ ὥρας δύο. See 13:31 on ἐπὶ ἡμέρας πλείους. The ὡς functions to make clear that an estimation of time is involved.

κραζόντων. Pres act ptc masc gen pl κράζω (attributive modifier of πάντων). Barrett (933) prefers the nominative κραζόντες (found in א and A) as the *lectio difficilior*, though it is unclear how a nominative participle could function here.

Μεγάλη. Predicate nominative.

19:35 καταστείλας δὲ ὁ γραμματεὺς τὸν ὄχλον φησίν, Ἄνδρες Ἐφέσιοι, τίς γάρ ἐστιν ἀνθρώπων ὃς οὐ γινώσκει τὴν Ἐφεσίων πόλιν νεωκόρον οὖσαν τῆς μεγάλης Ἀρτέμιδος καὶ τοῦ διοπετοῦς;

καταστείλας. Aor act ptc masc nom sg καταστέλλω (temporal).

γραμματεὺς. This term, which commonly refers to an expert in the Jewish law in the NT, here carries its secular sense of "a city official with responsibility for the records of a town or city and apparently certain responsibilities for maintaining law and order" (LN 37.94).

φησίν. Pres act ind 3rd sg φημί.

Ἄνδρες. See 1:11.

τίς γάρ ἐστιν ἀνθρώπων ὃς. This expression (lit. "For, who is there, among men who . . .?") carries a connotation of incredulity. The use of γάρ (emphatic: "after all") adds to this connotation.

ἐστιν. Pres act ind 3rd sg εἰμί.

ἀνθρώπων. Partitive genitive.

γινώσκει. Pres act ind 3rd sg γινώσκω.

νεωκόρον. Predicate accusative (see 1:22 on μάρτυρα).

οὖσαν. Pres act ptc fem acc sg εἰμί. The participle could either introduce indirect discourse with a verb of cognition (cf. 7:12; 24:10; codex D changes οὖσαν to εἶναι) or be attributive ("the city of Ephesus which is the keeper . . .").

διοπετοῦς. This term probably refers to a meteorite that was regarded as a sacred supernatural object (LN 2.48).

19:36 ἀναντιρρήτων οὖν ὄντων τούτων δέον ἐστὶν ὑμᾶς κατεσταλμένους ὑπάρχειν καὶ μηδὲν προπετὲς πράσσειν.

ἀναντιρρήτων. Predicate genitive adjective (see 1:16 on ὁδηγοῦ).

ὄντων. Pres act ptc neut gen pl εἰμί. Genitive absolute (see 1:8 on ἐπελθόντος), causal.

τούτων. Genitive substantival subject (see 1:8 on ἐπελθόντος).

δέον. Pres act ptc neut sg nom δεῖ (present periphrastic with the present tense of εἰμί). This is a rare example of the participial form of the verb δεῖ being used periphrastically (see 1 Pet 1:6 for the one other example in the NT).

ἐστὶν. Pres act ind 3rd sg εἰμί.

ὑμᾶς. Accusative subject of the infinitives (see 1:3 on αὐτὸν).

κατεσταλμένους. Prf pass ptc masc acc pl καταστέλλω (perfect periphrastic with ὑπάρχειν; see 2:13 on μεμεστωμένοι).

ὑπάρχειν. Pres act inf ὑπάρχω (complementary, modifying δέον).

πράσσειν. Pres act inf πράσσω (complementary, modifying δέον).

19:37 ἠγάγετε γὰρ τοὺς ἄνδρας τούτους οὔτε ἱεροσύλους οὔτε βλασφημοῦντας τὴν θεὸν ἡμῶν.

ἠγάγετε. Aor act ind 2nd pl ἄγω.

ἱεροσύλους. It is unclear whether the focus of the term is on desecration of temples (see LN 53.105) or robbing of temples (57.242).

βλασφημοῦντας. Pres act ptc acc masc pl βλασφημέω. The function of the participle depends on how the whole expression, οὔτε ἱεροσύλους οὔτε βλασφημοῦντας τὴν θεὸν ἡμῶν, is analyzed. If we posit an implicit ὄντας, then the adjective (ἱεροσύλους) and the participle become predicate accusatives (see 1:22 on μάρτυρα; cf. Wallace 1996, 619). This analysis may be necessary given the οὔτε . . . οὔτε construction. Alternatively, the adjective and participle may be viewed as standing in apposition to τοὺς ἄνδρας τούτους, and thus both be substantival.

τὴν θεὸν. The masculine form of θεός can be used with either a masculine or a feminine referent (cf. v. 27; Barrett, 926). The gender is made clear in this passage by the feminine article.

19:38 εἰ μὲν οὖν Δημήτριος καὶ οἱ σὺν αὐτῷ τεχνῖται ἔχουσι πρός τινα λόγον, ἀγοραῖοι ἄγονται καὶ ἀνθύπατοί εἰσιν, ἐγκαλείτωσαν ἀλλήλοις.

εἰ. Introduces a first class condition.

ἔχουσι. Pres act ind 3rd pl ἔχω.

λόγον. The expression, ἔχω λόγον appears to denote "to have a formal charge to file, to have a case."

ἀγοραῖοι. Lit. "the things pertaining to the market." According to BAGD (13) the expression, ἀγοραῖοι ἄγονται, means "the courts are in session."

ἄγονται. Pres pass ind 3rd pl ἄγω.

ἀνθύπατοί. Predicate nominative. The second accent comes from the enclitic εἰσιν (see 1:4 on ἠκούσατέ).

εἰσιν. Pres act ind 3rd pl εἰμί.

ἐγκαλείτωσαν. Pres act impv 3rd pl ἐγκαλέω.

ἀλλήλοις. Dative complement of ἐγκαλείτωσαν.

19:39 εἰ δέ τι περαιτέρω ἐπιζητεῖτε, ἐν τῇ ἐννόμῳ ἐκκλησίᾳ ἐπιλυθήσεται.

τι. Accusative object of ἐπιζητεῖτε.

περαιτέρω. As the harder reading (the adverb occurs only here in the NT), περαιτέρω ("further"; 𝔓[74] B 33 36 453 *al*) is preferable to περὶ ἑτέρων ("concerning other matters"; ℵ A D (E) Ψ *Byz* (vg) sy[h] co).

It is unlikely that the variation could have been accidental.

ἐπιζητεῖτε. Pres act ind 2nd pl ἐπιζητέω.

ἐκκλησία. See v. 32.

ἐπιλυθήσεται. Fut pass ind 3rd sg ἐπιλύω.

19:40–41 καὶ γὰρ κινδυνεύομεν ἐγκαλεῖσθαι στάσεως περὶ τῆς σήμερον, μηδενὸς αἰτίου ὑπάρχοντος περὶ οὗ [οὐ] δυνησόμεθα ἀποδοῦναι λόγον περὶ τῆς συστροφῆς ταύτης. καὶ ταῦτα εἰπὼν ἀπέλυσεν τὴν ἐκκλησίαν.

κινδυνεύομεν. Pres act ind 1st pl κινδυνεύω.

ἐγκαλεῖσθαι. Pres pass inf ἐγκαλέω (epexegetical).

στάσεως. The content of the accusation (ἐγκαλεῖσθαι) is expressed in the genitive case (Rogers and Rogers, 283; cf. Porter 1994, 97).

τῆς. The article functions as a nominalizer (see 1:3 on τὰ), changing the adverb into a noun.

μηδενὸς . . . ταύτης. Lit. "being no reason about which we are not able to give a word concerning this commotion." Barrett (940) notes that most scholars view this verse as corrupt or poorly edited and offers no viable resolution of the syntax. The problems relate, primarily, to the presence of the variant οὐ and the two prepositional phrases. Some scholars also debate the meaning of the term αἰτίου, which probably should be understood as "cause" or "source." It is likely that the "double negative" formed with οὐ and μηδενὸς reflected a colloquialism that, strictly speaking, was ungrammatical (and thus corrected by many scribes). The text could appropriately be rendered: "since there is no cause we can (readily) point to as an explanation for this commotion."

αἰτίου. Genitive subject (see 1:8 on ἐπελθόντος).

ὑπάρχοντος. Pres act ptc neut gen sg ὑπάρχω. Genitive absolute (see 1:8 on ἐπελθόντος), causal.

οὗ. The antecedent is αἰτίου.

[οὐ]. The manuscript evidence is fairly strong both with (א A B Ψ *Byz al*) and without ($\mathfrak{P}^{74}$ D E 33 *al*) the negative. The text with the negative is clearly the harder reading (see above).

δυνησόμεθα. Fut dep ind 1st pl δύναμαι.

ἀποδοῦναι. Aor act inf ἀποδίδωμι (complementary).

εἰπὼν. Aor act ptc masc nom sg λέγω (temporal).

ἀπέλυσεν. Aor act ind 3rd sg ἀπολύω.

Acts 20:1–6

[1]After the riot had ended, and Paul had sent for the disciples and encouraged (them), he said goodbye and then left for Macedonia. [2](Then,) After traveling through those regions and sharing many words of encouragement, he came into Greece [3]and stayed (there) for three months.

When there was a plot by the Jews against him as he was about to set sail for Syria, he decided to return (instead) through Macedonia. [4]Sopater the son of Pyrrhus, a Berean, accompanied him, as did Aristarchus and Secundus from Thessalonica, Gaius from Derbe, Timothy, and Tychicus and Trophimus, (two) Asians. [5]After going on ahead, these men waited for us in Troas. [6]After the days of unleavened bread, we sailed from Philippi and after five days caught up to them in Troas, where we stayed for seven days.

20:1 Μετὰ δὲ τὸ παύσασθαι τὸν θόρυβον μεταπεμψάμενος ὁ Παῦλος τοὺς μαθητὰς καὶ παρακαλέσας, ἀσπασάμενος ἐξῆλθεν πορεύεσθαι εἰς Μακεδονίαν.

παύσασθαι. Aor pass inf παύω. Used with μετά τό to indicate antecedent time (see 1:3 on μετὰ τὸ παθεῖν).

τὸν θόρυβον. Accusative subject of the infinitive (see 1:3 on αὐτὸν).

μεταπεμψάμενος. Aor mid ptc masc nom sg μεταπέμπω (attendant circumstance). The linking of the two participles (with καί) followed by a third participle that is not conjoined suggests that the first two introduce attendant circumstances of the temporal infinitive while the latter modifies ἐξῆλθεν.

παρακαλέσας. Aor act ptc masc nom sg παρακαλέω (attendant circumstance; see above).

ἀσπασάμενος. Aor mid dep ptc masc nom sg ἀσπάζομαι (temporal).

ἐξῆλθεν. Aor act ind 3rd sg ἐξέρχομαι.

πορεύεσθαι. Pres dep inf πορεύομαι (purpose; lit. "he left in order to go").

20:2 διελθὼν δὲ τὰ μέρη ἐκεῖνα καὶ παρακαλέσας αὐτοὺς λόγῳ πολλῷ ἦλθεν εἰς τὴν Ἑλλάδα

διελθὼν. Aor act ptc masc nom sg διέρχομαι (temporal).

παρακαλέσας. Aor act ptc masc nom sg παρακαλέω (temporal).

λόγῳ πολλῷ. Dative of instrument (lit. "with many words"). For an analogous use of this singular expression, see 15:32.

ἦλθεν. Aor act ind 3rd sg ἔρχομαι.

'Ελλάδα. Bruce (423) notes that this name is used as a synonym for (the province of) Achaia (see 18:12; 19:21).

20:3 ποιήσας τε μῆνας τρεῖς· γενομένης ἐπιβουλῆς αὐτῷ ὑπὸ τῶν 'Ιουδαίων μέλλοντι ἀνάγεσθαι εἰς τὴν Συρίαν, ἐγένετο γνώμης τοῦ ὑποστρέφειν διὰ Μακεδονίας.

ποιήσας . . . μῆνας τρεῖς. An idiom (lit. "making three months") meaning, "to stay for three months" (cf. 15:33; 18:23).

ποιήσας. Aor act ptc masc nom sg ποιέω (attendant circumstance). This participle modifies ἦλθεν in v. 2 while the following participle is part of the next clause.

μῆνας. Although the idiom as a whole indicates extent of time, the accusative noun serves as the direct object of the participle (contra Rogers and Rogers, 283).

γενομένης. Aor mid dep ptc fem gen sg γίνομαι. Genitive absolute (see 1:8 on ἐπελθόντος), temporal.

ἐπιβουλῆς. Genitive subject (see 1:8 on ἐπελθόντος).

αὐτῷ. Dative of (dis)advantage.

μέλλοντι. Pres act ptc masc dat sg μέλλω. Although a good English translation requires a temporal clause here, in terms of syntax, the participle is attributive (contra Rogers and Rogers, 283). On the force of μέλλω plus an infinitive, see 3:3 on μέλλοντας.

ἀνάγεσθαι. Pres pass inf ἀνάγω (complementary). On the meaning, see 13:13 on 'Αναχθέντες.

ἐγένετο γνώμης. Lit. "he was of a mind." The (descriptive) genitive noun functions like a predicate adjective.

ἐγένετο. Aor mid dep ind 3rd sg γίνομαι.

ὑποστρέφειν. Pres act inf ὑποστρέφω. The articular infinitive may be viewed as either epexegetical modifying γνώμης or as complementary if ἐγένετο γνώμης is viewed as a set idiomatic verb phrase (cf. 23.20 on ἐρωτῆσαι).

20:4 συνείπετο δὲ αὐτῷ Σώπατρος Πύρρου Βεροιαῖος, Θεσσαλονικέων δὲ Ἀρίσταρχος καὶ Σεκοῦνδος, καὶ Γάϊος Δερβαῖος καὶ Τιμόθεος, Ἀσιανοὶ δὲ Τυχικὸς καὶ Τρόφιμος.

συνείπετο. Impf dep ind 3rd sg συνέπομαι. Since the subject of this verb is, strictly speaking, only Σώπατρος Πύρρου Βεροιαῖος, the singular form is used.

δὲ. The use of this word to introduce what follows indicates that the subsequent names are part of a separate clause with an implicit συνείποντο (but see below for an alternative interpretation).

αὐτῷ. Verbs with a συν- prefix take a dative complement.

Πύρρου. Genitive of relationship.

Βεροιαῖος. Nominative in apposition to Σώπατρος.

Θεσσαλονικέων, Δερβαῖος. Genitives of place.

Ἀρίσταρχος, Σεκοῦνδος, Γάϊος, Τιμόθεος, Ἀσιανοὶ. Most renderings of this verse imply that these names are nominative subjects of an implicit συνείποντο (see above). It may be better, however, given the context of v. 5 and the use of οὗτοι there, to take these nominative names as the topic (see 2:22 on Ἰησοῦν τὸν Ναζωραῖον) of v. 5 that is picked up with the resumptive demonstrative pronoun: "Sopater . . . accompanied him. Aristarchus and Secundus from Thessalonica, Gaius from Derbe, Timothy, and Tychicus and Trophimus—Asians—these went on ahead." Otherwise, it is difficult to account for the use of οὗτοι.

Γάϊος. On the diaeresis over the *iota*, see 2:31 on προϊδὼν.

Τυχικὸς καὶ Τρόφιμος. Nominative in apposition to Ἀσιανοὶ.

20:5 οὗτοι δὲ προελθόντες ἔμενον ἡμᾶς ἐν Τρῳάδι,

οὗτοι. See v. 4.

προελθόντες. Aor act ptc masc nom pl προέρχομαι (temporal).

ἔμενον. Impf act ind 3rd pl μένω. Here the verb is transitive ("to wait for").

ἡμᾶς. Accusative direct object of ἔμενον. On the use of the plural, see 16:10 on ἐζητήσαμεν.

20:6 ἡμεῖς δὲ ἐξεπλεύσαμεν μετὰ τὰς ἡμέρας τῶν ἀζύμων ἀπὸ Φιλίππων, καὶ ἤλθομεν πρὸς αὐτοὺς εἰς τὴν Τρῳάδα ἄχρι ἡμερῶν πέντε, ὅπου διετρίψαμεν ἡμέρας ἑπτά.

ἐξεπλεύσαμεν. Aor act ind 1st pl ἐκπλέω.

ἤλθομεν πρὸς . . . ἄχρι. The verb with these prepositions (lit. "we came to . . . until") may form an idiomatic expression meaning, "to catch up to . . . *after*."

ἤλθομεν. Aor act ind 1st pl ἔρχομαι.

διετρίψαμεν. Aor act ind 1st pl διατρίβω.

ἡμέρας. Accusative indicating extent of time (see 7:20 on μῆνας).

Acts 20:7–12

[7]On the first day of the week, after we had gathered to break bread,
Paul addressed them, because he was about to leave the next day, and
he prolonged the conversation until midnight. [8]There were a number of
lamps in the upstairs room where we had gathered. [9]A young man named
Eutychus, who was sitting on the window sill and falling into a deep
sleep as Paul spoke on and on, was overcome by sleep and fell down
from the third story. When they picked him up he was dead. [10]But Paul
went down and knelt over him. Then, he put his arms around him and
said, "Don't worry! He's still alive!" [11]And so, after he had gone (back)
upstairs, broken bread and eaten, and then talked (with them) for a long
time—until dawn—he left. [12]Meanwhile, they brought the child (home)
alive and were extremely comforted.

20:7 Ἐν δὲ τῇ μιᾷ τῶν σαββάτων συνηγμένων ἡμῶν κλάσαι ἄρτον, ὁ Παῦλος διελέγετο αὐτοῖς μέλλων ἐξιέναι τῇ ἐπαύριον, παρέτεινέν τε τὸν λόγον μέχρι μεσονυκτίου.

μιᾷ. Substantival.

σαββάτων. Here, "week." On the use of the plural, see 13:14.

συνηγμένων. Prf pass ptc masc gen pl συνάγω. Genitive absolute (see 1:8 on ἐπελθόντος), temporal.

ἡμῶν. Genitive subject (see 1:8 on ἐπελθόντος).

κλάσαι. Aor act inf κλάω (purpose).

διελέγετο. Impf dep ind 3rd sg διαλέγομαι.

αὐτοῖς. Dative complement of διελέγετο.

μέλλων. Pres act ptc masc nom sg μέλλω (causal). On the force of μέλλω plus an infinitive, see 3:3 on μέλλοντας.

ἐξιέναι. Pres act inf ἔξειμι (complementary).

παρέτεινέν. Impf act ind 3rd sg παρατείνω. The second accent comes from the enclitic τε (see 1:4 on ἠκούσατέ).

20:8 ἦσαν δὲ λαμπάδες ἱκαναὶ ἐν τῷ ὑπερῴῳ οὗ ἦμεν συνηγμένοι.

ἦσαν. Impf ind 3rd pl εἰμί.

λαμπάδες. Predicate nominative.

οὗ. See 1:13.

ἦμεν. Impf ind 1st pl εἰμί.

συνηγμένοι. Prf pass ptc masc nom pl συνάγω (pluperfect periphrastic; see 1:17 on κατηριθμημένος).

20:9 καθεζόμενος δέ τις νεανίας ὀνόματι Εὔτυχος ἐπὶ τῆς θυρίδος, καταφερόμενος ὕπνῳ βαθεῖ διαλεγομένου τοῦ Παύλου ἐπὶ πλεῖον, κατενεχθεὶς ἀπὸ τοῦ ὕπνου ἔπεσεν ἀπὸ τοῦ τριστέγου κάτω καὶ ἤρθη νεκρός.

καθεζόμενος. Pres dep ptc masc nom sg καθέζομαι (attributive).

τις. See 8:9.

ὀνόματι. Dative of reference.

Εὔτυχος. Nominative in apposition to νεανίας.

καταφερόμενος. Pres pass ptc masc nom sg καταφέρω (attributive).

ὕπνῳ βαθεῖ. Page (212) argues that this expression indicates strong drowsiness rather than deep sleep. On the syntax, see below.

διαλεγομένου. Pres dep ptc masc gen sg διαλέγομαι. Genitive absolute (see 1:8 on ἐπελθόντος), temporal.

ἐπὶ πλεῖον. This idiom (lit. "upon much") indicates continuation of an action for "a relatively long duration of time" (LN 67.89).

τοῦ Παύλου. Genitive subject (see 1:8 on ἐπελθόντος).

κατενεχθεὶς. Aor pass ptc masc nom sg καταφέρω (attendant circumstance).

ἀπὸ τοῦ ὕπνου. Here, ἀπὸ introduces the agent of the passive verb. In the earlier expression, ὕπνῳ βαθεῖ, the dative case presumably marks the instrument of the participle.

ἔπεσεν. Aor act ind 3rd sg πίπτω.

τοῦ τριστέγου. Deer notes that τριστέγου refers to the third story of a building when the ground floor is counted as the first, as is done in the U.S. In Britain, however, where the ground floor is not counted, "second story" would be the appropriate translation.

ἤρθη νεκρός. Lit. "he was taken up dead."

ἤρθη. Aor pass ind 3rd sg αἴρω.

νεκρός. Used with the passive verb, the nominative noun functions as a complement in a subject-complement double nominative construction (cf. 4:36 on υἱὸς and 1:12 on Ἐλαιῶνος).

20:10 καταβὰς δὲ ὁ Παῦλος ἐπέπεσεν αὐτῷ καὶ συμπεριλαβὼν εἶπεν, Μὴ θορυβεῖσθε, ἡ γὰρ ψυχὴ αὐτοῦ ἐν αὐτῷ ἐστιν.

καταβὰς. Aor act ptc masc nom sg καταβαίνω (attendant circumstance).

ἐπέπεσεν. Aor act ind 3rd sg ἐπιπίπτω.

αὐτῷ. Dative complement of ἐπέπεσεν.

συμπεριλαβὼν. Aor act ptc masc nom sg συμπεριλαμβάνω (probably temporal). Although this participle could introduce an attendant circumstance of the verb εἶπεν, the use of καί to join the participle and main verb with what precedes suggests a slight temporal shift here.

εἶπεν. Aor act ind 3rd sg λέγω.

Μὴ θορυβεῖσθε. Although it is common to claim that μή with a present imperative indicates a command to stop action that is already in progress (cf. Rogers and Rogers, 284; Barrett, 955), McKay (1985) has clearly demonstrated the flaws of such a view. Moreover, Boyer (1987, 43) has argued that in 100 of the 174 occurrences of this construction in the NT there is no indication of time. Furthermore, there are clear examples, such as 22:10, where the construction is used to indicate that the addressee should undertake an action that has not yet begun. It is probably best, then, to acknowledge that (1) the state of the action must be derived from the context rather than the tense of the verb, (2) the tense of the verb indicates aspect rather than time with the aorist portraying the action as a whole and the present portraying it as a process (without concern for whether or not the action has already commenced), and (3) the choice of tense is probably governed by which material the writer/speaker wanted to highlight by using the present tense (cf. Porter 1989, 335–60).

θορυβεῖσθε. Pres pass impv 2nd pl θορυβέω.

ἐστιν. Pres act ind 3rd sg εἰμί.

20:11 ἀναβὰς δὲ καὶ κλάσας τὸν ἄρτον καὶ γευσάμενος ἐφ' ἱκανόν τε ὁμιλήσας ἄχρι αὐγῆς, οὕτως ἐξῆλθεν.

ἀναβὰς. Aor act ptc masc nom sg ἀναβαίνω (temporal). The referent of the participles is the same as the referent of the main verb: Paul.

κλάσας. Aor act ptc masc nom sg κλάω (temporal).

γευσάμενος. Aor mid dep ptc masc nom sg γεύομαι (temporal).

ἐφ' ἱκανόν. The position of the postpositive τε indicates that this temporal phrase goes with what follows.

ὁμιλήσας. Aor act ptc masc nom sg ὁμιλέω (temporal). This verb is used only in Luke-Acts (see also Luke 24:14, 15; Acts 24:26) in the NT.

οὕτως. The rare (classical) use of this adverb with a series of participles (elsewhere in the NT only in 27:17) probably serves to summarize the concluding events of this pericope and draw it to a close (cf. BDF §425.6).

ἐξῆλθεν. Aor act ind 3rd sg ἐξέρχομαι.

20:12 **ἤγαγον δὲ τὸν παῖδα ζῶντα καὶ παρεκλήθησαν οὐ μετρίως.**

ἤγαγον. Aor act ind 3rd pl ἄγω.

ζῶντα. Pres act ptc masc acc sg ζάω. The participle functions as the complement in an object-complement double accusative construction (see 1:3 on ζῶντα).

παρεκλήθησαν. Aor pass ind 3rd pl παρακαλέω.

οὐ μετρίως. Litotes (lit. "not moderately"; see 1:5 on οὐ μετὰ πολλὰς ταύτας ἡμέρας).

Acts 20:13–16

[13]We went on ahead to the boat and sailed to Assos where we were going to pick up Paul. For he had made such arrangements, since he himself was intending to go by land. [14]When he met us in Assos, we took him aboard and went to Mitylene. [15]After sailing from there, on the next day we arrived off Chios. On the following day we crossed over to Samos; and on the day after that we came to Miletus. [16]For Paul had decided to sail past Ephesus in order to avoid spending time in Asia. He was hurrying so that it might be possible for him to be in Jerusalem for the day of Pentecost.

20:13 **Ἡμεῖς δὲ προελθόντες ἐπὶ τὸ πλοῖον ἀνήχθημεν ἐπὶ τὴν Ἄσσον ἐκεῖθεν μέλλοντες ἀναλαμβάνειν τὸν Παῦλον· οὕτως γὰρ διατεταγμένος ἦν μέλλων αὐτὸς πεζεύειν.**

προελθόντες. Aor act ptc masc nom pl προέρχομαι (attendant circumstance).

ἐπί. On the directional use of ἐπί, cf. Mark 16:2.

ἀνήχθημεν. Aor pass ind 1st pl ἀνάγω. On the meaning, see 13:13.

μέλλοντες. Pres act ptc masc nom pl μέλλω (causal). On the force of μέλλω plus an infinitive, see 3:3 on μέλλοντας. Here the use of μέλλω with an infinitive may indicate future intention.

ἀναλαμβάνειν. Pres act inf ἀναλαμβάνω (complementary).

διατεταγμένος. Prf mid ptc masc nom sg διατάσσω. The participle could be part of a pluperfect periphrastic construction (with μέλλων then introducing the cause of his arrangements or an attendant circumstance), though in such constructions the participle typically follows the main verb (Boyer [1984, 172] identified 28 exceptions to this rule but did not list them). Alternatively, if the following participle were part of a periphrastic construction, διατεταγμένος would probably indicate the result of that construction. The choice has little effect on how the verse is translated.

ἦν. Impf ind 3rd sg εἰμί.

μέλλων. Pres act ptc masc nom sg μέλλω. On the syntax, see above on διατεταγμένος.

πεζεύειν. Pres act inf πεζεύω (complementary).

20:14 ὡς δὲ συνέβαλλεν ἡμῖν εἰς τὴν ᾿Ασσον, ἀναλαβόντες αὐτὸν ἤλθομεν εἰς Μιτυλήνην,

ὡς. Temporal (see 18:5).

συνέβαλλεν. Impf act ind 3rd sg συνβάλλω.

ἡμῖν. Verbs with a συν- prefix take a dative complement.

ἀναλαβόντες. Aor act ptc masc nom pl ἀναλαμβάνω (attendant circumstance or temporal).

ἤλθομεν. Aor act ind 1st pl ἔρχομαι.

20:15 κἀκεῖθεν ἀποπλεύσαντες τῇ ἐπιούσῃ κατηντήσαμεν ἄντικρυς Χίου, τῇ δὲ ἑτέρᾳ παρεβάλομεν εἰς Σάμον, τῇ δὲ ἐχομένῃ ἤλθομεν εἰς Μίλητον.

κἀκεῖθεν. A shortened form (crasis) of καὶ ἐκεῖθεν.

ἀποπλεύσαντες. Aor act ptc masc nom pl ἀποπλέω (attendant circumstance or temporal).

τῇ ἐπιούσῃ. Pres act ptc fem dat sg ἔπειμι (substantival). A shortened form of τῇ ἐπιούσῃ ἡμέρᾳ (cf. 7:26).

κατηντήσαμεν. Aor act ind 1st pl καταντάω.

ἄντικρυς. Only here in the NT ("a position directly opposite and implying some space between"; LN 83.44).

παρεβάλομεν. Aor act ind 1st pl παραβάλλω. According to Louw and Nida (54.12), this verb (a technical, nautical term) means "to sail up to or near."

τῇ δὲ ἐχομένῃ. Many manuscripts (D 181 614 1678 *Byz* it[d, gig] syr[p, h] *pc*) add the phrase καὶ μείναντες ἐν Τρωγυλλίῳ ("and remaining in Trogyllium") before the dative noun phrase.

τῇ . . . ἐχομένῃ. Pres mid ptc fem dat sg ἔχω. The dative substantival participle is used as a shortened form of τῇ ἐχομένῃ ἡμέρᾳ (see 21:26; cf. Luke 13:33).

ἤλθομεν. Aor act ind 1st pl ἔρχομαι.

20:16 κεκρίκει γὰρ ὁ Παῦλος παραπλεῦσαι τὴν Ἔφεσον, ὅπως μὴ γένηται αὐτῷ χρονοτριβῆσαι ἐν τῇ Ἀσίᾳ· ἔσπευδεν γὰρ εἰ δυνατὸν εἴη αὐτῷ τὴν ἡμέραν τῆς πεντηκοστῆς γενέσθαι εἰς Ἱεροσόλυμα.

κεκρίκει. Plprf act ind 3rd sg κρίνω. On the form, see 4:22 on γεγόνει.

παραπλεῦσαι. Aor act inf παραπλέω (indirect discourse with a verb of cognition).

τὴν Ἔφεσον. Accusative complement of παραπλεῦσαι.

ὅπως . . . Ἀσίᾳ. Lit. "in order that spending time in Asia not happen to him."

γένηται. Aor mid dep subj 3rd sg γίνομαι. The subjunctive is used with ὅπως to indicate purpose.

χρονοτριβῆσαι. Aor act inf χρονοτριβέω. The infinitival clause, χρονοτριβῆσαι ἐν τῇ Ἀσίᾳ, serves as the subject of γένηται (see also 9:32 on κατελθεῖν).

ἔσπευδεν. Impf act ind 3rd sg σπεύδω.

εἰ δυνατὸν εἴη αὐτῷ . . . γενέσθαι εἰς Ἱεροσόλυμα. It is probably best to take the infinitival clause, γενέσθαι εἰς Ἱεροσόλυμα, as the subject of εἴη (see also 9:32 on κατελθεῖν). The optative verb is used with εἰ in the protasis of a fourth class condition to express a remotely possible condition (lit. "if being in Jerusalem might somehow be possible for him."

εἴη. Pres act opt 3rd sg εἰμί.

αὐτῷ. Dative of reference or advantage.
τὴν ἡμέραν. Accusative indicating a point in time.
γενέσθαι. Aor mid dep inf γίνομαι (see above).

Acts 20:17–38

[17]From Miletus he sent (word) to Ephesus and summoned the elders of the church. [18]When they reached him he said to them, "You yourselves know how I lived during the whole time I was with you, from the first day that I set foot in Asia. [19](You know) how I served the Lord with great humility and sorrow (in the midst of) the trials that happened to me because of the plots of the Jews, [20]and how I held back nothing that was useful, lest I fail to announce to you and teach you both in public and from house to house, [21](and how) I testified to both Jews and Greeks about repentance toward God and faith in our Lord Jesus.

[22]And now, since I have been bound by the Spirit, I am going to Jerusalem even though I do not know what will happen to me there. [23](I only know) that the Holy Spirit, in every city, keeps testifying to me and saying that prison and suffering await me. [24]But on no account, do I regard my life as precious for myself so that I might finish my race and the ministry that I received from the Lord Jesus, to testify to the good news of the God's grace.

[25]And now I know that none of you among whom I traveled, preaching about the kingdom, will see my face again! [26]Therefore, I declare to you on this very day that I am innocent of the blood of all people. [27]For I did not hold back (anything) lest I fail to announce to you the whole plan of God.

[28]Guard yourselves and all the flock among whom the Holy Spirit has placed you as overseers to guide the church of God, which he acquired with his own blood. [29]I know that fierce wolves will come to you after my departure and will not spare the flock. [30]Even from among you yourselves men will rise up who will say misleading things in order to draw away disciples after themselves. [31]Therefore, be alert and remember that for three years, night and day, I never stopped warning each one of you with deep concern. [32]And now, I entrust you to God and to the message about his grace, which is able to build you up and give you an inheritance among all those who have been sanctified.

[33]I never wanted anyone's silver or gold or clothing. [34]You yourselves know that these hands (of mine) took care of my needs and those who were with me. [35]In everything (I did), I showed you that in this way, by

working hard, it is necessary to help the weak, and to remember the words of the Lord Jesus. (Remember) that he himself said, 'It is more blessed to give than to receive.'"

[36]After he had said these things he knelt with all of them and prayed.
[37]There was a lot of weeping among all of them and they began embracing Paul and kissing him. [38]They were upset the most by his statement that they were not going to see him again. Then they escorted him to the ship.

20:17 Ἀπὸ δὲ τῆς Μιλήτου πέμψας εἰς Ἔφεσον μετεκαλέσατο τοὺς πρεσβυτέρους τῆς ἐκκλησίας.

πέμψας. Aor act ptc masc nom sg πέμπω (attendant circumstance).

μετεκαλέσατο. Aor mid ind 3rd sg μετακαλέω.

20:18 ὡς δὲ παρεγένοντο πρὸς αὐτὸν εἶπεν αὐτοῖς, Ὑμεῖς ἐπίστασθε, ἀπὸ πρώτης ἡμέρας ἀφ' ἧς ἐπέβην εἰς τὴν Ἀσίαν πῶς μεθ' ὑμῶν τὸν πάντα χρόνον ἐγενόμην,

ὡς. Temporal (see 18:5).

παρεγένοντο. Aor mid dep 3rd pl παραγίνομαι.

εἶπεν. Aor act ind 3rd sg λέγω.

Ὑμεῖς. The explicit subject pronoun should probably be taken as intensive.

ἐπίστασθε. Pres dep ind 2nd pl ἐπίσταμαι.

ἐπέβην. Aor act ind 1st sg ἐπιβαίνω.

πῶς. Introduces the clausal complement of ἐπίστασθε. As with ὡς (see 10:38), the use of πῶς rather than ὅτι may suggest a focus on manner or point to general rather than specific knowledge (see also 9:27 on πῶς . . . πῶς). Here, given the participles that follow, the focus is almost certainly on manner.

τὸν πάντα χρόνον. Accusative indicating extent of time (see 7:20 on μῆνας).

ἐγενόμην. Aor mid dep ind 1st sg γίνομαι.

20:19 δουλεύων τῷ κυρίῳ μετὰ πάσης ταπεινοφροσύνης καὶ δακρύων καὶ πειρασμῶν τῶν συμβάντων μοι ἐν ταῖς ἐπιβουλαῖς τῶν Ἰουδαίων,

δουλεύων. Pres act ptc masc nom sg δουλεύω. The syntax of the participle is difficult to determine. It could be taken as a temporal modifier of ἐγενόμην ("as I served the Lord . . ."). It is probably better, however, to take the participle as standing in apposition to πῶς and thus epexegetical in nature: "You know how I lived, namely, how I served the Lord . . ." As such, the participle provides the answer to the indirect rhetorical question introduced by πῶς.

συμβάντων. Aor act ptc masc gen pl συμβαίνω. The participle should probably be taken as an articular attributive modifier of the anarthrous (see 3:3 on Πέτρον καὶ Ἰωάννην) noun preceding it.

ἐν ταῖς ἐπιβουλαῖς. Causal.

20:20 ὡς οὐδὲν ὑπεστειλάμην τῶν συμφερόντων τοῦ μὴ ἀναγγεῖλαι ὑμῖν καὶ διδάξαι ὑμᾶς δημοσίᾳ καὶ κατ' οἴκους,

ὡς. Introduces a second clausal complement of ἐπίστασθε (v. 18). See 10:38 on ὡς (cf. v. 18 on πῶς).

ὑπεστειλάμην. Aor mid ind 1st sg ὑποστέλλω.

τῶν συμφερόντων. Pres act ptc neut gen pl συμφέρω (substantival). Partitive genitive.

τοῦ μὴ ἀναγγεῖλαι. Aor act inf ἀναγγέλλω (purpose; see 3:2 on τοῦ αἰτεῖν).

(τοῦ μὴ) διδάξαι. Aor act inf διδάσκω (purpose; see 3:2 on τοῦ αἰτεῖν). See also above.

κατ' οἴκους. Distributive (see 2:46 on καθ' ἡμέραν). The use of the plural (only here) may make the expression more emphatic (cf. 5:42).

20:21 διαμαρτυρόμενος Ἰουδαίοις τε καὶ Ἕλλησιν τὴν εἰς θεὸν μετάνοιαν καὶ πίστιν εἰς τὸν κύριον ἡμῶν Ἰησοῦν.

διαμαρτυρόμενος. Pres dep ptc masc nom sg διαμαρτύρομαι (epexegetical to ὡς, v. 20; cf. v. 19 on δουλεύων).

τὴν . . . μετάνοιαν καὶ πίστιν. Wallace (1996, 289) argues that both Luke's theology of faith and the common usage of impersonal TSKS (article-substantive-καί-substantive) constructions to identify the first substantive as a subset of the second, support the view that this phrase portrays repentance as an integral component of saving faith.

20:22 καὶ νῦν ἰδοὺ δεδεμένος ἐγὼ τῷ πνεύματι πορεύομαι εἰς Ἰερουσαλὴμ τὰ ἐν αὐτῇ συναντήσοντά μοι μὴ εἰδώς,

καὶ νῦν. See 4:29 on καὶ τὰ νῦν. In this speech, there are several climactic statements (see vv. 25, 32).

ἰδού. See 1:10.

δεδεμένος ἐγὼ τῷ πνεύματι. This expression (lit. "I bound in the Spirit/spirit") could simply indicate an inner compulsion, but more likely indicates that the Spirit (τῷ πνεύματι, dative of instrument/agent) has compelled Paul to go to Jerusalem.

δεδεμένος. Prf pass ptc masc nom sg δέω. Structurally the participle could be either attributive or adverbial (causal or manner).

πορεύομαι. Pres dep ind 1st sg πορεύομαι.

τὰ συναντήσοντά. Fut act ptc neut acc pl συναντάω (substantival). Wallace (1996, 567) notes that this is one of only 12 future participles in the NT. The second accent comes from the enclitic μοι (see 1:4 on ἠκούσατέ).

εἰδώς. Prf act ptc masc nom sg οἶδα (concessive).

20:23 πλὴν ὅτι τὸ πνεῦμα τὸ ἅγιον κατὰ πόλιν διαμαρτύρεταί μοι λέγον ὅτι δεσμὰ καὶ θλίψεις με μένουσιν.

ὅτι. Introduces a clausal complement of an implicit εἰδώς.

κατὰ πόλιν. Distributive (see 2:46 on καθ' ἡμέραν).

διαμαρτύρεταί. Pres dep ind 3rd sg διαμαρτύρομαι. The second accent comes from the enclitic μοι (see 1:4 on ἠκούσατέ).

μοι. Dative complement of διαμαρτύρεταί.

λέγον. Pres act ptc neut nom sg λέγω (attendant circumstance; redundant, see 1:6 on λέγοντες).

ὅτι. Introduces a clausal complement (indirect discourse) of λέγον.

δεσμά. See 16:26.

μένουσιν. Pres act ind 3rd pl μένω.

20:24 ἀλλ' οὐδενὸς λόγου ποιοῦμαι τὴν ψυχὴν τιμίαν ἐμαυτῷ ὡς τελειῶσαι τὸν δρόμον μου καὶ τὴν διακονίαν ἣν ἔλαβον παρὰ τοῦ κυρίου Ἰησοῦ, διαμαρτύρασθαι τὸ εὐαγγέλιον τῆς χάριτος τοῦ θεοῦ.

οὐδενὸς λόγου. The precise sense and/or function of this phrase is difficult to determine. It is unlikely that it modifies τιμίαν (contra BAGD, 477). More likely, it functions as an adverbial expression (genitive of respect) meaning something like "on no account."

ποιοῦμαι. Pres mid ind 1st sg ποιέω.

τιμίαν. Accusative complement in a double accusative object complement construction (cf 1:3 on ζῶντα).

ἐμαυτῷ. Dative of advantage.

ὡς τελειῶσαι. The rare use of ὡς with an infinitive (the "harder" and better supported reading) denotes purpose as many scribes (E 33 323 614 945 1739 2495 *al*) indicated by replacing the adverb with the more common ὥστε (cf. BADG, 898; Luke 9:52; 3 Macc 1:2; 4 Macc 14:1) or του (D it[gig]). For more on the textual issues in this verse, see the excellent summary by Barrett, 971–72.

τελειῶσαι. Aor act inf τελειόω (see above).

ἔλαβον. Aor act ind 1st sg λαμβάνω.

διαμαρτύρασθαι. Aor mid dep inf διαμαρτύρομαι (epexegetical to τὴν διακονίαν).

χάριτος. Objective genitive.

20:25 Καὶ νῦν ἰδοὺ ἐγὼ οἶδα ὅτι οὐκέτι ὄψεσθε τὸ πρόσωπόν μου ὑμεῖς πάντες ἐν οἷς διῆλθον κηρύσσων τὴν βασιλείαν.

καὶ νῦν. See 4:29 on καὶ τὰ νῦν.

ἰδοὺ. See 1:10.

οἶδα. Prf act ind 1st sg οἶδα.

ὅτι. Introduces a clausal complement of οἶδα.

ὄψεσθε. Fut mid dep ind 2nd pl ὁράω.

τὸ πρόσωπόν μου. Synecdoche (see 1:22 on τοῦ βαπτίσματος Ἰωάννου) for "me."

ὑμεῖς πάντες ἐν οἷς διῆλθον κηρύσσων τὴν βασιλείαν. This entire construction serves as the subject of ὄψεσθε.

διῆλθον. Aor act ind 1st sg διέρχομαι.

κηρύσσων. Pres act ptc masc nom sg κηρύσσω (manner).

τὴν βασιλείαν. See 1:3 on τῆς βασιλείας τοῦ θεοῦ.

20:26 διότι μαρτύρομαι ὑμῖν ἐν τῇ σήμερον ἡμέρᾳ ὅτι καθαρός εἰμι ἀπὸ τοῦ αἵματος πάντων·

μαρτύρομαι. Pres dep ind 1st sg μαρτύρομαι.

ἐν τῇ σήμερον ἡμέρᾳ. A highly intensive expression: "this very day."

ὅτι. Introduces a clausal complement (indirect discourse) of μαρτύρομαι.

καθαρός. Predicate adjective.

εἰμι. Pres act ind 1st sg εἰμί.

20:27 οὐ γὰρ ὑπεστειλάμην τοῦ μὴ ἀναγγεῖλαι πᾶσαν τὴν βουλὴν τοῦ θεοῦ ὑμῖν.

ὑπεστειλάμην. Aor mid ind 1st sg ὑποστέλλω.

τοῦ μὴ ἀναγγεῖλαι. Aor act inf ἀναγγέλλω (purpose; see 3:2 on τοῦ αἰτεῖν).

20:28 προσέχετε ἑαυτοῖς καὶ παντὶ τῷ ποιμνίῳ, ἐν ᾧ ὑμᾶς τὸ πνεῦμα τὸ ἅγιον ἔθετο ἐπισκόπους ποιμαίνειν τὴν ἐκκλησίαν τοῦ θεοῦ, ἣν περιεποιήσατο διὰ τοῦ αἵματος τοῦ ἰδίου.

προσέχετε ἑαυτοῖς. See 5:35.

προσέχετε. Pres act impv 2nd pl προσέχω.

ἔθετο. Aor mid ind 3rd sg τίθημι.

ἐπισκόπους. The complement in an object-complement double accusative construction (see 1:3 on ζῶντα).

ποιμαίνειν. Pres act inf ποιμαίνω (purpose).

περιεποιήσατο. Aor mid ind 3rd sg περιποιέω. According to Louw and Nida (57.61), this verb means "to acquire possession of something, with the probable component of considerable effort."

τοῦ αἵματος τοῦ ἰδίου. In this phrase, τοῦ ἰδίου could indicate "his own blood" or "the blood of his own *Son.*" On the face of it, the former appears to be more natural, though theologically imprecise. Bruce (434; see also Omanson), on the other hand, argues that ἴδιος is used absolutely in the papyri as "a term of endearment to near relations." While the Byzantine textual tradition changes the word order (τοῦ ἰδίου αἵματος) to make it unambiguous, it also changes the referent of the expression from θεοῦ το κυρίου.

20:29 ἐγὼ οἶδα ὅτι εἰσελεύσονται μετὰ τὴν ἄφιξίν μου λύκοι βαρεῖς εἰς ὑμᾶς μὴ φειδόμενοι τοῦ ποιμνίου,

οἶδα. Prf act ind 1st sg οἶδα.

ὅτι. Introduces a clausal complement of οἶδα.

εἰσελεύσονται. Fut mid dep ind 3rd pl εἰσέρχομαι.

εἰς. See 1:8 on ἐφ᾽ ὑμᾶς.

φειδόμενοι. Pres dep ptc masc nom pl φείδομαι (attendant circumstance).

τοῦ ποιμνίου. Genitive object of φειδόμενοι.

20:30 καὶ ἐξ ὑμῶν αὐτῶν ἀναστήσονται ἄνδρες λαλοῦντες διεστραμμένα τοῦ ἀποσπᾶν τοὺς μαθητὰς ὀπίσω αὐτῶν.

αὐτῶν. Intensive.

ἀναστήσονται. Fut mid ind 3rd pl ἀνίστημι.

λαλοῦντες. Pres act ptc masc nom pl λαλέω (attributive or attendant circumstance).

διεστραμμένα. Prf pass ptc neut acc pl διαστρέφω (substantival direct object of λαλοῦντες). Barrett (979) notes that this expression refers to heretical teaching.

ἀποσπᾶν. Pres act inf ἀποστάω (purpose; see 3:2 on τοῦ αἰτεῖν).

20:31 διὸ γρηγορεῖτε μνημονεύοντες ὅτι τριετίαν νύκτα καὶ ἡμέραν οὐκ ἐπαυσάμην μετὰ δακρύων νουθετῶν ἕνα ἕκαστον.

γρηγορεῖτε. Pres act impv 2nd pl γρηγορέω.

μνημονεύοντες. Pres act ptc masc nom pl μνημονεύω (attendant circumstance).

ὅτι. Introduces a clausal complement of μνημονεύοντες.

τριετίαν. Accusative indicating extent of time (see 7:20 on μῆνας).

νύκτα καὶ ἡμέραν. Accusative in apposition to τριετίαν. On the author's use of hyperbole (cf. 1:18 on πάντα).

παυσάμην. Aor mid ind 1st sg παύω.

μετὰ δακρύων. Although formally the prepositional phrase indicates that tears accompanied Paul's actions, functionally it indicates the manner in which Paul warned or instructed them (see below).

νουθετῶν. Pres act ptc masc nom sg νουθετέω (complementary; see Wallace 1996, 646). It is unclear whether the focus is on instruction (LN 33.231) or warning of danger (33.424). The mention of tears may fit better with the latter and probably serves to emphasize the gravity of the "warning." Presumably, Paul was very concerned, even when he was with them, that false teachers would inevitably attempt to lead the Ephesians astray.

20:32 καὶ τὰ νῦν παρατίθεμαι ὑμᾶς τῷ θεῷ καὶ τῷ λόγῳ τῆς χάριτος αὐτοῦ, τῷ δυναμένῳ οἰκοδομῆσαι καὶ δοῦναι τὴν κληρονομίαν ἐν τοῖς ἡγιασμένοις πᾶσιν.

καὶ τὰ νῦν. See 4:29.

παρατίθεμαι. Pres mid ind 1st sg παρατίθημι.

τῷ λόγῳ τῆς χάριτος αὐτοῦ. This expression could conceivably be taken as a hendiadys: "his gracious message," in which case genitive χάριτος would be attributive and the genitive pronoun would modify τῷ λόγῳ rather than τῆς χάριτος.

τῷ δυναμένῳ. Pres dep ptc masc dat sg δύναμαι. The participle could be taken as an attributive modifier of τῷ λόγῳ or as a substantival dative in apposition to τῷ θεῷ ("to the one who is able").

οἰκοδομῆσαι. Aor act inf οικοδομέω (complementary).

δοῦναι. Aor act inf δίδωμι (complementary).

τοῖς ἡγιασμένοις. Prf pass ptc masc dat pl ἁγιάζω (substantival).

20:33 ἀργυρίου ἢ χρυσίου ἢ ἱματισμοῦ οὐδενὸς ἐπεθύμησα·

ἀργυρίου . . . χρυσίου . . . ἱματισμοῦ. Genitive objects (common with verbs of emotion; Robertson 1934, 508) of ἐπεθύμησα. The fronting (see 3:13 on ὑμεῖς) of the direct objects probably makes the statement more emphatic.

οὐδενός. Substantival possessive genitive.

ἐπεθύμησα. Aor act ind 1st sg ἐπιθυμέω.

20:34 αὐτοὶ γινώσκετε ὅτι ταῖς χρείαις μου καὶ τοῖς οὖσιν μετ' ἐμοῦ ὑπηρέτησαν αἱ χεῖρες αὗται.

αὐτοί. Intensive.

γινώσκετε. Pres act ind 2nd pl γινώσκω.

ὅτι. Introduces a clausal complement of γινώσκετε.

ταῖς χρείαις . . . τοῖς οὖσιν. Dative complements of ὑπηρέτησαν.

τοῖς οὖσιν. Pres act ptc masc dat pl εἰμί (substantival).

ὑπηρέτησαν. Aor act ind 3rd pl ὑπηρετέω.

αἱ χεῖρες αὗται. Synecdoche (see 1:22 on τοῦ βαπτίσματος Ἰωάννου) for "I, myself."

20:35 πάντα ὑπέδειξα ὑμῖν ὅτι οὕτως κοπιῶντας δεῖ ἀντιλαμβάνεσθαι τῶν ἀσθενούντων, μνημονεύειν τε τῶν λόγων τοῦ κυρίου Ἰησοῦ ὅτι αὐτὸς εἶπεν, Μακάριόν ἐστιν μᾶλλον διδόναι ἢ λαμβάνειν.

πάντα. Accusative of respect or accusative direct object (with an epexegetical ὅτι).

ὑπέδειξα. Aor act ind 1st sg ὑποδείκνυμι.

ὅτι. Introduces a clausal complement of ὑπέδειξα or epexegetical (see above).

κοπιῶντας. Pres act ptc masc acc pl κοπιάω (means).

δεῖ. Pres act ind 3rd sg δεῖ (impersonal).

ἀντιλαμβάνεσθαι. Pres dep inf ἀντιλαμβάνομαι (complementary; see 1:16 on ἔδει).

τῶν ἀσθενούντων. Pres act ptc masc gen pl ἀσθενέω (substantival).

μνημονεύειν. Pres act inf μνημονεύω (complementary to δεῖ).

τε. The use of τε rather than καί probably highlights the "close affinity" between the two infinitival clauses, i.e., the second infinitive adds something similar to the previous infinitive (cf. Levinsohn 1987, 122, 124).

τῶν λόγων. Genitive object of μνημονεύειν.

ὅτι. The ὅτι clause could stand in apposition to τῶν λόγων τοῦ κυρίου—and thus serve as a clausal complement of μνημονεύειν—or less likely, be causal: "It is necessary to remember the word of the Lord because he said."

αὐτὸς. Intensive.

εἶπεν. Aor act ind 3rd sg λέγω.

Μακάριόν. Predicate adjective. The second accent comes from the enclitic ἐστιν (see 1:4 on ἠκούσατέ).

ἐστιν. Pres act ind 3rd sg εἰμί.

μᾶλλον . . . ἢ. This construction is used to highlight a contrast in quality between two propositions.

διδόναι. Pres act inf δίδωμι (subject).

λαμβάνειν. Pres act inf λαμβάνω (subject).

20:36 Καὶ ταῦτα εἰπὼν θεὶς τὰ γόνατα αὐτοῦ σὺν πᾶσιν αὐτοῖς προσηύξατο.

εἰπών. Aor act ptc masc nom sg λέγω (temporal).
θεὶς τὰ γόνατα. See 7:60.
θείς. Aor act ptc masc nom sg τίθημι (attendant circumstance).
προσηύξατο. Aor mid dep ind 3rd sg προσεύχομαι.

20:37 ἱκανὸς δὲ κλαυθμὸς ἐγένετο πάντων καὶ ἐπιπεσόντες ἐπὶ τὸν τράχηλον τοῦ Παύλου κατεφίλουν αὐτόν,

κλαυθμός. Predicate adjective.
ἐγένετο. Aor mid dep ind 3rd sg γίνομαι (impersonal).
πάντων. Substantival genitive of source.
ἐπιπεσόντες . . . Παύλου. Lit. "falling on Paul's neck."
ἐπιπεσόντες. Aor act ptc masc nom pl ἐπιπίπτω (attendant circumstance or temporal).
κατεφίλουν. Impf act ind 3rd pl καταφιλέω.

20:38 ὀδυνώμενοι μάλιστα ἐπὶ τῷ λόγῳ ᾧ εἰρήκει ὅτι οὐκέτι μέλλουσιν τὸ πρόσωπον αὐτοῦ θεωρεῖν. προέπεμπον δὲ αὐτὸν εἰς τὸ πλοῖον.

ὀδυνώμενοι. Pres pass ptc masc nom pl ὀδυνάω (attendant circumstance).
τῷ λόγῳ ᾧ εἰρήκει. Lit. "the word that he had said."
ᾧ. Dative by attraction (see 1:1 on ὧν) to τῷ λόγῳ (it normally would have been accusative as the object of εἰρήκει).
εἰρήκει. Plprf act ind 3rd sg λέγω.
ὅτι. The ὅτι clause is epexegetical to τῷ λόγῳ.
μέλλουσιν. Pres act ind 3rd pl μέλλω. See 3:3 on μέλλοντας.
τὸ πρόσωπον αὐτοῦ. Synecdoche (see 1:22 on τοῦ βαπτίσματος Ἰωάννου) for "him."
θεωρεῖν. Pres act inf θεωρέω (complementary).
προέπεμπον. Impf act ind 3rd pl προπέμπω.

Acts 21:1–6

[1]When we set sail, after leaving them, we followed a straight course and came to Cos. On the next day (we sailed) to Rhodes, and from there (we sailed) to Patara. [2]After finding a ship that was crossing to Phoenicia,

we went aboard and set sail. [3]When we had sighted Cyprus and passed it on our left, we sailed on to Syria and landed at Tyre, because the ship was going to unload its cargo there.

[4]After we had located (some) disciples, we stayed there for seven days. They kept telling Paul through the Spirit not to go to Jerusalem. [5]When we had finished our time (there), we left and went on our way. All of them, along with (their) wives and children, escorted us until we were outside the city. After we had knelt upon the shore and prayed, [6]we said goodbye to one another. Then we boarded the ship and they returned to their own homes.

21:1 Ὡς δὲ ἐγένετο ἀναχθῆναι ἡμᾶς ἀποσπασθέντας ἀπ' αὐτῶν, εὐθυδρομήσαντες ἤλθομεν εἰς τὴν Κῶ, τῇ δὲ ἑξῆς εἰς τὴν Ῥόδον κἀκεῖθεν εἰς Πάταρα,

Ὡς. Temporal (see 18:5).

ἐγένετο. Aor mid dep ind 3rd sg γίνομαι. On the use of ἐγένετο with an infinitive and a temporal expression, see 4:5.

ἀναχθῆναι. Aor pass inf ἀνάγω. The infinitival clause, ἀναχθῆναι ἡμᾶς ἀποσπασθέντας ἀπ' αὐτῶν, functions as the subject of ἐγένετο (see also 9:32 on κατελθεῖν). On the meaning of the passive verb, see 13:13.

ἡμᾶς. Accusative subject of the infinitive (see 1:3 on αὐτὸν).

ἀποσπασθέντας. Aor pass ptc masc acc pl ἀποσπάω (temporal modifier of the infinitive). Accusative in agreement with the subject of the infinitive.

ἀπ'. See 1:8 on ἐφ' ὑμᾶς.

εὐθυδρομήσαντες. Aor act ptc masc nom pl εὐθυδρομέω (attendant circumstance of ἤλθομεν).

ἤλθομεν. Aor act ind 1st pl ἔρχομαι.

τῇ . . . ἑξῆς. Dative of time. The article functions as a nominalizer (see 1:3 on τὰ), changing the adverb into a substantive. This expression is used only by Luke in the NT (25:17; 27:18; Luke 7:11; 9:37).

κἀκεῖθεν. A shortened form (crasis) of καὶ ἐκεῖθεν.

21:2 καὶ εὑρόντες πλοῖον διαπερῶν εἰς Φοινίκην ἐπιβάντες ἀνήχθημεν.

εὑρόντες. Aor act ptc masc nom pl εὑρίσκω (temporal).

διαπερῶν. Pres act ptc neut acc sg διαπεράω (attributive).

ἐπιβάντες. Aor act ptc masc nom pl ἐπιβαίνω (attendant circumstance).

ἀνήχθημεν. Aor pass ind 1st pl ἀνάγω. On the meaning of the passive verb, see 13:13.

21:3 ἀναφάναντες δὲ τὴν Κύπρον καὶ καταλιπόντες αὐτὴν εὐώνυμον ἐπλέομεν εἰς Συρίαν καὶ κατήλθομεν εἰς Τύρον· ἐκεῖσε γὰρ τὸ πλοῖον ἦν ἀποφορτιζόμενον τὸν γόμον.

ἀναφάναντες. Aor act ptc masc nom pl ἀναφαίνω (temporal).

καταλιπόντες. Aor act ptc masc nom pl καταλείπω (temporal).

ἐπλέομεν. Impf act ind 1st pl πλέω.

κατήλθομεν. Aor act ind 1st pl κατέρχομαι.

ἐκεῖσε. This form is found only in Acts (see also 22:5).

τὸ πλοῖον. Neuter nominative subject of ἦν.

ἦν. Impf ind 3rd sg εἰμί.

ἀποφορτιζόμενον. Pres dep ptc neut nom sg ἀποφορτίζομαι (imperfect periphrastic; see 1:10 on ἀτενίζοντες).

21:4 ἀνευρόντες δὲ τοὺς μαθητὰς ἐπεμείναμεν αὐτοῦ ἡμέρας ἑπτά, οἵτινες τῷ Παύλῳ ἔλεγον διὰ τοῦ πνεύματος μὴ ἐπιβαίνειν εἰς Ἱεροσόλυμα.

ἀνευρόντες. Aor act ptc masc nom pl ἀνευρίσκω (temporal or causal). This verb appears to differ from the non-compounded form εὑρίσκω in that it carries the idea of intentional searching (cf. LN 27.28).

ἐπεμείναμεν. Aor act ind 1st pl ἐπιμένω.

αὐτοῦ. "There" (see 18:19).

ἡμέρας. Accusative indicating extent of time (see 7:20 on μῆνας).

οἵτινες. The relative clause modifies τοὺς μαθητάς.

ἔλεγον. Impf act ind 3rd pl λέγω.

ἐπιβαίνειν. Pres act inf ἐπιβαίνω (indirect discourse).

21:5 ὅτε δὲ ἐγένετο ἡμᾶς ἐξαρτίσαι τὰς ἡμέρας, ἐξελθόντες ἐπορευόμεθα προπεμπόντων ἡμᾶς πάντων σὺν γυναιξὶ καὶ τέκνοις ἕως ἔξω τῆς πόλεως, καὶ θέντες τὰ γόνατα ἐπὶ τὸν αἰγιαλὸν προσευξάμενοι

ἐγένετο. Aor mid dep ind 3rd sg γίνομαι. On the use of ἐγένετο with an infinitive and a temporal expression, see 4:5.

ἡμᾶς. Accusative subject of the infinitive (see 1:3 on αὐτὸν).

ἐξαρτίσαι. Aor act inf ἐξαρτίζω. The infinitival clause, ἡμᾶς ἐξαρτίσαι τὰς ἡμέρας, functions as the subject of ἐγένετο (see also 9:32 on κατελθεῖν).

ἐξελθόντες. Aor act ptc masc nom pl ἐξέρχομαι (attendant circumstance).

ἐπορευόμεθα. Impf dep ind 1st pl πορεύομαι.

προπεμπόντων. Pres act ptc masc gen pl προπέμπω. Genitive absolute (see 1:8 on ἐπελθόντος), attendant circumstance.

ἡμᾶς. Accusative direct object of προπεμπόντων.

πάντων. Genitive subject (see 1:8 on ἐπελθόντος).

θέντες τὰ γόνατα. See 7:60.

θέντες. Aor act ptc masc nom pl τίθημι (temporal).

προσευξάμενοι. Aor mid dep ptc masc nom pl προσεύχομαι (temporal).

21:6 ἀπησπασάμεθα ἀλλήλους καὶ ἀνέβημεν εἰς τὸ πλοῖον, ἐκεῖνοι δὲ ὑπέστρεψαν εἰς τὰ ἴδια.

ἀπησπασάμεθα. Aor mid dep ind 1st pl ἀπασπάζομαι.

ἀνέβημεν. Aor act ind 1st pl ἀναβαίνω.

ὑπέστρεψαν. Aor act ind 3rd pl ὑποστρέφω.

τὰ ἴδια. Robertson (1934, 691) notes that the use of this (neuter plural) expression for "one's home" is attested in the papyri.

Acts 21:7–16

[7]After completing our voyage from Tyre, we arrived in Ptolemais. And after greeting the believers (there), we spent a day with them. [8]The next day we departed and went to Caesarea. (There,) We went to the house of Philip the evangelist, who was a member of the Seven, and stayed with him. [9]He had four unmarried daughters who prophesied.

[10]After we had stayed (there) many days, a prophet came down from Judea, named Agabus. [11]After coming to us and taking Paul's belt, he tied up his own feet and hands (with it), and said, "Here is what the Holy Spirit says: 'This is the way that the Jews in Jerusalem will tie up the man to whom this belt belongs and hand him over to the Gentiles.'"

[12]When we heard these things both we and the local residents begged him not to go up to Jerusalem. [13]Then Paul responded, "What are you doing, crying and breaking my heart? For I am ready not only to be tied

up, but even to die in Jerusalem for the sake of the name of the Lord Jesus." [14]When he could not be persuaded we gave up and said, "The Lord's will be done!"

[15]After this time, we packed up and headed to Jerusalem. [16]Some of the disciples from Caesarea went with us in order to bring us to the one we were to stay with, Mnason, who was a Cypriot and an early disciple.

21:7 Ἡμεῖς δὲ τὸν πλοῦν διανύσαντες ἀπὸ Τύρου κατηντήσαμεν εἰς Πτολεμαΐδα καὶ ἀσπασάμενοι τοὺς ἀδελφοὺς ἐμείναμεν ἡμέραν μίαν παρ᾽ αὐτοῖς.

πλοῦν. Masc sg acc of πλόος (direct object of διανύσαντες).

διανύσαντες. Aor act ptc masc nom pl διανύω (temporal). Although the verb usually indicates "to complete" (thus, "after completing the voyage from Tyre"; LN 68.25), it may indicate "to continue" here (68.18; BAGD, 187).

κατηντήσαμεν. Aor act ind 1st pl καταντάω.

ἀσπασάμενοι. Aor mid dep ptc masc nom pl ἀσπάζομαι (temporal).

ἀδελφούς. See 1:15.

ἐμείναμεν. Aor act ind 1st pl μένω.

ἡμέραν. Accusative indicating extent of time (see 7:20 on μῆνας).

21:8 τῇ δὲ ἐπαύριον ἐξελθόντες ἤλθομεν εἰς Καισάρειαν καὶ εἰσελθόντες εἰς τὸν οἶκον Φιλίππου τοῦ εὐαγγελιστοῦ, ὄντος ἐκ τῶν ἑπτά, ἐμείναμεν παρ᾽ αὐτῷ.

ἐξελθόντες. Aor act ptc masc nom pl ἐξέρχομαι (attendant circumstance).

ἤλθομεν. Aor act ind 1st pl ἔρχομαι.

εἰσελθόντες. Aor act ptc masc nom pl εἰσέρχομαι (attendant circumstance).

εἰς. See 1:8 on ἐφ᾽ ὑμᾶς.

τοῦ εὐαγγελιστοῦ. Genitive in apposition to Φιλίππου.

ὄντος. Pres act ptc masc gen sg εἰμί (attributive).

ἐκ τῶν ἑπτα. Partitive.

ἐμείναμεν. Aor act ind 1st pl μένω.

21:9 τούτῳ δὲ ἦσαν θυγατέρες τέσσαρες παρθένοι προφητεύουσαι.

τούτῳ. Dative of possession (with εἰμί).

ἦσαν. Impf ind 3rd pl εἰμί.

θυγατέρες τέσσαρες παρθένοι προφητεύουσαι. Nominative subject of ἦσαν.

παρθένοι. Nominative in apposition to θυγατέρες.

προφητεύουσαι. Pres act ptc fem nom pl προφητεύω (attributive or substantival in apposition to θυγατέρες).

21:10 ἐπιμενόντων δὲ ἡμέρας πλείους κατῆλθέν τις ἀπὸ τῆς Ἰουδαίας προφήτης ὀνόματι Ἅγαβος,

ἐπιμενόντων. Pres act ptc masc gen pl ἐπιμένω. Genitive absolute (see 1:8 on ἐπελθόντος), temporal.

ἡμέρας. Accusative indicating extent of time (see 7:20 on μῆνας).

κατῆλθέν. Aor act ind 3rd sg κατέρχομαι.

τις. See 8:9.

προφήτης. Nominative subject of κατῆλθέν.

ὀνόματι. Dative of reference.

Ἅγαβος. Nominative in apposition to προφήτης.

21:11 καὶ ἐλθὼν πρὸς ἡμᾶς καὶ ἄρας τὴν ζώνην τοῦ Παύλου, δήσας ἑαυτοῦ τοὺς πόδας καὶ τὰς χεῖρας εἶπεν, Τάδε λέγει τὸ πνεῦμα τὸ ἅγιον, Τὸν ἄνδρα οὗ ἐστιν ἡ ζώνη αὕτη, οὕτως δήσουσιν ἐν Ἰερουσαλὴμ οἱ Ἰουδαῖοι καὶ παραδώσουσιν εἰς χεῖρας ἐθνῶν.

ἐλθὼν. Aor act ptc masc nom sg ἔρχομαι (temporal). The use of καί makes it clear that the participle modifies the following finite verb rather than the preceding one.

ἄρας. Aor act ptc masc nom sg αἴρω (temporal).

δήσας. Aor act ptc masc nom sg δέω (attendant circumstance). The lack of a καί suggests that this participle differs in function from the previous two that are conjoined.

εἶπεν. Aor act ind 3rd sg λέγω.

Τάδε. Wallace (1996, 328) notes that "the pronoun is used [in the expression τάδε λέγει] to add solemnity to the prophetic utterance that follows."

λέγει. Pres act ind 3rd sg λέγω.

Τὸν ἄνδρα. This noun phrase serves as the topicalized (see 2:22 on

᾽Ιησοῦν τὸν Ναζωραῖον) direct object of δήσουσιν and παραδώσουσιν.

οὗ. The relative pronoun functions as a possessive genitive predicate of ἐστιν.

ἐστιν. Pres act ind 3rd sg εἰμί.

δήσουσιν. Fut act ind 3rd pl δέω. There is no need to posit a new syntactic category, "causative active" (contra Wallace 1996; see 16:3 on περιέτεμεν).

παραδώσουσιν. Fut act ind 3rd pl παραδίδωμι.

χεῖρας ἐθνῶν. Synecdoche (see 1:22 on τοῦ βαπτίσματος ᾽Ιωάννου) for "the Gentiles."

21:12 ὡς δὲ ἠκούσαμεν ταῦτα, παρεκαλοῦμεν ἡμεῖς τε καὶ οἱ ἐντόπιοι τοῦ μὴ ἀναβαίνειν αὐτὸν εἰς ᾽Ιερουσαλήμ.

ὡς. Temporal (see 18:5).

ἠκούσαμεν. Aor act ind 1st pl ἀκούω.

παρεκαλοῦμεν. Impf act ind 1st pl παρακαλέω.

ἀναβαίνειν. Pres act inf ἀναβαίνω. On whether the articular infinitive introduces indirect discourse or a purpose clause, see 15:20 on ἀπέχεσθαι.

αὐτὸν Accusative subject of the infinitive (see 1:3 on αὐτὸν).

21:13 τότε ἀπεκρίθη ὁ Παῦλος, Τί ποιεῖτε κλαίοντες καὶ συνθρύπτοντές μου τὴν καρδίαν; ἐγὼ γὰρ οὐ μόνον δεθῆναι ἀλλὰ καὶ ἀποθανεῖν εἰς ᾽Ιερουσαλὴμ ἑτοίμως ἔχω ὑπὲρ τοῦ ὀνόματος τοῦ κυρίου ᾽Ιησοῦ.

τότε. In the reading favored by UBS[4]/NA[27], the adverb indicates a prompt response and emphasizes Paul's resolve (see 1:12). This reading is supported by B C[2] 36 307 453 1678 cop[bo] and by 𝔓[74] א A E *al*, which add καὶ εἶπεν. Many other manuscripts (Ψ *Byz*), however, take the adverb with the preceding clause (thus, "started begging him not to go up to Jerusalem at that time") and add a conjunction after ἀπεκρίθη. The fact that τότε appears always to precede the verb it modifies, however, provides strong support for the UBS[4]/NA[27] reading.

ἀπεκρίθη. Aor pass dep ind 3rd sg ἀποκρίνομαι.

Τί ποιεῖτε. Used with a participial modifier, this periphrastic expression is roughly analogous to "why?" but probably carries a connotation of surprise over the actions described.

ποιεῖτε Pres act ind 2nd pl ποιέω.

κλαίοντες Pres act ptc masc nom pl κλαίω. In terms of syntax, the participles cannot be complementary since ποιεῖτε has a direct object (τί), and they cannot be epexegetical to τί since they are nominative rather than accusative. It is best to take both participles as indicating means (cf. the English, "What are you trying to do by crying and breaking my heart?").

συνθρύπτοντές τὴν καρδίαν. An idiom meaning, "to cause great sorrow" (LN 25.282).

συνθρύπτοντές. Pres act ptc masc nom pl συνθρύπτω (means; see above). The second accent comes from the enclitic μου (see 1:4 on ἠκούσατέ).

ἐγὼ. Nominative subject of ἔχω, fronted for emphasis (see 2:15 on ὑμεῖς).

δεθῆναι. Aor pass inf δέω. The infinitive may be viewed as either epexegetical to ἑτοίμως or complementary to ἑτοίμως ἔχω if ἑτοίμως ἔχω is viewed as a unit (an idiomatic verb phrase).

ἀποθανεῖν. Aor act inf ἀποθνῄσκω (epexegetical/complementary to ἑτοίμως ἔχω; see above).

ἑτοίμως ἔχω. An idiom meaning "I am ready" (see 7:1 on οὕτως ἔχει).

ἔχω Pres act ind 1st sg ἔχω.

21:14 **μὴ πειθομένου δὲ αὐτοῦ ἡσυχάσαμεν εἰπόντες, Τοῦ κυρίου τὸ θέλημα γινέσθω.**

πειθομένου. Pres pass ptc masc gen sg πείθω. Genitive absolute (see 1:8 on ἐπελθόντος), temporal or causal.

αὐτοῦ. Genitive subject (see 1:8 on ἐπελθόντος).

ἡσυχάσαμεν. Aor act ind 1st pl ἡσυχάζω. Lit. "we were quiet."

εἰπόντες. Aor act ptc masc nom pl λέγω (attendant circumstance).

τὸ θέλημα. Nominative subject of γινέσθω.

γινέσθω. Pres dep impv 3rd sg γίνομαι.

21:15 **Μετὰ δὲ τὰς ἡμέρας ταύτας ἐπισκευασάμενοι ἀνεβαίνομεν εἰς Ἱεροσόλυμα·**

Μετὰ . . . τὰς ἡμέρας ταύτας. Lit. "after these days."

ἐπισκευασάμενοι. Aor mid dep ptc masc nom pl ἐπισκευάζομαι (attendant circumstance). Only here in the NT: "to be or to become ready for some purpose" (LN 77.8).

ἀνεβαίνομεν. Impf act ind 1st pl ἀναβαίνω.

21:16 συνῆλθον δὲ καὶ τῶν μαθητῶν ἀπὸ Καισαρείας σὺν ἡμῖν, ἄγοντες παρ' ᾧ ξενισθῶμεν Μνάσωνί τινι Κυπρίῳ, ἀρχαίῳ μαθητῇ.

συνῆλθον. Aor act ind 3rd pl συνέρχομαι.

τῶν μαθητῶν. Partitive genitive. τινες is left implicit (cf. 19:33 on ἐκ τοῦ ὄχλου).

σὺν. See 1:8 on ἐφ' ὑμᾶς.

ἄγοντες. Pres act ptc masc nom pl ἄγω (purpose). The participle should be viewed as adverbial rather than adjectival (contra Rogers and Rogers, 288). The position (following the main verb) and tense of the participle (present rather than aorist) both suggest that it does not introduce an attendant circumstance. The participial clause probably provides the reason the disciples accompanied Paul (cf. Barrett, 1002).

παρ' ᾧ ξενισθῶμεν Μνάσωνί. The construction can be analyzed in several ways. Most have argued that the dative Μνάσωνί is a "victim" of inverse attraction, i.e., the antecedent has been attracted (see 10:36 on τὸν λόγον [ὃν]) to the case of the relative pronoun (so BDF §294.5; Barrett, 1003; Wallace 1996, 339). The construction could be viewed as an internally headed relative clause (see 1:2 on ἄχρι ἧς ἡμέρας), though there seems to be little motivation for such a construction here. It is probably best to take ᾧ as introducing a headless relative clause (see 3:6 on ὃ): "to the one whom . . .," with the dative Μνάσωνί standing in apposition to the relative pronoun.

ξενισθῶμεν. Aor pass subj 1st pl ξενίζω. On the use of the subjunctive, see 23:12 on ἀποκτείνωσιν.

Μνάσωνί. The second accent comes from the enclitic τινι (see 1:4 on ἠκούσατέ).

τινι. See 8:9.

Κυπρίῳ, μαθητῇ. Datives in apposition to Μνάσωνί.

Acts 21:17–25

[17]When we arrived in Jerusalem, the believers (there) welcomed us gladly. [18]On the following day, Paul went with us to (visit) James, and all the elders were present. [19]After he had greeted them, he began explaining in detail each of the things that God had done among the

Gentiles through his ministry. [20]Those who heard glorified God and said (to Paul), "Brother, you can see how many thousands of believers there (now) are among the Jews, and all (of them) are strongly devoted to (keeping) the Law. [21]But they have been told about you that you teach all the Jews throughout the nations to abandon (the Law of) Moses by saying that they should not circumcise their children or live according to (our) customs. [22]So what should we do? They will certainly hear that you have come.

[23]Therefore, you must do what we tell you. We have four men who have taken a vow. [24]Take them and have yourself purified with them. Also, pay their expenses so that they may have their heads shaved. Then everyone will know that there is no (truth) to the things they were told about you, but that you yourself also live according to custom by keeping the Law. [25]And regarding Gentile believers, we sent word (to them), after reaching a decision, that they should avoid (eating) meat offered to idols, blood, (the meat of animals that have been) strangled, and sexual immorality."

21:17 Γενομένων δὲ ἡμῶν εἰς Ἱεροσόλυμα ἀσμένως ἀπεδέξαντο ἡμᾶς οἱ ἀδελφοί.

Γενομένων. Aor mid dep ptc masc gen pl γίνομαι. Genitive absolute (see 1:8 on ἐπελθόντος), temporal.

ἡμῶν. Genitive subject (see 1:8 on ἐπελθόντος).

ἀπεδέξαντο. Aor mid dep ind 3rd pl ἀποδέχομαι.

ἀδελφοί. See 1:15.

21:18 τῇ δὲ ἐπιούσῃ εἰσῄει ὁ Παῦλος σὺν ἡμῖν πρὸς Ἰάκωβον, πάντες τε παρεγένοντο οἱ πρεσβύτεροι.

τῇ ἐπιούσῃ. Pres act ptc fem dat sg ἔπειμι (substantival). A shortened form of τῇ ἐπιούσῃ ἡμέρᾳ (cf. 7:26).

εἰσῄει. Impf act ind 3rd sg εἴσειμι.

παρεγένοντο. Aor mid dep ind 3rd pl παραγίνομαι.

21:19 καὶ ἀσπασάμενος αὐτοὺς ἐξηγεῖτο καθ' ἓν ἕκαστον, ὧν ἐποίησεν ὁ θεὸς ἐν τοῖς ἔθνεσιν διὰ τῆς διακονίας αὐτοῦ.

ἀσπασάμενος. Aor mid dep ptc masc nom sg ἀσπάζομαι (temporal).

ἐξηγεῖτο. Impf dep ind 3rd sg ἐξηγέομαι.

καθ' ἓν ἕκαστον. In this expression (lit. "one by one, each thing"), ἕκαστον should probably be viewed as the substantival direct object of ἐξηγεῖτο, with the prepositional phrase, καθ' ἓν indicating the manner ("in detail"; BAGD, 236) in which Paul laid out the recent events of his ministry to the Gentiles (contra Barrett, 1006, who calls καθ' ἓν a "direct object accusative").

ὧν. The relative pronoun introduces a headless relative clause (see 3:6 on ὃ). The genitive case may indicate reference ("concerning the things God did"; cf. v. 24), or the relative pronoun may have been attracted to an unexpressed antecedent in the genitive case (so Rogers and Rogers, 288).

ἐποίησεν. Aor act ind 3rd sg ποιέω.

21:20 οἱ δὲ ἀκούσαντες ἐδόξαζον τὸν θεὸν εἶπόν τε αὐτῷ, Θεωρεῖς, ἀδελφέ, πόσαι μυριάδες εἰσὶν ἐν τοῖς Ἰουδαίοις τῶν πεπιστευκότων καὶ πάντες ζηλωταὶ τοῦ νόμου ὑπάρχουσιν·

ἀκούσαντες. Aor act ptc masc nom pl ἀκούω (substantival).

ἐδόξαζον. Impf act ind 3rd pl δοξάζω.

εἶπόν. Aor act ind 3rd pl λέγω. The second accent comes from the enclitic τε (see 1:4 on ἠκούσατέ). The exegetical insights that Barrett (1006) and BDF (§327: "they praised God for some time and in various ways until they finally said") derive from the verb tenses are unwarranted. It is better to simply recognize that the aorist portrays the hearing and speaking as a whole, while the imperfect portrays the glorifying as a process.

τε. The use of τε here probably gives prominence to the following statement, which provides the lead-in to what follows (cf. Levinsohn 1987, 122).

Θεωρεῖς. Pres act ind 2nd sg θεωρέω.

ἀδελφέ. See 1:15. On the position of the vocative, see 10:13.

πόσαι. Introduces an indirect question.

μυριάδες. Predicate nominative of an impersonal εἰσίν.

εἰσὶν. Pres act ind 3rd pl εἰμί.

τῶν πεπιστευκότων. Prf act ptc masc gen pl πιστεύω (substantival; partitive genitive modifying μυριάδες).

ζηλωταὶ. Predicate adjective.

νόμου. Genitive of reference.

ὑπάρχουσιν. Pres act ind 3rd pl ὑπάρχω.

21:21 κατηχήθησαν δὲ περὶ σοῦ ὅτι ἀποστασίαν διδάσκεις ἀπὸ Μωϋσέως τοὺς κατὰ τὰ ἔθνη πάντας Ἰουδαίους λέγων μὴ περιτέμνειν αὐτοὺς τὰ τέκνα μηδὲ τοῖς ἔθεσιν περιπατεῖν.

κατηχήθησαν. Aor pass ind 3rd pl κατηχέω.

ὅτι. Introduces a clausal complement (indirect discourse) of κατηχήθησαν.

διδάσκεις. Pres act ind 2nd sg διδάσκω.

τοὺς . . . Ἰουδαίους. On the use of the accusative case with the indirect object (of διδάσκεις), see 8:25 on πολλάς κώμας and 13:32 on ὑμᾶς.

κατὰ τὰ ἔθνη. The use of the distributive preposition with τὰ ἔθνη (only here in the NT) suggests that τὰ ἔθνη should be taken as "the nations" rather than "the Gentiles" (contra most or all scholars and versions). The accusation thus emphasizes the widespread nature of Paul's "heretical" teaching.

λέγων. Pres act ptc masc nom sg λέγω (means).

περιτέμνειν. Pres act inf περιτέμνω (indirect discourse).

αὐτοὺς. Accusative subject of the infinitive (see 1:3 on αὐτὸν).

ἔθεσιν. Dative of rule (see 2:23 on βουλῇ καὶ προγνώσει).

περιπατεῖν. Pres act inf περιπατέω (indirect discourse).

21:22 τί οὖν ἐστιν; πάντως ἀκούσονται ὅτι ἐλήλυθας.

τί οὖν ἐστιν;. Lit. "What is it, then?"

ἐστιν. Pres act ind 3rd sg εἰμί.

πάντως. "Pertaining to being in every respect certain" (LN 71.16).

ἀκούσονται. Fut mid ind 3rd pl ἀκούω.

ὅτι. Introduces a clausal complement (indirect discourse) of ἀκούσονται.

ἐλήλυθας. Prf act ind 2nd sg ἔρχομαι.

21:23 τοῦτο οὖν ποίησον ὅ σοι λέγομεν· εἰσὶν ἡμῖν ἄνδρες τέσσαρες εὐχὴν ἔχοντες ἐφ' ἑαυτῶν.

τοῦτο. Points forward to the topic.

ποίησον. Aor act impv 2nd sg ποιέω.

ὅ. The relative clause modifies τοῦτο.

λέγομεν. Pres act ind 1st pl λέγω.

εἰσὶν. Pres act ind 3rd pl εἰμί.

ἡμῖν. Dative of possession (with εἰμί).

εὐχὴν . . . ἑαυτῶν. Lit. "who have a vow upon themselves."

ἔχοντες. Pres act ptc masc nom pl ἔχω (attributive).

21:24 τούτους παραλαβὼν ἁγνίσθητι σὺν αὐτοῖς καὶ δαπάνησον ἐπ᾽ αὐτοῖς ἵνα ξυρήσονται τὴν κεφαλήν, καὶ γνώσονται πάντες ὅτι ὧν κατήχηνται περὶ σοῦ οὐδέν ἐστιν ἀλλὰ στοιχεῖς καὶ αὐτὸς φυλάσσων τὸν νόμον.

παραλαβὼν. Aor act ptc masc nom sg παραλαμβάνω (attendant circumstance).

ἁγνίσθητι. Aor pass impv 2nd sg ἁγνίζω.

δαπάνησον ἐπ' αὐτοῖς. Lit. "spend on them" = "pay their expenses" (LN 57.146).

δαπάνησον. Aor act impv 2nd sg δαπανάω.

ξυρήσονται. Fut mid ind 3rd pl ξυράω. The future tense is used with ἵνα (in place of an aorist subjunctive; cf. A B[2] C D[*]) to express purpose.

γνώσονται. Fut mid ind 3rd pl γινώσκω. This future indicative verb could either introduce a second purpose clause (with ἵνα) or be read as a simple future.

ὅτι. Introduces a clausal complement of γνώσονται.

ὧν. The relative pronoun introduces a headless relative clause (see 3:6 on ὅ). The genitive case probably indicates reference: "concerning the things that they have been informed concerning you, nothing is true."

κατήχηνται. Prf pass ind 3rd pl κατηχέω.

οὐδέν. Nominative subject or predicate nominative of an impersonal ἐστιν.

ἐστιν. Pres act ind 3rd sg εἰμί.

στοιχεῖς. Pres act ind 2nd sg στοιχέω ("to live in conformity with some presumed standard or set of customs"; LN 41.12).

καὶ. The conjunction is emphatic ("you *also*").

αὐτὸς. Intensive (modifying στοιχεῖς).

φυλάσσων. Pres act ptc masc nom sg φυλάσσω (means).

21:25 περὶ δὲ τῶν πεπιστευκότων ἐθνῶν ἡμεῖς ἐπεστείλαμεν

κρίναντες φυλάσσεσθαι αὐτοὺς τό τε εἰδωλόθυτον καὶ αἷμα καὶ πνικτὸν καὶ πορνείαν.

πεπιστευκότων. Prf act ptc neut gen pl πιστεύω (attributive).

ἐπεστείλαμεν. Aor act ind 1st pl ἐπιστέλλω.

κρίναντες. Aor act ptc masc nom pl κρίνω (temporal). It is unclear how the participle could give the content of the writing (contra Rogers and Rogers, 289).

φυλάσσεσθαι. Pres mid inf φυλάσσω (indirect discourse). The middle form indicates to "(be on one's) guard against, look out for, avoid" (BAGD, 868).

αὐτοὺς. Accusative subject of the infinitive (see 1:3 on αὐτὸν).

αἷμα . . . πνικτὸν . . . πορνείαν. On the meaning of these terms, see 15:20 on πορνείας. The thing that is to be guarded against may either be introduced using the active form of the verb along with the preposition ἀπό (see, e.g., 1 John 5:21), or by using the middle voice of the verb with an accusative complement as here (BAGD, 868).

Acts 21:26–40

26Then, on the following day, after Paul had taken the men and been
purified with them, he entered the temple in order to announce the time
when the period of purification would be complete, at which time a
sacrifice would be offered for each one of them. 27When the seven days
were almost over, after spotting him in the temple, the Jews from Asia
stirred up the whole crowd. They grabbed him 28and shouted, "Israelites, help! This is the man who teaches everyone everywhere against
(our) people, (our) law, and this (holy) place. Furthermore, he has even
brought Greeks into the temple and defiled this holy place!" 29For earlier they had seen Trophimus the Ephesian in the city with him, and
they thought that Paul had brought him into the temple.

30The whole city was in an uproar and a mob of people formed. After
seizing Paul, they dragged him outside the temple, and immediately the
gates were closed. 31As they were trying to kill him, news that all of
Jerusalem was in turmoil reached the commander of the regiment (sta-
tioned there). 32He immediately took soldiers and centurions and ran
down to them. When they saw the commander and the soldiers, they
stopped beating Paul. 33Then the commander came up and arrested him
and ordered him to be bound with two chains. He asked who he could
possibly be and what he had done.

[34]Now, some among the crowd were shouting one thing and some another. So when he was unable to determine what had really happened, because of the turmoil, he ordered that (Paul) be brought into the barracks. [35]When he reached the steps (of the barracks), Paul had to be carried by the soldiers because the crowd was so violent. [36]For a crowd of people were following and shouting, "Away with him!" [37]Then, as he was about to be taken into the barracks, Paul said to the commander, "May I say something to you?" And he replied, "Do you understand Greek? [38]Then you are not the Egyptian who started a rebellion some time ago and led four thousand terrorists out into the desert?" [39]Paul responded, "I am a Jewish man from Tarsus of Cilicia—a citizen of an important city! I beg you to allow me to speak to the people." [40]After (the commander) had given him permission, Paul stood on the steps and motioned with his hand to the people. When it was completely quiet, he addressed them in the Hebrew language:

21:26 τότε ὁ Παῦλος παραλαβὼν τοὺς ἄνδρας τῇ ἐχομένῃ ἡμέρᾳ σὺν αὐτοῖς ἁγνισθεὶς, εἰσῄει εἰς τὸ ἱερόν διαγγέλλων τὴν ἐκπλήρωσιν τῶν ἡμερῶν τοῦ ἁγνισμοῦ ἕως οὗ προσηνέχθη ὑπὲρ ἑνὸς ἑκάστου αὐτῶν ἡ προσφορά.

παραλαβὼν. Aor act ptc masc nom sg παραλαμβάνω (temporal).

ἐχομένῃ. Pres mid ptc fem dat sg ἔχω (attributive).

ἁγνισθεὶς. Aor pass ptc masc nom sg ἁγνίζω (temporal).

εἰσῄει. Impf act ind 3rd sg εἴσειμι.

διαγγέλλων. Pres act ptc masc nom sg διαγγέλλω (purpose).

τὴν . . . ἁγνισμοῦ. Lit. "the completion of the days of purification."

ἕως οὗ. The preposition and relative pronoun may be combined to form an idiomatic relative phrase (cf. Culy 1989, 43) meaning, "at which time."

προσηνέχθη. Aor pass ind 3rd sg προσφέρω.

21:27 ʽΩς δὲ ἔμελλον αἱ ἑπτὰ ἡμέραι συντελεῖσθαι, οἱ ἀπὸ τῆς ʼΑσίας ʼΙουδαῖοι θεασάμενοι αὐτὸν ἐν τῷ ἱερῷ συνέχεον πάντα τὸν ὄχλον καὶ ἐπέβαλον ἐπʼ αὐτὸν τὰς χεῖρας

ʽΩς. Temporal (see 18:5).

ἔμελλον Impf act ind 3rd pl μέλλω. See 3:3 on μέλλοντας.

συντελεῖσθαι. Pres pass inf συντελέω (complementary).

θεασάμενοι. Aor mid dep ptc masc nom pl θεάομαι (temporal or attendant circumstance). The participle is almost certainly not attributive since it is anarthrous (see 3:3 on Πέτρον καὶ' Ιωάννην) and would modify an articular noun (contra Rogers and Rogers, 289).

συνέχεον. Impf act ind 3rd pl συγχέω.

ἐπέβαλον ἐπ' αὐτὸν τὰς χεῖρας. Perhaps, "arrested" or "attacked" (see 4:3).

ἐπέβαλον. Aor act ind 3rd pl ἐπιβάλλω.

ἐπ'. See 1:8 on ἐφ' ὑμᾶς.

21:28 κράζοντες, Ἄνδρες Ἰσραηλῖται, βοηθεῖτε· οὗτός ἐστιν ὁ ἄνθρωπος ὁ κατὰ τοῦ λαοῦ καὶ τοῦ νόμου καὶ τοῦ τόπου τούτου πάντας πανταχῇ διδάσκων, ἔτι τε καὶ Ἕλληνας εἰσήγαγεν εἰς τὸ ἱερὸν καὶ κεκοίνωκεν τὸν ἅγιον τόπον τοῦτον.

κράζοντες. Pres act ptc masc nom pl κράζω (attendant circumstance).

Ἄνδρες. See 1:11.

Ἰσραηλῖται. Vocative.

βοηθεῖτε. Pres act impv 2nd pl βοηθέω.

οὗτός. The second accent comes from the enclitic ἐστιν (see 1:4 on ἠκούσατέ).

ἐστιν. Pres act ind 3rd sg εἰμί.

ὁ ἄνθρωπος. Predicate nominative.

πάντας. Accusative direct object of διδάσκων.

διδάσκων. Pres act ptc masc nom sg διδάσκω (attributive).

ἔτι τε καὶ. Although BAGD (316) renders this phrase and ἔτι δὲ καί as "furthermore," the context here and in Luke 14:26 (where the textual tradition varies between ἔτι τε καὶ and ἔτι δὲ καὶ) suggests a more intensive connotation: "moreover . . . *even* . . ."

εἰσήγαγεν. Aor act ind 3rd sg εἰσάγω.

κεκοίνωκεν. Prf act ind 3rd sg κοινόω.

21:29 ἦσαν γὰρ προεωρακότες Τρόφιμον τὸν Ἐφέσιον ἐν τῇ πόλει σὺν αὐτῷ, ὃν ἐνόμιζον ὅτι εἰς τὸ ἱερὸν εἰσήγαγεν ὁ Παῦλος.

ἦσαν. Impf ind 3rd pl εἰμί.

προεωρακότες. Prf act ptc masc nom pl προοράω (pluperfect periphrastic; see 1:17 on κατηριθμημένος).

τὸν Ἐφέσιον. Accusative in apposition to Τρόφιμον.

ἐνόμιζον. Impf act ind 3rd pl νομίζω.

ὅτι. Introduces a clausal complement of ἐνόμιζον.

εἰς. See 1:8 on ἐφ' ὑμᾶς.

εἰσήγαγεν. Aor act ind 3rd sg εἰσάγω.

21:30 ἐκινήθη τε ἡ πόλις ὅλη καὶ ἐγένετο συνδρομὴ τοῦ λαοῦ, καὶ ἐπιλαβόμενοι τοῦ Παύλου εἷλκον αὐτὸν ἔξω τοῦ ἱεροῦ καὶ εὐθέως ἐκλείσθησαν αἱ θύραι.

ἐκινήθη. Aor pass ind 3rd sg κινέω.

τε. The conjunction τε is sometimes used, as here, to introduce a response to a previous event (see Levinsohn 1987, 135–36; cf. 13:46; 24:10). Here, the crowd responds to the accusation in v. 28 by forming a mob.

ἐγένετο . . . λαοῦ. Lit. "there was a rushing together of people."

ἐγένετο. Aor mid dep ind 3rd sg γίνομαι (impersonal).

συνδρομή. Predicate nominative ("a tumultuous concourse of people"; LSJ 1703).

τοῦ λαοῦ. Subjective genitive.

ἐπιλαβόμενοι. Aor mid dep ptc masc nom pl ἐπιλαμβάνομαι (temporal).

τοῦ Παύλου. Genitive object of ἐπιλαβόμενοι.

εἷλκον. Impf act ind 3rd pl ἕλκω.

ἐκλείσθησαν. Aor pass ind 3rd pl κλείω.

21:31 ζητούντων τε αὐτὸν ἀποκτεῖναι ἀνέβη φάσις τῷ χιλιάρχῳ τῆς σπείρης ὅτι ὅλη συγχύννεται Ἰερουσαλήμ.

ζητούντων. Pres act ptc masc gen pl ζητέω. Genitive absolute (see 1:8 on ἐπελθόντος), temporal. The use of a genitive absolute without an overt subject is rare (cf. Luke 12:36).

ἀποκτεῖναι. Aor act inf ἀποκτείνω (complementary).

ἀνέβη φάσις τῷ χιλιάρχῳ. Lit. "a report went up to the commander."

ὅτι. The conjunction may be viewed as epexegetical modifying φάσις, or as introducing the clausal complement (indirect discourse) of a noun (φάσις) that implies communication.

ἀνέβη. Aor act ind 3rd sg ἀναβαίνω.

ὅλη. The fronted (see 3:13 on ὑμεῖς) adjective is emphatic (see 2:15 on ὑμεῖς).

συγχύννεται. Pres pass ind 3rd sg συγχέω/συγχύννω.

21:32 ὃς ἐξαυτῆς παραλαβὼν στρατιώτας καὶ ἑκατοντάρχας κατέδραμεν ἐπ' αὐτούς, οἱ δὲ ἰδόντες τὸν χιλίαρχον καὶ τοὺς στρατιώτας ἐπαύσαντο τύπτοντες τὸν Παῦλον.

ὃς. The antecedent is τῷ χιλιάρχῳ (v. 31).

ἐξαυτῆς. "Immediately."

παραλαβὼν. Aor act ptc masc nom sg παραλαμβάνω (attendant circumstance).

κατέδραμεν. Aor act ind 3rd sg κατατρέχω.

ἰδόντες. Aor act ptc masc nom pl ὁράω. The participle should be viewed as substantival rather than temporal, though a temporal translation may be preferable in English (cf. v. 20 on ἀκούσαντες).

ἐπαύσαντο. Aor mid ind 3rd pl παύω.

τύπτοντες. Pres act ptc masc nom pl τύπτω (complementary; see Wallace 1996, 646).

21:33 τότε ἐγγίσας ὁ χιλίαρχος ἐπελάβετο αὐτοῦ καὶ ἐκέλευσεν δεθῆναι ἁλύσεσι δυσί, καὶ ἐπυνθάνετο τίς εἴη καὶ τί ἐστιν πεποιηκώς.

ἐγγίσας. Aor act ptc masc nom sg ἐγγίζω (attendant circumstance).

ἐπελάβετο. Aor mid dep ind 3rd sg ἐπιλαμβάνομαι.

αὐτοῦ. Genitive object of ἐπελάβετο.

ἐκέλευσεν. Aor act ind 3rd sg κελεύω.

δεθῆναι. Aor pass inf δέω (indirect discourse).

ἁλύσεσι. Dative of instrument.

ἐπυνθάνετο. Impf dep ind 3rd sg πυνθάνομαι.

εἴη. Pres act opt 3rd sg εἰμί. Wallace (1996, 483) calls εἴη an oblique optative that "may be used in indirect questions after a secondary tense." The optative suggests that the commander was astounded that one man could cause such an uproar.

ἐστιν. Pres act ind 3rd sg εἰμί.

πεποιηκώς. Prf act ptc masc nom sg ποιέω (perfect periphrastic; see 2:13 on μεμεστωμένοι).

21:34 ἄλλοι δὲ ἄλλο τι ἐπεφώνουν ἐν τῷ ὄχλῳ. μὴ δυναμένου δὲ αὐτοῦ γνῶναι τὸ ἀσφαλὲς διὰ τὸν θόρυβον ἐκέλευσεν ἄγεσθαι αὐτὸν εἰς τὴν παρεμβολήν.

ἄλλοι . . . ἄλλο. See 19:32.

ἐπεφώνουν. Impf act ind 3rd pl ἐπιφωνέω.

δυναμένου. Pres pass ptc masc gen sg δύναμαι. Genitive absolute (see 1:8 on ἐπελθόντος), temporal. This passage represents one of only five instances in the NT where the genitive absolute construction is used to introduce a subject that appears to be the same as the subject of the main verb (the other passages are Matt 1:18; Mark 6:22; Acts 22:17; 28:6). Here, and at 28:6, the genitive absolute "is negative and expresses the failure of the subject to achieve his goal or see his expectation fulfilled. The following independent clause describes the alternative method or conclusion that he adopts. The change of direction implied in the adoption of this alternative may compensate for the failure to change the subject" (Levinsohn 1987, 68, n. 13). It is also possible that the use of the genitive absolute may be conditioned by the switch in semantic role of the two subjects: the first is an experiencer, while the second is an agent (cf. Levinsohn 1992, 178).

αὐτοῦ. Genitive subject (see 1:8 on ἐπελθόντος).

γνῶναι. Aor act inf γινώσκω (complementary).

τὸ ἀσφαλὲς. Lit. "the certainty."

ἐκέλευσεν. Aor act ind 3rd sg κελεύω.

ἄγεσθαι. Pres pass inf ἄγω (indirect discourse).

αὐτὸν. Accusative subject of the passive infinitive (see 1:3 on αὐτὸν).

21:35 ὅτε δὲ ἐγένετο ἐπὶ τοὺς ἀναβαθμούς, συνέβη βαστάζεσθαι αὐτὸν ὑπὸ τῶν στρατιωτῶν διὰ τὴν βίαν τοῦ ὄχλου,

ἐγένετο. Aor mid dep ind 3rd sg γίνομαι.

συνέβη. Aor act ind 3rd sg συμβαίνω.

βαστάζεσθαι. Pres pass inf βαστάζω. The whole infinitival clause, βαστάζεσθαι αὐτὸν ὑπὸ τῶν στρατιωτῶν διὰ τὴν βίαν τοῦ ὄχλου, serves as the subject of συνέβη. This construction commonly occurs with ἐγένετο (see 9:32 on κατελθεῖν).

αὐτὸν. Accusative subject of the passive infinitive (see 1:3 on αὐτὸν).

διὰ. Causal.

βίαν τοῦ ὄχλου. Lit. "the violence of the crowd."

21:36 ἠκολούθει γὰρ τὸ πλῆθος τοῦ λαοῦ κράζοντες, Αἶρε αὐτόν.

ἠκολούθει. Impf act ind 3rd sg ἀκολουθέω.

κράζοντες. Pres act ptc masc nom pl κράζω (attendant circumstance). The shift to the plural (the subject class noun πλῆθος and the main verb are singular) may emphasize that the entire crowd was shouting.

Αἶρε αὐτόν. This expression (lit. "Take him away!") serves as an idiom that calls for someone's execution.

Αἶρε. Pres act impv 2nd sg αἴρω.

21:37 Μέλλων τε εἰσάγεσθαι εἰς τὴν παρεμβολὴν ὁ Παῦλος λέγει τῷ χιλιάρχῳ, Εἰ ἔξεστίν μοι εἰπεῖν τι πρὸς σέ; ὁ δὲ ἔφη, Ἑλληνιστὶ γινώσκεις;

Μέλλων. Pres act ptc masc nom sg μέλλω (temporal). On the force of μέλλω plus an infinitive, see 3:3 on μέλλοντας.

τε. The use of τε here argues against the generally recognized paragraph break at v. 37. According to Levinsohn, the τε indicates that the events of v. 37 should be read against the background of the crowd's violence in v. 35. He then points out (1980, 503) that "if the incident is begun at v. 35 rather than at v. 37, it becomes clearer that this part of the story is orientated primarily, not around Paul and the tribune, but around Paul and the crowd."

εἰσάγεσθαι. Pres pass inf εἰσάγω (complementary).

λέγει. Pres act ind 3rd sg λέγω.

Εἰ. Introduces direct discourse.

ἔξεστίν. Pres act ind 3rd sg ἔξεστιν (impersonal). The second accent comes from the enclitic μοι (see 1:4 on ἠκούσατέ).

εἰπεῖν. Aor act inf λέγω (complementary; see 1:16 on ἔδει).

σέ. Enclitics are generally accented following a preposition, though the critical texts show some counter-examples (Matt 25:39). Elsewhere, it is sometimes unclear what led the critical text editors to retain or omit accents (see especially the three occurrences of σου in Matt 7:4–5; cf. Robertson 1934, 233–35).

ἔφη. Aor/Impf act ind 3rd sg φημί. On the tense, see 7:2.

Ἑλληνιστὶ γινώσκεις;. The use of the adverb Ἑλληνιστὶ (lit. "in Greek") with γινώσκω may be an idiomatic expression relating to comprehension ("Do you understand Greek?") or may be part of an elliptical construction in which λαλεῖν has been omitted (so Lake and Cadbury, 276).

γινώσκεις. Pres act ind 2nd sg γινώσκω.

21:38 οὐκ ἄρα σὺ εἶ ὁ Αἰγύπτιος ὁ πρὸ τούτων τῶν ἡμερῶν ἀναστατώσας καὶ ἐξαγαγὼν εἰς τὴν ἔρημον τοὺς τετρακισχιλίους ἄνδρας τῶν σικαρίων;

εἶ. Pres act ind 2nd sg εἰμί.
Αἰγύπτιος. Predicate nominative.
ἀναστατώσας. Aor act ptc masc nom sg ἀναστατόω (attributive).
ἐξαγαγὼν. Aor act ptc masc nom sg ἐξάγω (attributive).
ἄνδρας τῶν σικαρίων. Lit. "men of the assassins."

21:39 εἶπεν δὲ ὁ Παῦλος, Ἐγὼ ἄνθρωπος μέν εἰμι Ἰουδαῖος, Ταρσεὺς τῆς Κιλικίας, οὐκ ἀσήμου πόλεως πολίτης· δέομαι δέ σου, ἐπίτρεψόν μοι λαλῆσαι πρὸς τὸν λαόν.

εἶπεν. Aor act ind 3rd sg λέγω.
Ἐγὼ ἄνθρωπος μέν εἰμι Ἰουδαῖος, Ταρσεὺς . . . πολίτης. Strictly speaking, ἄνθρωπος is a predicate nominative while the following nominative nouns stand in apposition to it (lit. "I am a man—a Jew, a Tarsean . . . a citizen").
εἰμι. Pres act ind 1st sg εἰμί.
οὐκ ἀσήμου πόλεως πολίτης. Litotes (lit. "a citizen of a not insignificant city"; see 1:5 on οὐ μετὰ πολλὰς ταύτας ἡμέρας).
δέομαι. Pres dep ind 1st sg δέομαι.
σου. Genitive object of δέομαι.
ἐπίτρεψόν. Aor act impv 2nd sg ἐπιτρέφω. The second accent comes from the enclitic μοι (see 1:4 on ἠκούσατέ).
λαλῆσαι. Aor act inf λαλέω. The infinitive functions as the direct object of ἐπίτρεψόν (cf. 27:3), with μοι serving as the indirect object.

21:40 ἐπιτρέψαντος δὲ αὐτοῦ ὁ Παῦλος ἑστὼς ἐπὶ τῶν ἀναβαθμῶν κατέσεισεν τῇ χειρὶ τῷ λαῷ. πολλῆς δὲ σιγῆς γενομένης προσεφώνησεν τῇ Ἑβραΐδι διαλέκτῳ λέγων,

ἐπιτρέψαντος. Aor act ptc masc gen sg ἐπιτρέπω. Genitive absolute (see 1:8 on ἐπελθόντος), temporal.
αὐτοῦ. Genitive subject (see 1:8 on ἐπελθόντος). The antecedent is τῷ χιλιάρχῳ (v. 37).
ἑστὼς. Prf act ptc masc nom sg ἵστημι (attendant circumstance).
κατέσεισεν. Aor act ind 3rd sg κατασείω.

πολλῆς σιγῆς. Lit. "much silence." Genitive subject (see 1:8 on ἐπελθόντος).

γενομένης. Aor mid dep ptc fem gen sg γίνομαι. Genitive absolute (see 1:8 on ἐπελθόντος), temporal.

προσεφώνησεν. Aor act ind 3rd sg προσφωνέω.

τῇ 'Εβραΐδι. Dative of instrument. Either Hebrew or Aramaic. On the diaeresis over the *iota*, see 2:31 on προϊδὼν.

λέγων. Pres act ptc masc nom sg λέγω (attendant circumstance, redundant; see 1:6 on λέγοντες).

Acts 22:1–21

1"Brothers and fathers, listen now to my defense to you! 2When they
heard that he was addressing them in the Hebrew language, they became even quieter. Then he said, 3"I am a Jewish man, who was born in
Tarsus of Cilicia. I was raised in this (very) city and trained at the feet of
Gamiliel in accord with the precise nature of (our) ancestors' law. I am
deeply devoted to God just as all of you are today. 4I persecuted the
'Way,' even to the point of having them killed, by binding both men
and women and delivering them to prison, 5as even the high priest and
all the elders can attest for me. (They are the ones) from whom I also
received letters to fellow Jews in Damascus and I was going (there) in
order to take those (Christians) who were there in chains to Jerusalem
so that they might be punished.

6Now, as I was on my way and nearing Damascus at about noon, a
bright light from the sky suddenly flashed around me! 7I fell to the
ground and heard a voice saying to me, 'Saul, Saul, why are you persecuting me?' 8I answered, 'Who are you, Lord?' And he said to me, 'I am
Jesus, the Nazarene, whom you are persecuting.' 9Those who were with
me saw the light but did not hear the voice of the one who was speaking
to me. 10Then I said, 'What should I do, Lord?' And the Lord said to
me, 'Go at once into Damascus and there you will be told all that you
have been assigned to do.' 11When I could not see, because of the bril-
liance of the light, I entered Damascus with those who were with me
leading me by the hand.

12Now, a certain Ananias, a devout man by the Law's standards and
respected by all the Jews who lived there, 13came to me, stood beside
me and said, 'Brother Saul, see again!' And at that very moment I looked
up at him. 14Then he said, 'The God of our ancestors has chosen you to
know his will and to see the Righteous One and hear his voice. 15For

you will be his witness to all people of the things you have seen and heard. [16]So now, what are you waiting for? Be baptized and have your sins washed away as you call on his name.'

[17]Now, after I had returned to Jerusalem, while I was praying in the temple, I fell into a trance [18]and saw (the Lord) saying to me, 'Hurry, you must leave Jerusalem quickly because they will not accept your testimony about me!' [19]I replied, 'Lord, they themselves know that (I went) from synagogue to synagogue imprisoning and beating those who believe in you. [20]And when the blood of Stephen, your witness, was shed, I myself was standing there, approving (of what was happening) and guarding the outer garments of those who were killing him.' [21]Then he said to me, 'Go (now), for I will be sending you far away to the Gentiles!'"

22:1 Ἄνδρες ἀδελφοὶ καὶ πατέρες, ἀκούσατέ μου τῆς πρὸς ὑμᾶς νυνὶ ἀπολογίας.

Ἄνδρες See 1:11.

ἀδελφοὶ καὶ πατέρες Vocative (see also v. 5 on τοὺς ἀδελφοὺς).

ἀκούσατε. Aor act impv 2nd pl ἀκούω. The second accent comes from the enclitic μου (see 1:4 on ἠκούσατέ).

μου. The genitive pronoun is a possessive modifier of ἀπολογίας.

τῆς . . . ἀπολογίας. Genitive object of ἀκούσατέ.

22:2 ἀκούσαντες δὲ ὅτι τῇ Ἑβραΐδι διαλέκτῳ προσεφώνει αὐτοῖς μᾶλλον παρέσχον ἡσυχίαν. καὶ φησίν,

ἀκούσαντες. Aor act ptc masc nom pl ἀκούω (temporal).

ὅτι. Introduces a clausal complement (indirect discourse) of ἀκούσαντες.

Ἑβραΐδι. Dative of instrument. Either Hebrew or Aramaic. On the diaeresis over the *iota*, see 2:31 on προϊδὼν.

προσεφώνει. Impf act ind 3rd sg προσφωνέω.

παρέσχον ἡσυχίαν. "they kept silent" (LN 13.26).

παρέσχον. Aor act ind 3rd pl παρέχω.

ἡσυχίαν. Accusative direct object of παρέσχον.

φησίν. Pres act ind 3rd sg φημί.

22:3 Ἐγώ εἰμι ἀνὴρ Ἰουδαῖος, γεγεννημένος ἐν Ταρσῷ τῆς

Κιλικίας, ἀνατεθραμμένος δὲ ἐν τῇ πόλει ταύτῃ, παρὰ τοὺς πόδας Γαμαλιὴλ πεπαιδευμένος κατὰ ἀκρίβειαν τοῦ πατρῴου νόμου, ζηλωτὴς ὑπάρχων τοῦ θεοῦ καθὼς πάντες ὑμεῖς ἐστε σήμερον·

εἰμι. Pres act ind 1st sg εἰμί.

ἀνήρ. Predicate nominative.

᾽Ιουδαῖος. Attributive modifier of ἀνήρ.

γεγεννημένος. Prf pass ptc masc nom sg γεννάω (attributive).

ἀνατεθραμμένος. Prf pass ptc masc nom sg ἀνατρέφω (attributive).

ἐν τῇ πόλει ταύτῃ. There is some ambiguity concerning whether "this city" refers (back) to Tarsus or to Jerusalem (the home of Gamaliel and present location of Paul). On the whole, we prefer the latter view given the use of δέ, which appears to introduce a new piece of information that is not directly linked to the previous proposition.

παρὰ τοὺς πόδας Γαμαλιήλ. Given its common association with instruction, the prepositional phrase more naturally goes with πεπαιδευμένος than ἀνατεθραμμένος.

πεπαιδευμένος. Prf pass ptc masc nom sg παιδεύω (attributive).

ζηλωτής. Predicate nominative.

ὑπάρχων. Pres act ptc masc nom sg ὑπάρχω (attributive).

ἐστε. Pres act ind 2nd pl εἰμί.

22:4 **ὃς ταύτην τὴν ὁδὸν ἐδίωξα ἄχρι θανάτου δεσμεύων καὶ παραδιδοὺς εἰς φυλακὰς ἄνδρας τε καὶ γυναῖκας,**

ὅς. The relative clause modifies ἀνήρ (v. 3).

ταύτην τὴν ὁδὸν Lit. "this Way" (see also 9:2 on τῆς ὁδοῦ).

ἐδίωξα. Aor act ind 1st sg διώκω.

ἄχρι θανάτου. Although the similar phrase ἕως θανάτου is almost certainly used to form a hyperbolic idiom denoting the extreme nature of a feeling (see, e.g., Matt 26:38; LXX Jonah 4:9; Sir 37:2), the use of ἄχρι suggests a literal understanding for ἄχρι θανάτου.

δεσμεύων. Pres act ptc masc nom sg δεσμεύω (means).

παραδιδούς. Pres act ptc masc nom sg παραδίδωμι (means).

ἄνδρας τε καὶ γυναῖκας. Accusative direct object of the conjoined participles.

22:5 ὡς καὶ ὁ ἀρχιερεὺς μαρτυρεῖ μοι καὶ πᾶν τὸ πρεσβυτέριον, παρ' ὧν καὶ ἐπιστολὰς δεξάμενος πρὸς τοὺς ἀδελφοὺς εἰς Δαμασκὸν ἐπορευόμην, ἄξων καὶ τοὺς ἐκεῖσε ὄντας δεδεμένους εἰς Ἰερουσαλὴμ ἵνα τιμωρηθῶσιν.

μαρτυρεῖ. Pres act ind 3rd sg μαρτυρέω. Singular verbs are sometimes used with compound subjects.

μοι. Dative of advantage.

δεξάμενος. Aor mid dep ptc masc nom sg δέχομαι (temporal). In Greek relative clauses, the relative pronoun along with the preposition that governs it should introduce a finite verb. Since, however, παρά is not used with πορεύομαι elsewhere in the NT, παρ' ὧν must go with the participle even though, strictly speaking, it is an ungrammatical construction.

τοὺς ἀδελφοὺς. Here, as in v. 1, 7:2, 13:15, and 23:1, this expression is used to refer to fellow Jews rather than as a technical term for "believers" (cf. 1:15).

ἐπορευόμην. Impf dep ind 1st sg πορεύομαι.

ἄξων. Fut act ptc masc nom sg ἄγω (purpose; see 8:27 on προσκυνή σων; cf. 20:22 on τὰ . . . συναντήσοντά).

ἐκεῖσε. See 21:3.

τοὺς . . . ὄντας. Pres act ptc masc acc pl εἰμί (substantival).

δεδεμένους. Prf pass ptc masc acc pl δέω. The participle should probably be viewed a complement in an object-complement double accusative construction (see 1:3 on ζῶντα), with τοὺς ἐκεῖσε ὄντας serving as the object (cf. 9:2).

τιμωρηθῶσιν. Aor pass subj 3rd pl τιμωρέω. The subjunctive is used with ἵνα to indicate purpose.

22:6 Ἐγένετο δέ μοι πορευομένῳ καὶ ἐγγίζοντι τῇ Δαμασκῷ περὶ μεσημβρίαν ἐξαίφνης ἐκ τοῦ οὐρανοῦ περιαστράψαι φῶς ἱκανὸν περὶ ἐμέ,

Ἐγένετο. Aor mid dep ind 3rd sg γίνομαι.

πορευομένῳ. Pres dep ptc masc dat sg πορεύομαι. The use of participles rather than infinitives (see 9:3 where the same events are recounted using infinitives) is unusual. While there is no question that a good English translation will render the two participles using a temporal expression, strictly speaking the participles cannot be adverbial since they have no verb to modify (both 'Εγένετο and περιαστράψαι have different subjects). Instead, they are both clearly attributive modifiers of μοι (see Culy 2004; contra, e.g., Rogers and Rogers 291). The use of participles rather than the more usual infinitives probably serves to keep the focus on Paul himself rather than the background events: "There I was, going along and nearing Damascus at about noon, when a bright light from the sky suddenly flashed around me!"

ἐγγίζοντι. Pres act ptc masc dat sg ἐγγίζω (attributive; see above).

περιαστράψαι. Aor act inf περιαστράπτω. The infinitival clause, ἐκ τοῦ οὐρανοῦ περιαστράψαι φῶς ἱκανὸν περὶ ἐμε, functions as the subject of 'Εγένετο (see also 9:32 on κατελθεῖν).

φῶς. Accusative subject of the infinitive (see 1:3 on αὐτὸν).

περὶ ἐμέ. See 1:8 on ἐφ' ὑμᾶς.

22:7 ἔπεσά τε εἰς τὸ ἔδαφος καὶ ἤκουσα φωνῆς λεγούσης μοι, Σαοὺλ Σαούλ, τί με διώκεις;

ἔπεσά. Aor act ind 1st sg πίπτω.

ἤκουσα. Aor act ind 1st sg ἀκούω.

φωνῆς. Genitive object of ἤκουσα. On the significance of the shift fron accusative (at 9:4 and 26:14) to genitive here, see 9:7 on φωνῆς and Wallace 1996, 133–34.

λεγούσης. Pres act ptc fem gen sg λέγω. Although the participle could be viewed as attributive, since verbs of perception commonly take double accusatives it is better to take it as a genitive complement of ἤκουσα in an object-complement "double genitive" construction (see 2:6 on λαλούντων).

Σαοὺλ Σαούλ. See 9:4.

διώκεις. Pres act ind 2nd sg διώκω.

22:8 ἐγὼ δὲ ἀπεκρίθην, Τίς εἶ, κύριε; εἶπέν τε πρός με, 'Εγώ εἰμι 'Ιησοῦς ὁ Ναζωραῖος ὃν σὺ διώκεις.

ἀπεκρίθην. Aor pass dep ind 1st sg ἀποκρίνομαι.

εἶ. Pres act ind 2nd sg εἰμί.

κύριε. On the position of the vocative, see 10:13 on Πέτρε.

εἶπέν. Aor act ind 3rd sg λέγω. The second accent comes from the enclitic τε (see 1:4 on ἠκούσατέ).

εἰμι. Pres act ind 1st sg εἰμί.

'Ιησοῦς. Predicate nominative.

ὁ Ναζωραῖος. Nominative in apposition to 'Ιησοῦς.

διώκεις. Pres act ind 2nd sg διώκω.

22:9 οἱ δὲ σὺν ἐμοὶ ὄντες τὸ μὲν φῶς ἐθεάσαντο τὴν δὲ φωνὴν οὐκ ἤκουσαν τοῦ λαλοῦντός μοι.

ὄντες. Pres act ptc masc nom pl εἰμί (subtantival).

ἐθεάσαντο. Aor mid dep ind 3rd pl θεάομαι.

φωνὴν. Accusative object of ἤκουσαν. On the use of the accusative rather than the genitive and the apparent contradition between the statement here and the one in ch. 9, see 9:7 on φωνῆς.

ἤκουσαν. Aor act ind 3rd pl ἀκούω.

τοῦ λαλοῦντός. Pres act ptc masc gen sg λαλέω (substantival). The second accent comes from the enclitic μοι (see 1:4 on ἠκούσατέ).

22:10 εἶπον δέ, Τί ποιήσω, κύριε; ὁ δὲ κύριος εἶπεν πρός με, 'Αναστὰς πορεύου εἰς Δαμασκόν κἀκεῖ σοι λαληθήσεται περὶ πάντων ὧν τέτακταί σοι ποιῆσαι.

εἶπον δέ. On the use of this construction, see 19:4.

εἶπον. Aor act ind 1st sg λέγω.

ποιήσω. Aor act subj 1st sg ποιέω (deliberative subjunctive).

κύριε. On the position of the vocative, see 10:13 on Πέτρε.

εἶπεν. Aor act ind 3rd sg λέγω.

'Αναστὰς. Aor act ptc masc nom sg ἀνίστημι (with an imperative main verb an attendant circumstance participle carries imperatival force). Here, ἀνίστημι probably carries its literal sense (but see 8:26 on 'Ανάστηθι . . . πορεύου).

πορεύου. Pres dep impv 2nd sg πορεύομαι.

κἀκεῖ. A shortened form (crasis) of καί ἐκεῖ.

σοι . . . ποιῆσαι. Lit. "it will be told to you about everything that has been appointed to you to do."

λαληθήσεται. Fut pass ind 3rd sg λαλέω (impersonal).

πάντων. Substantival.

ὧν. Genitive by attraction (see 1:1 on ὧν) to πάντων. As the syntactic direct object of ποιῆσαι the relative pronoun would normally be accusative.

τέτακταί. Prf pass ind 3rd sg τάσσω. The second accent comes from the enclitic σοι (see 1:4 on ἠκούσατέ).

σοι. Dative indirect object of τέτακταί.

ποιῆσαι. Aor act inf ποιέω (indirect discourse; Rogers and Rogers, 291).

22:11 ὡς δὲ οὐκ ἐνέβλεπον ἀπὸ τῆς δόξης τοῦ φωτὸς ἐκείνου, χειραγωγούμενος ὑπὸ τῶν συνόντων μοι ἦλθον εἰς Δαμασκόν.

ὡς. Temporal (see 18:5).

ἐνέβλεπον. Impf act ind 1st sg ἐνβλέπω.

ἀπὸ. Causal.

χειραγωγούμενος. Pres pass ptc masc nom sg χειραγωγέω (means; cf. 9:8).

τῶν συνόντων. Pres act ptc masc gen pl σύνειμι (substantival).

μοι. Verbs with a συν- prefix take a dative complement.

ἦλθον. Aor act ind 1st sg ἔρχομαι.

22:12 ʽΑνανίας δέ τις, ἀνὴρ εὐλαβὴς κατὰ τὸν νόμον, μαρτυρούμενος ὑπὸ πάντων τῶν κατοικούντων ʼΙουδαίων,

ἀνὴρ. Nominative in apposition to ʽΑνανίας.

κατὰ. Introduces the standard against which Ananias' piety was measured.

μαρτυρούμενος. Pres pass ptc masc nom sg μαρτυρέω (attributive). On the meaning of the term, see 10:22.

τῶν κατοικούντων. Pres act ptc masc gen pl κατοικέω (attributive).

22:13 ἐλθὼν πρός με καὶ ἐπιστὰς εἶπέν μοι, Σαοὺλ ἀδελφέ, ἀνάβλεψον. κἀγὼ αὐτῇ τῇ ὥρᾳ ἀνέβλεψα εἰς αὐτόν.

ἐλθὼν. Aor act ptc masc nom sg ἔρχομαι (attendant circumstance).

ἐπιστὰς. Aor act ptc masc nom sg ἐφίστημι (attendant circumstance).

εἶπέν. Aor act ind 3rd sg λέγω. The second accent comes from the enclitic μοι (see 1:4 on ἠκούσατέ).

Σαοὺλ ἀδελφέ. Vocative.

ἀνάβλεψον. Aor act impv 2nd sg ἀναβλέπω. In light of the context of 9:17, it is likely that readers would understand the verb to mean "see again."

κἀγὼ. A shortened form (crasis) of καὶ ἐγώ.

ἀνέβλεψα. Aor act ind 1st sg ἀναβλέπω. Here, unlike in the previous clause, the prepositional phrase, εἰς αὐτόν, points the reader to a difference sense of ἀναβλέπω: "to look up."

22:14 ὁ δὲ εἶπεν, Ὁ θεὸς τῶν πατέρων ἡμῶν προεχειρίσατό σε γνῶναι τὸ θέλημα αὐτοῦ καὶ ἰδεῖν τὸν δίκαιον καὶ ἀκοῦσαι φωνὴν ἐκ τοῦ στόματος αὐτοῦ,

ὁ. The article functions like a personal pronoun here (cf. 3:5).

εἶπεν. Aor act ind 3rd sg λέγω.

προεχειρίσατό. Aor mid dep ind 3rd sg προχειρίζομαι. The second accent comes from the enclitic σε (see 1:4 on ἠκούσατέ).

σε. In light of the analogous structure in 26:16, the pronoun should be viewed as the accusative object of προεχειρίσατό rather than the accusative subject of the infinitive.

γνῶναι. Aor act inf γινώσκω (purpose).

ἰδεῖν. Aor act inf ὁράω (purpose).

ἀκοῦσαι. Aor act inf ἀκούω (purpose).

φωνὴν . . . αὐτοῦ. Lit. "the sound from his mouth."

22:15 ὅτι ἔσῃ μάρτυς αὐτῷ πρὸς πάντας ἀνθρώπους ὧν ἑώρακας καὶ ἤκουσας.

ὅτι. Causal.

ἔσῃ μάρτυς αὐτῷ . . . ὧν. Lit. "you will be a witness to/for him . . . of the things that."

ἔσῃ. Fut ind 2nd sg εἰμί.

μάρτυς. Predicate nominative.

αὐτῷ. Dative of possession (with εἰμί) or dative of advantage. The antecedent is Ὁ θεὸς (v. 14).

ὧν. The relative pronoun introduces a headless relative clause (see 3:6 on ὅ). The case should probably be viewed as either indicating reference (relating syntactically to ἑώρακας) or the genitive object of ἤκουσας, though conceptually the relative pronoun clearly has a relationship to both verbs. Theoretically, it would also be possible to argue that the genitive case resulted from attraction (see 1:1 on ὧν) to an unexpressed antecedent. In order to understand how a relative pronoun could "attract" to the case of an antecedent that does not exist, it is important to realize that attraction is a process that may occur precisely because the relative pronoun has been moved to a position in the syntactic structure of the sentence (preceding the clause to which it belongs) where it is vulnerable to case assignment from the word or structure that would have assigned case to its antecedent (see Culy 1989, 123–46).

ἑώρακας Prf act ind 2nd sg ὁράω.

ἤκουσας. Aor act ind 2nd sg ἀκούω.

22:16 καὶ νῦν τί μέλλεις; ἀναστὰς βάπτισαι καὶ ἀπόλουσαι τὰς ἁμαρτίας σου ἐπικαλεσάμενος τὸ ὄνομα αὐτοῦ.

καὶ νῦν. See 4:29 on καὶ τὰ νῦν.

τί μέλλεις. An idiom meaning, "Why are you delaying?" (BADG, 501).

μέλλεις. Pres act ind 2nd sg μέλλω.

ἀναστὰς. Aor act ptc masc nom sg ἀνίστημι (with an imperative main verb an attendant circumstance participle carries imperatival force). On the force of this verb, see 8:26 on ᾿Ανάστηθι πορεύου. That the Lord wanted Paul to be baptized at once is made clear by the preceding question (cf. the analogous construction and context at 9:11).

βάπτισαι. Aor mid impv 2nd sg βαπτίζω. Wallace (1996, 426) identifies both imperatives as permissive middles: "Rise, *have yourself baptized* and *allow* your sins *to be washed away.*"

ἀπόλουσαι τὰς ἁμαρτίας σου. Lit. "wash away your sins."

ἀπόλουσαι. Aor mid impv 2nd sg ἀπολούω. Since this word is conjoined with an unambiguous imperative, it should not be taken as an aorist active infinitive (contra Rogers and Rogers, 291).

ἐπικαλεσάμενος. Aor mid ptc masc nom sg ἐπικαλέω. While we cannot argue with the theology of taking ἐπικαλεσάμενος as a participle of means, the syntax and semantics, which closely link the two imperatives, disallow taking it as a modifier of ἀπόλουσαι alone and suggest that it instead introduces an attendant circumstance: the whole process of baptism, washing of sins, and calling on the Lord's name is portrayed as a single complex event (contra Barrett, 1029; Rogers and Rogers, 292; Fitzmyer 1998, 702).

22:17 ᾿Εγένετο δέ μοι ὑποστρέψαντι εἰς ᾿Ιερουσαλὴμ καὶ προσευχομένου μου ἐν τῷ ἱερῷ γενέσθαι με ἐν ἐκστάσει

BDF (§409.4) call this "a very clumsy sentence" and wonder if Luke really wrote it at all (§278). Similarly, Barrett (1043) remarks that "the construction of this verse is astounding." Quite the contrary, the whole construction follows the rules of Greek syntax (though it is somewhat complicated). We should, therefore, not be surprised that scribes made no attempt to improve the syntax (contra Barrett, 1043). The conjoined infinitival clause (γενέσθαι . . . καὶ ἰδεῖν . . .), which extends to the end of v. 18, functions as the subject of ᾿Εγένετο, which also has an indirect object (μοι) that is modified by an attributive participle (where English would prefer a temporal expression; cf. 22:6 on πορευομένῳ). This entire construction is modified by a temporal genitive absolute construction introduced by an epexegetical καί: lit. "It happened to me, who had returned to Jerusalem—specifically, while I was praying in the temple—that I was in a trance."

᾿Εγένετο. Aor mid dep ind 3rd sg γινόμαι.

ὑποστρέψαντι. Aor act ptc masc dat sg ὑποστρέφω (attributive; see above).

καὶ. Epexegetical.

προσευχομένου. Pres mid ptc masc gen sg προσεύχομαι. Genitive absolute (see 1:8 on ἐπελθόντος), temporal. The genitive absolute construction is required since the subject of the participle is different from the subject of the main clause (see Culy 2004; contra Bruce, 458).

μου. Genitive subject (see 1:8 on ἐπελθόντος).

γενέσθαι. Aor mid dep inf γίνομαι (subject; see above).

με. Accusative subject of the infinitive (see 1:3 on αὐτὸν).

22:18 καὶ ἰδεῖν αὐτὸν λέγοντά μοι, Σπεῦσον καὶ ἔξελθε ἐν τάχει ἐξ ᾿Ιερουσαλήμ, διότι οὐ παραδέξονταί σου μαρτυρίαν περὶ ἐμοῦ.

ἰδεῖν. Aor act inf ὁράω (subject; see v. 17).

αὐτὸν. The following context makes it clear that the antecedent is the Lord.

λέγοντά. Pres act ptc masc acc sg λέγω. The participle functions as the complement in an object-complement double accusative construction (see 1:3 on ζῶντα). The second accent comes from the enclitic μοι (see 1:4 on ἠκούσατέ).

Σπεῦσον. Aor act impv 2nd sg σπεύδω.

ἔξελθε. Aor act impv 2nd sg ἐξέρχομαι.

ἐν τάχει. See 12:7.

ἐξ. See 1:8 on ἐφ' ὑμᾶς.

παραδέξονταί. Fut mid dep ind 3rd pl παραδέχομαι. The second accent comes from the enclitic σου (see 1:4 on ἠκούσατέ).

22:19 κἀγὼ εἶπον, Κύριε, αὐτοὶ ἐπίστανται ὅτι ἐγὼ ἤμην φυλακίζων καὶ δέρων κατὰ τὰς συναγωγὰς τοὺς πιστεύοντας ἐπὶ σέ,

κἀγὼ. A shortened form (crasis) of καὶ ἐγώ.

εἶπον. Aor act ind 1st sg λέγω.

Κύριε. Vocative.

αὐτοὶ. Intensive (contra Wallace [1996, 323] who views it as redundant).

ἐπίστανται. Pres dep ind 3rd pl ἐπίσταμαι.

ὅτι. Introduces a clausal complement (indirect discourse) of ἐπίστανται.

ἤμην. Impf ind 1st sg εἰμί.

φυλακίζων. Pres act ptc masc nom sg φυλακίζω (imperfect periphrastic; see 1:10 on ἀτενίζοντες).

δέρων. Pres act ptc masc nom sg δέρω (imperfect periphrastic; see 1:10 on ἀτενίζοντες).

κατὰ. Distributive.

τοὺς πιστεύοντας. Pres act ptc masc acc pl πιστεύω (substantival).

22:20 καὶ ὅτε ἐξεχύννετο τὸ αἷμα Στεφάνου τοῦ μάρτυρός σου, καὶ αὐτὸς ἤμην ἐφεστὼς καὶ συνευδοκῶν καὶ φυλάσσων τὰ ἱμάτια τῶν ἀναιρούντων αὐτόν.

ἐξεχύννετο. Impf pass ind 3rd sg ἐκχέω/ἐκχύννω.

μάρτυρός. Genitive in apposition to Στεφάνου. The second accent comes from the enclitic σου (see 1:4 on ἠκούσατέ).

αὐτὸς. Intensive.

ἤμην. Impf ind 1st sg εἰμί.

ἐφεστὼς. Prf act ptc masc nom sg ἐφίστημι (pluperfect periphrastic; see 1:17 on κατηριθμημένος). The fact that the verb does not occur as a present participle suggests that no distinction should be read between it and the following present participles.

συνευδοκῶν. Pres act ptc masc nom sg συνευδοκέω (imperfect periphrastic; see 1:10 on ἀτενίζοντες).

φυλάσσων. Pres act ptc masc nom sg φυλάσσω (imperfect periphrastic; see 1:10 on ἀτενίζοντες).

τῶν ἀναιρούντων. Pres act ptc masc gen pl ἀναιρέω (substantival).

22:21 καὶ εἶπεν πρός με, Πορεύου, ὅτι ἐγὼ εἰς ἔθνη μακρὰν ἐξαποστελῶ σε.

εἶπεν. Aor act ind 3rd sg λέγω.

Πορεύου. Pres dep impv 2nd sg πορεύομαι.

ὅτι. Causal.

ἐξαποστελῶ. Fut act ind 1st sg ἐξαποστέλλω (predicative future).

Acts 22:22–29

22Now, they were listening to him until this statement, but (when they heard it) they shouted, "Away from the earth with such a person! For it is not right for him to live!" 23And since they were yelling, throwing off their outer garments, and flinging dirt into the air, 24the commander ordered him to be brought into the barracks and said that he should be interrogated using a whip so that he might learn the precise reason why they were shouting at him in this way.

25When they had tied him up with straps (to be beaten), Paul said to the centurion who was standing (there), "Is it lawful for you to beat a man who is a Roman citizen and has not been tried?" 26When the centurion heard (this) he went to the commander and reported it, saying, "What are you about to do? This man is a Roman citizen!"

27So the commander went (to Paul) and said to him, "Tell me, are you a Roman citizen?" And he replied, "Yes, (I am)." 28Then the commander responded, "My citizenship cost me a lot of money!" But Paul replied, "I was born (a citizen)."

29Immediately, those who were about to interrogate him moved away from him, and the commander was also afraid because he knew that he had bound a Roman citizen.

22:22 Ἤκουον δὲ αὐτοῦ ἄχρι τούτου τοῦ λόγου καὶ ἐπῆραν τὴν φωνὴν αὐτῶν λέγοντες, Αἶρε ἀπὸ τῆς γῆς τὸν τοιοῦτον, οὐ γὰρ καθῆκεν αὐτὸν ζῆν.

Ἤκουον. Impf act ind 3rd pl ἀκούω.

αὐτοῦ. Genitive object of Ἤκουον.

ἐπῆραν . . . λέγοντες. Lit. "they raised their voice saying."

ἐπῆραν. Aor act ind 3rd pl ἐπαίρω.

λέγοντες. Pres act ptc masc nom pl λέγω (attendant circumstance).

Αἶρε. Pres act impv 2nd sg αἴρω.

τὸν τοιοῦτον. Substantival direct object of Αἶρε.

καθῆκεν. Impf act ind 3rd sg καθήκω (impersonal). This verb (only here and in Rom 1:28) means, "to be fitting or right, with the implication of possible moral judgment involved" (LN 66.1).

αὐτὸν. Accusative subject of the infinitive (see 1:3 on αὐτὸν).

ζῆν. Pres act inf ζάω (complementary; see 1:16 on ἔδει).

22:23 κραυγαζόντων τε αὐτῶν καὶ ῥιπτούντων τὰ ἱμάτια καὶ κονιορτὸν βαλλόντων εἰς τὸν ἀέρα,

κραυγαζόντων. Pres act ptc masc gen pl κραυγάζω. Genitive absolute (see 1:8 on ἐπελθόντος), causal.

αὐτῶν. Genitive subject (see 1:8 on ἐπελθόντος) of the three participles.

ῥιπτούντων τὰ ἱμάτια καὶ κονιορτὸν βαλλόντων εἰς τὸν ἀέρα. The two symbolic actions indicate the intense anger of the crowd toward Paul.

ῥιπτούντων. Pres act ptc masc gen pl ῥίπτω. Genitive absolute (see 1:8 on ἐπελθόντος), causal.

βαλλόντων. Pres act ptc masc gen pl βάλλω. Genitive absolute (see 1:8 on ἐπελθόντος), causal.

22:24 ἐκέλευσεν ὁ χιλίαρχος εἰσάγεσθαι αὐτὸν εἰς τὴν παρεμβολήν, εἴπας μάστιξιν ἀνετάζεσθαι αὐτὸν ἵνα ἐπιγνῷ δι' ἣν αἰτίαν οὕτως ἐπεφώνουν αὐτῷ.

ἐκέλευσεν. Aor act ind 3rd sg κελεύω.

εἰσάγεσθαι. Pres pass inf εἰσάγω (indirect discourse).

αὐτὸν. Accusative subject of the infinitive (see 1:3 on αὐτὸν).

εἴπας. Aor act ptc masc nom sg λέγω (attendant circumstance).

μάστιξιν. The dative of instrument (in terms of syntax) is used to introduce the manner (in terms of semantics) in which Paul was to be interrogated.

ἀνετάζεσθαι. Pres pass inf ἀνετάζω.

αὐτὸν. Accusative subject of the infinitive (see 1:3 on αὐτὸν).

ἐπιγνῷ. Aor act subj 3rd sg ἐπιγινώσκω. The subjunctive is used with ἵνα to indicate purpose.

δι' ἣν αἰτίαν. The internally headed relative clause ("on account of which reason"; see 1:2 on ἄχρι ἧς ἡμέρας) probably produces an intensive expression: "the *precise* reason why." The more typical construction would be ἵνα ἐπιγνῷ τὴν αἰτίαν δι' ἣν οὕτως ἐπεφώνουν αὐτῷ ("in order that he might know the reason for which they were shouting at him in this way"; cf. 23:28) with αἰτίαν being the direct object of ἐπιγνῷ. A number of scholars have suggested that the commander made this statement because he had not understood the speech, which was given in Aramaic (cf. Bruce, 460; Barrett, 1047). Understanding the function of internally headed relative clauses, however, helps clarify that the commander was not concerned with the content of the speech, but rather with figuring out why the Jews had responded to the speech in such a manner (this reading is supported by the commander's use of οὕτως and the parallel account in 23:28).

ἐπεφώνουν. Impf act ind 3rd pl ἐπιφωνέω.

22:25 ὡς δὲ προέτειναν αὐτὸν τοῖς ἱμᾶσιν, εἶπεν πρὸς τὸν ἑστῶτα ἑκατόνταρχον ὁ Παῦλος, Εἰ ἄνθρωπον Ῥωμαῖον καὶ ἀκατάκριτον ἔξεστιν ὑμῖν μαστίζειν;

ὡς. Temporal (see 18:5).

προέτειναν . . . τοῖς ἱμᾶσιν. In light of the use of ἱμάς elsewhere in the NT to indicate a strap (Mark 1:7//Luke 3:16//John 1:27) and the fact that an instrumental use of the dative is natural in this context, we prefer the view that this expression refers to tying a prisoner using straps with his arms spread out (in preparation for whipping). Others (Barrett, 1047–48; BAGD, 376), prefer the view that the dative expression indicates purpose (a questionable function of the dative case): "for the lash."

προέτειναν. Aor act ind 3rd pl προτείνω.

τοῖς ἱμᾶσιν. Instrumental; see above.

εἶπεν. Aor act ind 3rd sg λέγω.

ἑστῶτα. Prf act ptc masc acc sg ἵστημι (attributive).

Εἰ. Introduces direct discourse.

ἄνθρωπον. The accusative direct object of μαστίζειν has been fronted (see 3:13 on ὑμεῖς) for emphasis (see 2:15 on ὑμεῖς).

'Ρωμαῖον καὶ ἀκατάκριτον. Substantival accusative adjectives in apposition to ἄνθρωπον or attributive.

ἔξεστιν. Pres act ind 3rd sg ἔξεστιν.

μαστίζειν. Pres act inf μαστίζω. The discontinuous infinitival clause, ἄνθρωπον 'Ρωμαῖον καὶ ἀκατάκριτον . . . μαστίζειν, functions as the subject of ἔξεστιν.

22:26 ἀκούσας δὲ ὁ ἑκατοντάρχης προσελθὼν τῷ χιλιάρχῳ ἀπήγγειλεν λέγων, Τί μέλλεις ποιεῖν; ὁ γὰρ ἄνθρωπος οὗτος 'Ρωμαῖός ἐστιν.

ἀκούσας. Aor act ptc masc nom sg ἀκούω (temporal).

προσελθὼν. Aor act ptc masc nom sg προσέρχομαι (attendant circumstance).

ἀπήγγειλεν. Aor act ind 3rd sg ἀπαγγέλλω.

λέγων. Pres act ptc masc nom sg λέγω (attendant circumstance).

Τί μέλλεις ποιεῖν; This expression probably did not carry the accusatory connotation of the English, "What are you about to do?" For this reason, the NCV's, "Do you know what you are doing?" is probably an appropriate English rendering, though the question may well be a mitigated command (appropriate in addressing a superior): "Stop what you're about to do!"

μέλλεις. Pres act ind 2nd sg μέλλω. On the force of μέλλω plus an infinitive, see 3:3 on μέλλοντας.

ποιεῖν. Pres act inf ποιέω (complementary).

'Ρωμαῖός. Predicate nominative. The second accent comes from the enclitic ἐστιν (see 1:4 on ἠκούσατέ).

ἐστιν. Pres act ind 3rd sg εἰμί.

22:27 προσελθὼν δὲ ὁ χιλίαρχος εἶπεν αὐτῷ, Λέγε μοι, σὺ 'Ρωμαῖος εἶ; ὁ δὲ ἔφη, Ναί.

προσελθὼν. Aor act ptc masc nom sg προσέρχομαι (attendant circumstance).

εἶπεν. Aor act ind 3rd sg λέγω.

Λέγε. Pres act impv 2nd sg λέγω.

Ρωμαῖος. Predicate nominative.

εἶ. Pres act ind 2nd sg εἰμί.

ὁ. The article functions like a personal pronoun here (cf. 3:5).

ἔφη. Aor/Impf act ind 3rd sg φημί. On the tense, see 7:2.

22:28 ἀπεκρίθη δὲ ὁ χιλίαρχος, Ἐγὼ πολλοῦ κεφαλαίου τὴν πολιτείαν ταύτην ἐκτησάμην. ὁ δὲ Παῦλος ἔφη, Ἐγὼ δὲ καὶ γεγέννημαι.

ἀπεκρίθη. Aor pass dep ind 3rd sg ἀποκρίνομαι. On the force of the verb, see 9:13.

Ἐγὼ . . . ἐκτησάμην. Lit. "I acquired this citizenship with a large sum of money."

Ἐγὼ. The fronted (see 3:13 on ὑμεῖς) explicit subject pronoun shifts the focus (see 2:15 on ὑμεῖς) to the commander.

κεφαλαίου. Genitive of price.

ἐκτησάμην. Aor mid dep ind 1st sg κτάομαι.

ἔφη. Aor/Impf act ind 3rd sg φήμι. On the tense, see 7:2.

Ἐγὼ. The fronted (see 3:13 on ὑμεῖς) explicit subject pronoun shifts the focus (see 2:15 on ὑμεῖς) back to Paul and highlights (along with the δὲ καὶ) the contrast. Barrett (1050) is probably correct in arguing that the two conjunctions emphasize the following word (cf. 1 Cor 15:15): "I, as a matter of fact, was *born* (a Roman citizen)."

γεγέννημαι. Prf pass ind 1st sg γεννάω.

22:29 εὐθέως οὖν ἀπέστησαν ἀπ' αὐτοῦ οἱ μέλλοντες αὐτὸν ἀνετάζειν, καὶ ὁ χιλίαρχος δὲ ἐφοβήθη ἐπιγνοὺς ὅτι Ῥωμαῖός ἐστιν καὶ ὅτι αὐτὸν ἦν δεδεκώς.

οὖν. The conjunction (omitted in D), along with the temporal adverb εὐθέως, "makes explicit the close consequential relationship between the conversation that established that Paul was a Roman citizen (vv 27-28) and the withdrawal of his torturers" (Levinsohn 1987, 140).

ἀπέστησαν. Aor act ind 3rd pl ἀφίστημι.

ἀπ'. See 1:8 on ἐφ' ὑμᾶς.

οἱ μέλλοντες. Pres act ptc masc nom pl μέλλω (substantival). On the force of μέλλω plus an infinitive, see 3:3 on μέλλοντας.

ἀνετάζειν. Pres act inf ἀνετάζω (complementary).

ἐφοβήθη. Aor pass dep ind 3rd sg φοβέομαι.

ἐπιγνοὺς. Aor act ptc masc nom sg ἐπιγινώσκω (causal).

ἐπιγνοὺς . . . δεδεκώς. Lit. "knowing that he was a Roman and that he had bound him."

ὅτι . . . ὅτι. Both conjunctions introduce clausal complements (indirect discourse) of ἐπιγνοὺς.

Ῥωμαῖός. Predicate nominative. The second accent comes from the enclitic ἐστιν (see 1:4 on ἠκούσατέ).

ἐστιν. Pres act ind 3rd sg εἰμί.

αὐτὸν. Accusative direct object of the participle.

ἦν. Impf ind 3rd sg εἰμί.

δεδεκώς. Prf act ptc masc nom sg δέω (pluperfect periphrastic; see 1:17 on κατηριθμημένος.

Acts 22:30–23:5

[30]The next day, because (the commander) wanted to know the facts—(specifically) why (Paul) was being accused by the Jews—he released him and ordered the chief priests along with the entire Council to assemble. Then he had Paul brought in and had him stand before them.

[23:1]Paul looked directly at the Council and said, "Brothers, up until this day I have lived in accord with God's standards with a completely clear conscience." [2](When he heard this,) The high priest Ananias gave orders to those standing next to him to slap his mouth. [3]Then Paul said to them, "God is about to strike you, you whitewashed wall! Do you (dare) sit there judging me according to the law and yet order me to be slapped even though it is against the law?" [4]Those standing next to him said, "Do you dare insult God's high priest?" [5]Paul replied, "I did not know, brothers, that he was the high priest! For it is written, 'You must not speak evil of your people's ruler.'"

22:30 Τῇ δὲ ἐπαύριον βουλόμενος γνῶναι τὸ ἀσφαλὲς, τὸ τί κατηγορεῖται ὑπὸ τῶν Ἰουδαίων, ἔλυσεν αὐτόν καὶ ἐκέλευσεν συνελθεῖν τοὺς ἀρχιερεῖς καὶ πᾶν τὸ συνέδριον, καὶ καταγαγὼν τὸν Παῦλον ἔστησεν εἰς αὐτούς.

βουλόμενος. Pres dep ptc masc nom sg βούλομαι (causal).

γνῶναι. Aor act inf γινώσκω (complementary).

τὸ τί κατηγορεῖται ὑπὸ τῶν Ἰουδαίων. The article functions as a nominalizer (see 1:3 on τὰ), changing the interrogative clause into a substantive that stands in apposition to the accusative direct object τὸ ἀσφαλὲς.

κατηγορεῖται. Pres pass ind 3rd sg κατηγορέω.

ἔλυσεν. Aor act ind 3rd sg λύω.

ἐκέλευσεν. Aor act ind 3rd sg κελεύω.

συνελθεῖν. Aor act inf συνέρχομαι (indirect discourse).

τοὺς ἀρχιερεῖς καὶ πᾶν τὸ συνέδριον. Accusative subject of the infinitive (see 1:3 on αὐτὸν).

καταγαγὼν. Aor act ptc masc nom sg κατάγω (temporal).

ἔστησεν. Aor act ind 3rd sg ἵστημι. In this context, it may *appear* that ἔστησεν could either be taken transitively ("to place, to stand"), with the commander as the subject and Paul as the unexpressed direct object, or intransitively ("to stand"), with Paul as the subject. Since the latter, however, would have required the preceding participle to be a genitive absolute, given the different subject, the syntax actually makes it clear that the transitive use of the verb is intended. The actual agent of the verb, the soldiers, is left implicit (the commander probably did not personally escort Paul).

23:1 ἀτενίσας δὲ ὁ Παῦλος τῷ συνεδρίῳ εἶπεν, Ἄνδρες ἀδελφοί, ἐγὼ πάσῃ συνειδήσει ἀγαθῇ πεπολίτευμαι τῷ θεῷ ἄχρι ταύτης τῆς ἡμέρας.

Ἄνδρες. See 1:11.

ἀδελφοί. Here, as in 7:2; 13:15; 22:1, 5; 23:5, 6, this vocative expression is used to refer to fellow Jews rather than as a technical term for "believers" (cf. 1:15).

ἀτενίσας. Aor act ptc masc nom sg ἀτενίζω (attendant circumstance).

εἶπεν. Aor act ind 3rd sg λέγω.

πάσῃ συνειδήσει ἀγαθῇ. This noun phrase (lit. "with all good conscience") indicates the manner in which Paul lived before God.

πεπολίτευμαι. Prf dep ind 1st sg πολιτεύομαι. Elsewhere in the NT, πολιτεύομαι ("to live") is found only in Phil 1:27. Most commentators suggest that it carries with it the notion of citizenship in Philippians (cf. Fee, 161; O'Brien, 147; Silva 1988, 91; Hawthorne, 55), though Hawthorne (55) recognizes that such a notion is unlikely in Acts. Given the numerous references in the LXX (2 Macc 6:1; 11:25; 3 Macc 3:4; 4 Macc 2:8, 23; 4:23; 5:16), however, where the more general notion is clearly intended, it is questionable whether the idea of citizenship is present in either NT passage. In the extrabiblical passages cited by Silva in support of the citizenship view, the nuance of citizenship is *always* made clear by an explicit reference to heaven in the context. Such contextual information is lacking in the present passage.

τῷ θεῷ. When the verb πολιτεύομαι is used in the LXX, it frequently is followed by a dative noun (usually νόμῳ/νόμοις; cf. Esth 8:17; 2 Macc 6:1; 3 Macc 3:4; 4 Macc 2:8; 4:23; 5:16) or κατά plus a noun phrase (2 Macc 11:25; 4 Macc 2:23) indicating the standard by which the person lived. It is possible that τῷ θεῷ is here equivalent to τῷ θεοῦ νόμῳ and thus a dative of rule (see 2:23 on βουλῇ καὶ προγνώσει). Or, the dative case may denote reference.

23:2 ὁ δὲ ἀρχιερεὺς Ἁνανίας ἐπέταξεν τοῖς παρεστῶσιν αὐτῷ τύπτειν αὐτοῦ τὸ στόμα.

Ἁνανίας. Nominative in apposition to ὁ ἀρχιερεὺς.

ἐπέταξεν. Aor act ind 3rd sg ἐπιτάσσω.

τοῖς παρεστῶσιν. Prf act ptc masc dat pl παρίστημι (substantival). Dative indirect object of ἐπέταξεν.

αὐτῷ. Dative complement of παρεστῶσιν. The antecedent is Paul.

τύπτειν. Pres act inf τύπτω (indirect discourse).

23:3 τότε ὁ Παῦλος πρὸς αὐτὸν εἶπεν, Τύπτειν σε μέλλει ὁ θεός, τοῖχε κεκονιαμένε· καὶ σὺ κάθῃ κρίνων με κατὰ τὸν νόμον καὶ παρανομῶν κελεύεις με τύπτεσθαι;

τότε. The adverb indicates a prompt (rash?) response (see 1:12).

εἶπεν. Aor act ind 3rd sg λέγω.

Τύπτειν. Pres act inf τύτπω (complementary).

μέλλει. Pres act ind 3rd sg μέλλω. On the force of μέλλω plus an infinitive, see 3:3 on μέλλοντας.

τοῖχε κεκονιαμένε. On the position of the vocative, see 10:13.

κεκονιαμένε. Prf pass ptc masc voc sg κονιάω (attributive). This is the only vocative participle in the NT or LXX.

καὶ σὺ . . . τύπτεσθαι; This sentence may well have been intended as a statement, rather than a question, that explains why Paul called the high priest a whitewashed wall. Such a reading may fit better both with the preceding vocative and with the following statement by those standing beside Paul: "You sit there judging me according to the law and yet violate the law by ordering me to be slapped!"

καὶ σὺ. The use of καί to introduce a question lends a note of indignation (cf. Rogers and Rogers, 293; Barrett, 1060).

κάθῃ. Pres dep ind 2nd sg κάθημαι.

κρίνων. Pres act ptc masc nom sg κρίνω (attendant circumstance).

παρανομῶν. Pres act ptc masc nom sg παρανομέω (concessive).

κελεύεις. Pres act ind 2nd sg κελεύω.

με. Accusative subject of the passive infinitive (see 1:3 on αὐτὸν).

τύπτεσθαι. Pres pass inf τύπτω (indirect discourse).

23:4 οἱ δὲ παρεστῶτες εἶπαν, Τὸν ἀρχιερέα τοῦ θεοῦ λοιδορεῖς;

παρεστῶτες. Prf act ptc masc nom pl παρίστημι (substantival).

εἶπαν. Aor act ind 3rd pl λέγω.

Τὸν ἀρχιερέα τοῦ θεοῦ. The fronting (see 3:13 on ὑμεῖς) of the direct object helps convey the incredulity of the speakers.

λοιδορεῖς. Pres act ind 2nd sg λοιδορέω.

23:5 ἔφη τε ὁ Παῦλος, Οὐκ ᾔδειν, ἀδελφοί, ὅτι ἐστὶν ἀρχιερεύς· γέγραπται γὰρ ὅτι Ἄρχοντα τοῦ λαοῦ σου οὐκ ἐρεῖς κακῶς.

ἔφη. Aor/Impf act ind 3rd sg φημί. On the tense, see 7:2.

Οὐκ ᾔδειν, ἀδελφοί, ὅτι ἐστὶν ἀρχιερεύς. According to Levinsohn (1987, 32), Paul's reply amounts to an apology. Such a view appears consistent with the following OT quotation. Others (cf. Marshall, 363–64), however, have noted that it is inconceivable that Paul would not have recognized the high priest and thus suggest that his reply should be taken as irony or sarcasm comparable to CEV's rendering: "Oh! I didn't know he was the high priest. The Scriptures do tell us not to speak evil about a leader of our people." In this view, the use of the OT quote involves further irony implying that the high priest was not qualified (in light of his behavior) to be a ruler of God's people.

ᾔδειν. Plprf act ind 1st sg οἶδα.

ἀδελφοί. See v. 1. On the position of the vocative, see 10:13.

ὅτι. Introduces a causal complement of ᾔδειν.

ἐστὶν. Pres act ind 3rd sg εἰμί.

ἀρχιερεύς. Predicate nominative.

γέγραπται. Prf pass ind 3rd sg γράφω.

ὅτι. Introduces direct discourse.

ἐρεῖς. Fut act ind 2nd sg λέγω (imperatival future; see 18:15 on ὄψεσθε).

Acts 23:6–11

6When Paul realized that part (of the group) was Sadducees and part Pharisees, he shouted out in the Council, "Brothers, I am a Pharisee, a son of Pharisees, (and) I am being tried for (my) hope in the resurrection from the dead!" 7When he said this, an argument began between the Pharisees and the Sadducees, and the group was divided. 8For the Sadducees say that there is no resurrection, or angels, or spirits; but the Pharisees profess them all. 9So there was a lot of shouting, and some of the scribes, who were members of the Pharisees, stood up and began strongly protesting, saying, "We find nothing wrong with this man. Did an angel or spirit (actually) speak to him? (Perhaps one did!)"

10When a terrible argument ensued, the commander became afraid that they would tear Paul to pieces so he ordered the troops to go down and take him away from them and then bring him (back) to the barracks. 11The next night, the Lord stood beside him and said, "Have courage! For just as you have testified about me in Jerusalem, in the same way you must also testify in Rome."

23:6 Γνοὺς δὲ ὁ Παῦλος ὅτι τὸ ἓν μέρος ἐστὶν Σαδδουκαίων τὸ δὲ ἕτερον Φαρισαίων ἔκραζεν ἐν τῷ συνεδρίῳ, Ἄνδρες ἀδελφοί, ἐγὼ Φαρισαῖός εἰμι, υἱὸς Φαρισαίων, περὶ ἐλπίδος καὶ ἀναστάσεως νεκρῶν [ἐγὼ] κρίνομαι.

Γνοὺς. Aor act ptc masc nom sg γινώσκω (temporal).

ὅτι. Introduces a clausal complement of Γνοὺς.

ἐστὶν. Pres act ind 3rd sg εἰμί.

Σαδδουκαίων . . . Φαρισαίων. Barrett (1063) calls these nouns "predicate partitive genitives" and argues that the expression should be rendered: "one part consisted of Sadducees, the other of Pharisees." While the rendering may not be completely inappropriate, in terms of syntax the nouns cannot be viewed as partitive genitives since they are independent predicates. Instead, they should simply be viewed as predicate genitives. The confusion stems from the fact that the part of the subject that these nouns modify is left implicit: "part *of them* were Sadducees . . ."

ἔκραζεν. Impf act ind 3rd sg κράζω.

Ἄνδρες. See 1:11.

ἀδελφοί. See v. 1.

Φαρισαῖός . . . Φαρισαίων. Wallace (1996, 103, n. 84) compares this expression to instances where a noun is modified by the same noun in the genitive and indicates that the first noun is a *par excellence* referent (e.g., "king of kings"). It is not clear, however, that the present expression is analogous.

Φαρισαῖός. Predicate nominative. The second accent comes from the enclitic εἰμι (see 1:4 on ἠκούσατέ).

υἱός. Nominative in apposition to Φαρισαῖός.

περὶ. Reference.

ἐλπίδος καὶ ἀναστάσεως. This phrase could either be taken as a hendiadys (see 1:25 on τῆς διακονίας καὶ ἀποστολῆς), with the coordination of the two nouns allowing the writer to avoid a series of dependent genitives (BDF §442.16), or the καὶ could be viewed as epexegetical and thus introduce a clarification of the "hope."

νεκρῶν. Objective genitive.

κρίνομαι. Pres pass ind 1st sg κρίνω.

23:7 τοῦτο δὲ αὐτοῦ εἰπόντος ἐγένετο στάσις τῶν Φαρισαίων καὶ Σαδδουκαίων καὶ ἐσχίσθη τὸ πλῆθος.

τοῦτο. Accusative direct object of εἰπόντος.

αὐτοῦ. Genitive subject (see 1:8 on ἐπελθόντος).

εἰπόντος. Aor act ptc masc gen sg λέγω. Genitive absolute (see 1:8 on ἐπελθόντος), temporal.

ἐγένετο. Aor mid dep ind 3rd sg γίνομαι.

στάσις. The noun should be viewed as the nominative subject of ἐγένετο rather than the predicate nominative of an impersonal ἐγένετο. The latter analysis would leave no reason for Luke to use a genitive absolute in the prior clause (see 1:8 on ἐπελθόντος).

τῶν Φαρισαίων καὶ Σαδδουκαίων. Wallace (1996, 135) notes that genitive substantives occasionally "occur after certain nouns whose lexical nature requires a genitive." He further notes that "the most common instances involve two genitives joined by καί, with the meaning 'between,'" as here.

ἐσχίσθη. Aor pass ind 3rd sg σχίζω.

23:8 Σαδδουκαῖοι μὲν γὰρ λέγουσιν μὴ εἶναι ἀνάστασιν μήτε ἄγγελον μήτε πνεῦμα, Φαρισαῖοι δὲ ὁμολογοῦσιν τὰ ἀμφότερα.

λέγουσιν. Pres act ind 3rd pl λέγω.

εἶναι. Pres act inf εἰμί (indirect discourse).

ἀνάστασιν . . . ἄγγελον . . . πνεῦμα. Predicate accusatives (see 1:22 on μάρτυρα) or accusative subjects of the infinitive (see 1:3 on αὐτὸν).

μήτε ἄγγελον μήτε πνεῦμα. Lit. "neither angel nor spirit."

ὁμολογοῦσιν. Pres act ind 3rd pl ὁμολογέω.

ἀμφότερα. See 19:16 on ἀμφοτέρων.

23:9 ἐγένετο δὲ κραυγὴ μεγάλη, καὶ ἀναστάντες τινὲς τῶν γραμματέων τοῦ μέρους τῶν Φαρισαίων διεμάχοντο λέγοντες, Οὐδὲν κακὸν εὑρίσκομεν ἐν τῷ ἀνθρώπῳ τούτῳ· εἰ δὲ πνεῦμα ἐλάλησεν αὐτῷ ἢ ἄγγελος;

ἐγένετο. Aor mid dep ind 3rd sg γίνομαι.

κραυγὴ. Nominative subject or predicate nominative of an impersonal ἐγένετο.

ἀναστάντες. Aor act ptc masc nom pl ἀνίστημι (attendant circumstance).

τινὲς. Substantival subject of διεμάχοντο.

γραμματέων. Partitive genitive.

διεμάχοντο. Impf dep ind 3rd pl διαμάχομαι.

λέγοντες. Pres act ptc masc nom pl λέγω (attendant circumstance or means).

εὑρίσκομεν. Pres act ind 1st pl εὑρίσκω.

εἰ δὲ πνεῦμα ἐλάλησεν αὐτῷ ἢ ἄγγελος; The particle εἰ may introduce a conditional statement that lacks an apodosis: "But if a spirit or an angel spoke to him . . ." Many scribes (*Byz* cop[sa]) understood the clause this way and sought to supply the implicit apodosis: μὴ θεομαχῶμεν ("then let us not fight against God"). The εἰ could also be taken as a conditional particle introducing a question (cf. UBS[4]/NA[27]): "(What) if a spirit or angel spoke to him?" Alternatively, we may follow UBS[4]/NA[27] punctuation and take εἰ as introducing direct discourse: "Did an angel or spirit (actually) speak to him? (Perhaps one did!)." In the end, the syntactic ambiguity has little effect on the obvious sense and force of the construction.

ἐλάλησεν. Aor act ind 3rd sg λαλέω.

23:10 Πολλῆς δὲ γινομένης στάσεως φοβηθεὶς ὁ χιλίαρχος μὴ διασπασθῇ ὁ Παῦλος ὑπ' αὐτῶν ἐκέλευσεν τὸ στράτευμα καταβὰν ἁρπάσαι αὐτὸν ἐκ μέσου αὐτῶν ἄγειν τε εἰς τὴν παρεμβολήν.

Πολλῆς. The adjective likely serves as a modifier of the subject στάσεως (see below) that has been fronted (see 3:13 on ὑμεῖς) to emphasize the seriousness of the argument (see 13:44 on σχεδὸν πᾶσα ἡ πόλις). Here, the intensification of the argument precipitates the commander's actions that follow. It would also be possible to view it as a predicate genitive: "when the argument became great."

γινομένης. Pres dep ptc fem gen sg γίνομαι. Genitive absolute (see 1:8 on ἐπελθόντος), temporal, or perhaps causal.

στάσεως. Genitive subject (see 1:8 on ἐπελθόντος), or perhaps predicate genitive of an impersonal γινομένης.

φοβηθεὶς. Aor pass dep ptc masc nom sg φοβέομαι (causal; Rogers and Rogers 294).

διασπασθῇ. Aor pass subj 3rd sg διασπάω. The subjunctive with μή is commonly used after verbs of warning or fearing (Wallace 1996, 477) and indicates a concern regarding a potential outcome (lit. "the commander was afraid lest Paul be torn apart by them"; cf. 13:40 on ἐπέλθῃ).

ἐκέλευσεν. Aor act ind 3rd sg κελεύω.

καταβὰν. Aor act ptc neut acc sg καταβαίνω (attendant circumstance of the infinitive).

ἁρπάσαι. Aor act inf ἁρπάζω (indirect discourse).

ἄγειν. Pres act inf ἄγω (indirect discourse).

23:11 Τῇ δὲ ἐπιούσῃ νυκτὶ ἐπιστὰς αὐτῷ ὁ κύριος εἶπεν, Θάρσει ὡς γὰρ διεμαρτύρω τὰ περὶ ἐμοῦ εἰς Ἰερουσαλὴμ, οὕτω σε δεῖ καὶ εἰς Ῥώμην μαρτυρῆσαι.

ἐπιούσῃ. Pres act ptc fem dat sg ἔπειμι (attributive).

νυκτὶ. Dative of time.

ἐπιστὰς. Aor act ptc masc nom sg ἐφίστημι (attendant circumstance).

εἶπεν. Aor act ind 3rd sg λέγω.

Θάρσει. Pres act impv 2nd sg θαρσέω.

ὡς. Introduces a comparison and is correlative with οὕτω.

διεμαρτύρω. Aor mid ind 2nd sg διαμαρτύρομαι.

τὰ. The article functions as a nominalizer (see 1:3 on τὰ), changing the prepositional phrase into a substantive.

σε. Accusative subject of the infinitive (see 1:3 on αὐτὸν).

δεῖ. Pres act ind 3rd sg δεῖ.

μαρτυρῆσαι. Aor act inf μαρτυρέω (complementary; see 1:16 on ἔδει).

Acts 23:12–15

[12]When it was day, the Jews made a plan and bound themselves (to it)
with an oath, saying that they would neither eat nor drink until they had
killed Paul. [13]There were more than forty who formed this conspiracy.
[14]They went to the chief priests and elders and said, "We have bound
ourselves with an oath to consume nothing until we have killed Paul. [15]So
now, you must report to the commander, along with the Council, so that
he will bring him down to you as if you are going to examine his case
more thoroughly. And we will be ready to kill him before he arrives!"

23:12 Γενομένης δὲ ἡμέρας ποιήσαντες συστροφὴν οἱ Ἰουδαῖοι ἀνεθεμάτισαν ἑαυτοὺς λέγοντες μήτε φαγεῖν μήτε πιεῖν ἕως οὗ ἀποκτείνωσιν τὸν Παῦλον.

Γενομένης. Aor mid dep ptc fem gen sg γίνομαι. Genitive absolute (see 1:8 on ἐπελθόντος), temporal. The use of the genitive absolute rather than a temporal adverbial clause indicates that the reader is to see continuity between what precedes and what follows: "there is a direct relationship between the Lord's promise of v. 11 that Paul is to be a witness in Rome and the plot of the Jews to kill him" (Levinsohn 1992, 184).

ἡμέρας. Genitive subject (see 1:8 on ἐπελθόντος) or predicate genitive of an impersonal Γενομένης.

ποιήσαντες συστροφὴν. Or, "formed a conspiracy" (LN 30.72).

ποιήσαντες. Aor act ptc masc nom pl ποιέω (attendant circumstance).

ἀνεθεμάτισαν. Aor act ind 3rd pl ἀναθεματίζω.

λέγοντες. Pres act ptc masc nom pl λέγω (means).

φαγεῖν. Aor act inf ἐσθίω (indirect discourse).

πιεῖν. Aor act inf πίνω (indirect discourse).

ἕως οὗ. Here, "until *the time* when" (cf. 21:26).

ἀποκτείνωσιν. Aor act subj 3rd pl ἀποκτείνω. The subjunctive is used since the speakers are envisioning or "projecting" an unrealized event (cf. 21:16 on ξενισθῶμεν).

23:13 ἦσαν δὲ πλείους τεσσεράκοντα οἱ ταύτην τὴν συνωμοσίαν ποιησάμενοι,

ἦσαν. Impf ind 3rd pl εἰμί.

πλείους. Predicate adjective.

οἱ ταύτην τὴν συνωμοσίαν ποιησάμενοι. Louw and Nida (30.73, n. 13) note that συνωμοσία may simply be a stylistic variant for συστροφή in v. 12.

οἱ ποιησάμενοι. Aor mid ptc masc nom pl ποιέω. In terms of syntax, we prefer to take the participle as the substantival subject of ἦσαν, though it is possible to take it as an attributive modifier of the predicate πλείους τεσσεράκοντα (as is required in a good English translation).

23:14 οἵτινες προσελθόντες τοῖς ἀρχιερεῦσιν καὶ τοῖς πρεσβυτέροις εἶπαν, Ἀναθέματι ἀνεθεματίσαμεν ἑαυτοὺς μηδενὸς γεύσασθαι ἕως οὗ ἀποκτείνωμεν τὸν Παῦλον.

προσελθόντες. Aor act ptc masc nom pl προσέρχομαι (attendant circumstance).

εἶπαν. Aor act ind 3rd pl λέγω.

Ἀναθέματι. The dative noun, which could be instrumental, should probably be taken as a (redundant) cognate dative that emphasizes the speakers' view that this was a very serious oath.

ἀνεθεματίσαμεν. Aor act ind 1st pl ἀναθεματίζω.

μηδενὸς. Genitive object of γεύσασθαι.

γεύσασθαι. Aor mid dep inf γεύομαι. The infinitive could be taken as epexegetical to Ἀναθέματι. It cannot serve as a clausal object of ἀνεθεματίσαμεν that introduces indirect discourse since ἀνεθεματίσαμεν already has a direct object (ἑαυτοὺς). It may, however, introduce indirect discourse following an implicit λέγοντες (cf. v. 12).

ἕως οὗ. See v. 12.

ἀποκτείνωμεν. Aor act subj 1st pl ἀποκτείνω. On the use of the subjunctive, see v. 12.

23:15 νῦν οὖν ὑμεῖς ἐμφανίσατε τῷ χιλιάρχῳ σὺν τῷ συνεδρίῳ ὅπως καταγάγῃ αὐτὸν εἰς ὑμᾶς ὡς μέλλοντας διαγινώσκειν ἀκριβέστερον τὰ περὶ αὐτοῦ· ἡμεῖς δὲ πρὸ τοῦ ἐγγίσαι αὐτὸν ἕτοιμοί ἐσμεν τοῦ ἀνελεῖν αὐτόν.

ἐμφανίσατε. Aor act impv 2nd pl ἐμφανίζω. Here, the verb may signify bringing formal charges against Paul (cf. 24:1; 25:15; LN 56.8).

καταγάγῃ. Aor act subj 3rd sg κατάγω. The subjunctive is used with ὅπως to introduce a purpose clause.

μέλλοντας. Pres act ptc masc acc pl μέλλω. On the force of μέλλω plus an infinitive, see 3:3 on μέλλοντας. On the use of the participle with ὡς, see 27:30 on μελλόντων.

διαγινώσκειν. Pres act inf διαγινώσκω (complementary).

τὰ περὶ αὐτοῦ. Lit. "the things concerning him." The article functions as a nominalizer (see 1:3 on τὰ), changing the prepositional phrase into a substantive.

ἐγγίσαι. Aor act inf ἐγγίζω. Used with πρὸ τοῦ to indicate subsequent time, i.e., the event of the main verb precedes the event of the infinitive (cf. Wallace 1996, 596). Here, the main verb and its predicate indicates a state: "ready."

αὐτὸν. Accusative subject of the infinitive (see 1:3 on αὐτὸν).

ἕτοιμοί. Predicate adjective. The second accent comes from the enclitic ἐσμεν (see 1:4 on ἠκούσατέ).

ἐσμεν. Pres act ind 1st pl εἰμί.

τοῦ ἀνελεῖν. Aor act inf ἀναιρέω (epexegetical to ἕτοιμοί).

Acts 23:16–22

16When Paul's nephew heard about the ambush, he went and entered the barracks and informed Paul.
17Then Paul called one of the centurions and said, "Take this young man to the commander, for he has something to report to him."
18So the one who took him brought him to the commander and said, "The prisoner (named) Paul called me and asked me to bring this young man to you, who has something to say to you."
19After the commander had taken him by the hand and moved away, he asked him privately, "What is it that you have to report to me?"
20He replied, "The Jews have agreed to petition you in order that you might bring Paul down to the Council tomorrow as if they are going to ask more thoroughly about something concerning him.
21Therefore, don't pay attention to them. For more than forty of their men are lying in ambush for Paul. They have bound themselves with an oath not to eat or drink until they have killed him, and now they are ready and waiting for your decision."
22Then the commander sent the young man away after giving him the following order: "Tell no one that you have reported these things to me."

23:16 Ἀκούσας δὲ ὁ υἱὸς τῆς ἀδελφῆς Παύλου τὴν ἐνέδραν παραγενόμενος καὶ εἰσελθὼν εἰς τὴν παρεμβολὴν ἀπήγγειλεν τῷ Παύλῳ.

Ἀκούσας. Aor act ptc masc nom sg ἀκούω (temporal).

ἐνέδραν. Only here and at 25:3 in the NT.

παραγενόμενος. Aor act ptc masc nom sg παραγίνομαι (attendant circumstance). The participle modifies the following main verb, not the preceding participle.

εἰσελθὼν. Aor act ptc masc nom sg εἰσέρχομαι (attendant circumstance).

εἰς. See 1:8 on ἐφ' ὑμᾶς.

ἀπήγγειλεν. Aor act ind 3rd sg ἀπαγγέλλω.

τῷ Παύλῳ. Dative indirect object of ἀπήγγειλεν.

23:17 προσκαλεσάμενος δὲ ὁ Παῦλος ἕνα τῶν ἑκατονταρχῶν ἔφη, Τὸν νεανίαν τοῦτον ἀπάγαγε πρὸς τὸν χιλίαρχον, ἔχει γὰρ ἀπαγγεῖλαί τι αὐτῷ.

προσκαλεσάμενος. Aor mid dep ptc masc nom sg προσκαλέομαι (attendant circumstance).

ἑκατονταρχῶν. Partitive genitive.

ἔφη. Aor/Impf act ind 3rd sg φημί. On the tense, see 7:2.

ἀπάγαγε. Aor act impv 2nd sg ἀπάγω.

ἔχει. Pres act ind 3rd sg ἔχω.

ἀπαγγεῖλαί. Aor act inf ἀπαγγέλλω (epexegetical to τι). The second accent comes from the enclitic τι (see 1:4 on ἠκούσατέ).

τι. Direct object of ἔχει, though it may appear to be part of the subordinate clause. The unusual word order—one would expect τι to fall before the infinitive (cf. v. 18) or be omitted altogether (see, e.g., John 8:6)—probably is the result of the fronting (see 3:13 on ὑμεῖς) of the infinitive to lend a sense of importance or urgency to the statement.

23:18 ὁ μὲν οὖν παραλαβὼν αὐτὸν ἤγαγεν πρὸς τὸν χιλίαρχον καὶ φησίν, Ὁ δέσμιος Παῦλος προσκαλεσάμενός με ἠρώτησεν τοῦτον τὸν νεανίσκον ἀγαγεῖν πρὸς σέ ἔχοντά τι λαλῆσαί σοι.

ὁ. The article functions as a nominalizer (see 1:3 on τὰ), rather than a personal pronoun (see 15:3 on Οἱ and 1:6 on οἱ and συνελθόντες), though an adverbial expression may be preferable as an English translation.

μὲν οὖν. See 1:6.

ὁ παραλαβὼν. Aor act ptc masc nom sg παραλαμβάνω (substantival; see above).

ἤγαγεν. Aor act ind 3rd sg ἄγω.

φησίν. Pres act ind 3rd sg φημί.

Παῦλος. Nominative in apposition to δέσμιος.

προσκαλεσάμενός. Aor mid dep ptc masc nom sg προσκαλέομαι (attendant circumstance). The second accent comes from the enclitic με (see 1:4 on ἠκούσατέ).

ἠρώτησεν. Aor act ind 3rd sg ἐρωτάω.

τὸν νεανίσκον. Accusative direct object of ἀγαγεῖν.

ἀγαγεῖν. Aor act inf ἄγω (indirect discourse).

ἔχοντά. Pres act ptc masc acc sg ἔχω. The participle cannot be adverbial since the accusative case indicates that it does not modify the main verb. Instead, it must be an attributive modifier of νεανίσκον (cf. 22:6 on πορευομένῳ). The second accent comes from the enclitic τι (see 1:4 on ἠκούσατέ).

λαλῆσαί. Aor act inf λαλέω (epexegetical to τι). The second accent comes from the enclitic σοι (see 1:4 on ἠκούσατέ).

23:19 ἐπιλαβόμενος δὲ τῆς χειρὸς αὐτοῦ ὁ χιλίαρχος καὶ ἀναχωρήσας κατ' ἰδίαν ἐπυνθάνετο, Τί ἐστιν ὃ ἔχεις ἀπαγγεῖλαί μοι;

ἐπιλαβόμενος. Aor mid dep ptc masc nom sg ἐπιλαμβάνομαι (temporal).

ἀναχωρήσας. Aor act ptc masc nom sg ἀναχωρέω (temporal).

κατ' ἰδίαν. "privately" (LN 28.67).

ἐπυνθάνετο. Impf dep ind 3rd sg πυνθάνομαι.

ἐστιν. Pres act ind 3rd sg εἰμί.

ὃ. The relative pronoun introduces a headless relative clause (see 3:6 on ὃ) that functions as the subject of ἐστιν. The relative pronoun itself is the direct object of ἔχεις.

ἔχεις. Pres act ind 2nd sg ἔχω.

ἀπαγγεῖλαί. Aor act inf ἀπαγγέλλω (epexegetical to ὃ). The second accent comes from the enclitic μοι (see 1:4 on ἠκούσατέ).

23:20 εἶπεν δὲ ὅτι Οἱ Ἰουδαῖοι συνέθεντο τοῦ ἐρωτῆσαί σε ὅπως αὔριον τὸν Παῦλον καταγάγης εἰς τὸ συνέδριον ὡς μέλλον τι ἀκριβέστερον πυνθάνεσθαι περὶ αὐτοῦ.

εἶπεν. Aor act ind 3rd sg λέγω.

ὅτι. Introduces direct discourse.

συνέθεντο. Aor mid ind 3rd pl συντίθημι/συντίθεμαι.

ἐρωτῆσαί. Aor act inf ἐρωτάω. The second accent comes from the enclitic σε (see 1:4 on ἠκούσατέ). Although Barrett (1076) argues that the articular infinitive introduces a purpose clause (cf. 15:20 on ἀπέχεσθαι and 21:12 on ἀναβαίνειν), it is difficult to see how a purpose clause could follow συντίθημι. Since genitive articular infinitives tend to follow verbs of deciding, exhorting, commanding, etc. (BAGD, 551), it is probably better to view the infinitive as complementary, even though complementary infinitives are normally anarthrous (see 3:3 on Πέτρον καὶ Ἰωάννην). This view is supported by LSJ who state that συντίθημι can be used with an infinitive to mean, "to agree to do something."

καταγάγης. Aor act subj 2nd sg κατάγω. The subjunctive is used with ὅπως to introduce a purpose clause.

ὡς. See v. 15.

μέλλον. Pres act ptc neut acc sg μέλλω. On the force of μέλλω plus an infinitive, see 3:3 on μέλλοντας. On the use of the participle with ὡς and its case, see 27:30 on μέλλοντων.

τι. Accusative direct object of πυνθάνεσθαι.

πυνθάνεσθαι. Pres mid inf πυνθάνομαι (complementary).

23:21 σὺ οὖν μὴ πεισθῇς αὐτοῖς· ἐνεδρεύουσιν γὰρ αὐτὸν ἐξ αὐτῶν ἄνδρες πλείους τεσσεράκοντα, οἵτινες ἀνεθεμάτισαν ἑαυτοὺς μήτε φαγεῖν μήτε πιεῖν ἕως οὗ ἀνέλωσιν αὐτόν, καὶ νῦν εἰσιν ἕτοιμοι προσδεχόμενοι τὴν ἀπὸ σοῦ ἐπαγγελίαν.

μὴ πεισθῇς. Aor pass subj 2nd sg πείθω (prohibitive subjunctive).

αὐτοῖς. On the use of the dative case with the passive form of πείθω, see 27:11 on τῷ κυβερνήτῃ.

ἐνεδρεύουσιν. Pres act ind 3rd pl ἐνεδρεύω.

ἀνεθεμάτισαν. Aor act ind 3rd pl ἀναθεματίζω.

φαγεῖν. Aor act inf ἐσθίω (epexegetical; see also 23:14 on γεύσασθαι).

πιεῖν. Aor act inf πίνω (epexegetical).

ἕως οὗ. See v. 12.

ἀνέλωσιν. Aor act subj 3rd pl ἀναιρέω. On the use of the subjunctive, see v. 12.

εἰσιν. Pres act ind 3rd pl εἰμί.

ἕτοιμοι. Predicate adjective.

προσδεχόμενοι. Pres dep ptc masc nom pl προσδέχομαι (attendant circumstance of εἰσιν ἕτοιμοι). It is unclear why Rogers and Rogers (295) call the participle adjectival since it has no substantive to modify. Moreover, the participle should not be viewed as part of a periphrastic construction since εἰσιν already has a complement (ἕτοιμοι).

23:22 ὁ μὲν οὖν χιλίαρχος ἀπέλυσε τὸν νεανίσκον παραγγείλας μηδενὶ ἐκλαλῆσαι ὅτι ταῦτα ἐνεφάνισας πρός με.

μὲν οὖν. See 1:6.

ἀπέλυσε. Aor act ind 3rd sg ἀπολύω.

παραγγείλας. Aor act ptc masc nom sg παραγγέλλω (temporal).

ἐκλαλῆσαι. Aor act inf ἐκλαλέω (indirect discourse).

ὅτι. The ὅτι, along with πρός με, marks a shift from indirect to direct discourse (cf. 1:4; 25:4–5; BDF §470.2).

ἐνεφάνισας. Aor act ind 2nd sg ἐμφανίζω.

Acts 23:23–30

[23]Then he summoned two of (his) centurions and said, "Have two hundred soldiers, along with seventy horsemen and two hundred spearmen, ready to go to Caesarea by nine o'clock tonight." [24]He also said to provide horses for Paul to ride so that they could take him safely to Felix the governor. [25]And he wrote the following letter:

> [26]*Claudius Lysias, to the most excellent Governor Felix.*
> *Greetings.*
> [27]*This man had been seized by the Jews and was about to be killed by them; but I arrived (on the scene) with (my) soldiers and rescued him, (after) learning that he was a Roman.* [28]*And since I wanted to determine the reason why they were accusing him, I had him brought down to their council.* [29]*I found him accused with respect to matters of their law, but he had no charge (against him) that was worthy of death or imprisonment.* [30]*When it was reported*

to me that there would be a plot against this man, I immediately sent (him) to you and also ordered his accusers to state the charges against him before you.

23:23 Καὶ προσκαλεσάμενος δύο [τινὰς] τῶν ἑκατονταρχῶν εἶπεν, Ἑτοιμάσατε στρατιώτας διακοσίους, ὅπως πορευθῶσιν ἕως Καισαρείας, καὶ ἱππεῖς ἑβδομήκοντα καὶ δεξιολάβους διακοσίους ἀπὸ τρίτης ὥρας τῆς νυκτός,

προσκαλεσάμενος. Aor mid dep ptc masc nom sg προσκαλέομαι (attendant circumstance).

ἑκατονταρχῶν. Partitive genitive.

εἶπεν. Aor act ind 3rd sg λέγω.

Ἑτοιμάσατε. Aor act impv 2nd pl ἑτοιμάζω.

πορευθῶσιν. Aor pass dep subj 3rd pl πορεύομαι. The subjunctive is used with ὅπως to introduce a purpose clause.

δεξιολάβους. The meaning of this term, which occurs only here in extant Greek literature, is uncertain. The expression literally refers to those who take something in their right hand. Most scholars follow Jerome and render the word, "spearmen." Other suggestions include "slingers" and "those who lead horses" (see Barrett, 1077–78).

ἀπὸ τρίτης ὥρας. Given the use of ἀπό with ὥρα elsewhere (Matt 9:22; 15:28; 17:18; 27:45; John 19:27), Barrett (1079) may be correct in arguing that this expression indicates that the soldiers were to be ready to go at any time *after* nine o'clock, rather than precisely *at* nine o'clock. This reading finds support in the use of ἑτοιμάζω with ἀπό in passages like Matt 25:34; 2 Chr 8:16; and Tobit 6:18, where the preposition appears to point to a starting point for a state of affairs.

23:24 κτήνη τε παραστῆσαι ἵνα ἐπιβιβάσαντες τὸν Παῦλον διασώσωσι πρὸς Φήλικα τὸν ἡγεμόνα,

κτήνη. Neuter plural accusative direct object of the infinitive.

παραστῆσαι. Aor act inf παρίστημι. The conjunction τε closely links this clause to the preceding command, while the infinitive indicates a shift to indirect discourse (cf. v. 22; 1:4; 25:5; BDF §470).

ἵνα . . . διασώσωσι. Lit. "in order that putting Paul on (them) they might rescue (him)."

ἐπιβιβάσαντες. Aor act ptc masc nom pl ἐπιβιβάζω (attendant circumstance).

διασώσωσι. Aor act subj 3rd pl διασῴζω. The subjunctive is used with ἵνα to indicate the purpose of the infinitive command.

ἡγεμόνα. Accusative in apposition to Φήλικα.

23:25 γράψας ἐπιστολὴν ἔχουσαν τὸν τύπον τοῦτον·

γράψας. Aor act ptc masc nom sg γράφω (attendant circumstance of εἶπεν, v. 23).

ἐπιστολὴν . . . τοῦτον. Lit. "a letter that had this character" (cf. "a letter that went like this:").

ἔχουσαν. Pres act ptc fem acc sg ἔχω (attributive).

23:26 Κλαύδιος Λυσίας τῷ κρατίστῳ ἡγεμόνι Φήλικι χαίρειν.

τῷ κρατίστῳ ἡγεμόνι Φήλικι. Given the presence of the article, in terms of syntax, it is probably best to take κρατίστῳ as an adjective (rather than a substantive: "His Excellency") modifying an articular ἡγεμόνι, with the anarthrous Φήλικι (see 3:3 on Πέτρον καὶ Ἰωάννην) standing in apposition to ἡγεμόνι.

κρατίστῳ. The superlative adjective denotes "pertaining to having noble status, with the implication of power and authority, often employed as a title" (LN 87.55).

χαίρειν. Pres act inf χαίρω (infinitive absolute; see 15:23).

23:27 Τὸν ἄνδρα τοῦτον συλλημφθέντα ὑπὸ τῶν Ἰουδαίων καὶ μέλλοντα ἀναιρεῖσθαι ὑπ' αὐτῶν ἐπιστὰς σὺν τῷ στρατεύματι ἐξειλάμην μαθὼν ὅτι Ῥωμαῖός ἐστιν.

Τὸν ἄνδρα. Accusative direct object of ἐξειλάμην, fronted (see 3:13 on ὑμεῖς) to place Paul in focus (see 2:15 on ὑμεῖς).

συλλημφθέντα. Aor pass ptc masc acc sg συλλαμβάνω (attributive; lit. "[this man] who had been seized").

μέλλοντα. Pres act ptc masc acc sg μέλλω (attributive). On the force of μέλλω plus an infinitive, see 3:3 on μέλλοντας.

ἀναιρεῖσθαι. Pres pass inf ἀναιρέω (complementary).

ἐπιστὰς. Aor act ptc masc nom sg ἐφίστημι (attendant circumstance of ἐξειλάμην).

ἐξειλάμην. Aor mid ind 1st sg ἐξαιρέω.

μαθὼν. Aor act ptc masc nom sg μανθάνω. It is unclear how the participle should be understood in light of the preceding story. It is possible that the participle simply introduces an additional piece of relevant information that is appended to the previous comments: "and (later) learned that he was a Roman." Fitzmyer (1998, 728), Witherington (1998, 700), and others, however, may be correct in reading the participle as part of the commander's careful effort to portray himself as the hero of the story, who guards the rights of Roman citizens. The participle would thus (erroneously) indicate that the commander's knowledge of Paul's citizenship was the *reason* for his timely intervention.

ὅτι. Introduces a clausal complement of μαθὼν.

Ῥωμαῖός. Predicate nominative. The second accent comes from the enclitic ἐστιν (see 1:4 on ἠκούσατέ).

ἐστιν. Pres act ind 3rd sg εἰμί.

23:28 βουλόμενός τε ἐπιγνῶναι τὴν αἰτίαν δι' ἣν ἐνεκάλουν αὐτῷ, κατήγαγον εἰς τὸ συνέδριον αὐτῶν

βουλόμενός. Pres dep ptc masc nom sg βούλομαι (causal). The second accent comes from the enclitic τε (see 1:4 on ἠκούσατέ).

τε. The conjunction introduces the specific lead-in to the next development in the story (see Levinsohn 1987, 129–35).

ἐπιγνῶναι. Aor act inf ἐπιγινώσκω (complementary).

τὴν αἰτίαν δι' ἣν. The use of the regular (postnominal) relative clause, rather than an internally headed relative clause (see 22:24), slightly changes the nuance.

ἐνεκάλουν. Impf act ind 3rd pl ἐγκαλέω.

κατήγαγον. Aor act ind 1st sg κατάγω. The actual agent, the soldiers, is left implicit (see also 16:3 on περιέτεμεν).

23:29 ὃν εὗρον ἐγκαλούμενον περὶ ζητημάτων τοῦ νόμου αὐτῶν, μηδὲν δὲ ἄξιον θανάτου ἢ δεσμῶν ἔχοντα ἔγκλημα.

ὃν. The antecedent is αὐτῷ (v. 28).

εὗρον. Aor act ind 1st sg εὑρίσκω.

ἐγκαλούμενον. Pres pass ptc masc acc sg ἐγκαλέω. The participle functions as the complement of ὃν (the direct object) in an object-complement double accusative construction (see 1:3 on ζῶντα).

μηδὲν. Accusative modifier of ἔγκλημα, fronted (see 3:13 on ὑμεῖς) for emphasis (see 2:15 on ὑμεῖς).

ἄξιον. The adjective is either attributive or functions as the complement of μηδὲν . . . ἔγκλημα (the direct object of ἔχοντα) in an object-complement double accusative construction (see 1:3 on ζῶντα).

ἔχοντα. Pres act ptc masc acc sg ἔχω. The participle functions as a second complement of ὃν in an object-complement double accusative construction (see 1:3 on ζῶντα).

23:30 μηνυθείσης δέ μοι ἐπιβουλῆς εἰς τὸν ἄνδρα ἔσεσθαι, ἐξαυτῆς ἔπεμψα πρὸς σέ παραγγείλας καὶ τοῖς κατηγόροις λέγειν [τὰ] πρὸς αὐτὸν ἐπὶ σοῦ.

μηνυθείσης δέ μοι ἐπιβουλῆς εἰς τὸν ἄνδρα ἔσεσθαι. In this unusual construction, the infinitival clause functions as the subject of the passive participle, μηνυθείσης. Because the participle is part of a genitive absolute construction, the subject of the subjective infinitival clause is placed in the genitive case (cf. 1:8 on ἐπελθόντος).

μηνυθείσης. Aor pass ptc fem gen sg μηνύω. Genitive absolute (see 1:8 on ἐπελθόντος), temporal.

μοι. Indirect object of the passive participle.

εἰς. Disadvantage/opposition.

ἐπιβουλῆς. Genitive subject (see above; see also 1:8 on ἐπελθόντος).

ἔσεσθαι. Fut mid inf εἰμί. Elsewhere, infinitival constructions that introduce indirect discourse virtually always serve as the syntactic direct object of the verb they modify (cf. Wallace 1996, 603). Here, however, the construction serves as the subject of the passive participle. On the tense, see 11:28.

ἐξαυτῆς. "Immediately."

ἔπεμψα. Aor act ind 1st sg πέμπω.

παραγγείλας. Aor act ptc masc nom sg παραγγέλλω (attendant circumstance).

τοῖς κατηγόροις. Dative indirect object of παραγγείλας.

λέγειν. Pres act inf λέγω (indirect discourse).

Acts 23:31–35

[31]So the soldiers, in accord with the orders that had been given to them, took Paul and brought him to Antipatris during the night. [32]The next day, after dismissing the mounted soldiers to go on with him, (the other soldiers) returned to the barracks. [33]When they had entered

Caesarea and delivered the letter to the governor, they also turned Paul over to him. [34]When (the governor) had read (the letter), asked what province he was from, and discovered that (he was) from Cilicia, [35]he said, "I will hear your case when your accusers have also arrived." He then ordered that Paul be kept under guard in Herod's palace.

23:31 Οἱ μὲν οὖν στρατιῶται κατὰ τὸ διατεταγμένον αὐτοῖς ἀναλαβόντες τὸν Παῦλον ἤγαγον διὰ νυκτὸς εἰς τὴν Ἀντιπατρίδα,

μὲν οὖν. See 1:6.

κατὰ. Standard (see 7:44).

τὸ διατεταγμένον. Prf pass ptc neut acc sg διατάσσω (substantival).

ἀναλαβόντες. Aor act ptc masc nom pl ἀναλαμβάνω (attendant circumstance).

ἤγαγον. Aor act ind 3rd pl ἄγω.

23:32 τῇ δὲ ἐπαύριον ἐάσαντες τοὺς ἱππεῖς ἀπέρχεσθαι σὺν αὐτῷ ὑπέστρεψαν εἰς τὴν παρεμβολήν·

ἐάσαντες. Aor act ptc masc nom pl ἐάω (temporal).

ἀπέρχεσθαι. Pres mid inf ἀπέρχομαι (complementary). This "surprising word" (Barrett, 1086) is perfectly appropriate since focus is not on where the cavalry is about to go (πορεύεσθαι; Ψ *Byz*) but rather on the fact that they are being "dismissed" or "allowed to leave" by their superior officers.

ὑπέστρεψαν. Aor act ind 3rd pl ὑποστρέφω. The plural subject of the main verb and the participle is clearly the στρατιῶται who had received orders in v. 31. More specifically, since the plural subject of v. 32 both issued the orders (ἐάσαντες) and returned to the barracks themselves (ὑπέστρεψαν), the soldiers in question were likely the centurions who commanded the infantry (cf. Barrett, 1086). Barrett also notes the possibility that ἐάω means "to leave" here: thus, "The next day, they left the mounted soldiers to go on with him and returned to the barracks."

23:33 οἵτινες εἰσελθόντες εἰς τὴν Καισάρειαν καὶ ἀναδόντες τὴν ἐπιστολὴν τῷ ἡγεμόνι παρέστησαν καὶ τὸν Παῦλον αὐτῷ.

εἰσελθόντες. Aor act ptc masc nom pl εἰσέρχομαι (temporal).

εἰς. See 1:8 on ἐφ' ὑμᾶς.

ἀναδόντες. Aor act ptc masc nom pl ἀναδίδωμι (temporal).

παρέστησαν καὶ τὸν Παῦλον αὐτῷ. Since the two participial clauses are conjoined (and thus bear the same function), and the main clause contains a καί, this clause must indicate what the soldiers did after entering the city and delivering the letter.

παρέστησαν. Aor act ind 3rd pl παρίστημι. Given the context (see above), the verb (lit. "they *presented* Paul to him") must refer to a relinquishing of control here (so LN 37.111).

23:34 ἀναγνοὺς δὲ καὶ ἐπερωτήσας ἐκ ποίας ἐπαρχείας ἐστὶν, καὶ πυθόμενος ὅτι ἀπὸ Κιλικίας,

ἀναγνοὺς. Aor act ptc masc nom sg ἀναγινώσκω (temporal).

ἐπερωτήσας. Aor act ptc masc nom sg ἐπερωτάω (temporal).

ἐστὶν. Pres act ind 3rd sg εἰμί. The use of the finite verb (with direct discourse), rather than an infinitive to indicate indirect discourse, indicates that the governor directed his question to his subordinates (lit. "What province is he from?") rather than to Paul (contra Fitzmyer 1998, 729; Witherington 1998, 701).

πυθόμενος ὅτι. In this rare use of πυνθάνομαι with ὅτι (introducing a clausal complement), the verb means "to learn/discover." The ὅτι thus does not introduce indirect discourse.

πυθόμενος. Aor mid dep ptc masc nom sg πυνθάνομαι (temporal).

23:35 Διακούσομαί σου, ἔφη, ὅταν καὶ οἱ κατήγοροί σου παραγένωνται· κελεύσας ἐν τῷ πραιτωρίῳ τοῦ Ἡρῴδου φυλάσσεσθαι αὐτόν.

Διακούσομαί. Fut mid ind 1st sg διακούω ("to give a judicial hearing in a legal matter"; LN 56.13). The second accent comes from the enclitic σου (see 1:4 on ἠκούσατέ).

σου. Genitive object of Διακούσομαί.

ἔφη. Aor/Impf act ind 3rd sg φημί. On the tense, see 7:2.

παραγένωνται. Aor mid dep subj 3rd pl παραγίνομαι. The subjunctive is used with ὅταν in an indefinite temporal clause.

κελεύσας. Aor act ptc masc nom sg κελεύω (attendant circumstance of ἔφη). There is no reason why the aorist participle cannot refer to an action that occurred subsequent to the main verb (cf. Porter 1989, 387; contra Moulton, 1.132f).

φυλάσσεσθαι. Pres pass inf φυλάσσω (indirect discourse).

αὐτόν. Accusative subject of the passive infinitive (see 1:3 on αὐτὸν).

Acts 24:1–9

[1]After five days, the high priest Ananias came down with some elders and a lawyer named Tertullus, and they presented charges against Paul to the governor. [2]After (Paul) had been called, Tertullus began to present the charges, saying, "Since we are experiencing much peace through you and since reforms are taking place in this nation through your foresight, [3]we welcome this in all ways and in every place, most excellent Felix, with great gratitude. [4]But so that I might not trouble you further, I urge you to listen to us briefly out of your graciousness. [5]For we have found this man (to be) a troublemaker and one who incites rebellion among all the Jews throughout the world, and a ringleader of the sect of the Nazarenes. [6]He also tried to desecrate the temple, so we arrested him. [8]By questioning (him) concerning all these things, you yourself will be able to find out from him about the things we are accusing him of (doing)." [9]The Jews also joined in the attack by insisting that these things were true.

24:1 Μετὰ δὲ πέντε ἡμέρας κατέβη ὁ ἀρχιερεὺς Ἁνανίας μετὰ πρεσβυτέρων τινῶν καὶ ῥήτορος Τερτύλλου τινός, οἵτινες ἐνεφάνισαν τῷ ἡγεμόνι κατὰ τοῦ Παύλου.

κατέβη. Aor act ind 3rd sg καταβαίνω.

Ἁνανίας. Nominative in apposition to ὁ ἀρχιερεὺς.

ῥήτορος. Genitive governed by μετά.

Τερτύλλου τινός. Genitive in apposition to ῥήτορος (lit. "a certain Tertullus").

οἵτινες. A good example of why ὅστις is inappropriately called an *indefinite* relative pronoun (see 2:21 on ὃς ἂν ἐπικαλέσηται).

ἐνεφάνισαν. Aor act ind 3rd pl ἐμφανίζω. Used with κατά, this verb indicates "to make a formal report before authorities on a judicial matter" (LN 56.8; cf. BAGD, 257).

24:2 κληθέντος δὲ αὐτοῦ ἤρξατο κατηγορεῖν ὁ Τέρτυλλος λέγων, Πολλῆς εἰρήνης τυγχάνοντες διὰ σοῦ καὶ διορθωμάτων γινομένων τῷ ἔθνει τούτῳ διὰ τῆς σῆς προνοίας,

κληθέντος. Aor pass ptc masc gen sg καλέω. Genitive absolute (see 1:8 on ἐπελθόντος), temporal.

αὐτοῦ. Genitive subject (see 1:8 on ἐπελθόντος). In light of the genitive absolute construction, the antecedent of the pronoun must be either Paul or the governor, not Tertullus (the subject of the main verb). For a possible explanation of why codex B omits the pronoun, see Barrett, 1094. On the whole, it is probably best to regard Paul as the antecedent and view the expression as a reference to Paul's case being announced.

ἤρξατο. Aor mid ind 3rd sg ἄρχω.

κατηγορεῖν. Pres act inf κατηγορέω (complementary).

λέγων. Pres act ptc nom masc sg λέγω (attendant circumstance).

εἰρήνης. Genitive object of τυγχάνοντες.

τυγχάνοντες. Pres act ptc nom masc pl τυγχάνω (causal).

διορθωμάτων. Genitive subject (see 1:8 on ἐπελθόντος).

γινομένων. Pres dep ptc neut gen pl γίνομαι. Genitive absolute (see 1:8 on ἐπελθόντος), causal. The shift in subject necessitates the use of the genitive absolute.

ἔθνει. Dative of advantage.

24:3 πάντῃ τε καὶ πανταχοῦ ἀποδεχόμεθα, κράτιστε Φῆλιξ, μετὰ πάσης εὐχαριστίας.

πάντῃ τε καὶ πανταχοῦ. This phrase could function as the end of v. 2 or the beginning of v. 3 (see Omanson).

ἀποδεχόμεθα. Pres dep ind 1st pl ἀποδέχομαι.

κράτιστε. See 23:26.

Φῆλιξ. On the position of the vocative, see 10:13.

μετὰ πάσης εὐχαριστίας. In terms of syntax, the prepositional phrase indicates that great gratitude accompanied the reception of Felix's reforms. In terms of semantics, it denotes the manner in which the reforms were received.

24:4 ἵνα δὲ μὴ ἐπὶ πλεῖόν σε ἐγκόπτω, παρακαλῶ ἀκοῦσαί σε ἡμῶν συντόμως τῇ σῇ ἐπιεικείᾳ.

ἐπὶ πλεῖόν. On the meaning, see 20:9. The second accent on πλεῖόν comes from the enclitic σε (see 1:4 on ἠκούσατέ).

ἐγκόπτω. Pres act subj 1st sg ἐγκόπτω. Used with ἵνα to introduce the purpose for the nature of the following request.

παρακαλῶ. Pres act ind 1st sg παρακαλέω.

ἀκοῦσαί. Aor act inf ἀκούω (indirect discourse). The second accent comes from the enclitic σε (see 1:4 on ἠκούσατέ).

σε. Accusative subject of the infinitive (see 1:3).

ἡμῶν. Genitive object of ἀκούω.

τῇ σῇ ἐπιεικείᾳ. This expression probably was used in formal contexts to show appropriate deference to a high official. Tertullus was either asking Felix to be gracious (as was his custom = dative of rule (see 2:23 on βουλῇ καὶ προγνώσει [cf. BAGD, 292], or was urging him to hear the case because of his graciousness (causal dative).

24:5 εὑρόντες γὰρ τὸν ἄνδρα τοῦτον λοιμὸν καὶ κινοῦντα στάσεις πᾶσιν τοῖς Ἰουδαίοις τοῖς κατὰ τὴν οἰκουμένην πρωτοστάτην τε τῆς τῶν Ναζωραίων αἱρέσεως,

εὑρόντες. Aor act ptc masc nom pl εὑρίσκω. Strictly speaking, the participle should be viewed as a nominative absolute since there is no main verb (in vv. 5–8) that it modifies. It is likely that this construction was used in a legal context to introduce a case formally (cf. 2:29 on ἐξὸν).

λοιμὸν. The substantival accusative adjective functions as the complement in an object-complement double accusative construction (see 1:3 on ζῶντα) with a compound complement.

κινοῦντα. Pres act ptc masc acc sg κινέω. The participial clause functions as the complement (conjoined with λοιμὸν) in an object-complement double accusative construction (see 1:3 on ζῶντα) with a compound complement.

πᾶσιν τοῖς Ἰουδαίοις τοῖς κατὰ τὴν οἰκουμένην. Hyperbole (cf. 1:18 on πάντα).

πρωτοστάτην. The noun functions as the complement in an object-complement double accusative elliptical construction (see below).

τε. The use of this conjunction suggests an elliptical construction: εὑρόντες γὰρ τὸν ἄνδρα τοῦτον λοιμὸν is understood.

Ναζωραίων. Genitive of identification.

αἱρέσεως. Genitive of subordination.

24:6 ὃς καὶ τὸ ἱερὸν ἐπείρασεν βεβηλῶσαι ὃν καὶ ἐκρατήσαμεν,

ὃς καὶ. The use of the relative pronoun with a καί fits well with a recitation of facts in a legal context.

ἐπείρασεν. Aor act ind 3rd sg πειράζω.

βεβηλῶσαι. Aor act inf βεβηλόω (complementary). This verb is used only here and in Matt 12:5 in the NT ("to cause something to become unclean, profane, or ritually unacceptable"; LN 53.33).

ὃν καὶ. See above.

ἐκρατήσαμεν. Aor act ind 1st pl κρατέω. A significant number of manuscripts (E Ψ 33 36 181 307 *Byz*[pt] *al*) have a much fuller text (with minor variations): ἐκρατήσαμεν καὶ κατὰ τὸν ἡμέτερον νόμον ἠθελήσαμεν κρῖναι. [7]παρελθὼν δὲ Λυσίας ὁ χιλίαρχος μετὰ πολλῆς βίας ἐκ τῶν χειρῶν ἡμῶν ἀπήγαγε, [8]κελεύσας τοὺς κατηγόρους αυτοῦ ἔρχεσθαι ἐπὶ σέ ("we arrested him and wanted to judge him according to our law, but Lysias the commander came and violently took him away from our hands and commanded his accusers to come to you"). The UBS[4]/NA[27] text is supported by 𝔓[74] א A B 81 1175 *Byz*[pt] *pc*.

24:8 παρ' οὗ δυνήσῃ αὐτὸς ἀνακρίνας περὶ πάντων τούτων ἐπιγνῶναι ὧν ἡμεῖς κατηγοροῦμεν αὐτοῦ.

δυνήσῃ. Fut mid dep ind 2nd sg δύναμαι.

αὐτὸς. Intensive.

ἀνακρίνας. Aor act ptc masc nom sg ἀνακρίνω (means).

περὶ πάντων τούτων. The prepositional phrase most likely goes with the participle ἀνακρίνας ("by questioning him about all the things") rather than the infinitive ἐπιγνῶναι ("to find out about all the things"), since the infinitive already has a relative clause denoting reference/respect as its complement (but see below).

ἐπιγνῶναι. Aor act inf ἐπιγινώσκω (complementary to δυνήσῃ).

ὧν. Depending on how the prepositional phrase περὶ πάντων τούτων is analyzed (see above), the relative pronoun could either introduce a headless relative clause (see 3:6 on ὅ), with the case denoting reference/respect (if περὶ πάντων τούτων goes with ἀνακρίνας), or the relative clause could modify περὶ πάντων τούτων with the relative pronoun being attracted to the case of its antecedent (if περὶ πάντων τούτων goes with ἐπιγνῶναι): "By questioning (him), you yourself will be able to find out about all these things that we are accusing him of (doing)." The fact that the relative pronoun is not contiguous with περὶ πάντων τούτων, however, makes the latter view unlikely.

κατηγοροῦμεν. Pres act ind 1st pl κατηγορέω.
αὐτοῦ. Genitive object of κατηγοροῦμεν.

24:9 συνεπέθεντο δὲ καὶ οἱ Ἰουδαῖοι φάσκοντες ταῦτα οὕτως ἔχειν.

συνεπέθεντο. Aor mid ind 3rd pl συνεπιτίθημι.
φάσκοντες. Pres act ptc masc nom pl φάσκω (means).
ταῦτα. Accusative subject of the infinitive (see 1:3 on αὐτὸν).
οὕτως ἔχειν. See 7:1.
ἔχειν. Pres act inf ἔχω (indirect discourse).

Acts 24:10–21

[10]When the governor motioned to him to speak, Paul answered, "Because I know that you have been a (good) judge for many years to this nation, I gladly defend myself. [11]Since you are able to determine that I have had no more than twelve days since I went up to worship in Jerusalem, [12]and they neither found me in the temple disputing with anyone nor causing a crowd of the people (to gather)—neither in the synagogues nor around the city—[13]nor are they able to provide proof to you concerning the things they are now accusing me of (doing), [14]I (now) admit this to you that in accordance with the Way, which they call a sect, I serve (our) ancestral God and believe everything that is in accord with the Law and that is written in the Prophets, [15]and I have the same hope in God that these men themselves embrace, namely, that there will soon be a resurrection of both the righteous and the wicked.

[16]With this in mind, I too strive to have a clear conscience before God and people at all times. [17]After many years, I came to present money for the poor to my people along with offerings (to God). [18–19]This is what I was doing when some Jews from Asia found me in the temple, ritually purified, associated with neither a crowd nor a disturbance. They should appear before you and state their accusations if they actually have anything against me. [20]Or let these men here either say what crime they found when I stood before (their) council, [21]or in regard to this one thing that I shouted out when I stood among them: 'I am being tried before you today concerning the resurrection of the dead!'"

24:10 Ἀπεκρίθη τε ὁ Παῦλος νεύσαντος αὐτῷ τοῦ ἡγεμόνος λέγειν, Ἐκ πολλῶν ἐτῶν ὄντα σε κριτὴν τῷ ἔθνει τούτῳ ἐπι-

στάμενος εὐθύμως τὰ περὶ ἐμαυτοῦ ἀπολογοῦμαι,

᾿Απεκρίθη. Aor pass dep ind 3rd sg ἀποκρίνομαι.

τε. The conjunction τε is sometimes used, as here, to introduce a response to a previous event (see Levinsohn 1987, 135–36; cf. 13:46; 21:30). Here, Paul responds to the charges that were brought against him in vv. 2–9.

νεύσαντος. Aor act ptc masc gen sg νεύω. Genitive absolute (see 1:8 on ἐπελθόντος), temporal.

ἡγεμόνος. Genitive subject (see 1:8 on ἐπελθόντος).

λέγειν. Pres act inf λέγω. The infinitive functions as the direct object of νεύσαντος. Since the physical gesture of motioning is a form of communication, as with other infinitival constructions the infinitive may be viewed as introducing indirect discourse (cf. John 13:24).

᾿Εκ πολλῶν ἐτῶν. Robertson (1934, 597) notes that "with expressions of time ἐκ gives the point of departure" (cf. 9:33 on ἐξ ἐτῶν ὀκτώ).

ὄντα. Pres act ptc masc acc sg εἰμί. The whole participial clause, ᾿Εκ πολλῶν ἐτῶν ὄντα σε κριτὴν τῷ ἔθνει τούτῳ, functions as a clausal complement of ἐπιστάμενος (indirect discourse with a verb of cognition). It cannot be causal (contra Rogers and Rogers, 297).

κριτὴν. Predicate accusative of ὄντα.

ἐπιστάμενος. Pres dep ptc masc nom sg ἐπίσταμαι (causal).

εὐθύμως. This term (a *hapax legomenon*) indicates that Paul is encouraged (LN 25.147) by the state of affairs.

τὰ περὶ ἐμαυτοῦ. The article functions as a nominalizer (see 1:3 on τά): lit. "the things concerning me." Accusative of respect ("I gladly defend myself with respect to my case").

ἀπολογοῦμαι. Pres dep ind 1st sg ἀπολογέομαι.

24:11 δυναμένου σου ἐπιγνῶναι ὅτι οὐ πλείους εἰσίν μοι ἡμέραι δώδεκα ἀφ᾿ ἧς ἀνέβην προσκυνήσων εἰς ᾿Ιερουσαλήμ.

δυναμένου. Pres dep ptc masc gen sg δύναμαι. Genitive absolute (see 1:8 on ἐπελθόντος), causal.

σου. Genitive subject (see 1:8 on ἐπελθόντος).

ἐπιγνῶναι. Aor act inf ἐπιγινώσκω (complementary).

ὅτι. Introduces a clausal complement of ἐπιγνῶναι. It is important to recognize (contra the punctuation of UBS[4]/NA[27]) that the complement clause extends all the way through v. 13, with the main verb of the sentence that began with the genitive absolute in this verse being introduced in v. 14.

πλείους. The fronting (see 3:13 on ὑμεῖς) of the comparative adjective probably allows the speaker to draw more attention to the shortness of time involved (for the more typical order, see 4:22; 23:13, 21; 25:6).

εἰσίν. Pres act ind 3rd pl εἰμί.

μοι. Dative of possession (with εἰμί).

ἀφ᾽ ἧς. A shortened (idiomatic) form of ἀφ᾽ ἡμέρας ἀφ᾽ ἧς (cf. 20:18).

ἀνέβην. Aor act ind 1st sg ἀναβαίνω.

προσκυνήσων. Fut act ptc masc nom sg προσκυνέω (purpose; see 8:27 on προσκυνήσων; cf. 20:22 on συναντήσοντά).

24:12 καὶ οὔτε ἐν τῷ ἱερῷ εὗρόν με πρός τινα διαλεγόμενον ἢ ἐπίστασιν ποιοῦντα ὄχλου οὔτε ἐν ταῖς συναγωγαῖς οὔτε κατὰ τὴν πόλιν,

καὶ. The conjunction marks what follows as a continuation of the complement clause (modifying ἐπιγνῶναι) begun in v. 11.

εὗρόν. Aor act ind 3rd pl εὑρίσκω. The second accent comes from the enclitic με (see 1:4 on ἠκούσατέ).

διαλεγόμενον. Pres dep ptc masc acc sg διαλέγομαι. The participle functions as the complement in an object-complement double accusative construction (see 1:3 on ζῶντα).

ἐπίστασιν. The whole construction, ἐπίστασιν ποιοῦντα ὄχλου, probably carries a negative connotation and refers to being the cause of a crowd forming (cf. v. 18; BAGD, 300; LN 39.34).

ποιοῦντα. Pres act ptc masc acc sg ποιέω (used in a causative sense; cf. 3:12; 5:34). The participle functions as the complement in an object-complement double accusative construction (see 1:3 on ζῶντα).

οὔτε . . . οὔτε. This correlative phrase modifies ἐπίστασιν ποιοῦντα ὄχλου rather than οὔτε ἐν τῷ ἱερῷ (contra Barrett, 1103).

24:13 οὐδὲ παραστῆσαι δύνανταί σοι περὶ ὧν νυνὶ κατηγοροῦσίν μου.

οὐδὲ. The complement clause (modifying ἐπιγνῶναι) begun in v. 11

continues through the end of this verse.

παραστῆσαι. Aor act inf παρίστημι (complementary). Fronted (see 3:13 on ὑμεῖς) for emphasis.

δύνανταί. Pres dep ind 3rd pl δύναμαι. The second accent comes from the enclitic σοι (see 1:4 on ἠκούσατέ).

περὶ ὧν. The relative pronoun introduces a headless relative clause (see 3:6 on ὃ).

κατηγοροῦσίν. Pres act ind 3rd pl κατηγορέω. The second accent comes from the enclitic μου (see 1:4 on ἠκούσατέ).

μου. Genitive object of κατηγοροῦσίν.

24:14 ὁμολογῶ δὲ τοῦτό σοι ὅτι κατὰ τὴν ὁδὸν ἣν λέγουσιν αἵρεσιν, οὕτως λατρεύω τῷ πατρῴῳ θεῷ πιστεύων πᾶσι τοῖς κατὰ τὸν νόμον καὶ τοῖς ἐν τοῖς προφήταις γεγραμμένοις,

ὁμολογῶ. Pres act ind 1st sg ὁμολογέω.

τοῦτό. Accusative direct object of ὁμολογῶ. The demonstrative pronoun is cataphoric (refers forward) here. The second accent comes from the enclitic σοι (see 1:4 on ἠκούσατέ).

ὅτι. Epexegetical to τοῦτό.

κατὰ. Standard (see 7:44).

ἣν. Accusative direct object of λέγουσιν.

λέγουσιν. Pres act ind 3rd pl λέγω.

αἵρεσιν. The complement (ἣν is the object) in an object-complement double accusative construction (see 1:3 on ζῶντα; cf. 10:28 on κοινὸν ἢ ἀκάθαρτον).

οὕτως. The adverb is resumptive for κατὰ τὴν ὁδὸν.

λατρεύω. Pres act ind 1st sg λατρεύω.

τῷ πατρῴῳ θεῷ. Dative object of λατρεύω.

πιστεύων. Pres act ptc masc nom sg πιστεύω (attendant circumstance).

πᾶσι τοῖς κατὰ τὸν νόμον καὶ τοῖς ἐν τοῖς προφήταις γεγραμμένοις. The adjective πᾶσι should probably be taken as attributive rather than substantival. The two dative articles (τοῖς) then function as nominalizers (see 1:3 on τὰ), changing the prepositional phrase and participial phrase into substantives (dative objects of πιστεύων).

κατὰ. Standard (see 7:44).

γεγραμμένοις. Prf pass ptc neut dat pl γράφω (substantival).

24:15 ἐλπίδα ἔχων εἰς τὸν θεὸν ἣν καὶ αὐτοὶ οὗτοι προσδέχονται, ἀνάστασιν μέλλειν ἔσεσθαι δικαίων τε καὶ ἀδίκων.

ἔχων. Pres act ptc masc nom sg ἔχω (attendant circumstance of λατρεύω, v. 14).

αὐτοὶ. Intensive.

προσδέχονται. Pres dep ind 3rd pl προσδέχομαι.

ἀνάστασιν. Predicate accusative of an impersonal ἔσεσθαι. Fronted (see 3:13 on ὑμεῖς) for emphasis.

μέλλειν. Pres act inf μέλλω (epexegetical to ἐλπίδα). On the force of μέλλω plus an infinitive, see 3:3 on μέλλοντας.

ἔσεσθαι. Fut mid dep inf εἰμί. On the tense, see 11:28.

δικαίων . . . ἀδίκων. Objective genitives modifying ἀνάστασιν.

24:16 ἐν τούτῳ καὶ αὐτὸς ἀσκῶ ἀπρόσκοπον συνείδησιν ἔχειν πρὸς τὸν θεὸν καὶ τοὺς ἀνθρώπους διὰ παντός.

ἐν τούτῳ. The prepositional phrase should probably be viewed as causal ("for this reason" or "with this in mind"; cf. BAGD, 261), with this construction being used to refer to a larger context than other causal constructions.

αὐτὸς. Intensive.

ἀσκῶ. Pres act ind 1st sg ἀσκέω. This verb (a *hapax legomenon*) indicates "to engage in some activity, with both continuity and effort" (LN 68.72).

ἔχειν. Pres act inf ἔχω (complementary or purpose).

διὰ παντός. An idiomatic expression meaning "always" (cf. 2:25; 10:2).

24:17 δι' ἐτῶν δὲ πλειόνων ἐλεημοσύνας ποιήσων εἰς τὸ ἔθνος μου παρεγενόμην καὶ προσφοράς,

δι'. On the temporal use of διά to mean "after," see Moule, 56.

πλειόνων. The comparative form is used as an elative in this context (see 13:31 on πλείους; cf. Barrett, 1107).

ποιήσων. Fut act ptc masc nom sg ποιέω (purpose; see 8:27 on προσκυνήσων; cf. 20:22 on συναντήσοντά).

παρεγενόμην. Aor mid dep ind 1st sg παραγίνομαι.

24:18–19 ἐν αἷς εὗρόν με ἡγνισμένον ἐν τῷ ἱερῷ οὐ μετὰ ὄχλου οὐδὲ μετὰ θορύβου, τινὲς δὲ ἀπὸ τῆς 'Ασίας 'Ιουδαῖοι, οὓς ἔδει ἐπὶ σοῦ παρεῖναι καὶ κατηγορεῖν εἴ τι ἔχοιεν πρὸς ἐμέ.

ἐν αἷς. The antecedent of the relative pronoun is προσφοράς. The preposition may indicate reference or, given the context, involvement in an activity.

εὗρόν. Aor act ind 3rd pl εὑρίσκω. The subject of the sentence is introduced in the next verse.

ἡγνισμένον. Prf pass ptc masc acc sg ἁγνίζω. The participle functions as the complement in an object-complement double accusative construction (see 1:3 on ζῶντα).

τινὲς . . . 'Ιουδαῖοι. Nominative subject of εὗρόν (v. 18; contra Rogers and Rogers, 298, and Barrett, 1109, who both claim that this noun phrase lacks a verb). The location of the subject is conditioned by the "heavy" or lengthy relative clause that modifies it (οὓς . . . ἐμέ).

οὓς ἔδει ἐπὶ σοῦ παρεῖναι καὶ κατηγορεῖν. Here, the apodosis precedes the protasis (cf. 26:32 on 'Απολελύσθαι . . . οὗτος).

οὓς. Accusative subject of the infinitive παρεῖναι (see 1:3 on αὐτὸν).

ἔδει. Impf act ind 3rd sg δεῖ.

παρεῖναι. Pres act inf πάρειμι (complementary; see 1:16 on ἔδει).

κατηγορεῖν. Pres act inf κατηγορέω (complementary).

ἔχοιεν. Pres act opt 3rd pl ἔχω. On the use of the optative, see 5:24 on τί ἂν γένοιτο τοῦτο).

24:20–21 ἢ αὐτοὶ οὗτοι εἰπάτωσαν τί εὗρον ἀδίκημα στάντος μου ἐπὶ τοῦ συνεδρίου, ἢ περὶ μιᾶς ταύτης φωνῆς ἧς ἐκέκραξα ἐν αὐτοῖς ἑστὼς ὅτι Περὶ ἀναστάσεως νεκρῶν ἐγὼ κρίνομαι σή μερον ἐφ' ὑμῶν.

ἢ . . . ἤ. Verses 20–21 could be viewed as a large "either . . . or" construction.

αὐτοὶ. Intensive.

εἰπάτωσαν. Aor act impv 3rd pl λέγω.

τί. Accusative modifier of ἀδίκημα.

εὗρον. Aor act ind 3rd pl εὑρίσκω. Many scribes (C E Ψ 36 307 453 *Byz al*) naturally added ἐν εμοὶ after the verb, which was implicit in Paul's statement.

στάντος. Aor act ptc masc gen sg ἵστημι. Genitive absolute (see 1:8

on ἐπελθόντος), temporal.

μου. Genitive subject (see 1:8 on ἐπελθόντος).

ἧς. Genitive by attraction to φωνῆς (see 1:1 on ὧν).

ἐκέκραξα. Aor act ind 1st sg ἐκκράζω. Rather than viewing this form as an example of a reduplicated aorist, it is better to posit the compound verb ἐκ-κράζω as the root, particularly since Luke is perfectly capable of using the aorist form of κράζω (see 7:60; contra Robertson 1934, 348).

ἑστὼς. Prf act ptc masc nom sg ἵστημι (temporal).

ὅτι. Epexegetical to φωνῆς.

νεκρῶν. Objective genitive.

κρίνομαι. Pres pass ind 1st sg κρίνω.

Acts 24:22–27

[22]Felix, now that he had a more accurate knowledge of the Way, dismissed them, saying, "When commander Lysias comes down, I will decide your case." [23]He gave orders to the centurion to keep Paul in custody, to allow him some freedom, and not to prevent any of his friends from taking care of him.

[24]Some days later, Felix arrived with his wife Drusilla, who was a Jew. He sent for Paul and listened to him (speak) about faith in Christ Jesus. [25]As he was speaking about righteousness, self-control, and the impending judgment, Felix became afraid and said, "For the time being, you may go. When I have more time, I will call for you." [26]Now, at the same time, he was also hoping that Paul would offer him a bribe. For this reason, he frequently sent for him and conversed with him.

[27]When two years had elapsed, Felix was succeeded by Porcius Festus. And since he wanted to gain favor with the Jews, he left Paul in prison.

24:22 Ἀνεβάλετο δὲ αὐτοὺς ὁ Φῆλιξ, ἀκριβέστερον εἰδὼς τὰ περὶ τῆς ὁδοῦ εἴπας, Ὅταν Λυσίας ὁ χιλίαρχος καταβῇ, διαγνώσομαι τὰ καθ' ὑμᾶς·

Ἀνεβάλετο. Aor mid ind 3rd sg ἀναβάλλω. According to Louw and Nida (56.18), this verb (only here in the NT) means "to adjourn a court proceeding until a later time" (cf. BAGD, 50). While such a sense is consistent with the context and reflects the end result of Felix's actions, two factors argue against this precise nuance here. First, it appears that elsewhere it is the passive form of the verb that carries this sense (see

LSJ, 52). Second, the verb has an animate direct object (αὐτοὺς) indicating that Felix's action was directed at those who had brought the complaint. We thus prefer a less technical rendering ("dismiss").

ἀκριβέστερον. It is unclear whether the adverb, which is comparative in form, carries comparative ("more accurately") or elative/superlative force (see 13:31 on πλείους): "knowing for certain," "knowing rather accurately" (Rogers and Rogers, 298; Bruce, 482). In the former case, it would indicate that Felix had learned more about the Way through the proceedings. (Witherington [1998, 713] argues for the comparative force but suggests that the adverb indicates that Felix had a more accurate understanding of the Way than the Jews who brought the complaint.) The latter, view, on the other hand, takes the whole clause as indicating that Felix already had a clear understanding of the Way *prior* to Paul's hearing (so Bruce). On the whole, the first option, which treats Felix's actions as a response to what he had learned from Paul, is the most natural reading. Moreover, there is no reason to assume that Luke records the entire exchange between Paul and Felix.

εἰδὼς. Prf act ptc masc nom sg οἶδα. The function of the participle depends on the interpretation of ἀκριβέστερον. If the adverb carries comparitive force, the participle is probably temporal. If the adverb is elative, the participle is probably causal.

τὰ περὶ τῆς ὁδοῦ. The accusative article functions as a nominalizer (see 1:3 on τὰ), changing the prepositional phrase into a substantive (lit. "the things concerning the Way").

εἴπας. Aor act ptc masc nom sg λέγω (attendant circumstance).

καταβῇ. Aor act subj 3rd sg καταβαίνω. The subjunctive is used with ὅταν in an indefinite temporal clause.

διαγνώσομαι. Fut mid dep ind 1st sg διαγινώσκω.

τὰ καθ' ὑμᾶς. The article functions as a nominalizer (see 1:3 on τὰ), changing the prepositional phrase into a substantive (lit. "the things corresponding to you [pl.]"). Our translation, which follows BAGD (182 s.v. διαγινώσκω), is probably appropriate given the legal context. Other biblical examples of this expression are non-legal (17:28; 18:15; Eph 1:15; Job 11:6; Tobit 10:9).

24:23 διαταξάμενος τῷ ἑκατοντάρχῃ τηρεῖσθαι αὐτὸν ἔχειν τε ἄνεσιν καὶ μηδένα κωλύειν τῶν ἰδίων αὐτοῦ ὑπηρετεῖν αὐτῷ.

διαταξάμενος. Aor mid ptc masc nom sg διατάσσω (attendant circumstance of ᾿Ανεβάλετο, v. 22).

τηρεῖσθαι. Pres pass inf τηρέω (indirect discourse).

αὐτὸν. Accusative subject of the passive infinitive (see 1:3 on αὐτὸν). The antecedent is Paul (lit. "for him to be guarded").

ἔχειν. Pres act inf ἔχω (indirect discourse). Paul is the subject (lit. "[for him] to have relief").

μηδένα. The accusative substantival adjective, which is modified by τῶν ἰδίων, is most likely the subject of the infinitive ὑπηρετεῖν (see 1:3 on αὐτὸν) rather than the direct object of κωλύειν (for an analogous example, see 8:36). Either way it has been fronted to add rhetorical force to Felix's instructions.

κωλύειν. Pres act inf κωλύω (indirect discourse). The implied subject of the infinitive is the centurion.

τῶν ἰδίων. Partitive genitive.

ὑπηρετεῖν. Pres act inf ὑπηρετέω. The infinitive should probably be viewed as complementary (assuming μηδένα is the subject; see also 8:36 on βαπτισθῆναι).

αὐτῷ. Dative complement of ὑπηρετεῖν.

24:24 Μετὰ δὲ ἡμέρας τινὰς παραγενόμενος ὁ Φῆλιξ σὺν Δρουσίλλῃ τῇ ἰδίᾳ γυναικὶ οὔσῃ ᾿Ιουδαίᾳ μετεπέμψατο τὸν Παῦλον καὶ ἤκουσεν αὐτοῦ περὶ τῆς εἰς Χριστὸν ᾿Ιησοῦν πίστεως.

παραγενόμενος. Aor mid dep ptc masc nom sg παραγίνομαι (attendant circumstance).

τῇ ἰδίᾳ γυναικὶ. Dative in apposition to Δρουσίλλῃ. The textual variants (τῇ γυναικί, τῇ γυναικὶ αὐτοῦ, τῇ ἰδίᾳ γυναικὶ αὐτοῦ) make it clear that this expression meant nothing more than "his wife" in the NT period.

οὔσῃ. Pres act ptc dat fem sg εἰμί (attributive).

᾿Ιουδαίᾳ. Predicate dative (cf. 1:16 on ὁδηγοῦ).

μετεπέμψατο. Aor mid dep ind 3rd sg μεταπέμπομαι.

ἤκουσεν. Aor act ind 3rd sg ἀκούω.

αὐτοῦ. Genitive object of ἤκουσεν.

24:25 διαλεγομένου δὲ αὐτοῦ περὶ δικαιοσύνης καὶ ἐγκρατείας καὶ τοῦ κρίματος τοῦ μέλλοντος, ἔμφοβος γενόμενος ὁ Φῆλιξ ἀπεκρίθη, Τὸ νῦν ἔχον πορεύου, καιρὸν δὲ μεταλαβὼν μετακαλέσομαί σε,

διαλεγομένου. Pres dep ptc masc gen sg διαλέγομαι. Genitive absolute (see 1:8 on ἐπελθόντος), temporal.

αὐτοῦ. Genitive subject (see 1:8 on ἐπελθόντος).

μέλλοντος. Pres act ptc neut gen sg μέλλω (attributive).

ἔμφοβος. Predicate nominative.

γενόμενος. Aor mid dep ptc masc nom sg γίνομαι (attendant circumstance).

ἀπεκρίθη. Aor pass dep ind 3rd sg ἀποκρίνομαι.

τὸ νῦν. The article functions as a nominalizer (see 1:3), changing the adverb into a substantive (direct object of ἔχον).

ἔχον. Pres act ptc neut acc sg ἔχω. The participle functions as part of an idiomatic temporal expression (thus the accusative case): "for the time being."

πορεύου. Pres dep impv 2nd sg πορεύομαι.

μεταλαβὼν. Aor act ptc masc nom sg μεταλαμβάνω (temporal).

μετακαλέσομαί. Fut mid ind 1st sg μετακαλέω. The second accent comes from the enclitic σε (see 1:4 on ἠκούσατέ).

24:26 ἅμα καὶ ἐλπίζων ὅτι χρήματα δοθήσεται αὐτῷ ὑπὸ τοῦ Παύλου· διὸ καὶ πυκνότερον αὐτὸν μεταπεμπόμενος ὡμίλει αὐτῷ.

ἐλπίζων. Pres act ptc masc nom sg ἐλπίζω. The participle is used with ἅμα to introduce an action or state that was coincident with the main verb (ἀπεκρίθη, v. 25; cf. Robertson 1934, 1139–40).

ὅτι. Introduces a clausal complement of ἐλπίζων.

δοθήσεται. Fut pass ind 3rd sg δίδωμι.

μεταπεμπόμενος. Pres dep ptc masc nom sg μεταπέμπομαι (attendant circumstance).

ὡμίλει. Impf act ind 3rd sg ὁμιλέω. See 20:11 on ὁμιλήσας.

αὐτῷ. Dative of association.

24:27 Διετίας δὲ πληρωθείσης ἔλαβεν διάδοχον ὁ Φῆλιξ Πόρκιον Φῆστον, θέλων τε χάριτα καταθέσθαι τοῖς Ἰουδαίοις ὁ Φῆλιξ κατέλιπε τὸν Παῦλον δεδεμένον.

Διετίας. Genitive subject (see 1:8 on ἐπελθόντος).

πληρωθείσης. Aor pass ptc fem gen sg πληρόω. Genitive absolute (see 1:8 on ἐπελθόντος), temporal.

ἔλαβεν διάδοχον. Lit. "received a successor."

ἔλαβεν. Aor act ind 3rd sg λαμβάνω.

Πόρκιον Φῆστον. Accusative in apposition to διάδοχον.

θέλων. Pres act ptc masc nom sg θέλω (causal).

τε. The conjunction indicates that "Felix's action provides the specific lead-in to the following incident" (Levinsohn 1987, 141).

χάριτα. Accusative direct object of καταθέσθαι and an alternative form of χάριν (cf. 25:9; see Barrett, 1119).

καταθέσθαι. Aor mid inf κατατίθημι (complementary).

τοῖς Ἰουδαίοις. Dative of reference.

κατέλιπε. Aor act ind 3rd sg καταλείπω.

δεδεμένον. Prf pass ptc masc acc sg δέω. The participle functions as the complement in an object-complement double accusative construction (see 1:3 on ζῶντα).

Acts 25:1–12

[1]Three days after Festus arrived in the province, he went up to Jerusalem from Caesarea, [2]and the chief priests and (other) leaders of the Jews presented (charges) against Paul to him. They appealed to him [3]and asked a favor that he might send Paul to Jerusalem because they were arranging an ambush to kill him along the way.

[4]Then Festus responded that Paul was being kept in custody in Caesarea and that he himself was going there right away. [5]"Therefore," he said, "let those among you who are influential go down with me and accuse him, if this man has done anything improper."

[6]After staying among them for eight or ten more days, he went down to Caesarea. On the following day, he sat on the judgment seat and ordered Paul to be brought. [7]When he arrived, those Jews who had come down from Jerusalem surrounded him and brought many serious charges against him that they had no way of proving. [8]Meanwhile, Paul defended himself (by saying): "I have not done anything wrong against the law of the Jews or against the temple or against Caesar." [9]But Festus, since he wanted to gain favor with the Jews, answered Paul, "Would you like to go up to Jerusalem so that you can stand trial there before me concerning these matters?" [10]Paul replied, "I am (now) standing before the judgment seat of Caesar, where I should be judged. I have not wronged the Jews in any way, as you well know. [11]Therefore, if I am guilty and have done something worthy of death, I do not refuse to die. But if there is no merit to the things of which these men are accusing

me, no one has the right to hand me over to them. I appeal to Caesar!"
12Then, after Festus had conferred with his council, he answered, "You
have appealed to Caesar; to Caesar you will go!"

25:1 Φῆστος οὖν ἐπιβὰς τῇ ἐπαρχείᾳ μετὰ τρεῖς ἡμέρας ἀνέβη εἰς Ἱεροσόλυμα ἀπὸ Καισαρείας,

ἐπιβὰς. Aor act ptc masc nom sg ἐπιβαίνω (attendant circumstance).

ἀνέβη. Aor act ind 3rd sg ἀναβαίνω.

25:2 ἐνεφάνισάν τε αὐτῷ οἱ ἀρχιερεῖς καὶ οἱ πρῶτοι τῶν Ἰουδαίων κατὰ τοῦ Παύλου καὶ παρεκάλουν αὐτὸν

ἐνεφάνισάν. Aor act ind 3rd pl ἐμφανίζω. The second accent comes from the enclitic τε (see 1:4 on ἠκούσατέ). On the sense of the verb, see 24:1.

τε. The conjunction τε is used because "the interaction between the Jewish leaders and Festus in Jerusalem is preliminary to the nuclear interaction in Caesarea which involves Paul" (Levinsohn 1987, 134).

παρεκάλουν. Impf act ind 3rd pl παρακαλέω.

25:3 αἰτούμενοι χάριν κατ᾽ αὐτοῦ ὅπως μεταπέμψηται αὐτὸν εἰς Ἰερουσαλήμ, ἐνέδραν ποιοῦντες ἀνελεῖν αὐτὸν κατὰ τὴν ὁδόν.

αἰτούμενοι. Pres mid ptc masc nom pl αἰτέω (means). Here, the middle voice indicates personal benefit for the speakers.

χάριν κατ᾽ αὐτοῦ. Lit. "a favor against him (i.e., Paul)."

μεταπέμψηται. Aor mid dep subj 3rd sg μεταπέμπομαι. The subjunctive is typically used with ὅπως to introduce a purpose clause. Here, there may be some basis for saying that it introduces the content (indirect discourse) of a verb of "beseeching" (cf. Matt 8:34; Luke 7:3; see Robertson 1934, 995, 1046; Wallace 1996, 678).

ἐνέδραν. Only here and at 23:16 in the NT.

ποιοῦντες. Pres act ptc masc nom pl ποιέω (causal, modifying αἰτούμενοι).

ἀνελεῖν. Aor act inf ἀναιρέω (purpose).

25:4 ὁ μὲν οὖν Φῆστος ἀπεκρίθη τηρεῖσθαι τὸν Παῦλον εἰς Καισάρειαν, ἑαυτὸν δὲ μέλλειν ἐν τάχει ἐκπορεύεσθαι·

μὲν οὖν. Levinsohn (1987, 142–43) points out that μὲν οὖν should not be taken as introducing a response in opposition to the plan of Paul's enemy. Rather, the use of οὖν indicates continuity with what precedes and thus suggests that Festus was responding favorably to their request by seeking to expedite the matter, while being unaware of their plot. He also notes (1992, 213) that "the prospective nature of μέν suggests that the speech of vv. 4–5 is of a preliminary nature with respect to the foreground events associated with the corresponding δέ (viz., those of vv. 6ff)."

ἀπεκρίθη. Aor pass dep ind 3rd sg ἀποκρίνομαι.

τηρεῖσθαι. Pres pass inf τηρέω (indirect discourse).

τὸν Παῦλον. Accusative subject of the passive infinitive (see 1:3 on αὐτὸν).

ἑαυτὸν. Accusative subject of the infinitive μέλλειν (see 1:3 on αὐτὸν).

μέλλειν. Pres act inf μέλλω (indirect discourse). On the force of μέλλω plus an infinitive, see 3:3 on μέλλοντας. This construction, combined with ἐν τάχει, emphasizes either Festus' intention to leave immediately or his rhetorical goals. The reality, however, was somewhat different (see v. 6).

ἐν τάχει. See 12:7.

ἐκπορεύεσθαι. Pres dep inf ἐκπορεύομαι (complementary).

25:5 Οἱ οὖν ἐν ὑμῖν, φησίν, δυνατοὶ συγκαταβάντες εἴ τί ἐστιν ἐν τῷ ἀνδρὶ ἄτοπον κατηγορείτωσαν αὐτοῦ.

Οἱ ἐν ὑμῖν . . . δυνατοὶ. Since φησίν separates the article from δυνατοὶ, Οἱ appears to modify ἐν ὑμῖν as a nominalizer (see 1:3 on τὰ): "those among you." The fact that δυνατοὶ would require an article if it stood in apposition to Οἱ ἐν ὑμῖν, however, suggests that Greek allowed a verb of speech to separate the head noun from its modifiers and the article thus modifies δυνατοὶ.

φησίν. Pres act ind 3rd sg φημί. On the shift from indirect to direct discourse, see 1:4 on ἣν ἠκούσατέ μου; 23:22 on ὅτι; BDF §470.2.

συγκαταβάντες. Aor act ptc masc nom pl συγκαταβαίνω (with an imperative main verb an attendant circumstance participle carries imperatival force).

εἴ . . . ἄτοπον. Lit. "if anything improper is in the man."

εἰ. Introduces a first class condition.

τί. This form should not be mistaken for an interrogative pronoun (the accent comes from the enclitic ἐστιν; see 1:4 on ἠκούσατέ). Rather, it is an indefinite adjective that modifies ἄτοπον and has been fronted (see 3:13 on ὑμεῖς) to place it in focus (see 2:15 on ὑμεῖς).

ἐστιν. Pres act ind 3rd sg εἰμί.

ἄτοπον. Neuter nominative subject of ἐστιν.

κατηγορείτωσαν. Pres act impv 3rd pl κατηγορέω.

αὐτοῦ. Genitive object of κατηγορείτωσαν.

25:6 Διατρίψας δὲ ἐν αὐτοῖς ἡμέρας οὐ πλείους ὀκτὼ ἢ δέκα, καταβὰς εἰς Καισάρειαν, τῇ ἐπαύριον καθίσας ἐπὶ τοῦ βήματος ἐκέλευσεν τὸν Παῦλον ἀχθῆναι.

Διατρίψας. Aor act ptc masc nom sg διατρίβω (temporal).

ἡμέρας οὐ πλείους ὀκτὼ ἢ δέκα. Accusative indicating extent of time (see 7:20 on μῆνας). Although this phrase should probably be taken as a comparative construction ("no more days than eight or ten"), ἡμέρας οὐ πλείους could be viewed as an example of litotes (lit. "not many days"; see 1:5 on οὐ μετὰ πολλὰς ταύτας ἡμέρας), with ὀκτὼ ἢ δέκα being appositional: "He stayed among them for a few more days, eight or ten that is, and then . . ."

καταβὰς. Aor act ptc masc nom sg καταβαίνω (attendant circumstance).

τῇ ἐπαύριον. Dative of time.

καθίσας. Aor act ptc masc nom sg καθίζω (attendant circumstance).

ἐκέλευσεν. Aor act ind 3rd sg κελεύω.

τὸν Παῦλον. Accusative subject of the passive infinitive (see 1:3 on αὐτὸν).

ἀχθῆναι. Aor pass inf ἄγω (indirect discourse).

25:7 παραγενομένου δὲ αὐτοῦ περιέστησαν αὐτὸν οἱ ἀπὸ Ἱεροσολύμων καταβεβηκότες Ἰουδαῖοι πολλὰ καὶ βαρέα αἰτιώματα καταφέροντες ἃ οὐκ ἴσχυον ἀποδεῖξαι,

παραγενομένου. Aor mid dep ptc masc gen sg παραγίνομαι. Genitive absolute (see 1:8 on ἐπελθόντος), temporal.

αὐτοῦ. Genitive subject (see 1:8 on ἐπελθόντος).

περιέστησαν. Aor act ind 3rd pl περιΐστημι.

καταβεβηκότες. Prf act ptc masc nom pl καταβαίνω (attributive).

πολλὰ καὶ βαρέα. The conjunction in this phrase (lit. "many and weighty") should probably be taken as epexegetical. Combined with βαρέα, it intensifies the expression.

καταφέροντες. Pres act ptc masc nom pl καταφέρω (attendant circumstance of περιέστησαν).

οὐκ ἴσχυον ἀποδεῖξαι. Lit. "which they were unable to prove." Our translation attempts to capture the semantic component of ἰσχύω (capability) that distinguishes it from δύναμαι.

ἴσχυον. Impf act ind 3rd pl ἰσχύω.

ἀποδεῖξαι. Aor act inf ἀποδείκνυμι (complementary).

25:8 τοῦ Παύλου ἀπολογουμένου ὅτι Οὔτε εἰς τὸν νόμον τῶν Ἰουδαίων οὔτε εἰς τὸ ἱερὸν οὔτε εἰς Καίσαρά τι ἥμαρτον.

τοῦ Παύλου. Genitive subject (see 1:8 on ἐπελθόντος).

ἀπολογουμένου. Pres dep ptc masc gen sg ἀπολογέομαι. Genitive absolute (see 1:8 on ἐπελθόντος), temporal or perhaps result (modifying the main verb in v. 7).

ὅτι. Introduces direct discourse.

εἰς. Disadvantage.

Καίσαρά. The second accent comes from the enclitic τι (see 1:4 on ἠκούσατέ).

τι. Accusative direct object of ἥμαρτον.

ἥμαρτον. Aor act ind 1st sg ἁμαρτάνω.

25:9 ὁ Φῆστος δὲ θέλων τοῖς Ἰουδαίοις χάριν καταθέσθαι ἀποκριθεὶς τῷ Παύλῳ εἶπεν, Θέλεις εἰς Ἱεροσόλυμα ἀναβὰς ἐκεῖ περὶ τούτων κριθῆναι ἐπ᾽ ἐμοῦ;

θέλων. Pres act ptc masc nom sg θέλω (causal).

τοῖς Ἰουδαίοις. Dative of reference.

καταθέσθαι. Aor mid inf κατατίθημι (complementary to θέλων).

ἀποκριθεὶς. Aor pass dep ptc masc nom sg ἀποκρίνομαι (attendant circumstance of εἶπεν).

εἶπεν. Aor act ind 3rd sg λέγω.

Θέλεις. Pres act ind 2nd sg θέλω.

ἀναβὰς. Aor act ptc masc nom sg ἀναβαίνω (attendant circumstance of the infinitive).

κριθῆναι. Aor pass inf κρίνω (complementary).

ἐπ' ἐμοῦ. Though many translations imply otherwise, the preposition does not introduce the agent of the passive verb, but rather is locative/spatial ("a position before, with the implication of a relationship of authority"; LN 83.35).

25:10 εἶπεν δὲ ὁ Παῦλος, Ἐπὶ τοῦ βήματος Καίσαρος ἑστὼς εἰμι, οὗ με δεῖ κρίνεσθαι. Ἰουδαίους οὐδὲν ἠδίκησα ὡς καὶ σὺ κάλλιον ἐπιγινώσκεις.

εἶπεν. Aor act ind 3rd sg λέγω.

ἑστὼς. Prf act ptc masc nom sg ἵστημι (perfect periphrastic; see 2:13 on μεμεστωμένοι).

εἰμι. Pres act ind 1st sg εἰμί.

οὗ. See 1:13.

με. Accusative subject of the infinitive κρίνεσθαι (see 1:3 on αὐτὸν).

δεῖ. Pres act ind 3rd sg δεῖ.

κρίνεσθαι. Pres pass inf κρίνω (complementary; see 1:16 on ἔδει).

οὐδὲν. Since it appears that ἀδικέω cannot take a double accusative construction, it is better to take οὐδὲν as an accusative of manner ("in no way"; cf. Gal 4:12; Phlm 18, and perhaps Luke 10:19) rather than as the second object in a double accusative construction (contra Plummer, 279).

ἠδίκησα. Aor act ind 1st sg ἀδικέω.

κάλλιον. The comparative adjective carries elative force (see 13:31 on πλείους; cf. Bruce, 488).

ἐπιγινώσκεις. Pres act ind 2nd sg ἐπιγινώσκω.

25:11 εἰ μὲν οὖν ἀδικῶ καὶ ἄξιον θανάτου πέπραχά τι, οὐ παραιτοῦμαι τὸ ἀποθανεῖν· εἰ δὲ οὐδέν ἐστιν ὧν οὗτοι κατηγοροῦσίν μου, οὐδείς με δύναται αὐτοῖς χαρίσασθαι· Καίσαρα ἐπικαλοῦμαι.

εἰ. Introduces a first class condition.

μὲν οὖν. See 1:6.

ἀδικῶ. Pres act ind 1st sg ἀδικέω.

ἄξιον. The adjective functions as the complement in an object-complement double accusative construction (see 1:3 on ζῶντα), with τι serving as the direct object.

πέπραχά. Prf act ind 1st sg πράσσω. The second accent comes from the enclitic τι (see 1:4 on ἠκούσατέ).

παραιτοῦμαι. Pres dep ind 1st sg παραιτέομαι. Although this verb typically indicates a request, here it means "to refuse" (see Barrett, 1130; cf. Heb 12:25).

τὸ ἀποθανεῖν. Aor act inf ἀποθνῄσκω (direct object).

εἰ. Introduces a first class condition.

οὐδέν. Predicate nominative of an impersonal ἐστιν (lit. "if there is nothing").

ἐστιν. Pres act ind 3rd sg εἰμί.

ὧν. The relative pronoun introduces a headless relative clause (see 3:6 on ὅ). The case could be taken as genitive of reference or genitive by attraction to an unexpressed antecedent (for how this can take place, see 22:15).

κατηγοροῦσίν. Pres act ind 3rd pl κατηγορέω. The second accent comes from the enclitic μου (see 1:4 on ἠκούσατέ).

μου. Genitive object of κατηγοροῦσίν.

με. Accusative direct object of the infinitive.

δύναται. Pres dep ind 3rd sg δύναμαι.

χαρίσασθαι. Aor mid dep inf χαρίζομαι (complementary).

ἐπικαλοῦμαι. Pres mid ind 1st sg ἐπικαλέω.

25:12 τότε ὁ Φῆστος συλλαλήσας μετὰ τοῦ συμβουλίου ἀπεκρίθη, Καίσαρα ἐπικέκλησαι, ἐπὶ Καίσαρα πορεύσῃ.

συλλαλήσας. Aor act ptc masc nom sg συλλαλέω (temporal).

συμβουλίου. Here, "an advisory council" (LN 11.86).

ἀπεκρίθη. Aor pass dep ind 3rd sg ἀποκρίνομαι.

ἐπικέκλησαι. Prf mid ind 2nd sg ἐπικαλέω.

πορεύσῃ. Fut mid dep ind 2nd sg πορεύομαι.

ἐπὶ. Used with the accusative form of Καῖσαρ, the preposition indicates the goal of Paul's impending journey.

Acts 25:13–22

[13]After some days had passed, King Agrippa and Bernice arrived in Caesarea and greeted Festus. [14]When they had been there for many days, Festus presented Paul's case to the king and said, "There is a man (here),

whom Felix left as a prisoner, [15]concerning whom, while I was in Jerusalem, the high priest and elders of the Jews presented charges and requested a ruling against him. [16]I answered them that it is not the custom of the Romans to hand over any man before the one who is accused has met his accusers face to face and received an opportunity to defend himself against the accusation.

[17]So after they came (back) here with (me), I did not delay at all, but on the next day I sat on the judgment seat and ordered the man to be brought. [18]But when his accusers stood up, they brought no accusation of the horrible things that I had suspected. [19]Instead, they had certain disagreements with him about their own religion and about a man named Jesus who had died, whom Paul claimed to be alive. [20]Since I was baffled by the dispute over these matters, I asked if he might want to go to Jerusalem and be tried there on these charges. [21]But when Paul requested that he be judged by the Emperor, I ordered him to be kept in custody until I could send him up to Caesar. [22]Agrippa (responded) to Festus, "I would like to hear this man myself." "Tomorrow," he replied, "you will hear him for yourself."

25:13 Ἡμερῶν δὲ διαγενομένων τινῶν Ἀγρίππας ὁ βασιλεὺς καὶ Βερνίκη κατήντησαν εἰς Καισάρειαν ἀσπασάμενοι τὸν Φῆστον.

Ἡμερῶν. Genitive subject (see 1:8 on ἐπελθόντος).

διαγενομένων. Aor mid dep ptc fem gen pl διαγίνομαι. Genitive absolute (see 1:8 on ἐπελθόντος), temporal.

ὁ βασιλεὺς. Nominative in apposition to Ἀγρίππας.

κατήντησαν. Aor act ind 3rd pl καταντάω.

ἀσπασάμενοι. Aor mid dep ptc masc nom pl ἀσπάζομαι (attendant circumstance). The participle should not be viewed as indicating purpose (contra Wallace 1996, 637), although such a sense is probably intended by the variant reading ἀσπασόμενοι (Ψ 36 81 323 1739 1891 2495 *pm* lat sy sa), which is future tense. Although a number of scholars have argued that the aorist participle cannot be used to express subsequent action (see Robertson 1934, 861–63), Porter (1992, 189) has demonstrated that "there are a number of examples in biblical and extra-biblical Greek where an aorist participle is used to refer to an action occurring after the action of the main verb. In virtually all of these examples, the aorist participle is placed after the main verb in syntactical order" (see also Porter 1989, 385–87).

25:14 ὡς δὲ πλείους ἡμέρας διέτριβον ἐκεῖ, ὁ Φῆστος τῷ βασιλεῖ ἀνέθετο τὰ κατὰ τὸν Παῦλον λέγων, Ἀνήρ τίς ἐστιν καταλελειμμένος ὑπὸ Φήλικος δέσμιος,

ὡς. Temporal (see 18:5).

ἡμέρας. Accusative indicating extent of time (see 7:20 on μῆνας).

διέτριβον. Impf act ind 3rd pl διατρίβω.

ἀνέθετο. Aor mid ind 3rd sg ἀνατίθημι. This verb occurs only here and at Gal 2:2.

τὰ κατὰ τὸν Παῦλον. The article functions as a nominalizer (see 1:3 on τὰ), changing the prepositional phrase into a substantive (lit. "the things corresponding to Paul").

λέγων. Pres act ptc masc nom sg λέγω (attendant circumstance or means).

τίς. See 8:9. The indefinite adjective/pronoun, which has received its accent from the enclitic ἐστιν (see 1:4 on ἠκούσατέ), should not be mistaken for an interrogative pronoun.

ἐστιν. Pres act ind 3rd sg εἰμί.

καταλελειμμένος. Prf pass ptc masc nom sg καταλείπω (perfect periphrastic; see 2:13 on μεμεστωμένοι).

δέσμιος. Used with the passive verb, the nominative noun functions as a complement in a subject-complement double nominative construction (cf. 4:36 on υἱὸς and 1:12 on Ἐλαιῶνος), in which Ἀνήρ τίς is the subject.

25:15 περὶ οὗ γενομένου μου εἰς Ἱεροσόλυμα ἐνεφάνισαν οἱ ἀρχιερεῖς καὶ οἱ πρεσβύτεροι τῶν Ἰουδαίων αἰτούμενοι κατ' αὐτοῦ καταδίκην.

γενομένου. Aor mid dep ptc masc gen sg γίνομαι. Genitive absolute (see 1:8 on ἐπελθόντος), temporal.

μου. Genitive subject (see 1:8 on ἐπελθόντος).

ἐνεφάνισαν. Aor act ind 3rd pl ἐμφανίζω. On the sense, see 24:1.

αἰτούμενοι. Pres mid ptc masc nom pl αἰτέω (attendant circumstance).

καταδίκην. Only here in the NT: "a guilty verdict."

25:16 πρὸς οὓς ἀπεκρίθην ὅτι οὐκ ἔστιν ἔθος Ῥωμαίοις χαρίζεσθαί τινα ἄνθρωπον πρὶν ἢ ὁ κατηγορούμενος κατὰ πρόσωπον

ἔχοι τοὺς κατηγόρους τόπον τε ἀπολογίας λάβοι περὶ τοῦ ἐγκλήματος.

ἀπεκρίθην. Aor pass dep ind 1st sg ἀποκρίνομαι.

ὅτι. Introduces indirect discourse. Although ὅτι can be used with ἀποκρίνομαι to introduce direct discourse, elsewhere in Acts ἀποκρίνομαι always occurs without a ὅτι when direct discourse follows.

ἔστιν. Pres act ind 3rd sg εἰμί. On the accent, see 4:12.

ἔθος. Predicate nominative.

Ῥωμαίοις. Dative of possession (with εἰμί).

χαρίζεσθαί. Pres dep inf χαρίζομαι (subject). The second accent comes from the enclitic τινα (see 1:4 on ἠκούσατέ).

ὁ κατηγορούμενος. Pres pass ptc masc nom sg κατηγορέω (substantival).

ἔχοι. Pres act opt 3rd sg ἔχω. Robertson (1934, 970) notes that the optative is probably used in place of the subjunctive in indirect speech—a construction found only in Luke's writings in the NT.

τόπον . . . ἐγκλήματος. Lit. "an opportunity of defense concerning the charge."

λάβοι. Aor act opt 3rd sg λαμβάνω.

25:17 **συνελθόντων οὖν [αὐτῶν] ἐνθάδε ἀναβολὴν μηδεμίαν ποιησάμενος τῇ ἑξῆς καθίσας ἐπὶ τοῦ βήματος ἐκέλευσα ἀχθῆναι τὸν ἄνδρα·**

συνελθόντων. Aor act ptc masc gen pl συνέρχομαι. Genitive absolute (see 1:8 on ἐπελθόντος), temporal. Given the context (vv. 5–6), the verb must indicate that the men accompanied Festus on his return to Caesarea (so BAGD, 788).

[αὐτῶν]. Genitive subject (see 1:8 on ἐπελθόντος). Metzger (492–93) notes three variants—αὐτῶν ἐνθάδε (𝔓[74] ℵ A E H L P Ψ and most miniscules), ἐνθάδε (B 0142 5 42 51 97 181 209* 234 453), and ἐνθά δε αὐτῶν (C 36 180 1518 2495)—and argues (his personal opinion) that the reading of B best explains the origin of the others. This is a good example of where an understanding of how information is processed is helpful for text-critical matters. All things being equal, the early and widespread testimony for αὐτῶν ἐνθάδε favors this reading. It would have been quite natural for some scribes, particularly those listening to a reader, to omit information that is implicit (leaving ἐνθάδε) or to alter the word order unconsciously (ἐνθάδε αὐτῶν). Therefore, the brackets in the UBS[4]/NA[27] text, in our view, are unwarranted.

ἀναβολὴν μηδεμίαν ποιησάμενος. Lit. "causing no delay."

ποιησάμενος. Aor mid ptc masc nom sg ποιέω (attendant circumstance of ἐκέλευσα). Here, the (negated) middle voice probably is used to highlight Festus' lack of "specific involvement" in causing a delay (cf. Porter 1992, 67).

τῇ ἑξῆς. See 21:1.

καθίσας. Aor act ptc masc nom sg καθίζω (attendant circumstance).

ἐκέλευσα. Aor act ind 1st sg κελεύω.

ἀχθῆναι. Aor pass inf ἄγω (indirect discourse).

τὸν ἄνδρα. Accusative subject of the passive infinitive (see 1:3 on αὐτὸν).

25:18 περὶ οὗ σταθέντες οἱ κατήγοροι οὐδεμίαν αἰτίαν ἔφερον ὧν ἐγὼ ὑπενόουν πονηρῶν,

περὶ . . . κατήγοροι. Lit. "Concerning whom the accusers stood."

σταθέντες. Aor pass ptc masc nom pl ἵστημι (temporal).

ἔφερον. Impf act ind 3rd pl φέρω.

ὧν . . . πονηρῶν. The internally headed relative clause (see 1:2 on ἄχρι ἧς ἡμέρας) probably intensifies the head noun: "no accusation of the *horrible* things" (for another internally headed relative clause where the antecdent is πονηρῶν, see Luke 3:19). Although the UBS[4]/NA[27] reading is not widely attested (א[c] B E 81 104 *pc*), it is the preferred reading since (1) it would have been natural for later scribes (*Byz*) to omit πονηρῶν to eliminate the (rare) internally headed relative clause; (2) although the feminine accusative form πονηράν (as an attributive modifier of αἰτίαν) is the best attested reading (𝔓[74] A C[*] Ψ 33[vid] 36 181 307 453 610 *al*), it is unlikely that scribes would have introduced the harder internally headed relative clause; (3) the accusative plural form πονηρά (א[*] C[2] it[w] vg[ms]) was probably simply a scribal error as the corrector of א recognized.

ὑπενόουν. Impf act ind 1st sg ὑπονοέω.

πονηρῶν. Objective genitive, modifying αἰτίαν (the content of the accusation). On its position, see above.

25:19 ζητήματα δέ τινα περὶ τῆς ἰδίας δεισιδαιμονίας εἶχον πρὸς αὐτὸν καὶ περί τινος Ἰησοῦ τεθνηκότος ὃν ἔφασκεν ὁ Παῦλος ζῆν.

εἶχον. Impf act ind 3rd pl ἔχω.

τεθνηκότος. Prf act ptc masc gen sg θνῄσκω (attributive).

ὃν. The accusative relative pronoun is the subject of the infinitive ζῆν (see 1:3 on αὐτὸν).

ἔφασκεν. Impf act ind 3rd sg φάσκω.

ζῆν. Pres act inf ζάω (indirect discourse).

25:20 ἀπορούμενος δὲ ἐγὼ τὴν περὶ τούτων ζήτησιν ἔλεγον εἰ βούλοιτο πορεύεσθαι εἰς Ἱεροσόλυμα κἀκεῖ κρίνεσθαι περὶ τούτων.

ἀπορούμενος. Pres mid ptc masc nom sg ἀπορέω (causal). According to Louw and Nida (32.9), this verb indicates a state of "perplexity, with the implication of serious anxiety."

ζήτησιν. Since ἀπορέω appears to be an intransitive verb, the accusative case must denote reference.

ἔλεγον. Impf act ind 1st sg λέγω.

βούλοιτο. Pres dep opt 3rd sg βούλομαι. While the optative in indirect discourse could simply be taken as a substitute for a direct discourse indicative or subjunctive (so Wallace 1996, 483), the somewhat "vague" connotation associated with the optative fits well in this context (cf. 5:24 on τί ἂν γένοιτο τοῦτο).

πορεύεσθαι. Pres dep inf πορεύομαι (complementary).

κρίνεσθαι. Pres pass inf κρίνω (complementary).

25:21 τοῦ δὲ Παύλου ἐπικαλεσαμένου τηρηθῆναι αὐτὸν εἰς τὴν τοῦ Σεβαστοῦ διάγνωσιν, ἐκέλευσα τηρεῖσθαι αὐτὸν ἕως οὗ ἀναπέμψω αὐτὸν πρὸς Καίσαρα.

Παύλου. Genitive subject (see 1:8 on ἐπελθόντος).

ἐπικαλεσαμένου . . . διάγνωσιν. Lit. "appealing that he be kept for the decision of the Emperor."

ἐπικαλεσαμένου. Aor mid ptc masc gen sg ἐπικαλέω. Genitive absolute (see 1:8 on ἐπελθόντος), temporal or causal.

τηρηθῆναι. Aor pass inf τηρέω (indirect discourse).

αὐτὸν. Accusative subject of the passive infinitive (see 1:3 on αὐτὸν).

ἐκέλευσα. Aor act ind 1st sg κελεύω.

τηρεῖσθαι. Pres pass inf τηρέω (indirect discourse).

αὐτὸν. Accusative subject of the passive infinitive (see 1:3 on αὐτὸν).

ἕως οὗ. See 23:12.
ἀναπέμψω. Aor act subj 1st sg ἀναπέμπω.

25:22 Ἀγρίππας δὲ πρὸς τὸν Φῆστον, Ἐβουλόμην καὶ αὐτὸς τοῦ ἀνθρώπου ἀκοῦσαι. Αὔριον, φησίν, ἀκούσῃ αὐτοῦ.

Ἐβουλόμην. Impf dep ind 1st sg βούλομαι.
αὐτὸς. Intensive.
τοῦ ἀνθρώπου. Genitive object of ἀκοῦσαι.
ἀκοῦσαι. Aor act inf ἀκούω (complementary).
φησίν. Pres act ind 3rd sg φημί.
ἀκούσῃ. Fut mid ind 2nd sg ἀκούω. The middle voice points to "more direct participation, specific involvement, or even some form of benefit of the subject doing the action" (Porter 1992, 67).
αὐτοῦ. Genitive object of ἀκούσῃ.

Acts 25:23–27

[23]So the next day, Agrippa and Bernice came with great pomp and entered the audience hall with both the commanders and the prominent men of the city; and when Festus had given the order, Paul was brought. [24]Then Festus said, "King Agrippa and all of you men present with us, you see this man concerning whom the entire Jewish populace appealed to me both in Jerusalem and here shouting that he must certainly not be allowed to live any longer. [25]I, on the other hand, realized that he had done nothing worthy of death; but since he himself appealed to the Emperor, I decided to send him. [26]I do not have anything definite to write to our Master about him. Therefore, I have brought him before you all, and especially before you, King Agrippa, so that after a hearing has occurred I will have something to write. [27]For it seems ridiculous to me to send a prisoner without indicating the charges against him."

25:23 Τῇ οὖν ἐπαύριον ἐλθόντος τοῦ Ἀγρίππα καὶ τῆς Βερνίκης μετὰ πολλῆς φαντασίας καὶ εἰσελθόντων εἰς τὸ ἀκροατήριον σύν τε χιλιάρχοις καὶ ἀνδράσιν τοῖς κατ' ἐξοχὴν τῆς πόλεως καὶ κελεύσαντος τοῦ Φήστου ἤχθη ὁ Παῦλος.

οὖν. The conjunction "makes explicit the close consequential relationship between Festus' reply to king Agrippa . . . and the elaborate ceremonial described in the [genitive absolutes] of v 23" (Levinsohn

1987, 139).

ἐλθόντος. Aor act ptc masc gen sg ἔρχομαι. Genitive absolute (see 1:8 on ἐπελθόντος), attendant circumstance or temporal. The singular participle focuses attention on the arrival of Agrippa, who happened to be accompanied by his wife.

τοῦ Ἀγρίππα καὶ τῆς Βερνίκης. Genitive subject (see 1:8 on ἐπελθόντος).

μετὰ πολλῆς φαντασίας. In terms of syntax the prepositional phrase indicates accompaniment; in terms of semantics it indicates the (ostentatious) manner in which the royals made their entrance.

εἰσελθόντων. Aor act ptc masc gen pl εἰσέρχομαι. Genitive absolute (see 1:8 on ἐπελθόντος), attendant circumstance or temporal. The plural participle shifts the attention to the group as a whole.

τοῖς κατ' ἐξοχήν. The article functions as an adjectivizer (see 2:5 on τῶν ὑπὸ τὸν οὐρανόν), changing the prepositional phrase into an attributive modifier of ἀνδράσιν.

ἐξοχήν. Only here in the NT: "a position of high status" (LN 87.19).

κελεύσαντος. Aor act ptc masc gen sg κελεύω. Genitive absolute (see 1:8 on ἐπελθόντος), temporal.

τοῦ Φήστου. Genitive subject (see 1:8 on ἐπελθόντος).

ἤχθη. Aor pass ind 3rd sg ἄγω.

25:24 **καί φησιν ὁ Φῆστος, Ἀγρίππα βασιλεῦ καὶ πάντες οἱ συμπαρόντες ἡμῖν ἄνδρες, θεωρεῖτε τοῦτον περὶ οὗ ἅπαν τὸ πλῆθος τῶν Ἰουδαίων ἐνέτυχόν μοι ἔν τε Ἱεροσολύμοις καὶ ἐνθάδε βοῶντες μὴ δεῖν αὐτὸν ζῆν μηκέτι.**

φησιν. Pres act ind 3rd sg φημί.

Ἀγρίππα. Vocative.

βασιλεῦ. Vocative in apposition to Ἀγρίππα.

συμπαρόντες. Pres act ptc masc voc pl συμπάρειμι (attributive).

ἡμῖν. Verbs with a συν- prefix take a dative complement.

ἄνδρες. Vocative.

θεωρεῖτε. Pres act ind (or perhaps impv) 2nd pl θεωρέω.

ἅπαν τὸ πλῆθος τῶν Ἰουδαίων. Hyperbole (cf. 1:18 on πάντα).

ἐνέτυχόν. Aor act ind 3rd pl ἐντυγχάνω. The second accent comes from the enclitic μοι (see 1:4 on ἠκούσατέ).

ἔν. The accent comes from the enclitic τε (see 1:4 on ἠκούσατέ).

βοῶντες. Pres act ptc masc nom pl βοάω (manner).

μὴ . . . μηκέτι. The double negative intensifies the demand.

δεῖν. Pres act inf δεῖ (indirect discourse/command).

αὐτὸν. Accusative subject of the infinitive ζῆν (see 1:3 on αὐτὸν).

ζῆν. Pres act inf ζάω (complementary).

25:25 ἐγὼ δὲ κατελαβόμην μηδὲν ἄξιον αὐτὸν θανάτου πεπραχέναι, αὐτοῦ δὲ τούτου ἐπικαλεσαμένου τὸν Σεβαστὸν ἔκρινα πέμπειν.

κατελαβόμην. Aor mid ind 1st sg καταλαμβάνω.

μηδὲν. The accusative direct object has been fronted (see 3:13 on ὑμεῖς) for emphasis.

ἄξιον. Attributive.

αὐτὸν. Accusative subject of the infinitive (see 1:3 on αὐτὸν).

πεπραχέναι. Prf act inf πράσσω (indirect discourse with a verb of cognition).

αὐτοῦ. Intensive.

τούτου. Substantival genitive subject (see 1:8 on ἐπελθόντος).

ἐπικαλεσαμένου. Aor mid ptc masc gen sg ἐπικαλέω. Genitive absolute (see 1:8 on ἐπελθόντος), causal or temporal.

ἔκρινα. Aor act ind 1st sg κρίνω.

πέμπειν. Pres act inf πέμπω (complementary).

25:26 περὶ οὗ ἀσφαλές τι γράψαι τῷ κυρίῳ οὐκ ἔχω, διὸ προήγαγον αὐτὸν ἐφ' ὑμῶν καὶ μάλιστα ἐπὶ σοῦ, βασιλεῦ Ἀγρίππα, ὅπως τῆς ἀνακρίσεως γενομένης σχῶ τί γράψω·

ἀσφαλές. Attributive.

γράψαι. Aor act inf γράφω (epexegetical to τι).

ἔχω. Pres act ind 1st sg ἔχω.

προήγαγον. Aor act ind 1st sg προάγω.

βασιλεῦ Ἀγρίππα. On the position of the vocative, see 10:13.

ἀνακρίσεως. Genitive subject (see 1:8 on ἐπελθόντος).

γενομένης. Aor mid dep ptc fem gen sg γίνομαι. Genitive absolute (see 1:8 on ἐπελθόντος), temporal or perhaps means (so Healey and Healey, 220).

σχῶ. Aor act subj 1st sg ἔχω. The subjunctive is used with ὅπως to introduce a purpose clause.

τί. The interrogative pronoun introduces an indirect question that serves as the clausal direct object of σχῶ.

γράψω. Aor act subj OR Fut act ind 1st sg γράφω. Since the future indicative and aorist subjunctive appear to be used "interchangeably" in some constructions, it is impossible to determine which form occurs here. The slight difference between the semantics of the subjunctive mood, which Porter identifies as [+projection] (1989, 321–34), and the future tense, which Porter identifies as [+expectation] (1989, 403–16), may, however, favor the future tense. Whereas a subjunctive statement would simply serve to project or visualize a state of affairs, a future tense statement would carry a sense of confident expectation that would be appropriate in making a request of one's superior.

25:27 ἄλογον γάρ μοι δοκεῖ πέμποντα δέσμιον μὴ καὶ τὰς κατ' αὐτοῦ αἰτίας σημᾶναι.

Because of the complexity of this construction, we will treat the syntax of the major constituents together. The case of ἄλογον and πέμποντα are ambiguous. Formally, the *singular* adjective could be either masculine accusative, neuter nominative, or neuter accusative, while the participle could be either masculine accusative singular, neuter nominative plural, or neuter accusative plural. Since ἄλογον and πέμποντα somehow modify one another, they must agree in gender, number, and case. Therefore, they both must be masculine accusative singular. To make sense of the syntax, the whole infinitival construction, πέμποντα δέσμιον μὴ καὶ τὰς κατ' αὐτοῦ αἰτίας σημᾶναι, must be considered the subject of δοκεῖ. The participle can then be viewed as a temporal modifier of the infinitive (not an attendant circumstance, given the presence of the καί). It must be in the accusative case to agree with the implicit subject of the infinitive (see 1:3 on αὐτὸν). The accusative adjective ἄλογον serves as a predicate adjective. Thus, "when sending a prisoner, not also to signify the charges seems ridiculous to me."

δοκεῖ. Pres act ind 3rd sg δοκέω.

πέμποντα. Pres act ptc masc acc sg πέμπω (temporal modifier of the infinitive; see above.).

σημᾶναι. Aor act inf σημαίνω (see above).

Acts 26:1–23

[1]So Agrippa said to Paul, "You are granted permission to speak for yourself." Then Paul gestured with his hand and began his defense.

2“King Agrippa, I consider myself fortunate to be about to make my defense before you today concerning all the things that I am accused of by the Jews. 3Therefore, I ask you, in particular, who are an expert in all the customs and disputes of the Jews, to listen to me patiently.

4Now, all the Jews know how I lived since my youth, living among my own people from the beginning, and also in Jerusalem; 5and they have known me for a long time, if they care to testify, that I—(as) a Pharisee—lived in accord with the strictest sect of our religion. 6And now I am standing trial because of my hope in the promise that God made to our ancestors. 7Our twelve tribes, by earnestly serving (God) day and night, themselves hope to receive this (same) promise; and this is the very hope of which the Jews are accusing me, Your Majesty! 8How can you people find it unbelievable that God raises the dead?

9Now, I myself thought that it was necessary to do many hostile things against the name of Jesus the Nazarene. 10And that is what I did in Jerusalem—after receiving authority from the chief priests to do so, I both locked up many of God’s people in prison and cast my vote against them when they were condemned to death. 11I punished them often in every last synagogue and forced them to blaspheme; and because I was absolutely furious with them I even pursued them to foreign cities.

12Meanwhile, as I was on my way to Damascus with authority and complete power from the chief priests, 13in the middle of the day along the road, Your Majesty, I saw a light from heaven, brighter than the sun, shining around me and those traveling with me. 14After all of us had fallen to the ground, I heard a voice saying to me in the Hebrew language, ‘Saul, Saul, why are you persecuting me? It is bad for you to kick against the goads!’ 15Then I said, ‘Who are you, Lord?’ And the Lord said, ‘I am Jesus whom you are persecuting. 16But get up and stand on your feet. For here is the reason that I have appeared to you: to choose you in advance to be a servant and witness of both the things you have seen and of the things I will reveal to you 17by rescuing you from (your own) people and from the Gentiles to whom I am sending you 18and to open their eyes so that they might turn from darkness to light and from the authority of Satan to God so that they might receive forgiveness of sins and an inheritance among those who have been sanctified by faith in me.’

19Therefore, King Agrippa, I did not disobey the heavenly vision. 20Instead, I preached—first to those in Damascus and Jerusalem, and then in all the region of Judea and among the Gentiles—that they should repent and turn to God, and do things that are consistent with repentance. [21]Because of these things, after the Jews had seized me in the temple, they were trying to kill me. [22]Therefore, since I have received help from God up until this day, I stand and testify to all people, speaking about nothing besides those things that both the prophets and Moses said were going to happen. [23]Was the Christ destined to suffer? Was he the first to rise from the dead? Then, of course, he is going to proclaim light to both the (Jewish) people and the Gentiles!"

26:1 'Αγρίππας δὲ πρὸς τὸν Παῦλον ἔφη, 'Επιτρέπεταί σοι περὶ σεαυτοῦ λέγειν. τότε ὁ Παῦλος ἐκτείνας τὴν χεῖρα ἀπελογεῖτο,

ἔφη. Aor/Impf act ind 3rd sg φημί. On the tense, see 7:2.

'Επιτρέπεταί. Pres pass ind 3rd sg ἐπιτρέπω. The second accent comes from the enclitic σοι (see 1:4 on ἠκούσατέ).

σοι. Indirect object of 'Επιτρέπεταί.

λέγειν. Pres act inf λέγω (subject of the passive infinitive).

ἐκτείνας. Aor act ptc nom masc sg ἐκτείνω (attendant circumstance). The expression ἐκτείνας τὴν χεῖρα indicates an oratorical gesture or respectful gesture to the king rather than a motion for silence (as with κατασείσας τῇ χειρί in 12:17 and 13:16; Bruce, 496).

ἀπελογεῖτο. Impf dep ind 3rd sg ἀπολογέομαι.

26:2 Περὶ πάντων ὧν ἐγκαλοῦμαι ὑπὸ 'Ιουδαίων, βασιλεῦ 'Αγρίππα, ἥγημαι ἐμαυτὸν μακάριον ἐπὶ σοῦ μέλλων σήμερον ἀπολογεῖσθαι

ὧν. Genitive object of ἐγκαλοῦμαι or genitive by attraction to πάντων (see 1:1 on ὧν).

ἐγκαλοῦμαι. Pres pass ind 1st sg ἐγκαλέω.

βασιλεῦ 'Αγρίππα. On the position of the vocative, see 10:13.

ἥγημαι. Prf dep ind 1st sg ἡγέομαι. The perfect is used with this verb at only one other place in the NT (Phil 3:7, where it is contrasted with the present form in 3:8). Following Porter's (1989, 92; 1994, 23) analysis of Greek tense, it is likely that the perfect is used either to draw special attention to Paul's statement (as the "frontground" tense) or—as the tense used to focus on a state of affairs or condition—to highlight the fact that the speaker is referring to his own state rather than to what he thinks about something else (the same holds true for Phil 3:8; contra

Fee 316, n. 14, 317, n. 16; O'Brien, 384; Hawthorne, 136).

ἐμαυτὸν. Direct object of ἥγημαι.

μακάριον. The accusative adjective functions as the complement in an object-complement double accusative construction (see 1:3 on ζῶντα).

μέλλων. Pres act ptc masc nom sg μέλλω (causal). On the force of μέλλω plus an infinitive, see 3:3 on μέλλοντας.

ἀπολογεῖσθαι. Pres dep inf ἀπολογέομαι (complementary).

26:3 μάλιστα γνώστην ὄντα σε πάντων τῶν κατὰ 'Ιουδαίους ἐθῶν τε καὶ ζητημάτων, διὸ δέομαι μακροθύμως ἀκοῦσαί μου.

μάλιστα. The adverb most likely modifies the participial clause as a whole rather than just γνώστην (cf. Bruce, 497).

γνώστην ὄντα σε. Although Robertson (1934, 490; cf. Porter 1994, 91) views γνώστην ὄντα σε as "the most certain example in the N.T." of the accusative absolute, it is better to argue that σε is really the accusative subject of ἀκοῦσαί that has been moved to the front of the sentence, along with all of its modifiers, to place it in focus (see 2:15 on ὑμεῖς; contra Barrett, 1150). The participle then functions as an attributive modifier of σε and the conjunction διὸ links Paul's request for a patient hearing with v. 2 rather than with the participial clause.

γνώστην. Predicate accusative (see 1:22 on μάρτυρα).

ὄντα. Pres act ptc masc acc sg εἰμί (attributive; not causal, contra Rogers and Rogers, 302).

τῶν . . . ἐθῶν τε καὶ ζητημάτων. Genitive of reference.

διὸ. See above.

δέομαι. Pres dep ind 1st sg δέομαι.

ἀκοῦσαί. Aor act inf ἀκούω (indirect discourse). The second accent comes from the enclitic μου (see 1:4 on ἠκούσατέ).

μου. Genitive object of ἀκοῦσαί.

26:4 Τὴν μὲν οὖν βίωσίν μου [τὴν] ἐκ νεότητος τὴν ἀπ' ἀρχῆς γενομένην ἐν τῷ ἔθνει μου ἔν τε 'Ιεροσολύμοις ἴσασι πάντες [οἱ] 'Ιουδαῖοι

μὲν οὖν. See 1:6.

βίωσίν. Lit. "way of life." The accusative direct object of ἴσασι has been fronted (see 3:13 on ὑμεῖς) to place it in focus (see 2:15 on ὑμεῖς). The second accent comes from the enclitic μου (see 1:4 on ἠκούσατέ).

[τὴν]. The article (omitted by B C* H 36 *pc*) functions as an adjectivizer (see 2:5 on τῶν ὑπὸ τὸν οὐρανόν), changing the prepositional phrase into an attributive modifier of βίωσίν.

γενομένην. Aor mid dep ptc fem acc sg γίνομαι (attributive modifier of βίωσίν in apposition to [τὴν] ἐκ νεότητος).

τε. This conjunction appears to be used to highlight the significance of Ἱεροσολύμοις over against ἐν τῷ ἔθνει μου (cf. Levinsohn 1992, 56).

ἴσασι. Prf act ind 3rd pl οἶδα. This is the only place in the NT (excluding textual variants) where the older literary form is used instead of οἴδασιν (cf. Luke 11:44; 23:34; Barrett, 1151).

26:5 προγινώσκοντές με ἄνωθεν, ἐὰν θέλωσι μαρτυρεῖν, ὅτι κατὰ τὴν ἀκριβεστάτην αἵρεσιν τῆς ἡμετέρας θρησκείας ἔζησα Φαρισαῖος.

προγινώσκοντές. Pres act ptc masc nom pl προγινώσκω (attendant circumstance). The second accent comes from the enclitic με (see 1:4 on ἠκούσατέ).

ἄνωθεν Here, this adverb indicates "for a relatively long period in the past" (LN 67.90).

ἐὰν. Introduces a third class condition.

θέλωσι. Pres act subj 3rd pl θέλω.

μαρτυρεῖν. Pres act inf μαρτυρέω (complementary).

ὅτι. Introduces a clausal complement of προγινώσκοντές that stands in apposition to με.

ἀκριβεστάτην. One of only a few examples in the NT of –τατος being used to form the superlative (cf. Jude 20; Rev 18:12; 21:11).

ἔζησα. Aor act ind 1st sg ζάω.

Φαρισαῖος. The nominative stands in apposition to the unexpressed subject of the verb ("I").

26:6 καὶ νῦν ἐπ' ἐλπίδι τῆς εἰς τοὺς πατέρας ἡμῶν ἐπαγγελίας γενομένης ὑπὸ τοῦ θεοῦ ἕστηκα κρινόμενος,

καὶ νῦν. See 4:29 on καὶ τὰ νῦν.

ἐπ'. Causal.

ἐπαγγελίας. Objective genitive, or perhaps source ("hope stemming from the promise").

γενομένης ὑπὸ. Occasionally, the participial form of γίνομαι is used with ὑπό in a passive-like construction, where ὑπό introduces the agent of the implied action (see also 12:5; Luke 13:17; Eph 5:12). This construction may serve to highlight the one responsible for the noun (here ἐπαγγελίας) that the participial phrase modifies. Here, Paul wants to emphasize that the promise that has gotten him into trouble was made by God.

γενομένης. Aor mid dep ptc fem gen sg γίνομαι (attributive).

ἕστηκα. Prf act ind 1st sg ἵστημι. On the use of the perfect, see 1:11 on ἑστήκατε.

κρινόμενος. Pres pass ptc masc nom sg κρίνω. The participle probably indicates an attendant circumstance ("I stand and am tried") rather than purpose ("I stand here in order to be judged").

26:7 εἰς ἣν τὸ δωδεκάφυλον ἡμῶν ἐν ἐκτενείᾳ νύκτα καὶ ἡμέραν λατρεῦον ἐλπίζει καταντῆσαι, περὶ ἧς ἐλπίδος ἐγκαλοῦμαι ὑπὸ Ἰουδαίων, βασιλεῦ.

εἰς . . . καταντῆσαι. Lit. "to which our twelve tribes hope to attain."

εἰς ἣν. The antecedent is ἐπαγγελίας (v. 6).

δωδεκάφυλον. Only here in the NT.

ἐν. In terms of syntax, the preposition introduces the instrument used for service, but in terms of semantics, the prepositional phrase indicates the manner in which the twelve tribes served God.

ἐκτενείᾳ. "A state of eagerness involving perseverance over a period of time" (LN 25.70; only here in the NT).

νύκτα καὶ ἡμέραν. Accusative indicating extent of time (see 7:20 on μῆνας); hyperbole (cf. 1:18 on πάντα).

λατρεῦον. Pres act ptc neut nom sg λατρεύω. Given its use with the verb καταντάω, the participle most likely introduces the means of reaching the goal rather than simply an attendant circumstance (contra Rogers and Rogers, 303).

ἐλπίζει. Pres act ind 3rd sg ἐλπίζω. The singular verb agrees with the singular form δωδεκάφυλον.

καταντῆσαι. Aor act inf καταντάω (complementary). The verb is used here of attaining an objective.

περὶ ἧς ἐλπίδος. The internally headed relative clause (see 1:2 on ἄχρι ἧς ἡμέρας) probably intensifies the expression: "concerning this *very* hope."

ἐγκαλοῦμαι ὑπὸ Ἰουδαίων. Lit. "I am being accused by the Jews."
ἐγκαλοῦμαι. Pres pass ind 1st sg ἐγκαλέω.
βασιλεῦ. On the position of the vocative, see 10:13.

26:8 τί ἄπιστον κρίνεται παρ᾽ ὑμῖν εἰ ὁ θεὸς νεκροὺς ἐγείρει;

τί ἄπιστον κρίνεται παρ᾽ ὑμῖν. Lit. "Why should it be judged unbelievable in your (pl.) view?"

ἄπιστον. The adjective should probably be viewed as neuter nominative rather than accusative. Used with the passive verb, the nominative adjective functions as a complement in a subject-complement double nominative construction (cf. 4:36 on υἱός and 1:12 on Ἐλαιῶνος).

κρίνεται. Pres pass ind 3rd sg κρίνω.

εἰ. Here, εἰ introduces an indirect question (cf. Moule, 151) that functions as the clausal subject of κρίνεται.

ἐγείρει. Pres act ind 3rd sg ἐγείρω.

26:9 ἐγὼ μὲν οὖν ἔδοξα ἐμαυτῷ πρὸς τὸ ὄνομα Ἰησοῦ τοῦ Ναζωραίου δεῖν πολλὰ ἐναντία πρᾶξαι,

ἐγὼ . . . ἔδοξα ἐμαυτῷ. The use of the explicit subject pronoun along with the reflexive pronoun (lit. "I thought in myself") places the focus strongly on the speaker.

μὲν οὖν. See 1:6.

ἔδοξα. Aor act ind 1st sg δοκέω.

δεῖν. Pres act inf δεῖ (indirect discourse with a verb of cognition).

πρᾶξαι. Aor act inf πράσσω (complementary).

26:10 ὃ καὶ ἐποίησα ἐν Ἱεροσολύμοις, καὶ πολλούς τε τῶν ἁγίων ἐγὼ ἐν φυλακαῖς κατέκλεισα τὴν παρὰ τῶν ἀρχιερέων ἐξουσίαν λαβὼν ἀναιρουμένων τε αὐτῶν κατήνεγκα ψῆφον.

ἐποίησα. Aor act ind 1st sg ποιέω.

καὶ πολλούς. The conjunction is epexegetical.

τε . . . τε. The significance of this "both . . . and" construction is missed by both Barrett (1155) and many scribes (it is omitted by B Ψ *Byz*) due to the distance between the two conjunctions.

τῶν ἁγίων. Partitive genitive.

κατέκλεισα. Aor act ind 1st sg κατακλείω.

λαβών. Aor act ptc masc nom sg λαμβάνω (temporal).

ἀναιρουμένων. Pres pass ptc masc gen pl ἀναιρέω. Genitive absolute (see 1:8 on ἐπελθόντος), temporal.

αὐτῶν. Genitive subject (see 1:8 on ἐπελθόντος).

κατήνεγκα ψῆφον. Lit. "I brought my stone against (them)."

κατήνεγκα. Aor act ind 1st sg καταφέρω.

26:11 καὶ κατὰ πάσας τὰς συναγωγὰς πολλάκις τιμωρῶν αὐτοὺς ἠνάγκαζον βλασφημεῖν περισσῶς τε ἐμμαινόμενος αὐτοῖς ἐδίωκον ἕως καὶ εἰς τὰς ἔξω πόλεις.

κατὰ πάσας. The combination of the distributive preposition and the adjective πᾶς may be emphatic: "every single synagogue" (cf. 17:17).

τιμωρῶν. Pres act ptc masc nom sg τιμωρέω (attendant circumstance, or perhaps means: "by punishing").

ἠνάγκαζον. Impf act ind 1st sg ἀναγκάζω.

βλασφημεῖν. Pres act inf βλασφημέω (complementary).

περισσῶς. Given the position of the clitic τε, the adverb must modify ἐμμαινόμενος.

ἐμμαινόμενος. Pres dep ptc masc nom sg ἐμμαίνομαι (causal).

ἐδίωκον. Impf act ind 1st sg διώκω.

ἕως καὶ εἰς. Lit. "as far as even into."

τὰς ἔξω πόλεις. In this expression, ἔξω (lit. "outside") probably indicates "non-Jewish" (see BAGD, 279).

26:12 Ἐν οἷς πορευόμενος εἰς τὴν Δαμασκὸν μετ' ἐξουσίας καὶ ἐπιτροπῆς τῆς τῶν ἀρχιερέων

Ἐν οἷς. The preposition ἐν with a dative plural relative pronoun forms a temporal idiomatic expression meaning "while" or "meanwhile" (cf. Luke 12:1; Culy 1989, 39–40, 160). The singular relative pronoun may also be used (Mark 2:19//Luke 5:34; Luke 19:13; John 5:7; 1 Pet 2:12; 3:16; and perhaps Rom 8:3).

πορευόμενος. Pres dep ptc masc nom sg πορεύομαι (temporal).

τῆς τῶν ἀρχιερέων. In this construction, where the first article, which is seemingly superfluous, serves as an adjectivizer (see 2:5 on τῶν ὑπὸ τὸν οὐρανόν), changing the genitive noun phrase into an attributive modifier of the preceding noun phrase, the genitive noun phrase is emphasized in some way. The adjectivizer (first article) may direct the reader to read the genitive noun phrase as indicating source rather than possession (cf. 11:23 on [τὴν] τοῦ ψεου).

26:13 ἡμέρας μέσης κατὰ τὴν ὁδὸν εἶδον, βασιλεῦ, οὐρανόθεν ὑπὲρ τὴν λαμπρότητα τοῦ ἡλίου περιλάμψαν με φῶς καὶ τοὺς σὺν ἐμοὶ πορευομένους.

ἡμέρας μέσης. Genitive of time.

εἶδον. Aor act ind 1st sg ὁράω.

βασιλεῦ. On the position of the vocative, see 10:13.

ὑπὲρ τὴν λαμπρότητα τοῦ ἡλίου. Lit. "beyond the brightness of the sun."

περιλάμψαν. Aor act ptc neut acc sg περιλάμπω. The participle functions as the complement in an object-complement double accusative construction (see 1:3 on ζῶντα) in which the neuter accusative φῶς is the direct object.

με . . . καὶ τοὺς σὺν ἐμοὶ πορευομένους. Accusative complement of περιλάμψαν.

πορευομένους. Pres dep ptc masc acc pl πορεύομαι (substantival).

26:14 πάντων τε καταπεσόντων ἡμῶν εἰς τὴν γῆν ἤκουσα φωνὴν λέγουσαν πρός με τῇ Ἑβραΐδι διαλέκτῳ, Σαοὺλ Σαούλ, τί με διώκεις; σκληρόν σοι πρὸς κέντρα λακτίζειν.

καταπεσόντων. Aor act ptc masc gen pl καταπίπτω. Genitive absolute (see 1:8 on ἐπελθόντος), temporal.

πάντων . . . ἡμῶν. Genitive subject (see 1:8 on ἐπελθόντος).

ἤκουσα. Aor act ind 1st sg ἀκούω.

φωνὴν. On the significance of the shift from accusative (also at 9:4) to genitive at 22:7, see 9:7 on φωνῆς and Wallace 1996, 133–34.

λέγουσαν. Pres ptc act fem acc sg λέγω. Although the participle could be viewed as attributive, since verbs of perception commonly take double accusatives it is better to take it as the complement in an object-complement double accusative construction (see 1:3 on ζῶντα).

τῇ Ἑβραΐδι διαλέκτῳ. Dative of means. On the diaeresis over the *iota*, see 2:31 on προϊδὼν.

Σαοὺλ Σαούλ. See 9:4.

διώκεις. Pres act ind 2nd sg διώκω.

σκληρόν. Predicate adjective with an implicit verb. Porter (1994,

85), however, argues that a nominative by itself can be used to form a "nominal clause" (cf. 8:32 on ἄφωνος).

σοι. Dative of disadvantage.

πρὸς κέντρα λακτίζειν. Louw and Nida define κέντρα as "a pointed stick used in driving draft animals" (6.9). The idiom, πρὸς κέντρα λακτίζειν (lit. "to kick against the goad"), means "to hurt oneself by active resistance" (6.9) or "to react against authority in such a way as to cause harm or suffering to oneself" (39.19).

λακτίζειν. Pres act inf λακτίζω (subject of the implicit verb).

26:15 ἐγὼ δὲ εἶπα, Τίς εἶ, κύριε; ὁ δὲ κύριος εἶπεν, Ἐγώ εἰμι Ἰησοῦς ὃν σὺ διώκεις.

εἶπα. Aor act ind 1st sg λέγω.

εἶ. Pres act ind 2nd sg εἰμί.

κύριε. On the position of the vocative, see 10:13 on Πέτρε.

εἶπεν. Aor act ind 3rd sg λέγω.

εἰμι. Pres act ind 1st sg εἰμί.

Ἰησοῦς. Predicate nominative.

διώκεις. Pres act ind 2nd sg διώκω.

26:16 ἀλλὰ ἀνάστηθι καὶ στῆθι ἐπὶ τοὺς πόδας σου· εἰς τοῦτο γὰρ ὤφθην σοι, προχειρίσασθαί σε ὑπηρέτην καὶ μάρτυρα ὧν τε εἶδές [με] ὧν τε ὀφθήσομαί σοι,

ἀλλὰ. The contrast (contraexpectation) suggested by the conjunction is left implicit: "In contrast to what you expect, now that you know who I am, I want you to stand and receive a commission from me." See also 10:20.

ἀνάστηθι. Aor act impv 2nd sg ἀνίστημι.

στῆθι. Aor act impv 2nd sg ἵστημι.

ὤφθην. Aor pass ind 1st sg ὁράω. In the passive voice, this verb means "to appear" (see Wallace 1996, 165, n. 72).

προχειρίσασθαι. Aor mid dep inf προχειρίζομαι (epexegetical to εἰς τοῦτο).

ὑπηρέτην καὶ μάρτυρα. The compound noun phrase functions as the complement in an object-complement double accusative construction (see 1:3 on ζῶντα) with προχειρίζομαι ("to choose someone in advance to be *something*").

ὧν . . . ὧν. The relative pronouns introduce headless relative clauses (see 3:6 on ὅ). The genitive case may stem from attraction (see 1:1 on ὧν) to an unexpressed antecedent (τουτῶν—objective genitive; for how this can take place see 22:15) or may denote reference.

εἶδές. Aor act ind 2nd sg ὁράω. The second accent comes from the enclitic με (see 1:4 on ἠκούσατέ).

[με]. The reading with the pronoun enjoys superior external support (𝔓[74] ℵ A C[2] E Ψ 096 *Byz pc*) and appears to be the harder reading (Omanson), while the reading without the pronoun is only supported by B C[*vid] 614 945 1175 *pc*. It is likely that some scribes omitted the pronoun because of the dissonance caused by its accusative case (presumably accusative of reference).

ὧν τε ὀφθήσομαί σοι. The syntax here is complex. The case of the relative pronoun has apparently been determined by attraction (see above). The problem, however, is determining what grammatical role the relative pronoun plays in the relative clause. Strictly speaking, it cannot be the direct object of the verb since the verb is passive. It is probably best to say that prior to attraction the relative pronoun was an accusative of reference: "you will be a witness of the things concerning which I will appear to you" (cf. Page, 248; Barrett, 1160), though it may also be possible to argue that the passive form is deponent (transitive) here and means something like "to reveal, show" (see Robertson 1934, 819).

ὀφθήσομαί. Fut pass ind 1st sg ὁράω (see also above). The second accent comes from the enclitic σοι (see 1:4 on ἠκούσατέ).

26:17 ἐξαιρούμενός σε ἐκ τοῦ λαοῦ καὶ ἐκ τῶν ἐθνῶν εἰς οὓς ἐγὼ ἀποστέλλω σε

ἐξαιρούμενός. Pres mid ptc masc nom sg ἐξαιρέω (means of ὀφθήσομαί). The second accent comes from the enclitic se (see 1:4 on ἠκούσατέ).

ἀποστέλλω Pres act ind 1st sg ἀποστέλλω.

26:18 ἀνοῖξαι ὀφθαλμοὺς αὐτῶν, τοῦ ἐπιστρέψαι ἀπὸ σκότους εἰς φῶς καὶ τῆς ἐξουσίας τοῦ Σατανᾶ ἐπὶ τὸν θεόν, τοῦ λαβεῖν αὐτοὺς ἄφεσιν ἁμαρτιῶν καὶ κλῆρον ἐν τοῖς ἡγιασμένοις πίστει τῇ εἰς ἐμέ.

ἀνοῖξαι. Aor act inf ἀνοίγω (purpose). The unexpressed subject is almost certainly Paul rather than God (a passive infinitive would have probably been used).

ἐπιστρέψαι. Aor act inf ἐπιστρέφω. The articular infinitive could express a purpose of ἀνοῖξαι (most likely given the shift to an articular construction) or an additional purpose of ἀποστέλλω. The unexpressed subject of this infinitive is probably those to whom Paul is being sent (with the infinitive being intransitive), though the infinitive could be transitive with either Paul ("in order that you might open their eyes and turn [them] from darkness") or God (unlikely) serving as the unexpressed subject.

λαβεῖν. Aor act inf λαμβάνω (purpose of ἀνοῖξαι). For more on the role of the three infinitives in this verse, see Barrett, 1161–62.

αὐτοὺς. Accusative subject of the infinitive (see 1:3 on αὐτὸν).

τοῖς ἡγιασμένοις. Prf pass ptc masc dat pl ἁγιάζω (substantival).

πίστει. Means.

τῇ εἰς ἐμέ. The article functions as an adjectivizer (see 2:5 on τῶν ὑπὸ τὸν οὐρανόν), changing the prepositional phrase into an attributive modifier of πίστει.

26:19 Ὅθεν, βασιλεῦ Ἀγρίππα, οὐκ ἐγενόμην ἀπειθὴς τῇ οὐρανίῳ ὀπτασίᾳ

βασιλεῦ Ἀγρίππα. Vocative.

οὐκ ἐγενόμην ἀπειθὴς. Litotes (lit. "I was not disobedient"; see 1:5 on οὐ μετὰ πολλὰς ταύτας ἡμέρας).

ἐγενόμην. Aor mid dep ind 1st sg γίνομαι.

ἀπειθὴς. Predicate adjective.

26:20 ἀλλὰ τοῖς ἐν Δαμασκῷ πρῶτόν τε καὶ Ἱεροσολύμοις, πᾶσάν τε τὴν χώραν τῆς Ἰουδαίας καὶ τοῖς ἔθνεσιν ἀπήγγελλον μετανοεῖν καὶ ἐπιστρέφειν ἐπὶ τὸν θεόν, ἄξια τῆς μετανοίας ἔργα πράσσοντας.

τοῖς ἐν Δαμασκῷ . . . τε καὶ Ἱεροσολύμοις. The article functions as a nominalizer (see 1:3 on τὰ), changing the prepositional phrase into a substantive.

πᾶσάν τε τὴν χώραν τῆς Ἰουδαίας καὶ τοῖς ἔθνεσιν. The syntax of the UBS⁴/NA²⁷ text (supported by 𝔓⁷⁴ א A B vg^mss) may not be as intolerable as most scholars contend (see, e.g., Bruce, 502–3; Barrett, 1163). Luke may have simply used two types of constructions to modify ἀπαγγέλλω. The datives clearly indicate the recipients (indirect objects) of the message (those in Damascus and Jerusalem, and the Gentiles), while the case of πᾶσάν τε τὴν χώραν τῆς Ἰουδαίας may be explained in a variety of ways (cf. πολλάς κώμας in 8:25). The accusative case may indicate location (see 1:19 on Ἰερουσαλήμ), extent of space (BDF §161; "as far as all the region of Judea"), or reflect a syntactic process in which the indirect object has "advanced" to the direct object position—a phenomenon that is not unusual with verbs of speech (see 13:32 ὑμᾶς). In the latter case, τὴν χώραν τῆς Ἰουδαίας would serve as a metonym (see 1:9 on τῶν ὀφθαλμῶν αὐτῶν) for "the people who live in the region of Judea." The advancement view, however, is weakened by the fact that there are no examples of advancement with this verb in the NT (though we are dealing with a limited corpus of data). The scribal addition of εἰς before the accusative noun phrase (E Ψ*Byz* lat; cf. Luke 8:34) to smooth out the text probably suggests that many scribes understood the expression as locative. Had they viewed τὴν χώραν τῆς Ἰουδαίας as the addressee they probably would have changed its case to dative or (less likely) added πρός (cf. 16:36) rather than εἰς.

πᾶσάν. Hyperbole (cf. 1:18 on πάντα). The second accent comes from the enclitic τε (see 1:4 on ἠκούσατέ).

ἀπήγγελλον. Impf act ind 1st sg ἀπαγγέλλω.

μετανοεῖν. Pres act inf μετανοέω (indirect discourse/command).

ἐπιστρέφειν. Pres act inf ἐπιστρέφω (indirect discourse/command).

ἄξια. Attributive.

πράσσοντας. Pres act ptc acc masc pl πράσσω (attendant circumstance of the conjoined infinitives). The accusative case is necessary since the subject of the participle is the unexpressed subject of the infinitive.

26:21 ἕνεκα τούτων με Ἰουδαῖοι συλλαβόμενοι [ὄντα] ἐν τῷ ἱερῷ ἐπειρῶντο διαχειρίσασθαι.

συλλαβόμενοι. Aor mid ptc masc nom pl συλλαμβάνω (temporal).

[ὄντα]. Pres act ptc masc acc sg εἰμί. The accusative participle ($\mathfrak{P}^{74}$ א E Ψ 33 36 81 614 945 1175 1739 1891 2495 *al* latt; omitted by A B 048 *Byz*) must be attributive rather than adverbial (contra, e.g., Rogers and Rogers, 304) since its subject is different than the subject of the main verb.

ἐπειρῶντο. Impf dep ind 3rd pl πειράομαι.

διαχειρίσασθαι. Aor mid inf διαχειρίζω (complementary).

26:22 ἐπικουρίας οὖν τυχὼν τῆς ἀπὸ τοῦ θεοῦ ἄχρι τῆς ἡμέρας ταύτης ἕστηκα μαρτυρόμενος μικρῷ τε καὶ μεγάλῳ οὐδὲν ἐκτὸς λέγων ὧν τε οἱ προφῆται ἐλάλησαν μελλόντων γίνεσθαι καὶ Μωϋσῆς,

τυχὼν. Aor act ptc masc nom sg τυγχάνω (causal).

τῆς ἀπὸ τοῦ θεοῦ. The seemingly superflous article functions as an adjectivizer (see 2:5 on τῶν ὑπὸ τὸν οὐρανόν), changing the prepositional phrase ("from God") into an attributive modifier of ἐπικουρίας ("which comes from God") and perhaps adding force to the expression: "since I have received *the kind of help that only God can give*."

ἕστηκα. Prf act ind 1st sg ἵστημι. On the use of the perfect, see 1:11 on ἑστήκατε.

μαρτυρόμενος. Pres dep ptc masc nom sg μαρτύρομαι (attendant circumstance or manner). There is no reason to take ἕστηκα μαρτυρόμενος as a periphrastic construction (contra Dietrich, 209–10; cf. 1:11 on [εμ]βλέποντες).

μικρῷ τε καὶ μεγάλῳ. Lit. "to both small and great." An example of merismus—a literary device in which the entirety of a group is referred to by mentioning the two extremes.

λέγων. Pres act ptc masc nom sg λέγω (attendant circumstance or means).

ὧν. The relative pronoun introduces a headless relative clause (see 3:6 on ὅ). The genitive case probably denotes reference (as a syntactic complement of ἐλάλησαν), though theoretically the case could have been attracted to the unexpressed antecedent (τουτῶν; for how this can take place see 22:15), which would have been genitive following ἐκτός.

ἐλάλησαν. Aor act ind 3rd pl λαλέω.

μελλόντων. Pres act ptc neut gen pl μέλλω (attributive modifying the relative pronoun: "the prophets spoke about the things which were about the happen"). On the force of μέλλω plus an infinitive, see 3:3 on μέλλοντας.

γίνεσθαι. Pres dep inf γίνομαι (complementary).

26:23 εἰ παθητὸς ὁ Χριστός, εἰ πρῶτος ἐξ ἀναστάσεως νεκρῶν φῶς μέλλει καταγγέλλειν τῷ τε λαῷ καὶ τοῖς ἔθνεσιν.

εἰ . . . εἰ. BAGD (219) treats εἰ as a complementizer equivalent to ὅτι here, noting that such a usage is attested elsewhere after verbs of emotion (see, e.g., Sirach 23:14), but failing to explain the lack of such a verb in the present context. Lake and Cadbury (321) take the same approach, arguing that εἰ may carry the implication that the proposition that follows is apt to be denied by some. Such an approach at least attempts to account for the use of εἰ rather than ὅτι. The fact that we are dealing with two appositional clauses, each of which is introduced by εἰ, however, makes it highly unlikely that the two particles function as complementizers. More likely, εἰ in both cases introduces either a conditional clause or a direct question (cf. 19:2). Though the end result would be roughly the same, the evidence favors the latter view. Given the fact that conditional clauses are distinguished, in part, by verb tense it would be highly unusual to omit the verb unless the protasis had the same verb as the apodosis. On the other hand, the omission of the verb in short questions is an effective rhetorical device used to make the question "sharper or more urgent" (McKay 1994, 91). The two questions lead to the inference that follows much like the protasis of a conditional construction leads to the apodosis: "If the Christ was destined to suffer, [and] if he was the first the rise from the dead, [then,] he would be eager to proclaim light to both the (Jewish) people and the Gentiles!"

παθητὸς. Predicate adjective ("subject to suffering," LN 24.85).

πρῶτος ἐξ ἀναστάσεως νεκρῶν. This expression (lit. "the first from the resurrection of the dead"), which is appropriately rendered "the first to rise from the dead" (Fitzmyer 1998, 761; contra Barrett, 1166), highlights the fact that Christ's resurrection was simply a foretaste of the resurrection in which Christians place their hope (cf. Dunn, 15–16; see also 23:6; 1 Cor 15:20).

πρῶτος. Predicate adjective.

νεκρῶν. Objective genitive.

μέλλει. Pres act ind 3rd sg μέλλω.

καταγγέλλειν. Pres act inf καταγγέλλω (complementary). On the force of μέλλω plus an infinitive, see 3:3 on μέλλοντας. Here, the use of μέλλω with an infinitive appears to highlight the close necessary temporal link between Jesus' death and resurrection, and the proclamation of the Good News.

Acts 26:24–32

[24]As Paul was saying these things in his defense, Festus in a loud voice said, "You're crazy, Paul! Your great learning is driving you insane!" [25]Paul replied, "I am not crazy, most excellent Festus. What I am saying is true and sensible. [26]The king, to whom I also speak frankly, knows about these matters. For I am not convinced, by any means, that he is ignorant of any of these things. For this matter was not carried out in a corner! [27]King Agrippa, do you believe the prophets? I know that you do." [28]Then Agrippa (said) to Paul, "Are you trying to persuade me to become a Christian so easily?" [29]Paul replied, "(If it were up to me,) I would pray to God that whether 'so easily' or with difficulty not only you, but also all those who hear me today would become just as I indeed am—except for these chains!"

[30]Then the king, along with the governor, Bernice, and those sitting with them, stood up, [31]and as they were leaving they spoke to one another, saying, "This man has done *nothing* worthy of death or imprisonment!" [32]Agrippa said to Festus, "This man would have been able to be released if he had not appealed to Caesar."

26:24 Ταῦτα δὲ αὐτοῦ ἀπολογουμένου ὁ Φῆστος μεγάλῃ τῇ φωνῇ φησιν, Μαίνῃ, Παῦλε· τὰ πολλά σε γράμματα εἰς μανίαν περιτρέπει.

Ταῦτα. Accusative direct object of ἀπολογουμένου.

αὐτοῦ. Genitive subject (see 1:8 on ἐπελθόντος).

ἀπολογουμένου. Pres dep ptc masc gen sg ἀπολογέομαι. Genitive absolute (see 1:8 on ἐπελθόντος), temporal.

φησίν. Pres act ind 3rd sg φημί.

Μαίνῃ. Pres dep ind 2nd sg μαίνομαι.

Παῦλε. On the position of the vocative, see 10:13 on Πέτρε.

τὰ πολλά . . . γράμματα. Neuter nominative subject of περιτρέπει.

σε. Accusative direct object of περιτρέπει. The unusual position of the pronoun probably adds rhetorical force to the statement.

περιτρέπει. Pres act ind 3rd sg περιτρέπω.

26:25 ὁ δὲ Παῦλος, Οὐ μαίνομαι, φησίν, κράτιστε Φῆστε, ἀλλὰ ἀληθείας καὶ σωφροσύνης ῥήματα ἀποφθέγγομαι.

μαίνομαι. Pres dep ind 1st sg μαίνομαι.

φησίν. Pres act ind 3rd sg φημί.

κράτιστε. See 23:26.

Φῆστε. On the position of the vocative, see 10:13 on Πέτρε.

ἀληθείας . . . ἀποφθέγγομαι. Lit. "I speak words of truth and sound judgment."

ἀληθείας καὶ σωφροσύνης. Attributive genitives (contra Barrett, 1168, who, following Page [250], takes the first as objective and the second as subjective).

ἀποφθέγγομαι. Pres dep 1st sg ἀποφθέγγομαι.

26:26 ἐπίσταται γὰρ περὶ τούτων ὁ βασιλεὺς πρὸς ὃν καὶ παρρησιαζόμενος λαλῶ, λανθάνειν γὰρ αὐτὸν [τι] τούτων οὐ πείθομαι οὐθέν· οὐ γάρ ἐστιν ἐν γωνίᾳ πεπραγμένον τοῦτο.

ἐπίσταται. Pres dep ind 3rd sg ἐπίσταμαι.

παρρησιαζόμενος. Pres dep ptc masc nom sg παρρησιάζομαι (manner).

λαλῶ. Pres act ind 1st sg λαλέω.

λανθάνειν. Pres act inf λανθάνω (indirect discourse with a verb of cognition).

αὐτὸν. Accusative subject of the infinitive (see 1:3 on αὐτὸν; contra Barrett, 1169, who calls it the direct object of a transitive λανθάνειν; cf. BDF §149).

[τι]. The neuter accusative indefinite adjective should probably be accepted as the harder reading (supported by 𝔓[74] א A E *Byz* syr[p]). It is omitted by B 36 614 1175 2495 *pc* syr[h], while it is changed to ἐγώ by 945 1739 1891 *pc* (cf. v. 31). The presence of the substantival adjective makes the function of the accusative οὐθέν difficult to determine, since they cannot both be direct objects, probably leading a number of scribes to omit τι. It is probably best to treat οὐδέν as an adverbial adjective. Such adjectives are typically neuter accusative singular (Wallace 1996, 293; cf. v. 31).

οὐ πείθομαι. Litotes (Barrett, 1169; see 1:5 on οὐ μετὰ πολλὰς ταύτας ἡμέρας).

πείθομαι. Pres pass ind 1st sg πείθω.

οὐθέν. On the form, see 15:9. On the syntax, see above.

ἐστιν. Pres act ind 3rd sg εἰμί.

πεπραγμένον. Prf pass ptc neut nom sg πράσσω (perfect periphrastic; see 2:13 on μεμεστωμένοι).

τοῦτο. Nominative substantival subject of the passive participle.

26:27 πιστεύεις, βασιλεῦ ᾿Αγρίππα, τοῖς προφήταις; οἶδα ὅτι πιστεύεις.

πιστεύεις. Pres act ind 2nd sg πιστεύω.

βασιλεῦ ᾿Αγρίππα. On the position of the vocative, see 10:13 on Πέτρε.

οἶδα. Prf act ind 1st sg οἶδα.

ὅτι. Introduces a clausal complement of οἶδα.

26:28 ὁ δὲ ᾿Αγρίππας πρὸς τὸν Παῦλον, ᾿Εν ὀλίγῳ με πείθεις Χριστιανὸν ποιῆσαι.

᾿Εν ὀλίγῳ με πείθεις Χριστιανὸν ποιῆσαι. This clause could be taken as either a (sarcastic) statement or as a rhetorical question. While the textual support for this reading (𝔓[74] ℵ A B 048 33 81 1175 *pc* syr[hmg]) makes its originality highly likely, the textual history of the clause makes it clear that later scribes found the syntax perplexing. The most important variation is the change from ποιῆσαι to γενέσθαι (E Ψ *Byz* latt syr CyrilJ).

᾿Εν ὀλίγῳ. This expression may either indicate "in a short time" (LN 67.106) or something like "with little effort, easily" (22:41). Barrett (1170) argues that the temporal interpretation is not likely given the collocation of this expression with ἐν μεγάλῳ in the following verse, since the latter would "hardly be used of time."

με. Accusative subject (see 1:3 on αὐτὸν) of the infinitive or direct object of πείθεις (see below).

πείθεις. Pres act ind 2nd sg πείθω.

Χριστιανὸν. If the infinitive is taken as indicating purpose (see below), with ποιέω being used in a causative sense (see 3:12; 5:34; 24:12), then Χριστιανὸν functions as the complement in a double accusative (causative) construction: "in order to make (me) a Christian" (with the direct object me being implicit).

ποιῆσαι. Aor act inf ποιέω. The infinitive probably indicates purpose (so Robertson 1934, 1923–24). Given the fact that many scribes viewed ποιῆσαι and γενέσθαι as roughly interchangeable, and the parallel statement in the following verse where γενέσθαι is used, it is likely that Agrippa's comment/question somehow refers to persuasion resulting in conversion to Christianity. The view of some that Χριστιανὸν ποιῆσαι is an idiom meaning "to play the Christian" or "to act like a Christian" (so NRSV; Bruce, 506; Conzelmann, 212; Haenchen, 689) suffers from the significant weakness that "one over-literal rendering of a Hebrew verb [in LXX 1 Kgs 21:7] is not sufficient to establish a Greek idiom" (Barrett, 1171).

26:29 ὁ δὲ Παῦλος, Εὐξαίμην ἂν τῷ θεῷ καὶ ἐν ὀλίγῳ καὶ ἐν μεγάλῳ οὐ μόνον σὲ ἀλλὰ καὶ πάντας τοὺς ἀκούοντάς μου σήμερον γενέσθαι τοιούτους ὁποῖος καὶ ἐγώ εἰμι παρεκτὸς τῶν δεσμῶν τούτων.

Εὐξαίμην. Aor mid dep opt 1st sg εὔχομαι. The optative is used with ἂν in the apodosis of an incomplete fourth class condition. Presumably, the implicit protasis would be something like, "If I could" or "If it were up to me." According to Turner (1963, 123), this is the only place in the NT where the deliberative (or "potential") optative is not part of a question.

καὶ ἐν ὀλίγῳ καὶ ἐν μεγάλῳ. The fact that this phrase does not appear to occur elsewhere in extant Greek literature suggests that Paul is using a creative play on words (based on Agrippa's comment; v. 28) rather than an established idiom. Taken with the final comment (παρεκτὸς τῶν δεσμῶν τούτων, and perhaps ὁποῖος καὶ ἐγώ εἰμι; see below), this verse suggests that Paul was enjoying the verbal sparring! Bruce (506) notes that the expression could mean "with few words or many," or "with ease or with difficulty." Although such an interpretation would typically require ἤ rather than καί, Barrett (1172) cites 10:14 as an example where καί is used like ἤ. The construction here, however, involves καί . . . καί, rather than simply being two constituents conjoined with καί. Moreover, it is far from certain that καί functions as a substitute for ἤ in 10:14 (see note).

σὲ . . . τοὺς ἀκούοντάς. Accusative subjects of the infinitive (see 1:3 on αὐτὸν).

τοὺς ἀκούοντάς. Pres act ptc acc masc pl ἀκούω (substantival). The second accent comes from the enclitic μου (see 1:4 on ἠκούσατέ).

μου. Genitive object of ἀκούοντάς.

γενέσθαι . . . εἰμι. Lit. "become such of whatever sort I indeed am."

γενέσθαι. Aor mid dep inf γίνομαι (indirect discourse).

τοιούτους. Predicate accusative (see 1:22 on μάρτυρα).

ὁποῖος. Predicate nominative of εἰμί. The parenthetical clause (ὁποῖος καὶ ἐγώ εἰμί) using the correlative pronoun (ὁποῖος is used in this manner only here in the NT; Robertson 1934, 732) may carry a nuance of self-deprecation.

εἰμι. Pres act ind 1st sg εἰμί.

26:30 Ἀνέστη τε ὁ βασιλεὺς καὶ ὁ ἡγεμὼν ἥ τε Βερνίκη καὶ οἱ συγκαθήμενοι αὐτοῖς,

Ἀνέστη. Aor act ind 3rd sg ἀνίστημι. The use of the singular verb with a compound subject probably keeps the focus on Festus (cf. 7:15; 11:14; 16:31, 33).

οἱ συγκαθήμενοι. Pres dep ptc masc nom pl συγκάθημαι (substantival).

αὐτοῖς. Verbs with a συν- prefix take a dative complement.

26:31 καὶ ἀναχωρήσαντες ἐλάλουν πρὸς ἀλλήλους λέγοντες ὅτι Οὐδὲν θανάτου ἢ δεσμῶν ἄξιον [τι] πράσσει ὁ ἄνθρωπος οὗτος.

ἀναχωρήσαντες. Aor act ptc masc nom pl ἀναχωρέω (temporal).

ἐλάλουν. Impf act ind 3rd pl λαλέω.

λέγοντες. Pres act ptc masc nom pl λέγω (attendant circumstance, redundant; see 1:6 on λέγοντες).

ὅτι. Introduces direct discourse.

Οὐδὲν θανάτου ἢ δεσμῶν ἄξιον [τι]. The fronted (see 3:13 on ὑμεῖς) construction is emphatic.

Οὐδὲν. In manuscripts that omit τι (see below) this substantival adjective functions as the direct object of πράσσει. If τι is included, however, Οὐδὲν must function as an adverbial adjective ("in no way"; see v. 26 on [τι]).

ἄξιον. The adjective functions as the complement in an object-complement double accusative construction (see 1:3 on ζῶντα), with the direct object being either τι or Οὐδὲν.

[τι]. The neuter accusative indefinite adjective, supported by 𝔓[74] ℵA Ψ 33 81 104 945 1175 1739 1891 *pc* vg, should probably be accepted as the harder reading (lit. "has in no way done anything worthy . . ."). It is omitted by B *Byz* it syr (cf. v. 26; lit. "has done nothing wrong").

πράσσει. Pres act ind 3rd sg πράσσω.

26:32 'Αγρίππας δὲ τῷ Φήστῳ ἔφη, 'Απολελύσθαι ἐδύνατο ὁ ἄνθρωπος οὗτος εἰ μὴ ἐπεκέκλητο Καίσαρα.

ἔφη. Aor/Impf act ind 3rd sg φημί. On the tense, see 7:2.

'Απολελύσθαι ἐδύνατο ὁ ἄνθρωπος οὗτος. Here, the apodosis precedes the protasis (24:19).

'Απολελύσθαι. Prf pass inf ἀπολύω (complementary).

ἐδύνατο. Impf dep ind 3rd sg δύναμαι.

εἰ. Used with the indicative to introduce an incomplete (lacking ἄν in the apodosis) second class condition.

ἐπεκέκλητο. Plprf mid ind 3rd sg ἐπικαλέω.

Acts 27:1–8

[1]When it was decided that we should set sail for Italy, they handed Paul over, along with some other prisoners, to a centurion of the Augustan Cohort named Julius. [2]We boarded a ship from Adramyttium that was about to sail to places along the coast of Asia and set sail. Aristarchus, a Macedonian from Thessalonica, was with us.

[3]On the next day we landed at Sidon, and Julius acted kindly toward Paul and allowed him to go to his friends and receive care. [4]From there we set sail and sailed under the shelter of Cyprus because the winds were against us. [5]After sailing across the open sea off Cilicia and Pamphilia we arrived at Myra of Lycia. [6]There the centurion found an Alexandrian ship sailing to Italy and put us aboard it.

[7]Over a period of many days, we sailed along slowly and with difficulty we made it as far as Cnidus—since the wind did not allow us to proceed—and then sailed under the shelter of Crete off Salome. [8]Sailing along its coast we came with difficulty to a place called Fair Havens, which is near the town of Lasea.

27:1 'Ως δὲ ἐκρίθη τοῦ ἀποπλεῖν ἡμᾶς εἰς τὴν 'Ιταλίαν, παρεδίδουν τόν τε Παῦλον καί τινας ἑτέρους δεσμώτας ἑκατοντάρχῃ ὀνόματι 'Ιουλίῳ σπείρης Σεβαστῆς.

'Ως. Temporal (see 18:5).

ἐκρίθη. Aor pass ind 3rd sg κρίνω.

ἀποπλεῖν. Pres act inf ἀποπλέω. The infinitival clause (τοῦ ἀποπλεῖν ἡμᾶς εἰς τὴν 'Ιταλίαν) functions as the subject of ἐκρίθη.

ἡμᾶς. Accusative subject of the infinitive (see 1:3 on αὐτὸν). On the use of the plural, see 16:10 on ἐζητήσαμεν.

παρεδίδουν. Impf act ind 3rd pl παραδίδωμι.

ὀνόματι. Dative of reference.

Ἰουλίῳ. Dative in apposition to ἑκατοντάρχῃ.

27:2 ἐπιβάντες δὲ πλοίῳ Ἀδραμυττηνῷ μέλλοντι πλεῖν εἰς τοὺς κατὰ τὴν Ἀσίαν τόπους ἀνήχθημεν ὄντος σὺν ἡμῖν Ἀριστάρχου Μακεδόνος Θεσσαλονικέως.

ἐπιβάντες. Aor act ptc masc nom pl ἐπιβαίνω (attendant circumstance).

μέλλοντι. Pres act ptc neut dat sg μέλλω (attributive). On the force of μέλλω plus an infinitive, see 3:3 on μέλλοντας.

πλεῖν. Pres act inf πλέω (complementary).

ἀνήχθημεν. Aor pass ind 1st pl ἀνάγω. On the meaning, see 13:13.

ὄντος. Pres act ptc masc gen sg εἰμί. Genitive absolute (see 1:8 on ἐπελθόντος), attendant circumstance. On the placement of the genitive absolute, see 5:2 on συνειδυίης.

Ἀριστάρχου. Genitive subject (see 1:8 on ἐπελθόντος).

Μακεδόνος. Genitive in apposition to Ἀριστάρχου.

Θεσσαλονικέως. Genitive of source.

27:3 τῇ τε ἑτέρᾳ κατήχθημεν εἰς Σιδῶνα, φιλανθρώπως τε ὁ Ἰούλιος τῷ Παύλῳ χρησάμενος ἐπέτρεψεν πρὸς τοὺς φίλους πορευθέντι ἐπιμελείας τυχεῖν.

τῇ . . . ἑτέρᾳ. Dative of time.

κατήχθημεν. Aor pass ind 1st pl κατάγω. In a nautical context, the passive form of the verb with εἰς is used to indicate "landing" at a destination (cf. BAGD, 410).

χρησάμενος. Aor mid dep ptc masc nom sg χράομαι (attendant circumstance).

ἐπέτρεψεν. Aor act ind 3rd sg ἐπιτρέπω.

πορευθέντι. Aor pass ptc masc dat sg πορεύομαι. Notwithstanding the requirements of a clear English translation, the participle cannot be adverbial since there is no verb with which it shares a subject (see Culy 2004; contra Rogers and Rogers, 306). Instead, it is either substantival or serves as an attributive modifier of the dative complement of ἐπέτρεψεν, which has been left out by ellipsis due to the nearness of its referent (Παύλῳ).

ἐπιμελείας τυχεῖν. Lit. "to obtain care."

τυχεῖν. Aor act inf τυγχάνω. The infinitive functions as the direct object of ἐπίτρεψεν (cf. 21:39 on λαλῆσαι).

27:4 κἀκεῖθεν ἀναχθέντες ὑπεπλεύσαμεν τὴν Κύπρον διὰ τὸ τοὺς ἀνέμους εἶναι ἐναντίους,

κἀκεῖθεν. A shortened form (crasis) of καί ἐκεῖθεν.

ἀναχθέντες. Aor pass ptc masc nom pl ἀνάγω (attendant circumstance). On the meaning, see 13:13.

ὑπεπλεύσαμεν. Aor act ind 1st pl ὑποπλέω ("to sail or move along beside some object which provides a degree of protection or shelter"; LN 54.10).

τοὺς ἀνέμους. Accusative subject of the infinitive (see 1:3 on αὐτὸν).

εἶναι. Pres act inf εἰμί. Used with διὰ τὸ to indicate cause.

ἐναντίους. Predicate accusative adjective (see 1:22 on μάρτυρα).

27:5 τό τε πέλαγος τὸ κατὰ τὴν Κιλικίαν καὶ Παμφυλίαν διαπλεύσαντες κατήλθομεν εἰς Μύρα τῆς Λυκίας.

τό . . . πέλαγος. Accusative direct object of διαπλεύσαντες.

τὸ κατὰ τὴν Κιλικίαν καὶ Παμφυλίαν. The article functions as an adjectivizer (see 2:5 on τῶν ὑπὸ τὸν οὐρανόν), changing the prepositional phrase into an attributive modifier of πέλαγος.

διαπλεύσαντες. Aor act ptc masc nom pl διαπλέω (temporal).

κατήλθομεν. Aor act ind 1st pl κατέρχομαι.

27:6 κἀκεῖ εὑρὼν ὁ ἑκατοντάρχης πλοῖον Ἀλεξανδρῖνον πλέον εἰς τὴν Ἰταλίαν ἐνεβίβασεν ἡμᾶς εἰς αὐτό.

κἀκεῖ. A shortened form (crasis) of καί ἐκεῖ.

εὑρὼν. Aor act ptc masc nom sg εὑρίσκω (attendant circumstance).

πλέον. Pres act ptc neut acc sg πλέω (attributive).

ἐνεβίβασεν. Aor act ind 3rd sg ἐμβιβάζω. Only here in the NT ("to cause to go aboard, to cause to embark"; LN 15.96).

27:7 ἐν ἱκαναῖς δὲ ἡμέραις βραδυπλοοῦντες καὶ μόλις γενόμενοι κατὰ τὴν Κνίδον, μὴ προσεῶντος ἡμᾶς τοῦ ἀνέμου ὑπεπλεύσαμεν τὴν Κρήτην κατὰ Σαλμώνην,

ἐν. Temporal. While Barrett (1186) cites this as an unusual case in which the preposition ἐν is used to denote extent of time (cf. 7:20 on μῆνας), the "extent" of the temporal reference comes from the expression ἱκαναῖς ἡμέραις. In vv. 7–8, "the first three participles describe the journey as far as Cnidos, ὑπεπλεύσαμεν takes the ship as far as the south coast of Crete, the next participle and the finite verb to Fair Havens" (Barrett, 1185–86).

βραδυπλοοῦντες. Pres act ptc masc nom pl βραδυπλοέω (attendant circumstance of ὑπεπλεύσαμεν). Only here in the NT ("to sail slowly").

γενόμενοι. Aor mid dep ptc masc nom pl γίνομαι (attendant circumstance of ὑπεπλεύσαμεν).

προσεῶντος. Pres act ptc masc gen sg προσεάω. Only here in the NT ("to allow to go farther"; LN 13.139). Genitive absolute (see 1:8 on ἐπελθόντος), causal. On the placement of the genitive absolute, see 5:2 on συνειδυίης.

τοῦ ἀνέμου. Genitive subject (see 1:8 on ἐπελθόντος).

ὑπεπλεύσαμεν. Aor act ind 1st pl ὑποπλέω.

27:8 μόλις τε παραλεγόμενοι αὐτὴν ἤλθομεν εἰς τόπον τινὰ καλούμενον Καλοὺς Λιμένας ᾧ ἐγγὺς πόλις ἦν Λασαία.

παραλεγόμενοι. Pres dep ptc masc nom pl παραλέγομαι (attendant circumstance of ἤλθομεν). Only here and at v. 13 in the NT ("to sail along the coast, to sail along thc shore"; LN 54.8).

αὐτὴν. Accusative direct object of παραλεγόμενοι. The antecedent is τὴν Κρήτην (v. 7).

ἤλθομεν. Aor act ind 1st pl ἔρχομαι.

τινὰ. See 8:9.

καλούμενον. Pres pass ptc masc acc sg καλέω (attributive).

Λιμένας. The accusative noun serves as a complement in a passive object-complement double case construction.

ἐγγὺς. Predicate adjective. Barrett (1187) notes that ἐγγύς is used with the dative only here and in 9:38 in the NT. Elsewhere it is used with the genitive (see also Robertson 1934, 639–40).

ἦν. Impf ind 3rd sg εἰμί.

Λασαία. Nominative in apposition to πόλις.

Acts 27:9–12

[9]Since a lot of time had passed and the voyage was already unsafe because the Fast had already passed, Paul urged [10]them, saying, "Men! I can see that this voyage is going to end in disaster and great loss of not only the cargo and the ship, but our lives as well!" [11]But the centurion paid attention to the helmsman and captain rather than to what Paul had said. [12]Since the harbor was not suitable for spending the winter, the majority made a plan to sail from there, (thinking that) somehow, if they could reach Phoenix—a harbor of Crete that faces southwest and northwest—they would be able to spend the winter (there).

27:9 Ἱκανοῦ δὲ χρόνου διαγενομένου καὶ ὄντος ἤδη ἐπισφαλοῦς τοῦ πλοὸς διὰ τὸ καὶ τὴν νηστείαν ἤδη παρεληλυθέναι παρῄνει ὁ Παῦλος

χρόνου. Genitive subject (see 1:8 on ἐπελθόντος).

διαγενομένου. Aor mid dep ptc masc gen sg διαγίνομαι. Genitive absolute (see 1:8 on ἐπελθόντος), causal.

ὄντος. Pres act ptc masc gen sg εἰμί. Genitive absolute (see 1:8 on ἐπελθόντος), causal.

ἐπισφαλοῦς. Predicate genitive (see 1:16 on ὁδηγοῦ) from ἐπισφαλής (only here in the NT): "dangerous, unsafe."

τοῦ πλοὸς. Genitive subject (see 1:8 on ἐπελθόντος).

τὴν νηστείαν. Accusative subject of the infinitive (see 1:3 on αὐτὸν).

παρεληλυθέναι. Prf act inf παρέρχομαι. Used with διὰ τὸ to indicate cause.

παρῄνει. Impf act ind 3rd sg παραινέω. Only here and in v. 22 in the NT ("to advise strongly, to urge"; LN 33.295).

27:10 λέγων αὐτοῖς, Ἄνδρες, θεωρῶ ὅτι μετὰ ὕβρεως καὶ πολλῆς ζημίας οὐ μόνον τοῦ φορτίου καὶ τοῦ πλοίου ἀλλὰ καὶ τῶν ψυχῶν ἡμῶν μέλλειν ἔσεσθαι τὸν πλοῦν.

λέγων. Pres act ptc masc nom sg λέγω (attendant circumstance).

Ἄνδρες. In this case, the vocative is not further qualified and should therefore be rendered "Men" (cf. v. 21; 1:11).

θεωρῶ. Pres act ind 1st sg θεωρέω.

ὅτι. Introduces indirect discourse.

μετὰ ὕβρεως καὶ πολλῆς ζημίας. The preposition denotes accompaniment. Lit. "([the voyage is about to take place] *with* damage and great loss").

τοῦ φορτίου . . . τοῦ πλοίου . . . τῶν ψυχῶν. Objective genitives.

μέλλειν. Pres act inf μέλλω (indirect discourse). Here the infinitive lends a note of certainty to Paul's claim (cf. 3:3 on μέλλοντας). This is the only place in the NT where both ὅτι and an infinitive verb are used in the same clause to introduce indirect discourse. The infinitive is probably used due to the heavy prepositional phrase that separates it from the main verb. For an example outside of the NT, see Xenophon, *Hell.* 2.2.2 (Moulton, 1.213).

ἔσεσθαι. Fut mid dep inf εἰμί (complementary). On the tense, see 11:28.

τὸν πλοῦν. Accusative subject of the infinitive (see 1:3 on αὐτὸν).

27:11 ὁ δὲ ἑκατοντάρχης τῷ κυβερνήτῃ καὶ τῷ ναυκλήρῳ μᾶλλον ἐπείθετο ἢ τοῖς ὑπὸ Παύλου λεγομένοις.

τῷ κυβερνήτῃ . . . τῷ ναυκλήρῳ . . . τοῖς λεγομένοις. Uncertainty regarding the semantics of πείθω in the passive voice makes it difficult to determine the function of the dative case here. Although some translations imply that the dative case indicates agency ("was persuaded by the helmsman and captain"), it might be more appropriate to say that the passive form of πείθω means something like "to pay attention to" or "to follow" (cf. BAGD, 639) and takes a dative complement.

κυβερνήτῃ . . . ναυκλήρῳ. Thomas (339) notes that the κυβερνήτης "was subordinate to the ναύκληρος . . ., the 'supreme commander' of the ship" (see also Plutarch, *Praec. ger. rei publ.* 807b). It remains unclear, however, whether the pair represents the helmsman and captain or the captain and ship owner.

ἐπείθετο. Impf pass ind 3rd sg πείθω.

τοῖς . . . λεγομένοις. Pres pass ptc neut dat pl λέγω (substantival). On the case, see above.

27:12 ἀνευθέτου δὲ τοῦ λιμένος ὑπάρχοντος πρὸς παραχειμασίαν οἱ πλείονες ἔθεντο βουλὴν ἀναχθῆναι ἐκεῖθεν, εἴ πως δύναιντο καταντήσαντες εἰς Φοίνικα παραχειμάσαι λιμένα τῆς Κρήτης

βλέποντα κατὰ λίβα καὶ κατὰ χῶρον.

ἀνευθέτου. Predicate genitive adjective (see 1:16 on ὁδηγοῦ).

τοῦ λιμένος. Genitive subject (see 1:8 on ἐπελθόντος).

ὑπάρχοντος. Pres act ptc masc gen sg ὑπάρχω. Genitive absolute (see 1:8 on ἐπελθόντος), causal.

οἱ πλείονες. Here, the comparative form is used substantivally to indicate "the majority," which may simply mean the centurion, "helmsman," and "captain," as opposed to Paul (see v. 11).

ἔθεντο. Aor mid ind 3rd pl τίθημι.

ἀναχθῆναι. Aor pass inf ἀνάγω (epexegetical). On the meaning, see 13:13.

εἴ πως δύναιντο. The use of εἰ with an optative verb forms a fourth class condition (always incomplete in the NT), which is normally used to express something that has only a remote possibility of happening in the future. The use of πως further emphasizes the sense of uncertainty (cf. 17:27). More specifically, in this context the incomplete fourth class condition serves to parenthetically introduce the hopeful reason behind the majority's decision (cf. 17:27).

δύναιντο. Pres pass opt 3rd pl δύναμαι.

καταντήσαντες. Aor act ptc masc nom pl καταντάω. Given the overall context, it is probably best to view this participle as expressing a condition, which turns out to be wishful thinking. As in many other cases (cf. Wallace 1996, 633), the putative conditional participle may express means.

παραχειμάσαι. Aor act inf παραχειμάζω (complementary).

λιμένα. Accusative in apposition to Φοίνικα.

βλέποντα κατὰ λίβα καὶ κατὰ χῶρον. For the problems associated with this expression, see Lake and Cadbury (330) or the briefer summary in Barrett (1192–93).

βλέποντα. Pres act ptc masc sg acc βλέπω (attributive modifier of λιμένα).

Acts 27:13–20

13When a south wind began to blow gently, thinking that they had
achieved their plan, they raised the anchor and were sailing as close as
possible along (the coast of) Crete. 14After a short time, a very strong
wind, called a Northeaster, came down from (the direction of Crete).
15When the ship was caught (by the wind) and unable to face into the

wind, we gave in (to the wind) and were carried along.

16As we ran under the shelter of a small island called Cauda, we were somehow able to gain control of the dinghy. 17After hoisting it aboard, they used ropes to undergird the ship. Since they were afraid they would run aground on the Syrtis, they lowered the (drift) anchor and were carried along.

18On the next day, since we were being battered by the storm, they began throwing things overboard. 19Then, on the third day, they threw the ship's gear overboard with their own hands. 20When neither sun nor stars appeared for many days, and a terrible storm persisted, finally, all hope of our being saved was (slowly) taken away.

27:13 Ὑποπνεύσαντος δὲ νότου δόξαντες τῆς προθέσεως κεκρατηκέναι, ἄραντες ἆσσον παρελέγοντο τὴν Κρήτην.

Ὑποπνεύσαντος. Aor act ptc masc gen sg ὑποπνέω. Genitive absolute (see 1:8 on ἐπελθόντος), temporal.

νότου. Genitive subject (see 1:8 on ἐπελθόντος).

δόξαντες. Aor act ptc masc nom pl δοκέω (causal).

τῆς προθέσεως. Genitive complement of κεκρατηκέναι. BDF (§170) argue that when κρατέω is used of physical touching it takes the accusative if a complete object is grasped and the genitive if only a part of an object is grasped. Not only does this analysis not always work with physical objects (compare Matt 9:25 and 28:9), it also cannot account for abstract objects (compare the present verse with Rev 2:14, 15). It is probable that when the verb is used in the sense of realizing a goal, as here, that it must take a genitive complement.

κεκρατηκέναι. Prf act inf κρατέω (indirect discourse with a verb of cognition).

ἄραντες. Aor act ptc masc nom pl αἴρω (attendant circumstance).

ἆσσον. "A position extremely close to another position" (LN 83.28). The comparative form is used as an elative (see 13:31 on πλείους): "as close as possible."

παρελέγοντο. Impf dep ind 3rd pl παραλέγομαι. See v. 8.

τὴν Κρήτην. Accusative complement of παρελέγοντο.

27:14 μετ' οὐ πολὺ δὲ ἔβαλεν κατ' αὐτῆς ἄνεμος τυφωνικὸς ὁ καλούμενος Εὐρακύλων·

μετ' οὐ πολύ. Litotes (lit. "after not much"; see 1:5 on οὐ μετὰ πολλὰς ταύτας ἡμέρας).

ἔβαλεν. Aor act ind 3rd sg βάλλω. Although typically used transitively, βάλλω may be used intransively, as here (cf. BAGD, 131). The language is reminscient of the account of the sea storm in Jonah (though a form of βάλλω is used only in 1:12, 15) where God throws (טול) a great wind upon the sea, the sailors respond by first throwing (טול) the cargo overboard, and then throwing (טול) Jonah overboard (1:12, 15).

κατ᾿ αὐτῆς. With the genitive, the preposition could mean either "against" or "down from." Since the former appears to require that the neuter πλοῖον ("ship") be the antecedent of the feminine αὐτῆς, many have suggested that the antecedent must be "Crete" (v. 13) and the preposition indicate "down from" (so Barrett, 1194; Bruce, 518). It is *possible*, that the use of βάλλω with ἄνεμος τυφωνικὸς would have signaled the reader that a sea storm is in view, making it plausible that the unexpressed (but understood) antecedent is the feminine θάλασσα: "against the sea" (cf. LXX Jonah 1:4).

ἄνεμος τυφωνικὸς. Nominative subject of ἔβαλεν.

καλούμενος. Pres pass ptc masc nom sg καλέω (attributive).

Εὐρακύλων. Nominative complement in a subject-object double nominative construction with the passive καλούμενος (cf. 4:36 on υἱὸς and 1:12 on ᾿Ελαιῶνος). Metzger (497) notes that this term appears to be a hybrid compound of Εὖρος (the east wind) and the Latin *Aquilo* (the north wind). The fact that the term does not occur elsewhere in extant Greek literature helps explain the variety of variant readings introduced by copyists (Omanson).

27:15 συναρπασθέντος δὲ τοῦ πλοίου καὶ μὴ δυναμένου ἀντοφθαλμεῖν τῷ ἀνέμῳ ἐπιδόντες ἐφερόμεθα.

συναρπασθέντος. Aor pass ptc neut gen sg συναρπάζω. Genitive absolute (see 1:8 on ἐπελθόντος), temporal.

τοῦ πλοίου. Genitive subject (see 1:8 on ἐπελθόντος).

δυναμένου. Pres dep ptc neut gen sg δύναμαι. Genitive absolute (see 1:8 on ἐπελθόντος), temporal.

ἀντοφθαλμεῖν. Pres act inf ἀντοφθαλμέω (complementary). Only here in the NT ("to face straight ahead"; LN 82.9).

τῷ ἀνέμῳ. Syntactically, the dative noun phrase probably modifies ἀντοφθαλμεῖν ("into the wind") and is then left implicit following ἐπιδόντες: "we yielded *to the wind*" (cf. Barrett, 1194–95).

ἐπιδόντες. Aor act ptc masc nom pl ἐπιδίδωμι (attendant circumstance).

ἐφερόμεθα. Impf pass ind 1st pl φέρω.

27:16 νησίον δέ τι ὑποδραμόντες καλούμενον Καῦδα ἰσχύσαμεν μόλις περικρατεῖς γενέσθαι τῆς σκάφης,

τι. See 8:9.

ὑποδραμόντες. Aor act ptc nom masc pl ὑποτρέχω (temporal). The term (lit. "to run under"; only here in the NT) is a synonym of ὑποπλέω (see vv. 4, 7; LN 54.10). In contrast with ὑποπλέω, however, this term probably suggests a lack of control. Therefore, while the participle could indicate means ("by sailing under the shelter"), such a function is less likely than a temporal function. Martín-Ascensio (212) argues that "a close reading of all the 'we' clauses in Acts 27 reveals that the fundamental feature they have in common is not primarily their referent, but rather, the sense of powerlessness created by their non-ergative structures" (which make no reference to causation on the part of the subject).

καλούμενον. Pres pass ptc neut acc sg καλέω (attributive).

Καῦδα. The accusative noun serves as a complement in a passive object-complement double case construction (cf. 1:12 on' Ελαιῶνος).

ἰσχύσαμεν . . . σκάφης. Lit. "we were with difficulty able to be in control of the dinghy."

ἰσχύσαμεν. Aor act ind 1st pl ἰσχύω.

περικρατεῖς. Predicate adjective. Only here in the NT ("pertaining to being in control"; LN 37.23).

γενέσθαι. Aor mid dep inf γίνομαι (complementary).

τῆς σκάφης. Objective genitive, modifying περικρατεῖς.

27:17 ἣν ἄραντες βοηθείαις ἐχρῶντο ὑποζωννύντες τὸ πλοῖον, φοβούμενοί τε μὴ εἰς τὴν Σύρτιν ἐκπέσωσιν, χαλάσαντες τὸ σκεῦος, οὕτως ἐφέροντο.

ἄραντες. Aor act ptc masc nom pl αἴρω (temporal).

βοηθείαις. Dative complement of ἐχρῶντο. In this context, the term may refer to interior braces or ropes that went around the outside of the hull to prevent the ship from being torn apart in heavy seas (see BAGD 144, 844).

ἐχρῶντο. Impf dep ind 3rd pl χράομαι.

ὑποζωννύντες. Pres act ptc masc nom pl ὑποζώννυμι (purpose).

φοβούμενοί. Pres dep ptc masc nom pl φοβέομαι (causal). The second accent comes from the enclitic τε (see 1:4 on ἠκούσατέ).

τὴν Σύρτιν. According to BAGD (794), "the Syrtis" was the name of "two gulfs along the Libyan coast which, because of their shallowness and shifting sand-banks, were greatly feared by mariners."

ἐκπέσωσιν. Aor act subj 3rd pl ἐκπίπτω. The subjunctive with μή is commonly used after verbs of warning or fearing (Wallace 1996, 477) and indicates concern regarding a potential outcome.

χαλάσαντες. Aor act ptc masc nom pl χαλάω (attendant circumstance).

τὸ σκεῦος. It is unclear whether this term refers to the anchor, which was lowered in hopes of slowing the ship, or the ship's gear associated with fair-weather sails (see Bruce, 520). Given v. 40, a reference to one or more (drift) anchors is most likely.

ἐφέροντο. Impf pass ind 3rd pl φέρω.

27:18 **σφοδρῶς δὲ χειμαζομένων ἡμῶν τῇ ἑξῆς ἐκβολὴν ἐποιοῦντο**

χειμαζομένων. Pres pass ptc masc gen pl χειμάζω. Genitive absolute (see 1:8 on ἐπελθόντος), causal.

ἡμῶν. Genitive subject (see 1:8 on ἐπελθόντος).

τῇ ἑξῆς. See 21:1.

ἐκβολὴν ἐποιοῦντο. A periphrastic expression for getting rid of something (lit. "they were causing a throwing out"). Noting that the ship's cargo of grain, which provided ballast in heavy seas, was not jettisoned until the ship was in dangerously shallow waters, and the otherwise redundant use of αὐτόχειρες with ἔρριψαν in the next verse, Clark (1975, 144–46) suggests that ἐκβολὴν ἐποιοῦντο indicates that the sailors attempted to hoist the ship's gear (τὴν σκευὴν τοῦ πλοίου; v. 19) overboard by mechanical means, but failed until the next day when they accomplished the feat "by hand." Thus the shift from the imperfect to the aorist tense and the specification of αὐτόχειρες in v. 19. It is also possible, however, that the sailors began by getting rid of non-essentials, or things that were readily at hand, and preserved their precious cargo (in the hold) until there was no hope of saving it (cf. Jonah 1:4–5).

ἐποιοῦντο. Impf mid ind 3rd pl ποιέω. The use of the middle voice appears to be a feature of this idiom (ἐκβολὴ ποιέω; see Jonah 1:5).

27:19 καὶ τῇ τρίτῃ αὐτόχειρες τὴν σκευὴν τοῦ πλοίου ἔρριψαν.

τῇ τρίτῃ. Dative of time. The noun ἡμέρᾳ is left implicit.

αὐτόχειρες. Nominative subject of ἔρριψαν. The term may represent a synecdoche (see 1:22 on τοῦ βαπτίσματος Ἰωάννου) for "they," it could lend weak emphasis to the means by which the gear was jettisoned (see v. 18 on ἐκβολὴν ἐποιοῦντο), or it could highlight that it was a deliberate act (Fitzmyer 1998, 777).

τὴν σκευὴν. According to Louw and Nida (6.2), the feminine noun σκεύη represents a collective expression for any kind of artifact that may be referred to using σκεῦος (cf. v. 17).

ἔρριψαν. Aor act ind 3rd pl ῥίπτω.

27:20 μήτε δὲ ἡλίου μήτε ἄστρων ἐπιφαινόντων ἐπὶ πλείονας ἡμέρας, χειμῶνός τε οὐκ ὀλίγου ἐπικειμένου, λοιπὸν περιῃρεῖτο ἐλπὶς πᾶσα τοῦ σῴζεσθαι ἡμᾶς.

ἡλίου . . . ἄστρων. Genitive subject (see 1:8 on ἐπελθόντος).

ἐπιφαινόντων. Pres act ptc neut gen pl ἐπιφαίνω. Genitive absolute (see 1:8 on ἐπελθόντος), temporal.

χειμῶνός . . . οὐκ ὀλίγου. Litotes (see 1:5 on οὐ μετὰ πολλὰς ταύ τας ἡμέρας).

χειμῶνός. Genitive subject (see 1:8 on ἐπελθόντος). The second accent comes from the enclitic τε (see 1:4 on ἠκούσατέ).

ἐπικειμένου. Pres dep ptc masc gen sg ἐπικείμαι. Genitive absolute (see 1:8 on ἐπελθόντος), temporal.

περιῃρεῖτο. Impf pass ind 3rd sg περιαιρέω. The choice of the imperfect may highlight that the evaporation of hope was a gradual process brought about by the duration and severity of the storm (cf. Bruce, 521; Fitzmyer 1998, 777).

τοῦ σῴζεσθαι. Pres pass inf σῴζω (epexegetical). While Wallace (1996, 234) views this as a substantival infinitive used with the objective genitive to indicate the object of their hope, it is unclear whether an infinitive can be used in this way. Wallace does not list other examples where a substantival infinitive bears no syntactic function (here he takes the function from the genitive article). Moreover, objective infinitives function as the direct object of a *finite verb*. Finally, in this case the infinitive fits quite well with Wallace's (607) definition of epexegetical infinitives (cf. 14:9).

ἡμᾶς. Accusative subject of the infinitive (see 1:3 on αὐτὸν).

Acts 27:21–26

[21]After they had gone without food for some time, Paul stood up among them and said, "Men, you could have paid attention to me and not set sail from Crete, and thus avoided this damage and loss. [22]But now, I urge you to cheer up, for there will be no loss of life among you; only the ship (will be lost). [23]For last night, an angel of God, to whom I belong and whom I worship, stood by me [24]and said, 'Don't be afraid, Paul! It is necessary for you to stand before Caesar; and God graciously promises you that he will protect all those who are sailing with you!' [25]So, cheer up, men! For I believe God—that things will happen in exactly the way that I have been told. [26]But it is necessary for us to run aground on a certain island."

27:21 Πολλῆς τε ἀσιτίας ὑπαρχούσης τότε σταθεὶς ὁ Παῦλος ἐν μέσῳ αὐτῶν εἶπεν, Ἔδει μέν, ὦ ἄνδρες, πειθαρχήσαντάς μοι μὴ ἀνάγεσθαι ἀπὸ τῆς Κρήτης κερδῆσαί τε τὴν ὕβριν ταύτην καὶ τὴν ζημίαν.

Πολλῆς . . . ἀσιτίας. The gender, number, and case of Πολλῆς make it clear that it serves as a modifier of ἀσιτίας rather than as the genitive subject itself (i.e., "many of them"). Technically, the noun ἀσιτίας could be viewed as either the genitive subject (lit. "after much fasting had occurred"; see 1:8 on ἐπελθόντος) or predicate genitive (lit. "after there had been much fasting"; see 1:16 on ὁδηγοῦ) of ὑπαρχούσης.

ὑπαρχούσης. Pres act ptc fem gen sg ὑπάρχω. Genitive absolute (see 1:8 on ἐπελθόντος), temporal.

σταθεὶς. Aor pass ptc masc nom sg ἵστημι (attendant circumstance).

εἶπεν. Aor act ind 3rd sg λέγω.

Ἔδει . . . τε. Lit. "It was necessary, O men, to obey me and not to set sail from Crete and so to avoid . . ."

Ἔδει. Impf act ind 3rd sg δεῖ (impersonal).

ὦ ἄνδρες. On the use of the the particle ὦ, see 13:10 on Ὦ πλήρης. On the position of the vocative, see 10:13 on Πέτρε. On the translation of ἄνδρες, see v. 10.

πειθαρχήσαντάς. Aor act ptc masc acc pl πειθαρχέω (attendant circumstance of the infinitives). The second accent comes from the enclitic μοι (see 1:4 on ἠκούσατέ).

ἀνάγεσθαι. Pres pass inf ἀνάγω (complementary). On the meaning, see 13:13.

κερδῆσαί. Aor act inf κερδαίνω (complementary). The second accent comes from the enclitic τε (see 1:4 on ἠκούσατέ). The use of τε, which indicates a close consequential relationship between the two infinitive clauses, to conjoin the infinitival clauses disallows taking the μή with both infinitives (contra Barrett, 1200). To make both infinitives negative Luke would have had to have written μὴ ἀνάγεσθαι ἀπὸ τῆς Κρήτης *καὶ* κερδῆσαί (cf. 20:20) or perhaps μὴ ἀνάγεσθαι ἀπὸ τῆς Κρήτης *μηδὲ* κερδῆσαί (cf. 4:18).

27:22 καὶ τὰ νῦν παραινῶ ὑμᾶς εὐθυμεῖν· ἀποβολὴ γὰρ ψυχῆς οὐδεμία ἔσται ἐξ ὑμῶν πλὴν τοῦ πλοίου.

καὶ τὰ νῦν. See 4:29.

παραινῶ. Pres act ind 1st sg παραινέω.

ὑμᾶς. Since παραινέω takes a dative complement, the accusative pronoun must be the subject of the infinitive (see 1:3 on αὐτὸν).

εὐθυμεῖν. Pres act inf εὐθυμέω (indirect discourse).

ἀποβολή. Nominative subject or predicate nominative of an impersonal ἔσται.

ψυχῆς. Objective genitive.

ἔσται. Fut ind 3rd sg εἰμί.

27:23 παρέστη γάρ μοι ταύτῃ τῇ νυκτὶ τοῦ θεοῦ, οὗ εἰμι [ἐγώ] ᾧ καὶ λατρεύω, ἄγγελος

παρέστη. Aor act ind 3rd sg παρίστημι. The position of the verb need not suggest emphasis (contra Barrett, 1200). Luke frequently uses γάρ clauses that begin with an indicative verb (see, e.g., 1:20; 4:27; 5:26; 6:14; 15:28; 19:37; 20:16; 23:21).

ταύτῃ τῇ νυκτὶ. Lit. "this night." Dative of time.

τοῦ θεοῦ. Genitive of source. Since relative clauses are generally roughly contiguous with the noun they modify, the fronting of τοῦ θεοῦ has resulted in the unusual word order, in which τοῦ θεοῦ both precedes and is separated from the noun (ἄγγελος) it modifies. The fronting (see 3:13 on ὑμεῖς) serves to emphasize the source and authority behind the angel and his message.

οὗ. Genitive of possession.

εἰμι. Pres act ind 1st sg εἰμί.

ᾧ. Dative complement of λατρεύω.

λατρεύω. Pres act ind 1st sg λατρεύω.

27:24 λέγων, Μὴ φοβοῦ, Παῦλε, Καίσαρί σε δεῖ παραστῆναι, καὶ ἰδοὺ κεχάρισταί σοι ὁ θεὸς πάντας τοὺς πλέοντας μετὰ σοῦ.

λέγων. Pres act ptc masc nom sg λέγω (attendant circumstance).

φοβοῦ. Aor mid dep impv 2nd sg φοβέω.

Παῦλε. On the position of the vocative, see 10:13 on Πέτρε.

Καίσαρί. Dative of location. The fronting (see 3:13 on ὑμεῖς) of this noun highlights the one before whom Paul must stand. The second accent comes from the enclitic σε (see 1:4 on ἠκούσατέ).

σε. Accusative subject of the infinitive (see 1:3 on αὐτὸν).

δεῖ. Pres act ind 3rd sg δεῖ.

παραστῆναι. Aor act inf παρίστημι (complementary; see 1:16 on ἔδει).

καὶ . . . σοῦ. Lit. "God has graciously granted to you all those who are sailing with you!"

ἰδοὺ. See 1:10.

κεχάρισταί. Prf dep ind 3rd sg χαρίζομαι ("to give or grant graciously and generously, with the implication of good will on the part of the giver"; LN 57.102). The second accent comes from the enclitic σοι (see 1:4 on ἠκούσατέ).

τοὺς πλέοντας. Pres act ptc masc acc pl πλέω (substantival).

27:25 διὸ εὐθυμεῖτε, ἄνδρες· πιστεύω γὰρ τῷ θεῷ ὅτι οὕτως ἔσται καθ' ὃν τρόπον λελάληταί μοι.

εὐθυμεῖτε. Pres act impv 2nd pl εὐθυμέω.

ἄνδρες. On the position of the vocative, see 10:13 on Πέτρε.

πιστεύω. Pres act ind 1st sg πιστεύω.

ὅτι. Introduces indirect discourse with a verb of cognition. The ὅτι clause stands in apposition to the dative complement of πιστεύω (τῷ θεῷ).

ἔσται. Fut ind 3rd sg εἰμί.

καθ' ὃν τρόπον. The internally headed relative clause (see 1:2 on ἄχρι ἧς ἡμέρας) is used with οὕτως to produce a highly intensified expression: "in the *very same* manner" (cf. 1:11).

λελάληταί. Prf pass ind 3rd sg λαλέω. The second accent comes from the enclitic μοι (see 1:4 on ἠκούσατέ).

μοι. The pronoun is the indirect object of the impersonal passive verb (lit. "it has been told *to me*").

27:26 εἰς νῆσον δέ τινα δεῖ ἡμᾶς ἐκπεσεῖν.

δεῖ. Pres act ind 3rd sg δεῖ.

ἡμᾶς. Accusative subject of the infinitive (see 1:3 on αὐτὸν).

ἐκπεσεῖν. Aor act inf ἐκπίπτω (complementary; see 1:16 on ἔδει).

Acts 27:27–32

[27]On the fourteenth night, as we were being driven across the Adriatic Sea, in the middle of the night the sailors suspected that they were approaching land. [28]They took soundings and found (the depth to be) twenty fathoms. Then, after going a little farther and taking soundings again, they found (the depth to be) fifteen fathoms. [29]Since they were afraid that we might run aground somewhere at a rocky place, they threw out four anchors from the stern and prayed for daylight.

[30]When the sailors tried to flee from the ship and lowered the dinghy into the sea, as if they were going to lower anchors from the bow, [31]Paul said to the centurion and the soldiers, "Unless these men remain on the ship, you cannot be saved." [32]Then the soldiers cut the ropes of the dinghy and allowed it to fall.

27:27 Ὡς δὲ τεσσαρεσκαιδεκάτη νὺξ ἐγένετο διαφερομένων ἡμῶν ἐν τῷ Ἀδρίᾳ, κατὰ μέσον τῆς νυκτὸς ὑπενόουν οἱ ναῦται προσάγειν τινὰ αὐτοῖς χώραν.

Ὡς . . . ἐγένετο. Lit. "When the fourteenth night had come."

ἐγένετο. Aor mid dep ind 3rd sg γίνομαι.

διαφερομένων. Pres pass ptc masc gen pl διαφέρω. Genitive absolute (see 1:8 on ἐπελθόντος), temporal. Here, "to cause to move in various directions by means of a force" (LN 15.163).

ἡμῶν. Genitive subject (see 1:8 on ἐπελθόντος).

ὑπενόουν. Impf act ind 3rd pl ὑπονοέω.

προσάγειν . . . χώραν. Lit. "some land was coming near to them."

προσάγειν. Pres act inf προσάγω (indirect discourse with a verb of cognition).

χώραν. Accusative subject of the infinitive (see 1:3 on αὐτὸν).

27:28 καὶ βολίσαντες εὗρον ὀργυιὰς εἴκοσι, βραχὺ δὲ διαστήσαντες καὶ πάλιν βολίσαντες εὗρον ὀργυιὰς δεκαπέντε·

βολίσαντες. Aor act ptc masc nom pl βολίζω (attendant circumstance).

εὗρον. Aor act ind 3rd pl εὑρίσκω.

ὀργυιὰς. Accusative direct object of εὗρον. One fathom is equivalent to about six feet.

διαστήσαντες. Aor act ptc masc nom pl διΐστημι (temporal).

βολίσαντες. Aor act ptc masc nom pl βολίζω (temporal).

27:29 φοβούμενοί τε μή που κατὰ τραχεῖς τόπους ἐκπέσωμεν, ἐκ πρύμνης ῥίψαντες ἀγκύρας τέσσαρας ηὔχοντο ἡμέραν γενέσθαι.

φοβούμενοί. Pres dep ptc masc nom pl φοβέομαι (causal). The second accent comes from the enclitic τε (see 1:4 on ἠκούσατέ).

ἐκπέσωμεν. Aor act subj 1st pl ἐκπίπτω. On the use of the subjunctive with μή, see 23:10 on διασπασθῇ.

ῥίψαντες. Aor act ptc masc nom pl ῥίπτω (attendant circumstance).

ηὔχοντο. Impf dep ind 3rd pl εὔχομαι. Moulton (2.324) argues that in contrast to προσεύχομαι, which was used of Christian prayer, εὔχομαι was used of either pagan prayer or generic wishing. While it may be possible, though unlikely, to view most NT uses of εὔχομαι as expressions of general wishes (Acts 26:29; Rom 9:3; 2 Cor 13:7, 9; 3 John 1:2), James 5:16 clearly uses εὔχομαι to refer to Christian prayer.

ἡμέραν. Accusative subject of the infinitive (see 1:3 on αὐτὸν).

γενέσθαι. Aor mid dep inf γίνομαι (indirect discourse).

27:30 τῶν δὲ ναυτῶν ζητούντων φυγεῖν ἐκ τοῦ πλοίου καὶ χαλασάντων τὴν σκάφην εἰς τὴν θάλασσαν προφάσει ὡς ἐκ πρῴρης ἀγκύρας μελλόντων ἐκτείνειν,

τῶν . . . ναυτῶν. Genitive subject (see 1:8 on ἐπελθόντος).

ζητούντων. Pres act ptc masc gen pl ζητέω. Genitive absolute (see 1:8 on ἐπελθόντος), temporal.

φυγεῖν. Aor act inf φεύγω (complementary).

χαλασάντων. Aor act ptc masc gen pl χαλάω. Genitive absolute (see 1:8 on ἐπελθόντος), temporal.

προφάσει. The dative case should probably be viewed as instrumental: lit. "using the pretext/excuse."

μελλόντων. Pres act ptc masc gen pl μέλλω. On the force of μέλλω plus an infinitive, see 3:3 on μέλλοντας. Bruce (524) argues that a participle can be used with ὡς to indicate a pretext: "as if." In such instances, the participle takes its case from the case of its referent in what precedes.

ἐκτείνειν. Pres act inf ἐκτείνω (complementary).

27:31 **εἶπεν ὁ Παῦλος τῷ ἑκατοντάρχῃ καὶ τοῖς στρατιώταις, Ἐὰν μὴ οὗτοι μείνωσιν ἐν τῷ πλοίῳ, ὑμεῖς σωθῆναι οὐ δύνασθε.**

εἶπεν. Aor act ind 3rd sg λέγω.

μείνωσιν. Aor act subj 3rd pl μένω. The subjunctive is used with ἐάν in the protasis of a third class condition.

ὑμεῖς. The nominative subject of δύνασθε has been fronted (see 3:13 on ὑμεῖς) for emphasis.

σωθῆναι. Aor pass inf σῴζω (complementary).

δύνασθε. Pres dep ind 2nd pl δύναμαι.

27:32 **τότε ἀπέκοψαν οἱ στρατιῶται τὰ σχοινία τῆς σκάφης καὶ εἴασαν αὐτὴν ἐκπεσεῖν.**

ἀπέκοψαν. Aor act ind 3rd pl ἀποκόπτω.

εἴασαν. Aor act ind 3rd pl ἐάω.

αὐτὴν. Accusative subject of the infinitive (see 1:3 on αὐτὸν).

ἐκπεσεῖν. Aor act inf ἐκπίπτω (complementary).

Acts 27:33–38

[33]Now, as the day was about to dawn, Paul started urging everyone to have some food, saying, "As of today, this is the fourteenth day you have been anxiously waiting and going without food—eating nothing at all. [34]Therefore, I urge you to have some food, since you need it to survive. For not one of you will be harmed in any way." [35]After he had

said these things, he took (some) bread and gave thanks to God in front of them all. Then he broke it and began to eat. [36]Then, all of them were encouraged and also had (some) food themselves. [37](There were 276 of us on the ship.) [38]When they had had their fill of food they began to lighten the ship by throwing the wheat overboard into the sea.

27:33 Ἄχρι δὲ οὗ ἡμέρα ἤμελλεν γίνεσθαι, παρεκάλει ὁ Παῦλος ἅπαντας μεταλαβεῖν τροφῆς λέγων, Τεσσαρεσκαιδεκάτην σήμερον ἡμέραν προσδοκῶντες ἄσιτοι διατελεῖτε μηθὲν προσλαβόμενοι.

Ἄχρι . . . οὗ. See 7:18.

ἡμέρα. Nominative subject of ἤμελλεν.

ἤμελλεν. Impf act ind 3rd sg μέλλω. On the force of μέλλω plus an infinitive, see 3:3 on μέλλοντας.

γίνεσθαι. Pres dep inf γίνομαι

παρεκάλει. Impf act ind 3rd sg παρακαλέω.

ἅπαντας. Accusative subject of the infinitive (see 1:3 on αὐτὸν).

μεταλαβεῖν. Aor act inf μεταλαμβάνω (indirect discourse). On the meaning, see 2:46.

τροφῆς. Genitive complement of μεταλαβεῖν.

λέγων. Pres act ptc masc nom sg λέγω (attendant circumstance, redundant; see 1:6 on λέγοντες).

ἡμέραν. Accusative indicating extent of time (see 7:20 on μῆνας).

προσδοκῶντες. Pres act ptc masc nom pl προσδοκάω (attendant circumstance). Louw and Nida (25.228, n. 16) note that "προσδοκάω includes two significant semantic features: (1) waiting over a period of time; and (2) apprehension and worry with regard to the outcome of the severe storm. It would be possible to classify προσδοκάω as simply continuing in a state over a period of time, but particularly in the context of Ac 27.33 the element of apprehension and worry seems to be dominant."

διατελεῖτε. Pres act ind 2nd pl διατελέω. Wallace's examples for the "extending-from-past present tense" (519–20), including διαλτελεῖτε here, demonstrate that such a notion comes from the context (Luke 15:29) or the semantics of the verb, as here, rather than from the tense itself.

προσλαβόμενοι. Aor mid ptc masc nom pl προσλαμβάνω (attendant circumstance; "to take hold of or grasp, with focus upon the goal of the motion"; LN 18.2).

27:34 διὸ παρακαλῶ ὑμᾶς μεταλαβεῖν τροφῆς· τοῦτο γὰρ πρὸς τῆς ὑμετέρας σωτηρίας ὑπάρχει, οὐδενὸς γὰρ ὑμῶν θρὶξ ἀπὸ τῆς κεφαλῆς ἀπολεῖται.

παρακαλῶ. Pres act ind 1st sg παρακαλέω.

ὑμᾶς. Accusative subject of the infinitive (see 1:3 on αὐτὸν).

μεταλαβεῖν. Aor act inf μεταλαμβάνω (indirect discourse).

τροφῆς. Genitive complement of μεταλαβεῖν.

τοῦτο . . . ὑπάρχει. Lit. "for this is for your deliverance."

τοῦτο. The antecedent of the neuter demonstrative pronoun must be "taking food" rather than the feminine τροφῆς.

πρὸς. The use of πρός with the genitive, only here in the NT, probably means something like, "from the point of view of your advantage" (Robertson 1934, 623) or "in the interest of" (BDF §240).

σωτηρίας. Louw and Nida (21.18, n. 2) note that this term implies "not only a rescue from danger but a restoration to a former state of safety and well being." Here, it is appropriately rendered, "survival."

ὑπάρχει. Pres act ind 3rd sg ὑπάρχω.

οὐδενὸς γὰρ ὑμῶν θρὶξ ἀπὸ τῆς κεφαλῆς ἀπολεῖται. An idiomatic expression denoting certainty regarding one's safety (lit. "For a hair from the head of none of you will be lost"; cf. Luke 21:18).

οὐδενὸς. The possessive genitive adjective, which has been fronted (see 3:13 on ὑμεῖς) for emphasis, modifies κεφαλῆς.

ὑμῶν. Partitive genitive.

θρὶξ. Nominative subject of ἀπολεῖται.

ἀπολεῖται. Fut mid ind 3rd sg απόλλυμι.

27:35 εἴπας δὲ ταῦτα καὶ λαβὼν ἄρτον εὐχαρίστησεν τῷ θεῷ ἐνώπιον πάντων καὶ κλάσας ἤρξατο ἐσθίειν.

εἴπας. Aor act ptc masc nom sg λέγω (temporal).

λαβὼν. Aor act ptc masc nom sg λαμβάνω (temporal). Strictly speaking, the conjoined participles carry the same function ("after he had said these things and taken bread"), though it is more natural in English to render the first temporally and the second as an attendant circumstance.

εὐχαρίστησεν. Aor act ind 3rd sg εὐχαριστέω.

κλάσας. Aor act ptc masc nom sg κλάω (attendant circumstance).

ἤρξατο. Aor mid ind 3rd sg ἄρχω.

ἐσθίειν. Pres act inf ἐσθίω (complementary).

27:36 εὔθυμοι δὲ γενόμενοι πάντες καὶ αὐτοὶ προσελάβοντο τροφῆς.

εὔθυμοι. Predicate adjective (only here in the NT: "encouraged").

γενόμενοι. Aor mid dep ptc masc nom pl γίνομαι (attendant circumstance).

πάντες. Nominative substantival subject of γενόμενοι.

αὐτοὶ. Intensive.

προσελάβοντο. Aor mid ind 3rd pl προσλαμβάνω.

τροφῆς. Genitive complement of προσελάβοντο.

27:37 ἤμεθα δὲ αἱ πᾶσαι ψυχαὶ ἐν τῷ πλοίῳ διακόσιαι ἑβδομήκοντα ἕξ.

ἤμεθα. Impf ind 1st pl εἰμί.

αἱ πᾶσαι ψυχαὶ. Synecdoche (see 1:22 on τοῦ βαπτίσματος Ἰωάννου) for "all the *people.*" A rare example of a non-pronomial subject with a first person verb: lit. "we were—all the souls in the ship—276."

διακόσιαι ἑβδομήκοντα ἕξ. Predicate adjective. On the textual variation related to the number, see Metzger (499–500).

27:38 κορεσθέντες δὲ τροφῆς ἐκούφιζον τὸ πλοῖον ἐκβαλλόμενοι τὸν σῖτον εἰς τὴν θάλασσαν.

κορεσθέντες. Aor pass ptc masc nom pl κορέννυμι (temporal).

τροφῆς. Genitive complement of κορεσθέντες.

ἐκούφιζον. Impf act ind 3rd pl κουφίζω.

ἐκβαλλόμενοι. Pres mid ptc masc nom pl ἐκβάλλω (means).

Acts 27:39–44

[39]Now, when the day dawned, they did not recognize the land but noticed a bay that had a beach onto which they decided to run the ship aground, if possible. [40]So, after abandoning the anchors, they let them (sink) into the sea. At the same time, after loosening the ropes that connected the rudders, and raising the (fore)sail to the wind, they headed for the beach. [41]When they encountered a sandbar, they ran the ship

aground. The bow got stuck and would not move, but the stern began to be broken up by the force of the waves.

[42]Now, the soldiers' plan was that they would kill the prisoners so that no one would swim away and escape; [43]but because the centurion wanted to spare Paul, he prevented them from carrying out their plan and ordered those who were able to swim to be the first to jump overboard and head for land. [44]The rest (he ordered to get to land by) some using boards and others using some of the other things from the ship. And in this way everyone made it safely to land.

27:39 Ὅτε δὲ ἡμέρα ἐγένετο, τὴν γῆν οὐκ ἐπεγίνωσκον, κόλπον δέ τινα κατενόουν ἔχοντα αἰγιαλὸν εἰς ὃν ἐβουλεύοντο εἰ δύναιντο ἐξῶσαι τὸ πλοῖον.

ἐγένετο. Aor mid dep ind 3rd sg γίνομαι.

ἐπεγίνωσκον. Impf act ind 3rd pl ἐπιγινώσκω.

τινα. See 8:9 on τις.

κατενόουν. Impf act ind 3rd pl κατανοέω. There is some debate regarding why Luke used the imperfect tense with this verb and the preceding one. Moulton (1.117) suggests that the sense here is "noticed one after the other" (so also Bruce, 526), while Barrett (1211) suggests that Luke simply chose a less suitable tense in this case. It is probably better to maintain that Luke used the imperfect because he viewed the "recognizing" and "noticing" as processes that were in progress as the sun rose: "they had no success in their efforts to identify the land, but were eventually able to make out a bay with a beach" (cf. Fitzmyer 1998, 773).

ἔχοντα. Pres act ptc masc acc sg ἔχω (attributive).

ἐβουλεύοντο. Impf dep ind 3rd pl βουλεύομαι.

εἰ. Used with the optative δύναιντο to form the protasis of an incomplete fourth class condition. Here the protasis, which is parenthetical in nature, is in the middle of the apodosis.

δύναιντο. Pres pass opt 3rd pl δύναμαι.

ἐξῶσαι. Aor act inf ἐξωθέω (complementary). The variant reading, ἐκσῶσαι ("to bring safely"), which is found in a few manuscripts (B* C cop[sa, bo] arm) and pronounced in the same ways as ἐξῶσαι, apparently arose from an error in hearing (Metzger, 500).

27:40 καὶ τὰς ἀγκύρας περιελόντες εἴων εἰς τὴν θάλασσαν,

ἅμα ἀνέντες τὰς ζευκτηρίας τῶν πηδαλίων καὶ ἐπάραντες τὸν ἀρτέμωνα τῇ πνεούσῃ κατεῖχον εἰς τὸν αἰγιαλόν.

περιελόντες. Aor act ptc masc nom pl περιαιρέω (temporal).

εἴων. Impf act ind 3rd pl ἐάω.

ἀνέντες. Aor act ptc masc nom pl ἀνίημι (temporal; see 24:26 on ἐλπίζων).

ἐπάραντες. Aor act ptc masc nom pl ἐπαίρω (temporal; see 24:26 on ἐλπίζων).

τῇ πνεούσῃ. Pres act ptc fem dat sg πνέω (substantival).

κατεῖχον. Impf act ind 3rd pl κατέχω.

27:41 **περιπεσόντες δὲ εἰς τόπον διθάλασσον ἐπέκειλαν τὴν ναῦν καὶ ἡ μὲν πρῷρα ἐρείσασα ἔμεινεν ἀσάλευτος, ἡ δὲ πρύμνα ἐλύετο ὑπὸ τῆς βίας [τῶν κυμάτων].**

περιπεσόντες. Aor act ptc masc nom pl περιπίπτω (attendant circumstance).

τόπον διθάλασσον. According to Louw and Nida (1.68), τόπος διθάλασσος refers to "a bar or reef produced in an area where two currents meet."

ἐπέκειλαν. Aor act ind 3rd pl ἐπικέλλω.

ἐρείσασα. Aor act ptc fem nom sg ἐρείδω (attendant circumstance).

ἔμεινεν. Aor act ind 3rd sg μένω.

ἀσάλευτος. Predicate adjective.

ἐλύετο. Impf pass ind 3rd sg λύω.

[τῶν κυμάτων]. The fact that the *corrector* of א, who presumably acted as a proofreader who checked the text against a master copy (cf. Silva 1996, 45), added τῶν κυμάτων suggests that it may have been natural for scribes (א* A B arm geo) to leave information implicit that was obvious from the context.

27:42 **τῶν δὲ στρατιωτῶν βουλὴ ἐγένετο ἵνα τοὺς δεσμώτας ἀποκτείνωσιν, μή τις ἐκκολυμβήσας διαφύγῃ.**

ἐγένετο ἵνα. Moulton (3.139) treats ἐγένετο ἵνα as a "Hebraistic figure of speech," presumably thinking of the common וַיְהִי כִּי (lit. "and it happened that"). Unlike in the present case, however, where the verb has a subject (βουλή), the Hebrew expression is impersonal. It is probably better, then, to say that the ἵνα introduces a clausal predicate, analogous to a predicate nominative/adjective: "the soldiers' plan was that *they would kill the prisoners*" (cf. John 4:32; see also Wallace's discussion of "content conjunctions," [1996, 678]).

ἐγένετο. Aor mid dep ind 3rd sg γίνομαι.

ἀποκτείνωσιν. Aor act subj 3rd pl ἀποκτείνω. The subjunctive is used with ἵνα in a clausal predicate (see above).

ἐκκολυμβήσας. Aor act ptc masc nom sg ἐκκολυμβάω (attendant circumstance or means).

διαφύγῃ. Aor act subj 3rd sg διαφεύγω. The subjunctive is used with μή to indicate concern regarding a potential outcome (cf. 23:10 on διασπασθῇ).

27:43 ὁ δὲ ἑκατοντάρχης βουλόμενος διασῶσαι τὸν Παῦλον ἐκώλυσεν αὐτοὺς τοῦ βουλήματος, ἐκέλευσέν τε τοὺς δυναμένους κολυμβᾶν ἀπορίψαντας πρώτους ἐπὶ τὴν γῆν ἐξιέναι

βουλόμενος. Pres dep ptc masc nom sg βούλομαι (causal).

διασῶσαι. Aor act inf διασῴζω (complementary).

ἐκώλυσεν. Aor act ind 3rd sg κωλύω. Although κωλύω is typically modified by an infinitival clause (8:36; 10:47; 16:6; 24:23), here it is used with two nouns—with the persons being hindered in the accusative (αὐτοὺς; cf. 11:17) and the thing being prevented in the genitive (genitive of reference; τοῦ βουλήματος; see BDF §180).

ἐκέλευσέν. Aor act ind 3rd sg κελεύω. The second accent comes from the enclitic τε (see 1:4 on ἠκούσατέ).

τοὺς δυναμένους. Pres dep ptc masc acc pl δύναμαι (substantival). Accusative subject of the infinitive ἐξιέναι (see 1:3 on αὐτὸν).

κολυμβᾶν. Pres act inf κολυμβάω (complementary).

ἀπορίψαντας. Aor act ptc acc masc pl ἀπορίπτω (attendant circumstance of ἐξιέναι = indirect discourse).

πρώτους. The adjective is used adverbially and takes its gender, case, and number from τοὺς δυναμένους.

ἐξιέναι. Pres act inf ἔξειμι (indirect discourse).

27:44 καὶ τοὺς λοιποὺς οὓς μὲν ἐπὶ σανίσιν, οὓς δὲ ἐπί τινων τῶν ἀπὸ τοῦ πλοίου. καὶ οὕτως ἐγένετο πάντας διασωθῆναι ἐπὶ τὴν γῆν.

οὓς μὲν . . . οὓς δε. "some . . . others . . ." Accusative in apposition to τοὺς λοιποὺς.

σανίσιν . . . τινων. There does not appear to be a distinction between the use of the dative and genitive cases with ἐπί here (cf. BDF §235).

τινων. Substantival or attributive (see below). It is unclear whether τινων is masculine, referring to people (so Barrett, 1177, 1215), or neuter, referring to things. On the whole, v. 43 seems to rule out the former since it implies that those who could swim were to make their way to land first. The phrase τῶν ἀπὸ τοῦ πλοίου thus likely refers to other items from the ship that would float.

τῶν ἀπὸ τοῦ πλοίου. The article functions as a nominalizer (see 1:3 on τὰ), changing the prepositional phrase into a substantive modified by τινων (though it would be possible to take the article as an adjectivizer [see 2:5 on τῶν ὑπὸ τὸν οὐρανόν] with a substantival τινων).

ἐγένετο . . . διασωθῆναι. See 4:5. Although Levinsohn (1992, 171) claims that this construction can be used to indicate that an expected event materialized, and cites this passage as the main example, such a notion comes from the adverb οὕτως rather than ἐγένετο plus the infinitive. Levinsohn's others examples (10:25; 21:1, 5), which use either ὡς or ὅτε, do not seem to support his analysis either.

ἐγένετο. Aor mid dep ind 3rd sg γίνομαι.

πάντας. Accusative subject of the infinitive (see 1:3 on αὐτὸν).

διασωθῆναι. Aor pass inf διασῴζω. The infinitival clause (πάντας διασωθῆναι ἐπὶ τὴν γῆν) functions as the subject of ἐγένετο (see also 9:32 on κατελθεῖν).

Acts 28:1–6

[1]When we had made it to safety, we then learned that the island was called Malta. [2]The local inhabitants showed us extraordinary kindness. They welcomed us all and built a fire because it had started to rain and was cold.

[3]After Paul had gathered a bundle of firewood and was putting it on the fire, a viper came out because of the heat and latched onto his hand. [4]When the local inhabitants saw the creature hanging from his hand, they started saying to one another, "Surely, this man is a murderer! Although he escaped from the sea, Justice won't allow him to live." [5]Paul, though, shook the beast into the fire and suffered no harm.

[6]Now, they were expecting him to become feverish at any time or to suddenly drop dead. But after they had waited a long time and seen nothing bad happening to him, they changed their minds and started saying that he was a god.

28:1 Καὶ διασωθέντες τότε ἐπέγνωμεν ὅτι Μελίτη ἡ νῆσος καλεῖται.

διασωθέντες. Aor pass ptc masc nom pl διασῴζω (temporal).

ἐπέγνωμεν. Aor act ind 1st pl ἐπιγινώσκω.

ὅτι. Introduces a clausal complement of ἐπέγνωμεν.

Μελίτη. Complement in a subject-complement double nominative construction with the passive καλεῖται (cf. 4:36 on υἱὸς and 1:12 on Ἐλαιῶνος).

καλεῖται. Pres pass ind 3rd sg καλέω.

28:2 οἵ τε βάρβαροι παρεῖχον οὐ τὴν τυχοῦσαν φιλανθρωπίαν ἡμῖν, ἅψαντες γὰρ πυρὰν προσελάβοντο πάντας ἡμᾶς διὰ τὸν ὑετὸν τὸν ἐφεστῶτα καὶ διὰ τὸ ψῦχος.

οἵ . . . βάρβαροι. Lit. "the foreigners." The article, which gets its accent from the enclitic τε (see 1:4 on ἠκούσατέ), should not be mistaken for a relative pronoun.

τε. See 12:12.

παρεῖχον. Impf act ind 3rd pl παρέχω.

οὐ τὴν τυχοῦσαν. Litotes (lit. "not the [kind normally] experienced"; see 19:11; 1:5 on οὐ μετὰ πολλὰς ταύτας ἡμέρας).

τυχοῦσαν. Aor act ptc fem acc sg τυγχάνω (attributive).

ἅψαντες. Aor act ptc masc nom pl ἅπτω (attendant circumstance). Used to indicate lighting a fire, ἅπτω takes an accusative complement.

προσελάβοντο. Aor mid ind 3rd pl προσλαμβάνω.

διὰ . . . ψῦχος. Lit. "because of the rain that had set in and because of the cold."

ἐφεστῶτα. Prf act ptc masc acc sg ἐφίστημι (attributive).

28:3 συστρέψαντος δὲ τοῦ Παύλου φρυγάνων τι πλῆθος καὶ ἐπιθέντος ἐπὶ τὴν πυράν, ἔχιδνα ἀπὸ τῆς θέρμης ἐξελθοῦσα καθῆψεν τῆς χειρὸς αὐτοῦ.

συστρέψαντος. Aor act ptc masc gen sg συστρέφω. Genitive absolute (see 1:8 on ἐπελθόντος), temporal.

τοῦ Παύλου. Genitive subject (see 1:8 on ἐπελθόντος).

φρυγάνων. Partitive genitive modifying τι πλῆθος.

τι. See 8:9 on τις.

ἐπιθέντος. Aor act ptc masc gen sg ἐπιτίθημι. Genitive absolute (see 1:8 on ἐπελθόντος), temporal.

ἐξελθοῦσα. Aor act ptc fem nom sg ἐξέρχομαι (attendant circumstance).

καθῆψεν. Aor act ind 3rd sg καθάπτω.

τῆς χειρὸς. Genitive object of καθῆψεν.

28:4 ὡς δὲ εἶδον οἱ βάρβαροι κρεμάμενον τὸ θηρίον ἐκ τῆς χειρὸς αὐτοῦ, πρὸς ἀλλήλους ἔλεγον, Πάντως φονεύς ἐστιν ὁ ἄνθρωπος οὗτος ὃν διασωθέντα ἐκ τῆς θαλάσσης ἡ δίκη ζῆν οὐκ εἴασεν.

ὡς. Temporal (see 18:5).

εἶδον. Aor act ind 3rd pl ὁράω.

οἱ βάρβαροι. See v. 2.

κρεμάμενον. Pres mid ptc neut acc sg κρεμάννυμι. The participle functions as the complement in an object-complement double accusative construction (see 1:3 on ζῶντα).

ἔλεγον. Impf act ind 3rd pl λέγω.

φονεύς. Predicate nominative.

ἐστιν. Pres act ind 3rd sg εἰμί. On the loss of its accent, see 1:7 on ἐστιν.

ὃν. The relative pronoun takes accusative case as the subject of the infinitive ζῆν (see 1:3 on αὐτὸν).

διασωθέντα. Aor pass ptc masc acc sg διασῴζω (attributive; lit. "Justice has not allowed him [ὃν] who escaped from the sea to live."). Although a concessive rendering may be appropriate, strictly speaking the participle cannot be adverbial since it has a different subject than the main verb (see Culy 2004).

ἡ δίκη. It is unclear whether this is a reference to a goddess (cf. Fitzmyer 1998, 783) or simply an example of personification—a figure of speech in which an abstract idea, or something not human, is treated as though it were a person.

ζῆν. Pres act inf ζάω (complementary).

εἴασεν. Aor act ind 3rd sg ἐάω.

28:5 ὁ μὲν οὖν ἀποτινάξας τὸ θηρίον εἰς τὸ πῦρ ἔπαθεν οὐδὲν κακόν,

ὁ. Although there would be good reasons for taking the article as a nominalizer (see 1:3 on τὰ), with ἀποτινάξας being substantival (cf. 1:6 on οἱ and συνελθόντες), given the use of the pronoun in v. 6, it is probably better to view it as functioning as a personal pronoun (cf. 3:5).

μὲν οὖν. See 1:6. It is probably better to say that an English translation works well with an adversative conjunction here than to claim that μὲν οὖν is used adversatively (contra Barrett, 1223; BAGD, 593; cf. Moule, 163).

ἀποτινάξας. Aor act ptc masc nom sg ἀποτινάσσω (attendant circumstance; see above).

ἔπαθεν. Aor act ind 3rd sg πάσχω.

28:6 οἱ δὲ προσεδόκων αὐτὸν μέλλειν πίμπρασθαι ἢ καταπίπτειν ἄφνω νεκρόν. ἐπὶ πολὺ δὲ αὐτῶν προσδοκώντων καὶ θεωρούντων μηδὲν ἄτοπον εἰς αὐτὸν γινόμενον μεταβαλόμενοι ἔλεγον αὐτὸν εἶναι θεόν.

οἱ. The article functions like a personal pronoun here (cf. 3:5).

προσεδόκων. Impf act ind 3rd pl προσδοκάω.

αὐτὸν. Accusative subject of the infinitive μέλλειν (see 1:3 on αὐτὸν).

μέλλειν. Pres act inf μέλλω (indirect discourse with a verb of cognition). On the force of μέλλω plus an infinitive, see 3:3 on μέλλοντας.

πίμπρασθαι. Pres pass inf πίμπρημι/πίμπραμαι (complementary). It is unclear whether this verb (only here in the NT) refers to burning with a fever (so LSJ) or swelling up (see LN 23.159, 163).

καταπίπτειν. Pres act inf καταπίπτω (complementary).

νεκρόν. Predicate adjective, with the case being dictated by the constituent that it modifies (αὐτὸν; cf. 20:9 on νεκρός; contra Rogers and Rogers [311] who take it as an accusative of manner).

αὐτῶν. Genitive subject (see 1:8 on ἐπελθόντος).

προσδοκώντων. Pres act ptc masc gen pl προσδοκάω. Genitive absolute (see 1:8 on ἐπελθόντος), temporal.

θεωρούντων. Pres act ptc masc gen pl θεωρέω. Genitive absolute (see 1:8 on ἐπελθόντος), temporal.

γινόμενον. Pres dep ptc neut acc sg γίνομαι. The participle functions as the complement in an object-complement double accusative construction (see 1:3 on ζῶντα), with ἄτοπον being the object.

μεταβαλόμενοι. Aor mid ptc masc nom pl μεταβάλλω (temporal).

ἔλεγον. Impf act ind 3rd pl λέγω. This appears to be an example where the subject of the genitive absolutes is also the subject of the main verb (see 21:34 on δυναμένου). The use of the genitive absolute may imply that after *all* of them had watched, *some* started saying that he was a god.

αὐτὸν. Accusative subject of the infinitive (see 1:3 on αὐτὸν).

εἶναι. Pres act inf εἰμί (indirect discourse).

θεόν. Predicate accusative (see 1:22 on μάρτυρα).

Acts 28:7–10

[7]The chief man of the island, named Publius, owned land in the areas around that place. He welcomed us and kindly treated us as guests for three days. [8]Now, it happened that the father of Publius was sick in bed, suffering with a fever and dysentery. Paul went to him and prayed, as he laid hands on him, and healed him. [9]When this happened, the rest of those on the island who had illnesses also started coming to (him) and were being cured. [10]They also greatly honored us, and when we were ready to sail, they put on board the things we needed.

28:7 Ἐν δὲ τοῖς περὶ τὸν τόπον ἐκεῖνον ὑπῆρχεν χωρία τῷ πρώτῳ τῆς νήσου ὀνόματι Ποπλίῳ, ὃς ἀναδεξάμενος ἡμᾶς τρεῖς ἡμέρας φιλοφρόνως ἐξένισεν.

τοῖς περὶ τὸν τόπον ἐκεῖνον. The article functions as a nominalizer (see 1:3 on τὰ), changing the prepositional phrase into a substantive.

ὑπῆρχεν . . . πρώτῳ. Lit. "lands were to the chief person."

ὑπῆρχεν. Impf act ind 3rd sg ὑπάρχω.

τῷ πρώτῳ. Substantival; dative of possession (with ὑπάρχω).

ὀνόματι. Dative of reference.

Ποπλίῳ. Dative in apposition to τῷ πρώτῳ.

ἀναδεξάμενος. Aor mid ptc masc nom sg ἀναδέχομαι (attendant circumstance).

ἡμέρας. Accusative indicating extent of time (see 7:20 on μῆνας).

ἐξένισεν. Aor act ind 3rd sg ξενίζω.

28:8 ἐγένετο δὲ τὸν πατέρα τοῦ Ποπλίου πυρετοῖς καὶ δυσεντερίῳ συνεχόμενον κατακεῖσθαι, πρὸς ὃν ὁ Παῦλος εἰσελθὼν καὶ προσευξάμενος ἐπιθεὶς τὰς χεῖρας αὐτῷ ἰάσατο αὐτόν.

ἐγένετο. Aor mid dep ind 3rd sg γίνομαι.

τὸν πατέρα. Accusative subject of the infinitive (see 1:3 on αὐτὸν).

πυρετοῖς καὶ δυσεντερίῳ. Verbs with a συν- prefix take a dative complement.

συνεχόμενον. Pres pass ptc masc acc sg συνέχω (attendant circumstance of the infinitive, or perhaps causal: "was resting in bed because he was sick"). Here, the adverbial participle is accusative in agreement with the subject of the infinitive.

κατακεῖσθαι. Pres mid inf κατάκειμαι. The infinitival clause, τὸν πατέρα τοῦ Ποπλίου πυρετοῖς καὶ δυσεντερίῳ συνεχόμενον κατακεῖσθαι, serves as the subject of ἐγένετο (see also 9:32 on κατελθεῖν).

εἰσελθὼν. Aor act ptc masc nom sg εἰσέρχομαι (attendant circumstance).

προσευξάμενος. Aor mid dep ptc masc nom sg προσεύχομαι (attendant circumstance).

ἐπιθεὶς. Aor act ptc masc nom sg ἐπιτίθημι. The conjoining of the preceding participles but not this one suggests that ἐπιθείς has a different function than εἰσελθὼν and προσευξάμενος. It is probably best to take ἐπιθείς as a modifier of προσευξάμενος that highlights the mode of the prayer.

ἰάσατο. Aor mid dep ind 3rd sg ἰάομαι.

28:9 τούτου δὲ γενομένου καὶ οἱ λοιποὶ οἱ ἐν τῇ νήσῳ ἔχοντες ἀσθενείας προσήρχοντο καὶ ἐθεραπεύοντο,

τούτου. Genitive subject (see 1:8 on ἐπελθόντος).

γενομένου. Aor mid dep ptc neut gen sg γίνομαι. Genitive absolute (see 1:8 on ἐπελθόντος), temporal.

οἱ ἐν τῇ νήσῳ ἔχοντες ἀσθενείας. The article functions as a nominalizer (see 1:3 on τὰ), changing the participle, which is modified by a prepositional phrase (ἐν τῇ νήσῳ) and a direct object (ἀσθενείας), into a substantive.

ἔχοντες. Pres act ptc masc nom pl ἔχω (substantival; see above).

προσήρχοντο. Impf dep ind 3rd pl προσέρχομαι.

ἐθεραπεύοντο. Impf pass ind 3rd pl θεραπεύω.

28:10 οἳ καὶ πολλαῖς τιμαῖς ἐτίμησαν ἡμᾶς καὶ ἀναγομένοις ἐπέθεντο τὰ πρὸς τὰς χρείας.

πολλαῖς τιμαῖς. Cognate dative (lit. "with many honors"). Bruce (533) prefers to take τιμή in the sense of compensation for their healings.

ἐτίμησαν. Aor act ind 3rd pl τιμάω.

ἀναγομένοις. Pres pass ptc dat masc pl ἀνάγω. On the meaning, see 13:13. Despite the translation, although the participle is anarthrous (see 3:3 on Πέτρον καὶ' Ιωάννην), it must be substantival rather adverbial given its dative case (see Culy 2004), which probably indicates advantage ("for those who were preparing to sail").

ἐπέθεντο. Aor mid ind 3rd pl ἐπιτίθημι.

τὰ πρὸς τὰς χρείας. The article functions as a nominalizer (see 1:3 on τὰ), changing the prepositional phrase into a substantive.

Acts 28:11–16

[11]So, after three months we set sail in an Alexandrian ship that had
spent the winter at the island and had the 'Heavenly Twins' as its emblem.
[12]We landed at Syracuse and stayed there for three days. [13]From there we
sailed around and arrived at Rhegium. After a day, a south wind came up
and we came to Puteoli on the second day, [14]where we found believers
and were invited to stay with them for seven days. So, in this way we
came to Rome.

[15]The believers from there had heard about our affairs and had come
as far as Appius' Market and the Three Taverns to meet us. When Paul
saw them, he gave thanks to God and took courage. [16]When we entered
Rome, Paul was allowed to live by himself with the soldier who guarded
him.

28:11 Μετὰ δὲ τρεῖς μῆνας ἀνήχθημεν ἐν πλοίῳ παρακεχειμακότι ἐν τῇ νήσῳ, 'Αλεξανδρίνῳ, παρασήμῳ Διοσκούροις.

ἀνήχθημεν. Aor pass ind 1st pl ἀνάγω. On the meaning, see 13:13.

παρακεχειμακότι. Prf act ptc neut dat sg παραχειμάζω (attributive).

'Αλεξανδρίνῳ. Dative in apposition to πλοίῳ.

παρασήμῳ. The adjective (or noun), which occurs only here in the NT, describes something as "being marked with a sign" (LN 33.479). It is unclear whether the marking indicates a figurehead or an emblem/ insignia.

Διοσκούροις. The Dioscuri, or "Heavenly Twins," were Castor and Pollux, who were "patrons of navigation, and were commonly worshipped by sailors" (Bruce, 534). The function of the dative is difficult to determine. W. M. Ramsay (cited in BDF §198.7) rendered the expression, "a ship, insignia the Dioscuri," with Διοσκούροις serving as a predicate expression used for identifying the registry of a ship. The dative could also be taken in a loose instrumental sense that complements the event idea in παρασήμῳ: "marked *with* the Dioscuri."

28:12 καὶ καταχθέντες εἰς Συρακούσας ἐπεμείναμεν ἡμέρας τρεῖς,

καταχθέντες. Aor pass ptc masc nom pl κατάγω (attendant circumstance).

ἐπεμείναμεν. Aor act ind 1st pl ἐπιμένω.

ἡμέρας. Accusative indicating extent of time (see 7:20 on μῆνας).

28:13 ὅθεν περιελόντες κατηντήσαμεν εἰς Ῥήγιον. καὶ μετὰ μίαν ἡμέραν ἐπιγενομένου νότου δευτεραῖοι ἤλθομεν εἰς Ποτιόλους,

περιελόντες. Aor act ptc masc nom pl περιαιρέω (attendant circumstance). Louw and Nida (54.24) argue that περιαιρέω is used here as a technical nautical term meaning "to raise the anchor in preparation for departing." There is little basis, however, for this meaning. Used with τὰς ἀγκύρας in 27:40, the expression seems to refer to getting rid of the anchors. Given the difficulty of making sense of περιελόντες in this context and its sparse textual support (it is found only in א* B Ψ *l* 597 cop[sa]), it may be better to view περιελόντες as a scribal error that resulted from the accidental omission of the θ from περιελθόντες (contra Metzger, 500–1). The latter (aor act ptc masc nom pl περιέρχομαι: "to move or go around some object or point of reference"; LN 15.33) has widespread and early support (𝔓[74] א[2] A 048 066 36 81 181 307 453 610 614 945 1175 1409 1678[vid] 1739 1891 2344 2464 *Byz al*). Moreover, the fact that the corrector of א adds the θ highlights the plausibility of accidental omission and calls into question the value of the textimony of א* (cf. Silva 1996, 45).

κατηντήσαμεν. Aor act ind 1st pl καταντάω.

ἐπιγενομένου. Aor mid dep ptc masc gen sg ἐπιγίνομαι. Genitive absolute (see 1:8 on ἐπελθόντος), attendant circumstance.

νότου. Genitive subject (see 1:8 on ἐπελθόντος).

ἤλθομεν. Aor act ind 1st pl ἔρχομαι.

28:14 οὗ εὑρόντες ἀδελφοὺς παρεκλήθημεν παρ᾽ αὐτοῖς ἐπιμεῖναι ἡμέρας ἑπτά· καὶ οὕτως εἰς τὴν Ῥώμην ἤλθαμεν.

οὗ. See 1:13.

εὑρόντες. Aor act ptc masc nom pl εὑρίσκω (attendant circumstance).

ἀδελφοὺς. See 1:15.

παρεκλήθημεν. Aor pass ind 1st pl παρακαλέω. Here, "to ask a person to accept offered hospitality" (LN 33.315).

ἐπιμεῖναι. Aor act inf ἐπιμένω (indirect discourse).

ἡμέρας. Accusative indicating extent of time (see 7:20 on μῆνας).

ἤλθαμεν. Aor act ind 1st pl ἔρχομαι. Elsewhere in Acts always ἤλθομεν (20:6, 14, 15; 21:1, 8, 27:8; 28:13; cf. v. 15 on ἦλθαν). Luke even uses the more typical form in the preceding verse.

28:15 κἀκεῖθεν οἱ ἀδελφοὶ ἀκούσαντες τὰ περὶ ἡμῶν ἦλθαν εἰς ἀπάντησιν ἡμῖν ἄχρι Ἀππίου Φόρου καὶ Τριῶν Ταβερνῶν, οὓς ἰδὼν ὁ Παῦλος εὐχαριστήσας τῷ θεῷ ἔλαβε θάρσος.

κἀκεῖθεν. A shortened form (crasis) of καὶ ἐκεῖθεν.

ἀδελφοὶ. See 1:15.

ἀκούσαντες. Aor act ptc masc nom pl ἀκούω (attendant circumstance).

τὰ περὶ ἡμῶν. The article functions as a nominalizer (see 1:3 on τὰ), changing the prepositional phrase into a substantive.

ἦλθαν. Aor act ind 3rd pl ἔρχομαι. Luke occasionally uses the less common spelling with the α (also at 12:10; see also ἐξῆλθαν in 16:40) rather than ο (see 4:23; 8:26; 11:12; 13:13, 51; 14:24; 17:1, 13; 28:23; cf. v. 14 on ἤλθαμεν). He switches back to ἦλθον in v. 23.

εἰς ἀπάντησιν ἡμῖν. Lit. "to/for a meeting with us."

Τριῶν Ταβερνῶν. Bruce (536) notes that the "Three Taverns" was "a station on the Appian Way about 33 miles south of Rome."

ἰδὼν. Aor act ptc masc nom sg ὁράω (temporal).

εὐχαριστήσας. Aor act ptc masc nom sg εὐχαριστέω (attendant circumstance).

ἔλαβε. Aor act ind 3rd sg λαμβάνω.

28:16 Ὅτε δὲ εἰσήλθομεν εἰς Ῥώμην, ἐπετράπη τῷ Παύλῳ μένειν καθ' ἑαυτὸν σὺν τῷ φυλάσσοντι αὐτὸν στρατιώτῃ.

εἰσήλθομεν. Aor act ind 1st pl εἰσέρχομαι. The last "we" statement in Acts (see 16:10).

εἰς. See 1:8 on ἐφ' ὑμᾶς.

ἐπετράπη. Aor pass ind 3rd sg ἐπιτρέπω.

μένειν. Pres act inf μένω (complementary). The infinitival clause, μένειν καθ' ἑαυτὸν σὺν τῷ φυλάσσοντι αὐτὸν στρατιώτῃ, functions as the subject of the passive ἐπετράπη (cf. 9:32 on κατελθεῖν).

φυλάσσοντι. Pres act ptc masc dat sg φυλάσσω (attributive).

Acts 28:17–22

[17]After three days Paul called together the leading men of the Jews. When they had gathered, he said to them, "Fellow Jews, although I had done nothing against the people or our ancestral customs, I was handed over to the Romans as a prisoner from Jerusalem. [18]After questioning me, they wanted to release me because there was no basis for imposing the death sentence. [19]But when the Jews objected, I was forced to appeal to Caesar—though I did not have any reason to accuse my own people.

[20]So for this reason I requested to see you and to speak to you. For I am wrapped in this chain because of the hope of Israel." [21]Then they said to him, "We neither received letters concerning you from Judea, nor has any of (our) fellow Jews come (from there) and reported or said anything bad about you. [22]So we think it best to hear from you what you think, for regarding this sect we are aware that it is spoken against everywhere."

28:17 Ἐγένετο δὲ μετὰ ἡμέρας τρεῖς συγκαλέσασθαι αὐτὸν τοὺς ὄντας τῶν Ἰουδαίων πρώτους· συνελθόντων δὲ αὐτῶν ἔλεγεν πρὸς αὐτούς, Ἐγώ, ἄνδρες ἀδελφοί, οὐδὲν ἐναντίον ποιήσας τῷ λαῷ ἢ τοῖς ἔθεσι τοῖς πατρῴοις δέσμιος ἐξ Ἱεροσολύμων παρεδόθην εἰς τὰς χεῖρας τῶν Ῥωμαίων,

Ἐγένετο. Aor mid dep ind 3rd sg γίνομαι.

συγκαλέσασθαι. Aor mid inf συγκαλέω. The infinitival clause, συγκαλέσασθαι αὐτὸν τοὺς ὄντας τῶν Ἰουδαίων πρώτους, functions as the subject of ἐγένετο (see also 9:32 on κατελθεῖν).

αὐτὸν. Accusative subject of the infinitive (see 1:3 on αὐτὸν).

τοὺς ὄντας τῶν Ἰουδαίων πρώτους. This construction may be understood in one of two ways: (1) the participle may be attributive and mean "local" (see 5:17 on οὖσα, where the feminine participle clearly agrees with the following noun rather than the subject), with the adjective πρώτους being substantival (with τοὺς; "the local leaders of the Jews"); or, more likely, (2) the participle may be substantival (with τοὺς) with πρώτους serving as a predicate accusative adjective (see 1:22 on μάρτυρα): "those who were first among the Jews."

τοὺς ὄντας. Pres act ptc masc acc pl εἰμί (see above).

τῶν Ἰουδαίων. Partitive genitive.

πρώτους. See above.

συνελθόντων. Aor act ptc masc gen pl συνέρχομαι. Genitive absolute (see 1:8 on ἐπελθόντος), temporal.

αὐτῶν. Genitive subject (see 1:8 on ἐπελθόντος).

ἔλεγεν. Impf act ind 3rd sg λέγω.

ἄνδρες. See 1:11.

ἀδελφοί. See 7:2.

ποιήσας. Aor act ptc masc nom sg ποιέω (concessive).

τῷ λαῷ ἢ τοῖς ἔθεσι τοῖς πατρῴοις. Dative complement of ἐναντίον.

δέσμιος. Nominative in apposition to Ἐγώ.

παρεδόθην. Aor pass ind 1st sg παραδίδωμι.

εἰς . . . Ῥωμαίων. Lit. "into the hands of the Romans."

28:18 οἵτινες ἀνακρίναντές με ἐβούλοντο ἀπολῦσαι διὰ τὸ μηδεμίαν αἰτίαν θανάτου ὑπάρχειν ἐν ἐμοί.

ἀνακρίναντές. Aor act ptc masc nom pl ἀνακρίνω (temporal). The second accent comes from the enclitic με (see 1:4 on ἠκούσατέ).

ἐβούλοντο. Impf dep ind 3rd pl βούλομαι.

ἀπολῦσαι. Aor act inf ἀπολύω (complementary).

μηδεμίαν . . . ἐμοι. Lit. "no reason of death was in me."

αἰτίαν. Accusative subject of the infinitive (see 1:3 on αὐτὸν).

ὑπάρχειν. Pres act inf ὑπάρχω. Used with διὰ τὸ to indicate cause.

28:19 ἀντιλεγόντων δὲ τῶν Ἰουδαίων ἠναγκάσθην ἐπικαλέσασθαι Καίσαρα οὐχ ὡς τοῦ ἔθνους μου ἔχων τι κατηγορεῖν.

ἀντιλεγόντων. Pres act ptc masc gen pl ἀντιλέγω. Genitive absolute (see 1:8 on ἐπελθόντος), temporal.

τῶν Ἰουδαίων. Genitive subject (see 1:8 on ἐπελθόντος).

ἠναγκάσθην. Aor pass ind 1st sg ἀναγκάζω.

ἐπικαλέσασθαι. Aor mid inf ἐπικαλέω (complementary).

οὐχ ὡς. Although BDF (§425.3) suggest that this phrase should be rendered "not as if," such a rendering masks the fact that ὡς probably functions, as it often does, to link two parts of a simile. Here, the "topic" of the simile is "I" and the "image" is τοῦ ἔθνους μου ἔχων τι κατηρεῖν. Given the syntactic nature of the topic (it is a substantive, though marked only on the verb), the image must also be a substantive: "one who has something to accuse my people of." The participle ἔχων should therefore be viewed as substantival even though it is anarthrous (see 3:3 on Πέτρων καὶ Ἰωάννην). For an analogous example, see Mark 1:22, where an anarthrous ἔχων is clearly linked with a noun (οἱ γραμματεῖς) in a negative simile. The whole construction, οὐχ ὡς . . . κατηγορεῖν (lit. "not as one who has anything to accuse my people of"), stands in apposition to the unexpressed subject, "I."

τοῦ ἔθνους. Genitive object of κατηγορεῖν.

ἔχων. Pres act ptc masc sg nom ἔχω (substantival; see above).

κατηγορεῖν. Pres act inf κατηγορέω (epexegetical to τι).

28:20 διὰ ταύτην οὖν τὴν αἰτίαν παρεκάλεσα ὑμᾶς ἰδεῖν καὶ προσλαλῆσαι, ἕνεκεν γὰρ τῆς ἐλπίδος τοῦ Ἰσραὴλ τὴν ἅλυσιν ταύτην περίκειμαι.

ταύτην τὴν αἰτίαν. The demonstrative pronoun most likely is anaphoric (referring backward) given the γάρ in the following clause, which would not be expected if ταύτην were cataphoric (cf. Barrett, 1240).

παρεκάλεσα. Aor act ind 1st sg παρακαλέω.

ὑμᾶς. Direct object of the infinitive(s).

ἰδεῖν. Aor act inf ὁράω (indirect discourse).

προσλαλῆσαι. Aor act inf προσλαλέω (indirect discourse).

τῆς ἐλπίδος τοῦ Ἰσραήλ. I.e., Israel's messianic hope.

τὴν ἅλυσιν. Accusative complement of περίκειμαι.

περίκειμαι. Pres dep ind 1st sg περίκειμαι. Here, "to have in a position around oneself" (LN 49.4; cf. BAGD, 648).

28:21 οἱ δὲ πρὸς αὐτὸν εἶπαν, Ἡμεῖς οὔτε γράμματα περὶ σοῦ

ἐδεξάμεθα ἀπὸ τῆς Ἰουδαίας οὔτε παραγενόμενός τις τῶν ἀδελφῶν ἀπήγγειλεν ἢ ἐλάλησέν τι περὶ σοῦ πονηρόν.

οἱ. The article functions like a personal pronoun here (cf. 3:5).

εἶπαν. Aor act ind 3rd pl λέγω.

ἐδεξάμεθα. Aor mid dep ind 1st pl δέχομαι.

παραγενόμενός. Aor mid dep ptc masc nom sg παραγίνομαι. The participle could be either attributive ("any of the brothers, who have arrived") or introduce an attendance circumstance. The second accent comes from the enclitic τις (see 1:4 on ἠκούσατέ).

ἀπήγγειλεν ἢ ἐλάλησέν. The use of the two verbs (Bruce [539] argues that the former has an official connotation while the latter refers to informal speech) emphasizes the fact that no news whatsoever about Paul had reached them.

ἀπήγγειλεν. Aor act ind 3rd sg ἀπαγγέλλω.

ἐλάλησέν. Aor act ind 3rd sg λαλέω. The second accent comes from the enclitic τι (see 1:4 on ἠκούσατέ).

τι περὶ σοῦ πονηρόν. The emphatic nature of the conjoined verbs (see above) makes it clear that this phrase does not imply that other reports about Paul, which were good or neutral, had been received (contra Barrett, 1241).

28:22 ἀξιοῦμεν δὲ παρὰ σοῦ ἀκοῦσαι ἃ φρονεῖς, περὶ μὲν γὰρ τῆς αἱρέσεως ταύτης γνωστὸν ἡμῖν ἐστιν ὅτι πανταχοῦ ἀντιλέγεται.

ἀξιοῦμεν. Pres act ind 1st pl ἀξιόω.

ἀκοῦσαι. Aor act inf ἀκούω. The infinitive could be viewed as (1) complementary, with ἀξιοῦμεν; or (2) objective (ἀξιόω appears to take a direct object at times: "to deem/think *something* best/worthy"; see Luke 7:7; cf. 15:38).

ἃ. Direct object of φρονεῖς.

φρονεῖς. Pres act ind 2nd sg φρονέω.

γνωστὸν. Predicate (neuter nominative) adjective.

ἐστιν. Pres act ind 3rd sg εἰμί.

ὅτι. In this relatively rare construction (cf. 1 Cor 6:7), the ὅτι clause may be viewed as (1) a clausal complement of the expression γνωστὸν ἡμῖν ἐστιν, which is analogous to γινώκομεν; or (2) a clausal subject of the equative clause: lit. "that it is spoken against everywhere is known to us" (cf. v. 28; 4:10; 13:38).

ἀντιλέγεται. Pres pass ind 3rd sg ἀντιλέγω.

Acts 28:23–31

[23]After setting a day to meet with him, they went to him, to the place where he was staying, in even greater numbers. From early in the day until quite late he explained (his position) to them as he testified about the kingdom of God and tried to convince them about Jesus from both the law of Moses and the prophets. [24]Some were convinced by what he said, but others would not believe. [25]Since they disagreed among themselves, they began leaving, as Paul said one (last) thing: "The Holy Spirit spoke appropriately through the prophet Isaiah to our ancestors, [26]and said,

> Go to this people and say, "You will listen carefully, but will never understand. You will look carefully, but will never perceive. [27]For the heart of this people has become insensitive, and their ears are plugged, and they have closed their eyes so that they might not see with their eyes, hear with their ears, perceive with their heart, and turn and I would heal them. [28]Therefore, let it be known to you that this salvation from God has been sent to the Gentiles; and they will listen!"

[30]So he lived (there) for two whole years at his own expense. He welcomed everyone who came to visit him, [31]and he boldly preached the kingdom of God and taught about the Lord Jesus Christ without hindrance.

28:23 Ταξάμενοι δὲ αὐτῷ ἡμέραν ἦλθον πρὸς αὐτὸν εἰς τὴν ξενίαν πλείονες οἷς ἐξετίθετο διαμαρτυρόμενος τὴν βασιλείαν τοῦ θεοῦ, πείθων τε αὐτοὺς περὶ τοῦ Ἰησοῦ ἀπό τε τοῦ νόμου Μωϋσέως καὶ τῶν προφητῶν, ἀπὸ πρωῒ ἕως ἑσπέρας.

Ταξάμενοι. Aor mid ptc masc nom pl τάσσω (temporal).

ἦλθον. Aor act ind 3rd pl ἔρχομαι.

εἰς τὴν ξενίαν. In accord with the usual meaning of ξενία, this expression could mean "for hospitality" rather than "to the place of lodging," though the latter is more likely given the context here (cf. Phlm 22; see LN 7.31, n. 7).

πλείονες. The form may be viewed as comparative (so BAGD, 689;

Fitzmyer 1998, 794) or elative (see 13:31 on πλείους): "they came in considerable numbers" (so Barrett, 1243).

ἐξετίθετο. Impf mid ind 3rd sg ἐκτίθημι. Here, "to explain, set forth" (BAGD, 245).

διαμαρτυρόμενος. Pres dep ptc masc nom sg διαμαρτύρομαι (attendant circumstance or means).

τὴν βασιλείαν τοῦ θεοῦ. See 1:3.

πείθων. Pres act ptc masc nom sg πείθω (attendant circumstance or means).

Μωϋσέως . . . πρωΐ. On the diaeresis over the *upsilon* and *iota*, see 2:31 on προϊδὼν.

28:24 καὶ οἱ μὲν ἐπείθοντο τοῖς λεγομένοις, οἱ δὲ ἠπίστουν·

οἱ μὲν . . . οἱ δὲ. See 17:32.

ἐπείθοντο. Impf pass ind 3rd pl πείθω.

τοῖς λεγομένοις. Pres pass ptc neut dat pl λέγω (substantival). On the use of the dative case with the passive form of πείθω, see 27:11.

ἠπίστουν. Impf act ind 3rd pl ἀπιστέω.

28:25 ἀσύμφωνοι δὲ ὄντες πρὸς ἀλλήλους ἀπελύοντο εἰπόντος τοῦ Παύλου ῥῆμα ἕν, ὅτι Καλῶς τὸ πνεῦμα τὸ ἅγιον ἐλάλησεν διὰ Ἠσαΐου τοῦ προφήτου πρὸς τοὺς πατέρας ὑμῶν

ἀσύμφωνοι. Predicate adjective. Only here in the NT ("to be in disagreement").

ὄντες. Pres act ptc masc nom pl εἰμί (causal).

ἀπελύοντο. Impf mid ind 3rd pl ἀπολύω. In the middle voice, "to leave."

εἰπόντος. Aor act ptc masc sg gen λέγω. Genitive absolute (see 1:8 on ἐπελθόντος), temporal or perhaps result ("so Paul said"). The aorist does not dictate that the action of the participle occurred prior to the action of the main verb (contra Barrett, 1244; see Porter 1989, 279–85).

τοῦ Παύλου. Genitive subject (see 1:8 on ἐπελθόντος).

ὅτι. Epexegetical.

ἐλάλησεν. Aor act ind 3rd sg λαλέω.

Ἠσαΐου. On the diaeresis over the *iota*, see 2:31 on προϊδὼν.

τοῦ προφήτου. Genitive in apposition to Ἠσαΐου.

ὑμῶν. Although many witnesses read ἡμῶν (36 307 453 610 614

1678 1891 *Byz al*), making the statement even more accusatory, the second person plural has better external support (𝔓[74] א A B Ψ 33 81 181 945 1175 1409 1739 2344 2464 *al*).

28:26 λέγων, Πορεύθητι πρὸς τὸν λαὸν τοῦτον καὶ εἰπόν, Ἀκοῇ ἀκούσετε καὶ οὐ μὴ συνῆτε καὶ βλέποντες βλέψετε καὶ οὐ μὴ ἴδητε·

λέγων. Pres act ptc masc nom sg λέγω (attendant circumstance, redundant; see 1:6 on λέγοντες). The quote from Isa 6:9–10 closely follows the LXX.

Πορεύθητι. Aor pass impv 2nd sg πορεύομαι.

εἰπόν. Aor act impv 2nd sg λέγω.

Ἀκοῇ ἀκούσετε. The use of ἀκούω with the cognate dative forms a Semitic idiom (lit. "you will hear with hearing") meaning "to listen intently and with presumed continuity" (LN 24.63).

ἀκούσετε. Fut act ind 2nd pl ἀκούω.

οὐ μὴ συνῆτε. Aor act subj 2nd pl συνίημι. The aorist subjunctive is used with οὐ μὴ to form an emphatic negative statement (cf. 13:41).

βλέποντες. Pres act ptc masc nom pl βλέπω. The use of the cognate participle with βλέψετε (lit. "looking, you will look") reflects a Semitic idiom (the infinitive absolute plus a finite verb) that intensifies the sense of the main verb (cf. 7:34 on ἰδὼν).

βλέψετε. Fut act ind 2nd pl βλέπω.

οὐ μὴ ἴδητε. Aor act subj 2nd pl ὁράω. The aorist subjunctive is used with οὐ μὴ to form an emphatic negative statement (cf. 13:41).

28:27 ἐπαχύνθη γὰρ ἡ καρδία τοῦ λαοῦ τούτου καὶ τοῖς ὠσὶν βαρέως ἤκουσαν καὶ τοὺς ὀφθαλμοὺς αὐτῶν ἐκάμμυσαν· μή ποτε ἴδωσιν τοῖς ὀφθαλμοῖς καὶ τοῖς ὠσὶν ἀκούσωσιν καὶ τῇ καρδίᾳ συνῶσιν καὶ ἐπιστρέψωσιν, καὶ ἰάσομαι αὐτούς.

ἐπαχύνθη. Aor pass ind 3rd sg παχύνω. According to Louw and Nida (32.4), παχύνω (lit. "to become thick/fat") here means "to become unable to understand or comprehend as the result of being mentally dull or spiritually insensitive."

βαρέως ἤκουσαν. "They are hard of hearing" (lit. "they hear with difficulty").

ἤκουσαν. Aor act ind 3rd pl ἀκούω.

ἐκάμμυσαν. Aor act ind 3rd pl καμμύω.

ἴδωσιν. Aor act subj 3rd pl ὁράω. The subjunctive verbs are used with μήποτε in a series of negative purpose clauses.

ἀκούσωσιν. Aor act subj 3rd pl ἀκούω.

συνῶσιν. Aor act subj 3rd pl συνίημι.

ἐπιστρέψωσιν. Aor act subj 3rd pl ἐπιστρέφω.

ἰάσομαι. Fut mid ind 1st sg ἰάομαι.

28:28 γνωστὸν οὖν ἔστω ὑμῖν ὅτι τοῖς ἔθνεσιν ἀπεστάλη τοῦτο τὸ σωτήριον τοῦ θεοῦ· αὐτοὶ καὶ ἀκούσονται.

γνωστὸν. Predicate (neuter nominative) adjective.

ἔστω. Pres act impv 3rd sg εἰμί.

ὅτι. See v. 22.

ἀπεστάλη. Aor pass ind 3rd sg ἀποστέλλω.

ἀκούσονται. Fut mid ind 3rd pl ἀκούω.

28:29 καὶ ταῦτα αὐτοῦ εἰπόντος ἀπῆλθον οἱ Ἰουδαῖοι, πολλὴν ἔχοντες ἐν ἑαυτοῖς συζήτησιν.

"When he had said these things, the Jews departed, arguing intensely among themselves." This verse (included by 36 307 453 610 614 945 1409 1678 1891 *Byz al*) is omitted by all early witnesses (𝔓[74] א A B E Ψ 048 33 81 181 1175 1739 2344 2464 *al*). Metzger (502) notes that it was probably added because of the abrupt transition from v. 28 to v. 30.

αὐτοῦ. Genitive subject (see 1:8 on ἐπελθόντος).

εἰπόντος. Aor act ptc masc gen sg λέγω. Genitive absolute (see 1:8 on ἐπελθόντος), temporal.

ἀπῆλθον. Aor act ind 3rd pl ἀπέρχομαι.

πολλὴν . . . συζήτησιν. Lit. "having much debate among themselves."

ἔχοντες. Pres act ptc masc nom pl ἔχω (manner).

πολλὴν . . . συζήτησιν. Direct object of ἔχοντες.

28:30 Ἐνέμεινεν δὲ διετίαν ὅλην ἐν ἰδίῳ μισθώματι καὶ ἀπεδέχετο πάντας τοὺς εἰσπορευομένους πρὸς αὐτόν,

Ἐνέμεινεν. Aor act ind 3rd sg ἐμμένω.

διετίαν. Accusative indicating extent of time (see 7:20 on μῆνας).

ἐν ἰδίῳ μισθώματι. Although Louw and Nida (57.175) follow most scholars in taking this as a reference to a "rented dwelling," Bruce (542), following Cadbury, argues that "at his own expense" is preferable since the alternative sense is unattested elsewhere. The traditional rendering may be attributed to the context, which speaks of Paul welcoming visitors, presumably at his own dwelling.

ἀπεδέχετο. Impf dep ind 3rd sg ἀποδέχομαι.

τοὺς εἰσπορευομένους. Pres dep ptc masc acc pl εἰσπορεύομαι (substantival).

28:31 κηρύσσων τὴν βασιλείαν τοῦ θεοῦ καὶ διδάσκων τὰ περὶ τοῦ κυρίου Ἰησοῦ Χριστοῦ μετὰ πάσης παρρησίας ἀκωλύτως.

κηρύσσων. Pres act ptc masc nom sg κηρύσσω (attendant circumstance).

τὴν βασιλείαν τοῦ θεοῦ. See 1:3.

διδάσκων. Pres act ptc masc nom sg διδάσκω (attendant circumstance).

τὰ περὶ τοῦ κυρίου Ἰησοῦ Χριστοῦ. The article functions as a nominalizer (see 1:3 on τὰ), changing the prepositional phrase into a substantive.

Bibliography

Alexander, Loveday. *The Preface to Luke's Gospel: Literary Convention and Social Context in Luke 1.1–4 and Acts 1.1*. Society for New Testament Studies, Monograph Series. Cambridge: Cambridge University Press, 1993.

Andersen, Francis I. *The Sentence in Biblical Hebrew*. New York: Mouton, 1974.

Arichea, Daniel C., Jr. "Some Notes on Acts 2.17–21." *The Bible Translator* 35 (1984): 442–43.

Arlandson, J. M. *Women, Class, and Society in Early Christianity: Models from Luke-Acts*. Peabody, Mass.: Hendrickson, 1997.

Barrett. C. K. 1994. *A Critical and Exegetical Commentary on the Acts of the Apostles*. International Critical Commentary. 2 vols. Edinburgh: T&T Clark, 1994, 1998.

Bauer, Walter. *A Greek-English Lexicon of the New Testament and Other Early Christian Literature*. Translated and adapted by W. F. Arndt, and F. W. Gingrich. 2nd ed. revised and augmented by F. W. Gingrich and F. W. Danker. Chicago: University of Chicago Press, 1979.

———. *A Greek-English Lexicon of the New Testament and Other Early Christian Literature*. Revised and edited by Frederick W. Danker. 3rd ed. Chicago: University of Chicago, 2000.

Blass, Friedrich W., Albert Debrunner, and Robert W. Funk. *A Greek Grammar of the New Testament Other Early Christian Literature*. Chicago: University of Chicago Press, 1961.

Bock, Darrell L. *Proclamation from Prophecy and Pattern: Lucan Old Testament Christology*. Journal for the Study of the New Testament, Suppl. Series 12. Sheffield: Sheffield Academic Press, 1987.

Boismard, M.-É. and A. Lamouille. *Les Actes des deux Apotres*. 3 vols. Paris: Gabalda, 1990.

Boyer, James L. "A Classification of Imperatives: A Statistical Study." *Grace Theological Journal* 8 (1987): 35–54.

———. "The Classification of Participles: A Statistical Study." *Grace Theological Journal* 5 (1984): 163–79.

———. "Second Class Conditions in New Testament Greek." *Grace Theological Journal* 3 (1982): 81–88.

Bratcher, R. G. "ἀκούω in Acts ix.7 and xxii.9." *Expository Times* 71 (1959–1960): 243–45.

Brawley, Robert L. *Text to Text Pours Forth Speech: Voices of Scripture in Luke-Acts*. Bloomington: Indiana University Press, 1995.

Brehm, H. Alan. "The Meaning of Ἑλληνιστής in Acts in Light of a Diachronic Analysis of ἑλληνίζειν." Pages 180–99 in *Discourse Analysis and Other Topics in Biblical Greek*. Edited by S. E. Porter and D. A. Carson. Journal for the Study of the New Testament, Suppl. Series 113. Sheffield: Sheffield Academic Press, 1995.

Bruce, F. F. *The Acts of the Apostles: The Greek Text with Introduction and Commentary*. 3rd rev. ed. Grand Rapids: Eerdmans, 1990.

Callow, Kathleen. *Discourse Considerations in Translating the Word of God.* Dallas: Summer Institute of Linguistics, 1974.

Carson, D. A. "Matthew." *The Expositor's Bible Commentary*. Vol. 8. Grand Rapids: Zondervan, 1984.

Chrysostom, St. John. *The Homilies of St. John Chrysostom, Archbishop of Constantinople, on the Acts of the Apostle.* Translated with notes and indices. Oxford: J. Parker, 1851–1852.

Clark, Albert C. *The Acts of the Apostles.* Oxford: Clarendon Press, 1933.

Clark, David J. "Vocative Displacement in Acts and Revelation." *The Bible Translator* 50 (1999): 101–10.

———. "What Went Overboard First?" *The Bible Translator* 26 (1975): 144–46.

Conzelmann, Hans. *Acts of the Apostles: A Commentary on the Acts of the Apostles*. Edited by Eldon Jay Epp and Christopher R. Matthews. Translated by James Limburg, A. Thomas Kraabel, and Donald H. Juel. Philadelphia: Fortress, 1987.

———. "Luke's Place in the Development of Early Christianity," Pages 298–316 in *Studies in Luke-Acts*. Edited by Leander E. Keck and J. Louis Martyn (Nashville: Abingdon, 1966).

Cotterell, Peter and Max Turner. *Linguistics & Biblical Interpretation.* Downers Grove, Ill.: Inter-Varsity, 1989.

Craigie, Peter C. *Psalms 1–50.* Word Biblical Commentary. Dallas: Word Books, 1983.

Culy, Martin M. "Relative Clauses in Koine Greek: A Transformational Approach." M.A. thesis, University of North Dakota, 1989.

———. "The Clue is in the Case: Distinguishing Adjectival and Adverbial Participlies." *Perspectives in Religious Studies* 2004, forthcoming.

Dana, H. E. and Julius R. Mantey. *A Manual Grammar of the Greek New Testament*. Upper Saddle River, N.J.: Prentice Hall, 1957.

Darr, John A. *On Character Building: the Reader and the Rhetoric of Characterization in Luke-Acts*. Louisville, Ky.: Westminster/John Knox, 1992.

Davies, W. D. and Dale C. Allison, Jr. *Matthew VII–XVIII*. Vol. 2 of *A Critical and Exegetical Commentary on the Gospel According to Saint Matthew*. Edinburgh: T&T Clark, 1991.

Dawsey, James. *The Lukan Voice*. Macon, Ga.: Mercer Universtiy Press, 1986.

Deer, Donald F. "Getting the 'Story' Straight in Acts 20.9." *The Bible Translator* 39 (1988): 246–47.

Deibler, Ellis. *An Index of Implicit Information in the New Testament*. Dallas: Summer Institute of Linguistics, 1995.

Dibelius, Martin. *Studies in the Acts of the Apostles*. London: SCM, 1956.

Dietrich, W. "Der periphrastische Verbalaspekt im Griechishen und Lateinischen." *Glotta* 51 (1973): 188–228.

Dunn, James D. G. *Romans 1–8*. World Biblical Commentary. Dallas: Word, 1988.

Ellingworth, Paul. *The Epistle to the Hebrews: A Commentary on the Greek Text*. New International Greek Testament Commentary. Grand Rapids: Eerdmans, 1993.

Esler, Phillip. *Community and Gospel in Luke-Acts: The Social and Political Motivations in Lucan Theology*. Society for New Testament Studies, Monograph Series 57. Cambridge: Cambridge University Press, 1987.

Evans, Craig and James A. Sanders. *Luke and Scripture: The Function of Sacred Tradition in Luke-Acts*. Minneapolis: Ausburg/Fortress, 1993.

Fearghail, Fearghus Ó. *The Introduction to Luke-Acts: A Study of the Role of Lk 1,1–4,44 in the Composition of Luke's Two-Volume Work*. Analecta Biblica 126. Rome: Pontifical Biblical Institute, 1991.

Fee, Gordon D. *Paul's Letter to the Philippians.* New International Commentary on the New Testament. Grand Rapids: Eerdmans, 1995.

Finley, Thomas J. *Joel, Amos, Obadiah.* Wycliffe Exegetical Commentary. Chicago: Moody, 1990.

Fitzmyer, Joseph A. *The Acts of the Apostles: A New Translation with Introduction and Commentary.* Anchor Bible. New York: Doubleday, 1998.

———. *Luke the Theologian: Aspects of His Teaching.* New York: Paulist, 1989.

Garrett, Susan R. *The Demise of the Devil: Magic and the Demonic in Luke's Writings.* Minneapolis: Fortress, 1989.

Gasque, W. Ward. "A Fruitful Field: Recent Study of the Acts of the Apostles." *Interpretation* 42 (1988): 117–31.

Gault, Jo Ann. "The Discourse Function of *Kai Egeneto* in Luke and Acts." *Occasional Papers in Translation and Textlinguistics* 4.4 (1990): 388–99.

Gowler, David B. *Host, Guest, Enemy and Friend: Portraits of the Pharisees in Luke and Acts.* Emory Studies in Early Christianity 2. New York: Peter Lang, 1991.

Haenchen, Ernst. *The Acts of the Apostles: A Commentary.* Louisville, Ky.: Westminster, 1971.

Hawthorne, Gerald. F. *Philippians.* World Bible Commentary. Dallas: Word, 1983.

Healey, Phillis and Alan Healey. "Greek Circumstantial Participles: Tracking Participants with Participles in the Greek New Testament." *Occasional Papers in Translation and Textlinguistics* 4.3 (1990): 177–257.

Hemer, Colin J. *Book of Acts in the Setting of Hellenistic History.* WUNT 49. Winona Lake, Ind.: Eisenbrauns, 1990.

Hewitt, James A. *New Testament Greek: A Beginning and Intermediate Grammar.* Peabody, Mass.: Hendrickson, 1986.

Jervell, Jacob. *The Theology of the Acts of the Apostles.* Cambridge: Cambridge University Press, 1996.

Johnson, Luke Timothy. *The Acts of the Apostles.* Sacra pagina 5. Collegeville, Minn.: Liturgical Press, 1992.

Käsemann, Ernst. *Perspectives on Paul.* Translated by Margaret Kohl. Philadelphia: Fortress, 1971.

Keck, Leander E. and J. Louis Martyn, eds. *Studies in Luke-Acts: Essays Presented in Honor of Paul Schubert.* Nashville: Abingdon, 1966.

Keathley, Naymond H., ed. *With Steadfast Purpose: Essays in Honor of Henry Jackson Flanders.* Waco, Tex.: Baylor University Press, 1990.

Knox, John. *Chapters in a Life of Paul.* Macon, Ga.: Mercer University Press, 1989.

Kruger, G. van W. "Conditionals in the NT: A Study of their Rationale." Ph.D. diss., University of Cambridge, 1966.

Kurz, William S. *Reading Luke-Acts: Dynamics of Biblical Narrative.* Louisville, Ky.: Westminster/John Knox, 1993.

Lake, Kirsopp and Henry L. Cadbury. *The Acts of the Apostles.* Part 1 of *The Beginnings of Christianity.* English Translation and Commentary. Vol. 4. London: Macmillan, 1933.

Lane, William L. *Hebrews 9–13.* Word Biblical Commentary. Dallas: Word, 1991.

Levinsohn, Stephen H. *Discourse Features of New Testament Greek.* Dallas: Summer Institute of Linguistics, 1992.

———. *Textual Connections in Acts.* Atlanta: Scholars Press, 1987.

———. "Relationships between Constituents and Beyond the Clause in the Acts of the Apostles." Ph.D. diss., University of Reading, 1980.

Liddell, Henry George and Robert Scott. *A Greek-English Lexicon.* 9th ed. Revised by Henry Stuart Jones. Oxford: Clarendon, 1968.

Longenecker, Richard N. *The Acts of the Apostles.* The Expositor's Bible Commentary. Vol. 9. Grand Rapids: Zondervan, 1981.

Louw, Johannes P. and Eugene A. Nida, eds. *Greek-English Lexicon of the New Testament Based on Semantic Domains.* 2 vols. New York: United Bible Societies, 1988.

Lüdemann, Gerd. *Early Christianity According to the Traditions in Acts: A Commentary.* Philadelphia: Fortress, 1989.

Marconi, Gilberto et al., eds. *Luke and Acts.* Translated by Matthew J. O'Connell. New York: Paulist, 1993.

Marshall, I. Howard. *The Acts of the Apostles.* Grand Rapids: Eerdmans, 1980.

Marshall, I. Howard and David Peterson, eds. *Witness to the Gospel: The Theology of Acts.* Grand Rapids: Eerdmans, 1998.

Martín-Ascensio, Gustavo. "Foregrounding and its Relevance for Interpretation and Translation, with Acts 27 as a Case Study." Pages 189–223 in *Translating the Bible: Problems and Prospects*. Edited by S. E. Porter and R. S. Hess. Sheffield: Sheffield Academic Press, 1999.

Matson, David L. *Household Conversion Narratives in Acts: Pattern and Interpretation*. Journal for the Study of the New Testament, Suppl. Series 123. Sheffield: Sheffield Academic Press, 1996.

McKay, K. L. *A New Syntax of the Verb in New Testament Greek: An Aspectual Approach*. Studies in Biblical Greek. Vol. 5. New York: Peter Lang, 1994.

———. "Aspect in Imperatival Constructions in New Testament Greek." *Novum Testamentum* (1985): 201–26.

Metzger, Bruce M. *A Textual Commentary on the Greek New Testament*. New York: United Bible Societies, 1971.

Moessner, David P. *Jesus and the Heritage of Israel: Luke's Narrative Claim upon Israel's Legacy*. Harrisburg: Trinity Press International, 1999.

Morganthaler, Robert. *Statistik des neutestamentlichen Wortschatzes*. Zurich: Gotthelf Verlag, 1958.

Moule, C. F. D. *An Idiom Book of New Testament Greek*. Cambridge: Cambridge University Press, 1959.

Moulton, J. H. *Prolegomena*. Vol. 1 of *A Grammar of NT Greek*. 3rd ed. Edinburgh: T&T Clark, 1908.

New, David. S. "The Injunctive Future and Existential Injunctions in the New Testament." *Journal for the Study of the New Testament* 44 (1991): 113–27.

Newman, Barclay M. and Eugene A. Nida. *A Translator's Handbook on the Acts of the Apostles*. New York: United Bible Societies, 1972.

Newsome, Carol A. and Sharon Ringe, eds. *The Women's Bible Commentary*. Louisville, Ky.: Westminster/John Knox, 1992.

Neyrey, Jorome H., ed. *The Social World of Luke-Acts: Models for Interpretation*. Peabody, Mass.: Hendrickson, 1991.

Niehaus, Jeff. "Amos." In *The Minor Prophets: An Exegetical and Expository Commentary*. Vol.1. Edited by Thomas E. McComiskey. Grand Rapids: Baker, 1992.

O'Brien, Peter T. *The Epistle to the Philippians: A Commentary on the Greek Text*. New International Greek Testament Commentary. Grand Rapids: Eerdmans, 1991.

Omanson, Roger L. Draft version and expansion of Metzger. Forthcoming.

Page, T. E. *The Acts of the Apostles, Being the Greek Text as Revised by Drs. Westcott and Hort, with Explanatory Notes*. London: Macmillan, 1886.

Parsons, Mikeal. "'Defiled AND Unclean': The Conjunction's Function in Acts 10:14." *Perspectives in Religious Studies* 27 (2000): 263–74.

———. "The Place of Jerusalem on the Lukan Landscape: An Exercise in Theological Cartography." Pages 155–72 in *Literary Studies in Luke-Acts*. Edited by Richard P. Thompson and Thomas E. Phillips. Macon, Ga.: Mercer University Press, 1998.

———. "Acts of the Apostles." Pages 1083–1122 in *Mercer Commentary on the Bible*. Edited by Watson Mills, Walter Harrelson, and Edgar McKnight. Macon, Ga.: Mercer University Press, 1994.

Parsons, Mikeal C. and Richard I. Pervo. *Rethinking the Unity of Luke and Acts*. Minneapolis: Ausburg/Fortress, 1993.

Parsons, Mikeal C. and Joseph B. Tyson, eds. *Cadbury, Knox, and Talbert: American Contributions to the Study of Acts*. Atlanta: Scholars , 1992.

Pervo, Richard I. *Profit with Delight: The Literary Genre of the Acts of the Apostles*. Philadelphia: Fortress, 1987.

Plummer, Alfred. *A Critical and Exegetical Commentary on the Gospel of S. Luke*. International Critical Commentary. 5th ed. Edinburgh: T&T Clark, 1922.

Pokorny, P. *Theologie der lukanischen Schriften*. Forschungen zur Religion und Literatur des Alten und Neuen Testament 174. Göttingen, 1998.

Polhill, John B. *Acts*. New American Commentary. Nashville: Broadman, 1992.

Porter, Stanley E. *Idioms of the Greek New Testament*. 2nd ed. Sheffield: Sheffield Academic Press, 1994.

———. *Verbal Aspect in the Greek of the New Testament, with Reference to Tense and Mood*. New York: Peter Lang, 1989.

Powell, Mark A. *What Are They Saying about Acts?* New York: Paulist, 1991.

Ramsay, William. *St. Paul the Traveler and the Roman Citizen*. Grand Rapids: Eerdmans, 1949.

Reimer, Ironi Richter. *Women in the Acts of the Apostles: A Feminist Liberation Prespective*. Translated by Linda M. Maloney. Minneapolis: Fortress, 1995.

Richard, Earl, ed. *New Views on Luke and Acts*. Collegeville, Minn.: Liturgical, 1990.

Robbins, Vernon K. "The Claims of the Prologues and Greco-Roman Rhetoric: The Prefaces to Luke and Acts in Light of Greco-Roman Rhetorical Strategies." Pages 63–83 in *Jesus and the Heritage of Israel: Luke's Narrative Claim upon Isreal's Legacy.* Edited by D. P. Moessner. Harrisburg, Pa.: Trinity Press International, 2000.

———. "The Social Location of the Implied Author of Luke-Acts." Pages 305–32 in *The Social World of Luke-Acts: Models for Interpretation.* Edited by Jorome H. Neyrey. Peabody, Mass.: Hendrickson, 1991.

Robertson, A. T. "The Meaning of Acts xxvi.28." *Expository Times* 35 (1923–1924): 185–86.

———. *A Grammar of the Greek New Testament in the Light of Historical Research.* Nashville: Broadman, 1934.

Rogers, Cleon L. Jr. and Cleon L. Rogers III. *The New Linguistic and Exegetical Key to the Greek New Testament*. Grand Rapids: Zondervan, 1998.

Schneider, G. *Die Apostelgeschichte*. Herderstheologischer Kommentar zum Neuen Testament 5/1-2. Freiburg im B.: Herder, 1980, 1982.

Scott, Julius M. "Luke's Geographical Horizon." Pages 483–544 in *The Book of Acts in Its Graeco-Roman Setting.* Edited by D. W. J. Gill and C. Gempf. Grand Rapids: Eerdmans, 1994.

Seim, Turid Karlsen. *The Double Message: Patterns of Gender in Luke-Acts*. Nashville: Abingdon, 1994.

Shepherd, William H., Jr. *The Narrative Function of the Holy Spirit as a Character in Luke-Acts*. Society of Biblical Literature, Dissertation Series 147. Atlanta: Scholars Press, 1994.

Silva, Moisés. *Explorations in Exegetical Method: Galatians as a Test Case*. Grand Rapids: Baker, 1996.

_________. *Philippians.* Wycliffe Exegetical Commentary. Chicago: Moody, 1988.

Smyth, Herbert Weir. *Greek Grammar*. Cambridge: Harvard University Press, 1959.

Soards, Marion L. *The Speeches in Acts: Their Content, Context, and Concerns.* Louisville, Ky.: Westminster/John Knox, 1994.

Squires, John T. *The Plan of God in Luke-Acts*. Society for New Testament Studies, Monograph Series 76. Cambridge: Cambridge University Press, 1993.

Strange, W. A. *The Problem of the Text of Acts*. Society for New Testament Studies, Monograph Series 71. Cambridge: Cambridge University Press, 1992.

Sterling, Gregory L. *Historiography and Self-Definition: Josephos, Luke-Acts and Apologetic Historiography*. Novum Testamentum Supplements 64. Leiden: E. J. Brill, 1992.

Sweeney, Michael L. "The Identity of 'They' in Acts 2.1." *The Bible Translator* 46 (1995): 245–48.

Talbert, Charles H. *Reading Acts: A Literary and Theological Commentary on the Acts of the Apostles*. New York: Crossroad, 1997.

———. "Once Again: Gospel Genre." *Semeia* 43 (1988): 53–73.

———. "Shifting Sands: The Recent Study of the Gospel of Luke." *Interpretation* 30 (1976): 381–95.

Tannehill, Robert C. *The Acts of the Apostles*. Vol. 2 of *The Narrative Unity of Luke-Acts: A Literary Interpretation*. Minneapolis: Fortress, 1990.

Thomas, Robert L. *Luke, Judaism, and the Scholars: Critical Approaches to Luke-Acts*. Columbia: University of South Carolina Press, 1999.

———. *Revelation 8–22: An Exegetical Commentary*. Chicago: Moody, 1995.

Thompson, Richard P. and Thomas E. Phillips, eds. *Literary Studies in Luke-Acts: Essays in Honor of Joseph B. Tyson*. Macon, Ga.: Mercer University Press, 1998.

Tuckett, Christopher M., ed. *Luke's Literary Achievement: Collected Essays*. Journal for the Study of the New Testament, Suppl. Series 116. Sheffield: Sheffield Academic Press, 1996.

Turner, Nigel. *Grammatical Insights into the New Testament*. Edinburgh: T&T Clark, 1965.

———. *A Grammar of New Testament Greek*. Vol. 3: *Syntax*. Ed. J. H. Moulton. Edinburgh: T&T Clark, 1963.

Tyson, Joseph B. *Luke-Acts and the Jewish People: Eight Critical Perspectives*. Minneapolis, Augsburg, 1988.

———. *Luke, Judaism, and the Scholars: Critical Approaches to Luke-Acts*. Columbia: University of South Carolina Press, 1999.

Unnik, W. C. van. "Luke-Acts, a Storm Center in Contempaory Scholarship." Pages 15–32 in *Studies in Luke-Acts: Essays Presented in Honor of Paul Schubert.* Edited by Leander E. Keck and J. Louis Martyn. Nashville: Abingdon, 1966.

Verheyden, Jozef, ed. *The Unity of Luke-Acts.* Leuven: Leuven University Press; Peeters, 1999.

Vielhauer, Philipp, "On the 'Paulinism' of Acts." Pages 33–50 in *Studies in Luke-Acts: Essays Presented in Honor of Paul Schubert.* Edited by Leander E. Keck and J. Louis Martyn. Nashville: Abingdon, 1966.

Wallace, Daniel B. *Greek Grammar Beyond the Basics: An Exegetical Syntax of the New Testament.* Grand Rapids: Zondervan, 1996.

———. "The Semantics and Exegetical Significance of the Object-Complement Construction in the New Testament." *Grace Theological Journal* 6 (1985): 91–112.

Winter, Bruce, ed. *The Book of Acts in Its First-Century Setting.* 6 vols. Grand Rapids: Eerdmans, 1993–1998.

Witherington, Ben, III. *The Acts of the Apostles: A Socio-Rhetorical Commentary.* Grand Rapids: Eerdmans, 1998.

———. *History, Literature, and Society in the Book of Acts.* Cambridge & New York: Cambridge University Press, 1996.